INDIA'S 500
BEST RECIPES

INDIA'S 500
BEST RECIPES

A vibrant collection of spicy appetizers, tangy meat, fish and vegetable dishes, breads, rices and delicious chutneys from India and South-East Asia, with over 500 photographs

SHEHZAD HUSAIN, RAFI FERNANDEZ,
MRIDULA BALJEKAR AND MANISHA KANANI

HERMES HOUSE

This edition is published by Hermes House

Hermes House is an imprint of
Anness Publishing Ltd
Hermes House
88–89 Blackfriars Road
London SE1 8HA
tel. 020 7401 2077; fax 020 7633 9499
info@anness.com

A CIP catalogue record for this book
is available from the British Library.

Publisher: Joanna Lorenz
Editorial Director: Judith Simons
Project Editor: Felicity Forster
Additional recipes: Becky Johnson, Sallie Morris and Deh-Ta Hsiung
Copy Editor: Jan Cutler
Cover Design: Chloë Steers
Designer: SMI
Editorial Reader: Rosie Fairhead
Production Controller: Steve Lang

Recipes in this book were previously published in *Complete Indian, Best-Ever Curry Cookbook* and *Fat-Free Indian*

1 3 5 7 9 10 8 6 4 2

Notes
Bracketed terms are intended for American readers.

For all recipes, quantities are given in both metric and imperial measures and, where appropriate,
in standard cups and spoons. Follow one set, but not a mixture, because they are not interchangeable.

Standard spoon and cup measures are level. 1 tsp = 5ml, 1 tbsp = 15ml, 1 cup = 250ml/8fl oz.

Australian standard tablespoons are 20ml. Australian readers should use
3 tsp in place of 1 tbsp for measuring small quantities of gelatine, flour, salt etc.

The nutritional analysis given for each recipe is calculated per portion (i.e. serving or item),
unless otherwise stated. If the recipe gives a range, such as Serves 4–6, then the
nutritional analysis will be for the smaller portion size, i.e. 6 servings.

Medium (US large) eggs are used unless otherwise stated.

Contents

Introduction

Perhaps the most popularly enjoyed cuisines in the world come from India and South-east Asia. Brightly coloured vegetables in richly flavoured sauces, tender meat and poultry, fresh fish, nutty-flavoured beans and lentils, and, of course, the array of spices, epitomize these most exciting foods that warm the body and soothe the spirit. Indeed, many

of us live in towns and cities where restaurants that specialize in Indian food flourish, and, because cuisine from South-east Asia has also become more widespread than ever before, food enthusiasts now have a wealth of choice when it comes to adventurous cooking using spices and flavourings. If you enjoy creating Indian and Asian food, look no further than this volume for a comprehensive selection of the most exciting eating ever. In these pages there are quick-and-easy dishes as well as a huge and imaginative variety of recipes that involve blending aromatic spices and flavourings to achieve a truly authentic taste of the East.

The beauty of Indian cooking is in its variety. Different areas and traditions have developed their own regional specialities, and recipes have been handed down through the generations as various combinations of spices and ingredients have been explored and enjoyed. Although many Indian dishes are fiery with chillies, there are others that are mellow. Balti cuisine, which is Kashmiri cooking from the area that is now north Pakistan, is beautifully aromatic, but does not use chillies excessively, so it is not too hot. Many of the most familiar regional dishes we enjoy come from northern India. These include koftas, mild kormas and tandoori recipes. The most fiery spice blends, however, such as the famous vindaloo, come from southern India, as well as an abundance of vegetarian dishes using lentils, beans and chickpeas. Fragrant jasmine rice is another speciality of southern India. Coconuts are favourite ingredients of eastern India, and are used for making both sweet and savoury dishes, including deliciously creamy sauces. From western India there are recipes using dairy products, including yogurt and buttermilk, and the meals are also accompanied by all kinds of unusual pickles. As many Indian people are vegetarian, there is no shortage of delectable meat-free recipes to choose from, which utilize nuts, beans, peas and lentils, making substantial and nutritious meals that are guaranteed to appeal to vegetarians and meat-eaters alike.

Dishes from South-east Asia use a different combination of flavours from those of India. They are scented with lemon grass and kaffir lime leaves and use delicate curry pastes made from herbs and spices. This cuisine owes part of its heritage to the influences of China as well as India. Another new dimension was introduced to Indian food when the Portuguese brought the fiery chilli from the Americas in the 16th century.

All of these fabulous cuisines are brought together here in one collection of recipes, with their diverse cooking styles and creative combinations of herbs, spices and flavourings. The book is divided into sections that offer everything the enthusiast could ask for, from soups and appetizers to fish and shellfish dishes, meat, poultry, vegetable and Balti dishes. It also includes a variety of side dishes, salads, relishes and chutneys, as well as breads, desserts and drinks – in fact everything you need to create the perfect meal, whether it be a quick evening supper or a dinner party for friends and family. Cook's Tips throughout the book explain some of the more unusual ingredients and how they are used.

Many recipes are quick to prepare with the simplest of spice combinations, whereas others call for a more varied store of spices and flavourings, including some lesser-known ingredients, such as mango powder (amchur) and compressed tamarind. Today, however, most of these special ingredients are easily available from supermarkets, Asian stores and markets, and sometimes even health-food stores. Fresh herbs such as coriander (cilantro) are sold cheaply in large bunches in Asian stores and markets, so you will have plenty to use to flavour your dishes. You will also be able to buy fresh fenugreek and, occasionally, fresh curry leaves, which taste superior to the dried ones that are readily available. It's well worth visiting an Asian store or market if you have one nearby – large bags of

whole spices are often sold cheaply, and these are ideal if you enjoy preparing spicy food regularly.

For the best flavour, always grind your spices just before you use them. You will immediately notice the strength of their aroma compared to spices that are bought ready ground. However, most of us want to take advantage of making quick spicy meals without a fuss and long periods of preparation, so ground spices might therefore be the best bet for busy people. Always buy ground spices in small quantities from a reputable supplier who has a quick turnover of stock, because once a spice has been ground it begins to lose its aroma and flavour. So don't be tempted to buy large quantities of ground spices, as you will lose out on taste.

To add an authentic touch to your Indian meal, try cooking and serving it in a karahi. This piece of equipment is a little like a wok but is more rounded in shape and is made of heavier metal. Traditionally the karahi is made of cast iron, although a variety of metals are now used. Karahis are available in various sizes, including small ones for cooking single portions. Before you buy a karahi, however, check whether you can use it on your particular type of stove. You can use a wok or large frying pan in place of a karahi for cooking most types of Indian dish. Another piece of equipment that is useful for cooking Indian meals is a heat diffuser. This is placed between the pan and the heat source, its function being to reduce the heat so that curries can simmer at the lowest possible temperature.

Once you have sourced your Indian and South-east Asian ingredients and chosen your cooking vessel, you are ready to create some of the tantalizing dishes contained in this book. Whether it's a speedy weekday meal or a special dinner, your family and friends are in for a gastronomic treat.

Tomato & Coriander Soup

Although soups are not often eaten in India or Pakistan, tomato soup bucks the trend and is very popular. This is excellent on a cold winter's day.

Serves 4
675g/1½lb tomatoes, peeled and chopped
15ml/1 tbsp oil
1 bay leaf

4 spring onions (scallions), chopped
5ml/1 tsp salt
2.5ml/½ tsp crushed garlic
5ml/1 tsp crushed black peppercorns
30ml/2 tbsp chopped fresh coriander (cilantro)
750ml/1¼ pints/3 cups water
15ml/1 tbsp cornflour (cornstarch)
30ml/2 tbsp single (light) cream, to garnish (optional)

1 To peel the tomatoes, plunge them in very hot water, leave for 30 seconds, then take them out. The skin should now peel off easily. If not, put the tomatoes back in the water for a little longer. Once they have been peeled, roughly chop the tomatoes.

2 In a medium, heavy pan, heat the oil and fry the tomatoes, bay leaf and spring onions for a few minutes until soft.

3 Gradually add the salt, garlic, peppercorns and coriander. Pour in the water. Stir, then simmer gently over a low heat for 15–20 minutes.

4 Meanwhile, dissolve the cornflour in a little cold water to form a thick creamy paste.

5 Remove the soup from the heat and leave to cool slightly for a few minutes. Press through a sieve (strainer), or purée in a blender or food processor.

6 Return the puréed soup to the pan, add the cornflour mixture and stir over a gentle heat for about 3 minutes until thickened.

7 Pour the soup into individual serving dishes and garnish with a swirl of cream, if using. Serve hot.

Energy 76kcal/315kJ; Fat 3.4g; Saturated fat 0.43g; Carbohydrate 10.1g; Fibre 1.9g.

Curried Carrot & Apple Soup

The combination of carrot, curry powder and apple is a highly successful one. Curried fruit is delicious.

Serves 4
10ml/2 tsp sunflower oil
15ml/1 tbsp mild korma curry powder
500g/1¼lb carrots, chopped
1 large onion, chopped

1 tart cooking apple, chopped
750ml/1¼ pints/3 cups chicken stock
salt and ground black pepper
plain yogurt and carrot curls, to garnish

1 Heat the oil in a large, heavy pan. Add the curry powder and fry for 2–3 minutes.

2 Add the carrots, onion and cooking apple and stir well until coated with the curry powder. Cover the pan.

3 Cook over low heat for about 15 minutes, shaking the pan occasionally, until soft. Spoon the vegetable mixture into a food processor or blender, then add half the stock and process until the mixture is smooth.

4 Return to the pan and pour in the remaining stock. Bring the soup to the boil and adjust the seasoning before serving in bowls, garnished with a swirl of yogurt and a few curls of raw carrot.

Variations
• Parsnips also taste great in a curried soup. Simply replace the carrots with chopped parsnips, or, if you prefer, use half the amount of carrots and half of parsnips.
• If you don't have any korma powder you can make up your own with 5ml/1 tsp each ground turmeric, cumin, coriander and cinnamon. Add 10ml/2 tsp grated fresh root ginger if you want to give your soup a little more kick.

Energy 89kcal/371kJ; Fat 2g; Saturated fat 0.3g; Carbohydrate 17.2g; Fibre 4.3g.

Spiced Cauliflower Soup

Light and tasty, this creamy, mildly spicy vegetable soup is multi-purpose. It makes a wonderful warming first course, an appetizing quick meal and is delicious chilled.

Serves 4–6
1 large potato, diced
1 small cauliflower, chopped
1 onion, chopped
15ml/1 tbsp oil
1 garlic clove, crushed
15ml/1 tbsp grated fresh root ginger
10ml/2 tsp ground turmeric
5ml/1 tsp cumin seeds
5ml/1 tsp black mustard seeds
10ml/2 tsp ground coriander
1 litre/1¾ pints/4 cups vegetable stock
300ml/½ pint/1¼ cups natural (plain) low-fat yogurt
salt and ground black pepper
fresh coriander (cilantro) or parsley, to garnish

1 Put the potato, cauliflower and onion into a large, heavy pan with the oil and 45ml/3 tbsp water. Heat until hot and bubbling, then stir well, cover the pan and turn the heat down. Continue cooking the mixture for about 10 minutes.

2 Add the garlic, ginger and spices. Stir well, and cook for another 2 minutes, stirring occasionally. Pour in the stock and season well. Bring to the boil, then cover and simmer for about 20 minutes. Purée in a food processor and return to the pan. Stir in the yogurt, adjust the seasoning, and serve garnished with coriander or parsley.

> **Cook's Tip**
> A freshly made stock always tastes best. To make home-made vegetable stock, add to 3.5 litres/6 pints/15 cups of water: 2 sliced leeks, 3 chopped celery sticks, 1 chopped onion, 1 chopped parsnip, 1 seeded and chopped yellow (bell) pepper, 3 crushed garlic cloves, fresh herbs and 45ml/3 tbsp light soy sauce. Season, then slowly bring to the boil. Lower the heat and simmer for 30 minutes, stirring from time to time. Leave to cool. Strain, discard the vegetables, and use the stock as indicated in the recipe.

Energy 188kcal/789kJ; Fat 5.4g; Saturated fat 0.77g; Carbohydrate 24.6g; Fibre 3g.

Fiery Hot Yogurt & Chilli Soup

Hot chillies, cool yogurt – this is an unusual and tasty soup with a real punch.

Serves 2–3
450ml/¾ pint/scant 2 cups natural (plain) low-fat yogurt, beaten
60ml/4 tbsp gram flour
2.5ml/½ tsp chilli powder
2.5ml/½ tsp ground turmeric
2 fresh green chillies, finely chopped
30ml/2 tbsp vegetable oil
4 whole dried red chillies
5ml/1 tsp cumin seeds
3 or 4 curry leaves
3 garlic cloves, crushed
5cm/2in piece fresh root ginger, crushed
salt
fresh coriander (cilantro) leaves, chopped, to garnish

1 Mix the yogurt, gram flour, chilli powder, turmeric and salt to taste in a bowl. Press the mixture through a strainer into a pan. Add the green chillies and simmer for 10 minutes, stirring occasionally.

2 Heat the vegetable oil in a heavy pan and fry the remaining spices, crushed garlic and fresh ginger until the dried chillies turn black.

3 Pour the oil and the spices over the yogurt soup, cover the pan and leave to rest for 5 minutes off the heat. Mix well and gently reheat for a further 5 minutes. Ladle into warmed soup bowls and serve hot, garnished with the coriander leaves.

> **Cook's Tips**
> • For a lower fat version drain off some of the oil before adding it to the yogurt. Low-fat yogurt makes this a healthy soup.
> • Adjust the amount of chilli according to how hot you want the soup to be.

Energy 321kcal/1344kJ; Fat 13.7g; Saturated fat 2.5g; Carbohydrate 33.8g; Fibre 1.5g.

Lentil Soup

This is a simple, mildly spiced lentil soup, which is a good accompaniment to heavily spiced meat dishes.

Serves 4–6
50g/½oz/1 tbsp ghee
1 large onion, finely chopped
2 garlic cloves, crushed
1 fresh green chilli, chopped
2.5ml/½ tsp turmeric
75g/3oz/⅓ cup split red lentils (masoor dhal)
250ml/8fl oz/1 cup water

400g/14oz canned tomatoes, chopped
2.5ml/½ tsp sugar
lemon juice, to taste
200g/7oz/1¾ cups plain boiled rice or 2 boiled potatoes (optional)
salt
fresh coriander (cilantro), chopped, to garnish (optional)

1 Heat the ghee in a large pan and fry the onion, garlic, chilli and turmeric until the onion is translucent.

2 Add the lentils and water, and bring to the boil. Reduce the heat, cover and cook until all the water is absorbed.

3 Mash the lentils with the back of a wooden spoon until you have a smooth paste. Add salt to taste and mix well.

4 Add the tomatoes, sugar and lemon, and reheat the soup. To provide extra texture, fold in the plain boiled rice or potatoes cut into small cubes. Garnish with coriander, if you like, and serve hot.

Cook's Tips
• When using lentils, first rinse in cold water and pick over to remove any small stones or loose skins.
• Fresh coriander (cilantro) is used in so many Indian dishes it is worth growing some in a window box or in several pots on your kitchen windowsill. If you have a garden you could grow some in a raised well-drained bed, so that you have a good supply.

South Indian Pepper Water

This soothing broth is perfect for winter evenings.

Serves 4–6
30ml/2 tbsp vegetable oil
2.5ml/½ tsp black pepper
5ml/1 tsp cumin seeds
2.5ml/½ tsp mustard seeds
1.5ml/¼ tsp asafoetida
2.5ml/½ tsp ground turmeric

2 dried red chillies
4–6 curry leaves
2 garlic cloves, crushed
300ml/½ pint/1¼ cups tomato juice
juice of 2 lemons
120ml/4fl oz/½ cup water
salt
fresh coriander (cilantro), to garnish

Heat the oil in a large pan and fry the pepper, spices, curry leaves and garlic until the chillies are nearly black and the garlic is golden brown. Lower the heat and pour in the tomato juice, lemon juice and water. Bring to the boil then simmer for 10 minutes. Season to taste with salt. Pour into heated bowls, garnish with the chopped coriander if you like, and serve.

Indian Pea Soup

This is a delicate and tasty cream soup.

Serves 6
115g/4oz potato, chopped
75g/3oz onion, chopped
1.2 litres/2 pints/5 cups chicken stock
2cm/¾in piece fresh root ginger

2.5ml/½ tsp ground cumin
75ml/5 tbsp chopped fresh coriander (cilantro)
½ green chilli
275g/10oz fresh or frozen peas
15ml/1 tbsp lemon juice
150ml/¼ pint/⅔ cup double (heavy) cream
salt

Put the potato, onion, stock, ginger and cumin in a pan and bring to the boil. Simmer for 30 minutes. Remove the ginger. Add the coriander, chilli, peas and lemon juice, and add salt to taste. Simmer for 2–3 minutes. Purée in a food processor or blender, then reheat. Add the cream and heat through before serving.

Energy 123kcal/520kJ; Fat 3.4g; Saturated fat 2g; Carbohydrate 18.7g; Fibre 2.6g.

Top: Energy 76kcal/315kJ; Fat 3.4g; Saturated fat 0.43g; Carbohydrate 10.1g; Fibre 1.9g.
Above: Energy 180kcal/744kJ; Fat 14.2g; Saturated fat 8.5g; Carbohydrate 9.7g; Fibre 2.5g.

Chicken Mulligatawny

This world-famous broth hails from the days of the British Raj. It is full of flavour and makes a substantial main-course soup.

Serves 4–6
900g/2lb boneless chicken portions, skinned
600ml/1 pint/2 ½ cups water
6 green cardamom pods
5cm/2in piece cinnamon stick
4–6 curry leaves
15ml/1 tbsp ground coriander
5ml/1 tsp ground cumin
2.5ml/½ tsp ground turmeric
3 garlic cloves, crushed
1 onion, finely chopped
115g/4oz creamed coconut (120ml/4fl oz/½ cup coconut cream)
juice of 2 lemons
deep-fried onions, to garnish

1 Place the chicken portions in a large pan with the water. Bring to the boil, then simmer for about 1 hour, or until the chicken is tender.

2 Skim the surface, then remove the chicken pieces with a slotted spoon and keep warm.

3 Reheat the stock in the pan. Add all the remaining ingredients, except the chicken and deep-fried onions. Simmer for 10–15 minutes, then strain and return the chicken to the soup. Reheat the soup and serve garnished with the deep-fried onions.

Variation
To make a delicious Chicken Mulligatawny Soup with Lentils, cook the chicken portions as step 1. Remove from the stock and keep warm. Now cook 175g/6oz/⅔ cup red lentils in the reserved stock for 30 minutes until tender. Add 115g/4oz diced potato and cook for a further 20 minutes. Add the remaining ingredients and cook as step 3. Cut the chicken into bitesize pieces and add to the strained soup. Serve garnished as before.

Spicy Chicken & Mushroom Soup

This creamy chicken soup has just enough spice to make it a great winter warmer, but not so much that it overwhelms the flavour of the mushrooms.

Serves 4
225g/8oz boneless chicken, skinned
75g/3oz/6 tbsp ghee or unsalted (sweet) butter
2.5ml/½ tsp crushed garlic
5ml/1 tsp garam masala
5ml/1 tsp crushed black peppercorns
5ml/1 tsp salt
1.5ml/¼ tsp grated nutmeg
1 medium leek, sliced
75g/3oz/1 cup mushrooms, sliced
50g/2oz/⅓ cup corn
300ml/½ pint/1¼ cups water
250ml/8fl oz/1 cup single (light) cream
15ml/1 tbsp chopped fresh coriander (cilantro)
5ml/1 tsp crushed dried red chillies (optional)

1 Cut the chicken pieces into very fine strips.

2 Melt the ghee or butter in a medium pan. Lower the heat slightly and add the garlic and garam masala. Lower the heat even further and add the black peppercorns, salt and nutmeg. Finally, add the chicken pieces, sliced leek, mushrooms and corn, and cook, stirring constantly, for 5–7 minutes, or until the chicken is cooked through.

3 Remove from the heat and leave to cool slightly. Transfer three-quarters of the mixture into a food processor or blender. Add the water and process for about 1 minute.

4 Pour the resulting purée back into the pan and stir with the rest of the mixture. Bring to the boil over a medium heat. Lower the heat and stir in the cream.

5 Add the fresh coriander and taste for seasoning. Serve hot, garnished with the crushed red chillies, if you like.

Energy 444kcal/1860kJ; Fat 22.3g; Saturated fat 17.7g; Carbohydrate 5g; Fibre 0.5g.

Energy 342kcal/1417kJ; Fat 28.5g; Saturated fat 17.6g; Carbohydrate 4.8g; Fibre 1g.

Hot-&-sour Prawn Soup

This is a classic Thai seafood soup – *Tom Yam Kung* – and it is fragrant with lemon grass, coriander and kaffir lime leaves.

Serves 4–6
450g/1lb raw king prawns (jumbo shrimp), thawed if frozen
1 litre/1¾ pints/4 cups chicken stock or water
3 lemon grass stalks, roots trimmed
10 kaffir lime leaves, torn in half
225g/8oz can straw mushrooms, drained
45ml/3 tbsp Thai fish sauce
60ml/4 tbsp fresh lime juice
30ml/2 tbsp chopped spring onion (scallion)
15ml/1 tbsp fresh coriander (cilantro) leaves
4 fresh red chillies, seeded and thinly sliced
salt and ground black pepper

1 Peel the prawns, reserving the shells. Devein the prawns and set aside.

2 Rinse the shells under cold water, then put them in a large pan with the stock or water. Bring to the boil.

3 Bruise the lemon grass stalks and add them to the stock with half the lime leaves. Simmer gently for 5–6 minutes, until the stock is fragrant.

4 Strain the stock, return it to the clean pan and reheat. Add the drained mushrooms and the prawns, then cook until the prawns turn pink.

5 Stir the fish sauce, lime juice, spring onion, coriander, chillies and the remaining lime leaves into the soup. Taste and adjust the seasoning if necessary. The soup should be sour, salty, spicy and hot.

> **Cook's Tip**
> *Removing the vein improves the appearance and taste of the prawn.*

Energy 96kcal/403kJ; Fat 1g; Saturated fat 0.2g; Carbohydrate 0.8g; Fibre 0.7g.

Pumpkin & Coconut Soup

The natural sweetness of the pumpkin is heightened by the addition of a little sugar in this attractive soup, but this is balanced by the chillies, shrimp paste and dried shrimp. Coconut cream blurs the boundaries beautifully.

Serves 4–6
450g/1lb pumpkin, cut into 2cm/¾in chunks
2 garlic cloves, crushed
4 shallots, finely chopped
2.5ml/½ tsp shrimp paste
1 lemon grass stalk, chopped
2 fresh green chillies, seeded
15ml/1 tbsp dried shrimp soaked for 10 minutes in warm water
600ml/1 pint/2½ cups chicken stock
600ml/1 pint/2½ cups coconut cream
30ml/2 tbsp Thai fish sauce
5ml/1 tsp granulated sugar
115g/4oz small cooked prawns (shrimp), peeled
salt and ground black pepper

To garnish
2 fresh red chillies, seeded and thinly sliced
10–12 fresh basil leaves

1 Put the garlic, shallots, shrimp paste, lemon grass, green chillies and salt to taste in a mortar. Drain the dried shrimp, discarding the soaking liquid, and add them, then use a pestle to grind the mixture into a paste. Alternatively, place all the ingredients in a food processor and process to a paste.

2 Bring the chicken stock to the boil in a large pan. Add the ground paste and stir well to dissolve.

3 Add the pumpkin chunks and bring to a simmer. Simmer for 10–15 minutes, or until the pumpkin is tender.

4 Stir in the coconut cream, then bring the soup back to simmering point. Do not let it boil. Add the fish sauce, sugar and ground black pepper to taste.

5 Add the prawns and cook for a further 2–3 minutes, until they are heated through. Serve in warm soup bowls, garnished with chillies and basil leaves.

Energy 79kcal/336kJ; Fat 0.9g; Saturated fat 0.5g; Carbohydrate 12.1g; Fibre 1.3g.

Northern Thai Squash Soup with Banana Flower

As the title of the recipe suggests, this comes from northern Thailand. It is quite hearty, something of a cross between a soup and a stew. Butternut squash has a full flavour that works very well in this dish. The banana flower isn't essential, but it does add a unique and authentic flavour.

Serves 4
1 butternut squash, about 300g/11oz
1 litre/1¾ pints/4 cups vegetable stock
90g/3½oz/scant 1 cup green beans, cut into 2.5cm/1in pieces
45g/1¾oz dried banana flower (optional)
15ml/1 tbsp Thai fish sauce
225g/8oz raw prawns (shrimp)
small bunch fresh basil
cooked rice, to serve

For the chilli paste
115g/4oz shallots, sliced
10 drained bottled green peppercorns
1 small fresh green chilli, seeded and finely chopped
2.5ml/½ tsp shrimp paste

1 Peel the butternut squash and cut it in half. Scoop out the seeds with a teaspoon and discard, then cut the flesh into neat cubes. Set aside.

2 To make the chilli paste, pound the shallots, peppercorns, chilli and shrimp paste together using a mortar and pestle, or purée them in a spice blender.

3 Heat the stock gently in a large pan, then stir in the chilli paste. Add the squash, beans and banana flower, if using. Bring to the boil and cook for 15 minutes.

4 Add the fish sauce, prawns and basil. Bring to simmering point, then simmer for 3 minutes. Serve in warmed bowls, accompanied by rice.

Energy 68kcal/287kJ; Fat 0.7g; Saturated fat 0.2g; Carbohydrate 4.7g; Fibre 1.7g.

Aromatic Galangal, Chicken & Coconut Soup

This beautiful soup is rich with coconut milk and intensely flavoured with galangal, lemon grass and kaffir lime leaves.

Serves 4–6
4 lemon grass stalks, roots trimmed
2 x 400ml/14fl oz cans coconut milk
475ml/16fl oz/2 cups chicken stock
2.5cm/1in piece fresh galangal, peeled and thinly sliced
10 black peppercorns, crushed
10 kaffir lime leaves, torn
300g/11oz skinned chicken breast fillet, cut into thin strips
115g/4oz/1 cup button (white) mushrooms, halved if large
50g/2oz/½ cup baby corn, quartered lengthways
60ml/4 tbsp fresh lime juice
45ml/3 tbsp Thai fish sauce
chopped fresh red chillies, spring onions (scallions) and fresh coriander (cilantro) leaves, to garnish

1 Cut off the lower 5cm/2in from each lemon grass stalk and chop it finely. Bruise the remaining pieces of stalk. Bring the coconut milk and chicken stock to the boil in a large pan over a medium heat.

2 Add the chopped and bruised lemon grass, the sliced galangal, peppercorns and half the kaffir lime leaves. Reduce the heat to low and simmer gently for 10 minutes. Strain the soup into a clean pan.

3 Return the soup to a low heat, then stir in the chicken strips, halved mushrooms and baby corn. Simmer the soup gently, stirring occasionally, for 5–7 minutes, or until the chicken is cooked through.

4 Stir in the lime juice and Thai fish sauce, then add the remaining kaffir lime leaves. Ladle into warm soup bowls and serve, garnished with chopped chillies, spring onions and fresh coriander leaves.

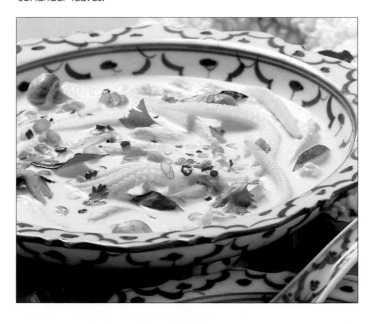

Energy 130kcal/555kJ; Fat 1.6g; Saturated fat 0.7g; Carbohydrate 10.2g; Fibre 0.5g.

Coconut & Seafood Soup

The long list of ingredients could mislead you into thinking that this soup is complicated and very time-consuming to prepare. In fact, it is extremely easy to put together and the flavours work beautifully.

Serves 4
600ml/1 pint/2 ½ cups fish stock
5 thin slices fresh galangal or fresh root ginger
2 lemon grass stalks, chopped
3 kaffir lime leaves, shredded
bunch garlic chives, about 25g/1oz
small bunch fresh coriander (cilantro), about 15g/½oz
15ml/1 tbsp vegetable oil

4 shallots, chopped
400ml/14fl oz can coconut milk
30–45ml/2–3 tbsp Thai fish sauce
45–60ml/3–4 tbsp Thai green curry paste
450g/1lb raw large prawns (shrimp), peeled and deveined
450g/1lb prepared squid
a little fresh lime juice (optional)
salt and ground black pepper
60ml/4 tbsp crisp fried shallot slices, to serve

1 Pour the fish stock into a large pan and add the slices of galangal or ginger, the lemon grass and half the shredded kaffir lime leaves.

2 Reserve a few garlic chives for the garnish, then chop the remainder. Add half the chopped garlic chives to the pan. Strip the coriander leaves from the stalks and set the leaves aside. Add the stalks to the pan. Bring to the boil, reduce the heat to low and cover the pan, then simmer gently for 20 minutes. Strain the stock into a bowl.

3 Rinse and dry the pan. Add the oil and shallots. Cook over a medium heat for 5–10 minutes, until the shallots are just beginning to brown.

4 Stir in the strained stock, coconut milk, the remaining kaffir lime leaves and 30ml/2 tbsp of the fish sauce. Heat gently until simmering and cook over a low heat for 5–10 minutes.

5 Stir in the curry paste and prawns, then cook for 3 minutes. Add the squid and cook for a further 2 minutes. Add the lime juice, if using, and season, adding more fish sauce to taste. Stir in the remaining chives and the reserved coriander leaves. Serve in bowls and sprinkle each portion with fried shallots and whole garlic chives.

Variations
• Instead of squid, you could add 400g/14oz firm white fish, such as monkfish, cut into small pieces.
• You could also replace the squid with mussels. Steam 675g/1½lb live mussels in a tightly covered pan for 3–4 minutes, or until they have opened. Discard any that remain shut, then remove them from their shells and add to the soup.

Chicken & Almond Soup

This soup makes an excellent appetizer and, served with naan bread, will also make a satisfying lunch or supper dish.

Serves 4
75g/3oz/6 tbsp ghee or unsalted (sweet) butter
1 medium leek, chopped
2.5ml/½ tsp shredded fresh root ginger
75g/3oz/¾ cup ground almonds
5ml/1 tsp salt
2.5ml/½ tsp crushed black peppercorns

1 fresh green chilli, chopped
1 medium carrot, sliced
50g/2oz/½ cup frozen peas
115g/4oz/¾ cup chicken breast fillet, cubed and skinned
15ml/1 tbsp chopped fresh coriander (cilantro), plus extra to garnish
450ml/¾ pint/scant 2 cups water
250ml/8fl oz/1 cup single (light) cream

1 Melt the ghee or butter in a large karahi, wok or deep pan, and sauté the leek with the ginger until softened.

2 Lower the heat and add the ground almonds, salt, crushed peppercorns, chopped chilli, sliced carrot, peas and cubed chicken to the pan.

3 Fry for about 10 minutes or until the chicken is completely cooked, stirring constantly. Add the chopped fresh coriander.

4 Remove from the heat and leave to cool slightly. Transfer the mixture to a food processor or blender and process for about 1½ minutes.

5 Pour in the water and blend the mixture for a further 30 seconds until smooth.

6 Pour back into the pan and bring to the boil, stirring. Lower the heat and gradually stir in the cream. Cook gently for a further 2 minutes, stirring occasionally. Serve garnished with more coriander.

Energy 229kcal/967kJ; Fat 5.7g; Saturated fat 1.1g; Carbohydrate 7.4g; Fibre 0.2g.

Energy 429kcal/1777kJ; Fat 39.2g; Saturated fat 18.4g; Carbohydrate 5.5g; Fibre 2.7g.

Thai-style Chicken Soup

A fragrant blend of coconut milk, lemon grass, ginger and lime makes a delicious soup, with just a hint of chilli.

Serves 4
5ml/1 tsp oil
1–2 fresh red chillies, seeded and chopped
2 garlic cloves, crushed
1 large leek, finely sliced
550ml/18fl oz/2½ cups chicken stock
450ml/¾ pint/scant 2 cups coconut milk
450g/1lb skinless, boneless chicken thighs, cut into bitesize pieces
30ml/2 tbsp Thai fish sauce
1 lemon grass stalk, split
2.5cm/1in piece fresh root ginger, peeled and crushed
5ml/1 tsp sugar
4 kaffir lime leaves (optional)
75g/3oz/¾ cup frozen peas, thawed
3 tbsp chopped fresh coriander (cilantro)

1 Heat the oil in a large pan. Add the chillies and garlic and cook for about 2 minutes. Add the leek and cook for 2 minutes longer.

2 Stir in the stock and coconut milk and bring to a boil over medium-high heat.

3 Add the chicken, fish sauce, lemon grass, ginger, sugar and lime leaves, if using. Lower the heat and simmer, covered, for 15 minutes until the chicken is tender, stirring occasionally.

4 Add the peas and cook for 3 minutes longer. Remove the lemon grass and stir in the coriander just before serving.

Cook's Tip
Whenever you have a roast chicken it is worth using the carcass to make stock. Remove all the skin from the remains of the bird and put the carcass into a large pan. Add a roughly chopped onion, carrot and celery stick, and a bouquet garni. Cover with water and bring to the boil. Skim off the scum and then simmer the stock for 1 hour. Strain through muslin (cheesecloth). Skim off the fat when the stock is cold.

Energy 212kcal/894kJ; Fat 4.7g; Saturated fat 1.5g; Carbohydrate 15.7g; Fibre 3.4g.

Beef & Berry Soup

The fresh berries give this soup an unexpected kick and the tender beef makes a filling meal.

Serves 4
30ml/2 tbsp vegetable oil
450g/1lb tender beef steak
2 onions, finely sliced
25g/1oz/2 tbsp butter
1.2 litres/2 pints/5 cups good beef stock or bouillon
2.5ml/½ tsp salt
115g/4oz/1 cup fresh huckleberries, blueberries or blackberries, lightly mashed
about 15ml/1 tbsp honey

1 Heat the oil in a heavy pan until almost smoking. Add the steak and brown on both sides over medium-high heat. Remove the steak from the pan and set aside.

2 Turn the heat to low and add the sliced onions and butter to the pan. Stir well, scraping up the meat juices. Cook over low heat for 8–10 minutes until the onions are soft.

3 Add the beef stock or bouillon and salt, and bring to the boil, stirring well. Stir in the mashed berries and the honey, and simmer for 20 minutes.

4 Meanwhile, cut the steak into thin, bitesize slivers. Taste the soup and add more salt or honey if necessary. Add the steak to the pan. Simmer for 30 seconds, stirring all the time. Serve the soup piping hot.

Cook's Tip
To make beef stock, boil 450g/1lb beef bones in water for 10 minutes, then put them in a roasting pan with 900g/2lb shin of beef and 40g/1½oz butter. Brown in the oven for 40 minutes at 220°C/425°F/Gas 7, turning. Transfer to a pan and add a bouquet garni, a chopped leek, onion, celery stick and 2 carrots. Cover with cold water. Bring to the boil and remove any scum. Simmer for 4 hours. Strain through muslin (cheesecloth). Skim off the fat when the stock is cold.

Energy 344kcal/1432kJ; Fat 21.3g; Saturated fat 8.2g; Carbohydrate 12g; Fibre 2g.

Onion Bhajias

A favourite snack in India, bhajias consist of a savoury vegetable mixture in a crisp and spicy batter. They can be served as an appetizer or as a side dish with curries.

Makes 20–25
2 large onions
225g/8oz/2 cups gram flour
2.5ml/½ tsp chilli powder
5ml/1 tsp ground turmeric
5ml/1 tsp baking powder
1.5ml/¼ tsp asafoetida

2.5ml/½ tsp each nigella, fennel, cumin and onion seeds, coarsely crushed
2 fresh green chillies, finely chopped
50g/2oz/2 cups fresh coriander (cilantro), chopped
vegetable oil, for deep-frying
salt

1 Using a sharp knife, slice the onions into thin rounds. Separate the slices and set them aside on a plate.

2 In a bowl mix together the flour, chilli powder, ground turmeric, baking powder and asafoetida. Add salt to taste. Sift the mixture into a large mixing bowl.

3 Add the coarsely crushed seeds, onion slices, green chillies and fresh coriander and toss together well.

4 Add enough cold water to make a paste, then stir in more water to make a thick batter that coats the onions and spices.

5 Heat enough oil in a karahi or wok for deep-frying. Drop spoonfuls of the mixture into the hot oil and fry the bhajias until they are golden brown. Leave enough space to turn the bhajias. Drain well and serve hot.

> **Variation**
> This versatile batter can be used with other vegetables, including okra, cauliflower and broccoli.

Energy 157kcal/650kJ; Fat 12.7g; Saturated fat 1.5g; Carbohydrate 8.2g; Fibre 0.9g.

Vegetable Samosas

A selection of highly spiced vegetables in a pastry casing makes these samosas a delicious snack at any time of the day.

Makes 28
14 sheets of filo pastry, thawed and wrapped in a damp dish towel
oil, for brushing the pastries

For the filling
3 large potatoes, boiled and roughly mashed
75g/3oz/¾ cup frozen peas, thawed
50g/2oz/⅓ cup canned corn, drained

5ml/1 tsp ground coriander
5ml/1 tsp ground cumin
5ml/1 tsp dry mango powder (amchur)
1 small onion, finely chopped
2 fresh green chillies, finely chopped
30ml/2 tbsp coriander (cilantro) leaves, chopped
30ml/2 tbsp chopped fresh mint leaves
juice of 1 lemon
salt

1 Preheat the oven to 200°C/400°F/Gas 6. Cut each sheet of filo pastry in half lengthways and fold each piece in half lengthways to give 28 thin strips. Lightly brush with oil.

2 Toss all the filling ingredients together in a large mixing bowl until they are well blended. Adjust the seasoning with salt and lemon juice if necessary.

3 Using one strip of the pastry at a time, place 15ml/1 tbsp of the filling mixture at one end and fold the pastry diagonally over. Continue folding to form a triangle shape. Brush the samosas with oil. Bake for 10–15 minutes, until golden brown.

> **Cook's Tip**
> Work with one or two sheets of filo pastry at a time and keep the rest covered with a damp dish towel to prevent it drying out.

Energy 50kcal/205kJ; Fat 0.78g; Saturated fat 0.1g; Carbohydrate 9.4g; Fibre 0.5g.

Spicy Toasts

These crunchy toasts make an ideal snack or part of a brunch. They are especially delicious served with grilled tomatoes.

Makes 4
4 eggs
300ml/¹/₂ pint/1¹/₄ cups milk
2 fresh green chillies, finely chopped
30ml/2 tbsp chopped fresh coriander (cilantro)
75g/3oz/³/₄ cup grated Cheddar or mozzarella cheese
2.5ml/¹/₂ tsp salt
1.5ml/¹/₄ tsp ground black pepper
4 slices bread
corn oil, for frying

1 Break the eggs into a medium bowl and whisk together. Slowly add the milk and whisk again. Add the chillies, coriander, cheese, salt and pepper, and mix well.

2 Cut the bread slices in half diagonally, and soak them, one at a time, in the egg mixture.

3 Heat the oil in a medium frying pan and fry the bread slices over a medium heat, turning them once or twice, until they are golden brown.

4 Drain off any excess oil as you remove the toasts from the pan, and serve immediately.

Variations
• You can also use these ingredients to make a spicy topping for toasted bread. Toast the sliced and halved bread on one side. Mix 115g/4oz cheese with the flavourings and spread on the untoasted side. Grill (broil) until bubbling and golden.
• Try garlic and wholegrain mustard in place of the chillies for toasting.
• Make it a creamy spread for toasting by adding 75g/3oz cubed and steamed butternut squash mashed with the cheese and flavourings.

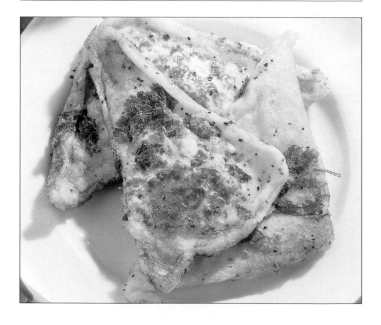

Cauliflower Samosas

Throughout the East, these tasty snacks are sold by street vendors, and eaten at any time of day.

Makes about 20
1 packet 25cm/10in square spring roll wrappers, thawed if frozen
30ml/2 tbsp plain (all-purpose) flour, mixed to a paste with water
vegetable oil, for deep-frying
coriander (cilantro) leaves, to garnish

For the filling
25g/1oz/2 tbsp ghee or unsalted (sweet) butter
1 small onion, finely chopped
1cm/¹/₂in piece fresh root ginger, chopped
1 garlic clove, crushed
2.5ml/¹/₂ tsp chilli powder
1 large potato, about 225g/8oz, cooked and finely diced
50g/2oz/¹/₂ cup cauliflower florets, lightly cooked and chopped into small pieces
50g/2oz/¹/₂ cup frozen peas, thawed
5–10ml/1–2 tsp garam masala
15ml/1 tbsp chopped fresh coriander (leaves and stems)
squeeze of lemon juice
salt

1 Heat the ghee or butter in a wok and fry the onion, ginger and garlic for 5 minutes until softened. Add the chilli powder, cook for 1 minute, then stir in the potato, cauliflower and peas. Sprinkle with garam masala and set aside to cool. Stir in the coriander, lemon juice and salt.

2 Cut the spring roll wrappers into three strips. Brush the edges with flour paste. Place a small spoonful of filling about 2cm/³/₄in in from the edge of one strip. Fold one corner over the filling to make a triangle and continue this folding until the entire strip has been used and a triangular pastry has been formed. Seal any open edges with more flour and water paste, adding more water if the paste is very thick.

3 Heat the oil for deep-frying to 190°C/375°F and fry the samosas until golden and crisp. Drain well on kitchen paper and serve hot garnished with coriander leaves and accompanied by cucumber, carrot and celery matchsticks, if you like.

Energy 105kcal/437kJ; Fat 6.8g; Saturated fat 1.3g; Carbohydrate 10.1g; Fibre 0.6g.

Energy 267kcal/1118kJ; Fat 4.5g; Saturated fat 6.9g; Carbohydrate 17.8g; Fibre 0.9g

Crisp-baked Coconut Chips

Coconut chips are a tasty nibble to serve with drinks. The chips can be sliced ahead of time and frozen on open trays.

Serves 8 as a snack
1 fresh coconut
salt

1 Preheat the oven to 160°C/325°F/Gas 3. First drain the coconut juice, either by piercing one of the coconut eyes with a sharp instrument or by breaking it carefully.

2 Lay the coconut on a board and hit the centre sharply with a hammer. The shell should break cleanly in two.

3 Having opened the coconut, use a broad-bladed knife to ease the flesh away from the hard outer shell. Taste a piece of the flesh just to make sure it is fresh. Peel away the brown skin with a potato peeler, if you like.

4 Slice the coconut flesh into wafer-thin shavings, using a food processor, mandoline or sharp knife. Sprinkle these evenly all over one or two baking sheets and sprinkle with salt. Bake for about 25–30 minutes or until crisp, turning them from time to time. Cool and serve. Any leftover chips can be stored in airtight containers.

Cook's Tips
• Coconuts are available all year round, but before buying always check for freshness. Simply shake the coconut to make sure it has liquid inside. The flesh will then be moist and flavoursome.
• This is the kind of recipe where the slicing blade on a food processor comes into its own. It is worth preparing two or three coconuts at a time, and freezing surplus chips. The chips can be cooked from frozen, but will need to be spread out well on the baking sheets, before being salted. Allow a little longer for frozen chips to cook.

Energy 83kcal/356kJ; Fat 1.1g; Saturated fat 0.8g; Carbohydrate 18.4g; Fibre 0g.

Roasted Coconut Cashew Nuts

Serve these hot and sweet cashew nuts in paper or cellophane cones at parties. Not only do they look enticing and taste terrific, but the cones help to keep clothes and hands clean and can simply be thrown away afterwards.

Serves 6–8
15ml/1 tbsp groundnut (peanut) oil
30ml/2 tbsp clear honey
225g/8oz/2 cups cashew nuts
115g/4oz/1⅓ cups desiccated (dry unsweetened shredded) coconut
2 small fresh red chillies, seeded and finely chopped
salt and ground black pepper

1 Heat the oil in a wok or large frying pan and then stir in the honey. After a few seconds add the nuts and coconut, and stir-fry until both are golden brown.

2 Add the chillies, with salt and pepper to taste. Toss until all the ingredients are well mixed. Serve warm or cooled in paper cones or on saucers.

Cook's Tip
For Deep-fried Cashew Nuts, mix 225g/8oz cashew nuts with 2.5ml/½ tsp paprika, 2.5ml/½ tsp turmeric, 2.5ml/½ tsp salt and 5ml/1 tsp water in a bowl. Leave the nuts to soak in the spices for 1 hour. Heat oil for deep-frying in a large pan or wok and fry the nuts until evenly browned. Remove with a slotted spoon and drain on kitchen paper. Transfer to a serving dish and sprinkle with a little chilli powder.

Variations
Almonds also work well, or choose peanuts for a more economical snack.

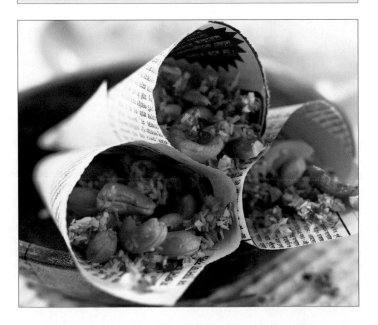

Energy 411kcal/1702kJ; Fat 35g; Saturated fat 14.7g; Carbohydrate 15.2g; Fibre 4g.

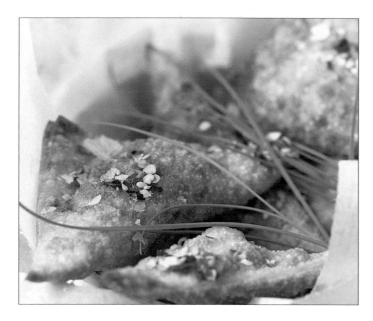

Green Curry Puffs

Shrimp paste and green curry sauce, used judiciously, give these puffs their distinctive, spicy, savoury flavour, and the addition of chilli steps up the heat.

Makes 24

24 small wonton wrappers, about 8cm/3¼in square, thawed if frozen
15ml/1 tbsp cornflour (cornstarch), mixed to a paste with 30ml/2 tbsp water
oil, for deep-frying

For the filling

1 small potato, about 115g/4oz, boiled and mashed
25g/1oz/¼ cup cooked petits pois (baby peas)
25g/1oz/¼ cup cooked corn
few sprigs fresh coriander (cilantro), chopped
1 small fresh red chilli, seeded and finely chopped
½ lemon grass stalk, finely chopped
15ml/1 tbsp soy sauce
5ml/1 tsp shrimp paste or Thai fish sauce
5ml/1 tsp Thai green curry paste

1 Combine the filling ingredients. Lay out one wonton wrapper and place a teaspoon of the filling in the centre. (Wonton wrappers dry out quickly, so keep them covered using clear film (plastic wrap) until you are ready to use them.)

2 Brush a little of the cornflour paste along two sides of the square. Fold the other two sides over to meet them, then press together to make a triangular pastry and seal in the filling. Make more pastries in the same way.

3 Heat the oil in a karahi, wok or deep-fryer to a temperature of 190°C/375°F or until a cube of bread, dropped in the oil, browns in about 45 seconds.

4 Add the pastries to the oil, a few at a time, and fry them for about 5 minutes, until golden brown.

5 Remove the puffs from the fryer or wok and drain on kitchen paper. If you intend to serve the puffs hot, place them in a low oven to keep warm while cooking successive batches. The puffs also taste good cold.

Energy 126kcal/524kJ; Fat 10.1g; Saturated fat 1.2g; Carbohydrate 8.3g; Fibre 0.4g.

Crisp Fried Aubergine

The spicy gram flour coating on these slices is deliciously crisp, revealing the succulent aubergine beneath. Choose a firm aubergine with a glossy skin.

Serves 4

50g/2oz/½ cup gram flour
15ml/1 tbsp semolina or ground rice
2.5ml/½ tsp onion seeds
5ml/1 tsp cumin seeds
2.5ml/½ tsp fennel seeds or aniseeds
2.5–5ml/½–1 tsp hot chilli powder
2.5ml/½ tsp salt, or to taste
1 large aubergine (eggplant)
vegetable oil, for deep-frying

1 Sift the gram flour into a large mixing bowl and add the semolina or ground rice with the onion and cumin seeds, fennel or aniseeds, and the hot chilli powder and salt.

2 Halve the aubergine lengthways and cut each half into 5mm/¼in thick slices. Rinse them and shake off the excess water, but do not pat dry. With some of the water still clinging to the slices, add them to the spiced gram flour mixture. Toss them around until they are evenly coated with the flour. Use a spoon if necessary to ensure that all the flour is used.

3 Heat the oil in a karahi, wok or deep-fryer to a temperature of 190°C/375°F, or until a cube of bread dropped in the oil browns in about 45 seconds. If it floats immediately, the oil has reached the right temperature.

4 Fry the spice-coated aubergine slices in a single layer. Avoid overcrowding the pan as this will lower the oil temperature, resulting in a soggy texture. Fry until the aubergines are crisp and well browned. Drain on kitchen paper and serve with a chutney.

Cook's Tip
Fennel and aniseeds aid digestion, and most deep-fried Indian recipes use them.

Energy 288kcal/1192kJ; Fat 25.4g; Saturated fat 3.1g; Carbohydrate 13.7g; Fibre 1.4g.

Potato Cakes with Stuffing

Only a few communities in India make these unusual potato cakes known as *petis*. They can also be served as a main meal with a fresh tomato salad.

Makes 8–10

15ml/1 tbsp vegetable oil
1 large onion, finely chopped
2 garlic cloves, finely crushed
5cm/2in piece fresh root ginger, finely crushed
5ml/1 tsp ground coriander
5ml/1 tsp ground cumin
2 fresh green chillies, finely chopped
30ml/2 tbsp each chopped fresh coriander (cilantro) and mint

225g/8oz lean minced (ground) beef or lamb
50g/2oz/⅓ cup frozen peas, thawed
juice of 1 lemon
900g/2lb potatoes, boiled and mashed
2 eggs, beaten
dry breadcrumbs, for coating
vegetable oil, for shallow-frying
salt
lemon wedges and salad leaves, to serve

1 Heat the oil and fry the onion, garlic, ginger, coriander, cumin, chillies and fresh coriander until the onion is translucent. Add the meat and peas and fry well until the meat is cooked, then season to taste with salt and lemon juice. The mixture should be very dry.

2 Divide the mashed potato into 8–10 portions, take one portion at a time and flatten into a pancake in the palm of your hand. Place a spoonful of the meat in the centre and gather the sides together to enclose the meat. Flatten it slightly to make a round.

3 Dip the cakes in beaten egg and then coat in breadcrumbs. Set aside to chill in the refrigerator for about 1 hour.

4 Heat the oil in a frying pan and shallow-fry the cakes until brown and crisp all over. Serve them hot with lemon wedges on a bed of salad leaves.

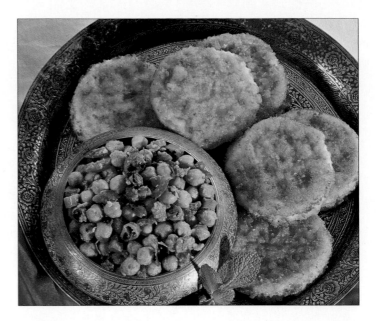

Spiced Potato Cakes with Chickpeas

Fragrant and spicy chickpeas go very well with these fiery potato cakes.

Makes 10–12

30ml/2 tbsp vegetable oil
30ml/2 tbsp ground coriander
30ml/2 tbsp ground cumin
2.5ml/½ tsp ground turmeric
2.5ml/½ tsp salt
2.5ml/½ tsp granulated sugar
30ml/2 tbsp gram flour, mixed with a little water to make a paste
450g/1lb/3 cups cooked chickpeas, drained
2 fresh green chillies, chopped
5cm/2in piece fresh root ginger, crushed

75g/3oz/1½ cups fresh coriander (cilantro), chopped
2 firm tomatoes, chopped
fresh mint sprigs, to garnish

For the potato cakes

450g/1lb potatoes, boiled and mashed
4 fresh green chillies, finely chopped
50g/2oz/2 cups chopped fresh coriander
7.5ml/1½ tsp ground cumin
5ml/1 tsp dry mango powder (amchur)
vegetable oil, for frying
salt

1 Heat the oil in a karahi, wok or large pan. Add the coriander, cumin, turmeric, salt, sugar and gram flour paste and cook until the water has evaporated and the oil has separated.

2 Add the chickpeas to the spices in the pan, and stir in the chopped chillies, ginger, fresh coriander and tomatoes. Toss the ingredients well and simmer gently for about 5 minutes. Transfer to a serving dish and keep warm.

3 To make the potato cakes, place the mashed potato in a large bowl and add the green chillies, chopped fresh coriander, cumin, dry mango powder and salt. Mix together until all the ingredients are well blended.

4 Using your hands, shape the potato mixture into little cakes. Heat the oil in a shallow frying pan and fry the cakes on both sides until golden brown. Transfer to a serving dish, garnish with mint sprigs and serve with the spicy chickpeas.

Energy 260kcal/1086kJ; Fat 15.4g; Saturated fat 3.6g; Carbohydrate 21.3g; Fibre 1.9g.

Energy 91kcal/383kJ; Fat 3.3g; Saturated fat 0.4g; Carbohydrate 11.9g; Fibre 2.2g.

Fish Cakes

Goan fish and shellfish are skilfully prepared with spices to make cakes of all shapes and sizes, whereas the rest of India makes fish kababs. Although haddock is used in this recipe, you can use other less expensive white fish, such as coley or whiting.

Makes 20
450g/1lb skinned haddock or cod
2 potatoes, peeled, boiled and coarsely mashed
4 spring onions (scallions), finely chopped
4 fresh green chillies, finely chopped
5cm/2in piece fresh root ginger, crushed
a few fresh coriander (cilantro) and mint sprigs, chopped
2 eggs
dry breadcrumbs, for coating
vegetable oil, for shallow-frying
salt and ground black pepper
lemon wedges and chilli sauce, to serve

1 Place the skinned fish in a lightly greased steamer and steam gently until cooked. Remove the steamer from the heat but leave the fish on the steaming tray until cool.

2 When the fish is cool, crumble it coarsely into a large bowl, using a fork. Mix in the mashed potatoes.

3 Add the spring onions, chillies, crushed ginger, chopped coriander and mint, and one of the eggs. Mix well and season to taste with salt and pepper.

4 Shape into cakes. Beat the remaining egg and dip the cakes in it, then coat with the breadcrumbs. Heat the oil and fry the cakes until brown on all sides. Serve as an appetizer or side dish, with the lemon wedges and chilli sauce.

Cook's Tip
For a quick version, used canned tuna in brine and omit step 1. Make sure the tuna is thoroughly drained before use.

Fish Cakes with Cucumber Relish

These wonderful small fish cakes are a very familiar and popular appetizer in Thailand and increasingly throughout South-east Asia.

Makes about 12
8 kaffir lime leaves
300g/11oz cod fillet, cut into chunks
30ml/2 tbsp red curry paste
1 egg
30ml/2 tbsp Thai fish sauce
5ml/1 tsp granulated sugar
30ml/2 tbsp cornflour (cornstarch)
15ml/1 tbsp chopped fresh coriander (cilantro)
50g/2oz/1/2 cup green beans, thinly sliced
vegetable oil, for deep-frying

For the cucumber relish
60ml/4 tbsp coconut or rice vinegar
50g/2oz/1/4 cup granulated sugar
60ml/4 tbsp water
1 head pickled garlic
1cm/1/2in piece fresh root ginger, chopped
1 cucumber, cut into thin batons
4 shallots, thinly sliced

1 To make the cucumber relish, mix the coconut or rice vinegar, sugar and water in a pan. Heat gently, stirring constantly until the sugar has dissolved. Remove from the heat and leave to cool.

2 Place the garlic and ginger in a bowl. Add the cucumber and shallots. Mix in the vinegar and stir lightly. Cover and set aside.

3 Reserve 2 or 3 kaffir lime leaves for the garnish and thinly slice the remainder. Put the fish, curry paste and egg in a food processor and process to a smooth paste. Transfer to a bowl and stir in the fish sauce, sugar, cornflour, sliced kaffir lime leaves, coriander and green beans. Shape the mixture into thick cakes.

4 Heat the oil in a deep-frying pan or wok to 190°C/375°F or until a cube of bread, added to the oil, browns in about 45 seconds. Fry the fish cakes, a few at a time, for 4–5 minutes, until cooked and evenly brown.

5 Lift out the fish cakes and drain them on kitchen paper. Keep each batch hot while frying successive batches. Garnish with the reserved kaffir lime leaves and serve with the cucumber relish.

Energy 56kcal/234kJ; Fat 3.3g; Saturated fat 0.5g; Carbohydrate 1.5g; Fibre 0.1g.

Energy 168kcal/696kJ; Fat 13.2g; Saturated fat 1.6g; Carbohydrate 7.4g; Fibre 0.2g.

Spicy Fried Fish Cubes

Firm white fish cubes, coated in a spicy tomato mixture and deep-fried, make an excellent appetizer. They are slightly messy for eating with the fingers, but taste so good that guests will waste no time in popping them into their mouths. Have plenty of paper napkins handy.

Serves 4–6

675g/1½lb cod fillet, or any other firm white fish

1 medium onion
15ml/1 tbsp lemon juice
5ml/1 tsp salt
5ml/1 tsp grated garlic
5ml/1 tsp crushed dried red chillies
7.5ml/1½ tsp garam masala
30ml/2 tbsp chopped fresh coriander (cilantro)
2 medium tomatoes
30ml/2 tbsp cornflour (cornstarch)
150ml/¼ pint/⅔ cup corn oil

1 Skin the fish and remove any remaining bones. Cut it into small cubes. Place in a bowl, cover and put in the refrigerator to chill.

2 Using a sharp knife, cut the onion into thin slices. Put in a bowl and add the lemon juice and salt.

3 Add the garlic, crushed dried red chillies, garam masala and fresh coriander. Mix well.

4 Peel the tomatoes by dropping them into boiling water for a few seconds. Remove with a slotted spoon and gently peel off the skins. Chop the tomatoes roughly and add to the onion mixture in the bowl.

5 Tip the contents of the bowl into a food processor or blender and process for about 30 seconds. Remove the fish from the refrigerator. Pour the contents of the food processor or blender over the fish and mix well.

6 Add the cornflour and mix again until the fish pieces are well coated with the onion mixture.

7 Heat the oil in a wok, karahi or deep pan. Lower the heat slightly and add the fish pieces, a few at a time. Turn them gently with a slotted spoon as they are liable to break easily. Cook for about 5 minutes until the fish is lightly browned.

8 Remove the fish pieces from the pan and drain on kitchen paper. Keep warm and continue frying the remaining fish. This dish is delicious served with Apricot Chutney and Parathas.

Corn Fritters

Sometimes it is the simplest dishes that taste the best. These fritters, packed with crunchy corn, are very easy to prepare and understandably popular.

Makes 12

3 corn cobs, total weight about 250g/9oz
1 garlic clove, crushed
small bunch fresh coriander (cilantro), chopped

1 small fresh red or green chilli, seeded and finely chopped
1 spring onion (scallion), finely chopped
15ml/1 tbsp soy sauce
75g/3oz/¾ cup rice flour or plain (all-purpose) flour
2 eggs, lightly beaten
60ml/4 tbsp water
oil, for shallow frying
salt and ground black pepper
sweet chilli sauce, to serve

1 Using a sharp knife, slice the kernels from the cobs and place them in a large bowl. Add the garlic, chopped coriander, red or green chilli, spring onion, soy sauce, flour, beaten eggs and water, and mix well. Season with salt and pepper to taste and mix again. The mixture should be firm enough to hold its shape, but not stiff.

2 Heat the oil in a large frying pan. Add spoonfuls of the corn mixture, gently spreading each one out with the back of the spoon to make a roundish fritter. Cook for 1–2 minutes on each side.

3 Drain on kitchen paper and keep hot while frying more fritters in the same way. Serve hot with sweet chilli sauce.

Variation

For onion fritters, mix together 115g/4oz gram flour, 1 egg, 75g/3oz/scant ½ cup yogurt, 15ml/1 tbsp lemon juice, 5ml/1 tsp salt, 10ml/2 tsp garam masala, 5ml/1 tsp fenugreek and 2.5ml/½ tsp chilli powder. Add 1 large chopped onion and 15ml/1 tbsp chopped fresh coriander (cilantro). Leave to stand for 10 minutes. Deep-fry until golden.

Cook's Tip

Other suitable white fish includes haddock. You could even use smoked haddock (choose the natural-coloured undyed haddock for the best flavour). Monkfish is also suitable; it is a firm-fleshed fish that tastes similar to shellfish. Ask your fishmonger to remove the bone and fine membrane that covers the fish, or remove it yourself with a sharp knife. Whiting can also be used, but be careful to remove any bones.

Energy 106kcal/443kJ; Fat 7.8g; Saturated fat 1.1g; Carbohydrate 7.4g; Fibre 0.7g.

Energy 434kcal/1809kJ; Fat 26.5g; Saturated fat 3.2g; Carbohydrate 18.2g; Fibre 1g.

Prawn & Vegetable Kebabs

This light and refreshing first course, with its delicate tang of coriander and lemon juice, looks great on a bed of lettuce leaves, and makes a perfect appetizer at a summer barbecue. To upgrade the recipe to a light lunch dish, simple add some naan and follow with a fresh mango sorbet.

Serves 4
30ml/2 tbsp chopped fresh
    coriander (cilantro)
5ml/1 tsp salt
2 fresh green chillies

45ml/3 tbsp lemon juice
30ml/2 tbsp oil
20 cooked king prawns (jumbo
    shrimp), peeled
1 medium courgette (zucchini),
    thickly sliced
1 medium onion, cut into
    8 chunks
8 cherry tomatoes
8 baby corn cobs
mixed salad leaves, to serve

1 Place the chopped coriander, salt, green chillies, lemon juice and oil in a food processor or blender and process for a few seconds to form a paste.

2 Scrape the spice paste from the food processor and transfer it to a medium mixing bowl.

3 Devein the peeled prawns (see Cook's Tip below right), add to the spices and stir to coat well. Cover the bowl and set aside for the prawns to marinate for about 30 minutes.

4 Preheat the grill (broiler) to very hot. Arrange the vegetables and prawns alternately on four skewers.

5 Reduce the temperature of the grill to medium, and grill (broil) the prawn kebabs for 5–7 minutes until cooked and browned, turning once.

6 Serve the prawn and vegetable kebabs immediately on a bed of mixed salad leaves.

Energy 183kcal/767kJ; Fat 7.7g; Saturated fat 1.04g; Carbohydrate 4.5g; Fibre 1.3g.

Glazed Garlic Prawns

It is best to peel the prawns for this dish as it helps them to absorb maximum flavour. Serve with salad as a first course or with rice and accompaniments for a more substantial meal.

Serves 4
15ml/1 tbsp oil
3 garlic cloves, roughly chopped
15–20 cooked king prawns
    (jumbo shrimp)

3 tomatoes, chopped
2.5ml/½ tsp salt
5ml/1 tsp crushed dried
    red chillies
5ml/1 tsp lemon juice
15ml/1 tbsp mango chutney
1 fresh green chilli, chopped
fresh coriander (cilantro) sprigs,
    to garnish

1 Heat the oil in a medium, heavy pan. Add the garlic and cook gently for a few minutes.

2 Set aside 4 whole prawns for the garnish. Peel the remainder and remove the black vein (see Cook's Tip).

3 Lower the heat and add the chopped tomatoes to the pan with the salt, crushed red chillies, lemon juice, mango chutney and fresh green chilli. Stir gently to mix and cook for 2–3 minutes.

4 Add the peeled prawns, increase the heat and stir-fry until heated through. Transfer the prawns to a serving dish.

5 Serve garnished with fresh coriander sprigs. Add a whole cooked prawn, in the shell, to each portion.

Cook's Tip
Larger prawns have a black intestinal vein that runs down the back of the prawn. As this can affect the taste and appearance of the dish it is best to remove it. It is easily picked out using a skewer or the point of a knife.

Energy 73kcal/302kJ; Fat 3.3g; Saturated fat 0.38g; Carbohydrate 4.9g; Fibre 0.8g.

Prawn & Sesame Toasts

These attractive little toast triangles are ideal for serving with pre-dinner drinks and are always a favourite hot snack at parties. They are surprisingly easy to prepare and you can cook them in just a few minutes.

Serves 4
225g/8oz peeled raw prawns (shrimp)
15ml/1 tbsp sherry
15ml/1 tbsp soy sauce
30ml/2 tbsp cornflour (cornstarch)
2 egg whites
4 slices white bread
115g/4oz/½ cup sesame seeds
oil, for deep-frying
sweet chilli sauce, to serve

1 Process the prawns, sherry, soy sauce and cornflour in a food processor.

2 In a grease-free bowl, whisk the egg whites until stiff. Fold them into the prawn and cornflour mixture.

3 Cut each slice of bread into four triangular quarters. Spread out the sesame seeds on a large plate. Spread the prawn paste over one side of each bread triangle, then press the coated sides into the sesame seeds so that they stick and cover the prawn paste.

4 Heat the oil in a karahi, wok or deep-fryer to a temperature of 190°C/375°F, or until a cube of bread dropped in the oil browns in about 45 seconds. Add the coated toasts, a few at a time, prawn side down, and deep-fry for 2–3 minutes, then turn and fry on the other side until golden.

5 Drain on kitchen paper and serve the toasts hot with sweet chilli sauce.

Cook's Tip
If you're catering for a party, process the prawns with the flavourings and cornflour in advance and chill until ready to cook.

Prawn & Spinach Pancakes

Serve these delicious filled pancakes hot. They can be eaten in the hand, but are rather messy, so do provide plenty of paper napkins if you choose the casual approach. Try to use red onions for this recipe if you can, although they are not essential.

Makes 4–6 pancakes
For the pancakes
175g/6oz/1½ cups plain (all-purpose) flour
2.5ml/½ tsp salt
3 eggs
350ml/12fl oz/1½ cups semi-skimmed (low-fat) milk
15g/½oz/1 tbsp low-fat spread

1 tomato, quartered, fresh coriander (cilantro) sprigs and lemon wedges, to garnish

For the filling
30ml/2 tbsp oil
2 medium red onions, sliced
2.5ml/½ tsp crushed garlic
2.5cm/1in piece fresh root ginger, shredded
5ml/1 tsp chilli powder
5ml/1 tsp garam masala
5ml/1 tsp salt
2 tomatoes, sliced
225g/8oz frozen leaf spinach, thawed and drained
115g/4oz/1 cup frozen cooked peeled prawns (shrimp), thawed
30ml/2 tbsp chopped fresh coriander

1 To make the pancakes, sift the flour and salt together. Beat the eggs and add to the flour, beating continuously. Gradually stir in the milk. Leave the batter to stand for 1 hour.

2 Make the filling. Heat the oil in a deep frying pan and fry the sliced onions until golden.

3 Gradually add the crushed garlic, ginger, chilli powder, garam masala and salt, followed by the sliced tomatoes and spinach, stirring constantly.

4 Add the prawns and chopped coriander. Cook for a further 5–7 minutes or until any excess liquid has been absorbed. Keep warm.

5 Heat about 2.5ml/½ tsp of the low-fat spread in a 25cm/10in non-stick frying pan. Pour in about one-quarter of the pancake batter, tilting the pan so that the batter spreads well, coats the bottom of the pan and is evenly distributed.

6 When fine bubbles begin to appear on the surface, flip the pancake over using a spatula and cook for a further minute or so. Transfer to a plate and keep warm. Cook the remaining pancakes in the same way.

7 Fill the pancakes with the spinach and prawns. Serve warm, garnished with the tomato, coriander sprigs and lemon wedges.

Cook's Tip
To keep the pancakes warm while cooking the remainder, pile them on top of each other on a plate with a sheet of baking parchment between them to prevent them sticking. Place in a low oven.

Energy 389kcal/1617kJ; Fat 28.5g; Saturated fat 3.7g; Carbohydrate 13.9g; Fibre 2.7g.

Energy 389kcal/1633kJ; Fat 14.7g; Saturated fat 2.83g; Carbohydrate 48.8g; Fibre 4g.

Prawns with Pomegranate Seeds

This pretty dish makes an impressive appetizer, and is delicious served with a mixed salad. Exotic flavourings of garlic, ginger, pomegranate and coriander make the butterflied prawns extra special.

Serves 4
5ml/1 tsp crushed garlic
5ml/1 tsp grated fresh root ginger
5ml/1 tsp coarsely ground
    pomegranate seeds
5ml/1 tsp ground coriander
5ml/1 tsp salt
5ml/1 tsp chilli powder
30ml/2 tbsp tomato purée
    (paste)
60ml/4 tbsp water
45ml/3 tbsp chopped fresh
    coriander (cilantro)
30ml/2 tbsp corn oil
12 large cooked prawns (shrimp)
1 medium onion, sliced into rings

1 Put the garlic, ginger, pomegranate seeds, ground coriander, salt, chilli powder, tomato purée and water in a bowl. Stir in 30ml/2 tbsp of the chopped coriander. Add the oil and mix well.

2 Peel the prawns, rinse them gently and pat them dry on kitchen paper. Using a sharp knife, make a small slit at the back of each prawn and remove the black vein. Open out each prawn to make a butterfly shape.

3 Add the prawns to the spice mixture, making sure they are all well coated. Leave to marinate for about 2 hours.

4 Meanwhile, cut four squares of foil, about 20 x 20cm/8 x 8in. Preheat the oven to 230°C/450°F/Gas 8. When the prawns are ready, place 3 prawns and a few onion rings on to each square of foil, garnishing each with a little fresh coriander, and fold up into little packets.

5 Bake the prawns for 12–15 minutes. Put the foil packets on individual serving plates and open them up at the table so that the delicious fragrance from the prawns is sealed until the last minute.

Energy 88kcal/364kJ; Fat 5.8g; Saturated fat 0.8g; Carbohydrate 4g; Fibre 0.7g.

Grilled Prawns

Prawns taste delicious when grilled, especially if they are first flavoured with spices.

Serves 4–6
18 large cooked prawns (shrimp)
60ml/4 tbsp lemon juice
5ml/1 tsp salt
5ml/1 tsp chilli powder
5ml/1 tsp crushed garlic
7.5ml/1½ tsp soft light brown
    sugar
45ml/3 tbsp corn oil, plus extra
    for basting
30ml/2 tbsp chopped fresh
    coriander (cilantro)
1 fresh green chilli, sliced
1 tomato, sliced
1 small onion, cut into rings
lemon wedges, to garnish

1 Peel the prawns and rinse them gently under cold water. Pat dry. Make a slit at the back of each prawn and remove the black vein. Open each prawn out into a butterfly shape.

2 Mix the lemon juice with the salt, chilli powder, crushed garlic and light brown sugar in a bowl. Add the corn oil and chopped coriander, and mix well. Stir in the prawns and leave to marinate for 1 hour.

3 Preheat the grill (broiler) to the maximum setting. Place the green chilli, tomato slices and onion rings in a flameproof dish. Add the prawn mixture.

4 Grill (broil) for 10–15 minutes, basting several times with a brush dipped in oil.

5 Serve immediately, garnished with the lemon wedges.

Cook's Tip
Although the recipe requires the prawns to be peeled, always buy prawns with their shells on and peel them yourself, as the flavour will be much better than that of prawns bought ready-peeled.

Energy 122kcal/504kJ; Fat 8.7g; Saturated fat 1.3g; Carbohydrate 1.9g; Fibre 0.4g.

Quick-fried Prawns with Spices

These spicy prawns are stir-fried in moments to make a wonderful appetizer. This is fabulous finger food, so be sure to provide your guests with finger bowls.

Serves 4
450g/1lb large raw prawns (shrimp)
2.5cm/1in fresh root ginger, grated
2 garlic cloves, crushed
5ml/1 tsp hot chilli powder
5ml/1 tsp ground turmeric
10ml/2 tsp black mustard seeds
seeds from 4 green cardamom pods, crushed
50g/2oz/¼ cup ghee or butter
120ml/4fl oz/½ cup coconut milk
salt and ground black pepper
30–45ml/2–3 tbsp chopped fresh coriander (cilantro), to garnish
naan bread, to serve

1 Peel the prawns carefully, leaving the tails attached.

2 Using a small, sharp knife, make a slit along the back of each prawn and remove the dark vein. Rinse under cold running water, drain and pat dry.

3 Put the ginger, garlic, chilli powder, turmeric, mustard seeds and cardamom seeds in a bowl. Add the prawns and toss to coat completely in the spice mixture.

4 Heat a karahi or wok until hot. Add the ghee or butter and swirl it around until foaming.

5 Add the spiced prawns and stir-fry for 1–1½ minutes until they are just turning pink.

6 Stir in the coconut milk and simmer for 3–4 minutes until the prawns are just cooked through. Season to taste with salt and black pepper.

7 Sprinkle with the chopped fresh coriander and serve immediately, with naan bread.

Energy 196kcal/817kJ; Fat 11.5g; Saturated fat 7g; Carbohydrate 2.1g; Fibre 0g.

Goan-style Mussels

Mussels make a marvellous appetizer. Serve them Goan-style, in a fragrant coconut sauce. They take only minutes to cook, and the wonderful aroma will stimulate even the most jaded appetite.

Serves 4
900g/2lb live mussels
115g/4oz creamed coconut (120ml/4fl oz/½ cup coconut cream)
450ml/¾ pint/scant 2 cups boiling water
45ml/3 tbsp oil
1 onion, finely chopped
3 garlic cloves, crushed
2.5cm/1in piece fresh root ginger, peeled and finely chopped
2.5ml/½ tsp ground turmeric
5ml/1 tsp ground cumin
5ml/1 tsp ground coriander
1.5ml/¼ tsp salt
chopped fresh coriander (cilantro), to garnish

1 Scrub the mussels under cold water and pull off any beards that remain attached to the shells. Discard any mussels that are open and which fail to snap shut when tapped.

2 Put the creamed coconut in a measuring jug or cup and pour in the boiling water. Stir with a wooden spoon until all the coconut has dissolved, then set aside until required. Heat the oil in a karahi, wok or heavy pan. Add the onion and fry for 5 minutes, stirring frequently.

3 Add the garlic and ginger and fry for 2 minutes. Stir in the turmeric, cumin, coriander and salt and fry for 2 minutes. Pour in the coconut liquid, stir well and bring to the boil. Reduce the heat and simmer for 5 minutes.

4 Add the mussels, cover the pan and cook over medium heat for 6–8 minutes, by which time all the mussels should have opened. Spoon the mussels on to a serving platter. If any of the mussels have failed to open, discard them immediately.

5 Pour the sauce over the mussels, garnish with the chopped fresh coriander, and serve.

Energy 339kcal/1405kJ; Fat 29.5g; Saturated fat 18.3g; Carbohydrate 5g; Fibre 0.5g.

Spicy Crab with Coconut

This simple appetizer looks pretty and tastes absolutely delicious. Have all the ingredients ready and cook it just before calling your guests to the table. It needs no accompaniment other than some warmed plain naan bread.

Serves 4

40g/1½oz/½ cup desiccated (dry unsweetened shredded) coconut
2 garlic cloves
5cm/2in piece fresh root ginger, grated
2.5ml/½ tsp cumin seeds
1 small cinnamon stick
2.5ml/½ tsp ground turmeric
2 dried red chillies
15ml/1 tbsp coriander seeds
2.5ml/½ tsp poppy seeds
15ml/1 tbsp vegetable oil
1 medium onion, sliced
1 small green (bell) pepper, seeded and cut into strips
16 crab claws
fresh coriander (cilantro) sprigs, to garnish
150ml/¼ pint/⅔ cup natural (plain) low-fat yogurt, to serve

1 Put the desiccated coconut in a food processor and add the garlic, ginger, cumin seeds, cinnamon stick, turmeric, red chillies, coriander and poppy seeds. Process until well blended.

2 Heat the oil in a karahi, wok or heavy pan. Add the onion slices and fry over a medium heat for 2–3 minutes, until softened but not coloured.

3 Stir in the green pepper strips and toss over the heat for 1 minute. Using a slotted spoon, remove the vegetables from the pan and place them in a bowl.

4 Place the pan over a high heat. When it is hot, add the crab claws and stir-fry for 2 minutes. Return the vegetables to the pan with the coconut mixture. Toss over the heat until the mixture is fragrant and the crab claws and vegetables are coated in the spices. Serve on individual plates, garnished with the coriander. Offer the cooling yogurt separately.

Chilli Crabs

The essential ingredients of this delicious crab dish owe more to South-east Asian cuisine than India, and it is not surprising to discover that it comes from the eastern part of the country.

Serves 4

2 cooked crabs, about 675g/1½lb altogether
1cm/½in cube shrimp paste
2 garlic cloves
2 fresh red chillies, seeded, or 5ml/1 tsp chopped chilli from a jar
1cm/½in fresh root ginger, peeled and sliced
60ml/4 tbsp sunflower oil
300ml/½ pint/1¼ cups tomato ketchup
15ml/1 tbsp soft dark brown sugar
150ml/¼ pint/⅔ cup warm water
4 spring onions (scallions), chopped
cucumber chunks and hot toast, to serve (optional)

1 Remove the large claws of one crab and turn it on to its back, with the head facing away from you. Use your thumbs to push the body up from the main shell. Discard the stomach sac and "dead men's fingers", that is, lungs and any green matter. Leave the creamy brown meat in the shell, and cut the shell in half with a cleaver or strong knife. Cut the body section in half and crack the claws with a sharp blow from a hammer or cleaver. Avoid splintering the claws. Repeat with the other crab.

2 Grind the shrimp paste, garlic, chillies and ginger to a paste in a food processor or with a pestle and mortar.

3 Heat a karahi or wok and add the oil. Fry the spice paste, stirring constantly, without browning.

4 Stir in the tomato ketchup, sugar and water and mix the sauce well. When just boiling, add all the crab pieces and toss in the sauce until well coated and hot. Serve in a large bowl, sprinkled with the chopped spring onions. Place in the centre of the table for everyone to help themselves. Accompany this dish with cool cucumber chunks and hot toast for mopping up the sauce, if you like.

Energy 276kcal/1152kJ; Fat 14.3g; Saturated fat 1.7g; Carbohydrate 25.4g; Fibre 0.7g.

Energy 186kcal/777kJ; Fat 10.1g; Saturated fat 5.8g; Carbohydrate 4.8g; Fibre 2.6g.

Crisp-fried Crab Claws

Crab claws are readily available from the freezer cabinet of many Asian stores and supermarkets. Thaw them thoroughly and dry on kitchen paper before coating them.

Serves 4

50g/2oz/⅓ cup rice flour
15ml/1 tbsp cornflour (cornstarch)
2.5ml/½ tsp sugar
1 egg
60ml/4 tbsp cold water
1 lemon grass stalk, root trimmed
2 garlic cloves, finely chopped
15ml/1 tbsp chopped fresh coriander (cilantro)

1–2 fresh red chillies, seeded and finely chopped
5ml/1 tsp Thai fish sauce
vegetable oil, for deep-frying
12 half-shelled crab claws, thawed if frozen
ground black pepper

For the chilli vinegar dip

45ml/3 tbsp granulated sugar
120ml/4fl oz/½ cup water
120ml/4fl oz/½ cup red wine vinegar
15ml/1 tbsp Thai fish sauce
2–4 fresh red chillies, seeded and chopped

1 First make the chilli vinegar dip. Mix the sugar and water in a pan. Heat gently, stirring until the sugar has dissolved, then bring to the boil. Lower the heat and simmer for 5–7 minutes. Stir in the rest of the ingredients, pour into a serving bowl and set aside.

2 Combine the rice flour, cornflour and sugar in a bowl. Beat the egg with the cold water, then stir the egg and water mixture into the flour mixture and beat well until it forms a light batter.

3 Cut off the lower 5cm/2in of the lemon grass stalk and chop it finely. Add the lemon grass to the batter, with the garlic, coriander, red chillies and fish sauce. Stir in pepper to taste.

4 Heat the oil in a deep-fryer or wok to 190°C/375°F or until a cube of bread browns in 45 seconds. Dip the crab claws into the batter, then fry, in batches, until golden. Serve with the dip.

Ginger Chicken Wings

Many people regard chicken wings as the best part of the bird. Served this way, they are certainly delicious, and exactly the right size for an appetizer with drinks, or as a first course.

Serves 4

10–12 chicken wings, skinned
175ml/6fl oz/¾ cup natural (plain) low-fat yogurt
7.5ml/1½ tsp crushed fresh root ginger
5ml/1 tsp salt
5ml/1 tsp Tabasco sauce

15ml/1 tbsp tomato ketchup
5ml/1 tsp crushed garlic
15ml/1 tbsp lemon juice
15ml/1 tbsp fresh coriander (cilantro) leaves
15ml/1 tbsp oil
2 medium onions, sliced
15ml/1 tbsp shredded fresh root ginger

1 Place the chicken wings in a non-metallic bowl. Pour the yogurt into a separate bowl along with the ginger pulp, salt, Tabasco sauce, tomato ketchup, garlic pulp, lemon juice and half the fresh coriander leaves. Whisk everything together, then pour the mixture over the chicken wings and stir gently to coat the chicken completely.

2 Heat the oil in a wok or heavy frying pan and fry the onions until soft.

3 Pour in the chicken wings and cook over a medium heat, stirring occasionally, for 10–15 minutes.

4 Add the remaining coriander and the shredded ginger and serve hot.

Cook's Tip
You can substitute drumsticks or other chicken portions for the wings in this recipe, but remember to increase the cooking time.

Energy 224kcal/933kJ; Fat 12.9g; Saturated fat 1.7g; Carbohydrate 16.9g; Fibre 0.3g.

Energy 224kcal/936kJ; Fat 9g; Saturated fat 2.23g; Carbohydrate 12.64g; Fibre 1.24g.

Chicken Kofta Balti with Paneer

This rather unusual appetizer looks most elegant when served in small individual karahis.

Serves 6

For the koftas
450g/1lb boneless chicken, skinned and cubed
5ml/1 tsp crushed garlic
5ml/1 tsp shredded fresh root ginger
7.5ml/1½ tsp ground coriander
7.5ml/1½ tsp chilli powder
7.5ml/1½ tsp ground fenugreek
1.5ml/¼ tsp ground turmeric
5ml/1 tsp salt
30ml/2 tbsp chopped fresh coriander (cilantro)
2 fresh green chillies, chopped
600ml/1 pint/2½ cups water
corn oil, for frying

For the paneer mixture
1 medium onion, sliced
1 red (bell) pepper, seeded and cut into strips
1 green (bell) pepper, seeded and cut into strips
175g/6oz paneer, cubed
175g/6oz/1½ cups corn
fresh mint sprigs

1 Put all the kofta ingredients, apart from the oil, into a medium pan. Bring to the boil slowly over medium heat, and cook until all the liquid has evaporated. Remove from the heat and leave to cool slightly. Put the mixture into a food processor or blender and process for 2 minutes.

2 Transfer the mixture to a large mixing bowl. Taking a little of the mixture at a time, shape it into small balls, using your hands. You should be able to make about 12 koftas. Heat the corn oil in a karahi, wok or deep pan over a high heat. Reduce the heat slightly and drop the koftas carefully into the oil. Move them around gently to ensure that they cook evenly.

3 When the koftas are lightly browned, remove them from the oil with a slotted spoon and drain on kitchen paper. Set aside.

4 Heat the oil still remaining in the karahi, and flash-fry all the ingredients for the paneer mixture. This should take about 3 minutes over high heat. Divide the paneer mixture evenly between six individual karahis. Add two koftas to each serving, and garnish with mint sprigs.

Chicken Tikka

This extremely popular Indian first course is quick and easy to cook. The dish can also be served as a main course for four.

Serves 6 as an appetizer
450g/1lb boneless chicken, skinned and cubed
5ml/1 tsp crushed fresh root ginger
5ml/1 tsp crushed garlic
5ml/1 tsp chilli powder
1.5ml/¼ tsp ground turmeric
5ml/1 tsp salt
150ml/¼ pint/⅔ cup natural (plain) low-fat yogurt
60ml/4 tbsp lemon juice
15ml/1 tbsp chopped fresh coriander (cilantro)
15ml/1 tbsp oil

For the garnish
mixed salad leaves
1 small onion, cut into rings
lime wedges
fresh coriander (cilantro)

1 In a medium bowl, mix together the chicken pieces, ginger, garlic, chilli powder, turmeric and salt.

2 Stir in the yogurt, lemon juice and fresh coriander and leave to marinate for at least 2 hours.

3 Place in a grill (broiler) pan or in a flameproof dish lined with foil and baste with the oil.

4 Preheat the grill to medium. Grill (broil) the chicken for 15–20 minutes until cooked, turning and basting several times. Serve on a bed of mixed salad leaves, garnished with onion rings, lime wedges and coriander.

Cook's Tip
To make the turning and basting of the chicken easier, thread the chicken pieces on to six soaked wooden skewers before placing under the grill (broiler).

Energy 134kcal/561kJ; Fat 5.5g; Saturated fat 1.49g; Carbohydrate 3.9g; Fibre 0.3g.

Energy 235kcal/984kJ; Fat 10.3g; Saturated fat 2.1g; Carbohydrate 12.3g; Fibre 1.9g.

Pineapple Chicken Kebabs

This chicken dish has a delicate tang and the meat is very tender. The pineapple not only tenderizes the chicken but also gives it a slight sweetness.

Serves 6

225g/8oz can pineapple
  chunks
5ml/1 tsp ground cumin
5ml/1 tsp ground coriander
5ml/1 tsp chilli powder
2.5ml/½ tsp crushed garlic
5ml/1 tsp salt
30ml/2 tbsp natural (plain)
  low-fat yogurt
15ml/1 tbsp chopped fresh
  coriander (cilantro)
few drops of orange food
  colouring, optional
275g/10oz boneless chicken,
  skinned and cubed
½ red (bell) pepper, seeded
½ yellow or green (bell) pepper,
  seeded
1 large onion
6 cherry tomatoes
15ml/1 tbsp oil
salad leaves, to serve

1 Drain the pineapple juice into a bowl. Reserve 8 large chunks of pineapple and squeeze the juice from the remaining chunks into the bowl and set aside. You should have about 120ml/4fl oz/½ cup pineapple juice.

2 In a large bowl, mix together the spices, garlic, salt, yogurt, fresh coriander and food colouring, if using. Mix in the reserved pineapple juice.

3 Add the chicken to the yogurt and spice mixture, cover and leave to marinate in a cool place for about 1–1½ hours.

4 Cut the peppers and onion into bitesize chunks.

5 Preheat the grill (broiler) to medium. Arrange the chicken pieces, vegetables and reserved pineapple chunks alternately on 6 metal skewers.

6 Brush the kebabs lightly with the oil, then place the skewers on a flameproof dish or in a grill pan, turning the chicken pieces and basting with the marinade regularly, for about 15 minutes until cooked through. Serve with salad leaves.

Energy 183kcal/768kJ; Fat 6.6g; Saturated fat 1.47g; Carbohydrate 15.4g; Fibre 1.8g.

Chicken & Pasta Balti

This is not a traditional Balti dish, as pasta is not eaten widely in India or Pakistan, however, it is included here as it is truly delicious! The crushed pomegranate seeds give this dish an unusual tangy flavour.

Serves 4–6

75g/3oz/¾ cup small pasta shells
  (the coloured ones look most
  attractive)
75ml/5 tbsp corn oil
4 curry leaves
4 whole dried red chillies
1 large onion, sliced
5ml/1 tsp garlic pulp
5ml/1 tsp chilli powder
5ml/1 tsp shredded fresh
  root ginger
5ml/1 tsp crushed pomegranate
  seeds
5ml/1 tsp salt
2 medium tomatoes, chopped
175g/6oz chicken, skinned, boned
  and cubed
225g/8oz/1½ cups canned
  chickpeas, drained
115g/4oz/1 cup corn
50g/2oz mangetouts (snow peas),
  diagonally sliced
15ml/1 tbsp chopped fresh
  coriander (cilantro)

1 Cook the pasta in boiling water, following the directions on the pack. Add 15ml/1 tbsp of the oil to the water to prevent the pasta from sticking together. When it is cooked, drain and set to one side in a sieve (strainer).

2 Heat the remaining oil in a deep round frying pan or a large karahi, and add the curry leaves, whole dried chillies and the onion. Fry for about 5 minutes.

3 Add the garlic, chilli powder, ginger, pomegranate seeds, salt and tomatoes. Stir-fry for about 3 minutes.

4 Next add the cubed chicken, chickpeas, corn and mangetouts to the onion mixture. Cook over a medium heat for about 5 minutes, stirring constantly.

5 Add the pasta and stir well. Cook for a further 7–10 minutes, until the chicken is cooked through.

6 Serve garnished with the fresh coriander if you wish.

Energy 350kcal/1468kJ; Fat 17.6g; Saturated fat 2.7g; Carbohydrate 29.5g; Fibre 4.2g.

Stuffed Aubergines with Lamb

Lamb and aubergines go really well together. This dish uses different coloured peppers in the lightly spiced filling mixture.

Serves 4
2 medium aubergines (eggplants)
15ml/1 tbsp oil, plus extra for brushing
1 medium onion, sliced
5ml/1 tsp shredded fresh root ginger
5ml/1 tsp chilli powder
5ml/1 tsp crushed garlic
1.5ml/¼ tsp ground turmeric
5ml/1 tsp salt
5ml/1 tsp ground coriander
1 medium tomato, chopped
350g/12oz lean leg of lamb, minced (ground)
1 medium green (bell) pepper, seeded and roughly chopped
1 medium orange (bell) pepper, seeded and roughly chopped
30ml/2 tbsp chopped fresh coriander (cilantro)
plain rice, to serve

For the garnish
½ onion, sliced
2 cherry tomatoes, quartered
fresh coriander (cilantro)

1 Cut the aubergines in half lengthways, and scoop out and discard most of the flesh. Preheat the oven to 180°C/350°F/Gas 4. Place the aubergine shells cut side up in a lightly greased ovenproof dish.

2 In a medium heavy pan, heat the oil and fry the onion until golden brown. Gradually stir in the ginger, chilli powder, garlic, turmeric, salt and ground coriander. Add the chopped tomato, lower the heat and cook for about 5 minutes, stirring frequently.

3 Add the minced lamb and cook for 7–10 minutes more.

4 Add the chopped peppers and chopped fresh coriander to the lamb mixture and stir well.

5 Spoon the lamb mixture into the aubergine shells and brush the edge of the shells with a little oil. Bake in the oven for 1 hour or until cooked through and browned on top.

6 Serve with the garnish ingredients, on a bed of plain rice.

Energy 238kcal/997kJ; Fat 11.7g; Saturated fat 4.08g; Carbohydrate 12.6g; Fibre 5.9g.

Koftas in a Spicy Sauce

Little meatballs are called koftas in Indian cooking and are usually served in a spicy curry sauce. This curry is popular in most Indian homes.

Serves 4
225g/8oz/1 cup lean minced (ground) lamb
10ml/2 tsp poppy seeds
1 medium onion, chopped
5ml/1 tsp shredded fresh root ginger
5ml/1 tsp crushed garlic
5ml/1 tsp salt
5ml/1 tsp chilli powder
7.5ml/1½ tsp ground coriander
30ml/2 tbsp fresh coriander (cilantro) leaves
1 small egg, beaten

For the sauce
75ml/2fl oz/½ cup natural (plain) low-fat yogurt
30ml/2 tbsp tomato purée (paste)
5ml/1 tsp chilli powder
5ml/1 tsp salt
5ml/1 tsp crushed garlic
5ml/1 tsp crushed fresh root ginger
5ml/1 tsp garam masala
10ml/2 tsp oil
1 cinnamon stick
400ml/14fl oz/1⅔ cups water

1 Place the lamb in a food processor and mince (grind) it further for about 1 minute. Scrape the meat into a bowl, sprinkle the poppy seeds on top and set aside.

2 Place the onion in the food processor with the next 5 ingredients and half the fresh coriander. Grind for about 30 seconds, then add it to the lamb. Add the egg and mix well. Leave to stand for about 1 hour.

3 To make the sauce, whisk together the yogurt, tomato purée, chilli powder, salt, crushed garlic, ginger and garam masala. Heat the oil with the cinnamon stick in a pan for about 1 minute, then pour in the sauce. Lower the heat and cook for 1 minute. Remove from the heat and set aside.

4 Roll small balls of the meat mixture using your hands. Return the sauce to the heat and stir in the water. Drop in the koftas one by one. Add the remaining coriander, cover with a lid and cook for 7–10 minutes, stirring occasionally. Serve hot.

Energy 155kcal/647kJ; Fat 9.24g; Saturated fat 2.79g; Carbohydrate 7.56g; Fibre 1.16g.

Curried Lamb Samosas

Filo pastry is perfect for making samosas. Once you've mastered folding them, you'll be amazed at how quick they are to make. These lamb samosas have a simple filling that is tasty and quick to make – perfect for party fare.

Makes 12
25g/1oz/2 tbsp butter
225g/8oz/1 cup minced (ground) lamb
30ml/2 tbsp mild curry paste
12 sheets of filo pastry, thawed and wrapped in a damp dish towel
salt and ground black pepper

1 Heat a little of the butter in a large pan and add the lamb. Fry for 5–6 minutes, stirring occasionally until browned. Stir in the curry paste and cook for 1–2 minutes. Season and set aside. Preheat the oven to 200°C/400°F/Gas 6.

2 Melt the remaining butter in a pan. Cut the pastry sheets in half lengthways. Brush one strip of pastry with butter, then lay another strip on top and brush with more butter.

3 Place a spoonful of lamb in the corner of the strip and fold over to form a triangle at one end. Keep folding over in the same way to form a triangular shape.

4 Brush with butter and place on a baking sheet. Repeat using the remaining pastry and filling. Bake for 10–15 minutes until golden. Serve hot.

> **Variation**
> *For Cashew Nut Samosas, mix together 225g/8oz cooked and mashed potato, 15ml/1 tbsp chopped cashew nuts, 5ml/1 tsp coconut milk powder, ½ chopped green chilli, 5ml/1 tsp mustard seeds, 5ml/1 tsp cumin seeds, 15ml/ 1 tbsp chopped fresh coriander (cilantro) and 5ml/1 tsp soft light brown sugar. Use to fill the samosas in place of the lamb filling. If you like, the mustard and cumin seeds can be dry-roasted first.*

Energy 81kcal/341kJ; Fat 5.2g; Saturated fat 2.4g; Carbohydrate 4.9g; Fibre 0.2g.

Tandoori Masala Spring Lamb Chops

These spicy, lean and trimmed lamb chops are marinated for three hours and then cooked in the oven using very little oil. They make a tasty appetizer, served with a salad garnish, and would also serve three as a main course if served with rice.

Serves 6 as an appetizer
6 small lean spring lamb chops
30ml/2 tbsp natural (plain) low-fat yogurt
15ml/1 tbsp tomato purée (paste)

10ml/2 tsp ground coriander
5ml/1 tsp crushed fresh root ginger
5ml/1 tsp crushed garlic
5ml/1 tsp chilli powder
a few drops of red food colouring (optional)
5ml/1 tsp salt
15ml/1 tbsp oil, plus extra for basting
45ml/3 tbsp lemon juice

For the salad garnish
lettuce leaves (optional)
lime wedges
1 small onion, sliced
fresh coriander (cilantro)

1 Rinse the chops and pat dry. Trim off all excess fat.

2 In a medium bowl, mix together the yogurt, tomato purée, ground coriander, ginger and garlic, chilli powder, food colouring (if using), salt, oil and lemon juice.

3 Rub this spice mixture over the lamb chops, using your hands, and leave the chops to marinate in a cool place for at least 3 hours.

4 Preheat the oven to 240°C/475°F/Gas 9. Place the marinated chops in an ovenproof dish.

5 Using a brush, baste the chops with about 5ml/1 tsp oil and cook in the oven for 15 minutes. Lower the heat to 180°C/350°F/Gas 4 and cook for a further 10–15 minutes.

6 Check that the chops are cooked and serve immediately on a bed of lettuce leaves, if you like, garnished with lime wedges, sliced onion and fresh coriander.

Energy 117kcal/488kJ; Fat 6.6g; Saturated fat 2.42g; Carbohydrate 3.1g; Fibre 0.3g.

Lamb Kebabs

First introduced by the Muslims, kebabs have now become a favourite Indian dish and are often sold at open stalls; the wonderful aroma of the spicy meat is guaranteed to stop passers-by in their tracks to buy one.

Serves 8

For the kebabs
900g/2lb lean minced (ground) lamb
1 large onion, roughly chopped
5cm/2in piece fresh root ginger, chopped
2 garlic cloves, crushed
1 fresh green chilli, finely chopped
5ml/1 tsp chilli powder
30ml/2 tbsp chopped fresh coriander (cilantro)
5ml/1 tsp garam masala
10ml/2 tsp ground coriander
5ml/1 tsp ground cumin
5ml/1 tsp salt
1 egg
15ml/1 tbsp natural (plain) low-fat yogurt
15ml/1 tbsp oil
mixed salad, to serve

For the raita
250ml/8fl oz/1 cup natural (plain) low-fat yogurt
½ cucumber, finely chopped
30ml/2 tbsp chopped fresh mint
1.5ml/¼ tsp salt

1 Put all the ingredients for the kebabs, except the yogurt and oil, into a food processor or blender and process until the mixture binds together. Spoon into a bowl, cover and leave to marinate for 1 hour.

2 To make the raita, mix together all the ingredients and chill for at least 15 minutes in a refrigerator.

3 Preheat the grill (broiler). Divide the lamb mixture into eight equal portions with lightly floured hands and mould into long sausage shapes. Thread on to skewers and chill.

4 Brush the kebabs lightly with the yogurt and oil and cook under a hot grill for 8–10 minutes, turning occasionally, until brown all over. Serve the kebabs on a bed of mixed salad, accompanied by the raita.

Energy 249kcal/1045kJ; Fat 12.75g; Saturated fat 5.3g; Carbohydrate 7g; Fibre 0.6g.

Shammi Kebabs

These Indian treats are derived from the kebabs of the Middle East. They can be served either as appetizers or side dishes with a raita or chutney.

Serves 5–6
2 onions, finely chopped
250g/9oz lean lamb, boned and cubed
50g/2oz/¼ cup chana dhal or yellow split peas
5ml/1 tsp cumin seeds
5ml/1 tsp garam masala
4–6 fresh green chillies
5cm/2in piece fresh root ginger, grated
175ml/6fl oz/¾ cup water
juice of 1 lemon
a few fresh coriander (cilantro) and mint leaves, chopped, plus extra coriander sprigs to garnish
15ml/1 tbsp gram flour
2 eggs, beaten
vegetable oil, for shallow-frying
salt

1 Put the first seven ingredients and the water into a large pan with salt, and bring to the boil. Simmer, covered, until the meat and dhal are cooked. Remove the lid and continue to cook for a few more minutes, to reduce the excess liquid. Set aside to cool.

2 Transfer the cooled meat mixture to a food processor or blender and process well until the mixture becomes a rough, gritty paste.

3 Put the paste into a large mixing bowl and add the chopped coriander and mint leaves, lemon juice and gram flour. Knead well with your fingers for a good couple of minutes, to ensure that all ingredients are evenly distributed through the mixture, and any excess liquid has been thoroughly absorbed. When the colour appears even throughout, and the mixture has taken on a semi-solid, sticky rather than powdery consistency, the kebabs are ready for shaping into portions.

4 Divide the mixture into 10–12 equal portions and use your hands to roll each into a ball, then flatten slightly. Chill for 1 hour. Dip the kebabs in the beaten egg and shallow-fry each side until golden brown. Pat dry on kitchen paper.

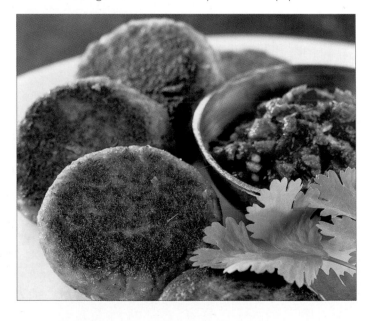

Energy 179kcal/750kJ; Fat 8.5g; Saturated fat 3.4g; Carbohydrate 10.4g; Fibre 1.3g.

Fish with Mango Sauce

This salad is best served during the summer months, preferably out of doors. The dressing combines the flavour of rich mango with hot chilli, ginger and lime.

Serves 4
1 French loaf
4 redfish, black bream or porgy, about 275g/10oz each

15ml/1 tbsp vegetable oil
1 mango
1cm/½in piece fresh root ginger
1 fresh red chilli, seeded and finely chopped
30ml/2 tbsp lime juice
30ml/2 tbsp chopped fresh coriander (cilantro)
175g/6oz young spinach
150g/5oz pak choi (bok choy)
175g/6oz cherry tomatoes, halved

1 Preheat the oven to 180°C/350°F/Gas 4. Cut the French loaf into 20cm/8in lengths. Slice lengthways, then cut the bread into thick fingers.

2 Place the bread on a baking sheet and leave to dry in the oven for 15 minutes.

3 Preheat the grill (broiler) or light the barbecue and allow the embers to settle. Slash the fish deeply on both sides and moisten with oil. Cook the fish on the barbecue for 6 minutes, turning once.

4 Peel the mango and cut in half, discarding the stone (pit). Thinly slice one half and set aside. Place the other half in a food processor or blender.

5 Peel the ginger, grate finely, then add to the mango with the chilli, lime juice and fresh coriander. Process until smooth. Adjust to a pouring consistency with 30–45ml/2–3 tbsp water.

6 Wash the spinach and pak choi leaves and spin dry, then distribute them among four serving plates.

7 Place the fish on the leaves. Spoon on the mango dressing and finish with the reserved slices of mango and the tomato halves. Serve with the fingers of crisp French bread.

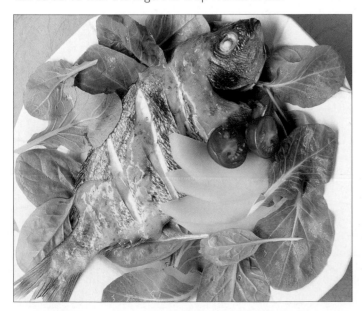

Energy 512kcal/2164kJ; Fat 12.3g; Saturated fat 0.8g; Carbohydrate 50g; Fibre 4.9g.

Braised Whole Fish in Chilli & Garlic Sauce

In India there are an increasing number of unusual dishes that borrow from other cultures. The vinegar in the sauce for this fish dish is typical of Goa, but the rice wine and bean sauce reveal a distinct Sichuan influence.

Serves 4–6
1 carp, bream, sea bass, trout, grouper or grey mullet, about 675g/1½lb, gutted
15ml/1 tbsp light soy sauce
15ml/1 tbsp rice wine or dry sherry
vegetable oil, for deep-frying

For the sauce
2 garlic cloves, finely chopped
2 or 3 spring onions (scallions), finely chopped, the white and green parts separated
5ml/1 tsp finely chopped fresh root ginger
30ml/2 tbsp chilli bean sauce
15ml/1 tbsp tomato purée (paste)
10ml/2 tsp light brown sugar
15ml/1 tbsp rice vinegar
120ml/4fl oz/½ cup chicken stock
15ml/1 tbsp cornflour (cornstarch), mixed to a paste with 10ml/2 tsp water
a few drops of sesame oil

1 Rinse and dry the fish well. Using a sharp knife, score both sides of the fish down to the bone with diagonal cuts about 2.5cm/1in apart. Rub both sides of the fish with the soy sauce and rice wine or sherry. Set aside for 10–15 minutes to marinate.

2 Heat sufficient oil for deep-frying in a wok. When it is hot, carefully add the fish and fry for 3–4 minutes on both sides, until golden brown.

3 To make the sauce pour away all but about 15ml/1 tbsp of the oil. Push the fish to one side of the wok and add the garlic, the white part of the spring onions, the ginger, chilli bean sauce, tomato purée, sugar, vinegar and chicken stock. Bring to the boil and braise the fish in the sauce for 4–5 minutes, turning it over once. Add the green of the spring onions. Stir in the cornflour paste to thicken the sauce. Sprinkle over a little sesame oil and serve immediately.

Energy 292kcal/1222kJ; Fat 16.1g; Saturated fat 2.5g; Carbohydrate 10.7g; Fibre 0.4g.

Sweet-&-sour Fish

When fish is cooked in this way the skin becomes crispy on the outside, while the flesh remains moist and juicy inside. The delicious sweet-and-sour sauce, with its colourful cherry tomatoes, complements the fish beautifully.

Serves 4–6

1 large or 2 medium fish such as snapper or mullet, heads removed
20ml/4 tsp cornflour (cornstarch)
120ml/4fl oz/½ cup vegetable oil
15ml/1 tbsp chopped garlic
15ml/1 tbsp chopped fresh root ginger
30ml/2 tbsp chopped shallots
225g/8oz cherry tomatoes
30ml/2 tbsp red wine vinegar
30ml/2 tbsp granulated sugar
30ml/2 tbsp tomato ketchup
45ml/3 tbsp water
salt and ground black pepper
fresh coriander (cilantro) leaves and shredded spring onions (scallions), to garnish

1 Thoroughly rinse and clean the fish. Score the skin diagonally on both sides of the fish.

2 Coat the fish lightly on both sides with 15ml/3 tsp of the cornflour. Shake off any excess.

3 Heat the oil in a karahi or wok and slide the fish into the pan. Reduce the heat to medium and fry the fish until crisp and brown, about 6–7 minutes on each side.

4 Remove the fish with a spatula and place on a large platter.

5 Pour off all but about 30ml/2 tbsp of the oil and add the garlic, ginger and shallots. Fry until golden.

6 Add the cherry tomatoes and cook until they burst open. Stir in the vinegar, sugar and tomato ketchup. Simmer gently for 1–2 minutes and adjust the seasoning.

7 Mix the remaining 5ml/1 tsp cornflour with the water. Stir into the sauce and heat until it thickens. Pour the sauce over the fish and garnish with coriander leaves and shredded spring onions.

Spicy Grilled Fish Fillets

The good thing about fish is that it can be grilled beautifully without sacrificing any flavour.

Serves 4

4 medium flat-fish fillets, such as plaice, sole or flounder, about 115g/4oz each
5ml/1 tsp crushed garlic
5ml/1 tsp garam masala
5ml/1 tsp chilli powder
1.5ml/¼ tsp ground turmeric
2.5ml/½ tsp salt
15ml/1 tbsp finely chopped fresh coriander (cilantro)
15ml/1 tbsp oil
30ml/2 tbsp lemon juice
tomato wedges, lime slices and grated carrot, to garnish

1 Line a flameproof dish or grill (broiler) pan with foil. Rinse the fish fillets, pat dry and put them in the foil-lined dish or pan.

2 In a bowl, mix the garlic, garam masala, chilli powder, turmeric, salt, coriander, oil and lemon juice.

3 Brush the fish fillets evenly all over with the spice mixture.

4 Preheat the grill to very hot, then lower the heat. Grill (broil) the fish for about 5 minutes, basting with the spice mixture, until it is cooked.

5 Serve immediately with a garnish of tomato wedges, lime slices and grated carrot.

Cook's Tip
Fish can easily be spoiled through over-cooking, so it is essential to grill (broil) it for just the right amount of time. No more than 5 minutes is usually sufficient to cook fillets of flat fish, such as plaice and sole. Test by lifting the flesh carefully with the tip of a knife. It should separate into flakes easily and should have lost that clear, milky appearance of raw fish. There is no need to turn flat fish over, as grilling on one side will be sufficient.

Energy 297kcal/1236kJ; Fat 21.5g; Saturated fat 2.8g; Carbohydrate 6g; Fibre 0.7g.

Energy 152kcal/641kJ; Fat 5.9g; Saturated fat 0.88g; Carbohydrate 3.7g; Fibre 0.7g.

Trout with Tamarind & Chilli Sauce

Sometimes trout can taste rather bland, but this spicy sauce really gives it a zing. If you like your food very spicy, add an extra chilli.

Serves 4
4 trout, cleaned
6 spring onions (scallions), sliced
60ml/4 tbsp soy sauce
15ml/1 tbsp vegetable oil
30ml/2 tbsp chopped fresh coriander (cilantro) and strips of fresh red chilli, to garnish

For the sauce
50g/2oz tamarind pulp
105ml/7 tbsp boiling water
2 shallots, coarsely chopped
1 fresh red chilli, seeded and chopped
1cm/½in piece fresh root ginger, peeled and chopped
5ml/1 tsp soft light brown sugar
45ml/3 tbsp Thai fish sauce

1 Slash the trout diagonally four or five times on each side. Place them in a shallow dish that is large enough to hold them all in a single layer.

2 Fill the cavity of each trout with spring onions and douse each fish with soy sauce. Carefully turn the fish over to coat both sides with the sauce. Sprinkle any remaining spring onions over the top.

3 To make the sauce, put the tamarind pulp in a small bowl and pour on the boiling water. Mash well with a fork until softened.

4 Transfer the tamarind mixture to a food processor or blender, and add the shallots, fresh chilli, ginger, sugar and fish sauce. Process to a coarse pulp. Scrape into a bowl.

5 Heat the oil in a large frying pan or wok and cook the trout, one at a time if necessary, for about 5 minutes on each side, until the skin is crisp and browned and the flesh cooked.

6 Transfer the trout to warmed serving plates and spoon over some of the sauce. Sprinkle with the coriander and chilli and serve with the remaining sauce.

Energy 252kcal/1061kJ; Fat 9.8g; Saturated fat 2g; Carbohydrate 4.7g; Fibre 0.6g.

Steamed Fish with Chilli Sauce

By leaving the fish whole and on the bone, maximum flavour is retained and the flesh remains beautifully moist and succulent.

Serves 4
1 large or 2 medium firm fish such as sea bass or grouper, scaled and cleaned
30ml/2 tbsp rice wine
3 fresh red chillies, seeded and thinly sliced
2 garlic cloves, finely chopped
2cm/¾in piece fresh root ginger, peeled and finely shredded

2 lemon grass stalks, crushed and finely chopped
2 spring onions (scallions), chopped
30ml/2 tbsp Thai fish sauce
juice of 1 lime
1 fresh banana leaf

For the chilli sauce
10 fresh red chillies, seeded and chopped
4 garlic cloves, chopped
60ml/4 tbsp Thai fish sauce
15ml/1 tbsp granulated sugar
75ml/5 tbsp fresh lime juice

1 Thoroughly rinse the fish under cold running water. Pat it dry with kitchen paper. With a sharp knife, slash the skin of the fish a few times on both sides.

2 Mix together the rice wine, chillies, garlic, shredded ginger, lemon grass and spring onions in a non-metallic bowl. Add the fish sauce and lime juice and mix to a paste. Place the fish on the banana leaf and spread the spice paste evenly over it, rubbing it in well where the skin has been slashed.

3 Put a rack or a small upturned plate in the base of a wok. Pour in boiling water to a depth of 5cm/2in. Lift the banana leaf, together with the fish, and place it on the rack or plate. Cover with a lid and steam for 10–15 minutes, or until the fish is cooked.

4 Meanwhile, make the sauce. Place all the ingredients in a food processor and process until smooth. If the mixture seems to be too thick, add a little cold water. Scrape into a serving bowl.

5 Serve the fish hot, on the banana leaf if you like, with the sweet chilli sauce to spoon over the top.

Energy 158kcal/665kJ; Fat 3.4g; Saturated fat 0.6g; Carbohydrate 7.3g; Fibre 1g.

Hot & Fragrant Trout

This wickedly hot spice paste could be used as a marinade for any fish or meat. It also makes a wonderful spicy dip for grilled meat.

Serves 4
2 large fresh green chillies, seeded
    and coarsely chopped
5 shallots, peeled
5 garlic cloves, peeled
30ml/2 tbsp fresh lime juice
30ml/2 tbsp Thai fish sauce
15ml/1 tbsp palm sugar or light
    muscovado (brown) sugar
4 kaffir lime leaves, rolled into
    cylinders and thinly sliced
2 trout or similar firm-fleshed fish,
    about 350g/12oz each, cleaned
fresh garlic chives, to garnish
boiled rice, to serve

1 Wrap the chillies, shallots and garlic in a foil package. Place under a hot grill (broiler) for 10 minutes, until softened.

2 When the package is cool enough to handle, tip the contents into a mortar or food processor and pound with a pestle or process to a paste.

3 Add the lime juice, fish sauce, sugar and lime leaves and mix well. With a teaspoon, stuff this paste inside the fish. Smear a little on the skin too. Grill (broil) the fish for about 5 minutes on each side, until just cooked through. Lift the fish on to a platter, garnish with garlic chives and serve with rice.

Cook's Tip
Farmed rainbow trout is available all year. The better-flavoured wild brown trout, however, is rarely available and more expensive. Salmon trout is also suitable for this dish; as it is a large fish, one will probably be sufficient for four people. For an economical dish, try mackerel. You can use one for each person or buy two larger fish; the larger fish will be easier to stuff.

Marinated Fried Fish with Ginger & Chilli

Fish and shellfish are a strong feature of the cuisine in the coastal region of southern India. Kerala, in the southernmost part of the country, produces some of the finest fish and shellfish dishes. These are flavoured with local spices, grown in the fabulous spice plantations that are the pride and joy of the state.

Serves 4–6
1 small onion, coarsely chopped
4 garlic cloves, crushed
5cm/2in piece fresh root ginger,
    chopped
5ml/1 tsp ground turmeric
10ml/2 tsp chilli powder
4 red mullet or snapper
vegetable oil, for shallow-frying
5ml/1 tsp cumin seeds
3 fresh green chillies, finely sliced
salt
lemon or lime wedges, to serve

1 In a food processor, grind the first five ingredients with salt to a smooth paste.

2 Make several slashes on both sides of the fish and rub them with the paste. Leave to rest for 1 hour. Excess fluid will be released as the salt dissolves, so lightly pat the fish dry with kitchen paper, without removing the paste.

3 Heat the vegetable oil and fry the cumin seeds and sliced chillies for 1 minute.

4 Add the fish, in batches if necessary, and fry on one side. When the first side is sealed, turn them over very gently to ensure they do not break. Fry until golden brown on both sides and fully cooked. Drain and serve hot, with lemon or lime wedges.

Variation
To enhance the flavour, add 15ml/1 tbsp chopped fresh coriander (cilantro) leaves to the spice paste in step 1.

Energy 171kcal/719kJ; Fat 5.3g; Saturated fat 1.2g; Carbohydrate 3.9g; Fibre 0g.

Energy 336kcal/1403kJ; Fat 20.1g; Saturated fat 1.5g; Carbohydrate 1.2g; Fibre 0.2g.

Vinegar Fish

Fish cooked in a spicy mixture that includes chillies, ginger and vinegar is delicious. The method lends itself particularly well to strong-flavoured oily fish, such as the mackerel that are regularly caught off the coast of Goa.

Serves 2–3

2 or 3 mackerel, filleted
2 or 3 fresh red chillies, seeded
4 macadamia nuts or 8 almonds
1 red onion, quartered
2 garlic cloves, crushed
1cm/½in piece fresh root ginger, sliced
5ml/1 tsp ground turmeric
45ml/3 tbsp coconut oil or vegetable oil
45ml/3 tbsp wine vinegar
150ml/¼ pint/⅔ cup water
salt
deep-fried onions and finely chopped fresh chilli, to garnish
rice, to serve (optional)

1 Rinse the mackerel fillets in cold water and dry well on kitchen paper. Set aside.

2 Put the chillies, macadamia nuts or almonds, onion, garlic, ginger, turmeric and 15ml/1 tbsp of the oil in a food processor and process to form a paste. Alternatively, pound them together in a mortar with a pestle.

3 Heat the remaining oil in a karahi, wok or pan. Add the spice and nut paste to the pan and cook for 1–2 minutes without browning. Stir in the wine vinegar and water, and season with salt to taste. Bring the sauce to the boil, then lower the heat.

4 Add the mackerel fillets to the sauce and simmer for 6–8 minutes, or until the fish is tender and cooked.

5 Transfer the mackerel to a warm serving platter. Bring the spicy sauce to the boil and cook for 1 minute, or until it has reduced slightly.

6 Pour the sauce over the fish, garnish with the deep-fried onions and chopped chilli and serve with rice, if you like.

Energy 659kcal/2727kJ; Fat 54.8g; Saturated fat 8.1g; Carbohydrate 7.7g; Fibre 2.9g.

Stuffed Fish

Every community in India prepares stuffed fish but the Parsee version must rank top of the list. The most popular fish in India is the pomfret. These are available from Indian and Chinese grocers or large supermarkets.

Serves 4

2 large pomfrets, or Dover or lemon sole
10ml/2 tsp salt
juice of 1 lemon

For the masala

115g/4oz/1⅓ cups desiccated (dry unsweetened shredded) coconut
115g/4oz/4 cups fresh coriander (cilantro), including the tender stalks
8 fresh green chillies, or to taste
5ml/1 tsp cumin seeds
6 garlic cloves
10ml/2 tsp granulated sugar
10ml/2 tsp lemon juice

1 Scale the fish and cut off the fins. Gut the fish and remove the heads, if you wish. Using a sharp knife, make two diagonal gashes on each side, then pat dry with kitchen paper.

2 Rub the fish inside and out with salt and lemon juice. Cover and leave to stand in a cool place for about 1 hour. Pat dry.

3 For the masala, grind all the ingredients together using a pestle and mortar or food processor. Stuff the fish with most of the masala mixture. Rub the rest into the gashes and all over the fish on both sides.

4 Place each fish on a separate piece of greased foil. Tightly wrap the foil over each fish. Place in a steamer and steam for 20 minutes, or bake in a preheated oven for 30 minutes at 200°C/400°F/Gas 6 or until cooked. Remove the fish from the foil and serve hot.

Cook's Tip
Try this fish steamed in banana leaves, as it is served in India.

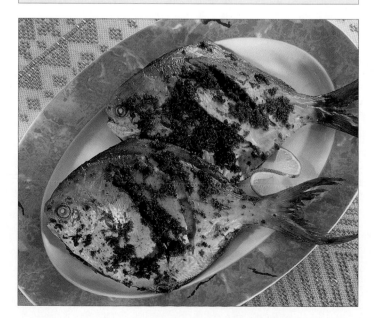

Energy 247kcal/1028kJ; Fat 14.3g; Saturated fat 10g; Carbohydrate 1.2g; Fibre 2.6g.

Pickled Fish Steaks

This dish is served cold, often as an appetizer. It also makes an ideal lunch when served with salad on a hot summer's day. Prepare it a day or two in advance, to allow the flavours to blend.

Serves 4–6
juice of 4 lemons
2.5cm/1in piece fresh root ginger, finely sliced
2 garlic cloves, crushed
2 fresh red chillies, finely chopped
3 fresh green chillies, finely chopped
4 thick, firm fish steaks
60ml/4 tbsp vegetable oil
4–6 curry leaves
1 onion, finely chopped
2.5ml/½ tsp ground turmeric
15ml/1 tbsp ground coriander
150ml/¼ pint/⅔ cup pickling vinegar
15ml/1 tbsp granulated sugar
salt
salad leaves and fresh tomato, to garnish

1 In a bowl, mix the lemon juice with the ginger, garlic and chillies. Pat the fish dry and rub the mixture over all sides of the fish. Cover and marinate for 3–4 hours in the refrigerator.

2 Heat the oil in a frying pan and fry the curry leaves, onion, turmeric and coriander until the onion is translucent.

3 Place the fish steaks and their marinade in the frying pan and spoon the onion mixture over them. Cook for 5 minutes, then turn the fish over gently to avoid damaging the steaks.

4 Pour in the vinegar and add the sugar and salt. Bring to the boil, then lower the heat and simmer until the fish is cooked. Carefully transfer the steaks to a large platter or individual serving dishes and pour over the vinegar mixture. Cool, then chill for 24 hours before serving, garnished with the salad leaves and tomato.

> **Cook's Tip**
> Cod or haddock work particularly well for this dish but you could also try hake, swordfish or even firm and meaty tuna.

Energy 233kcal/968kJ; Fat 12.1g; Saturated fat 1.5g; Carbohydrate 3g; Fibre 0.5g.

Fish & Vegetable Skewers

Threading firm fish cubes and colourful vegetables on skewers scores on several fronts. Not only does the food look good, but it is also easy to cook and serve.

Serves 4
275g/10oz firm white fish fillets, such as cod
45ml/3 tbsp lemon juice
5ml/1 tsp grated fresh root ginger
2 fresh green chillies, chopped
15ml/1 tbsp chopped fresh coriander (cilantro)
15ml/1 tbsp chopped fresh mint
5ml/1 tsp ground coriander
5ml/1 tsp salt
1 red (bell) pepper
1 green (bell) pepper
½ medium cauliflower
8–10 button (white) mushrooms
8 cherry tomatoes
15ml/1 tbsp oil
1 lime, quartered, to garnish (optional)
yellow rice, to serve

1 Cut the fish fillets into large and even-sized chunks.

2 In a large bowl, stir together the lemon juice, ginger, chopped green chillies, fresh coriander, mint, ground coriander and salt.

3 Add the fish chunks, cover and leave to marinate for about 30 minutes.

4 Cut the red and green peppers into large squares and divide the cauliflower into individual florets.

5 Preheat the grill (broiler) to hot. Arrange the peppers, cauliflower florets, button mushrooms and cherry tomatoes alternately with the fish pieces on four skewers.

6 Brush the kebabs with the oil and any remaining marinade. Transfer to a flameproof dish and grill (broil) for 7–10 minutes, turning occasionally, until the fish is cooked right through.

7 Garnish with lime quarters, if you like, and serve the kebabs on a bed of yellow rice.

Energy 131kcal/551kJ; Fat 4.4g; Saturated fat 0.51g; Carbohydrate 7.2g; Fibre 3g.

Green Fish Curry with Coconut

This dish combines all the delicious flavours of the East. A subtle blend of spices and a hint of coconut complement the flavour of the cod perfectly.

Serves 4
1.5ml/¼ tsp ground turmeric
30ml/2 tbsp lime juice
pinch of salt
4 cod fillets, skinned and cut into 5cm/2in chunks
1 onion, chopped
1 fresh green chilli, sliced
1 garlic clove, crushed
25g/1oz/¼ cup cashew nuts
2.5ml/½ tsp fennel seeds

30ml/2 tbsp desiccated (dry unsweetened shredded) coconut
30ml/2 tbsp oil
1.5ml/¼ tsp cumin seeds
1.5ml/¼ tsp ground coriander
1.5ml/¼ tsp ground cumin
1.5ml/¼ tsp salt
150ml/¼ pint/⅔ cup water
175ml/6fl oz/¾ cup natural (plain) low-fat yogurt
45ml/3 tbsp finely chopped fresh coriander (cilantro), plus extra to garnish

1 Mix together the turmeric, lime juice and salt, and rub over the fish. Cover and marinate for 15 minutes.

2 Meanwhile, grind the onion, chilli, garlic, cashew nuts, fennel seeds and coconut to a paste. Spoon the paste into a bowl and set aside.

3 Heat the oil in a large, heavy pan and fry the cumin seeds for 2 minutes or until they begin to splutter. Add the paste and fry for 5 minutes, then stir in the ground coriander, cumin, salt and water and cook for 2–3 minutes.

4 Stir in the yogurt and chopped fresh coriander. Simmer gently for 5 minutes. Gently stir in the fish pieces. Cover and cook gently for 10 minutes until the fish is tender. Garnish with more coriander. This curry is particularly good served with a vegetable pilau.

Cod in a Tomato Sauce

Dusting cod with spices before cooking gives it a delectable coating.

Serves 4
30ml/2 tbsp cornflour (cornstarch)
5ml/1 tsp salt
5ml/1 tsp garlic powder
5ml/1 tsp chilli powder
5ml/1 tsp ground ginger
5ml/1 tsp ground fennel seeds
5ml/1 tsp ground coriander
2 medium cod fillets, each cut into 2 pieces
15ml/1 tbsp oil
mashed potatoes, to serve

For the sauce
30ml/2 tbsp tomato purée (paste)
5ml/1 tsp garam masala
5ml/1 tsp chilli powder
5ml/1 tsp crushed garlic
5ml/1 tsp grated fresh root ginger
2.5ml/½ tsp salt
175ml/6fl oz/¾ cup water
15ml/1 tbsp oil
1 bay leaf
3 or 4 black peppercorns
1cm/½in piece cinnamon stick
15ml/1 tbsp chopped fresh coriander (cilantro)
15ml/1 tbsp chopped fresh mint

1 Mix together the cornflour, salt, garlic powder, chilli powder, ground ginger, ground fennel seeds and ground coriander. Use to coat the four cod pieces.

2 Preheat the grill (broiler) to very hot, then reduce the heat slightly and place the cod under the heat. After about 5 minutes spoon the oil over the cod. Turn the cod over and repeat the process. Cook for a further 5 minutes, check that the fish is cooked through and set aside.

3 Make the sauce by mixing together the tomato purée, garam masala, chilli powder, garlic, ginger, salt and water. Set aside.

4 Heat the oil in a karahi or wok and add the bay leaf, peppercorns and cinnamon. Pour the sauce into the pan and reduce the heat to low. Bring slowly to the boil, stirring occasionally, then simmer for about 5 minutes. Gently slide the pieces of fish into this mixture and cook for a further 2 minutes. Add the chopped fresh coriander and mint and serve the dish with mashed potatoes.

Energy 244kcal/1016kJ; Fat 14.3g; Saturated fat 5.21g; Carbohydrate 5.4g; Fibre 1.7g.

Energy 122kcal/509kJ; Fat 6.65g; Saturated fat 0.89g; Carbohydrate 4.73g; Fibre 0.48g.

Fish Fillets with a Chilli Sauce

For this recipe, the fish fillets are first marinated with fresh coriander and lemon juice, then cooked quickly before being served with a chilli sauce.

Serves 4
4 flat-fish fillets, such as plaice, sole or flounder, about 115g/4oz each
30ml/2 tbsp lemon juice
15ml/1 tbsp finely chopped fresh coriander (cilantro)
15ml/1 tbsp oil

lime wedges and a fresh coriander sprig, to garnish
yellow rice, to serve

For the sauce
5ml/1 tsp grated fresh root ginger
30ml/2 tbsp tomato purée (paste)
5ml/1 tsp granulated sugar
5ml/1 tsp salt
15ml/1 tbsp chilli sauce
15ml/1 tbsp malt vinegar
300ml/½ pint/1¼ cups water

1 Rinse and pat dry the fish fillets and place in a medium bowl. Add the lemon juice, coriander and oil and rub into the fish. Leave to marinate for at least 1 hour.

2 Make the sauce. Mix the grated ginger, tomato purée, sugar, salt and chilli sauce in a bowl. Stir in the vinegar and water.

3 Pour into a small pan and simmer gently over a low heat for about 6 minutes, stirring occasionally.

4 Meanwhile, preheat the grill (broiler) to medium. Lift the fish fillets out of the marinade and place them in a grill pan. Grill (broil) for about 5–7 minutes.

5 When the fish is cooked, arrange it on a warmed serving dish.

6 The chilli sauce should now be fairly thick – about the consistency of a thick chicken soup. Spoon the sauce over the fish fillets, garnish with the lime wedges and coriander sprig and serve immediately with yellow rice.

Cod with a Spicy Mushroom Sauce

Grilling fish before adding it to a sauce helps to prevent it from breaking up during the cooking process.

Serves 4
4 cod fillets
15ml/1 tbsp lemon juice
15ml/1 tbsp oil
1 medium onion, chopped
1 bay leaf
4 black peppercorns, crushed

115g/4oz/1 cup mushrooms
175ml/6fl oz/¾ cup natural (plain) low-fat yogurt
5ml/1 tsp grated fresh root ginger
5ml/1 tsp crushed garlic
2.5ml/½ tsp garam masala
2.5ml/½ tsp chilli powder
5ml/1 tsp salt
15ml/1 tbsp fresh coriander (cilantro) leaves, to garnish
lightly cooked green beans, to serve

1 Preheat the grill (broiler). Remove the skin and any bones from the cod fillets. Sprinkle with lemon juice, then par-cook under the grill for 5 minutes on each side. Remove the fillets from the heat and set aside.

2 Heat the oil in a karahi or wok and fry the chopped onion with the bay leaf and peppercorns for 2–3 minutes. Lower the heat, add the whole mushrooms and stir-fry for a further 4–5 minutes.

3 In a bowl mix together the natural yogurt, crushed ginger and grated garlic, garam masala, chilli powder and salt. Pour this over the onions and stir-fry for 3 minutes.

4 Add the cod fillets to the sauce and cook for a further 2 minutes. Serve garnished with the fresh coriander and accompanied by lightly cooked green beans.

> **Cook's Tip**
> If you can find tiny button (white) mushrooms they look particularly attractive in this fish dish. Alternatively, choose from the many other pretty coloured varieties, such as ceps and oyster mushrooms.

Energy 149kcal/627kJ; Fat 5.4g; Saturated fat 0.81g; Carbohydrate 3.9g; Fibre 0.2g.

Energy 170kcal/715kJ; Fat 4.32g; Saturated fat 0.79g; Carbohydrate 7.67g; Fibre 1g.

Fish Stew with Potatoes & Chilli

Cooking fish with vegetables is a tradition in eastern regions of India. This hearty dish with potatoes, peppers and tomatoes is perfect served with breads such as chapatis or parathas. You can try other combinations, such as green beans and spinach, but you do need a starchy vegetable in order to thicken the sauce.

Serves 4
30ml/2 tbsp vegetable oil
5ml/1 tsp cumin seeds
1 onion, chopped
1 red (bell) pepper,
    thinly sliced
1 garlic clove, crushed
2 fresh red chillies,
    finely chopped
2 bay leaves
2.5ml/½ tsp salt
5ml/1 tsp ground cumin
5ml/1 tsp ground coriander
5ml/1 tsp chilli powder
400g/14oz can chopped
    tomatoes
2 large potatoes, cut into
    2.5cm/1in chunks
300ml/½ pint/1¼ cups
    fish stock
4 cod fillets
chapatis, to serve

1 Heat the oil in a karahi, wok or large pan over a medium heat and fry the cumin seeds for 30–40 seconds until they begin to splutter. Add the chopped onion, red pepper, garlic, chillies and bay leaves, and fry for 5–7 minutes more until the onions have softened and browned.

2 Add the salt, ground cumin, ground coriander and chilli powder to the onion and red pepper mixture. Cook for 1–2 minutes, stirring occasionally.

3 Stir in the tomatoes, potatoes and fish stock. Bring to the boil, then lower the heat and simmer for a further 10 minutes, or until the potatoes are almost tender.

4 Add the fish fillets, then cover the pan and leave to simmer for 5–6 minutes until the fish is just cooked. Serve the fish piping hot, with chapatis.

Energy 251kcal/1053kJ; Fat 7.2g; Saturated fat 0.9g; Carbohydrate 8.4g; Fibre 1.8g.

Fish in a Tomato & Onion Sauce

It is difficult to imagine the cuisine of eastern India without fish. Bengal is as well known for its fish and shellfish dishes as Goa on the west coast. In both regions, coconut is used extensively, and the difference in the taste, as always, lies in the spicing. This onion-rich dish is known as *kalia* in Bengal, and a firm-fleshed fish such as monkfish is essential.

Serves 4
675g/1½lb firm-textured fish
    steaks, such as tuna or
    monkfish, skinned
30ml/2 tbsp lemon juice
5ml/1 tsp salt
5ml/1 tsp ground turmeric
vegetable oil, for shallow-frying
40g/1½oz/⅓ cup plain
    (all-purpose) flour
2.5ml/¼ tsp ground black pepper
60ml/4 tbsp vegetable oil
10ml/2 tsp granulated sugar
1 large onion, finely chopped
15ml/1 tbsp grated fresh
    root ginger
15ml/1 tbsp crushed garlic
5ml/1 tsp ground coriander
2.5–5ml/½–1 tsp hot chilli
    powder
175g/6oz canned chopped
    tomatoes, including the juice
300ml/½ pint/1¼ cups
    warm water
30ml/2 tbsp chopped fresh
    coriander (cilantro) leaves,
    to garnish
plain boiled rice, to serve

1 Cut the fish into 7.5cm/3in pieces and put it in a large bowl. Add the lemon juice and sprinkle with half the salt and half the turmeric. Mix gently with your fingertips, then cover and set aside for 15 minutes.

2 Pour enough oil into a 23cm/9in frying pan to cover the base to a depth of 1cm/½in and heat over a medium setting. Mix the flour and pepper and dust the fish in the seasoned flour. Add to the oil in a single layer and fry until browned on both sides and a light crust has formed. Drain on kitchen paper.

3 In a karahi, wok or large pan, heat 60ml/4 tbsp oil. When the oil is hot, but not smoking, add the sugar and let it caramelize. As soon as the sugar is brown, add the finely chopped onion, ginger and garlic and fry for 7–8 minutes, until just beginning to colour. Stir regularly.

4 Add the ground coriander, chilli powder and the remaining turmeric. Stir-fry for about 30 seconds and add the tomatoes. Cook until the tomatoes are mushy and the oil separates from the spice paste, stirring regularly.

5 Pour the warm water and remaining salt into the pan, and bring to the boil. Carefully add the fried fish, reduce the heat to low and simmer, uncovered, for 5–6 minutes.

6 Transfer to a serving dish and garnish with the coriander leaves. Serve with plain boiled rice.

> **Cook's Tip**
> *Choose fresh rather than frozen fish for the best flavour.*

Energy 435kcal/1811kJ; Fat 30.7g; Saturated fat 3.8g; Carbohydrate 12.5g; Fibre 1.2g.

Tuna Curry

This not-very-authentic fish curry can be made in minutes. It's the ideal dish for a wannabe Bollywood star on a tight schedule.

Serves 4

1 onion
1 red (bell) pepper
1 green (bell) pepper
30ml/2 tbsp oil
1.5ml/¼ tsp cumin seeds
2.5ml/½ tsp ground cumin
2.5ml/½ tsp ground coriander
2.5ml/½ tsp chilli powder
1.5ml/¼ tsp salt
2 garlic cloves, crushed
400g/14oz can tuna in brine, drained and flaked
1 fresh green chilli, finely chopped
2.5cm/1in piece fresh root ginger, grated
1.5ml/¼ tsp garam masala
5ml/1 tsp lemon juice
30ml/2 tbsp chopped fresh coriander (cilantro)
fresh coriander sprig, to garnish
pitta bread and cucumber raita, to serve

1 Thinly slice the onion and the red and green peppers, discarding the seeds from the peppers.

2 Heat the oil in a karahi, wok or heavy pan and stir-fry the cumin seeds for 2–3 minutes until they begin to spit and splutter.

3 Add the ground cumin, coriander, chilli powder and salt and cook for 2–3 minutes. Then add the garlic, onion and peppers.

4 Fry the vegetables, stirring from time to time, for 5–7 minutes until the onion has browned. Stir in the tuna, chopped green chilli and grated ginger and cook for 5 minutes.

5 Add the garam masala, lemon juice and chopped fresh coriander and continue to cook the curry for a further 3–4 minutes.

6 Meanwhile, place the pitta breads on a grill (broiler) rack and grill (broil) until they just puff up. Split with a sharp knife. Serve the curry in the pitta breads with the cucumber raita, garnished with a coriander sprig.

Energy 165kcal/690kJ; Fat 6.8g; Saturated fat 0.97g; Carbohydrate 8.7g; Fibre 1.8g.

Monkfish & Okra Curry

Okra, when cut into short lengths, releases a liquid that helps to thicken this tasty sauce surrounding tender morsels of monkfish.

Serves 4

450g/1lb monkfish
5ml/1 tsp ground turmeric
2.5ml/½ tsp chilli powder
2.5ml/½ tsp salt
5ml/1 tsp cumin seeds
2.5ml/½ tsp fennel seeds
2 dried red chillies
30ml/2 tbsp oil
1 onion, finely chopped
2 garlic cloves, crushed
4 tomatoes, peeled and finely chopped
150ml/¼ pint/⅔ cup water
225g/8oz okra, trimmed and cut into 2.5cm/1in lengths
5ml/1 tsp garam masala
plain rice, to serve

1 Remove the membrane and bones from the monkfish, cut into 2.5cm/1in cubes and place in a dish. Mix together the ground turmeric, chilli powder and 1.5ml/¼ tsp of the salt, and rub the mixture all over the fish. Cover and marinate for 15 minutes.

2 Put the cumin seeds, fennel seeds and chillies in a large, heavy pan and dry-roast the spice mixture for 3–4 minutes. Put the spices into a blender or use a pestle and mortar to grind to a coarse powder.

3 Heat 15ml/1 tbsp of the oil in the frying pan and fry the monkfish cubes for about 4–5 minutes. Remove with a slotted spoon and drain on kitchen paper.

4 Add the remaining oil to the pan and fry the onion and garlic for about 5 minutes. Add the roasted spice powder and the remaining salt and fry for 2–3 minutes. Stir in the tomatoes and water and simmer for 5 minutes.

5 Add the prepared okra and cook for about 5–7 minutes.

6 Return the fish to the pan together with the garam masala. Cover and simmer for 5–6 minutes or until the fish is tender. Serve immediately with plain rice.

Energy 193kcal/805kJ; Fat 8.8g; Saturated fat 1.31g; Carbohydrate 9.4g; Fibre 3.6g.

Stir-fried Monkfish with Vegetables

Monkfish is fabulous stir-fried, as it holds its shape well during cooking. Here it is partnered with tomatoes and courgette in a mildly spiced sauce that complements the sweet flavour of the monkfish perfectly.

Serves 4
30ml/2 tbsp oil
2 medium onions, sliced
5ml/1 tsp crushed garlic
5ml/1 tsp ground cumin
5ml/1 tsp ground coriander
5ml/1 tsp chilli powder
900g/2lb monkfish, filleted and
    cut into cubes
30ml/2 tbsp fresh fenugreek
    leaves
2 tomatoes, seeded and sliced
1 courgette (zucchini), sliced
salt
15ml/1 tbsp lime juice

1 Heat the oil in a karahi, wok or heavy pan and fry the onions over a low heat until soft.

2 Meanwhile mix together the garlic, cumin, coriander and chilli powder. Add this spice mixture to the onions and stir-fry for about 1 minute.

3 Add the fish and continue to stir-fry for 3–5 minutes until the fish is well cooked throughout.

4 Add the fenugreek, tomatoes and courgette, followed by salt to taste, and stir-fry for a further 2 minutes. Sprinkle with lime juice before serving.

Cook's Tip
Monkfish is ideal here as it has firm flesh that does not disintegrate during cooking. It can be quite expensive, but is well worth using for this dish. As it has only one central bone, there are no fiddly bones to worry about. However, the dish would also work with cubed cod or uncooked, peeled prawns (shrimp). Watch the cooking times for both cod and prawns as overcooked cod will disintegrate and overcooked prawns will be tough. The prawns are cooked as soon as they turn pink.

Goan Fish Casserole

The cooking of Goa is a mixture of Portuguese and Indian; the addition of tamarind gives a slightly sour note to the spicy coconut sauce.

Serves 4
7.5ml/1½ tsp ground turmeric
5ml/1 tsp salt
450g/1lb monkfish fillet, cut
    into pieces
15ml/1 tbsp lemon juice
5ml/1 tsp cumin seeds
5ml/1 tsp coriander seeds
5ml/1 tsp black peppercorns
1 garlic clove, chopped
5cm/2in piece fresh root ginger,
    finely chopped
25g/1oz tamarind paste
150ml/¼ pint/⅔ cup hot water
30ml/2 tbsp vegetable oil
2 onions, halved and sliced
    lengthways
400ml/14fl oz/1⅔ cups coconut
    milk
4 mild fresh green chillies,
    seeded and cut into thin
    strips
16 large raw prawns (shrimp),
    peeled
30ml/2 tbsp chopped fresh
    coriander (cilantro) leaves,
    to garnish

1 Mix together the ground turmeric and salt in a small bowl. Place the monkfish in a shallow dish and sprinkle over the lemon juice, then rub the turmeric and salt mixture over the fish fillets to coat them completely. Cover and chill until you are ready to cook them.

2 Put the cumin seeds, coriander seeds and black peppercorns in a blender or small food processor and grind to a powder. Add the chopped garlic and ginger and process together for a few seconds more.

3 Preheat the oven to 200°C/400°F/Gas 6. Mix the tamarind paste with the hot water and set aside.

4 Heat the oil in a frying pan, add the onions and cook for 5–6 minutes, until softened and golden. Transfer the onions to a shallow earthenware dish.

5 Add the monkfish fillets to the oil remaining in the frying pan, and fry briefly over a high heat, turning them to seal on all sides. Remove the monkfish from the pan and place on top of the fried onions.

6 Add the ground spice mixture to the frying pan and cook over a medium heat, stirring constantly, for 1–2 minutes. Stir in the tamarind liquid, coconut milk and chilli strips and bring to the boil.

7 Pour the sauce into the earthenware dish to coat the fish completely.

8 Cover the earthenware dish and cook the fish casserole in the preheated oven for about 10 minutes.

9 Add the prawns, pushing them down so that they are completely immersed in the liquid, then cover the dish again and return it to the oven for 5 minutes, or until the prawns turn pink. Be careful not to overcook them or they will toughen. Check the seasoning and add more salt if necessary, then sprinkle with chopped coriander leaves and serve.

Energy 86kcal/360kJ; Fat 2.38g; Saturated fat 0.35g; Carbohydrate 8.32g; Fibre 1.87g.

Energy 211kcal/889kJ; Fat 6.7g; Saturated fat 1g; Carbohydrate 10.8g; Fibre 1.1g.

Mackerel in Tamarind

Coconut cream makes a heavenly sauce flavoured with ginger, chillies, coriander and turmeric in this delicious dish originating from Western India. Mackerel has a superbly rich flesh and yet it is a surprisingly inexpensive fish.

Serves 6–8

1kg/2¼ lb fresh mackerel
  fillets, skinned
30ml/2 tbsp tamarind pulp,
  soaked in 200ml/7fl oz/
  scant 1 cup water
1 onion
1cm/½in piece fresh root ginger
2 garlic cloves
1 or 2 fresh red chillies, seeded,
  or 5ml/1 tsp chilli powder
5ml/1 tsp ground coriander
5ml/1 tsp ground turmeric
2.5ml/½ tsp ground fennel
  seeds
15ml/1 tbsp dark brown sugar
90–105ml/6–7 tbsp oil
200ml/7fl oz/scant 1 cup
  coconut cream
fresh chilli shreds, to garnish

1 Rinse the fish fillets in cold water and dry them well on kitchen paper. Put into a shallow dish and sprinkle with a little salt. Strain the tamarind and pour the juice over the fish fillets. Leave for 30 minutes.

2 Quarter the onion, peel and slice the ginger and peel the garlic. Grind the onion, ginger, garlic and chillies or chilli powder to a paste in a food processor or with a pestle and mortar. Add the ground coriander, turmeric, fennel seeds and sugar.

3 Heat half the oil in a frying pan. Drain the fish fillets and fry for 5 minutes, or until cooked. Set aside.

4 Wipe out the pan and heat the remaining oil. Fry the spice paste, stirring all the time, until it gives off a spicy aroma. Do not let it brown. Add the coconut cream and simmer gently for a few minutes. Add the fish fillets and gently heat through.

5 Taste for seasoning and serve sprinkled with shredded chilli.

Energy 482kcal/1999kJ; Fat 38g; Saturated fat 6.9g; Carbohydrate 3.6g; Fibre 0.4g.

Fish & Prawns in Herb Sauce

Bengalis are famous for their seafood dishes and like to use mustard oil in recipes because it imparts a unique taste, flavour and aroma. No feast in Bengal is complete without one of these celebrated fish dishes.

Serves 4–6

3 garlic cloves
5cm/2in piece fresh root ginger
1 large leek, roughly chopped
4 fresh green chillies
60ml/4 tbsp mustard oil or
  vegetable oil
15ml/1 tbsp ground coriander
2.5ml/½ tsp fennel seeds
15ml/1 tbsp crushed yellow
  mustard seeds, or 5ml/1 tsp
  mustard powder
175ml/6fl oz/¾ cup thick
  coconut milk
225g/8oz huss or monkfish fillets,
  cut into thick chunks
225g/8oz king prawns (jumbo
  shrimp), peeled and deveined,
  with tails intact
salt
115g/4oz/4 cups fresh coriander
  (cilantro), chopped
2 fresh green chillies, to garnish

1 In a food processor, grind the garlic, ginger, leek and chillies to a coarse paste. Add a little vegetable oil if the mixture is too dry and process the mixture again.

2 In a large frying pan, heat the mustard or vegetable oil with the paste until it is well blended. Keep the window open and take care not to overheat the mixture as any smoke from the mustard oil will sting the eyes.

3 Stir the ground coriander, fennel seeds, mustard and coconut milk into the pan. Gently bring the mixture to the boil and then lower the heat and simmer, uncovered, for about 5 minutes.

4 Add the fish chunks. Simmer for 2 minutes, then fold in the king prawns and cook until the prawns turn a bright orange/pink colour. Season with salt, fold in the chopped fresh coriander and serve immediately, garnished with the fresh green chillies.

Energy 204kcal/852kJ; Fat 12.1g; Saturated fat 1.6g; Carbohydrate 3.7g; Fibre 1.4g.

FISH DISHES

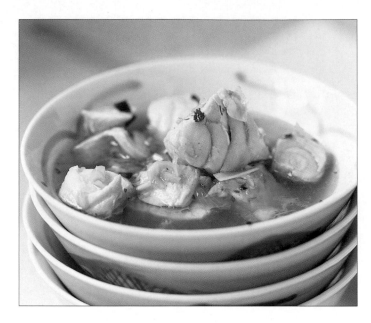

Northern Thai Fish Curry with Shallots & Lemon Grass

This is a thin, soupy curry with wonderfully strong flavours. Serve it with sticky rice to soak up the juices.

Serves 4
450g/1lb salmon fillet
500ml/17fl oz/2¼ cups vegetable stock
4 shallots, finely chopped

2 garlic cloves, finely chopped
2.5cm/1in piece fresh galangal, finely chopped
1 lemon grass stalk, finely chopped
2.5ml/½ tsp dried chilli flakes
15ml/1 tbsp Thai fish sauce
5ml/1 tsp palm sugar or light muscovado (brown) sugar
sticky rice, to serve

1 Place the salmon in the freezer for 30–40 minutes to firm up the flesh slightly. Remove and discard the skin, then use a sharp knife to cut the fish into 2.5cm/1in cubes, removing any stray bones with your fingers or with tweezers as you do so.

2 Pour the stock into a large, heavy pan and bring it to the boil over medium heat. Add the shallots, garlic, galangal, lemon grass, chilli flakes, fish sauce and sugar. Bring back to the boil, stir well, then reduce the heat and simmer gently for 15 minutes.

3 Add the fish, bring back to the boil, then turn off the heat. Leave the curry to stand for 10–15 minutes until the fish is cooked through, then serve with sticky rice.

Cook's Tip
Sticky rice is sometimes called "sweet" or "glutinous" rice. For four people put 400g/14oz/2 cups sticky rice into a large bowl and fill with cold water. Rub the rice with your hands until the water turns cloudy. Strain the rice and wash again in fresh water. Repeat until the water runs clear. Soak the rice in clean water for 3 hours or preferably overnight. Line a steamer basket or a colander with muslin (cheesecloth) and add the drained rice. Steam for 30 minutes until tender.

Energy 225kcal/936kJ; Fat 12.5g; Saturated fat 2.2g; Carbohydrate 5g; Fibre 0.7g.

Salmon Marinated with Thai Spices

The raw fish is marinated for several days in a brine flavoured with Thai spices, which effectively "cooks" it.

Serves 4–6
tail piece of 1 salmon, weighing about 675g/1½lb, cleaned, scaled and filleted
20ml/4 tsp coarse sea salt
20ml/4 tsp granulated sugar
2.5cm/1in piece fresh root ginger, grated
2 lemon grass stalks, coarse outer leaves removed, thinly sliced
4 kaffir lime leaves, finely chopped or shredded

grated rind of 1 lime
1 fresh red chilli, seeded and finely chopped
5ml/1 tsp black peppercorns, coarsely crushed
30ml/2 tbsp chopped fresh coriander (cilantro)
fresh coriander sprigs and quartered kaffir limes, to garnish

For the dressing
150ml/¼ pint/⅔ cup mayonnaise
juice of ½ lime
10ml/2 tsp chopped fresh coriander (cilantro)

1 Remove any remaining bones from the salmon using a pair of tweezers. Put the coarse sea salt, sugar, ginger, lemon grass, lime leaves, lime rind, chopped chilli, crushed black peppercorns and chopped coriander in a bowl and mix together.

2 Place one-quarter of the spice mixture in a shallow dish. Place one salmon fillet, skin down, on top. Spread two-thirds of the remaining mixture over the flesh, then place the remaining fillet on top, flesh side down. Sprinkle the rest of the spice mixture over the fish.

3 Cover with foil, then place a board on top. Add some weights, such as clean cans of fruit. Chill for 2–5 days, turning the fish daily in the spicy brine.

4 Make the dressing by mixing the mayonnaise, lime juice and chopped coriander in a bowl. Scrape the spices off the fish. Slice it as thinly as possible. Garnish with the coriander and kaffir limes, and serve with the lime dressing.

Energy 567kcal/2350kJ; Fat 47.1g; Saturated fat 7.5g; Carbohydrate 1g; Fibre 0.6g.

Fish Moolie

Choose a firm-textured fish for this dish so that the pieces stay intact during the brief cooking process.

Serves 4

500g/1¼lb monkfish or other firm-textured fish fillets, skinned and cut into 2.5cm/1in cubes
2.5ml/½ tsp salt
50g/2oz/⅔ cup desiccated (dry unsweetened shredded) coconut
6 shallots or small onions, roughly chopped
6 blanched almonds
2 or 3 garlic cloves, roughly chopped
2.5cm/1in piece fresh root ginger, peeled and sliced
2 lemon grass stalks, trimmed
10ml/2 tsp ground turmeric
45ml/3 tbsp vegetable oil
2 x 400ml/14fl oz cans coconut milk
1–3 fresh chillies, seeded and sliced
salt and ground black pepper
fresh chives, to garnish
boiled rice, to serve

1 Sprinkle the fish with the salt. Dry-fry the coconut in a wok or large frying pan over medium to low heat, turning all the time until it is crisp and golden. Transfer to a food processor and process to an oily paste. Scrape into a bowl and reserve.

2 Add the shallots or onions, almonds, garlic and ginger to the food processor. Cut off the lower 5cm/2in of the lemon grass stalks, chop them roughly and add to the processor. Process the mixture to a paste. Add the turmeric to the mixture in the processor and process briefly to mix. Bruise the remaining lemon grass and set the stalks aside.

3 Heat the oil in a wok. Add the onion mixture and cook for a few minutes without browning. Stir in the coconut milk and bring to the boil, stirring constantly to prevent curdling. Add the cubes of fish, most of the sliced chilli and the bruised lemon grass stalks. Cook for 3–4 minutes. Stir in the coconut paste and cook for a further 2–3 minutes only. Do not overcook the fish. Taste and adjust the seasoning.

4 Remove the lemon grass. Transfer to a hot serving dish and sprinkle with the remaining slices of chilli. Garnish with chopped and whole chives and serve with boiled rice.

Energy 334kcal/1400kJ; Fat 19.4g; Saturated fat 8.4g; Carbohydrate 18.4g; Fibre 3.5g.

Escabeche

This dish of pickled fish and vegetables is eaten wherever there are – or have been – Spanish settlers.

Serves 6

900g/2lb white fish fillets, such as sole or plaice
45–60ml/3–4 tbsp seasoned flour
vegetable oil, for shallow-frying

For the sauce

2.5cm/1in piece fresh root ginger, peeled and thinly sliced
2–3 garlic cloves, crushed
1 onion, cut into thin rings
30ml/2 tbsp vegetable oil
½ large green (bell) pepper, seeded and cut into small squares
½ large red (bell) pepper, seeded and cut into small squares
1 carrot, cut into matchsticks
25ml/1½ tbsp cornflour (cornstarch)
450ml/¾ pint/scant 2 cups water
45–60ml/3–4 tbsp herb or cider vinegar
15ml/1 tbsp soft light brown sugar
5–10ml/1–2 tsp Thai fish sauce
salt and ground black pepper
1 small chilli, seeded and sliced, and spring onions (scallions), finely shredded, to garnish
boiled rice, to serve

1 Wipe the fish and pat them dry on kitchen paper, then dust them lightly with seasoned flour. Heat the oil in a frying pan and fry the fish in batches until golden and almost cooked. Transfer to an ovenproof dish and keep warm.

2 Make the sauce in a wok or large frying pan. Fry the ginger, garlic and onion in the oil for 5 minutes or until the onion is softened but not browned. Add the pepper squares and carrot strips and stir-fry for 1 minute.

3 Put the cornflour in a small bowl and add a little of the water to make a paste. Stir in the remaining water, the vinegar and the sugar. Pour the cornflour mixture over the vegetables in the wok and stir until the sauce boils and thickens a little. Season with fish sauce and salt and pepper if needed.

4 Add the fish to the sauce and reheat briefly without stirring. Transfer to a warmed serving platter and garnish with chilli and spring onions, if you like. Serve with boiled rice.

Energy 272kcal/1133kJ; Fat 13.9g; Saturated fat 1.7g; Carbohydrate 15.6g; Fibre 1.4g.

Prawns with Chayote in Turmeric Sauce

This delicious, attractively coloured dish contains the squash chayote, but courgette also works well.

Serves 4
1 or 2 chayotes or 2 or 3
  courgettes (zucchini)
2 fresh red chillies, seeded
1 onion, quartered
5ml/1 tsp grated fresh root ginger
1 lemon grass stalk, lower
  5cm/2in sliced, top bruised

2.5cm/1in fresh turmeric, peeled
200ml/7fl oz/scant 1 cup water
lemon juice
400ml/14fl oz can coconut milk
450g/1lb cooked, peeled prawns
  (shrimp)
salt
fresh red chilli shreds, to garnish
boiled rice, to serve

1 Peel the chayotes, remove the seeds and cut into strips. If using courgettes, cut into 5cm/2in strips.

2 Grind the fresh red chillies, onion, ginger, sliced lemon grass and the fresh turmeric to a paste in a food processor or with a pestle and mortar. Add the water to the paste mixture, with a squeeze of lemon juice and salt to taste.

3 Pour into a pan. Add the top of the lemon grass stem. Bring to the boil and cook for 1–2 minutes. Add the chayote or courgette pieces and cook for 2 minutes. Stir in the coconut milk. Taste and adjust the seasoning.

4 Stir in the prawns and cook gently for 2–3 minutes. Remove the lemon grass stalk. Garnish with shreds of chilli and serve with rice.

Cook's Tip
The chayote is a small, green pear-shaped squash, whose mild taste is rather like a cross between a cucumber and an apple.

Pineapple Curry with Prawns & Mussels

The delicate sweet-and-sour flavour of this curry comes from the pineapple and although it seems an odd combination, it is rather delicious. Use the freshest shellfish that you can find.

Serves 4–6
600ml/1 pint/2½ cups coconut
  milk
30ml/2 tbsp curry paste
15ml/1 tbsp granulated sugar

225g/8oz king prawns (jumbo
  shrimp), peeled and deveined
450g/1lb mussels, cleaned
  (see Cook's Tip)
175g/6oz fresh pineapple, finely
  crushed or chopped
2 bay leaves
2 fresh red chillies, chopped,
  and coriander (cilantro) leaves,
  to garnish

1 In a large pan, bring half the coconut milk to the boil and heat, stirring, until it separates.

2 Add the curry paste and cook until fragrant. Add the sugar and continue to cook for 1 minute.

3 Stir in the remainder of the coconut milk and bring back to the boil. Add the king prawns, mussels, chopped pineapple and bay leaves.

4 Reheat until boiling and then simmer for 3–5 minutes, until the prawns are cooked and the mussels have opened. Remove any mussels that have not opened and throw them away. Discard the bay leaves if you like. Serve the curry garnished with chopped red chillies and coriander leaves.

Cook's Tip
To clean mussels, scrub the shells with a stiff brush and rinse them under cold running water. Scrape off any barnacles and remove the "beards" with a small knife. Rinse well.

Curried Prawns in Coconut Milk

This is a curry-like dish where the prawns are cooked in a spicy coconut gravy. It is a simple but flavoursome dish that is quick to prepare.

Serves 4–6
600ml/1 pint/2½ cups coconut milk
30ml/2 tbsp yellow curry paste
2.5ml/½ tsp salt
5ml/1 tsp granulated sugar
450g/1lb king prawns (jumbo shrimp), peeled, tails left intact, deveined
225g/8oz cherry tomatoes
juice of ½ lime, to serve
red chilli strips and coriander (cilantro) leaves, to garnish

1 Put half the coconut milk into a pan or wok and bring to the boil.

2 Add the curry paste to the coconut milk, stir until it disperses, then simmer for about 10 minutes.

3 Add the salt, sugar and remaining coconut milk. Simmer for another 5 minutes.

4 Add the prawns and cherry tomatoes. Simmer very gently for about 5 minutes until the prawns are pink and tender.

5 Serve sprinkled with lime juice and garnished with chillies and fresh coriander.

Cook's Tip
Curry paste is a useful standby, but if you prefer a more authentic flavour you can make your own curry powder and mix 30ml/2 tbsp of it with a little water to form a paste. Dry roast 75g/3oz/1 cup coriander seeds, 15ml/1 tbsp cumin seeds, 8 dried red chillies, 12 cardamom pods and 12 cloves gently for 10 minutes. Cool and add 5ml/1 tsp turmeric and 15ml/ 1 tbsp ground cinnamon. Grind to a fine powder and store in an airtight jar.

Prawns with Okra

This dish has a sweet taste with a strong chilli flavour. It should be cooked fast to prevent the okra from breaking up and releasing its distinctive, sticky juice.

Serves 4–6
4–6 tbsp oil
225g/8oz okra, washed, dried and left whole
4 cloves garlic, crushed
1 piece fresh ginger, 5cm/2in long, crushed
4–6 fresh green chillies, cut diagonally
2.5ml/½ tsp turmeric
4–6 curry leaves
5ml/1 tsp cumin seeds
450g/1lb fresh king prawns (jumbo shrimp), peeled and deveined
10ml/2 tsp brown sugar
juice of 2 lemons
salt

1 Heat the oil in a frying pan and fry the okra over a fairly high heat until they are slightly crisp and browned on all sides. Remove from the oil and put to one side on a piece of kitchen paper.

2 In the same oil, gently fry the garlic, ginger, chillies, turmeric, curry leaves and cumin seeds for 2–3 minutes. Add the prawns and mix well. Cook until the prawns are tender.

3 Add the salt, sugar, lemon juice and fried okra. Increase the heat and quickly fry for a further 5 minutes, stirring gently to prevent the okra from breaking. Adjust the seasoning, if necessary. Serve hot.

Cook's Tip
Okra, sometimes known as "lady's fingers" is a small, long seed pod that exudes a sticky liquid when the pod is cut. This liquid is useful for dishes that require a thick sauce, but for other dishes, such as this one, the pod must be left whole. Remove the stalk using a sharp knife but do not cut into the pod itself.

Energy 129kcal/547kJ; Fat 1.4g; Saturated fat 0.5g; Carbohydrate 9g; Fibre 0.6g.

Energy 215kcal/895kJ; Fat 12.3g; Saturated fat 1.6g; Carbohydrate 4.6g; Fibre 2.5g.

King Prawns with Onions & Fenugreek Leaves

An excellent partner for this mildly spiced prawn dish would be basmati rice with vegetables.

Serves 4
3 medium onions
15ml/1 tbsp oil
6–8 curry leaves
1.5ml/¼ tsp onion seeds
1 fresh green chilli, seeded
   and diced
1 fresh red chilli, seeded
   and diced

12–16 frozen cooked king
   prawns (jumbo shrimp),
   thawed and peeled
5ml/1 tsp shredded fresh
   root ginger
5ml/1 tsp salt
15ml/1 tbsp fresh fenugreek
   leaves

1 Cut the onions into thin slices, using a sharp knife.

2 Heat the oil in a karahi, wok or heavy pan and gently fry the sliced onions with the curry leaves and onion seeds for about 3 minutes.

3 Add the diced green and red chillies, followed by the prawns. Cook for about 5–7 minutes before adding the shredded root ginger and salt.

4 Finally, add the fenugreek leaves, cover and cook for a further 2–3 minutes before serving.

> **Cook's Tip**
> Small prawns (shrimp) will also work well in this recipe and are less expensive than king prawns. Buy unpeeled ones for the better flavour, but for a quicker meal use cooked, peeled prawns and just toss them in for long enough to warm them through. Allow 115g/4oz prawns per person.

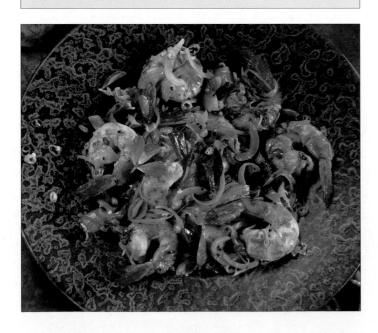

Energy 97kcal/403kJ; Fat 3.29g; Saturated fat 0.45g; Carbohydrate 9.39g; Fibre 1.58g.

Prawns with Green Vegetables

Mangetouts are superb crisply stir-fried with prawns in this fresh-tasting dish.

Serves 4–6
450g/1lb raw prawns (shrimp),
   peeled and deveined
½ egg white
15ml/1 tbsp cornflour
   (cornstarch), mixed to a paste
   with 10ml/2 tsp water
about 600ml/1 pint/2½ cups
   vegetable oil

175g/6oz mangetouts (snow
   peas), trimmed
5ml/1 tsp light brown sugar
15ml/1 tbsp finely chopped spring
   onion (scallion)
5ml/1 tsp finely chopped fresh
   root ginger
15ml/1 tbsp light soy sauce
15ml/1 tbsp Chinese rice wine
   or dry sherry
5ml/1 tsp chilli bean sauce
15ml/1 tbsp tomato purée
   (paste)
salt

1 Place the prawns in a bowl and mix with the egg white, cornflour paste and a pinch of salt. Heat 30–45ml/2–3 tbsp of the oil in a preheated wok and stir-fry the mangetouts for about 1 minute.

2 Add the sugar and a little salt and continue stirring for 1 more minute. Remove and place in the centre of a warmed serving platter.

3 Add the remaining oil to the wok and cook the prawns for 1 minute. Remove and drain.

4 Pour off all but about 15ml/1 tbsp of the oil. Add the spring onion and ginger to the wok.

5 Return the prawns to the wok and stir-fry for 1 minute, then add the soy sauce and rice wine or dry sherry. Blend the mixture thoroughly. Transfer half the prawns to one end of the serving platter.

6 Add the chilli bean sauce and tomato purée to the remaining prawns in the wok, blend well and place the "red" prawns at the other end of the platter. Serve.

Energy 551kcal/2275kJ; Fat 50.7g; Saturated fat 6.1g; Carbohydrate 1.8g; Fibre 1g.

Stir-fried Chilli-garlic Prawns

Prawns have a particular affinity with garlic. To enhance the flavour of the garlic, fry it very gently without letting it brown completely. The spice-coated prawns make a mouthwatering appetizer or light lunch, when served with a salad, or they can be transformed into a main meal with the addition of warm naan bread.

Serves 4
16–20 peeled, cooked king
    prawns (jumbo shrimp)
1 fresh green chilli
15ml/1 tbsp vegetable oil
3 garlic cloves, roughly halved
3 tomatoes, chopped
2.5ml/½ tsp salt
5ml/1 tsp crushed dried red chillies
5ml/1 tsp lemon juice
Mango Chutney, to taste
fresh coriander (cilantro) sprigs
    and chopped spring onions
    (scallions), to garnish

1 Devein the prawns by making a shallow cut down the centre of the curved back of the prawn. Pull out the black vein with a cocktail stick (toothpick) or your fingers, then rinse the prawn thoroughly. Set aside.

2 Slice through the fresh green chilli and scrape out the seeds. Wash your hands thoroughly afterwards as the juice can sting open cuts or your eyes if you rub them. Chop the chilli and set aside.

3 In a wok, karahi or large pan, heat the vegetable oil over a low heat and fry the garlic halves gently until they are tinged with golden brown.

4 Add the chopped tomatoes, salt, crushed red chillies, lemon juice, Mango Chutney and the chopped fresh chilli. Stir the ingredients well.

5 Add the prawns to the pan, then increase the heat and stir-fry briskly, mixing the prawns with the other ingredients until they are thoroughly heated through. Transfer the prawns in the sauce to a warm serving dish and garnish with fresh coriander sprigs and chopped spring onions. Serve immediately.

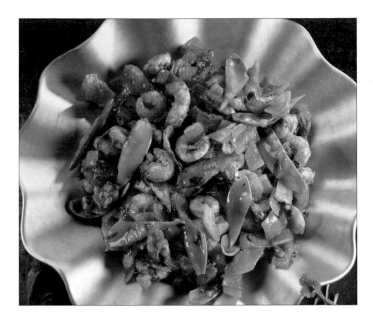

Prawn & Mangetout Stir-fry

Nothing beats a stir-fry for a quick and tasty midweek meal, especially when it's spiced up with ginger, garlic and Tabasco. If you keep some prawns in the freezer most of this dish can be made with store-cupboard ingredients.

Serves 4
15ml/1 tbsp oil
2 medium onions, diced
15ml/1 tbsp tomato purée
    (paste)
5ml/1 tsp Tabasco sauce

5ml/1 tsp lemon juice
5ml/1 tsp grated fresh root ginger
5ml/1 tsp crushed garlic
5ml/1 tsp chilli powder
5ml/1 tsp salt
15ml/1 tbsp chopped fresh
    coriander (cilantro)
175g/6oz/1½ cups frozen
    cooked peeled prawns (shrimp),
    thawed
12 mangetouts (snow peas),
    halved

1 Heat the oil in a karahi, wok or heavy pan and fry the onions until golden brown.

2 Mix the tomato purée with 30ml/2 tbsp water in a bowl. Stir in the Tabasco sauce, lemon juice, ginger and garlic, chilli powder and salt.

3 Lower the heat, pour the sauce over the onions and stir-fry for a few seconds until well mixed in.

4 Add the coriander, prawns and mangetouts to the pan and stir-fry for 5–7 minutes, or until the sauce is thick. Serve immediately.

> **Cook's Tip**
> Mangetouts, being small and almost flat, are perfect for stir-frying and are a popular ingredient in Indian cooking. They are particularly good stir-fried with prawns which need only minutes to heat through.

Energy 118kcal/495kJ; Fat 3.9g; Saturated fat 0.5g; Carbohydrate 3g; Fibre 0.4g.

Energy 108kcal/451kJ; Fat 3.48g; Saturated fat 0.49g; Carbohydrate 7.96g; Fibre 1.6g.

King Prawn Bhoona

The unusual and delicious flavour of this dish is achieved by grilling the marinated prawns to give them a chargrilled taste and then adding them to stir-fried onions and peppers.

Serves 4
45ml/⅓ tbsp natural (plain) low-fat yogurt
5ml/1 tsp paprika
5ml/1 tsp grated fresh root ginger
salt
12–16 cooked king prawns (jumbo shrimp), peeled and deveined

15ml/1 tbsp oil
3 medium onions, sliced
2.5ml/½ tsp fennel seeds, crushed
5cm/2in piece cinnamon stick
5ml/1 tsp crushed garlic
5ml/1 tsp chilli powder
1 medium yellow (bell) pepper, seeded and roughly chopped
1 medium red (bell) pepper, seeded and roughly chopped
15ml/1 tbsp fresh coriander (cilantro) leaves, to garnish

1 In a bowl, mix the yogurt, paprika, ginger and salt to taste. Pour this mixture over the prawns and leave to marinate for 30–45 minutes.

2 Heat the oil in a karahi, wok or heavy pan over medium heat and fry the sliced onions with the crushed fennel seeds and the piece of cinnamon stick.

3 Lower the heat and add the garlic and chilli powder. Stir over the heat until well mixed.

4 Add the peppers and stir-fry gently for 3–5 minutes.

5 Remove from the heat and transfer to a warm serving dish, discarding the cinnamon.

6 Preheat the grill (broiler) to medium. Put the prawns in a grill pan or flameproof dish and place under the heat to darken their tops and get a chargrilled effect. Add to the onion mixture, garnish with the coriander and serve.

Energy 1321kcal/552kJ; Fat 3.94g; Saturated fat 0.58g; Carbohydrate 15.95g; Fibre 3.11g.

Prawns with Fenugreek & Seeds

Tender shellfish, crunchy vegetables and a thick curry sauce combine to produce a dish rich in flavour and texture.

Serves 4
30ml/2 tbsp oil
5ml/1 tsp mixed fenugreek, mustard and onion seeds
2 curry leaves
½ medium cauliflower, cut into small florets
8 baby carrots, halved lengthways
6 new potatoes, thickly sliced
50g/2oz/½ cup frozen peas
2 medium onions, sliced

30ml/2 tbsp tomato purée (paste)
2.5ml/1½ tsp chilli powder
5ml/1 tsp ground coriander
5ml/1 tsp grated fresh root ginger
5ml/1 tsp crushed garlic
5ml/1 tsp salt
30ml/2 tbsp lemon juice
450g/1lb cooked peeled prawns (shrimp)
30ml/2 tbsp chopped fresh coriander (cilantro)
1 fresh red chilli, seeded and sliced
120ml/4fl oz/½ cup natural (plain) low-fat yogurt

1 Heat the oil in a karahi, wok or heavy pan. Lower the heat slightly and add the fenugreek, mustard and onion seeds and the curry leaves.

2 Increase the heat and add the cauliflower, carrots, potatoes and peas. Stir-fry quickly until browned, then remove the vegetables from the pan with a slotted spoon and drain on kitchen paper. Add the onions to the oil left in the pan and fry over a medium heat until golden brown.

3 While the onions are cooking, mix together the tomato purée, chilli powder, ground coriander, ginger, garlic, salt and lemon juice and pour the paste on to the onions.

4 Add the prawns and stir-fry over a low heat for about 5 minutes or until they are heated through.

5 Add the fried vegetables to the pan and mix together well. Add the fresh coriander and red chilli and pour in the yogurt. Warm through and serve.

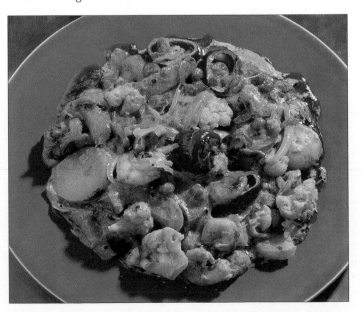

Energy 288kcal/1208kJ; Fat 9.2g; Saturated fat 1.34g; Carbohydrate 20.1g; Fibre 3.1g.

Parsi Prawn Curry

This dish comes from the west coast of India, where fresh seafood is eaten in abundance. Fresh king prawns or "tiger" prawns are ideal.

Serves 4–6

60ml/4 tbsp vegetable oil
1 medium onion, finely sliced
6 garlic cloves, finely crushed
5ml/1 tsp chilli powder
7.5ml/1½ tsp turmeric
2 medium onions, finely chopped
60ml/4 tbsp tamarind juice
5ml/1 tsp mint sauce
15ml/1 tbsp demerara (raw) sugar
450g/1lb fresh king prawns (jumbo shrimp), peeled and deveined
75g/3oz/3 cups fresh coriander (cilantro), chopped
salt

1 Heat the oil in a frying pan and fry the sliced onion until golden brown. In a bowl, mix the garlic, chilli powder and turmeric with a little water to form a paste. Add to the browned onion and simmer for 3 minutes.

2 Add the chopped onions to the pan and fry until they become translucent, stirring frequently. Stir in the tamarind juice, mint sauce, sugar and salt, and gently simmer for a further 3 minutes.

3 Pat the prawns dry with kitchen paper. Add to the spice mixture with a small amount of water and stir-fry until the prawns turn a bright orange-pink colour.

4 When the prawns are cooked, add the fresh coriander and stir-fry over a high heat for a few minutes to thicken the sauce. Serve immediately, while piping hot.

> **Cook's Tip**
> *Tamarind is usually sold in blocks of mashed pods or pulp or as a concentrated juice. It is used to sour the flavour of food.*

Energy 244kcal/1015kJ; Fat 12g; Saturated fat 1.4g; Carbohydrate 13.2g; Fibre 1.6g.

Masala Prawns & Rice

Fragrant saffron rice and king prawns are combined with mushrooms, peas and spices for this delicious one-pot meal.

Serves 4–6

2 large onions, sliced and boiled
300ml/½ pint/1¼ cups natural (plain) low-fat yogurt
30ml/2 tbsp tomato purée (paste)
60ml/4 tbsp green masala paste
30ml/2 tbsp lemon juice
5ml/1 tsp black cumin seeds
5cm/2in piece cinnamon stick
4 green cardamom pods
1.5ml/¼ tsp salt
450g/1lb raw king prawns (jumbo shrimp), peeled and deveined
225g/8oz/3 cups button (white) mushrooms
225g/8oz/2 cups frozen peas, thawed
450g/1lb/generous 2⅓ cups basmati rice
300ml/½ pint/1¼ cups water
1 sachet saffron powder mixed with 90ml/6 tbsp milk
15ml/1 tbsp oil, plus extra for greasing

1 Mix the onions, yogurt, tomato purée, green masala paste, lemon juice, black cumin seeds, cinnamon stick and cardamom pods together in a large bowl and add salt to taste. Mix the prawns, mushrooms and peas into the marinade and leave to absorb the spices for at least 2 hours.

2 Wash the rice well, cover with boiling water and leave to soak for 5 minutes, then drain.

3 Grease the base of a heavy pan and add the prawns, vegetables and any marinade juice. Cover with the drained rice and smooth the surface gently until you have an even layer.

4 Pour the water all over the surface of the rice. Make random holes through the rice with the handle of a spoon and pour in the saffron milk.

5 Sprinkle the oil over the surface of the rice and place a circular piece of foil directly on top. Cover and steam gently over a low heat for 45–50 minutes until the rice is cooked. Gently toss the rice, prawns and vegetables together and serve hot.

Energy 724kcal/3036kJ; Fat 9.8g; Saturated fat 3.32g; Carbohydrate 121.5g; Fibre 4.7g.

King Prawn Korma

This korma has a light, mild, creamy texture, and makes a good introduction to Indian cuisine for people who claim not to like spicy food.

Serves 4

12–16 cooked king prawns
(jumbo shrimp), peeled
and deveined
45ml/3 tbsp natural (plain)
low-fat yogurt
45ml/3 tbsp low-fat fromage
frais or ricotta cheese
5ml/1 tsp ground paprika
5ml/1 tsp garam masala
15ml/1 tbsp tomato purée
(paste)
45ml/3 tbsp coconut milk
5ml/1 tsp chilli powder
150ml/¼ pint/⅔ cup water
15ml/1 tbsp oil
5ml/1 tsp crushed garlic
5ml/1 tsp grated fresh root ginger
½ cinnamon stick
2 green cardamom pods
salt
15ml/1 tbsp chopped fresh
coriander (cilantro), to garnish

1 Rinse the prawns and drain them thoroughly to ensure that all excess liquid is removed.

2 Place the yogurt, fromage frais or ricotta, paprika, garam masala, tomato purée, coconut milk, chilli powder and water in a bowl.

3 Stir the yogurt and coconut mixture together well and set aside.

4 Heat the oil in a karahi, wok or heavy pan, add the crushed garlic, ginger, cinnamon stick, cardamoms and salt to taste and fry over low heat.

5 Increase the heat and pour in the yogurt and coconut mixture. Bring to the boil, stirring occasionally.

6 Add the drained king prawns to the spices and continue to stir-fry until the prawns are thoroughly heated through and the sauce is quite thick. Serve the korma garnished with the chopped fresh coriander.

Goan Prawn Curry

Cardamom, cloves and cinnamon are the essential flavourings for this dish.

Serves 4

15g/½oz/1 tbsp ghee or butter
2 garlic cloves, crushed
450g/1lb small raw prawns
(shrimp), peeled and deveined
15ml/1 tbsp groundnut (peanut)
oil
4 cardamom pods
4 cloves
5cm/2in piece cinnamon stick
15ml/1 tbsp mustard seeds
1 large onion, finely chopped
½–1 fresh red chilli, seeded
and sliced
4 tomatoes, peeled, seeded
and chopped
175ml/6fl oz/¾ cup fish stock
or water
350ml/12fl oz/1½ cups coconut
milk
45ml/3 tbsp Fragrant Spice Mix
(see Cook's Tip)
10–20ml/2–4 tsp chilli powder
salt
turmeric-coloured basmati rice,
to serve

1 Melt the ghee or butter in a wok, karahi or large pan, add the garlic and stir over a low heat for a few seconds. Add the prawns and stir-fry briskly to coat. Transfer to a plate. In the same pan, heat the oil and fry the cardamom, cloves and cinnamon for 2 minutes. Add the mustard seeds and fry for 1 minute. Add the onion and chilli and fry for 7–8 minutes or until softened and lightly browned.

2 Add the remaining ingredients except the prawns and bring to a slow simmer. Cook gently for 6–8 minutes and add the prawns. Simmer for 5–8 minutes until the prawns are cooked through. Serve the curry with basmati rice cooked with turmeric so that it is tinted a pale yellow colour, and lightly flavoured with the spice.

Cook's Tip
To make a Fragrant Spice Mix, dry-fry 25ml/1½ tbsp coriander seeds, 15ml/1 tbsp mixed peppercorns, 5ml/1 tsp cumin seeds, 1.5ml/¼ tsp fenugreek seeds and 1.5ml/¼ tsp fennel seeds until aromatic, then grind finely in a spice mill.

Energy 93kcal/391kJ; Fat 4.1g; Saturat.   0.57g; Carbohydrate 7.2g; Fibre 0.4g.

Energy 187kcal/784kJ; Fat 7g; Saturated fat 2.8g; Carbohydrate 10.5g; Fibre 1.3g.

Cod & Prawn Green Coconut Curry

This quick curry involves very little preparation, and takes just minutes to cook, so it's ideal if friends spring a surprise visit. If you can't find green masala curry paste at your local grocer or super-market, simply substitute another variety – the curry will taste just as good.

Serves 4
675g/1½lb cod fillets, skinned
90ml/6 tbsp green masala
   curry paste
175ml/6fl oz/¾ cup canned
   coconut milk
175g/6oz raw or cooked, peeled
   prawns (shrimp)
fresh coriander (cilantro),
   to garnish
basmati rice, to serve

1 Using a sharp knife, cut the skinned cod fillets into 4cm/ 1½in pieces.

2 Put the green masala curry paste and coconut milk in a frying pan. Heat to simmering and simmer gently for 5 minutes, stirring occasionally.

3 Add the cod pieces and prawns (if raw) to the cream mixture and cook gently for 5 minutes. If using ready-cooked prawns rather than raw shellfish, add them to the pan after this time has elapsed, and heat through.

4 Spoon into a serving dish, garnish the curry with fresh coriander and serve immediately with basmati rice.

> **Variation**
> Any firm fish, such as monkfish, can be used instead of cod. Whole fish steaks can be cooked in the sauce, but allow an extra 5 minutes' cooking time and baste them with the sauce from time to time.

Rich Prawn Curry

A rich, flavoursome curry made with tiger prawns and a delicious blend of aromatic spices.

Serves 4
675g/1½lb tiger prawns (shrimp)
4 dried red chillies
25g/1oz/⅓ cup desiccated
   (dry unsweetened shredded)
   coconut
5ml/1 tsp black mustard seeds
1 large onion, chopped
30ml/2 tbsp oil
4 bay leaves
2.5cm/1in piece fresh root ginger,
   finely chopped
2 garlic cloves, crushed
15ml/1 tbsp ground coriander
5ml/1 tsp chilli powder
5ml/1 tsp salt
4 tomatoes, finely chopped
plain rice, to serve

1 Peel the prawns and discard the shells. Run a sharp knife along the centre back of each prawn to make a shallow cut and carefully remove the thin black intestinal vein. Set aside.

2 Put the dried red chillies, coconut, mustard seeds and onion in a large, heavy frying pan and dry-fry for 8–10 minutes or until the spices begin to brown. The onion should turn a deep golden brown but do not let it burn or it will taste bitter.

3 Tip the mixture into a food processor or blender and process to a coarse paste.

4 Heat the oil in the frying pan and fry the bay leaves for 1 minute. Add the chopped ginger and the garlic and fry for 2–3 minutes. Add the coriander, chilli powder, salt and the coconut paste and fry gently for 5 minutes.

5 Stir in the chopped tomatoes and about 175ml/6fl oz/ ¾ cup water and simmer gently for 5–6 minutes or until the sauce has thickened.

6 Add the prawns and cook for about 4–5 minutes or until they turn pink and the edges are curling slightly. Serve with plain boiled rice.

Energy 227kcal/954kJ; Fat 7.1g; Saturated fat 1g; Carbohydrate 2.2g; Fibre 0g.

Energy 289kcal/1212kJ; Fat 12.13g; Saturated fat 4.18g; Carbohydrate 12.77g; Fibre 2.65g.

Prawns & Vegetables with Basmati Rice

This is an excellent combination of prawns and vegetables which is lightly flavoured with whole spices. Using frozen mixed vegetables speeds up the preparation time. Serve with a cool and refreshing raita.

Serves 4

300g/11oz/1½ cups basmati rice
15ml/1 tbsp oil
2 medium onions, sliced
3 green cardamom pods
2.5cm/1in cinnamon stick
4 black peppercorns
1 bay leaf
1.5ml/¼ tsp black cumin seeds
2.5cm/1in piece root ginger, grated
2 garlic cloves, roughly chopped
2 green chillies, seeded and chopped
30ml/2 tbsp chopped fresh coriander (cilantro)
30ml/2 tbsp lemon juice
115g/4oz/1 cup frozen vegetables (carrots, beans, corn and peas)
175–225g/6–8oz/1½–2 cups cooked peeled prawns (shrimp)
475ml/16fl oz/2 cups water

1 Wash the rice well in cold water and leave it to soak in plenty of water in a bowl for 30 minutes.

2 Heat the oil in a heavy pan and fry the sliced onions, cardamom pods, cinnamon stick, peppercorns, bay leaf, black cumin seeds, ginger, garlic and chillies for about 3 minutes, stirring continuously.

3 Add half the fresh coriander, the lemon juice, mixed vegetables and prawns. Stir for a further 3 minutes.

4 Drain the rice and add it to the pan. Gently stir in the water and bring to the boil. Lower the heat, add the remaining fresh coriander and cook, covered with a lid, for 15–20 minutes or until all the liquid has been absorbed and the rice is cooked. Allow to stand, still covered, for 5–7 minutes before serving.

Energy 410kcal/1737kJ; Fat 6.33g; Saturated fat 1.13g; Carbohydrate 72.33g; Fibre 1.37g.

Prawns with Basmati Mushroom Rice

Warm spices complement the flavour of mushrooms well in this tasty prawn dish.

Serves 4

150g/5oz/⅔ cup basmati rice
15ml/1 tbsp oil
1 medium onion, chopped
4 black peppercorns
2.5cm/1in cinnamon stick
1 bay leaf
1.5ml/¼ tsp cumin seeds
2 cardamom pods
5ml/1 tsp crushed garlic
5ml/1 tsp grated fresh root ginger
5ml/1 tsp garam masala
5ml/1 tsp chilli powder
7.5ml/1½ tsp salt
115g/4oz/1 cup cooked peeled prawns (shrimp)
115g/4oz/1½ cups mushrooms, cut into large pieces
30ml/2 tbsp chopped fresh coriander (cilantro)
120ml/4fl oz/½ cup natural (plain) low-fat yogurt
15ml/1 tbsp lemon juice
50g/2oz/½ cup frozen peas
250ml/8fl oz/1 cup water
1 fresh red chilli, seeded and sliced, to garnish

1 Wash the rice well and leave to soak in water for 30 minutes.

2 Heat the oil in a heavy pan and add the chopped onion, peppercorns, cinnamon, bay leaf, cumin seeds, cardamom pods, garlic, ginger, garam masala, chilli powder and salt. Lower the heat and stir-fry for 2–3 minutes. Add the prawns to the spice mixture and cook for 2 minutes, then add the mushrooms.

3 Stir in the coriander and yogurt, followed by the lemon juice and peas, and cook for 2 more minutes.

4 Drain the rice and add it to the prawn mixture. Pour in the water, cover the pan and cook over a medium heat for about 15 minutes, checking once to make sure that the rice has not stuck to the base of the pan.

5 Remove the pan from the heat and leave to stand, still covered, for about 5 minutes. Transfer to a serving dish and serve garnished with the sliced red chilli.

Energy 248kcal/1050kJ; Fat 5.20g; Saturated fat 0.99g; Carbohydrate 40.04g; Fibre 1.85g.

Satay Prawns

This delicious dish is inspired by the classic Indonesian satay. The combination of mild peanuts, aromatic spices, sweet coconut milk and zesty lemon juice in the spicy dip is perfect and is guaranteed to have guests coming back for more.

Serves 4–6
450g/1lb raw king prawns
   (jumbo shrimp)
25ml/1½ tbsp vegetable oil

For the peanut sauce
25ml/1½ tbsp vegetable oil
15ml/1 tbsp chopped garlic
1 small onion, chopped
3–4 fresh red chillies, seeded
   and chopped
3 kaffir lime leaves, torn
1 lemon grass stalk, bruised
   and chopped

5ml/1 tsp medium curry paste
250ml/8fl oz/1 cup coconut
   milk
1cm/½in piece cinnamon stick
75g/3oz/⅓ cup crunchy
   peanut butter
45ml/3 tbsp tamarind juice,
   made by mixing tamarind
   paste with warm water
30ml/2 tbsp Thai fish sauce
30ml/2 tbsp palm sugar or light
   muscovado (brown) sugar
juice of ½ lemon

For the garnish
½ bunch fresh coriander
   (cilantro) leaves
4 fresh red chillies, finely sliced
spring onions (scallions),
   cut diagonally

1 Remove the heads from the prawns and peel the bodies, leaving the tail ends intact. Slit each prawn along the back with a small, sharp knife and remove the black intestinal vein. Rinse under cold running water, pat completely dry on kitchen paper and set the prawns aside.

2 To make the peanut sauce, heat half the oil in a wok or large, heavy frying pan. Add the garlic and onion and cook over a medium heat, stirring occasionally, for 3–4 minutes, until the mixture has softened but not browned.

3 Add the chillies, kaffir lime leaves, lemon grass and curry paste. Stir well and cook for a further 2–3 minutes, then stir in the coconut milk, cinnamon stick, peanut butter, tamarind juice, fish sauce, sugar and lemon juice. Cook, stirring constantly, until well blended.

4 Bring to the boil, then reduce the heat to low and simmer gently for 15–20 minutes, until the sauce thickens. Stir occasionally with a wooden spoon to prevent the sauce from sticking to the base of the wok or frying pan.

5 Thread the prawns on to skewers and brush with a little oil. Cook under a preheated grill (broiler) for 2 minutes on each side until they turn pink and are firm to the touch. Alternatively, pan-fry the prawns, then thread on to skewers.

6 Remove the cinnamon stick from the sauce and discard. Arrange the skewered prawns on a warmed platter, garnish with spring onions, coriander leaves and sliced red chillies, and serve with the sauce.

Energy 291kcal/1215kJ; Fat 15.4g; Saturated fat 3.2g; Carbohydrate 14.6g; Fibre 1.2g.

Prawn Salad with Curry Dressing

Curry spices add an unexpected twist to this salad. The warm flavours combine especially well with the sweet shellfish and grated apple. Curry paste is needed here rather than curry powder as there is no cooking, which is necessary to bring out the flavours of powdered spices.

1 small bunch fresh coriander
   (cilantro)
15ml/1 tbsp lemon juice
450g/1lb shelled cooked
   prawns (shrimp)
1 apple
8 whole cooked prawns,
   8 lemon wedges and
   4 fresh coriander sprigs,
   to garnish
salt

Serves 4
1 ripe tomato, peeled
½ iceberg lettuce
1 small onion

For the curry dressing
75ml/5 tbsp mayonnaise
5ml/1 tsp mild curry paste
15ml/1 tbsp tomato ketchup

1 Cut the tomato in half and squeeze each half gently to remove the seeds. Discard them, then cut each tomato half into large dice.

2 Shred the lettuce leaves finely and put in a large bowl. Finely chop the onion and coriander. Add to the bowl together with the tomato, moisten with lemon juice and season with salt.

3 To make the dressing, combine the mayonnaise, curry paste and tomato ketchup in a small bowl. Add 30ml/2 tbsp water to thin the dressing and season to taste with salt.

4 Combine the prawns with the curry dressing and stir gently so that all the prawns are evenly coated with the dressing. Quarter and core the apple and coarsely grate the flesh into the prawn and dressing mixture.

5 Distribute the shredded lettuce mixture among four serving plates or bowls. Pile the prawn mixture in the centre of each and decorate each with two whole prawns, two lemon wedges and a sprig of coriander.

Energy 73kcal/311kJ; Fat 0.6g; Saturated fat 0.1g; Carbohydrate 6.8g; Fibre 1.3g.

Prawns with Fried Jasmine Rice & Thai Basil

Thai basil (bai grapao), also known as holy basil, has a unique, pungent flavour that is both spicy and sharp. It can be found in most Asian food markets.

Serves 4–6

1 onion
45ml/3 tbsp vegetable oil
1 egg, beaten
15ml/1 tbsp chopped garlic
15ml/1 tbsp shrimp paste
1kg/2¼lb/4 cups cooked jasmine rice
350g/12oz cooked shelled prawns (shrimp)
50g/2oz/½ cup thawed frozen peas
oyster sauce, to taste
2 spring onions (scallions), chopped
15–20 Thai basil leaves, roughly chopped, plus an extra sprig, to garnish

1 Chop the onion, and set it aside while you make the pancakes.

2 Heat 15ml/1 tbsp of the oil in a wok or frying pan. Add the beaten egg and swirl it around to set like a thin pancake.

3 Cook the pancake (on one side only) over a gentle heat until golden. Slide the pancake on to a board, roll up and cut into thin strips. Set aside.

4 Heat the remaining oil in the wok or pan, add the onion and garlic and stir-fry for 2–3 minutes.

5 Stir in the shrimp paste and mix well until thoroughly combined.

6 Add the rice, prawns and peas and toss and stir together, until everything is heated through.

7 Season with oyster sauce to taste, taking great care as the shrimp paste is salty. Mix in the spring onions and basil leaves.

8 Transfer to a serving dish and top with the strips of egg pancake. Serve, garnished with a sprig of basil.

Stir-fried Prawns with Tamarind

The sour, tangy flavour that is characteristic of many Thai dishes comes from tamarind. Fresh tamarind pods from the tamarind tree can sometimes be bought, but preparing them for cooking is a laborious process. It is much easier to use a block of tamarind paste.

Serves 4–6

6 dried red chillies
30ml/2 tbsp vegetable oil
30ml/2 tbsp chopped onion
30ml/2 tbsp palm sugar or light muscovado (brown) sugar
30ml/2 tbsp chicken stock or water
15ml/1 tbsp Thai fish sauce
90ml/6 tbsp tamarind juice, made by mixing tamarind paste with warm water
450g/1lb raw prawns (shrimp), peeled
15ml/1 tbsp fried chopped garlic
30ml/2 tbsp fried sliced shallots
2 spring onions (scallions), chopped, to garnish

1 Heat a wok or large frying pan, but do not add any oil at this stage. Add the dried chillies and dry-fry them by pressing them against the surface of the wok or pan with a spatula, turning them occasionally. Do not let them burn. Set them aside to cool slightly.

2 Add the oil to the wok or pan and reheat. Add the chopped onion and cook over a medium heat, stirring occasionally, for 2–3 minutes, until softened and a light golden brown.

3 Add the sugar, chicken stock or water, fish sauce, dry-fried red chillies and the tamarind juice, stirring constantly until the sugar has dissolved. Bring to the boil, then lower the heat slightly.

4 Add the prawns, garlic and shallots. Toss over the heat for 3–4 minutes, until the prawns are cooked. Garnish with the spring onions and serve.

> **Cook's Tip**
> Peel a few of the prawns but leave their tails intact to use as a garnish, if you like.

Energy 524kcal/2213kJ; Fat 13.8g; Saturated fat 2.2g; Carbohydrate 80.2g; Fibre 1.7g.

Energy 175kcal/736kJ; Fat 6.2g; Saturated fat 0.8g; Carbohydrate 10.2g; Fibre 0.4g.

Prawn Fritters

Ukoy, or prawn fritters, are a favourite snack or appetizer. Unusually, they are first shallow-fried, then deep-fried.

Serves 2–4
16 raw prawns (shrimp) in the shell
225g/8oz/2 cups plain (all-purpose) flour
5ml/1 tsp baking powder
2.5ml/½ tsp salt
1 egg, beaten
1 small sweet potato
1 garlic clove, crushed
115g/4oz/1½ cups beansprouts, soaked in cold water and well drained
vegetable oil, for shallow- and deep-frying
4 spring onions (scallions), chopped

For the dipping sauce
1 garlic clove, sliced
45ml/3 tbsp rice or wine vinegar
15–30ml/1–2 tbsp water
salt
6–8 small red chillies

1 To make the dipping sauce, mix the sliced garlic clove with the rice or wine vinegar in a bowl. Add the water, salt and red chillies. Divide the dipping sauce between two serving bowls.

2 Put the whole prawns in a pan with water to cover. Bring to the boil, then simmer for 4–5 minutes or until the prawns are pink and tender. Lift the prawns from the pan with a slotted spoon. Discard the heads and the body shell, but leave the tails on. Strain and reserve the cooking liquid. Allow to cool.

3 Sift the flour, baking powder and salt into a bowl. Add the beaten egg and about 300ml/½ pint/1¼ cups of the prawn stock to make a batter that has the consistency of double (heavy) cream.

4 Peel and grate the sweet potato using the large holes on a grater, and add it to the batter, then stir in the crushed garlic and the drained beansprouts.

5 Pour the oil for shallow-frying into a large frying pan. It should be about 5mm/¼in deep. Pour more oil into a wok for deep-frying. Heat the oil in the frying pan. Taking a generous spoonful of the batter, drop it carefully into the frying pan so that it forms a fritter, about the size of a large drop scone.

6 Make more fritters in the same way. As soon as the fritters have set, top each one with a single prawn and a few chopped spring onions. Continue to cook over a medium heat for 1 minute, then remove with a fish slice or metal spatula.

7 Heat the oil in a karahi, wok or deep-fryer to a temperature of 190°C/375°F, or until a cube of bread dropped in the oil browns in about 45 seconds. Deep-fry the prawn fritters in batches until they are crisp and golden brown. Drain the fritters on absorbent kitchen paper and then arrange them on a serving plate or platter. Offer a bowl of the sauce for dipping.

Energy 711kcal/2996kJ; Fat 21.9g; Saturated fat 3.2g; Carbohydrate 101g; Fibre 5.9g.

Salt & Pepper Prawns

These succulent and piquant shellfish beg to be eaten with the fingers, so provide finger bowls or hot cloths for your guests.

Serves 3–4
15–18 large raw prawns (shrimp), in the shell, about 450g/1lb
vegetable oil, for deep-frying
3 shallots or 1 small onion, very finely chopped
2 garlic cloves, crushed
1cm/½in piece fresh root ginger, peeled and very finely grated
1–2 fresh red chillies, seeded and finely sliced
2.5ml/½ tsp sugar, or to taste
3–4 spring onions (scallions), shredded, to garnish

For the fried salt
10ml/2 tsp salt
5ml/1 tsp Sichuan peppercorns

1 Make the fried salt by dry-frying the salt and peppercorns in a heavy frying pan over medium heat until the peppercorns begin to release their aroma. Cool the mixture, then tip into a mortar and crush with a pestle.

2 Carefully remove the heads and legs from the raw prawns and discard. Leave the body shells and the tails in place. Pat the prepared prawns dry with sheets of kitchen paper.

3 Heat the oil in a karahi, wok or deep-fryer to a temperature of 190°C/375°F, or until a cube of bread dropped in the oil browns in about 45 seconds. Fry the prawns for 1 minute, then lift them out and drain thoroughly on kitchen paper. Spoon 30ml/2 tbsp of the hot oil into a large frying pan, leaving the rest of the oil to one side to cool.

4 Heat the oil in the frying pan. Add the fried salt, with the shallots or onion, garlic, ginger, chillies and sugar. Toss the mixture together for 1 minute, then add the prawns and toss them over the heat for 1 minute more until they are coated and the shells are impregnated with the seasonings. Serve at once, garnished with the spring onions.

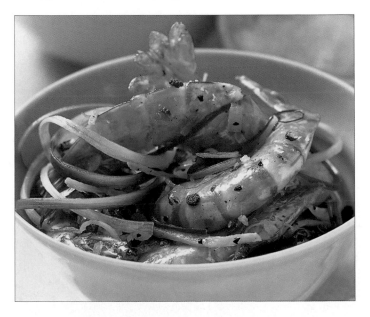

Energy 204kcal/844kJ; Fat 15.8g; Saturated fat 2g; Carbohydrate 1.7g; Fibre 0.3g.

Prawn Stew

Kangkong (or swamp cabbage) has delicate leaves and stems, which are delicious lightly cooked. It is similar to spinach, which can be used instead in this bright stew of vegetables, prawns and strips of fish fillet. Serve with noodles or rice to make a substantial and tasty meal.

Serves 4–6
15ml/1 tbsp tamarind pulp
150ml/1/4 pint/ 2/3 cup warm
  water
2 tomatoes
115g/4oz Chinese kangkong
  leaves or spinach
115g/4oz cooked large prawns
  (shrimp)
1.2 litres/2 pints/5 cups prepared
  fish or vegetable stock
1/2 mooli (daikon), peeled and
  finely diced
115g/4oz green beans, cut into
  1cm/1/2in lengths
225g/8oz piece of cod or
  haddock fillet, skinned and
  cut into strips
Thai fish sauce, to taste
squeeze of lemon juice,
  to taste
salt and ground black pepper
boiled rice or noodles,
  to serve

1 Put the tamarind pulp in a bowl and pour over the warm water. Set aside while you peel and chop the tomatoes, discarding the seeds. Strip the spinach or kangkong leaves from the stems and tear into small pieces.

2 Remove the heads and shells from the prawns, leaving the tails intact.

3 Pour the prepared fish stock into a large pan and add the diced mooli. Cook the mooli for 5 minutes, then add the beans and continue to cook for 3–5 minutes more.

4 Add the fish strips, tomato and spinach. Strain in the tamarind juice and cook for 2 minutes. Stir in the prawns and cook for 1–2 minutes to heat. Season with salt and pepper and add a little fish sauce and lemon juice to taste. Transfer to individual serving bowls and serve immediately, with boiled rice or noodles.

Energy 93kcal/389kJ; Fat 1.2g; Saturated fat 0.2g; Carbohydrate 3.4g; Fibre 2g.

Shellfish with Coconut Milk

Green curry paste, made with green chillies and plenty of fresh coriander, is what gives this seafood dish its unique flavour. This recipe recalls the days when the French were influential in India, first through their trading interests, and later when they ruled Pondicherry.

Serves 4–6
450g/1lb mussels in their shells,
  cleaned
60ml/4 tbsp water
225g/8oz medium cuttlefish
  or squid
400ml/14fl oz/1 2/3 cups
  coconut milk
300ml/1/2 pint/1 1/4 cups chicken
  or vegetable stock
350g/12oz monkfish, hoki or
  red snapper, skinned
150g/5oz raw or cooked prawn
  (shrimp) tails, peeled and deveined
75g/3oz green beans, trimmed
  and cooked
1 tomato, peeled, seeded and
  roughly chopped
torn basil leaves, to garnish
boiled rice, to serve

For the green curry paste
10ml/2 tsp coriander seeds
2.5ml/1/2 tsp cumin seeds
3 or 4 medium fresh green chillies,
  finely chopped
20ml/4 tsp granulated sugar
10ml/2 tsp salt
2cm/3/4in piece fresh root ginger,
  peeled and finely chopped
3 garlic cloves, crushed
1 medium onion, finely chopped
50g/2oz/2 cups fresh coriander
  (cilantro) leaves, finely chopped
2.5ml/1/2 tsp grated nutmeg
30ml/2 tbsp vegetable oil

1 Scrub the mussels in cold running water and pull off the "beards". Discard any that do not shut when sharply tapped. Put them in a pan with the water, cover and cook for 6–8 minutes. Discard any mussels that remain closed and remove three-quarters of the mussels from their shells. Set aside. Strain the cooking liquid and set aside.

2 To prepare the cuttlefish or squid, trim off the tentacles and discard the gut. Remove the cuttle shell from inside the body and rub off the skin. Cut the body open and score in a criss-cross pattern with a sharp knife. Cut into strips and set aside.

3 To make the green curry paste, dry-fry the coriander and cumin seeds in a karahi or wok. Grind the chillies with the sugar and salt in a pestle with a mortar or in a food processor. Add the coriander and cumin seeds, ginger, garlic and onion and grind to a paste. Add the fresh coriander, nutmeg and oil and combine thoroughly.

4 Strain the coconut milk and pour the thin liquid into a karahi or wok with the stock and reserved cooking liquid from the mussels. Reserve the thick part of the coconut milk. Add 60–75ml/4–5 tbsp of the green curry paste to the wok and bring the mixture to the boil. Boil rapidly for a few minutes, until the liquid has reduced completely.

5 Add the thick part of the coconut milk. Stir well, then add the cuttlefish or squid and monkfish, hoki or red snapper. Simmer for 15–20 minutes. Then add the prawns, mussels, beans and tomato. Simmer for 2–3 minutes until heated through. Transfer to a warmed serving dish, garnish with torn basil leaves and serve immediately with boiled rice.

Energy 270kcal/1142kJ; Fat 8.6g; Saturated fat 1.5g; Carbohydrate 9g; Fibre 0.9g.

Nasi Goreng

This is a marvellous way to use up leftover rice, chicken and meats. Cook the rice the day before, if possible.

Serves 4–6

2 eggs
30ml/2 tbsp water
105ml/7 tbsp oil
2 fresh red chillies, halved and seeded
1cm/½in cube shrimp paste
2 garlic cloves, crushed
1 onion, roughly chopped
225g/8oz pork fillet or fillet of beef, cut into neat strips
115g/4oz cooked prawns (shrimp)
175–225g/6–8oz cooked chicken, finely chopped
675g/1½lb/6 cups cold cooked long grain rice, preferably basmati (about 350g/12oz/ 1¾ cups raw rice)
30ml/2 tbsp dark soy sauce or 45ml/3 tbsp tomato ketchup
salt and ground black pepper
deep-fried onions, celery leaves and fresh coriander (cilantro) sprigs, to garnish

1 Put the eggs in a bowl and beat in the water, with salt and pepper to taste. Using a non-stick frying pan make two or three omelettes using as little oil as possible. Roll up each omelette and cut into strips when cold. Set aside. Shred one of the chillies and reserve it.

2 Put the shrimp paste in a food processor. Add the remaining chilli, the garlic and onion. Process to a fine paste. Heat the remaining oil in a wok and fry the paste, without browning, until it gives off a rich, spicy aroma. Add the pork or beef and toss over the heat to seal in the juices, then cook for 2 minutes more, stirring constantly.

3 Add the prawns and stir-fry for 2 minutes. Finally, stir in the chicken, cold rice, dark soy sauce or ketchup and seasoning to taste. Reheat the rice fully, stirring all the time to keep the rice light and fluffy and prevent it from sticking to the base of the pan.

4 Spoon into individual dishes and arrange the omelette strips and reserved chilli on top. Garnish with the deep-fried onions, celery leaves and coriander sprigs.

Mussels & Clams with Lemon Grass & Coconut Cream

Lemon grass has an incomparable aromatic flavour and is widely used with all kinds of seafood in Thailand as the flavours marry so perfectly.

Serves 6

1.8kg/4lb fresh mussels
450g/1lb baby clams
120ml/4fl oz/½ cup dry white wine
1 bunch spring onions (scallions), chopped
2 lemon grass stalks, chopped
6 kaffir lime leaves, chopped
10ml/2 tsp Thai green curry paste
200ml/7fl oz/scant 1 cup coconut cream
30ml/2 tbsp chopped fresh coriander (cilantro)
salt and ground black pepper
garlic chives, to garnish

1 Scrub the mussels' shells with a stiff brush and rinse under cold running water. Scrape off any barnacles and remove the "beards" with a small knife. Rinse well. Scrub the clams. Discard any mussels or clams that are damaged or broken or which do not close immediately when tapped sharply.

2 Put the wine in a large pan with the spring onions, lemon grass and lime leaves. Stir in the curry paste. Simmer until the wine has almost evaporated.

3 Add the mussels and clams to the pan and increase the heat to high. Cover tightly and steam the shellfish for 5–6 minutes, until they open.

4 Using a slotted spoon, transfer the mussels and clams to a heated serving bowl, cover and keep hot. Discard any shellfish that remain closed. Strain the cooking liquid into a clean pan through a sieve (strainer) lined with muslin (cheesecloth) and simmer briefly to reduce to about 250ml/8fl oz/1 cup.

5 Stir the coconut cream and chopped coriander into the sauce and season to taste. Heat through. Pour the sauce over the shellfish, garnish with the garlic chives and serve.

Energy 596kcal/2502kJ; Fat 27.2g; Saturated fat 4.5g; Carbohydrate 55.6g; Fibre 0.8g.

Energy 130kcal/551kJ; Fat 2.3g; Saturated fat 0.5g; Carbohydrate 3g; Fibre 0.5g.

Pan-steamed Mussels with Thai Herbs

Like so many Thai dishes, this is very easy to prepare. The lemon grass and kaffir lime leaves add a refreshing tang to the mussels.

Serves 4–6
1kg/2¼lb fresh mussels
2 lemon grass stalks, finely chopped
4 shallots, chopped
4 kaffir lime leaves, coarsely torn
2 fresh red chillies, sliced
15ml/1 tbsp Thai fish sauce
30ml/2 tbsp fresh lime juice
thinly sliced spring onions (scallions) and coriander (cilantro) leaves, to garnish

1 Scrub the mussels' shells with a stiff brush and rinse under cold running water. Scrape off any barnacles and remove the "beards" with a small knife. Rinse well. Discard any mussels that are broken or which do not close when tapped sharply.

2 Place the mussels in a large, heavy pan and add the lemon grass, shallots, kaffir lime leaves, chillies, fish sauce and lime juice. Mix well. Cover the pan tightly and steam the mussels over a high heat, shaking the pan occasionally, for 5–7 minutes, until the shells have opened.

3 Using a slotted spoon, transfer the cooked mussels to a warmed serving dish or individual bowls. Discard any mussels that have failed to open.

4 Garnish the mussels with the thinly sliced spring onions and coriander leaves. Serve immediately.

Cook's Tip
Mussels are bought alive. They can sometimes be a little gritty, so it is worth putting them into a bucket of cold salted water as soon as you get home. Sprinkle a little oatmeal or flour over the water so that the mussels can feed on this and excrete the grit.

Energy 73kcal/310kJ; Fat 1.6g; Saturated fat 0.3g; Carbohydrate 1.5g; Fibre 0.4g.

Spicy Squid

This aromatically spiced squid dish, *Cumi Cumi Smoor*, is simple yet delicious. For speed, buy ready-cleaned squid.

Serves 3–4
675g/1½lb squid
45ml/3 tbsp groundnut oil
1 onion, finely chopped
2 garlic cloves, crushed
1 beefsteak tomato, peeled and chopped
15ml/1 tbsp dark soy sauce
2.5ml/½ tsp grated nutmeg
6 cloves
150ml/¼ pint/⅔ cup water
juice of ½ lemon or lime
salt and ground black pepper
fresh coriander (cilantro) leaves and shredded spring onion (scallion), to garnish
boiled rice, to serve

1 Rinse and drain the squid, then slice lengthways along one side and open it out flat. Score the inside of the squid in a lattice pattern, using the blunt side of a sharp knife, then cut it crossways into long thin strips.

2 Heat a wok and add 15ml/1 tbsp of the oil. When hot, toss in the squid strips and stir-fry for 2–3 minutes, by which time the squid will have curled into attractive shapes or into firm rings. Lift out and set aside.

3 Wipe out the wok, add the remaining oil and heat it. Stir-fry the onion and garlic until soft and beginning to brown. Stir in the tomato, soy sauce, nutmeg, cloves, water and lemon or lime juice. Bring to the boil, lower the heat and add the squid with seasoning to taste.

4 Cook the mixture gently for a further 3–5 minutes, stirring from time to time to prevent sticking. Take care not to overcook the squid.

5 Divide boiled rice among 3–4 serving plates and spoon the spicy squid on top. Garnish with coriander leaves and shredded spring onions, and serve.

Energy 297kcal/1247kJ; Fat 15g; Saturated fat 2.2g; Carbohydrate 5.8g; Fibre 0.8g.

Curried Seafood with Coconut Milk

Fresh herbs and flavourings such as green chillies, kaffir lime leaves and lemon grass give this beautiful curry its green colour and fragrant flavour. The curry mixture is cooked for only a short while so that it retains its freshness.

Serves 4
225g/8oz small ready-prepared squid
225g/8oz raw tiger prawns (jumbo shrimp)
400ml/14fl oz/1²/₃ cups coconut milk
2 kaffir lime leaves, finely shredded
30ml/2 tbsp Thai fish sauce
450g/1lb firm white fish fillets, skinned, boned and cut into chunks

2 fresh green chillies, seeded and finely chopped
30ml/2 tbsp torn fresh basil or coriander (cilantro) leaves
squeeze of fresh lime juice
cooked Thai jasmine rice, to serve

For the curry paste
6 spring onions (scallions), coarsely chopped
4 fresh coriander (cilantro) stems, coarsely chopped, plus 45ml/ 3 tbsp chopped fresh coriander
4 kaffir lime leaves, shredded
8 fresh green chillies, seeded and coarsely chopped
1 lemon grass stalk, coarsely chopped
2.5cm/1in piece fresh root ginger, peeled and coarsely chopped
45ml/3 tbsp chopped fresh basil
15ml/1 tbsp vegetable oil

1 To make the curry paste, put all the ingredients except the oil in a food processor and process to a paste. Alternatively, pound together in a mortar with a pestle. Stir in the oil.

2 Rinse the squid and pat dry with kitchen paper. Cut the bodies into rings and halve the tentacles, if necessary.

3 Heat a wok until hot, add the prawns and stir-fry, without any oil, for about 4 minutes, until they turn pink.

4 Remove the prawns from the wok and leave to cool slightly, then peel off the shells, leaving a few unshelled for the garnish. Make a shallow slit along the back of each one and remove the black intestinal vein.

5 Pour the coconut milk into the wok, then bring to the boil over a medium heat, stirring constantly. Add 30ml/2 tbsp of the curry paste, the shredded lime leaves and fish sauce and stir well to mix. Reduce the heat to low and simmer gently for about 10 minutes.

6 Add the squid, prawns and chunks of fish and cook for about 2 minutes, until the seafood is tender. Take care not to overcook the squid as it will become tough very quickly.

7 Just before serving, stir in the chillies and basil or coriander. Taste and adjust the flavour with a squeeze of lime juice. Garnish with prawns in their shells, and serve with jasmine rice.

Variation
You can use any firm-fleshed white fish for this curry, such as monkfish, cod, haddock or John Dory.

Stir-fried Squid with Ginger

The abundance of fish around the Gulf of Thailand sustains thriving markets for the restaurant and hotel trade, and every market naturally features stalls where delicious, freshly caught seafood is cooked and served. This recipe is popular among street traders. Squid needs the minimum of cooking and tastes great with garlic, lemon and ginger.

Serves 2
4 ready-prepared baby squid, total weight about 250g/9oz
15ml/1 tbsp vegetable oil
2 garlic cloves, finely chopped
30ml/2 tbsp soy sauce
2.5cm/1in piece fresh root ginger, peeled and finely chopped
juice of ¹/₂ lemon
5ml/1 tsp granulated sugar
2 spring onions (scallions), chopped

1 Rinse the squid well and pat dry with kitchen paper. Cut the bodies into rings and halve the tentacles, if necessary.

2 Heat the oil in a wok or frying pan and cook the garlic until golden brown, but do not let it burn. Add the squid and stir-fry for 30 seconds over a high heat.

3 Add the soy sauce, ginger, lemon juice, sugar and spring onions. Stir-fry for a further 30 seconds, then serve.

Cook's Tips
• *Squid has an undeserved reputation for being rubbery in texture. This is always a result of overcooking it.*
• *Small squid generally have a sweeter flavour than those that are larger, and are usually more tender, too.*

Variations
This dish is often prepared with fresh galangal rather than ginger and works well with most kinds of seafood, including prawns (shrimp) and scallops.

Energy 282kcal/1186kJ; Fat 10.9g; Saturated fat 1.6g; Carbohydrate 6.4g; Fibre 0.9g.

Energy 161kcal/677kJ; Fat 7.7g; Saturated fat 1.2g; Carbohydrate 3.9g; Fibre 0.2g.

Spicy Tandoori Chicken

A delicious and popular Indian–Pakistani chicken dish which is traditionally cooked in a clay oven called a tandoor, this is extremely popular in the West and appears on the majority of restaurant menus.

Serves 4

4 chicken quarters, skinned
175ml/6fl oz/³⁄₄ cup natural
  (plain) low-fat yogurt
5ml/1 tsp garam masala
5ml/1 tsp grated fresh root ginger
5ml/1 tsp crushed garlic
7.5ml/1¹⁄₂ tsp chilli powder
1.5ml/¹⁄₄ tsp ground turmeric
5ml/1 tsp ground coriander
15ml/1 tbsp lemon juice
5ml/1 tsp salt
few drops of red food
  colouring
15ml/1 tbsp oil
mixed salad leaves, to serve
lime wedges, to garnish

1 Rinse and pat dry the chicken quarters. Make two deep slits in the flesh of each piece, place in a dish and set aside.

2 Mix together the yogurt, garam masala, ginger, garlic, chilli powder, turmeric, coriander, lemon juice, salt, red food colouring and oil, and beat so that all the ingredients are well combined.

3 Cover the chicken quarters with the spice mixture, cover and leave to marinate for about 3 hours.

4 Preheat the oven to 240°C/475°F/Gas 9. Transfer the chicken pieces to an ovenproof dish.

5 Bake the chicken in the oven for 20–25 minutes or until the chicken is cooked right through and evenly browned on top.

6 Remove from the oven, arrange on salad leaves on a serving dish and garnish with lime wedges.

> **Cook's Tip**
> *The traditional bright red colour is derived from food colouring. This is only optional and may be omitted if you prefer.*

Classic Tandoori Chicken

This is probably the most famous of all the Indian dishes. Marinate the chicken well and cook in an extremely hot oven for a clay-oven-baked taste. If you want authentic "burnt" spots on the chicken, place the dish under a hot grill for a few minutes after baking.

Serves 4–6

1.5kg/3lb oven-ready chicken
250ml/8fl oz/1 cup natural
  (plain) yogurt, beaten
60ml/4 tbsp tandoori
  masala paste
75g/3oz/6 tbsp ghee
salt
salad leaves, to serve
lemon twist and onion slices,
  to garnish

1 Using a sharp knife or scissors, remove the skin from the chicken and trim off any excess fat. Using a fork, beat the flesh at random.

2 Cut the chicken in half down the centre and through the breast. Cut each piece in half again. Make a few deep gashes diagonally into the flesh. Mix the yogurt with the masala paste and salt. Spread the chicken evenly with the yogurt mixture, spreading some into the gashes. Leave for at least 2 hours, but preferably overnight.

3 Preheat the oven to maximum heat. Place the chicken quarters on a wire rack in a deep baking tray. Spread the chicken with any excess marinade, reserve a little for basting halfway through cooking time.

4 Melt the ghee and pour over the chicken to seal the surface. This helps to keep the centre moist during the roasting period. Cook in the preheated oven for 10 minutes, then remove, leaving the oven on.

5 Baste the chicken pieces with the remaining marinade. Return to the oven and switch off the heat. Leave the chicken in the oven for about 15–20 minutes without opening the door. Serve on a bed of salad leaves and garnish with the lemon twist and onion slices.

Energy 610kcal/2530kJ; Fat 44.6g; Saturated fat 12.2g; Carbohydrate 3.8g; Fibre 0g.

Energy 300kcal/1256kJ; Fat 12g; Saturated fat 3.39g; Carbohydrate 5.9g; Fibre 0.2g.

Tandoori Chicken Kebabs

This dish originates from the plains of the Punjab at the foot of the Himalayas. Allow the chicken to marinate for about three hours to absorb the tandoori flavourings.

Serves 4
4 skinned chicken breast fillets, about 175g/6oz each
15ml/1 tbsp lemon juice
45ml/3 tbsp tandoori paste
45ml/3 tbsp natural (plain) low-fat yogurt
1 garlic clove, crushed
30ml/2 tbsp chopped fresh coriander (cilantro)
salt and ground black pepper
1 small onion, cut into wedges and separated into layers
a little oil, for brushing
fresh coriander sprigs, to garnish
pilau rice and naan bread, to serve

1 Chop the chicken breast fillets into 2.5cm/1in cubes, place in a mixing bowl and add the lemon juice, tandoori paste, yogurt, garlic, chopped coriander and seasoning. Cover and leave the chicken to marinate in the refrigerator for 2–3 hours.

2 Preheat the grill (broiler) to high. Thread alternate pieces of marinated chicken and onion on to four skewers.

3 Brush the onions with a little oil, place on a grill rack and cook under a high heat for 10–12 minutes, or until the chicken is cooked through, turning once midway through. Garnish the kebabs with fresh coriander sprigs and serve with pilau rice and naan bread.

> **Cook's Tip**
> Use chopped, boned and skinned chicken thighs, or turkey breasts, for a tasty and less expensive alternative.

Energy 257kcal/1078kJ; Fat 9.4g; Saturated fat 2.31g; Carbohydrate 3.5g; Fibre 2.9g.

Stuffed Roast Chicken

At one time this dish was cooked only in royal palaces and the ingredients varied according to individual chefs. The saffron and the rich stuffing make it a truly royal dish.

Serves 4–6
1 sachet saffron powder
2.5ml/1/2 tsp ground nutmeg
15ml/1 tbsp warm milk
1.3kg/3lb whole chicken
75g/3oz/6 tbsp ghee
75ml/5 tbsp hot water

For the stuffing
3 medium onions, finely chopped
2 fresh green chillies, chopped
50g/2oz/1/3 cup sultanas (golden raisins)
50g/2oz/1/2 cup ground almonds
50g/2oz dried apricots, soaked until soft
3 hard-boiled eggs, coarsely chopped
salt

For the masala
4 spring onions (scallions), chopped
2 cloves garlic, crushed
5ml/1 tsp five-spice powder
4–6 green cardamom pods
2.5ml/1/2 tsp turmeric
5ml/1 tsp ground black pepper
30ml/2 tbsp natural (plain) yogurt
50g/2oz/1 cup desiccated (dry unsweetened shredded) coconut, toasted

1 Mix together the saffron, nutmeg and milk. Use to brush the inside of the chicken and over the skin. Heat 50g/2oz/4 tbsp of the ghee in a large frying pan and fry the chicken on all sides to seal it. Remove and keep warm.

2 To make the stuffing, in the same ghee, fry the onions, chillies, and sultanas for 2–3 minutes. Allow to cool and add the ground almonds, apricots, chopped eggs and salt. Use to stuff the chicken.

3 Heat the remaining ghee in a large, heavy pan and gently fry all the masala ingredients except the coconut for 2–3 minutes. Add the water. Place the chicken on the bed of masala, cover the pan and cook until the chicken is tender. Remove the chicken from the pan. Cook the liquid to reduce excess fluids in the masala. When the mixture thickens, pour over the chicken. Sprinkle with toasted coconut and serve hot.

Energy 823kcal/3420kJ; Fat 57.9g; Saturated fat 19.7g; Carbohydrate 21.1g; Fibre 4.9g.

Jeera Chicken

An aromatic dish with a delicious, distinctive taste of cumin. Serve simply with a cooling cucumber raita.

Serves 4

45ml/3 tbsp cumin seeds
15ml/1 tbsp oil
2.5ml/¹⁄₂ tsp black peppercorns
4 green cardamom pods
2 fresh green chillies,
   finely chopped
2 garlic cloves, crushed
2.5cm/1in piece fresh root
   ginger, grated
5ml/1 tsp ground coriander
10ml/2 tsp ground cumin
2.5ml/¹⁄₂ tsp salt
8 chicken pieces, skinned
5ml/1 tsp garam masala
fresh coriander (cilantro)
   and chilli powder,
   to garnish
cucumber raita, to serve

1 Dry-roast 15ml/1 tbsp of the cumin seeds for 5 minutes and then set aside.

2 Heat the oil in a large, heavy pan or wok and fry the remaining cumin seeds, black peppercorns and cardamoms for about 2–3 minutes.

3 Add the chillies, garlic and ginger and fry for about 2 minutes.

4 Add the ground coriander, ground cumin and salt. Stir well, then cook for a further 2–3 minutes.

5 Add the chicken and stir to coat the pieces in the sauce. Cover with a lid and simmer for 20–25 minutes.

6 Add the garam masala and reserved toasted cumin seeds and cook for a further 5 minutes. Garnish with fresh coriander and chilli powder and serve with cucumber raita.

> **Cook's Tip**
> *Dry-roast the cumin seeds in a small, heavy frying pan over a medium heat, stirring them until they turn a few shades darker and give off a wonderful roasted aroma.*

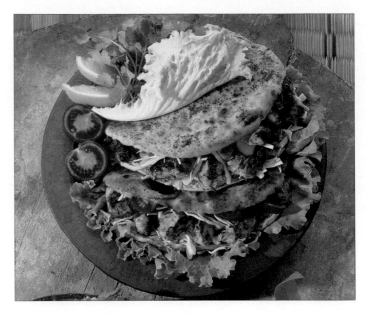

Chicken Naan Pockets

This easy dish is ideal for a light snack lunch or supper. For speed, use the ready-baked naans available in most of today's supermarkets and Asian stores, but beware that as they are larger than typical home-cooked naan they will contain more fat.

Serves 4

4 small naan, about 90g/3¹⁄₂oz
   each
45ml/3 tbsp natural (plain)
   low-fat yogurt
7.5ml/1¹⁄₂ tsp garam masala
5ml/1 tsp chilli powder
5ml/1 tsp salt
45ml/3 tbsp lemon juice
15ml/1 tbsp chopped fresh
   coriander (cilantro)
1 fresh green chilli, chopped
450g/1lb skinned boneless
   chicken, cubed
8 onion rings
2 tomatoes, quartered
¹⁄₂ white cabbage, shredded

For the garnish
mixed salad leaves
2 small tomatoes, halved
lemon wedges
fresh coriander (cilantro)

1 Cut into the middle of each naan to make a pocket, then set them aside.

2 Mix together the yogurt, garam masala, chilli powder, salt, lemon juice, fresh coriander and chopped green chilli.

3 Pour the marinade over the chicken, cover and leave to marinate for about 1 hour.

4 Preheat the grill (broiler) to very hot, then lower the heat to medium. Put the chicken pieces in a pan or flameproof dish lined with foil.

5 Grill (broil) for 15–20 minutes until tender and fully cooked, turning the chicken twice.

6 Remove from the heat and fill each naan with the chicken and then with the onion rings, tomatoes and cabbage. Serve garnished with mixed salad leaves, tomato halves, lemon wedges and coriander.

Energy 286kcal/1198kJ; Fat 14.1g; Saturated fat 3.19g; Carbohydrate 7.6g; Fibre 0.1g.

Energy 472kcal/1986kJ; Fat 15.3g; Saturated fat 6.46g; Carbohydrate 53.4g; Fibre 4.2g.

Goan Chicken Curry

Coconut in all its forms is widely used to enrich Goan cuisine.

Serves 4
75g/3oz/1 cup desiccated (dry unsweetened shredded) coconut
30ml/2 tbsp vegetable oil
2.5ml/½ tsp cumin seeds
4 black peppercorns
15ml/1 tbsp fennel seeds
15ml/1 tbsp coriander seeds
2 onions, finely chopped
2.5ml/½ tsp salt
8 small chicken pieces, such as thighs and drumsticks, skinned
fresh coriander (cilantro) sprigs and lemon wedges, to garnish

1 Put the desiccated coconut in a bowl with 45ml/3 tbsp water. Leave to soak for 15 minutes.

2 Heat 15ml/1 tbsp of the oil in a karahi, wok or large pan and fry the cumin seeds, peppercorns, fennel and coriander seeds over a low heat for 3–4 minutes until they begin to splutter.

3 Add the finely chopped onions and fry for about 5 minutes without browning, stirring occasionally, until the onion has softened and turned opaque.

4 Stir in the coconut, along with the soaking water and salt, and continue to fry for a further 5 minutes, stirring occasionally to prevent the mixture from sticking to the pan.

5 Put the coconut mixture into a food processor or blender and process to form a coarse paste. Spoon into a bowl and set aside until required.

6 Heat the remaining oil and fry the chicken for 10 minutes. Add the coconut paste and cook over a low heat for 15–20 minutes, or until the coconut mixture is golden brown and the chicken is tender.

7 Transfer the curry to a warmed serving plate, and garnish with sprigs of fresh coriander and lemon wedges. Mint and Coconut Chutney, rice or lentils make good accompaniments.

Energy 305kcal/1271kJ; Fat 21.4g; Saturated fat 12.1g; Carbohydrate 1.2g; Fibre 2.6g.

Chicken Dopiaza

Dopiaza translates literally as "two onions" and describes this chicken dish in which two types of onion – large and small – are used at different stages.

Serves 4
30ml/2 tbsp oil
8 small onions, halved
2 bay leaves
8 green cardamom pods
4 cloves
3 dried red chillies
8 black peppercorns
2 medium onions, finely chopped
2 garlic cloves, crushed
2.5cm/1in piece fresh root ginger, finely chopped
5ml/1 tsp ground coriander
5ml/1 tsp ground cumin
2.5ml/½ tsp ground turmeric
5ml/1 tsp chilli powder
2.5ml/½ tsp salt
4 tomatoes, peeled and finely chopped
120ml/4fl oz/½ cup water
8 chicken pieces, such as thighs and drumsticks, skinned
plain rice, to serve

1 Heat half the oil in a wok or large heavy pan and fry the small onions for 10 minutes, or until golden brown. Remove and set aside.

2 Add the remaining oil and fry the bay leaves, cardamoms, cloves, chillies and peppercorns for 2 minutes. Add the medium onions, garlic and ginger and fry for 5 minutes. Stir in the ground spices and salt and cook for 2 minutes.

3 Add the tomatoes and water and simmer for 5 minutes until the sauce thickens. Add the chicken and cook for 15 minutes.

4 Add the reserved small onions, then cover and cook for a further 10 minutes, or until the chicken is cooked through. Spoon the mixture on to a serving dish or individual plates. Serve with plain boiled rice.

> **Cook's Tip**
> Soak the small onions in boiling water for 2–3 minutes to make them easier to peel.

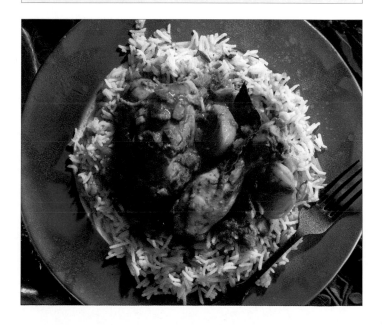

Energy 352kcal/1469kJ; Fat 15.1g; Saturated fat 3.67g; Carbohydrate 22.6g; Fibre 3.9g.

Chicken Dhansak

Dhansak curries originally came from Iran with the Parsee community. The curries traditionally include lentils, which make the dish substantial and flavoursome.

Serves 4
75g/3oz/⅓ cup green lentils
475ml/16fl oz/2 cups chicken stock
15ml/1 tbsp oil
5ml/1 tsp cumin seeds
2 curry leaves
1 onion, finely chopped
2.5cm/1in piece fresh root ginger, chopped
1 fresh green chilli, finely chopped
5ml/1 tsp ground cumin
5ml/1 tsp ground coriander
1.5ml/¼ tsp salt
1.5ml/¼ tsp chilli powder
400g/14oz can chopped tomatoes
8 chicken pieces, skinned
90ml/6 tbsp chopped fresh coriander (cilantro)
5ml/1 tsp garam masala
boiled plain and yellow rice, to serve

1 Rinse the lentils under cold running water. Put into a pan with the stock. Bring to the boil, cover and simmer for about 15–20 minutes. Put the lentils and stock to one side.

2 Heat the oil in a large, heavy pan and fry the cumin seeds and curry leaves for 2 minutes. Add the onion, ginger and chilli and fry for about 5 minutes. Stir in the cumin, ground coriander, salt and chilli powder with 30ml/2 tbsp water.

3 Add the tomatoes and the chicken pieces to the spices. Cover and cook for 10–15 minutes.

4 Add the lentils and stock, half the chopped fresh coriander and the garam masala. Cook for a further 10 minutes or until the chicken is tender. Garnish with the remaining fresh coriander and serve with spiced plain and yellow rice.

> **Cook's Tip**
> Before cooking green lentils, always pick them over and remove any small sticks or stones that might be hidden.

Energy 328kcal/1376kJ; Fat 10.8g; Saturated fat 2.54g; Carbohydrate 19.7g; Fibre 3.5g.

Hot Chilli Chicken

Not for the faint-hearted, this fiery hot curry is made with a spicy chilli masala paste.

Serves 4
30ml/2 tbsp tomato purée (paste)
2 garlic cloves, roughly chopped
2 fresh green chillies, roughly chopped
5 dried red chillies
2.5ml/½ tsp salt
1.5ml/¼ tsp granulated sugar
5ml/1 tsp chilli powder
2.5ml/½ tsp paprika
15ml/1 tbsp curry paste
15ml/1 tbsp oil
2.5ml/½ tsp cumin seeds
1 onion, finely chopped
2 bay leaves
5ml/1 tsp ground coriander
5ml/1 tsp ground cumin
1.5ml/¼ tsp ground turmeric
400g/14oz can chopped tomatoes
150ml/¼ pint/⅔ cup water
8 chicken thighs, skinned
5ml/1 tsp garam masala
sliced fresh green chillies, to garnish
chapatis and natural (plain) low-fat yogurt, to serve

1 Put the tomato purée, chopped garlic cloves, fresh green chillies and the dried red chillies into a food processor or blender.

2 Add the salt, sugar, chilli powder, paprika and curry paste. Process all the ingredients to a smooth paste, stopping once or twice to scrape down any of the mixture that has stuck to the sides of the bowl.

3 Heat the oil in a large, heavy pan and fry the cumin seeds for 2 minutes. Add the onion and bay leaves and fry for about 5 minutes.

4 Add the chilli paste and fry the mixture for 2–3 minutes. Add the ground coriander, cumin and turmeric and cook for 2 minutes. Add the tomatoes.

5 Pour in the water and stir to mix. Bring to the boil and simmer for 5 minutes until the sauce thickens. Add the chicken and garam masala. Cover and simmer for 25–30 minutes, until the chicken is tender. Garnish with sliced green chillies and serve with chapatis and natural low-fat yogurt.

Energy 290kcal/1212kJ; Fat 13g; Saturated fat 3.5g; Carbohydrate 11.6g; Fibre 1.4g.

Chicken in Cashew Nut Sauce

This strongly flavoured chicken dish has a deliciously thick and nutty sauce, and is best served with plain boiled rice.

Serves 4

2 medium onions
30ml/2 tbsp tomato purée (paste)
50g/2oz/1/2 cup cashew nuts
7.5ml/1 1/2 tsp garam masala
5ml/1 tsp crushed garlic
5ml/1 tsp chilli powder
15ml/1 tbsp lemon juice
1.5ml/1/4 tsp ground turmeric
5ml/1 tsp salt
15ml/1 tbsp natural (plain) low-fat yogurt
30ml/2 tbsp oil
30ml/2 tbsp chopped fresh coriander (cilantro)
15ml/1 tbsp sultanas (golden raisins)
450g/1lb boneless chicken, skinned and cubed
175g/6oz/2 1/2 cups button (white) mushrooms
300ml/1/2 pint/1 1/4 cups water

1 Cut the onions into quarters, place in a food processor or blender and process for about 1 minute. Add the tomato purée, cashew nuts, garam masala, garlic, chilli powder, lemon juice, turmeric, salt and yogurt. Process the spiced onion mixture in the food processor for a further 1–1 1/2 minutes.

2 In a heavy pan or karahi, heat the oil, lower the heat to medium and pour in the spice mixture from the food processor. Fry the mixture for 2 minutes, lowering the heat a little more if necessary.

3 When the spice mixture is lightly cooked, add half the chopped fresh coriander, the sultanas and the chicken cubes and continue to stir-fry for a further 1 minute.

4 Add the mushrooms, pour in the water and simmer. Cover the pan and cook over a low heat for about 10 minutes.

5 After this time, check that the chicken is cooked through and the sauce is thick. Cook for a little longer if necessary, then spoon into a serving bowl. Garnish with the remaining fresh coriander and serve.

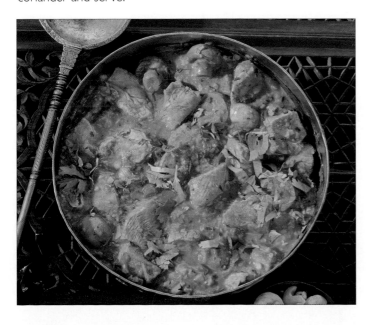

Energy 283kcal/1182kJ; Fat 12.70g; Saturated fat 3.48g; Carbohydrate 9.70g; Fibre 3.10g.

Chicken Saag

A mildly spiced dish using a popular combination of spinach and chicken. This recipe is best made using fresh spinach.

Serves 4

225g/8oz fresh spinach leaves, washed but not dried
2.5cm/1in piece fresh root ginger, grated
2 garlic cloves, crushed
1 fresh green chilli, roughly chopped
200ml/7fl oz/scant 1 cup water
15ml/1 tbsp oil
2 bay leaves
1.5ml/1/4 tsp black peppercorns
1 onion, finely chopped
4 tomatoes, peeled and finely chopped
10ml/2 tsp curry powder
5ml/1 tsp salt
5ml/1 tsp chilli powder
45ml/3 tbsp natural (plain) low-fat yogurt
8 chicken thighs, skinned
naan bread, to serve
natural low-fat yogurt and chilli powder, to garnish

1 Cook the spinach leaves, without extra water, in a tightly covered pan for 5 minutes. Put the cooked spinach, ginger, garlic and chilli with 50ml/2fl oz/1/4 cup of the measured water into a food processor or blender and process to a thick purée. Set aside.

2 Heat the oil in a large, heavy pan, add the bay leaves and black peppercorns and fry for 2 minutes. Stir in the onion and fry for a further 6–8 minutes or until the onion has browned.

3 Add the tomatoes and simmer for about 5 minutes.

4 Stir in the curry powder, salt and chilli powder. Cook for 2 minutes over medium heat, stirring once or twice. Stir in the spinach purée and the remaining measured water, then simmer for 5 minutes. Add the yogurt, 15ml/1 tbsp at a time, and simmer for 5 minutes.

5 Add the chicken thighs and stir to coat them in the sauce. Cover and cook for 25–30 minutes until the chicken is tender. Serve on naan bread, drizzle over some natural yogurt and dust with chilli powder.

Energy 283kcal/1182kJ; Fat 12.7g; Saturated fat 3.48g; Carbohydrate 9.7g; Fibre 3.1g.

Chicken Tikka Masala

This is said to be the UK's favourite chicken dish. In this version, tender chicken pieces are cooked in a creamy, spicy tomato sauce and served on naan bread.

Serves 4
675g/1½lb skinned chicken breast portions
90ml/6 tbsp tikka paste
120ml/4fl oz/½ cup natural (plain) low-fat yogurt
15ml/1 tbsp oil
1 onion, chopped
1 garlic clove, crushed
1 fresh green chilli, seeded and chopped
2.5cm/1in piece fresh root ginger, grated
15ml/1 tbsp tomato purée (paste)
250ml/8fl oz/1 cup water
a little melted ghee or butter
15ml/1 tbsp lemon juice
fresh coriander (cilantro) sprigs, natural (plain) low-fat yogurt and toasted cumin seeds, to garnish
naan bread, to serve

1 Cut the chicken into 2.5cm/1in cubes. Mix 45ml/3 tbsp of the tikka paste and 60ml/4 tbsp of the yogurt into a bowl. Add the chicken and leave to marinate for 20 minutes.

2 Heat the oil in a heavy pan and fry the onion, garlic, chilli and ginger for 5 minutes. Add the remaining tikka paste and fry for 2 minutes. Stir in the tomato purée and water, bring to the boil and simmer for 15 minutes.

3 Meanwhile, thread the chicken pieces on to wooden kebab skewers. Preheat the grill (broiler).

4 Brush the chicken pieces with melted ghee or butter and cook under a medium heat for 15 minutes, turning occasionally.

5 Put the tikka sauce into a food processor or blender and process until smooth. Return to the pan.

6 Add the remaining yogurt and the lemon juice, remove the chicken from the skewers and add to the pan, then simmer for 5 minutes. Garnish with the fresh coriander, yogurt and toasted cumin seeds and serve on naan bread.

Energy 315kcal/1321kJ; Fat 12.5g; Saturated fat 4g; Carbohydrate 7.5g; Fibre 0.6g.

Chicken with Green Mango

Green, unripe mango is used for making various dishes on the Indian subcontinent, including pickles, chutneys and some meat, chicken and vegetable dishes. This is a fairly simple chicken dish to prepare and is good served with rice and dhal.

Serves 4
1 medium green mango
450g/1lb skinned boneless chicken, cubed
1.5ml/¼ tsp onion seeds
5ml/1 tsp grated fresh root ginger
2.5ml/½ tsp crushed garlic
5ml/1 tsp chilli powder
1.5ml/¼ tsp ground turmeric
5ml/1 tsp salt
5ml/1 tsp ground coriander
30ml/2 tbsp oil
2 medium onions, sliced
4 curry leaves
300ml/½ pint/1¼ cups water
2 medium tomatoes, quartered
2 fresh green chillies, chopped
30ml/2 tbsp chopped fresh coriander (cilantro)

1 To prepare the mango, peel off the skin and slice the flesh thickly. Discard the stone (pit) from the middle. Place the mango slices in a small bowl, cover and set aside.

2 Place the chicken cubes in a bowl and add the onion seeds, ginger, garlic, chilli powder, turmeric, salt and ground coriander. Mix to coat the chicken with the spices, then add half the mango slices.

3 In a medium, heavy pan, heat the oil and fry the sliced onions until golden brown. Add the curry leaves and stir lightly.

4 Gradually add the chicken pieces and mango to the onions in the pan, stirring all the time.

5 Pour in the water, lower the heat and cook for about 12–15 minutes, stirring occasionally, until the chicken is cooked through and the water has been absorbed.

6 Add the remaining mango slices, the quartered tomatoes, chopped green chillies and fresh coriander. Serve the curry piping hot.

Energy 281kcal/1172kJ; Fat 11.2g; Saturated fat 2.44g; Carbohydrate 20.6g; Fibre 3.6g.

Chicken in Orange & Black Pepper Sauce

This is a low-fat version of a favourite Indian dish which is very creamy and full of flavour.

Serves 4
225g/8oz low-fat fromage frais or ricotta cheese
50ml/2fl oz/¼ cup natural (plain) low-fat yogurt
120ml/4fl oz/½ cup orange juice
7.5ml/1½ tsp grated fresh root ginger
5ml/1 tsp crushed garlic
5ml/1 tsp ground black pepper
5ml/1 tsp salt
5ml/1 tsp ground coriander
1 small chicken, about 675g/1½lb, skinned and cut into 8 pieces
15ml/1 tbsp oil
1 bay leaf
1 large onion, chopped
15ml/1 tbsp fresh mint leaves
1 fresh green chilli, seeded and chopped

1 In a small mixing bowl whisk the fromage frais or ricotta cheese with the yogurt, orange juice, ginger, garlic, pepper, salt and coriander.

2 Pour the fromage frais and orange mixture over the chicken, cover, and set aside for 3–4 hours.

3 Heat the oil with the bay leaf in a wok or heavy frying pan and fry the chopped onion for about 5 minutes or until just beginning to become soft.

4 Pour the chicken mixture into the pan with the onions and bay leaf and stir-fry for 3–5 minutes over a medium heat. Lower the heat, cover and cook for 7–10 minutes, adding a little water if the sauce is too thick. Add the fresh mint and chilli and serve.

> **Cook's Tip**
> If you prefer the spicy taste of curry leaves, you can use them instead of the bay leaf, but you will need to double the quantity.

Energy 199kcal/836kJ; Fat 5.11g; Saturated fat 1.06g; Carbohydrate 14.4g; Fibre 1.02g.

Spicy Masala Chicken

These tender chicken pieces have a sweet-and-sour taste. Serve cold with a salad and rice or hot with potatoes.

Serves 6
12 chicken thighs, skinned
90ml/6 tbsp lemon juice
5ml/1 tsp grated fresh root ginger
5ml/1 tsp crushed garlic
5ml/1 tsp crushed dried red chillies
5ml/1 tsp salt
5ml/1 tsp soft brown sugar
30ml/2 tbsp clear honey
30ml/2 tbsp chopped fresh coriander (cilantro)
1 fresh green chilli, finely chopped
30ml/2 tbsp vegetable oil
fresh coriander, to garnish
yellow rice and salad, to serve

1 Prick the chicken thighs with a fork, rinse them, pat dry with kitchen paper and set aside in a bowl.

2 In a large mixing bowl, mix together the lemon juice, grated ginger, garlic, crushed dried red chillies, salt, sugar and honey.

3 Transfer the chicken thighs to the spice mixture and coat well. Cover and set aside for about 45 minutes.

4 Preheat the grill (broiler) to medium. Add the fresh coriander and chopped chilli to the chicken thighs and place them in a flameproof dish.

5 Pour any remaining marinade over the chicken and brush with the oil.

6 Grill (broil) the chicken thighs for 15–20 minutes, turning and basting with the marinade occasionally, until cooked through and browned.

7 Serve cold, garnished with fresh coriander and accompanied by yellow rice and salad.

Energy 243kcal/1017kJ; Fat 12g; Saturated fat 3.18g; Carbohydrate 5.3g; Fibre 0g.

Chicken Korma

Although kormas are traditionally rich and high in fat, this recipe uses low-fat yogurt instead of cream, which gives the sauce a delicious creamy flavour while keeping down the fat content.

Serves 4
675g/1½lb skinned chicken
   breast portions
2 garlic cloves, crushed
2.5cm/1in piece fresh root ginger,
   roughly chopped
15ml/1 tbsp oil
3 green cardamom pods
1 onion, finely chopped
10ml/2 tsp ground cumin
1.5ml/¼ tsp salt
300ml/½ pint/1¼ cups natural
   (plain) low-fat yogurt
toasted flaked or sliced almonds
   (optional) and a fresh coriander
   (cilantro) sprig, to garnish
plain rice, to serve

1 Using a sharp knife, remove any visible fat from the chicken and cut the meat into 2.5cm/1in cubes.

2 Put the crushed garlic and ginger into a food processor or blender with 30ml/2 tbsp water and process to a smooth, creamy paste.

3 Heat the oil in a large, heavy pan and cook the chicken cubes for 8–10 minutes until browned on all sides. Remove the chicken cubes with a slotted spoon and set aside.

4 Add the cardamom pods and fry for 2 minutes. Add the finely chopped onion and fry for a further 5 minutes. Stir in the garlic and ginger paste, cumin and salt and cook, stirring, for a further 5 minutes. Add half the yogurt, stirring in a spoonful at a time, and cook over a low heat until it has all been absorbed.

5 Return the chicken to the pan. Cover and simmer over a low heat for 5–6 minutes or until the chicken is tender.

6 Add the remaining yogurt and simmer for a further 5 minutes. Garnish with toasted almonds and coriander and serve with rice.

Energy 288kcal/1211kJ; Fat 9.3g; Saturated fat 2.54g; Carbohydrate 9.8g; Fibre 0.5g.

Mild Chicken Curry with Lentils

In this low-fat dish, the mildly spiced sauce is thickened using low-fat lentils rather than the traditional onions fried in ghee. The resulting dish is delicious and filling as well as healthy.

Serves 4–6
75g/3oz/⅓ cup red lentils
30ml/2 tbsp mild curry
   powder
10ml/2 tsp ground coriander
5ml/1 tsp cumin seeds
475ml/16fl oz/2 cups
   vegetable stock
8 chicken thighs, skinned
225g/8oz fresh spinach, shredded,
   or frozen spinach, thawed and
   well drained
15ml/1 tbsp chopped fresh
   coriander (cilantro), plus extra
   to garnish
salt and ground black pepper
white or brown basmati rice and
   grilled (broiled) poppadums,
   to serve

1 Put the red lentils in a large, heavy pan and add the mild curry powder, ground coriander, cumin seeds and vegetable stock.

2 Bring the mixture to the boil, then lower the heat. Cover and simmer for 10 minutes, stirring often.

3 Add the chicken thighs and spinach. Replace the cover and simmer gently for a further 40 minutes, or until the chicken is cooked through.

4 Stir in the chopped coriander and season with salt and ground black pepper to taste. Serve garnished with fresh coriander sprigs and accompanied by white or brown basmati rice and poppadums.

> **Cook's Tip**
> *Nourishing lentils are an excellent low-fat source of vitamins, protein and fibre. Yellow and red lentils, in particular, are very popular in Indian cooking, adding subtle colour and texture to dishes.*

Energy 296kcal/1244kJ; Fat 10.2g; Saturated fat 2.83g; Carbohydrate 15.1g; Fibre 3.8g.

Chicken Jalfrezi

A jalfrezi is a stir-fried curry which features onions, ginger and garlic in a rich pepper sauce.

Serves 4

675g/1½lb chicken breast
   portions
15ml/1 tbsp oil
5ml/1 tsp cumin seeds
1 onion, finely chopped
1 green (bell) pepper, seeded
   and finely chopped
1 red (bell) pepper, seeded
   and finely chopped

1 garlic clove, crushed
2cm/¾in piece fresh root ginger,
   finely chopped
15ml/1 tbsp curry paste
1.5ml/¼ tsp chilli
   powder
5ml/1 tsp ground coriander
5ml/1 tsp ground cumin
2.5ml/½ tsp salt
400g/14oz can chopped
   tomatoes
30ml/2 tbsp chopped fresh
   coriander (cilantro), plus extra
   to garnish
plain rice, to serve

1 Skin the chicken breast portions and remove any visible fat. Cut the meat into 2.5cm/1in cubes.

2 Heat the oil in a karahi, wok or heavy pan and fry the cumin seeds for 2 minutes until they splutter. Add the onion, peppers, garlic and ginger and fry for 6–8 minutes.

3 Add the curry paste and fry for about 2 minutes. Stir in the chilli powder, ground coriander, cumin and salt and add 15ml/ 1 tbsp water; fry for a further 2 minutes.

4 Add the chicken cubes and fry for about 5 minutes. Add the canned tomatoes and chopped fresh coriander. Cover the pan tightly with a lid and cook for about 15 minutes or until the chicken cubes are tender. Garnish with sprigs of fresh coriander and serve with rice.

> **Cook's Tip**
> *Removing the skin and any visible fat from the chicken makes a healthier dish which is low in fat.*

Energy 291kcal/1224kJ; Fat 9.8g; Saturated fat 2.24g; Carbohydrate 11.7g; Fibre 3.5g.

Karahi Chicken with Fresh Fenugreek

Fresh fenugreek is a flavour that many people are unfamiliar with and this recipe is a good introduction to this delicious herb. The chicken is boiled before being quickly stir-fried, to make sure that it is cooked all the way through.

Serves 4

115g/4oz boneless chicken thigh
   meat, skinned and cut into strips
115g/4oz chicken breast fillet,
   skinned and cut into strips

2.5ml/½ tsp crushed garlic
5ml/1 tsp chilli powder
2.5ml/½ tsp salt
10ml/2 tsp tomato purée
   (paste)
30ml/2 tbsp oil
1 bunch fresh fenugreek leaves
15ml/1 tbsp chopped fresh
   coriander (cilantro)
300ml/½ pint/1¼ cups water
pilau rice and wholemeal
   (whole-wheat) chapatis,
   to serve (optional)

1 Bring a pan of water to the boil, add the chicken strips and cook for about 5–7 minutes. Drain the chicken and set aside.

2 In a mixing bowl, combine the garlic, chilli powder and salt with the tomato purée.

3 Heat the oil in a large, heavy pan. Lower the heat and stir in the tomato purée and spice mixture.

4 Add the chicken pieces to the spices and stir-fry for 5–7 minutes, then lower the heat further.

5 Add the fenugreek leaves and chopped fresh coriander. Continue to stir-fry for 5–7 minutes until all the ingredients are well mixed.

6 Pour in the water, cover and cook for about 5 minutes, stirring several times, until the dish is simmering. Serve hot with pilau rice and warm wholemeal chapatis, if you like.

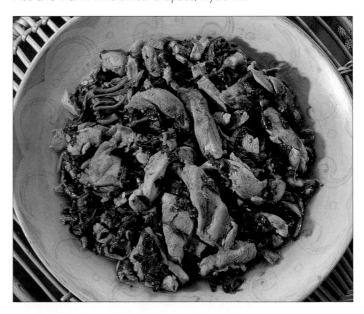

Energy 127kcal/528kJ; Fat 7.9g; Saturated fat 1.51g; Carbohydrate 1.2g; Fibre 0.1g.

Karahi Chicken & Tomatoes with Mint

A traditional herb that goes deliciously well with spicy chicken is mint, which has cooling qualities to counter the heat of ginger and chillies. This is mildly spiced recipe is perfect for children or those who like a piquant flavour without heat.

Serves 4
275g/10oz skinned chicken breast fillets, cut into strips
300ml/1/2 pint/1 1/4 cups water
30ml/2 tbsp oil
2 small bunches spring onions (scallions), roughly chopped
5ml/1 tsp shredded fresh root ginger
5ml/1 tsp crushed dried red chillies
30ml/2 tbsp lemon juice
15ml/1 tbsp chopped fresh coriander (cilantro)
15ml/1 tbsp chopped fresh mint
3 tomatoes, peeled, seeded and roughly chopped
5ml/1 tsp salt
fresh mint and coriander sprigs, to garnish

1 Put the strips of chicken breast and water into a pan, bring to the boil and lower the heat to medium. Cook for about 10 minutes, uncovered, or until the water has evaporated and the chicken is cooked. Remove the pan from the heat and set aside.

2 Heat the oil in a heavy pan and stir-fry the spring onions for 2 minutes until soft but not browned.

3 Add the cooked chicken strips and stir-fry for about 3 minutes over a medium heat.

4 Gradually add the shredded ginger, dried red chillies, lemon juice, chopped coriander and mint, tomatoes and salt and gently stir to blend all the flavours.

5 Transfer the spicy chicken mixture to a serving dish and garnish with a few sprigs of fresh mint and coriander before serving piping hot.

Energy 157kcal/655kJ; Fat 8.2g; Saturated fat 1.5g; Carbohydrate 4.2g; Fibre 1.4g.

Red Hot Chicken Curry

This curry has a satisfyingly thick sauce, and uses sweet red and green peppers for extra colour and flavour.

Serves 4
2 medium onions
1/2 red (bell) pepper
1/2 green (bell) pepper
30ml/2 tbsp oil
1.5ml/1/4 tsp fenugreek seeds
1.5ml/1/4 tsp onion seeds
2.5ml/1/2 tsp crushed garlic
2.5ml/1/2 tsp grated fresh root ginger
5ml/1 tsp ground coriander
5ml/1 tsp chilli powder
5ml/1 tsp salt
400g/14oz can tomatoes
30ml/2 tbsp lemon juice
350g/12oz chicken, skinned and cubed
30ml/2 tbsp chopped fresh coriander (cilantro)
3 fresh green chillies, chopped
fresh coriander, to garnish

1 Using a sharp knife, dice the onions. Seed the peppers and cut them into chunks.

2 In a medium, heavy pan, heat the oil and fry the fenugreek and onion seeds until they turn a shade darker. Add the chopped onions, crushed garlic and fresh ginger. Fry for about 5 minutes until the onions turn golden brown. Reduce the heat to very low.

3 In a bowl, mix together the ground coriander, chilli powder, salt, canned tomatoes and lemon juice. Stir well.

4 Pour this mixture into the pan and increase the heat to medium. Stir-fry for about 3 minutes.

5 Add the chicken cubes and stir-fry for 5–7 minutes.

6 Add the chopped fresh coriander and green chillies and the red and green pepper chunks.

7 Lower the heat, cover the pan and allow to simmer for about 10 minutes, until the chicken cubes are cooked.

8 Serve the curry hot, garnished with fresh coriander.

Energy 214kcal/895kJ; Fat 10g; Saturated fat 2.08g; Carbohydrate 11g; Fibre 2.2g.

Kashmiri Chicken Curry

Surrounded by the snow-capped Himalayas, Kashmir is popularly known as the "Switzerland of the East". The state is also renowned for its rich culinary heritage, and this aromatic dish is one of the simplest among the region's repertoire.

Serves 4–6

20ml/4 tsp Kashmiri masala
   paste
60ml/4 tbsp tomato ketchup
5ml/1 tsp Worcestershire sauce
5ml/1 tsp five-spice powder
5ml/1 tsp granulated sugar
8 chicken joints, skinned
5cm/2in piece fresh
   root ginger
45ml/3 tbsp vegetable oil
4 garlic cloves, crushed
juice of 1 lemon
15ml/1 tbsp coriander (cilantro)
   leaves, finely chopped
salt

1 To make the marinade, mix the masala paste, tomato ketchup, Worcestershire sauce and five-spice powder with the sugar and a little salt. Leave the mixture to rest in a warm place until the sugar has dissolved.

2 Rub the chicken pieces with the marinade and set aside in a cool place for at least 2 hours, or preferably in the refrigerator overnight. Bring the chicken to room temperature before cooking.

3 Thinly peel the ginger, using a sharp knife or vegetable peeler. Grate the peeled root finely.

4 Heat the oil in a karahi, wok or large pan and fry half the ginger and all the garlic until golden.

5 Add the chicken and fry until both sides are sealed. Cover and cook until the chicken is tender, and the oil has separated from the sauce.

6 Sprinkle the chicken with the lemon juice, remaining grated ginger and chopped coriander leaves, and mix in well. Serve the chicken piping hot. Plain boiled rice would make a good accompaniment.

Mughlai-style Chicken

The cuisine of Andhra Pradesh is renowned for its pungency because the hottest variety of chilli is grown there. In contrast, however, the region is also home to the subtle flavours of a style of cooking known as *nizami*, which has a distinct Mughal influence. This recipe, with the heady aroma of saffron and the captivating flavour of a silky almond sauce, is a good example.

Serves 4–6

1 large onion
2 eggs
4 skinned chicken breast fillets
15–30ml/1–2 tbsp garam masala
90ml/6 tbsp ghee or vegetable oil
5cm/2in piece fresh root ginger,
   finely crushed
4 garlic cloves, finely crushed
4 cloves
4 green cardamom pods
5cm/2in piece cinnamon stick
2 bay leaves
15–20 saffron threads
150ml/¼ pint/⅔ cup natural
   (plain) yogurt, beaten with
   5ml/1 tsp cornflour
   (cornstarch)
75ml/2½fl oz/⅓ cup double
   (heavy) cream
50g/2oz/½ cup ground almonds
salt and ground black pepper

1 Chop the onion finely. Break the eggs into a bowl and season with salt and pepper.

2 Rub the chicken fillets with the garam masala, then brush with the beaten egg. In a karahi, wok, or large pan, heat the ghee or vegetable oil and fry the chicken until cooked through and browned on both sides. Remove from the pan and keep warm.

3 In the same pan, fry the chopped onion, ginger, garlic, cloves, cardamom pods, cinnamon and bay leaves. When the onion turns golden, remove the pan from the heat, allow the contents to cool a little and add the saffron and yogurt mixture. Stir well to prevent the yogurt from curdling.

4 Return the chicken to the pan, along with any juices, and gently cook until the chicken is tender. Adjust the seasoning. Just before serving, pour in the cream. Fold it in then repeat the process with the ground almonds. Serve when piping hot.

Energy 483kcal/2009kJ; Fat 34.9g; Saturated fat 8.2g; Carbohydrate 5.7g; Fibre 0.2g.

Energy 514kcal/2141kJ; Fat 32.3g; Saturated fat 9.9g; Carbohydrate 7.9g; Fibre 0.9g.

Chicken Curry with Sliced Apples

This mild yet flavoursome dish is pleasantly flavoured with a warming combination of spices and chilli. Yogurt and almonds make a creamy sauce, which is given an additional lift by the use of sliced apples.

Serves 4
10ml/2 tsp oil
2 medium onions, diced
1 bay leaf
2 cloves
2.5cm/1in piece cinnamon stick
4 black peppercorns
1 baby chicken, about 675g/1½lb, skinned and cut into 8 pieces
5ml/1 tsp garam masala
5ml/1 tsp grated fresh root ginger
5ml/1 tsp crushed garlic
5ml/1 tsp salt
5ml/1 tsp chilli powder
15ml/1 tbsp ground almonds
150ml/¼ pint/⅔ cup natural (plain) low-fat yogurt
2 green eating apples, peeled, cored and roughly sliced
15ml/1 tbsp chopped fresh coriander (cilantro)
15g/½oz flaked (sliced) almonds, lightly toasted, and fresh coriander leaves, to garnish

1 Heat the oil in a karahi, wok or heavy pan and fry the onions with the bay leaf, cloves, cinnamon and peppercorns for about 3–5 minutes until the onions are beginning to soften but have not yet begun to brown.

2 Add the chicken pieces to the onions and continue to stir-fry for at least another 3 minutes.

3 Lower the heat and add the garam masala, ginger, garlic, salt, chilli powder and ground almonds and cook, stirring constantly, for 2–3 minutes.

4 Pour in the yogurt and stir for a couple more minutes.

5 Add the apples and chopped coriander, cover and cook for about 10–15 minutes.

6 Check that the chicken is cooked through and serve immediately, garnished with the flaked almonds and whole coriander leaves.

Energy 237kcal/994kJ; Fat 8.25g; Saturated fat 1.31g; Carbohydrate 17.21g; Fibre 2.88g.

Chicken & Potatoes with Rice

This dish, *Murgh Biryani*, is mainly prepared for important occasions in India, and is truly fit for royalty. Every cook in India has a subtle variation which is kept a closely guarded secret.

Serves 4–6
1.3kg/3lb skinned chicken breast portions, cut into large pieces
60ml/4 tbsp biryani masala paste
2 fresh green chillies, chopped
15ml/1 tbsp grated fresh root ginger
15ml/1 tbsp crushed garlic
50g/2oz/2 cups fresh coriander (cilantro), chopped
6–8 fresh mint leaves, chopped
150ml/¼ pint/⅔ cup natural (plain) yogurt, beaten
30ml/2 tbsp tomato purée (paste)
4 onions, finely sliced, deep-fried and crushed

450g/1lb/2¼ cups basmati rice, washed and drained
5ml/1 tsp black cumin seeds
5cm/2in piece cinnamon stick
4 green cardamom pods
2 black cardamom pods
vegetable oil, for shallow-frying
4 large potatoes, peeled and quartered
175ml/6fl oz/¾ cup milk, mixed with 90ml/6 tbsp water
1 sachet saffron powder, mixed with 90ml/6 tbsp milk
25g/1oz/2 tbsp ghee or unsalted (sweet) butter
1 tomato, sliced
salt

For the garnish
ghee or unsalted (sweet) butter, for shallow-frying
50g/2oz/½ cup cashew nuts
50g/2oz/⅓ cup sultanas (golden raisins)

1 Mix the chicken pieces with the next 9 ingredients and salt in a large bowl and marinate, covered, in a cool place for about 2 hours. Place in a large heavy pan and cook over a low heat for about 10 minutes. Set aside.

2 Boil a large pan of water and soak the rice with the cumin seeds, cinnamon stick and green and black cardamom pods for about 5 minutes. Drain well. If you prefer, some of the whole spices may be removed and discarded at this stage.

3 Heat the oil for shallow-frying and fry the quartered potatoes until they are evenly browned on all sides. Drain the potatoes and set them aside.

4 Place half the rice on top of the chicken in the pan in an even layer. Then make an even layer with the potatoes. Put the remaining rice on top of the potatoes and spread to make an even layer.

5 Sprinkle the water mixed with milk all over the rice. Make random holes through the rice with the handle of a spoon and pour into each a little saffron milk. Place a few knobs (pats) of ghee or butter on the surface, cover the pan and cook over a low heat for 35–45 minutes.

6 While the biryani is cooking, make the garnish. Heat a little ghee or butter and fry the cashew nuts and sultanas until they swell. Drain and set aside. When the biryani is ready, gently toss the rice, chicken and potatoes together, garnish with the nut mixture and serve hot.

Energy 1032kcal/4349kJ; Fat 9.8g; Saturated fat 2.4g; Carbohydrate 131.1g; Fibre 2.9g.

Chicken Biryani

Biryanis originated in Persia and are traditionally made with a combination of meat and rice. They are often served at dinner parties and on festive occasions.

Serves 4
275g/10oz/1½ cups basmati rice
30ml/2 tbsp oil
1 onion, thinly sliced
2 garlic cloves, crushed
1 green chilli, finely chopped
2.5cm/1in piece fresh root ginger, finely chopped
675g/1½lb skinned chicken breast fillets, cut into 2.5cm/ 1in cubes
45ml/3 tbsp curry paste
1.5ml/¼ tsp salt
1.5ml/¼ tsp garam masala
3 tomatoes, cut into thin wedges
1.5ml/¼ tsp ground turmeric
2 bay leaves
4 green cardamom pods
4 cloves
1.5ml/¼ tsp saffron strands
Tomato and Fresh Chilli Chutney, to serve

1 Wash the rice in several changes of cold water. Put into a bowl, cover with water and leave to soak for 30 minutes.

2 Meanwhile, heat the oil in a large heavy frying pan and fry the onion for about 5–7 minutes until lightly browned. Add the garlic, chilli and ginger and fry for about 2 minutes. Add the chicken and fry for 5 minutes, stirring occasionally.

3 Add the curry paste, salt and garam masala and cook for 5 minutes. Stir in the tomato wedges and continue cooking for another 3–4 minutes, then remove from the heat and set aside.

4 Preheat the oven to 190°C/375°F/Gas 5. Bring a pan of water to the boil. Drain the rice and add it to the pan with the turmeric. Cook for about 10 minutes, or until the rice is almost tender. Drain the rice and toss together with the bay leaves, cardamoms, cloves and saffron.

5 Layer the rice and chicken in a shallow, ovenproof dish until all the mixture has been used, finishing off with a layer of rice. Cover and bake in the oven for 15–20 minutes or until the chicken is tender. Serve with Tomato and Fresh Chilli Chutney.

Chicken Pilau

Like biryanis, pilaus that include cooked meat and poultry make a convenient one-pot meal. A vegetable curry makes a good accompaniment, although for a simpler meal, such as supper, you could serve the pilau with a simple raita.

Serves 4
400g/14oz/2 cups basmati rice
75g/3oz/6 tbsp ghee or unsalted (sweet) butter
1 onion, sliced
1.5ml/¼ tsp mixed onion seeds and mustard seeds
3 curry leaves
5ml/1 tsp grated fresh root ginger
5ml/1 tsp crushed garlic
5ml/1 tsp ground coriander
5ml/1 tsp chilli powder
7.5ml/1½ tsp salt
2 tomatoes, sliced
1 potato, cubed
50g/2oz/½ cup frozen peas, thawed
175g/6oz skinned chicken breast fillets, cubed
60ml/4 tbsp chopped fresh coriander (cilantro)
2 fresh green chillies, chopped
750ml/1¼ pints/3 cups water

1 Wash the rice thoroughly under running water, then leave to soak for 30 minutes. Drain in a strainer or colander and set aside.

2 In a pan, melt the ghee or butter and fry the sliced onion until golden.

3 Add the onion and mustard seeds, the curry leaves, ginger, garlic, ground coriander, chilli powder and salt. Stir-fry for about 2 minutes over a low heat.

4 Add the sliced tomatoes, cubed potato, peas and chicken cubes and mix everything together well.

5 Add the rice and stir to combine with the other ingredients.

6 Add the coriander and chillies. Mix and stir-fry for 1 minute. Pour in the water, bring to the boil and then lower the heat. Cover tightly and cook for 20 minutes. Remove from the heat, leaving the lid in place, and leave the pilau to stand for 6–8 minutes. Serve hot.

Energy 531kcal/2224kJ; Fat 14.1g; Saturated fat 2.77g; Carbohydrate 61.3g; Fibre 3.7g.

Energy 603kcal/2515kJ; Fat 16.8g; Saturated fat 10g; Carbohydrate 91.9g; Fibre 2.1g.

Chicken Biryani with Almonds

Biryani is a meal in itself and needs no accompaniment.

Serves 4

275g/10oz/1½ cups basmati rice
10 whole green cardamom pods
2.5ml/½ tsp salt
2 or 3 whole cloves
5cm/2in piece cinnamon stick
45ml/3 tbsp vegetable oil
3 onions, sliced
4 skinned chicken breast fillets,
  about 175g/6oz each, cubed
1.5ml/¼ tsp ground cloves
1.5ml/¼ tsp hot chilli powder
5ml/1 tsp ground cumin
5ml/1 tsp ground coriander

2.5ml/½ tsp ground black pepper
3 garlic cloves, chopped
5ml/1 tsp finely chopped fresh
  root ginger
juice of 1 lemon
4 tomatoes, sliced
30ml/2 tbsp chopped fresh
  coriander (cilantro)
150ml/¼ pint/⅔ cup natural
  (plain) yogurt, plus extra
  to serve
4–5 saffron threads, soaked in
  10ml/2 tsp warm milk
150ml/¼ pint/⅔ cup water
toasted flaked (sliced) almonds
  and fresh coriander sprigs,
  to garnish

1 Wash the rice well and leave to soak in water for 30 minutes. Drain. Preheat the oven to 190°C/375°F/Gas 5. Remove the seeds from half the cardamom pods and grind them finely, using a mortar and pestle. Set aside the ground seeds.

2 Bring a pan of water to the boil. Add the rice with the salt, cardamoms, cloves and cinnamon stick. Boil for 2 minutes, then drain. Keep the rice hot in a covered pan.

3 Heat the oil in another pan, and fry the onions for 8 minutes, until browned. Add the chicken and the ground spices, including the ground cardamom. Mix well, then add the garlic, ginger and lemon juice. Stir-fry for 5 minutes. Transfer to a casserole and arrange the tomatoes on top. Sprinkle on the coriander, spoon the yogurt on top and cover with the rice.

4 Drizzle the saffron milk over the rice and pour over the water. Cover, then bake in the oven for 1 hour. Transfer to a serving platter and discard the whole spices. Garnish with almonds and coriander and serve immediately.

Energy 548kcal/2298kJ; Fat 11.1g; Saturated fat 1.7g; Carbohydrate 67.5g; Fibre 2.2g.

Chicken with Spicy Onions

Chunky onion slices infused with toasted cumin seeds and shredded ginger add a delicious contrast to the flavour of the chicken.

Serves 4–6

1.3kg/3lb chicken, jointed
  and skinned
17.5ml/½ tsp turmeric
2.5ml/½ tsp chilli powder
60ml/4 tbsp oil
4 small onions, finely chopped
175g/6oz/6 cups fresh coriander
  (cilantro), coarsely chopped

5cm/2in piece fresh root ginger,
  finely shredded
2 fresh green chillies,
  finely chopped
10ml/2 tsp cumin seeds,
  dry-roasted
75ml/5 tbsp natural
  (plain) yogurt
75ml/5 tbsp double
  (heavy) cream
2.5ml/½ tsp cornflour
  (cornstarch)
salt

1 With a sharp knife, make a few slashes in the chicken joints and then rub the meat with the turmeric, chilli powder and salt to taste. Heat the oil in a large frying pan and fry the chicken pieces in batches until both sides are sealed. Remove to a plate and keep hot.

2 Reheat the oil remaining in the pan and add three-quarters of the chopped onions, most of the fresh coriander, half the ginger, the green chillies and the cumin seeds and fry until the onions are translucent.

3 Return the chicken to the pan with any juices and mix well. Cover and cook gently for 15 minutes.

4 Remove the pan from the heat and leave to cool a little. Mix the yogurt, cream and cornflour in a bowl and gradually fold into the chicken, mixing well.

5 Return the pan to the heat and cook gently until the chicken is tender. Just before serving, stir in the reserved chopped onion, coriander and ginger. Spoon into a serving bowl and serve hot.

Energy 819kcal/3391kJ; Fat 65.4g; Saturated fat 23.4g; Carbohydrate 8.2g; Fibre 0.9g.

Fragrant Chicken Curry

This dish is perfect for a party as the chicken and sauce can be prepared in advance and combined and heated at the last minute.

Serves 4
45ml/3 tbsp oil
1 onion, coarsely chopped
2 garlic cloves, crushed
15ml/1 tbsp Thai red curry paste
1 litre/1¾ pints/4 cups
  coconut milk
2 lemon grass stalks, coarsely
  chopped
6 kaffir lime leaves, chopped
150ml/¼ pint/⅔ cup Greek
  (US strained plain) yogurt
30ml/2 tbsp apricot jam
1 cooked chicken, about
  1.6kg/3–3½lb
30ml/2 tbsp chopped fresh
  coriander (cilantro)
salt and ground black pepper
kaffir lime leaves, shredded,
  toasted coconut and fresh
  coriander, to garnish
boiled rice, to serve

1 Heat the oil in a large pan. Add the onion and garlic and cook over a low heat for 5–10 minutes until soft. Stir in the red curry paste. Cook, stirring constantly, for 2–3 minutes.

2 Stir in the coconut milk, then add the lemon grass, lime leaves, yogurt and apricot jam. Stir well. Cover and simmer for 30 minutes.

3 Remove the pan from the heat and leave to cool slightly. Transfer the sauce to a food processor or blender and process to a smooth purée, then strain it back into the rinsed-out pan, pressing as much of the puréed mixture as possible through the sieve (strainer) with the back of a wooden spoon. Set aside while you prepare the chicken.

4 Remove the skin from the chicken, slice the meat off the bones and cut it into bitesize pieces. Add to the sauce.

5 Bring the sauce back to simmering point. Stir in the fresh coriander and season with salt and pepper. Garnish with extra lime leaves, shredded coconut and coriander. Serve with rice.

Energy 531kcal/2216kJ; Fat 34.3g; Saturated fat 20.6g; Carbohydrate 4.3g; Fibre 0.8g.

Green Chicken Curry

Use fresh green chillies in this dish, if you like your curry hot. The mild aromatic flavour of the rice is a good foil for the spicy chicken.

Serves 3–4
4 spring onions (scallions),
  trimmed and coarsely
  chopped
1 or 2 fresh green chillies, seeded
  and coarsely chopped
2cm/¾in piece fresh root
  ginger, peeled
2 garlic cloves
5ml/1 tsp Thai fish sauce
large bunch fresh coriander
  (cilantro)
small handful of fresh parsley
30–45ml/2–3 tbsp water
30ml/2 tbsp sunflower oil
4 boneless chicken breast
  portions, skinned and diced
1 green (bell) pepper, seeded
  and thinly sliced
600ml/1 pint/2½ cups
  coconut milk
salt and ground black pepper
hot coconut rice, to serve

1 Put the spring onions, green chillies, ginger, garlic, fish sauce, coriander and parsley in a food processor or blender. Pour in 30ml/2 tbsp of the water and process to a smooth paste, adding a further 15ml/1 tbsp water if required.

2 Heat half the oil in a large frying pan. Cook the diced chicken until evenly browned. Transfer to a plate. Heat the remaining oil in the pan. Add the green pepper and stir-fry for 3–4 minutes, then add the chilli and ginger paste. Stir-fry for a further 3–4 minutes, until the mixture becomes fairly thick.

3 Return the chicken to the pan and add the coconut milk. Season with salt and pepper and bring to the boil, then reduce the heat, half-cover the pan and simmer for 8–10 minutes. When the chicken is cooked, transfer it, with the green pepper, to a plate. Boil the cooking liquid remaining in the pan for 10–12 minutes, until it is well reduced and fairly thick.

4 Return the chicken and pepper to the green curry sauce, stir well and cook gently for 2–3 minutes to heat through. Spoon the curry over the coconut rice, and serve immediately.

Energy 387kcal/1632kJ; Fat 11.1g; Saturated fat 2g; Carbohydrate 14.5g; Fibre 2.3g.

Yellow Chicken Curry

The combination of slightly sweet coconut milk and fruit with savoury chicken and spices is at once a comforting, refreshing and exotic combination.

Serves 4
300ml/½ pint/1¼ cups chicken stock
30ml/2 tbsp thick tamarind juice, made by mixing tamarind paste with warm water
15ml/1 tbsp granulated sugar
200ml/7fl oz/scant 1 cup coconut milk
1 green papaya, peeled, seeded and thinly sliced
250g/9oz boneless chicken breast portions, skinned and diced
juice of 1 lime
lime slices, to garnish

For the curry paste
1 fresh red chilli, seeded and coarsely chopped
4 garlic cloves, coarsely chopped
3 shallots, coarsely chopped
2 lemon grass stalks, sliced
5cm/2in piece fresh turmeric, coarsely chopped, or
5ml/1 tsp ground
5ml/1 tsp shrimp paste
5ml/1 tsp salt

1 To make the yellow curry paste, put the red chilli, garlic, shallots, lemon grass and turmeric in a mortar or food processor. Add the shrimp paste and salt. Pound or process to a paste, adding a little water if necessary.

2 Pour the stock into a wok or medium pan and bring it to the boil. Stir in the curry paste. Bring back to the boil and add the tamarind juice, sugar and coconut milk. Add the papaya and chicken and cook over medium to high heat for about 15 minutes, stirring frequently, until the chicken is cooked.

3 Stir in the lime juice, transfer to a warm dish and serve immediately, garnished with lime slices.

Cook's Tip
Fresh turmeric is a member of the root ginger family. When preparing it, wear gloves to protect your hands from staining.

Energy 135kcal/574kJ; Fat 1g; Saturated fat 0.3g; Carbohydrate 16.8g; Fibre 2.5g.

Coconut Chicken Curry

A mild coconut curry flavoured with turmeric, coriander and cumin seeds and typical south-east Asian flavourings of fish sauce and shrimp paste.

Serves 4
60ml/4 tbsp vegetable oil
1 large garlic clove, crushed
1 chicken, about 1.5kg/3lb 5oz, chopped into 12 large pieces
400ml/14fl oz/1¾ cups coconut cream
250ml/8fl oz/1 cup chicken stock
30ml/2 tbsp Thai fish sauce
30ml/2 tbsp sugar
juice of 2 limes
1 bunch of spring onions (scallions), thinly sliced
2 small fresh red chillies, seeded and finely chopped, to garnish

For the curry paste
5ml/1 tsp dried chilli flakes
2.5ml/½ tsp salt
5cm/2in piece fresh turmeric, coarsely chopped, or
5ml/1 tsp ground
2.5ml/½ tsp coriander seeds
2.5ml/½ tsp cumin seeds
5ml/1 tsp dried shrimp paste

1 First make the curry paste. Put all the ingredients in a mortar, food processor or spice grinder and pound, process or grind to a smooth paste.

2 Heat the oil in a wok or frying pan and cook the garlic until golden. Add the chicken and cook until golden. Remove the chicken and set aside.

3 Reheat the oil in the wok and add the curry paste and then half the coconut cream. Cook for a few minutes until fragrant.

4 Return the chicken to the wok or pan, add the stock, mixing well, then add the remaining coconut cream, the fish sauce, sugar and lime juice. Stir well and bring to the boil, then lower the heat and simmer for 15 minutes.

5 Divide the curry between four warm serving bowls and sprinkle with the chopped fresh chillies and spring onions to garnish. Serve immediately.

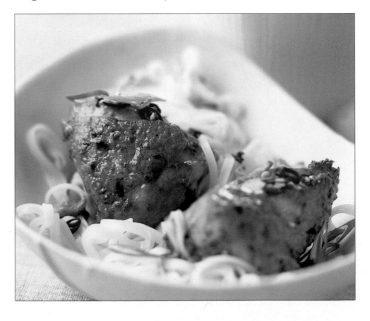

Energy 706kcal/2935kJ; Fat 50.4g; Saturated fat 12.8g; Carbohydrate 15.8g; Fibre 1.5g.

Red Chicken Curry with Bamboo Shoots

Bamboo shoots have a lovely crunchy texture, and it is quite acceptable to use canned ones instead of fresh. The unused curry paste will keep in the refrigerator for 3 months.

Serves 4–6

1 litre/1¾ pints/4 cups
   coconut milk
450g/1lb chicken breast fillet,
   skinned and cut into
   bitesize pieces
30ml/2 tbsp Thai fish sauce
15ml/1 tbsp sugar
225g/8oz drained canned
   bamboo shoots, rinsed
   and sliced
5 kaffir lime leaves, torn
salt and ground black pepper
chopped fresh red chillies
   and kaffir lime leaves,
   to garnish

For the red curry paste
5ml/1 tsp coriander seeds
2.5ml/½ tsp cumin seeds
12–15 fresh red chillies, seeded
   and roughly chopped
4 shallots, thinly sliced
2 garlic cloves, chopped
15ml/1 tbsp chopped
   galangal
2 lemon grass stalks,
   chopped
3 kaffir lime leaves, chopped
4 fresh coriander (cilantro)
   roots
10 black peppercorns
a good pinch of ground
   cinnamon
5ml/1 tsp ground turmeric
2.5ml/½ tsp shrimp paste
5ml/1 tsp salt
30ml/2 tbsp vegetable oil

1 To make the curry paste, dry-fry the coriander and cumin seeds for 1–2 minutes, then put in a mortar or food processor with the remaining ingredients except the oil and pound or process to a paste.

2 Add the oil, a little at a time, mixing or processing well after each addition. Transfer to a jar and keep in the refrigerator until ready to use.

3 Pour half the coconut milk into a large, heavy pan. Bring the milk to the boil, stirring constantly until it has separated.

4 Stir in 30ml/2 tbsp of the red curry paste and cook the mixture for 2–3 minutes, stirring constantly. Remaining red curry paste can be kept in the refrigerator for up to 3 months.

5 Add the chicken pieces, fish sauce and sugar to the pan. Stir well, then cook for 5–6 minutes until the chicken changes colour and is cooked through, stirring constantly to prevent the mixture from sticking to the bottom of the pan.

6 Add the remaining coconut milk to the chicken in the pan, then add the sliced bamboo shoots and torn kaffir lime leaves. Bring back to the boil over a medium heat, stirring constantly to prevent the mixture sticking, then taste and add salt and pepper if necessary.

7 To serve, spoon the curry into a warmed serving dish and garnish with chopped chillies and kaffir lime leaves.

Energy 244kcal/1032kJ; Fat 7.5g; Saturated fat 1.5g; Carbohydrate 17.4g; Fibre 0.2g.

Fragrant Grilled Chicken

If you have time, prepare the chicken in advance and leave it to marinate in the refrigerator for several hours – or even overnight.

Serves 4

450g/1lb chicken breast fillet,
   with skin
30ml/2 tbsp sesame oil
2 garlic cloves, crushed
2 coriander (cilantro) roots,
   finely chopped
2 small fresh red chillies, seeded
   and finely chopped
30ml/2 tbsp Thai fish sauce

5ml/1 tsp sugar
cooked rice, to serve
lime wedges, to garnish

For the sauce
90ml/6 tbsp rice vinegar
60ml/4 tbsp sugar
2.5ml/½ tsp salt
2 garlic cloves, crushed
1 small fresh red chilli, seeded
   and finely chopped
115g/4oz/4 cups fresh coriander
   (cilantro), finely chopped

1 Lay the chicken breast fillets between two sheets of clear film (plastic wrap), baking parchment or foil and beat with the side of a rolling pin or the flat side of a meat tenderizer until the meat is about half its original thickness. Place in a large, shallow dish or bowl.

2 Mix together the sesame oil, garlic, coriander roots, red chillies, fish sauce and sugar in a jug (pitcher), stirring until the sugar has dissolved. Pour the mixture over the chicken and turn to coat. Cover with clear film and set aside to marinate in a cool place for at least 20 minutes.

3 To make the sauce, heat the vinegar in a small pan, add the sugar and stir until dissolved. Add the salt and stir until the mixture begins to thicken. Add the remaining sauce ingredients, stir well, then spoon into a serving bowl.

4 Preheat the grill (broiler) and cook the chicken for 5 minutes. Turn over and baste with the marinade, then cook for 5 minutes more, or until cooked through and golden. Serve with rice and the sauce, garnished with lime wedges.

Energy 284kcal/1195kJ; Fat 8.3g; Saturated fat 1.5g; Carbohydrate 16.4g; Fibre 1.3g.

Barbecue Chicken with Lemon Grass

This is the perfect dish for a summer party, but you can also cook this tasty chicken in the oven if the weather proves disappointing.

Serves 4–6
1 chicken, about 1.6kg/3–3½lb, cut into 8–10 pieces
lime wedges and fresh red chillies, to garnish

For the marinade
2 lemon grass stalks, roots trimmed
2.5cm/1in piece fresh root ginger, peeled and thinly sliced
6 garlic cloves, coarsely chopped
4 shallots, coarsely chopped
½ bunch coriander (cilantro) roots, chopped
15ml/1 tbsp palm sugar or light muscovado (brown) sugar
120ml/4fl oz/½ cup coconut milk
30ml/2 tbsp Thai fish sauce
30ml/2 tbsp light soy sauce

1 To make the marinade, cut off the lower 5cm/2in of the lemon grass stalks and chop them coarsely. Put into a food processor with the ginger, garlic, shallots, coriander, sugar, coconut milk and sauces and process until smooth.

2 Place the chicken pieces in a dish, pour over the marinade and stir to mix well. Cover the dish and leave in a cool place to marinate for at least 4 hours, or preferably leave it in the refrigerator overnight.

3 Prepare the barbecue or preheat the oven to 200°C/400°F/ Gas 6. Drain the chicken, reserving the marinade. If you are cooking in the oven, arrange the chicken pieces in a single layer on a rack set over a roasting pan.

4 Cook the chicken on the barbecue over moderately hot coals or on medium heat for a gas barbecue, or bake in the oven for 20–30 minutes. Turn the pieces and brush with the reserved marinade once or twice during cooking.

5 As soon as the chicken pieces are golden brown and cooked through, transfer them to a serving platter, garnish with the lime wedges and red chillies and serve immediately.

Energy 572kcal/2375kJ; Fat 38.8g; Saturated fat 11.3g; Carbohydrate 9.4g; Fibre 0.7g.

Roast Lime Chicken with Sweet Potatoes

This chicken, delicately flavoured with garlic, turmeric and coriander, would traditionally be spit-roasted. However, it works very well as a conventional roast, and, cooked this way, it can be accompanied by the succulent addition of sweet potatoes flavoured with the delicious juices from the chicken.

Serves 4
4 garlic cloves, 2 finely chopped and 2 bruised but left whole
small bunch coriander (cilantro), with roots, coarsely chopped
10ml/2 tsp salt
5ml/1 tsp ground turmeric
5cm/2in piece fresh turmeric
1 roasting chicken, about 1.5kg/3¼lb
1 lime, cut in half
4 medium/large sweet potatoes, peeled and cut into thick wedges
300ml/½ pint/1¼ cups chicken or vegetable stock
30ml/2 tbsp soy sauce
salt and ground black pepper

1 Preheat the oven to 190°C/375°F/Gas 5. Calculate the cooking time for the chicken, allowing 20 minutes per 500g/1¼lb, plus 20 minutes. Using a mortar and pestle or food processor, grind the chopped garlic, coriander, salt and turmeric to a paste.

2 Place the chicken in a roasting pan and smear it with the herb and spice paste. Squeeze the lime juice over and place the lime halves and garlic cloves in the cavity. Cover with foil and roast in the oven.

3 Meanwhile, bring a pan of water to the boil and par-boil the sweet potatoes for 10–15 minutes, until just tender. Drain well and place them around the chicken in the roasting pan. Baste with the cooking juices and sprinkle with salt and pepper. Replace the foil and return the chicken to the oven.

4 About 20 minutes before the end of cooking, remove the foil and baste the chicken. Turn the sweet potatoes over.

5 At the end of the calculated roasting time, check that the chicken is cooked. Lift it out of the roasting pan, tip it so that all the juices collected in the cavity drain into the pan, then place the bird on a carving board. Cover it with tented foil and leave it to rest before carving. Transfer the sweet potatoes to a serving dish and keep them hot in the oven while you make the gravy.

6 Pour away the oil from the roasting pan but keep the juices. Place the roasting pan on top of the stove and heat until the juices are bubbling. Pour in the stock. Bring the mixture to the boil, stirring constantly with a wooden spoon and scraping the base of the pan to incorporate the residue.

7 Stir in the soy sauce and check the seasoning before straining the gravy into a jug (pitcher). Serve it with the carved meat and the sweet potatoes.

Energy 620kcal/2581kJ; Fat 38.9g; Saturated fat 11.4g; Carbohydrate 21.3g; Fibre 2.4g.

Curried Chicken & Rice

This simple but flavourful one-pot meal is the perfect choice for casual entertaining. The dish is delicately spiced and would be perfect accompanied by a salad or, if you have time, a curried vegetable side dish.

Serves 4
60ml/4 tbsp vegetable oil
4 garlic cloves, finely chopped
1 chicken, about 1.6kg/3–3½lb
   or chicken pieces, skin and
   bones removed and meat
   cut into bitesize pieces
5ml/1 tsp garam masala
450g/1lb/2⅓ cups jasmine rice,
   rinsed and drained
10ml/2 tsp salt
1 litre/1¾ pints/4 cups
   chicken stock
small bunch fresh coriander
   (cilantro), chopped,
   to garnish

1 Heat the oil in a wok or flameproof casserole that has a lid. Add the garlic and cook over low to medium heat until golden brown. Add the chicken, increase the heat and brown the pieces on all sides (see Cook's Tip).

2 Add the garam masala, stir well to coat the chicken all over in the spice, then tip in the drained rice. Add the salt and stir to mix.

3 Pour in the stock, stir well, then cover the wok or casserole and bring to the boil. Reduce the heat to low and simmer gently for 10 minutes, until the rice is cooked and tender.

4 Lift the wok or casserole off the heat, leaving the lid on, and leave for 10 minutes. Fluff up the rice grains with a fork and spoon on to a platter. Sprinkle with the coriander and serve immediately.

> **Cook's Tip**
> *You will probably need to brown the chicken in batches, so don't be tempted to add too much at once.*

Cashew Chicken

Although it is not native to South-east Asia, the cashew tree is highly prized in Thailand and the classic partnership of these slightly sweet nuts with chicken is immensely popular throughout the region.

Serves 4–6
450g/1lb boneless chicken breast
   portions
1 red (bell) pepper
2 garlic cloves, thinly sliced
4 dried red chillies, chopped
30ml/2 tbsp vegetable oil
30ml/2 tbsp oyster sauce
15ml/1 tbsp soy sauce
pinch of granulated sugar
1 bunch spring onions (scallions),
   cut into 5cm/2in lengths
175g/6oz/1½ cups cashew
   nuts, roasted
coriander (cilantro) leaves,
   to garnish

1 Remove and discard the skin from the chicken breasts and trim off any excess fat. With a sharp knife, cut the chicken into bitesize pieces and set aside.

2 Halve the red pepper, scrape out the seeds and membranes and discard, then cut the flesh into 2cm/¾in dice.

3 Preheat a wok and then heat the oil. The best way to do this is to drizzle a "necklace" of oil around the inner rim of the wok, so that it drops down to coat the entire inner surface. Make sure the coating is even by swirling the wok.

4 Add the garlic and dried chillies to the wok and stir-fry over a medium heat until golden. Do not let the garlic burn, otherwise it will taste bitter.

5 Add the chicken to the wok and stir-fry until it is cooked through, then add the red pepper. If the mixture is very dry, add a little water.

6 Stir in the oyster sauce, soy sauce and sugar. Add the spring onions and cashew nuts. Stir-fry for 1–2 minutes more, until heated through. Spoon into a warm dish and serve immediately, garnished with the coriander leaves.

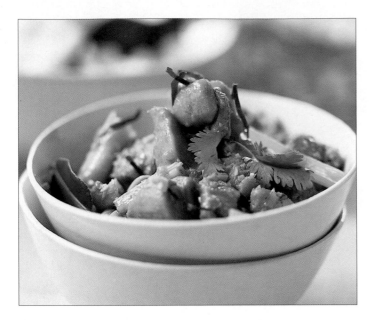

Chicken & Lemon Grass Curry

This truly delicious curry is exceptionally easy and takes less than 20 minutes to prepare and cook.

Serves 4
45ml/3 tbsp vegetable oil
2 garlic cloves, crushed
500g/1¼lb boneless chicken
    thighs, skinned and chopped
    into small pieces
45ml/3 tbsp Thai fish sauce
120ml/4fl oz/½ cup chicken stock
5ml/1 tsp granulated sugar
1 lemon grass stalk, chopped into
    4 pieces and lightly crushed
5 kaffir lime leaves, rolled into
    cylinders and thinly sliced
    across, plus extra to garnish

chopped roasted peanuts and
    chopped fresh coriander
    (cilantro), to garnish

For the curry paste
1 lemon grass stalk, coarsely
    chopped
2.5cm/1in piece fresh
    galangal, peeled and
    coarsely chopped
2 kaffir lime leaves, chopped
3 shallots, coarsely chopped
6 coriander roots, coarsely
    chopped
2 garlic cloves
2 fresh green chillies, seeded
    and coarsely chopped
5ml/1 tsp shrimp paste
5ml/1 tsp ground turmeric

1 To make the curry paste, place all the ingredients in a large mortar, or food processor and pound with a pestle or process to a smooth paste.

2 Heat the vegetable oil in a wok or large frying pan, add the garlic and cook over a low heat, stirring frequently, until golden brown. Be careful not to let the garlic burn or it will taste bitter. Add the curry paste and stir-fry for about 30 seconds more.

3 Add the chicken pieces and stir until coated with the curry paste. Stir in the fish sauce and stock, with the sugar, and cook, stirring constantly, for 2 minutes more. Add the lemon grass and lime leaves, reduce the heat and simmer for 10 minutes. If the mixture begins to dry out, add a little more stock or water.

4 Remove the lemon grass, if you like. Spoon the curry into four dishes, garnish with the lime leaves, peanuts and fresh coriander and serve immediately.

Energy 220kcal/923kJ; Fat 9.7g; Saturated fat 1.4g; Carbohydrate 3g; Fibre 0.5g.

Hot Sweet-&-sour Duck Casserole

This tasty recipe can be made with any game bird, or even rabbit. It is a distinctively sweet, sour and hot dish best eaten with rice as an accompaniment.

Serves 4–6
1.3kg/3lb duck, jointed
    and skinned
4 bay leaves
10ml/2 tsp salt

75ml/5 tbsp vegetable oil
juice of 5 lemons
8 medium onions, finely chopped
4 or 5 garlic cloves, crushed
15ml/1 tbsp chilli powder
300ml/½ pint/1¼ cups
    pickling vinegar
5cm/2in piece fresh root
    ginger, shredded
115g/4oz/generous ½ cup
    granulated sugar
15ml/1 tbsp garam masala

1 Place the prepared duck, bay leaves and salt in a large pan and cover with cold water. Bring to the boil, then simmer for 30–45 minutes, or until the duck is fully cooked. Remove the pieces of duck and keep warm. Reserve the liquid as a base for stock or soup.

2 In a large pan, heat the oil and lemon juice until it reaches smoking point. Add the onions, garlic and chilli powder and fry the onions until they are golden brown.

3 Add the vinegar, ginger and sugar and simmer until the sugar dissolves and the oil has separated from the mixture.

4 Return the duck to the pan and add the garam masala. Mix well, then reheat until the masala clings to the pieces of duck and the sauce is thick. Adjust the seasoning if necessary. If you prefer a thinner sauce, add a little of the reserved stock.

> **Cook's Tip**
> Be very careful when adding the onions and garlic to the oil and lemon juice mixture. Stand well back and use a spoon to scrape the onions into the pan, a few at a time. The hot mixture is likely to spit and splutter.

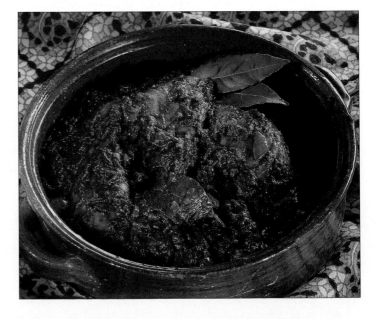

Energy 444kcal/1860kJ; Fat 17.5g; Saturated fat 3.3g; Carbohydrate 53.8g; Fibre 4.2g.

Duck Curry

Robust spices, coconut milk and chillies combined with orange make this a mouthwatering curry. The duck is best marinated for as long as possible, although it tastes good even if you only have time to marinate it briefly.

Serves 4

4 duck breast portions, skinned and boned
30ml/2 tbsp five-spice powder
30ml/2 tbsp sesame oil
grated rind and juice of 1 orange
1 medium butternut squash, peeled and cubed
10ml/2 tsp Thai red curry paste
30ml/2 tbsp Thai fish sauce
15ml/1 tbsp palm sugar or light muscovado (brown) sugar
300ml/½ pint/1¼ cups coconut milk
2 fresh red chillies, seeded
4 kaffir lime leaves, torn
small bunch coriander (cilantro), chopped, to garnish

1 Cut the duck meat into bitesize pieces and place in a bowl with the five-spice powder, sesame oil and grated orange rind and juice. Stir well to mix all the ingredients and coat the duck in the marinade.

2 Cover the bowl with clear film (plastic wrap) and set aside in a cool place to marinate for at least 15 minutes but preferably overnight.

3 Meanwhile, bring a pan of water to the boil. Add the butternut squash and cook for 10–15 minutes, until just tender. Drain well and set aside.

4 Pour the marinade from the duck into a wok and heat until boiling. Stir in the curry paste and cook for 2–3 minutes, until well blended and fragrant. Add the duck and cook for 3–4 minutes, stirring constantly, until browned on all sides.

5 Add the fish sauce and palm sugar and cook for 2 minutes more. Stir in the coconut milk until the mixture is smooth, then add the cooked squash, with the chillies and lime leaves.

6 Simmer gently, stirring frequently, for 5 minutes, then spoon into a dish, sprinkle with the coriander and serve.

Energy 306kcal/1282kJ; Fat 15.8g; Saturated fat 4.1g; Carbohydrate 10.9g; Fibre 1.5g.

Duck & Sesame Stir-fry

Wild duck is beautifully lean and full of flavour, and it is the best meat to use for this incredibly quick but tasty stir-fry. If you can't find any wild duck, use farmed duck but be sure to remove the skin and fat layer otherwise the meat will be too fatty for this recipe.

Serves 4

250g/9oz boneless wild duck meat
15ml/1 tbsp sesame oil
15ml/1 tbsp vegetable oil
4 garlic cloves, finely sliced
2.5ml/½ tsp dried chilli flakes
15ml/1 tbsp Thai fish sauce
15ml/1 tbsp light soy sauce
120ml/4fl oz/½ cup water
1 head broccoli, cut into small florets
coriander (cilantro) and 15ml/ 1 tbsp toasted sesame seeds, to garnish

1 Cut the duck meat into bitesize pieces. Heat the sesame and vegetable oils in a wok or large, heavy frying pan and stir-fry the sliced garlic over a medium heat until it is golden brown – do not let it burn.

2 Add the duck to the pan and stir-fry for a further 2 minutes, until the meat begins to brown.

3 Stir in the chilli flakes, fish sauce, soy sauce and water.

4 Add the broccoli and continue to stir-fry for about 2 minutes, until the duck is just cooked through.

5 Serve the stir-fry on warmed plates, garnished with coriander and sesame seeds.

> **Variations**
> • Partridge, pheasant and pigeon are all suitable game birds for this recipe.
> • Pak choi (bok choy) or Chinese flowering cabbage can be used instead of broccoli.

Energy 172kcal/718kJ; Fat 10.6g; Saturated fat 2.2g; Carbohydrate 2g; Fibre 2.9g.

Spicy Lamb Tikka

One of the best ways of tenderizing meat is to marinate it in papaya, which must be unripe or it will lend its sweetness to what should be a savoury dish.

Serves 4
675g/1½lb lean lamb, cubed
1 unripe papaya
45ml/3 tbsp natural (plain) yogurt
5ml/1 tsp grated fresh root ginger
5ml/1 tsp chilli powder
5ml/1 tsp crushed garlic
1.5ml/¼ tsp turmeric
10ml/2 tsp ground coriander
5ml/1 tsp ground cumin
5ml/1 tsp salt
30ml/2 tbsp lemon juice
15ml/1 tbsp chopped fresh
    coriander (cilantro), plus extra
    to garnish
1.5ml/¼ tsp red food colouring
300ml/½ pint/1¼ cups corn oil
lemon wedges and onion rings,
    to garnish

1 Place the lamb in a large bowl. Peel the papaya, cut it in half and scoop out the seeds. Cut the flesh into cubes and place in a food processor or blender. Process in bursts until the papaya forms a purée, adding about 15ml/1 tbsp water if necessary.

2 Pour 30ml/2 tbsp of the papaya over the lamb and rub it in well with your fingers. Cover and set aside for at least 3 hours.

3 Meanwhile, mix the yogurt, ginger, chilli powder, garlic, turmeric, ground coriander, ground cumin, salt and lemon juice in a bowl. Add the fresh coriander, red food colouring and 30ml/2 tbsp of the oil and mix well. Pour the spicy yogurt mixture over the lamb and mix well.

4 Heat the remaining oil in a karahi, wok or deep pan. Lower the heat slightly and add the lamb cubes, a few at a time.

5 Deep-fry each batch for 5–7 minutes or until the lamb is thoroughly cooked and tender. Keep the cooked pieces warm while frying the remainder.

6 Transfer to a serving dish and garnish with lemon wedges, onion rings and fresh coriander. Serve with raita and freshly baked naan bread.

Energy 438kcal/1820kJ; Fat 32.7g; Saturated fat 10.4g; Carbohydrate 2.4g; Fibre 0.7g.

Indian Lamb Burgers

Serve this spicy Indian burger in a bun with chilli sauce and a salad of tomatoes, onion and lettuce, or unaccompanied as an appetizer.

Serves 4–6
50g/2oz/⅓ cup chickpeas,
    soaked overnight in water
2 onions, finely chopped
250g/9oz lean lamb, cut into
    small cubes
5ml/1 tsp cumin seeds
5ml/1 tsp garam masala
4–6 fresh green chillies,
    roughly chopped
5cm/2in piece fresh ginger,
    crushed
175ml/6fl oz/¾ cup water
a few fresh coriander (cilantro)
    and mint leaves, chopped
juice of 1 lemon
15ml/1 tbsp gram flour
2 eggs, beaten
vegetable oil, for shallow-frying
½ lime
salt

1 Drain the chickpeas and cook them in a pan of boiling water for 1 hour. Drain again, return to the pan and add the onions, lamb, cumin seeds, garam masala, chillies, ginger and water, and salt to taste. Bring to the boil. Simmer, covered, until the meat and chickpeas are cooked.

2 Remove the lid and cook uncovered to reduce the excess liquid. Cool, and grind to a paste in a food processor.

3 Scrape the mixture into a mixing bowl and add the fresh coriander (cilantro) and mint, lemon juice and flour. Knead well. Divide into 10–12 portions and roll each into a ball, then flatten slightly. Chill for 1 hour.

4 Dip the burgers in the beaten egg and shallow-fry each side until golden brown. Serve hot, with the lime.

Variation
Chicken or lean pork would work well instead of the lamb in this recipe.

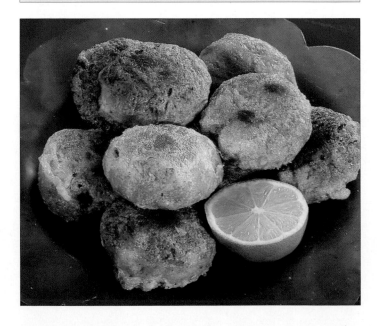

Energy 357kcal/1485kJ; Fat 25.1g; Saturated fat 6g; Carbohydrate 15.6g; Fibre 1.5g.

Lamb Meatballs in a Spicy Sauce

The word "meatballs" conjures up something quite humdrum, but these spicy little patties, with their delectable sauce, are exciting and full of flavour.

Serves 6

For the meatballs
675g/1½lb lean minced (ground) lamb
1 fresh green chilli, roughly chopped
1 garlic clove, chopped
2.5cm/1in piece fresh root ginger, chopped
1.5ml/¼ tsp garam masala
1.5ml/¼ tsp salt
45ml/3 tbsp chopped fresh coriander (cilantro), plus extra to garnish
pilau rice, to serve

For the sauce
15ml/1 tbsp oil
1.5ml/¼ tsp mustard seeds
2.5ml/½ tsp cumin seeds
1 onion, chopped
1 garlic clove, chopped
2.5cm/1in piece fresh root ginger, finely chopped
5ml/1 tsp ground cumin
5ml/1 tsp ground coriander
2.5ml/½ tsp salt
2.5ml/½ tsp chilli powder
15ml/1 tbsp tomato purée (paste)
400g/14oz can chopped tomatoes

1 To make the meatballs, put all the ingredients into a food processor or blender and process until the mixture binds together. Shape the mixture into 18 balls. Cover and chill in the refrigerator for 10 minutes.

2 To make the sauce, heat the oil in a heavy pan and fry the mustard and cumin seeds until they splutter.

3 Add the onion, garlic and ginger and fry for 5 minutes. Stir in the remaining sauce ingredients and simmer for 5 minutes.

4 Add the meatballs to the spicy sauce. Bring to the boil, cover and simmer for 25–30 minutes, or until the meatballs are cooked through. Serve on a bed of pilau rice and garnish with chopped fresh coriander.

Energy 231kcal/968kJ; Fat 12.3g; Saturated fat 5g; Carbohydrate 5.4g; Fibre 0.9g.

Lamb Chops Kashmiri-style

These chops are cooked in a unique way, being boiled in milk and then fried.

Serves 4
8–12 lamb chops, about 50–75g/2–3oz each
1 piece cinnamon bark
1 bay leaf
2.5ml/½ tsp fennel seeds
2.5ml/½ tsp black peppercorns
3 green cardamom pods
5ml/1 tsp salt
600ml/1 pint/2½ cups milk
150ml/¼ pint/⅔ cup evaporated milk
150ml/¼ pint/⅔ cup natural (plain) yogurt
30ml/2 tbsp plain (all-purpose) flour
5ml/1 tsp chilli powder
5ml/1 tsp grated fresh root ginger
2.5ml/½ tsp garam masala
2.5ml/½ tsp crushed garlic
pinch of salt
300ml/½ pint/1¼ cups corn oil
fresh mint sprigs and lime quarters, to garnish

1 Trim the lamb chops to remove any excess fat, and place them in a large pan. Add the cinnamon bark, bay leaf, fennel seeds, peppercorns, cardamoms and salt. Pour in the milk. Bring to the boil over a high heat.

2 Lower the heat and cook for 12–15 minutes, or until the milk has reduced to about half its original volume. At this stage, pour in the evaporated milk and lower the heat further. Simmer until the chops are cooked through and all the milk has evaporated.

3 While the chops are cooking, blend together the yogurt, flour, chilli powder, ginger, garam masala, crushed garlic and a pinch of salt in a mixing bowl.

4 Remove the chops from the pan and discard the whole spices. Add the chops to the spicy yogurt mixture.

5 Heat the oil in a deep pan, wok or medium karahi. Lower the heat slightly and add the chops. Fry until they are golden brown, turning them once or twice as they cook.

6 Transfer the chops to a serving dish, and garnish with mint sprigs and lime quarters. Serve immediately.

Energy 484kcal/2022kJ; Fat 29g; Saturated fat 9.3g; Carbohydrate 17.6g; Fibre 0.2g.

Lamb Korma with Mint

This superb dish of lamb cooked in a creamy sauce flavoured with mint, coconut, chillies and a subtle blend of spices is quick to cook because the lamb is sliced into thin strips.

Serves 4
2 fresh green chillies
120ml/4fl oz/½ cup natural (plain) low-fat yogurt
50ml/2fl oz/¼ cup coconut milk
15ml/1 tbsp ground almonds
5ml/1 tsp salt
5ml/1 tsp crushed garlic
5ml/1 tsp grated fresh root ginger
5ml/1 tsp garam masala
1.5ml/¼ tsp ground cardamom
large pinch of ground cinnamon
15ml/1 tbsp chopped fresh mint
15ml/1 tbsp oil
2 medium onions, diced
1 bay leaf
4 black peppercorns
225g/8oz lean lamb, cut into strips
150ml/¼ pint/⅔ cup water
fresh mint leaves, to garnish

1 Finely chop the chillies. Whisk the yogurt with the chillies, coconut milk, ground almonds, salt, garlic, ginger, garam masala, cardamom, cinnamon and mint.

2 Heat the oil in a karahi, wok or heavy pan and fry the onions with the bay leaf and peppercorns for about 5 minutes.

3 When the onions are soft and golden brown, add the lamb and stir-fry for about 2 minutes.

4 Pour in the yogurt and coconut mixture and the water, lower the heat, cover and cook for about 15 minutes or until the lamb is cooked through, stirring occasionally. Using two spoons, toss the mixture over the heat for a further 2 minutes. Serve garnished with fresh mint leaves.

> **Cook's Tip**
> Rice with peas and curry leaves goes very well with this korma.

Energy 193kcal/803kJ; Fat 10.14g; Saturated fat 2.91g; Carbohydrate 11.5g; Fibre 1.6g.

Spiced Lamb with Tomatoes & Peppers

Select lean tender lamb from the leg for this lightly spiced curry with juicy peppers and wedges of onion. Serve warm naan bread to mop up the tomato-rich juices.

Serves 6
2.5cm/1in piece fresh root ginger
1.5kg/3¼lb lean boneless lamb, cubed
250ml/8fl oz/1 cup natural (plain) yogurt
30ml/2 tbsp sunflower oil
3 onions
2 red (bell) peppers, seeded and cut into chunks
3 garlic cloves, finely chopped
1 fresh red chilli, seeded and chopped
30ml/2 tbsp mild curry paste
2 × 400g/14oz cans chopped tomatoes
large pinch of saffron threads
800g/1¾lb plum tomatoes, halved, seeded and cut into chunks
salt and ground black pepper
chopped fresh coriander (cilantro), to garnish

1 Thinly peel the fresh root ginger, using a sharp knife or a vegetable peeler, then grate the peeled root finely. Set the grated ginger aside.

2 Mix the lamb with the yogurt in a bowl. Cover and chill for about 1 hour.

3 Heat the oil in a large pan. Drain the lamb and reserve the yogurt, then cook the lamb in batches until it is golden on all sides – this will take about 15 minutes in total. Remove the lamb from the pan using a slotted spoon and set aside.

4 Cut two of the onions into wedges (six from each onion) and add to the oil remaining in the pan. Fry the onions over a medium heat for 10 minutes, or until they soften and are beginning to colour.

5 Add the peppers and cook for 5 minutes. Use a slotted spoon to remove the vegetables from the pan and set aside.

6 Meanwhile, chop the remaining onion. Add it to the rest of the oil in the pan with the chopped garlic, chilli and grated ginger, and cook for 4–5 minutes, stirring frequently, until the onion has softened.

7 Stir in the curry paste and canned chopped tomatoes with the reserved yogurt. Return the lamb to the pan, season and stir well. Bring to the boil, then reduce the heat and simmer for 30 minutes.

8 Pound the saffron to a powder in a mortar, then stir in a little boiling water to dissolve the saffron. Add this liquid to the curry and stir well.

9 Return the onion and pepper mixture to the pan, then stir in the fresh tomatoes. Bring the curry back to simmering point and cook for 15 minutes. Garnish with chopped fresh coriander and serve hot.

Energy 594kcal/2445kJ; Fat 32.8g; Saturated fat 13.8g; Carbohydrate 19.7g; Fibre 4.3g.

Lamb with Spinach

Serve this Punjabi dish with plain boiled rice, naan bread or parathas.

Serves 4–6
5ml/1 tsp grated fresh root ginger
5ml/1 tsp crushed garlic
7.5ml/1½ tsp chilli powder
5ml/1 tsp salt
5ml/1 tsp garam masala
90ml/6 tbsp corn oil
2 medium onions, sliced

675g/1½lb lean lamb, cut into
  5cm/2in cubes
600–900ml/1–1½
  pints/2½–3¾ cups water
400g/14oz fresh spinach
1 large red (bell) pepper, seeded
  and chopped
3 fresh green chillies, chopped
45ml/3 tbsp chopped fresh
  coriander (cilantro)
15ml/1 tbsp lemon juice
  (optional)

1 Mix together the ginger, garlic, chilli powder, salt and garam masala in a bowl. Set to one side.

2 Heat the oil in a medium pan. Add the onions and fry for 10–12 minutes or until well browned. Add the cubed lamb to the sizzling onion slices and fry for about 2 minutes, stirring frequently. Add the spice mixture and stir thoroughly until the meat pieces are well coated.

3 Pour in the water and bring to the boil. As soon as it is boiling, cover the pan and lower the heat. Cook gently for 25–35 minutes without letting the contents of the pan burn. If there is still a lot of water in the pan when the meat has become tender, remove the lid and boil briskly to evaporate any excess.

4 Meanwhile, wash and chop the spinach roughly, then blanch it for about 1 minute in a pan of boiling water. Drain well. Add the spinach to the lamb as soon as the water has evaporated. Fry over a medium heat for 7–10 minutes, using a wooden spoon in a semi-circular motion.

5 Add the red pepper, green chillies and fresh coriander to the pan and stir over a medium heat for 2 minutes. Sprinkle over the lemon juice (if using) and serve immediately.

Spring Lamb Chops

Tender spring lamb has the best flavour. Here, quick-cooking chops are finely spiced to enhance the flavour without masking the sweetness of the lamb.

Serves 4
8 small lean spring lamb chops
1 large fresh red chilli, seeded
30ml/2 tbsp chopped fresh
  coriander (cilantro)

15ml/1 tbsp chopped fresh mint
5ml/1 tsp salt
5ml/1 tsp soft brown sugar
5ml/1 tsp garam masala
5ml/1 tsp crushed garlic
5ml/1 tsp grated fresh root ginger
175ml/6fl oz/¾ cup low-fat
  natural (plain) yogurt
10ml/2 tsp oil
mixed salad, to serve

1 Trim any excess fat from each of the lamb chops. Place them in a large bowl.

2 Finely chop the chilli, then place in a bowl and mix with the chopped fresh coriander, mint, salt, brown sugar, garam masala, crushed garlic and ginger.

3 Pour the yogurt into the chilli mixture and, using a small whisk or a fork, mix together thoroughly.

4 Pour this mixture over the top of the chops and turn them with your fingers to make sure that they are completely covered. Cover and marinate overnight in the refrigerator.

5 Heat the oil in a karahi, wok or heavy pan and add the chops. Cook over a medium heat for about 20 minutes or until cooked right through, turning the chops from time to time. Alternatively, grill (broil) the chops, basting often with oil. Serve with the mixed salad.

Cook's Tip
You can freeze peeled fresh root ginger and grate it from frozen as you need it.

Energy 500kcal/2079kJ; Fat 36.4g; Saturated fat 11.3g; Carbohydrate 6.8g; Fibre 3.2g.

Energy 207kcal/864kJ; Fat 10.29g; Saturated fat 4.26g; Carbohydrate 6.63g; Fibre 0.27g.

Lamb with Courgettes

For this simple supper dish, lamb is cooked first with yogurt and then the sliced courgettes, which have already been browned, are added to the mixture.

Serves 4

15ml/1 tbsp oil
2 medium onions, chopped
225g/8oz lean lamb steaks, cut into strips
120ml/4fl oz/½ cup natural (plain) low-fat yogurt
5ml/1 tsp garam masala
5ml/1 tsp chilli powder
5ml/1 tsp crushed garlic
5ml/1 tsp grated fresh root ginger
2.5ml/½ tsp ground coriander
2 medium courgettes (zucchini), sliced
15ml/1 tbsp chopped fresh coriander (cilantro), to garnish

1 Heat the oil in a karahi, wok or heavy pan and fry the onions until golden brown (see Cook's Tip).

2 Add the lamb strips and stir-fry with the onions for 1 minute to seal the meat.

3 Put the yogurt, garam masala, chilli powder, garlic, ginger and ground coriander into a bowl. Whisk the mixture together.

4 Pour the yogurt mixture over the lamb and stir-fry for 2 minutes. Cover and cook over medium to low heat for 12–15 minutes.

5 Preheat the grill (broiler). Put the courgettes in a flameproof dish and brown lightly under the heat for about 3 minutes, turning once.

6 Check that the lamb is cooked through and the sauce is quite thick, then add the courgettes and serve garnished with the fresh coriander.

> **Cook's Tip**
> *Stir the onions only occasionally so that their moisture will be retained.*

Stir-fried Lamb with Baby Onions

The baby onions are stir-fried whole before being added to the lamb and pepper mixture in this recipe. Serve this dish with rice, lentils or naan bread.

Serves 4

15ml/1 tbsp oil
8 baby onions
225g/8oz boned lean lamb, cut into strips
5ml/1 tsp ground cumin
5ml/1 tsp ground coriander
15ml/1 tbsp tomato purée (paste)
5ml/1 tsp chilli powder
5ml/1 tsp salt
15ml/1 tbsp lemon juice
2.5ml/½ tsp onion seeds
4 curry leaves
300ml/½ pint/1¼ cups water
1 small red (bell) pepper, seeded and roughly sliced
1 small green (bell) pepper, seeded and roughly sliced
15ml/1 tbsp chopped fresh coriander (cilantro)
15ml/1 tbsp chopped fresh mint

1 Heat the oil in a karahi, wok or heavy pan and stir-fry the whole baby onions for about 3 minutes. Using a slotted spoon, remove the onions from the pan and set aside to drain. Set the pan aside, with the oil remaining in it.

2 Mix together the lamb strips, cumin, ground coriander, tomato purée, chilli powder, salt and lemon juice in a bowl until the lamb is well coated. Set aside.

3 Reheat the oil and briskly stir-fry the onion seeds and curry leaves for 2–3 minutes.

4 Add the lamb and spice mixture, and stir-fry for about 5 minutes, then pour in the measured water. Lower the heat and cook the lamb mixture gently for about 10 minutes, until the lamb is cooked through.

5 Add the peppers and half the fresh coriander and mint. Stir-fry for a further 2 minutes.

6 Finally, add the baby onions and the remaining chopped fresh coriander and mint, and serve immediately.

Energy 178kcal/742kJ; Fat 8.36g; Saturated fat 2.78g; Carbohydrate 10.83g; Fibre 1.99g.

Energy 155kcal/644kJ; Fat 9.48g; Saturated fat 2.82g; Carbohydrate 5.74g; Fibre 1.49g.

Spiced Lamb with Chillies

This is a fairly hot stir-fry dish, although you can, of course, make it less so by either discarding the seeds from the chillies, or using just one of each colour.

Serves 4
225g/8oz lean lamb fillet
120ml/4fl oz/½ cup natural (plain) low-fat yogurt
1.5ml/¼ tsp ground cardamom
5ml/1 tsp grated fresh root ginger
5ml/1 tsp crushed garlic
5ml/1 tsp chilli powder
5ml/1 tsp garam masala
5ml/1 tsp salt
15ml/1 tbsp oil
2 medium onions, chopped
1 bay leaf
300ml/½ pint/1¼ cups water
2 fresh green chillies, sliced lengthways
2 fresh red chillies, sliced lengthways
30ml/2 tbsp fresh coriander (cilantro) leaves

1 Using a sharp knife, remove any excess fat from the lamb and cut the meat into even strips.

2 In a bowl, mix the yogurt, cardamom, ginger, garlic, chilli powder and garam masala. Stir in the salt. Add the lamb strips. Mix well in the spicy yogurt to coat evenly. Leave for about 1 hour to marinate.

3 Heat the oil in a karahi, wok or heavy pan and fry the onions for 3–5 minutes until golden.

4 Add the bay leaf, then add the lamb with the yogurt and spice mixture. Stir-fry for 2–3 minutes.

5 Pour the water over the spicy lamb mixture, cover and cook for 15–20 minutes over a low heat, checking and stirring occasionally. Once the water has evaporated, stir-fry the mixture for 1 further minute.

6 Stir in the red and green chillies and the fresh coriander. Spoon into a serving dish and serve hot.

Khara Masala Lamb

This is a dish which involves a cooking technique called bhooning – stirring with a semi-circular motion.

Serves 4
15ml/1 tbsp oil
3 small onions, chopped
5ml/1 tsp shredded fresh root ginger
5ml/1 tsp sliced garlic
6 dried red chillies
3 cardamom pods
2 cinnamon sticks
6 black peppercorns
3 cloves
2.5ml/½ tsp salt
450g/1lb boned lean leg of lamb, cubed
600ml/1 pint/2½ cups water
2 fresh green chillies, sliced
30ml/2 tbsp chopped fresh coriander (cilantro)

1 Heat the oil in a large pan and add the onions. Lower the heat and fry the onions until they are lightly browned, stirring occasionally.

2 Add half the ginger and half the garlic, and stir well. Drop in half the red chillies, the cardamom pods, cinnamon, peppercorns, cloves and salt.

3 Add the lamb and fry over a medium heat. Stir continuously with a semi-circular movement, using a wooden spoon to scrape the bottom of the pan and prevent the meat from burning. Cook for about 5 minutes.

4 Stir in the water, cover with a lid and cook slowly over a medium-low heat for 35–40 minutes, or until the water has evaporated and the meat is tender, stirring from time to time to prevent the mixture from burning on the bottom of the pan.

5 Add the remaining ginger, garlic and dried red chillies, with the fresh green chillies and the chopped coriander. Continue to stir the mixture over the heat until some free oil is visible on the sides of the pan. Transfer the curry to a serving dish and serve immediately.

Energy 169kcal/706kJ; Fat 8.13g; Saturated fat 2.71g; Carbohydrate 10.01g; Fibre 1.32g.

Energy 242kcal/1012kJ; Fat 13.2g; Saturated fat 5.19g; Carbohydrate 6.7g; Fibre 0.9g.

Spicy Lamb & Potato Stew

Indian spices transform a simple lamb and potato stew into a mouthwatering dish fit for princes.

Serves 6
675g/1½lb lean lamb fillet
  (tenderloin)
15ml/1 tbsp oil
1 onion, finely chopped
2 bay leaves
1 fresh green chilli, seeded and
  finely chopped
2 garlic cloves, finely chopped
10ml/2 tsp ground coriander

5ml/1 tsp ground cumin
2.5ml/½ tsp ground turmeric
2.5ml/½ tsp chilli powder
2.5ml/½ tsp salt
2 tomatoes, peeled and chopped
600ml/1 pint/2½ cups chicken
  stock
2 large potatoes, cut in large
  chunks
chopped fresh coriander (cilantro),
  to garnish

1 Remove any visible fat from the lamb and cut the meat into neat 2.5cm/1in cubes.

2 Heat the oil in a large, heavy pan and fry the onion, bay leaves, chilli and garlic for 5 minutes.

3 Add the cubed meat and cook for about 6–8 minutes until lightly browned.

4 Add the ground coriander, ground cumin, ground turmeric, chilli powder and salt and cook the spices for 3–4 minutes, stirring all the time to prevent the spices from sticking to the bottom of the pan.

5 Add the tomatoes and stock and simmer for 5 minutes. Bring to the boil, cover and simmer for 1 hour.

6 Add the bitesize chunks of potato to the simmering mixture, stir in, and cook for a further 30–40 minutes, or until the meat is tender and much of the excess juices have been absorbed, leaving a thick but minimal sauce. Garnish with chopped fresh coriander and serve piping hot.

Energy 283kcal/1187kJ; Fat 12.4g; Saturated fat 5.02g; Carbohydrate 17.2g; Fibre 1.7g.

Lamb Dhansak

This is time-consuming to make, but the excellent flavour is just reward.

Serves 4–6
90ml/6 tbsp vegetable oil
5 fresh green chillies, chopped
2.5cm/1in piece fresh root
  ginger, grated
3 garlic cloves, crushed, plus
  1 garlic clove, sliced
2 bay leaves
5cm/2in piece cinnamon stick
900g/2lb lean lamb, cut into pieces
600ml/1 pint/2½ cups water
175g/6oz/¾ cup whole red
  lentils, washed and drained
50g/2oz/¼ cup each chana dhal
  or yellow split peas, husked
  moong dhal and split red
  lentils, washed and drained

2 potatoes, diced, soaked in water
1 aubergine (eggplant), chopped,
  soaked in water
4 onions, finely sliced, deep-fried
  and drained
50g/2oz fresh spinach, trimmed,
  washed and chopped
25g/1oz fresh or dried fenugreek
  leaves
2 carrots, sliced
115g/4oz fresh coriander
  (cilantro), chopped
50g/2oz fresh mint, chopped
30ml/2 tbsp dhansak masala
30ml/2 tbsp sambhar masala
5ml/1 tsp salt
10ml/2 tsp soft brown sugar
60ml/4 tbsp tamarind juice

1 Heat 45ml/3 tbsp of the oil in a wok, karahi or large pan, and gently fry the fresh chillies, ginger, crushed garlic, bay leaves and cinnamon for 2 minutes. Add the lamb pieces and the measured water. Bring to the boil, then simmer, covered, until the lamb is half cooked.

2 Drain the meat stock into another pan and put the lamb aside. Add the whole red lentils, chana dhal or split peas, moong dhal and split red lentils to the stock and cook gently for 25–30 minutes at a low temperature until they are tender. Mash the lentils with the back of a spoon.

3 Drain the potatoes and aubergine and add to the lentils. Reserve a little of the deep-fried onions and stir the remainder into the pan, along with the spinach, fenugreek and carrot. Add some hot water to the pan if the mixture seems too thick. Cook until the vegetables are tender, then mash again with a spoon, keeping the vegetables a little coarse.

4 Heat 15ml/1 tbsp of the remaining oil in a large frying pan. Reserve a few coriander and mint leaves to use as a garnish, and gently fry the remaining leaves with the dhansak and sambhar masala, salt and sugar. Add the lamb pieces and fry gently for 5 minutes.

5 Add the lamb and spices to the lentil mixture and stir. Cover, reduce the heat to low and cook until the lamb is tender. The lentils will absorb liquid, so add more water if needed. Mix in the tamarind juice.

6 Heat the remaining vegetable oil in a small pan and fry the sliced garlic until golden brown. Sprinkle the fried garlic slices over the dhansak. Garnish with the remaining deep-fried onion and the reserved fresh coriander and mint leaves. Serve the dish hot, with Caramelized Basmati Rice if you like.

Energy 720kcal/3017kJ; Fat 34.8g; Saturated fat 10g; Carbohydrate 58.6g; Fibre 7.6g.

Lahore-style Lamb Curry

This hearty dish of braised lamb with chana dhal has a wonderfully aromatic flavour imparted by the winter spices.

Serves 4
60ml/4 tbsp vegetable oil
1 bay leaf
2 cloves
4 black peppercorns
1 onion, sliced
450g/1lb lean boneless lamb, cubed
1.5ml/¼ tsp ground turmeric
7.5ml/1½ tsp chilli powder
5ml/1 tsp crushed coriander seeds
2.5cm/1in piece cinnamon stick
5ml/1 tsp crushed garlic
7.5ml/1½ tsp salt
1.5 litres/2½ pints/6 cups water
50g/2oz/⅓ cup chana dhal (yellow split peas)
2 tomatoes, quartered
2 fresh green chillies, chopped
15ml/1 tbsp chopped fresh coriander (cilantro)

1 Heat the oil in a karahi, wok or large pan. Lower the heat slightly and add the bay leaf, cloves, peppercorns and onion. Fry for about 5 minutes, or until the onion is golden brown.

2 Add the cubed lamb, turmeric, chilli powder, coriander seeds, cinnamon stick, garlic and most of the salt, and stir-fry for about 5 minutes over a medium heat. Pour in 900ml/ 1½ pints/3¾ cups of the water and cover the pan with a lid or foil, making sure the foil does not come into contact with the food. Simmer for 35–40 minutes or until the lamb is tender.

3 Put the chana dhal into a large pan with the remaining measured water and a good pinch of salt and boil for 12–15 minutes, or until the water has almost evaporated and the dhal is soft enough to be mashed. If the mixture is too thick, add up to 150ml/¼ pint/⅔ cup water.

4 When the lamb is tender, remove the lid or foil and stir-fry the mixture using a wooden spoon, until some free oil begins to appear on the sides of the pan.

5 Add the cooked lentils to the lamb and mix together well. Stir in the tomatoes, chillies and chopped coriander and serve.

Energy 362kcal/1508kJ; Fat 24g; Saturated fat 7.3g; Carbohydrate 11.5g; Fibre 1.6g.

Glazed Lamb

Lemon and honey make a classic stir-fry combination in sweet dishes, and this lamb recipe shows how well they work together in savoury dishes, too. Serve with a fresh mixed salad to complete this delicious dish.

Serves 4
450g/1lb boneless lean lamb
15ml/1 tbsp grapeseed oil
175g/6oz mangetouts (snow peas), trimmed
3 spring onions (scallions), sliced
30ml/2 tbsp clear honey
juice of ½ lemon
30ml/2 tbsp chopped fresh coriander (cilantro)
15ml/1 tbsp sesame seeds
salt and ground black pepper

1 Using a cleaver, cut the lamb into thin strips.

2 Heat the wok, then add the oil. When the oil is hot, stir-fry the lamb until browned all over. Remove and keep warm.

3 Add the mangetouts and spring onions to the hot wok and stir-fry for 30 seconds.

4 Return the lamb to the wok and add the honey, lemon juice, chopped coriander and sesame seeds and season well. Stir thoroughly to mix. Bring to the boil, then allow to bubble vigorously for 1 minute until the lamb is completely coated in the honey mixture. Serve immediately.

> **Cook's Tip**
> Use a tender cut of lamb such as leg for this recipe.

> **Variations**
> This recipe would work just as well made with pork or chicken instead of lamb. You could substitute chopped fresh basil for the coriander if using chicken.

Energy 268kcal/1119kJ; Fat 17.8g; Saturated fat 6.5g; Carbohydrate 2.4g; Fibre 2g.

Creamy Lamb Korma

A heritage of the talented cooks who served the Mughal emperors, this is a rich and luxurious dish. Mild in flavour, it is ideal for serving when you are unsure about how hot your guests like their curries to be.

Serves 4–6

15ml/1 tbsp white sesame seeds
15ml/1 tbsp white poppy seeds
50g/2oz/1/2 cup blanched almonds
2 fresh green chillies, seeded
6 garlic cloves, sliced
5cm/2in piece fresh root ginger, sliced
1 onion, finely chopped
45ml/3 tbsp ghee or vegetable oil
6 green cardamom pods
5cm/2in piece cinnamon stick
4 cloves
900g/2lb lean lamb, boned and cubed
5ml/1 tsp ground cumin
5ml/1 tsp ground coriander
300ml/1/2 pint/1 1/4 cups double (heavy) cream mixed with 2.5ml/1/2 tsp cornflour (cornstarch)
salt
roasted sesame seeds, to garnish

1 Preheat a karahi, wok or large pan over a medium heat without any fat, and add the first seven ingredients. Stir until they begin to change colour. They should go just a shade darker.

2 Leave the mixture to cool, then grind to a fine paste using a pestle and mortar or in a food processor. Heat the ghee or oil in the pan over a low heat.

3 Fry the cardamoms, cinnamon and cloves until the cloves swell. Add the lamb, ground cumin and coriander and the prepared paste, and season with salt to taste. Increase the heat to medium and stir well. Reduce the heat to low, then cover the pan and cook until the lamb is almost done.

4 Remove from the heat, leave to cool a little and gradually fold in the cream, reserving 5ml/1 tsp to garnish.

5 When ready to serve, gently reheat the lamb, uncovered. Spoon into a dish and garnish with the sesame seeds and the reserved cream. This korma is very good served with pilau rice.

Energy 939kcal/3892kJ; Fat 80.8g; Saturated fat 38.3g; Carbohydrate 5.1g; Fibre 1.5g.

Lamb Curry with Cardamom Rice

This Indian-style lamb biryani, with the meat and rice cooked together in a clay pot, is a delicious meal in itself.

Serves 4

1 large onion, quartered
2 garlic cloves
1 fresh green chilli, halved and seeded
5cm/2in piece fresh root ginger
15ml/1 tbsp ghee
15ml/1 tbsp vegetable oil
675g/1 1/2lb boned shoulder or leg of lamb, cut into chunks
15ml/1 tbsp ground coriander
10ml/2 tsp ground cumin
1 cinnamon stick, broken into 3 pieces
150ml/1/4 pint/2/3 cup thick natural (plain) yogurt
150ml/1/4 pint/2/3 cup water
75g/3oz/1/3 cup ready-to-eat dried apricots, cut into chunks
salt and ground black pepper

For the rice
250g/9oz/1 1/3 cups basmati rice
6 cardamom pods, split open
25g/1oz/2 tbsp butter, cut into small pieces
45ml/3 tbsp toasted cashew nuts or flaked (sliced) almonds

For the garnish
1 onion, sliced and fried until golden
a few sprigs of fresh coriander (cilantro)

1 Soak a large clay pot or chicken brick in cold water for 20 minutes, then drain. Place the onion, garlic, chilli and ginger in a food processor or blender and process with 15ml/1 tbsp water to a smooth paste.

2 Heat the ghee and vegetable oil in a heavy frying pan. Fry the lamb chunks in batches over a high heat until golden brown. Remove from the pan using a slotted spoon and set aside. Scrape the onion paste into the remaining oil left in the frying pan, stir in the ground coriander and cumin, add the cinnamon stick pieces and fry for 1–2 minutes, stirring constantly with a wooden spoon.

3 Return the meat to the frying pan, then gradually add the yogurt, a spoonful at a time, stirring well between each addition with a wooden spoon. Season the meat well with plenty of salt and pepper and stir in the water.

4 Transfer the contents of the frying pan to the prepared clay pot, cover with the lid and place in an unheated oven. Set the oven to 180°C/350°F/Gas 4 and cook for 45 minutes.

5 Meanwhile, prepare the basmati rice. Place it in a bowl, cover with cold water and leave to soak for 20 minutes. Drain the rice and place it in a large pan of boiling salted water, bring back to the boil and cook for 10 minutes. Drain and stir in the split cardamom pods.

6 Remove the clay pot from the oven and stir in the chopped ready-to-eat apricots. Pile the cooked rice on top of the lamb and dot with the butter. Drizzle over 60ml/4 tbsp water, then sprinkle the cashew nuts or flaked almonds on top. Cover the pot, reduce the oven temperature to 150°C/300°F/Gas 2 and cook the meat and rice for 30 minutes. Remove the lid from the pot and fluff up the rice with a fork. Garnish with the fried onion and coriander, and serve.

Energy 427kcal/1784kJ; Fat 25.3g; Saturated fat 11.3g; Carbohydrate 14.4g; Fibre 2g.

Rogan Josh

This is one of the most popular lamb dishes to have originated in Kashmir. Traditionally, fatty meat on the bone is slow-cooked until most of the fat is separated from the meat. The fat that escapes from the meat is known as rogan, and josh refers to the red colour. This recipe, however, uses lean lamb.

Serves 4–6
45ml/3 tbsp lemon juice
250ml/8fl oz/1 cup natural (plain) yogurt
5ml/1 tsp salt
2 garlic cloves, crushed
2.5cm/1in piece fresh root ginger, finely grated
900g/2lb lean lamb fillet, cubed
60ml/4 tbsp vegetable oil
2.5ml/½ tsp cumin seeds
2 bay leaves
4 green cardamom pods
1 onion, finely chopped
10ml/2 tsp ground coriander
10ml/2 tsp ground cumin
5ml/1 tsp chilli powder
400g/14oz can chopped tomatoes
30ml/2 tbsp tomato purée (paste)
150ml/¼ pint/⅔ cup water
toasted cumin seeds and bay leaves, to garnish
plain boiled rice, to serve

1 In a large bowl, mix together the lemon juice, yogurt, salt, half the crushed garlic and the ginger. Add the lamb, cover and marinate in the refrigerator overnight.

2 Heat the oil in a karahi, wok or large pan and fry the cumin seeds for 2 minutes. Add the bay leaves and cardamom pods and fry for a further 2 minutes.

3 Add the onion and remaining garlic and fry for 5 minutes. Add the coriander, cumin and chilli powder. Fry for 2 minutes.

4 Add the marinated lamb to the pan and cook for a further 5 minutes, stirring occasionally to prevent the mixture from sticking to the base of the pan and starting to burn.

5 Stir in the tomatoes, tomato purée and water. Cover and simmer for 1–1½ hours. Garnish with toasted cumin seeds and bay leaves, and serve with the rice.

Energy 566kcal/2362kJ; Fat 37g; Saturated fat 13.3g; Carbohydrate 10.7g; Fibre 1.2g.

Karahi Lamb

In this version of karahi lamb, the sautéed dried apricots flavoured with cinnamon and cardamom add an irresistible touch.

Serves 4
15ml/1 tbsp tomato purée (paste)
175ml/6fl oz/¾ cup natural (plain) yogurt
5ml/1 tsp garam masala
1.5ml/¼ tsp cumin seeds
5ml/1 tsp salt
5ml/1 tsp crushed garlic
5ml/1 tsp grated fresh root ginger
5ml/1 tsp chilli powder
450g/1lb lean spring lamb, cut into strips
30ml/2 tbsp vegetable oil
2 onions, finely sliced
25g/1oz/2 tbsp ghee, butter or margarine
2.5cm/1in piece cinnamon stick
2 green cardamom pods
5 dried apricots, quartered
15ml/1 tbsp chopped fresh coriander (cilantro)

1 In a bowl, blend the tomato purée, yogurt, garam masala, cumin seeds, salt, garlic, ginger and chilli powder. Add the lamb and leave to marinate for 1 hour.

2 Heat 10ml/2 tsp of the oil in a wok, karahi or large pan and fry the onions until crisp and golden brown. Remove the onions using a slotted spoon, allow them to cool and then grind them down by processing briefly in a food processor or blender, or with a pestle in a mortar. Reheat the oil and return the onions to the pan.

3 Add the lamb and stir-fry for about 2 minutes. Cover the pan, lower the heat and cook, stirring occasionally, for 15 minutes, or until the meat is cooked through. If required, add up to 150ml/¼ pint/⅔ cup water during the cooking. Remove from the heat and set aside.

4 Heat the ghee, butter or margarine with the remaining oil and add the cinnamon stick and cardamoms. Stir in the apricots and cook over a low heat for 2 minutes. Pour this sauce over the lamb.

5 Garnish with the chopped coriander and serve immediately.

Energy 369kcal/1536kJ; Fat 23.9g; Saturated fat 10g; Carbohydrate 13.8g; Fibre 1.8g.

Minced Lamb with Curry Leaves & Chilli

The whole chillies pack quite a punch, but can be removed from the dish before serving.

Serves 4
10ml/2 tsp oil
2 medium onions, chopped
10 curry leaves
6 fresh green chillies
350g/12oz lean minced (ground) lamb
5ml/1 tsp crushed garlic
5ml/1 tsp grated fresh root ginger
5ml/1 tsp chilli powder
1.5ml/¼ tsp ground turmeric
5ml/1 tsp salt
2 tomatoes, peeled and quartered
15ml/1 tbsp chopped fresh coriander (cilantro)

1 Heat the oil in a karahi, wok or heavy pan and fry the onions with the curry leaves and 3 of the whole green chillies.

2 Put the lamb into a bowl. Mix with the crushed garlic, grated ginger and spices.

3 Add the minced lamb and salt to the onions and stir-fry for 7–10 minutes.

4 Add the tomatoes, coriander and remaining chillies and stir-fry for 2 minutes. Serve hot.

Cook's Tips
• *This aromatic curry also makes a terrific brunch if served with fried eggs.*
• *Curry leaves are available from Indian grocers and are best used fresh rather than dried as their flavour diminishes when dried. They will keep for several days in a plastic bag in the refrigerator. You can also freeze them.*

Energy 197kcal/821kJ; Fat 9.37g; Saturated fat 3.59g; Carbohydrate 8.57g; Fibre 1.63g.

Lamb with Peas & Mint

A simple dish for a family meal, this is easy to prepare and very versatile. It is equally delicious whether served with plain boiled rice or chapatis. Another excellent use for the lamb mixture is for filling samosas.

Serves 4
15ml/1 tbsp oil
1 medium onion, chopped
2.5ml/½ tsp crushed garlic
2.5ml/½ tsp grated fresh root ginger
2.5ml/½ tsp chilli powder
1.5ml/¼ tsp ground turmeric
5ml/1 tsp ground coriander
5ml/1 tsp salt
2 medium tomatoes, sliced
275g/10oz lean leg of lamb, minced (ground)
1 large carrot, sliced or cut into batons
75g/3oz/½ cup petits pois (baby peas)
15ml/1 tbsp chopped fresh mint
15ml/1 tbsp chopped fresh coriander (cilantro)
1 fresh green chilli, chopped
fresh coriander, to garnish

1 In a deep, heavy frying pan, heat the oil and fry the chopped onion over a medium heat for 5 minutes until golden.

2 Meanwhile, in a small mixing bowl, mix the garlic, ginger, chilli powder, turmeric, ground coriander and salt. Stir well.

3 Add the sliced tomatoes and the spice mixture to the onions in the frying pan and fry for 2–3 minutes, stirring continuously.

4 Add the minced lamb to the mixture and stir-fry for about 7–10 minutes to seal.

5 Break up any lumps of meat which may form in the pan, using a potato masher if necessary.

6 Finally add the carrot, petits pois, chopped fresh mint and coriander and the chopped green chilli and mix well.

7 Cook, stirring for 2–3 minutes until the carrot slices or batons and the petits pois are cooked, then serve immediately, garnished with fresh coriander sprigs.

Energy 178kcal/742kJ; Fat 9.4g; Saturated fat 3.32g; Carbohydrate 7.2g; Fibre 2.1g.

Rezala

This delectable lamb recipe is a legacy of the Muslim Mughal era. It comes from Bengal where there is a tradition of Muslim cuisine.

Serves 4

1 large onion, roughly chopped
10ml/2 tsp grated fresh root ginger
10ml/2 tsp crushed garlic
4 or 5 cloves
2.5ml/½ tsp black peppercorns
6 green cardamom pods
5cm/2in piece cinnamon stick, halved
8 lamb rib chops
60ml/4 tbsp vegetable oil
1 large onion, finely sliced
175ml/6fl oz/¾ cup natural (plain) yogurt
50g/2oz/¼ cup butter
2.5ml/1 tsp salt
2.5ml/½ tsp ground cumin
2.5ml/½ tsp hot chilli powder
whole nutmeg
2.5ml/½ tsp granulated sugar
15ml/1 tbsp lime juice
pinch of saffron, steeped in 15ml/1 tbsp hot water for 10–15 minutes
15ml/1 tbsp rose water
rose petals, to garnish
naan bread or boiled basmatic rice, to serve (optional)

1 Process the onion in a blender or food processor. Add a little water if necessary to form a purée.

2 Put the purée in a glass bowl and add the grated ginger, crushed garlic, cloves, peppercorns, cardamom pods and cinnamon. Mix well.

3 Put the lamb chops in a large shallow glass dish and add the spice mixture. Mix thoroughly, cover the bowl and leave the lamb to marinate for 3–4 hours or overnight in the refrigerator. Bring back to room temperature before cooking.

4 In a karahi, wok or large pan, heat the oil over medium-high heat and fry the sliced onion for 6–7 minutes, until golden brown. Remove the onion slices with a slotted spoon, squeezing out as much oil as possible on the side of the pan. Drain the onions on kitchen paper.

5 In the remaining oil, fry the marinated lamb chops for 4–5 minutes, stirring frequently. Reduce the heat to low, cover and cook for 5–7 minutes.

6 Meanwhile, mix the yogurt and butter together in a small pan and place over a low heat. Cook for 5–6 minutes, stirring constantly, then stir into the lamb chops along with the salt. Add the cumin and chilli powder and cover the pan. Cook for 45–50 minutes until the chops are tender.

7 Using a nutmeg grater, or the finest cutting surface on a large, stainless steel grater, grate about 2.5ml/½ tsp nutmeg.

8 Add the nutmeg and sugar to the pan containing the lamb, cook for 1–2 minutes and add the lime juice, saffron and rose water. Stir and mix well, simmer for 2–3 minutes and remove from the heat. Spoon into a dish and garnish with the fried onion and rose petals. Serve with naan bread or boiled basmati rice, if you like.

Energy 637kcal/2630kJ; Fat 57.4g; Saturated fat 25.7g; Carbohydrate 12.8g; Fibre 1.7g.

Lamb with Apricots

Dried apricots are a useful store-cupboard ingredient and can really transform a curry or stew. Here they are combined with cinnamon, cardamom, cumin and coriander to make a delicious sauce with a hint of sweetness for lamb.

Serves 6

900g/2lb lean stewing lamb
15ml/1 tbsp oil
2.5cm/1in cinnamon stick
4 green cardamom pods
1 onion, chopped
15ml/1 tbsp curry paste
5ml/1 tsp ground cumin
5ml/1 tsp ground coriander
1.5ml/¼ tsp salt
175g/6oz/⅔ cup ready-to-eat dried apricots
350ml/12fl oz/1½ cups lamb stock
fresh coriander (cilantro), to garnish
saffron rice and mango chutney, to serve

1 Remove all the visible fat from the stewing lamb and cut into 2.5cm/1in cubes.

2 Heat the oil in a large, heavy pan and fry the cinnamon stick and cardamoms for 2 minutes. Add the onion and gently fry for about 6–8 minutes, stirring occasionally.

3 Add the curry paste and fry for 2 minutes. Stir in the ground cumin and coriander and the salt and stir-fry for a further 2–3 minutes.

4 Add the meat, apricots and the stock. Cover and cook for 1–1½ hours. Serve, garnished with fresh coriander, on yellow rice, with mango chutney in a separate bowl.

Cook's Tip
It is best to buy green cardamom pods from an Indian grocer or health food store, as the cardamoms sold in supermarkets are often bleached and do not have as full a flavour. Cardamom is a versatile spice in Indian cuisine, used in savoury and sweet dishes.

Energy 327kcal/1368kJ; Fat 16g; Saturated fat 6.59g; Carbohydrate 13.3g; Fibre 2.7g.

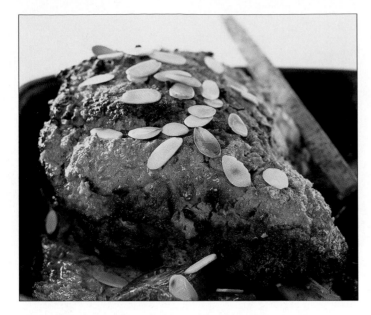

Mughlai-style Leg of Lamb

Legend has it that roasting a whole leg of lamb was first popularized by the Mongolian warrior Genghis Khan. Here the meat is permeated with spices.

Serves 4–6

4 large onions, chopped
4 garlic cloves
5cm/2in piece fresh root
    ginger, chopped
45ml/3 tbsp ground almonds
10ml/2 tsp ground cumin
10ml/2 tsp ground coriander
10ml/2 tsp ground turmeric
10ml/2 tsp garam masala
4–6 fresh green chillies
juice of 1 lemon
300ml/½ pint/1¼ cups natural
    (plain) yogurt, beaten
1.8kg/4lb leg of lamb
8–10 cloves
salt
15ml/1 tbsp flaked (sliced)
    almonds, to garnish
4 firm tomatoes, halved and
    grilled (broiled), to serve

1 Preheat the oven to 190°C/375°F/Gas 5. Place the onions, garlic, ginger, ground almonds, dry spices, chillies and lemon juice in a food processor or blender. Add salt to taste, and process to a smooth paste. Gradually add the yogurt and blend briefly to mix. Grease a large, deep roasting pan.

2 Remove most of the fat and skin from the lamb. Using a sharp knife, make deep pockets above the bone at each side of the thick end. Make deep diagonal gashes on both sides of the lamb.

3 Push the cloves firmly into the meat, spaced evenly on all sides.

4 Push some of the spice mixture into the pockets and gashes and spread the remainder evenly all over the meat. Place the meat on the roasting pan and loosely cover the whole pan with foil. Roast for 2–2½ hours, or until the meat is cooked, removing the foil for the last 10 minutes of cooking time.

5 Remove from the oven and leave to rest for about 10 minutes before carving. Garnish the roast with the almonds and serve with the tomatoes.

Energy 852kcal/3549kJ; Fat 51.2g; Saturated fat 17g; Carbohydrate 25.4g; Fibre 3.5g.

Kashmiri-style Lamb

This red-coloured, hot curry can be made milder by simply replacing the chilli powder with paprika and tomato purée.

Serves 4–6

60ml/4 tbsp vegetable oil
1.5ml/¼ tsp asafoetida
900g/2lb lean lamb, cubed
piece fresh root ginger,
    crushed
2 garlic cloves, crushed
60ml/4 tbsp rogan josh
    masala paste
5ml/1 tsp chilli powder, or
    10ml/2 tsp sweet paprika
    plus 10ml/2 tsp tomato
    purée (paste)
8–10 strands saffron (optional),
    plus extra to garnish
salt
about 150ml/¼ pint/⅔ cup
    natural (plain) yogurt, beaten

1 Heat the oil in a pan and fry the asafoetida and lamb, stirring well to seal the meat. Reduce the heat, cover and cook for about 10 minutes.

2 Add the ginger, garlic, rogan josh masala paste, chilli powder or paprika and tomato purée (if you want a milder curry), and saffron. Mix well and add salt. If the meat is too dry, add a very small amount of boiling water. Cover the pan and cook on a low heat for a further 10 minutes.

3 Remove the pan from the heat and leave to cool a little. Add the yogurt 15ml/1 tbsp at a time, stirring constantly to avoid curdling. Return to a low heat and cook uncovered until thick. Garnish with a spoonful of yogurt and a few saffron strands.

Cook's Tip
Asafoetida is made from the sap of the roots and stem of a large plant similar to fennel in appearance. The sap dries into a resin, which is ground for culinary use. As it has a strong aroma it is used in only small amounts.

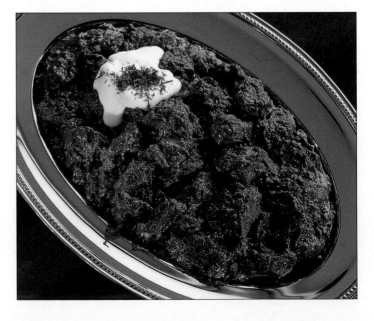

Energy 547kcal/2280kJ; Fat 39.3g; Saturated fat 13.5g; Carbohydrate 2.8g; Fibre 0g.

Hot-&-sour Lamb & Lentil Curry

This dish has a hot, sweet-and-sour flavour, through which should rise the slightly bitter flavour of fenugreek leaves.

Serves 4–6
90ml/6 tbsp vegetable oil
2 fresh red chillies, chopped
2 fresh green chillies, chopped
2.5cm/1in piece fresh root ginger, crushed
3 garlic cloves, crushed
2 bay leaves
5cm/2in piece cinnamon stick
900g/2lb lean lamb, cubed
600ml/1 pint/2½ cups water
350g/12oz/1½ cups mixed lentils (see Cook's Tip)
2 potatoes, cubed
1 aubergine (eggplant), cubed
2 courgettes (zucchini), cubed
4 onions, thinly sliced, deep-fried and drained
115g/4oz frozen spinach, thawed and drained
25g/1oz fenugreek leaves, fresh or dried
115g/4oz pumpkin, cubed
115g/4oz/4 cups fresh coriander (cilantro), chopped
50g/2oz/2 cups fresh mint, chopped, or 15ml/1 tbsp mint sauce
45ml/3 tbsp garam masala
10ml/2 tsp brown sugar
lemon juice, to taste
1 garlic clove, sliced
salt

1 Heat 45ml/3 tbsp of the oil in a pan, wok or karahi and fry the chillies, ginger and garlic for 2 minutes. Add the bay leaves, cinnamon, lamb and water. Bring to the boil, then reduce the heat and simmer until the lamb is half cooked.

2 Drain the water into another pan and put the lamb aside. Add the lentils to the water and cook until they are tender. Mash the lentils with the back of a spoon.

3 Add the cubes of potatoes and aubergine and stir into the mashed lentils, then add the courgette cubes and deep-fried onions. Stir in the spinach, fenugreek and pumpkin. Add some hot water if the mixture is too thick. Cook until the vegetables are tender, then mash again with a spoon, keeping the vegetables a little coarse.

4 Heat 15ml/1 tbsp of the oil in a frying pan, and gently fry the fresh coriander and mint (saving a little to garnish) with the masala, sugar and salt. Add the reserved lamb and fry gently for about 5 minutes.

5 Return the lamb and spices to the lentil and vegetable mixture and stir well. If the mixture seems dry, add more water. Heat gently until the lamb is fully cooked.

6 Add the lemon juice and mix well. Heat the remaining oil and fry the sliced clove of garlic until golden brown. Pour over the curry. Garnish with the remaining deep-fried onion slices and the reserved coriander and mint. Serve hot.

Hot Dry Meat Curry

This dish is nearly as hot as phaal (India's hottest curry) but the spices can still be distinguished above the fiery chilli.

Serves 4–6
30ml/2 tbsp vegetable oil
1 large onion, finely sliced
5cm/2in piece fresh root ginger, crushed
4 garlic cloves, crushed
6–8 curry leaves
45ml/3 tbsp extra-hot curry paste
15ml/1 tbsp chilli powder
5ml/1 tsp Indian five-spice powder
5ml/1 tsp ground turmeric
900g/2lb lean lamb, beef or pork, cubed
175ml/6fl oz/¾ cup thick coconut milk
salt
chopped tomato and coriander (cilantro) leaves, to garnish

1 Heat the oil in a large pan and fry the sliced onion, crushed ginger and garlic and the curry leaves until the onion is soft, stirring occasionally.

2 Stir in the curry paste, chilli, five-spice powder, turmeric and salt, and cook for a few moments, stirring frequently.

3 Add the meat and stir well over a medium heat to seal and evenly brown the meat pieces. Keep stirring until the oil separates. Cover and cook for about 20 minutes.

4 Add the coconut milk, mix well and simmer until the meat is cooked.

5 Towards the end of cooking, uncover the pan to reduce the excess liquid. Garnish and serve hot.

Cook's Tip
You might like to include bengal gram (a type of chickpea), moong dhal (small split yellow lentils) and masoor dhal (red split lentils). Cooking times will depend on the types chosen.

Cook's Tip
Indian five-spice powder contains aniseed, cumin, fenugreek, mustard and nigella. If you are unable to find it you can substitute garam masala or curry powder instead.

Energy 1040kcal/4359kJ; Fat 53.5g; Saturated fat 14.9g; Carbohydrate 73.5g; Fibre 9.8g.

Energy 558kcal/2323kJ; Fat 39.2g; Saturated fat 13.4g; Carbohydrate 6.9g; Fibre 0.9g.

Spicy Spring Lamb Roast

Coating a leg of lamb with a spicy, fruity rub gives it a wonderful flavour.

Serves 6

1.6kg/3–3½lb lean leg of spring lamb
5ml/1 tsp chilli powder
5ml/1 tsp crushed garlic
5ml/1 tsp ground coriander
5ml/1 tsp ground cumin
5ml/1 tsp salt
15ml/1 tbsp dried breadcrumbs
45ml/3 tbsp natural (plain) low-fat yogurt
30ml/2 tbsp lemon juice
30ml/2 tbsp sultanas (golden raisins)
15ml/1 tbsp oil

For the garnish

mixed salad leaves
fresh coriander (cilantro)
2 tomatoes, quartered
1 large carrot, shredded
lemon wedges

1 Preheat the oven to 180°C/350°F/Gas 4. Trim any excess fat from the lamb. Rinse the joint, pat it dry and set aside on a sheet of foil large enough to enclose it completely.

2 In a medium bowl, mix together the chilli powder, garlic, ground coriander, ground cumin and salt.

3 Mix together in a food processor the breadcrumbs, yogurt, lemon juice and sultanas.

4 Add the contents of the food processor to the spice mixture together with the oil and mix together well. Pour this on to the leg of lamb and rub all over the meat.

5 Enclose the meat in the foil and place in an ovenproof dish. Cook in the oven for about 1½ hours.

6 Remove the lamb from the oven, open the foil and, using the back of a spoon, spread the mixture evenly over the meat. Return the lamb, uncovered, to the oven for another 45 minutes or until it is cooked right through and tender.

7 Slice the meat and serve with the mixed salad leaves, fresh coriander, tomatoes, carrot and lemon wedges.

Lamb Pilau

A pilau is a rice dish containing whole spices, which can either be plain or combined with meat, chicken or vegetables.

Serves 4–6

30ml/2 tbsp corn oil
15ml/1 tbsp unsalted (sweet) butter or ghee
2 medium onions, sliced
5ml/1 tsp crushed garlic
5ml/1 tsp chilli powder
1.5ml/¼ tsp crushed fresh root ginger
1.5ml/¼ tsp ground turmeric
5ml/1 tsp garam masala
5ml/1 tsp salt
30ml/2 tbsp natural (plain) yogurt
2 medium tomatoes, sliced
450g/1lb lean minced (ground) lamb
30ml/2 tbsp chopped fresh coriander (cilantro)
2 medium fresh chillies, chopped
tomato slices

For the rice

450g/1lb/2¼ cups basmati rice
1.2 litres/2 pints/5 cups water
4 cloves
4 green cardamom pods
2.5ml/½ tsp black cumin seeds
6 black peppercorns
7.5ml/1½ tsp salt
15ml/1 tbsp chopped fresh coriander (cilantro)
2 fresh green chillies, chopped
15ml/1 tbsp lime juice
2.5ml/½ tsp saffron strands soaked in 30ml/2 tbsp milk (optional)

1 Wash the rice twice, drain and set aside in a sieve (strainer).

2 Heat the oil and ghee in a deep, round-bottomed frying pan or a large karahi. Add the onions and fry until golden brown.

3 Lower the heat to medium and add the garlic, chilli powder, ginger, turmeric, garam masala, salt, yogurt and tomatoes and stir-fry gently for about 1 minute.

4 Add the minced lamb and turn up the heat to high. Use a slotted spoon to fry the lamb, scraping the bottom of the pan to prevent it from burning.

5 Add the fresh coriander and chillies, and continue to stir, breaking up any lumps in the meat as you work. Once the lamb is throughly cooked, set it to one side.

6 Put the rinsed and drained rice into a large pan with the water, cloves, cardamom pods, cumin seeds, peppercorns and salt, and bring to the boil. When the rice has boiled for 2 minutes, drain off the water along with half the rice, leaving the rest in the pan.

7 Spread the cooked lamb over the rice in the pan and cover with the rice left in the strainer.

8 Add the fresh coriander, green chillies, lime juice and saffron in milk, if using.

9 Cover the pan with a tight-fitting lid and cook over a very low heat for 15–20 minutes.

10 Check that the rice is cooked through and mix gently with a slotted spoon before serving. Garnish with slices of tomato if you like.

Energy 265kcal/1109kJ; Fat 13.4g; Saturated fat 5.59g; Carbohydrate 8.9g; Fibre 0.7g.

Energy 704kcal/2939kJ; Fat 22.1g; Saturated fat 8.7g; Carbohydrate 93.4g; Fibre 1.2g.

Pork with Vegetables

This is a basic recipe for stir-frying any meat with any vegetables, according to seasonal availability.

Serves 4
225g/8oz pork fillet (tenderloin)
15ml/1 tbsp light soy sauce
5ml/1 tsp soft light brown sugar
5ml/1 tsp Chinese rice wine or
  dry sherry
10ml/2 tsp cornflour (cornstarch)
  mixed to a paste with a
  little water
115g/4oz/1²/₃ cups mangetouts
  (snow peas)
115g/4oz button (white)
  mushrooms
1 carrot
1 spring onion (scallion)
60ml/4 tbsp vegetable oil
5ml/1 tsp salt
stock (optional)
few drops sesame oil

1 Cut the pork into thin slices. Marinate with about 5ml/1 tsp of the soy sauce, the sugar, rice wine or sherry and cornflour paste.

2 Trim the mangetouts. Thinly slice the mushrooms. Cut the carrot into pieces roughly the same size as the pork and cut the spring onion into short sections.

3 Heat the oil in a preheated wok or large, heavy pan, and stir-fry the pork for about 1 minute or until its colour changes. Remove with a slotted spoon and keep warm while you cook the vegetables.

4 Add the vegetables to the wok and stir-fry for about 2 minutes. Add the salt and the partly cooked pork, and a little stock or water if necessary. Continue cooking and stirring for about 1 minute, then add the remaining soy sauce and blend well. Sprinkle with the sesame oil and serve.

Cook's Tip
When preparing vegetables for stir-frying, cut them to even sizes so that they will take the same amount of time to cook.

Energy 199kcal/826kJ; Fat 13.6g; Saturated fat 2.1g; Carbohydrate 5.7g; Fibre 1.6g.

Portuguese Pork

The Portuguese expanded their empire during the 15th century, establishing outposts in India and Malaysia. In these days, before refrigeration, spices were extremely valuable, and the Portuguese were keen to control the main trade routes both between Asia and Europe, and among different regions of Asia such as India, Indonesia, China and Japan. One major result of this Portuguese colonization was the influence of Portuguese cooking on Indian cuisine, as shown in this fiery pork curry recipe.

Serves 4–6
115g/4oz deep-fried onions,
  crushed
4 fresh red chillies
60ml/4 tbsp vindaloo curry paste
90ml/6 tbsp white wine vinegar
90ml/6 tbsp tomato purée
  (paste)
2.5ml/½ tsp fenugreek seeds
5ml/1 tsp ground turmeric
5ml/1 tsp crushed mustard seeds,
  or 2.5ml/½ tsp mustard
  powder
7.5ml/1½ tsp granulated
  sugar
900g/2lb boneless pork spare
  ribs, cubed
250ml/8fl oz/1 cup water
salt
plain boiled rice, to serve

1 Place the crushed onions, chillies, curry paste, vinegar, tomato purée, fenugreek seeds, turmeric and mustard seeds or powder in a bowl, with sugar and salt to taste.

2 Add the pork cubes and mix well. Cover and marinate for 2 hours, then transfer to a large, heavy pan.

3 Stir in the water. Bring to the boil and simmer gently for 2 hours. Serve hot with the rice.

Cook's Tip
When preparing fresh chillies, it is a good idea to wear rubber gloves, especially if using the hotter varieties. Never touch your eyes, nose or mouth while handling them, and wash both the gloves and your hands with soap and warm water afterwards.

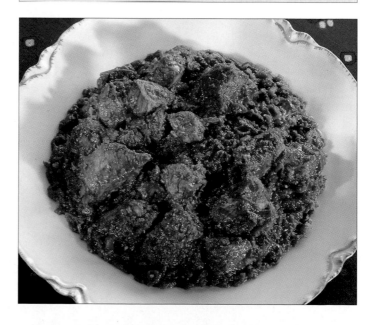

Energy 322kcal/1349kJ; Fat 12.2g; Saturated fat 3.6g; Carbohydrate 4.1g; Fibre 0.9g.

Chilli Pork with Curry Leaves

Curry leaves and chillies are two of the hallmark ingredients used in the southern states of India. This recipe is from the state of Andhra Pradesh, where the hottest chillies, known as *guntur* after the region where they are produced, are grown in abundance.

Serves 4–6
30ml/2 tbsp vegetable oil
1 large onion, finely sliced
5cm/2in piece fresh root ginger, grated
4 garlic cloves, crushed
12 curry leaves
45ml/3 tbsp extra-hot curry paste, or 60ml/4 tbsp hot curry powder
15ml/1 tbsp chilli powder
5ml/1 tsp five-spice powder
5ml/1 tsp ground turmeric
900g/2lb pork, cubed
175ml/6fl oz/¾ cup thick coconut milk
salt
red onion, finely sliced, to garnish
Indian bread and fruit raita, to serve

1 Heat the oil in a karahi, wok or large pan, and fry the onion, ginger, garlic and curry leaves until the onion is soft. Add the curry paste or powder, chilli and five-spice powder, turmeric and salt. Stir well.

2 Add the pork and stir well over a medium heat to seal and evenly brown the meat pieces. Keep stirring until the oil separates. Cover the pan and cook for about 20 minutes.

3 Stir in the coconut milk and simmer, covered, until the meat is cooked. Towards the end of cooking, uncover the pan to reduce the excess liquid. Garnish with onions and serve with any Indian bread, and with fruit raita, for a cooling effect.

> **Cook's Tip**
> For extra flavour, reserve half the curry leaves and add with the coconut milk in step 3.

Energy 484kcal/2018kJ; Fat 31g; Saturated fat 12.5g; Carbohydrate 6.9g; Fibre 0.9g.

Pork Balchao

This spicy stew is flavoured with vinegar and sugar, a combination that immediately identifies it as Goan.

Serves 4
60ml/4 tbsp vegetable oil
15ml/1 tbsp grated fresh root ginger
15ml/1 tbsp crushed garlic
2.5cm/1in piece cinnamon stick, broken up
2–4 dried red chillies, chopped or torn
4 cloves
10ml/2 tsp cumin seeds
10 black peppercorns
675g/1½lb cubed leg of pork, crackling and other visible fat removed
5ml/1 tsp ground turmeric
200ml/7fl oz/scant 1 cup warm water
25ml/1½ tbsp tomato purée (paste)
2.5ml/½ tsp chilli powder (optional)
1 large onion, finely sliced
5ml/1 tsp salt
5ml/1 tsp granulated sugar
10ml/2 tbsp cider vinegar
fresh chillies, to garnish

1 Heat 30ml/2 tbsp of the oil in a karahi, wok or large pan, and add the ginger and garlic. Fry for 30 seconds.

2 Grind the cinnamon stick, dried chillies, cloves, cumin seeds and peppercorns to a fine powder, using a spice mill or coffee grinder reserved for spices. Add the spice mix to the pan and fry for a further 30 seconds, stirring.

3 Add the pork and turmeric and increase the heat slightly. Fry for 5–6 minutes or until the meat starts to release its juices, stirring regularly. Add the water, tomato purée and chilli powder, if using, and bring to the boil. Cover the pan and simmer gently for 35–40 minutes.

4 Heat the remaining oil and fry the sliced onion for 8–9 minutes until browned, stirring regularly. Add the fried onion to the pork along with the salt, sugar and cider vinegar. Stir, cover and simmer for 30–35 minutes or until the pork is tender. Remove from the heat and spoon into a serving dish. Garnish with fresh chillies and serve.

Energy 326kcal/1361kJ; Fat 17.9g; Saturated fat 3.7g; Carbohydrate 4.8g; Fibre 0.9g.

Curried Pork with Pickled Garlic

This very rich curry is best accompanied by lots of plain rice and perhaps a light vegetable dish. It could serve four if accompanied by a vegetable curry. Asian stores sell pickled garlic. It is well worth investing in a jar, as the taste is sweet and delicious.

Serves 2
130g/4½oz lean pork steaks
30ml/2 tbsp vegetable oil
1 garlic clove, crushed
15ml/1 tbsp Thai red curry paste
130ml/4½fl oz/generous ½ cup coconut cream
2.5cm/1in piece fresh root ginger, finely chopped
30ml/2 tbsp vegetable or chicken stock
30ml/2 tbsp Thai fish sauce
5ml/1 tsp granulated sugar
2.5ml/½ tsp ground turmeric
10ml/2 tsp lemon juice
4 pickled garlic cloves, finely chopped
strips of lemon and lime rind, to garnish

1 Place the pork steaks in the freezer for 30–40 minutes, until firm, then, using a sharp knife, cut the meat into fine slivers, trimming off any excess fat.

2 Heat the oil in a wok or large, heavy frying pan and cook the garlic over low to medium heat until golden brown. Do not let it burn. Add the curry paste and stir it in well.

3 Add the coconut cream and stir until the liquid begins to reduce and thicken. Stir in the pork. Cook for 2 minutes more, until the pork is cooked through.

4 Add the ginger, stock, fish sauce, sugar and turmeric, stirring constantly, then add the lemon juice and pickled garlic. Spoon into bowls, garnish with strips of rind, and serve.

Cook's Tip
Thai red curry paste is a fiery curry paste made with hot red chillies, garlic, lemon grass, shrimp paste and turmeric.

Energy 193kcal/801kJ; Fat 13.8g; Saturated fat 2.3g; Carbohydrate 3.2g; Fibre 0g.

Sweet-&-sour Pork, Thai-style

It was the Chinese who originally created sweet-and-sour cooking, but the Thais also do it very well. This version has a fresher and cleaner flavour than the original. It makes a good one-dish meal when served over rice.

Serves 4
350g/12oz lean pork
30ml/2 tbsp vegetable oil
4 garlic cloves, thinly sliced
1 small red onion, sliced
30ml/2 tbsp Thai fish sauce
15ml/1 tbsp granulated sugar
1 red (bell) pepper, seeded and diced
½ cucumber, seeded and sliced
2 plum tomatoes, cut into wedges
115g/4oz piece of fresh pineapple, cut into small chunks
2 spring onions (scallions), cut into short lengths
ground black pepper

For the garnish
coriander (cilantro) leaves
spring onions (scallions), shredded

1 Place the pork in the freezer for 30–40 minutes, until firm. Using a sharp knife, cut it into thin strips.

2 Heat the oil in a wok or large frying pan. Add the thinly sliced garlic. Cook over a medium heat until golden, then add the pork and stir-fry for 4–5 minutes. Add the red onion slices and toss to mix.

3 Add the fish sauce, sugar and ground black pepper to taste. Toss the mixture over the heat for 3–4 minutes more.

4 Stir in the diced red pepper, cucumber, tomatoes, pineapple and spring onions. Stir-fry for 3–4 minutes more, then spoon into a bowl. Garnish with the coriander and shredded spring onions, and serve.

Cook's Tip
Freezing the pork slightly ensures extra-thin slices when you slice it.

Energy 202kcal/845kJ; Fat 9.5g; Saturated fat 2g; Carbohydrate 9.4g; Fibre 2.1g.

Lemon Grass Pork

Chillies and lemon grass flavour this simple stir-fry, while peanuts add an interesting contrast in texture. Look for jars of chopped lemon grass, which are handy when the fresh herb isn't available.

Serves 4

675g/1½lb boneless pork loin
2 lemon grass stalks, finely
   chopped
4 spring onions (scallions),
   thinly sliced
5ml/1 tsp salt
12 black peppercorns, coarsely
   crushed
30ml/2 tbsp groundnut
   (peanut) oil
2 garlic cloves, chopped
2 fresh red chillies, seeded
   and chopped
5ml/1 tsp soft light brown sugar
30ml/2 tbsp Thai fish sauce
25g/1oz/¼ cup roasted unsalted
   peanuts, chopped
ground black pepper
cooked rice noodles, to serve
coarsely torn coriander (cilantro)
   leaves, to garnish

1 Trim any excess fat from the pork. Cut the meat across into 5mm/¼in thick slices, then cut each slice into 5mm/¼in strips. Put the pork into a bowl with the lemon grass, spring onions, salt and crushed peppercorns; mix well. Cover with clear film (plastic wrap) and leave to marinate in a cool place for 30 minutes.

2 Preheat a wok, add the oil and swirl it around. Add the pork mixture and stir-fry over a medium heat for about 3 minutes, until browned all over.

3 Add the garlic and red chillies and stir-fry for a further 5–8 minutes over a medium heat, until the pork is cooked through and tender.

4 Add the sugar, fish sauce and chopped peanuts and toss to mix, then season to taste with black pepper. Serve immediately on a bed of rice noodles, garnished with the coarsely torn coriander leaves.

Pork & Pineapple Coconut Curry

The heat of this curry balances out the sweetness of the pineapple, and the coconut cream and spices make a smooth and fragrant dish. It takes very little time to cook, so is ideal for a quick supper before going out or for a midweek family meal on a busy evening.

Serves 4

400ml/14fl oz can coconut milk
10ml/2 tsp Thai red curry paste
400g/14oz pork loin steaks,
   trimmed and thinly sliced
15ml/1 tbsp Thai fish sauce
5ml/1 tsp palm sugar or light
   muscovado (brown) sugar
15ml/1 tbsp tamarind juice, made
   by mixing tamarind paste with
   warm water
2 kaffir lime leaves, torn
½ medium pineapple, peeled
   and chopped
1 fresh red chilli, seeded and
   finely chopped

1 Pour the coconut milk into a bowl and let it settle, so that the cream rises to the surface. Scoop the cream into a measuring jug (cup). You should have about 250ml/8fl oz/ 1 cup. If necessary, add a little of the coconut milk.

2 Pour the measured coconut cream into a large pan and bring it to the boil.

3 Cook the coconut cream for about 10 minutes, until it separates, stirring frequently to prevent it from sticking to the base of the pan and scorching. Add the red curry paste and stir until well mixed. Cook, stirring occasionally, for about 4 minutes, until the paste is fragrant.

4 Add the sliced pork and stir in the fish sauce, sugar and tamarind juice. Cook, stirring constantly, for 1–2 minutes, until the sugar has dissolved and the pork is no longer pink.

5 Add the reserved coconut milk and the lime leaves. Bring to the boil, then stir in the pineapple. Reduce the heat and simmer gently for 3 minutes, or until the pork is fully cooked. Sprinkle over the chilli and serve.

Energy 297kcal/1240kJ; Fat 15.2g; Saturated fat 3.6g; Carbohydrate 2.1g; Fibre 0.5g.

Energy 169kcal/712kJ; Fat 4.4g; Saturated fat 1.6g; Carbohydrate 11g; Fibre 0.6g.

Pork Belly with Five Spices

The Chinese influence on Thai cuisine stems from the early years of its history, when colonists from southern China settled in the country, bringing with them dishes like this, although Thai cooks have provided their own unique imprint. Lime and the whole of the coriander plant adds a full flavour to the spices used in this dish.

Serves 4
1 large bunch fresh coriander (cilantro) with roots
30ml/2 tbsp vegetable oil
1 garlic clove, crushed
30ml/2 tbsp five-spice powder
500g/1¼lb pork belly, cut into 2.5cm/1in pieces
400g/14oz can chopped tomatoes
150ml/¼ pint/⅔ cup hot water
30ml/2 tbsp dark soy sauce
45ml/3 tbsp Thai fish sauce
30ml/2 tbsp granulated sugar
1 lime, halved

1 Cut off the coriander roots. Chop five of them finely and freeze the remainder for another occasion. Chop the coriander stalks and leaves and set them aside. Keep the roots separate.

2 Heat the oil in a large pan and cook the garlic until golden brown. Stirring constantly, add the chopped coriander roots and then the five-spice powder.

3 Add the pork and stir-fry until the meat is thoroughly coated in spices and has browned. Stir in the tomatoes and hot water. Bring to the boil, then stir in the soy sauce, fish sauce and sugar.

4 Reduce the heat, cover the pan and simmer for 30 minutes. Stir in the chopped coriander stalks and leaves, squeeze over the lime juice and serve.

> **Cook's Tip**
> Make sure that you buy Chinese five-spice powder, as the Indian variety is made up from quite different spices.

Energy 581kcal/2405kJ; Fat 50.5g; Saturated fat 17.1g; Carbohydrate 11.6g; Fibre 2.3g.

Pork Chops with Field Mushrooms

These fabulous pork chops are great favourites with everyone and are delicious served with noodles or rice.

Serves 4
4 pork chops
4 large field (portabello) mushrooms
45ml/3 tbsp vegetable oil
4 fresh red chillies, seeded and thinly sliced
45ml/3 tbsp Thai fish sauce
90ml/6 tbsp fresh lime juice
4 shallots, chopped
5ml/1 tsp roasted ground rice

30ml/2 tbsp spring onions (scallions), chopped, plus shredded spring onions to garnish
coriander (cilantro) leaves, to garnish

For the marinade
2 garlic cloves, chopped
15ml/1 tbsp granulated sugar
15ml/1 tbsp Thai fish sauce
30ml/2 tbsp soy sauce
15ml/1 tbsp sesame oil
15ml/1 tbsp whisky or dry sherry
2 lemon grass stalks, finely chopped
2 spring onions, chopped

1 To make the marinade, combine the garlic, sugar, sauces, oil and whisky or sherry in a large, shallow dish. Stir in the lemon grass and spring onions. Add the pork chops, turning to coat them in the marinade. Cover and leave to marinate for 1–2 hours.

2 Lift the chops out of the marinade and place them on a barbecue over hot coals or on a grill (broiler) rack. Add the mushrooms and brush them with 15ml/1 tbsp of the oil. Cook the pork chops for 5–7 minutes on each side and the mushrooms for about 2 minutes. Brush both with the marinade while cooking.

3 Heat the remaining oil in a wok or small frying pan, then remove the pan from the heat and stir in the chillies, fish sauce, lime juice, shallots, ground rice and chopped spring onions. Put the pork chops and mushrooms on a large serving plate and spoon over the sauce. Garnish with the coriander leaves and shredded spring onion.

Energy 342kcal/1423kJ; Fat 22.1g; Saturated fat 5.3g; Carbohydrate 1.7g; Fibre 1.2g.

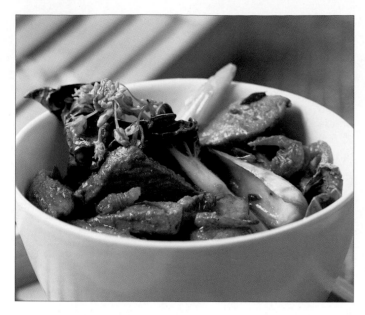

Stir-fried Pork with Dried Shrimp

You might expect the dried shrimp to give this dish a fishy flavour, but instead it simply imparts a delicious savoury taste.

Serves 4
250g/9oz pork fillet (tenderloin), sliced
30ml/2 tbsp vegetable oil
2 garlic cloves, finely chopped
45ml/3 tbsp dried shrimp
10ml/2 tsp dried shrimp paste or 5mm/¼in piece from block of shrimp paste
30ml/2 tbsp soy sauce
juice of 1 lime
15ml/1 tbsp palm sugar or light muscovado (brown) sugar
1 small fresh red or green chilli, seeded and finely chopped
4 pak choi (bok choy) or 450g/1lb spring greens (collards), shredded

1 Place the pork in the freezer for about 30 minutes, until firm. Using a sharp knife, cut it into thin slices.

2 Heat the oil in a wok or frying pan and cook the garlic until golden brown. Add the pork and stir-fry for about 4 minutes, until just cooked through.

3 Add the dried shrimp, then stir in the shrimp paste, with the soy sauce, lime juice and sugar.

4 Add the chilli and pak choi or spring greens and toss over the heat until the vegetables are just wilted. Transfer the stir-fried pork to warm individual bowls and serve immediately.

> **Cook's Tip**
> *Pork fillet, or tenderloin, is the lean and tender muscle from the back loin of the pig. It is a prime cut of meat that is tender with little fat and is ideal for quick cooking such as here. It has a thin membrane that covers the meat and which needs to be removed before cooking.*

Energy 342kcal/1423kJ; Fat 22.1g; Saturated fat 5.3g; Carbohydrate 1.7g; Fibre 1.2g.

Fragrant Pork on Lemon Grass Sticks

This simple pork recipe makes a substantial snack or unusual appetizer, and the lemon grass sticks not only add a subtle flavour but also make a good talking point while enjoying the food.

4 fresh coriander (cilantro) roots, finely chopped
2.5ml/½ tsp granulated sugar
15ml/1 tbsp soy sauce
salt and ground black pepper
8 × 10cm/4in lengths of lemon grass stalk
sweet chilli sauce, to serve

Serves 4
300g/11oz minced (ground) pork
4 garlic cloves, crushed

1 Place the minced pork, crushed garlic, chopped coriander root, sugar and soy sauce in a large bowl.

2 Season with salt and pepper to taste and mix well.

3 Divide into eight portions and mould each one into a ball. It may help to dampen your hands before shaping the mixture to prevent it from sticking.

4 Stick a length of lemon grass halfway into each ball, then press the meat mixture around the lemon grass to make a shape like a chicken leg.

5 Cook the pork sticks under a hot grill (broiler) for 3–4 minutes on each side, until golden and cooked through.

6 Serve with the chilli sauce for dipping.

> **Variation**
> *Slimmer versions of these pork sticks are perfect for parties. The quantities given above will be enough for 12 lemon grass sticks if you use the mixture sparingly.*

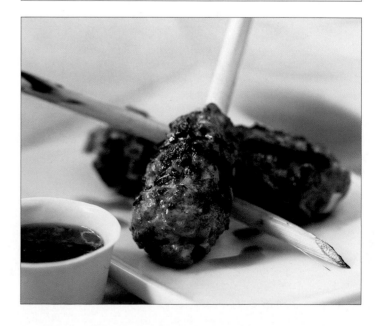

Energy 102kcal/428kJ; Fat 3.3g; Saturated fat 1.1g; Carbohydrate 1.2g; Fibre 1.3g.

Pork with Fried Rice

Bitesize cubes of pork cooked with eggs taste fantastic in this classic rice dish. If you like, you can garnish the dish with strips of omelette, made by rolling up a thin omelette and cutting across the roll into narrow sections.

Serves 4–6
45ml/3 tbsp vegetable oil
1 onion, chopped
15ml/1 tbsp chopped garlic

115g/4oz pork, cut into
  small cubes
2 eggs, beaten
1kg/2¼lb/4 cups cooked rice
30ml/2 tbsp Thai fish sauce
15ml/1 tbsp dark soy sauce
2.5ml/½ tsp caster (superfine)
  sugar
4 spring onions (scallions), finely
  sliced, 2 red chillies, sliced, and
  1 lime, cut into wedges,
  to garnish

1 Heat the oil in a wok or large frying pan. Add the chopped onion and garlic and cook for about 2 minutes until softened but not browned.

2 Add the pork to the softened onion and garlic. Stir-fry until the pork changes colour and is cooked.

3 Add the eggs and cook until scrambled into small lumps.

4 Add the rice and continue to stir and toss, to coat it with the oil and prevent it from sticking.

5 Add the fish sauce, soy sauce and caster sugar and mix well. Continue to fry the pork mixture until the rice is thoroughly heated. Spoon into warmed individual bowls and serve, garnished with sliced spring onions, chillies and lime wedges.

Cook's Tip
To make 1kg/2¼lb/9 cups cooked rice, you will need approximately 400g/14oz/2 cups uncooked rice.

Energy 497kcal/2095kJ; Fat 15.5g; Saturated fat 2.9g; Carbohydrate 78.4g; Fibre 0.5g.

Madras Beef Curry

Although Madras is renowned for the best vegetarian food in India, meat-based recipes such as this beef curry are also extremely popular there.

Serves 4–6
60ml/4 tbsp vegetable oil
1 large onion, finely sliced
3 or 4 cloves
4 green cardamom pods
2 whole star anise
4 fresh green chillies,
  chopped

2 fresh or dried red chillies,
  chopped
45ml/3 tbsp Madras masala
  paste
5ml/1 tsp ground turmeric
450g/1lb lean beef, cubed
60ml/4 tbsp tamarind juice
granulated sugar, to taste
salt
a few fresh coriander (cilantro)
  leaves, chopped, to garnish

1 Heat the oil in a karahi, wok or large pan over a medium heat and fry the onion slices for about 8 minutes until they turn golden brown.

2 Lower the heat, add all the spice ingredients, and fry for a further 2–3 minutes.

3 Add the cubed beef and mix well with the spices. Cover and cook over a low heat until the beef is tender and fully cooked. Cook uncovered on a higher heat for the last few minutes to reduce any excess liquid.

4 Fold in the tamarind juice, sugar and salt. Reheat the dish and garnish with the chopped coriander leaves. Pilau rice and a tomato and onion salad would make excellent accompaniments for this dish.

Cook's Tip
To tenderize the meat, add 60ml/4 tbsp white wine vinegar in step 2, along with the meat, and omit the tamarind juice.

Energy 317kcal/1318kJ; Fat 21.6g; Saturated fat 5.6g; Carbohydrate 4.8g; Fibre 0.9g.

Pork Fillet with Eggs & Mushrooms

Traditionally, this dish is served as a filling wrapped in thin pancakes, but it can also be served on its own with plain rice. The beauty of this dish is that once the ingredients are prepared, it takes moments to cook.

Serves 4

15g/½oz dried Chinese
　mushrooms
175–225g/6–8oz pork fillet
　(tenderloin)
225g/8oz Chinese leaves
　(Chinese cabbage)
115g/4oz bamboo shoots,
　drained
2 spring onions (scallions)
3 eggs
5ml/1 tsp salt
60ml/4 tbsp vegetable oil
15ml/1 tbsp light soy sauce
15ml/1 tbsp Chinese rice wine
　or dry sherry
few drops sesame oil

1 Rinse the mushrooms thoroughly in cold water and then soak in warm water for 25–30 minutes.

2 Rinse thoroughly again and discard the hard stalks, if any. Dry the mushrooms and thinly shred them.

3 Cut the pork fillet into matchstick-size shreds. Thinly shred the Chinese leaves, bamboo shoots and spring onions.

4 Beat the eggs with a pinch of salt. Heat a little oil in a wok, add the eggs and lightly scramble, but do not allow to become too dry. Remove from the wok.

5 Heat the remaining oil in the wok and stir-fry the pork for about 1 minute, or until the colour changes.

6 Add the vegetables to the wok and stir-fry for 1 minute. Add the remaining salt, the soy sauce and rice wine or sherry. Stir for 1 further minute before adding the scrambled eggs. Break up the scrambled eggs and blend well. Sprinkle with sesame oil and serve.

Spicy Meat Loaf

This mixture is baked in the oven and provides a hearty meal on a cold winter day.

Serves 4–6

5 eggs
450g/1lb lean minced
　(ground) beef
30ml/2 tbsp grated fresh
　root ginger
30ml/2 tbsp crushed garlic
6 fresh green chillies, chopped
2 small onions, finely chopped
2.5ml/½ tsp ground turmeric
50g/2oz/2 cups fresh coriander
　(cilantro), chopped
175g/6oz potato, grated
salt
salad leaves, to serve
lemon twist, to garnish

1 Preheat the oven to 180°C/350°F/ Gas 4. Beat 2 eggs until fluffy and pour into a greased 900g/2lb loaf tin (pan).

2 Knead together the meat, ginger and garlic, 4 green chillies, 1 chopped onion, 1 beaten egg, the turmeric, fresh coriander, potato and salt.

3 Pack into the loaf tin and smooth the surface. Cook in the preheated oven for 45 minutes.

4 Meanwhile, beat the remaining eggs and fold in the remaining green chillies and onion. Remove the loaf tin from the oven and pour the mixture all over the meat.

5 Return to the oven and cook until the eggs have set. Serve the loaf hot on a bed of salad leaves, garnished with a twist of lemon.

Cook's Tip
It is always best to buy meat for mincing (grinding) by the piece if possible so that you can choose some with little fat and remove any remaining fat before you mince (grind) it.

Energy 232kcal/961kJ; Fat 17.5g; Saturated fat 3.2g; Carbohydrate 2.2g; Fibre 1.7g.

Energy 394kcal/1637kJ; Fat 25.4g; Saturated fat 9.8g; Carbohydrate 10.1g; Fibre 1g.

Stewing-beef Curry

Madras curries originate from southern India and are aromatic, robust and pungent in flavour. This recipe uses stewing beef, but you can replace it with lean lamb if you prefer.

Serves 4
900g/2lb lean stewing beef
15ml/1 tbsp oil
1 large onion, finely chopped
4 cloves
4 green cardamom pods
2 green chillies, finely chopped
2.5cm/1in piece fresh root ginger, finely chopped
2 garlic cloves, crushed
2 dried red chillies
15ml/1 tbsp curry paste
10ml/2 tsp ground coriander
5ml/1 tsp ground cumin
2.5ml/½ tsp salt
150ml/¼ pint/⅔ cup beef stock
fresh coriander (cilantro), to garnish
boiled rice, to serve

1 Remove any visible fat from the beef and cut the meat into 2.5cm/1in cubes.

2 Heat the oil in a large, heavy frying pan and stir-fry the onion, cloves and cardamom pods for about 5 minutes. Add the fresh green chillies, ginger, garlic and dried red chillies and fry for a further 2 minutes.

3 Add the curry paste and fry for about 2 minutes. Add the cubed beef and fry for 5–8 minutes until all the meat pieces are lightly browned.

4 Add the coriander, cumin, salt and stock. Cover and simmer gently for 1–1½ hours or until the meat is tender. Serve with Tomato Rice and garnish with fresh coriander.

> **Cook's Tip**
> When whole cardamom pods are used as a flavouring, they are not meant to be eaten. In India, they are left on the side of the plate, along with any bones.

Beef Koftas with Coriander & Mint

Serve these tasty treats piping hot with naan bread, raita and a salad. Leftover koftas can be chopped coarsely and packed into pitta bread.

Makes 20–25
450g/1lb lean minced (ground) beef
30ml/2 tbsp grated fresh root ginger
30ml/2 tbsp crushed garlic
4 fresh green chillies, finely chopped
1 small onion, finely chopped
1 egg
2.5ml/½ tsp ground turmeric
5ml/1 tsp garam masala
50g/2oz/2 cups fresh coriander (cilantro), chopped
4–6 fresh mint leaves, chopped
175g/6oz potato
vegetable oil, for deep-frying
salt

1 Mix the minced meat, ginger, garlic, chillies, onion, egg, spices and herbs in a large bowl.

2 Grate the potato into the bowl, and season with salt to taste. Knead together to blend well and form a soft dough.

3 Shape the mixture into portions the size of golf balls. Place on a plate, cover and leave the koftas to rest for about 25 minutes.

4 In a karahi, wok or frying pan, heat the oil to medium-hot and fry the koftas in small batches until they are golden brown in colour. Drain well and serve hot.

> **Variation**
> This dish works equally well with lamb, but make sure it is lean. As always it is best to buy lean meat and mince (grind) it yourself if you are able to.

Energy 355kcal/1487kJ; Fat 14.8g; Saturated fat 4.66g; Carbohydrate 7.7g; Fibre 1.8g.

Energy 63kcal/263kJ; Fat 4g; Saturated fat 1.7g; Carbohydrate 1.8g; Fibre 0.2g.

Beef Vindaloo

A fiery dish originally from Goa, a vindaloo is made using a unique blend of hot aromatic spices and vinegar to give it a distinctive flavour.

Serves 6
15ml/1 tbsp cumin seeds
4 dried red chillies
5ml/1 tsp black peppercorns
seeds from 5 green cardamom pods
5ml/1 tsp fenugreek seeds
5ml/1 tsp black mustard seeds
2.5ml/½ tsp salt
2.5ml/½ tsp demerara (raw) sugar
60ml/4 tbsp white wine vinegar
30ml/2 tbsp oil
1 large onion, finely chopped
900g/2lb lean stewing beef, cut
    into 2.5cm/1in cubes
2.5cm/1in piece fresh root ginger,
    finely chopped
1 garlic clove, crushed
10ml/2 tsp ground coriander
2.5ml/½ tsp ground turmeric
plain and yellow rice, to serve

1 Put the cumin seeds, chillies, peppercorns, cardamom seeds, fenugreek seeds and mustard seeds into a spice grinder (or a pestle and mortar) and grind to a fine powder.

2 Spoon into a bowl, add the salt, sugar and white wine vinegar and mix to a thin paste. Heat 15ml/1 tbsp of the oil in a large, heavy pan and fry the onion for 10 minutes.

3 Put the onions and the spice mixture into a food processor or blender and process to a coarse paste.

4 Heat the remaining oil in the frying pan and fry the meat cubes for about 10 minutes until lightly browned. Remove with a slotted spoon.

5 Add the ginger and garlic to the oil remaining in the pan and fry for 2 minutes. Stir in the ground coriander and turmeric and fry for a further 2 minutes.

6 Add the spice and onion paste and fry for about 5 minutes.

7 Return the beef cubes to the pan with 300ml/½ pint/ 1¼ cups water. Cover and simmer for about 1–1½ hours or until the meat is tender. Serve with plain and yellow rice.

Energy 269kcal/1127kJ; Fat 11.6g; Saturated fat 3.28g; Carbohydrate 7.3g; Fibre 0.6g.

Beef with Green Beans

Green beans cooked with beef is a variation on the traditional recipe which uses lamb. The sliced red pepper provides a contrast to the colour of the beans and chillies, and adds extra flavour.

Serves 4
275g/10oz fine green beans,
    cut into 2.5cm/1in pieces
15ml/1 tbsp oil
1 medium onion, sliced
5ml/1 tsp grated fresh root ginger
5ml/1 tsp crushed garlic
5ml/1 tsp chilli powder
6.5ml/1¼ tsp salt
1.5ml/¼ tsp ground turmeric
2 tomatoes, chopped
450g/1lb lean beef, cubed
475ml/16fl oz/2 cups water
1 red (bell) pepper, seeded
    and sliced
15ml/1 tbsp chopped fresh
    coriander (cilantro)
2 fresh green chillies, chopped
warm chapatis, to serve (optional)

1 Blanch the beans in boiling water for 3–4 minutes, then rinse under cold running water, drain and set aside.

2 Heat the oil in a large, heavy pan and gently fry the onion slices until golden brown.

3 In a bowl, mix the ginger, garlic, chilli powder, salt, turmeric and chopped tomatoes. Spoon the ginger and garlic mixture into the pan and stir-fry with the onion for 5–7 minutes.

4 Add the beef and stir-fry for a further 3 minutes. Pour in the water, bring to the boil and lower the heat. Half-cover the pan and cook for 1–1¼ hours until most of the water has evaporated and the meat is tender.

5 Add the green beans and mix everything together well.

6 Finally, add the red pepper, fresh coriander and green chillies. Cook the mixture, stirring, for a further 7–10 minutes, or until the beans are tender.

7 Spoon into a large bowl or individual plates. Serve the beef hot, with warm chapatis if you like.

Energy 242kcal/1012kJ; Fat 11.6g; Saturated fat 2.91g; Carbohydrate 9.3g; Fibre 3g.

Beef Biryani

Biryani is one of the easiest and most relaxing ways of cooking when entertaining.

Serves 4

2 large onions
2 garlic cloves, chopped
2.5cm/1in piece fresh root ginger, peeled and roughly chopped
1/2–1 fresh green chilli, seeded and chopped
small bunch of fresh coriander (cilantro)
60ml/4 tbsp flaked (sliced) almonds
30–45ml/2–3 tbsp water
15ml/1 tbsp ghee or butter, plus 25g/1oz/2 tbsp butter for the rice
45ml/3 tbsp vegetable oil

30ml/2 tbsp sultanas (golden raisins)
500g/1¼lb braising or stewing steak, cubed
5ml/1 tsp ground coriander
15ml/1 tbsp ground cumin
2.5ml/½ tsp ground turmeric
2.5ml/½ tsp ground fenugreek
good pinch of ground cinnamon
175ml/6fl oz/¾ cup natural (plain) yogurt, whisked
275g/10oz/1½ cups basmati rice
about 1.2 litres/2 pints/5 cups hot chicken stock or water
salt and ground black pepper
2 hard-boiled eggs, quartered, to garnish
chapatis, to serve

1 Roughly chop one onion and place it in a food processor or blender. Add the garlic, ginger, chilli, fresh coriander and half the flaked almonds. Pour in the water and process to a smooth paste. Transfer the paste to a small bowl and set aside.

2 Finely slice the remaining onion into rings. Heat half the ghee or butter with half the oil in a heavy flameproof casserole and fry the onion for 10–15 minutes until a deep golden brown. Transfer to a plate. Fry the remaining almonds briefly until golden. Set aside. Quickly fry the sultanas until they swell. Transfer to the plate.

3 Heat the remaining ghee or butter in the casserole with a further 15ml/1 tbsp of the oil. Fry the meat, in batches, until browned. Transfer to a plate. Wipe the casserole clean with kitchen paper, heat the remaining oil and pour in the spice paste. Cook over a medium heat for 2–3 minutes, stirring, until the mixture begins to brown lightly. Stir in all the spices, season and cook for 1 minute more.

4 Lower the heat, then stir in the yogurt, a little at a time. Return the meat to the casserole. Stir to coat, cover tightly and simmer for 40–45 minutes until the meat is tender. Meanwhile, soak the rice in a bowl of cold water for 20 minutes.

5 Preheat the oven to 160°C/325°F/Gas 3. Drain the rice, place in a pan and add the hot chicken stock or water, with a little salt. Bring back to the boil, cover and cook for 5 minutes.

6 Drain the rice, and pile it on top of the meat. Using the handle of a spoon, make a hole through the rice and meat mixture, to the bottom of the pan. Place the fried onions, almonds and sultanas over the top and dot with butter.

7 Cover the casserole tightly with a double layer of foil and a lid. Cook in the oven for 30–40 minutes. Garnish and serve with chapatis.

Energy 741kcal/3090kJ; Fat 29.3g; Saturated fat 10.9g; Carbohydrate 79.1g; Fibre 3.1g.

Beef & Kidney with Spinach

Here, spinach is coarsely chopped and added towards the end of cooking, which retains the nutritional value of the spinach and gives the dish a lovely appearance.

Serves 4–6

5cm/2in piece fresh root ginger
30ml/2 tbsp vegetable oil
1 large onion, finely chopped
4 garlic cloves, crushed

60ml/4 tbsp mild curry paste, or 60ml/4 tbsp mild curry powder
1.5ml/¼ tsp ground turmeric
salt
900g/2lb steak and kidney, cubed
450g/1lb fresh spinach, trimmed, washed and chopped, or 450g/1lb frozen spinach, thawed and drained
60ml/4 tbsp tomato purée (paste)
2 large tomatoes, finely chopped

1 Using a sharp knife or vegetable peeler, remove the skin from the ginger. Grate it on the fine side of a metal grater.

2 Heat the oil in a frying pan, wok or karahi and fry the onion, ginger and garlic until the onion is soft and the ginger and garlic turn golden brown.

3 Lower the heat and add the curry paste or powder, turmeric and salt. Add the steak and kidney to the pan and mix well. Cover and cook, stirring frequently to prevent the mixture from sticking to the pan, for 20–30 minutes over a medium heat, until the meat is just tender.

4 Add the spinach and tomato purée and mix well. Cook uncovered until the spinach is softened and most of the liquid has evaporated.

5 Fold in the chopped tomatoes. Increase the heat, as the tomatoes will have a cooling effect on the other ingredients, and cook the mixture for a further 5 minutes, until they are soft.

6 Spoon into shallow bowls and serve piping hot with a simple accompaniment to offset the rich, gamey flavour of the dish, like plain boiled basmati rice. Go easy on any side portions though, as this is a very rich and filling dish.

Energy 362kcal/1515kJ; Fat 13.5g; Saturated fat 3.5g; Carbohydrate 11.7g; Fibre 4.4g.

Citrus Beef Curry

This superbly aromatic curry is not exceptionally hot but it is full of flavour.

Serves 4
450g/1lb rump (round) steak
30ml/2 tbsp vegetable oil
30ml/2 tbsp medium curry paste
2 bay leaves
400ml/14fl oz/1²⁄₃ cups coconut milk
300ml/¹⁄₂ pint/1¹⁄₄ cups beef stock
30ml/2 tbsp lemon juice
grated rind and juice of ¹⁄₂ orange
15ml/1 tbsp granulated sugar
115g/4oz baby (pearl) onions, peeled but left whole
225g/8oz new potatoes, halved
115g/4oz/1 cup unsalted roasted peanuts, roughly chopped
115g/4oz fine green beans, halved
1 red (bell) pepper, seeded and thinly sliced
unsalted roasted peanuts, to garnish (optional)

1 Trim any visible fat from the beef and cut the meat into 5cm/2in strips.

2 Heat the vegetable oil in a large, heavy pan, add the medium curry paste and cook over medium heat for 30 seconds, stirring constantly.

3 Add the beef and cook, stirring, for 2 minutes until it is beginning to brown and is thoroughly coated with the spices.

4 Stir in the bay leaves, coconut milk, stock, lemon juice, orange rind and juice, and sugar. Bring to the boil, stirring frequently.

5 Add the onions and potatoes, then bring back to the boil, reduce the heat and simmer, uncovered, for 5 minutes.

6 Stir in the peanuts, beans and pepper and simmer for a further 10 minutes, or until the beef and potatoes are tender. Serve in shallow bowls, with a spoon and fork, to enjoy all the rich and creamy juices. Sprinkle with extra unsalted roasted peanuts, if you like.

Energy 444kcal/1858kJ; Fat 24.2g; Saturated fat 5.4g; Carbohydrate 23.5g; Fibre 4.2g.

Chilli Beef with Basil

This is a dish for chilli lovers! It is very easy to prepare – all you need is a karahi or a wok.

Serves 2
about 90ml/6 tbsp vegetable oil
16–20 large fresh basil leaves
275g/10oz rump steak
30ml/2 tbsp Worcestershire sauce
5ml/1 tsp soft dark brown sugar
1 or 2 fresh red chillies, sliced into rings
3 garlic cloves, chopped
5ml/1 tsp chopped fresh root ginger
1 shallot, thinly sliced
30ml/2 tbsp finely chopped fresh basil leaves, plus extra to garnish
squeeze of lemon juice
salt and ground black pepper
rice, to serve

1 Heat the oil in a karahi or wok. Add the whole basil leaves and fry for about 1 minute until crisp and golden. Drain on kitchen paper. Remove the pan from the heat and pour off all but 30ml/2 tbsp of the oil.

2 Cut the steak across the grain into thin strips. Mix the Worcestershire sauce and sugar in a bowl. Add the beef, mix well, then cover and leave to marinate for about 30 minutes.

3 Reheat the oil until hot, add the chilli, garlic, ginger and shallot and stir-fry for 30 seconds. Add the beef and chopped basil, then stir-fry for about 3 minutes. Flavour with lemon juice, and add salt and pepper to taste.

4 Transfer the chilli beef to a warmed serving plate, sprinkle over the basil leaves to garnish and serve immediately with rice.

> **Cook's Tip**
> Although Worcestershire sauce is often thought of as archetypally English, it is actually based on an Indian recipe. Ingredients include molasses, anchovies and tamarind extract.

Energy 469kcal/1943kJ; Fat 38.6g; Saturated fat 9g; Carbohydrate 0g; Fibre 0g.

Spicy Meatballs

Serve these spicy little meat patties – pergedel djawa – with egg noodles and chilli sauce.

Serves 4–6

1cm/½in cube shrimp paste
1 large onion, roughly chopped
1 or 2 fresh red chillies, seeded and chopped
2 garlic cloves, crushed
15ml/1 tbsp coriander seeds
5ml/1 tsp cumin seeds
450g/1lb lean minced (ground) beef
10ml/2 tsp dark soy sauce
5ml/1 tsp dark brown sugar
juice of 1½ lemons
a little beaten egg
vegetable oil, for shallow-frying
salt and ground black pepper
chilli sambal, to serve
1 green and 2 red chillies, to garnish

1 Wrap the shrimp paste in a piece of foil and warm in a frying pan for 5 minutes, turning a few times. Unwrap and put in a food processor.

2 Add the onion, chillies and garlic to the food processor and process until finely chopped. Set aside. Dry-fry the coriander and cumin seeds in a hot frying pan for 1 minute, to release the aroma. Tip the seeds into a mortar and grind with a pestle.

3 Put the meat in a large bowl. Stir in the onion mixture. Add the ground spices, soy sauce, brown sugar, lemon juice and beaten egg. Season to taste.

4 Shape the meat mixture into small, even-size balls, and chill these for 5–10 minutes to firm them up.

5 Heat the oil in a wok or large frying pan and fry the meat balls for 4–5 minutes, turning often, until cooked through and browned. You may have to do this in batches.

6 Drain the meatballs on kitchen paper, and then pile them on to a warm serving platter or into a large serving bowl. Finely slice the green chilli and one of the red chillies and sprinkle over the meat balls. Garnish with the remaining red chilli, if you like.

Energy 379kcal/1568kJ; Fat 29.4g; Saturated fat 9.1g; Carbohydrate 6g; Fibre 0.9g.

Green Beef Curry with Aubergines

This is a very quick curry so be sure to use good-quality meat. Sirloin is recommended, but tender rump (round) steak could be used instead.

Serves 4–6

15ml/1 tbsp vegetable oil
45ml/3 tbsp Thai green curry paste (see Cook's Tip)
600ml/1 pint/2½ cups coconut milk
450g/1lb beef sirloin, trimmed and cut into thin strips
4 kaffir lime leaves, torn
15–30ml/1–2 tbsp Thai fish sauce
5ml/1 tsp palm sugar or light muscovado (brown) sugar
150g/5oz small Thai aubergines (eggplants), halved
a small handful of fresh Thai basil
2 fresh green chillies, shredded, to garnish

1 Heat the oil in a large, heavy pan or wok. Add the curry paste and cook for 1–2 minutes, until it is fragrant. Stir in half the coconut milk, a little at a time. Cook, stirring frequently, for about 5–6 minutes, until an oily sheen appears on the surface of the liquid.

2 Add the beef to the pan with the lime leaves, Thai fish sauce, sugar and aubergine. Cook for 2–3 minutes, then stir in the remaining coconut milk. Bring back to a simmer and cook until the meat and aubergines are tender. Stir in the basil just before serving. Garnish with the shredded green chillies.

Cook's Tip
To make the Thai green curry paste, put 15 fresh green chillies, 2 chopped lemon grass stalks, 3 sliced shallots, 2 garlic cloves, 15ml/1 tbsp chopped galangal, 4 chopped kaffir lime leaves, 2.5ml/½ tsp grated kaffir lime rind, 5ml/1 tsp chopped coriander root, 6 black peppercorns, 5ml/1 tsp each roasted coriander and cumin seeds, 15ml/1 tbsp granulated sugar, 5ml/1 tsp salt and 5ml/1 tsp shrimp paste into a food processor and process until smooth. Gradually add 30ml/2 tbsp vegetable oil, processing after each addition.

Energy 264kcal/1106kJ; Fat 13.8g; Saturated fat 4.9g; Carbohydrate 9.2g; Fibre 0.8g.

Mussaman Curry

This dish is traditionally based on beef, but chicken, lamb or tofu can be used instead.

Serves 4–6
675g/1½lb stewing steak
600ml/1 pint/2½ cups coconut milk
250ml/8fl oz/1 cup coconut cream
45ml/3 tbsp Mussaman curry paste
30ml/2 tbsp Thai fish sauce
15ml/1 tbsp palm sugar or light muscovado (brown) sugar
60ml/4 tbsp tamarind juice, made by soaking tamarind paste in warm water
6 green cardamom pods
1 cinnamon stick
1 large potato, about 225g/8oz, cut into even chunks
1 onion, cut into wedges
50g/2oz/½ cup roasted peanuts

1 Trim off any excess fat from the stewing steak, then, using a sharp knife, cut it into 2.5cm/1in chunks.

2 Pour the coconut milk into a large, heavy pan and bring to the boil over a medium heat. Add the chunks of beef, reduce the heat to low, partially cover the pan and simmer gently for about 40 minutes, or until tender.

3 Pour the coconut cream into a separate pan. Cook over a medium heat, stirring constantly, for about 5 minutes, or until it separates. Stir in the Mussaman curry paste and cook rapidly for 2–3 minutes, until fragrant and thoroughly blended.

4 Add the coconut cream and curry paste mixture to the pan with the beef and stir until thoroughly blended. Simmer for a further 4–5 minutes, stirring occasionally.

5 Stir the fish sauce, sugar, tamarind juice, cardamom pods, cinnamon stick, potato chunks and onion wedges into the beef curry. Continue to simmer for a further 15–20 minutes, or until the potato is cooked and tender. Add the roasted peanuts to the pan and mix well to combine. Cook for about 5 minutes more, then transfer to warmed individual serving bowls and serve immediately.

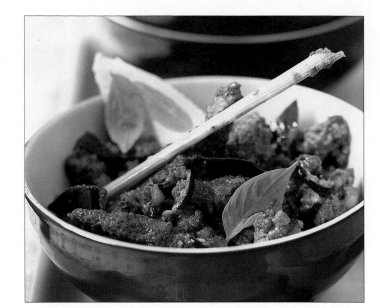

Thick Beef Curry in Sweet Peanut Sauce

This curry is deliciously rich and thicker than most other Thai curries. Serve it with boiled jasmine rice and salted duck's eggs, if you like.

Serves 4–6
600ml/1 pint/2½ cups coconut milk
45ml/3 tbsp Thai red curry paste
45ml/3 tbsp Thai fish sauce
30ml/2 tbsp palm sugar or light muscovado (brown) sugar
2 lemon grass stalks, bruised
450g/1lb rump (round) steak, cut into thin strips
75g/3oz/¾ cup roasted peanuts, ground
2 fresh red chillies, sliced
5 kaffir lime leaves, torn
salt and ground black pepper
2 salted duck's eggs, cut in wedges, and 10–15 Thai basil leaves, to garnish

1 Pour half the coconut milk into a large, heavy pan. Place over a medium heat and bring to the boil, stirring constantly until the milk separates.

2 Stir in the red curry paste and cook for 2–3 minutes until the mixture is fragrant and thoroughly blended. Add the fish sauce, sugar and bruised lemon grass stalks. Mix well.

3 Continue to cook until the colour deepens. Gradually add the remaining coconut milk, stirring constantly. Bring back to the boil.

4 Add the beef and peanuts. Cook, stirring constantly, for 8–10 minutes, or until most of the liquid has evaporated. Add the chillies and lime leaves. Season to taste and serve, garnished with wedges of salted eggs and Thai basil leaves.

> **Cook's Tip**
> You can use the red curry paste recipe given opposite or you can buy a ready-made Thai curry paste. There is a wide range available in most Asian stores and large supermarkets.

Energy 626kcal/2610kJ; Fat 39.3g; Saturated fat 22.7g; Carbohydrate 24.8g; Fibre 1.6g.

Energy 365kcal/1528kJ; Fat 19.6g; Saturated fat 6.2g; Carbohydrate 17.5g; Fibre 1.2g.

Dry Beef Curry with Peanut & Lime

Originating from the mountainous northern regions of Thailand, dry curries are now popular throughout the country. This dry beef curry is usually served with a moist dish such as Northern Thai Fish Curry with Shallots and Lemon Grass.

Serves 4–6
400g/14oz can coconut
   milk
900g/2lb stewing steak,
   finely chopped
300ml/½ pint/1¼ cups
   beef stock
30ml/2 tbsp crunchy
   peanut butter
juice of 2 limes
lime slices, fresh shredded
   coriander (cilantro) and
   fresh red chilli slices,
   to garnish

For the red curry paste
30ml/2 tbsp coriander
   seeds
5ml/1 tsp cumin seeds
seeds from 6 green cardamom
   pods
2.5ml/½ tsp grated or ground
   nutmeg
1.5ml/¼ tsp ground cloves
2.5ml/½ tsp ground cinnamon
20ml/4 tsp paprika
pared rind of 1 mandarin orange,
   finely chopped
4 or 5 small fresh red chillies,
   seeded and finely chopped
25ml/1½ tbsp granulated sugar
2.5ml/½ tsp salt
1 piece lemon grass, about
   10cm/4in long, shredded
3 garlic cloves, crushed
2cm/¾in piece fresh galangal,
   peeled and finely chopped
4 red shallots, finely chopped
1 piece shrimp paste, 2cm/
   ¾in square
50g/2oz coriander (cilantro) root
   or stem, chopped
Juice of ½ lime
30ml/2 tbsp vegetable oil

1 Strain the coconut milk into a bowl, retaining the thicker coconut milk in the strainer or sieve.

2 Pour the thin coconut milk from the bowl into a large, heavy pan, then scrape in half the residue from the sieve. Reserve the remaining thick coconut milk. Add the chopped steak. Pour in the beef stock and bring to the boil. Reduce the heat, cover the pan and simmer gently for 50 minutes.

3 Make the curry paste. Dry-fry all the seeds for 1–2 minutes. Transfer to a bowl and add the nutmeg, cloves, cinnamon, paprika and orange rind. Pound the chillies with the sugar and salt. Add the spice mixture, lemon grass, garlic, galangal, shallots and shrimp paste and pound to a paste. Work in the coriander, lime juice and oil.

4 Strain the beef, reserving the cooking liquid, and place a cupful of liquid in a wok. Stir in 30–45ml/2–3 tbsp of the curry paste, according to taste. Boil rapidly until all the liquid has evaporated. Stir in the reserved thick coconut milk, the peanut butter and the beef. Simmer, uncovered, for 15–20 minutes, adding a little more cooking liquid if the mixture starts to stick to the pan, but keep the curry dry.

5 Just before serving, stir in the lime juice. Serve in warmed bowls, garnished with the lime slices, shredded coriander and sliced red chillies.

Energy 559kcal/2328kJ; Fat 32.3g; Saturated fat 10.4g; Carbohydrate 10.5g; Fibre 6.9g.

Stir-fried Beef in Oyster Sauce

Mouthwatering tender rump steak is cooked here in a delicious combination with shiitake, oyster and straw mushrooms flavoured with garlic, ginger and chilli.

Serves 4–6
450g/1lb rump (round) steak
30ml/2 tbsp soy sauce
15ml/1 tbsp cornflour
   (cornstarch)
45ml/3 tbsp vegetable oil
15ml/1 tbsp chopped garlic
15ml/1 tbsp chopped fresh root
   ginger
225g/8oz/3¼ cups mixed
   mushrooms, such as shiitake,
   oyster and straw
30ml/2 tbsp oyster sauce
5ml/1 tsp granulated sugar
4 spring onions (scallions), cut into
   short lengths
ground black pepper
2 fresh red chillies, seeded and
   cut into strips, to garnish

1 Place the steak in the freezer for 30–40 minutes, until firm, then, using a sharp knife, slice it on the diagonal into thin strips.

2 Mix together the soy sauce and cornflour in a large bowl. Add the steak, turning to coat well, cover with clear film (plastic wrap) and leave to marinate at room temperature for 1–2 hours.

3 Heat half the oil in a wok or large, heavy frying pan. Add the garlic and ginger and cook for 1–2 minutes, until fragrant. Drain the steak, add it to the wok or pan and stir well to separate the strips. Cook, stirring frequently, for a further 1–2 minutes, until the steak is browned all over and tender. Remove from the wok or pan and set aside.

4 Heat the remaining oil in the wok or pan. Add the mushrooms and stir-fry over a medium heat until golden brown.

5 Return the steak to the wok and mix it with the mushrooms. Spoon in the oyster sauce and sugar, mix well, then add ground black pepper to taste. Toss over the heat until all the ingredients are thoroughly combined. Stir in the spring onions. Tip the mixture on to a serving platter, garnish with the strips of red chilli and serve.

Energy 298kcal/1240kJ; Fat 19.1g; Saturated fat 5.3g; Carbohydrate 5g; Fibre 0.8g.

Beef with Fried Rice

One of the joys of stir-fry cooking is the ease and speed with which a really good meal can be prepared. This one can be on the table in 15 minutes.

Serves 4
200g/7oz beef steak
15ml/1 tbsp vegetable oil
2 garlic cloves, finely chopped
1 egg
250g/9oz/2¼ cups cooked
 jasmine rice
½ medium head broccoli,
 coarsely chopped
30ml/2 tbsp dark soy sauce
15ml/1 tbsp light soy sauce
5ml/1 tsp palm sugar or light
 muscovado (brown) sugar
15ml/1 tbsp Thai fish sauce
ground black pepper
chilli sauce, to serve

1 Trim the steak and cut into very thin strips with a sharp knife.

2 Heat the oil in a wok or frying pan and cook the garlic over a low to medium heat until golden. Do not let it burn. Increase the heat to high, add the steak and stir-fry for 2 minutes.

3 Move the pieces of beef to the edges of the wok or pan and break the egg into the centre. When the egg starts to set, stir-fry it with the meat.

4 Add the rice and toss all the contents of the wok together, scraping up any residue on the base, then add the broccoli, soy sauces, sugar and fish sauce and stir-fry for 2 minutes more. Season to taste with pepper and serve immediately with chilli sauce.

Cook's Tip
Soy sauce is made from fermented soya beans. The first extraction is sold as light soy sauce and has a delicate, "beany" fragrance. Dark soy sauce has been allowed to mature for longer and has a fuller flavour.

Energy 242kcal/1013kJ; Fat 10.2g; Saturated fat 2.9g; Carbohydrate 21.5g; Fibre 1.7g.

Spicy Shredded Beef

The beef in this recipe is cut into very fine strips. Freezing the beef briefly before preparation makes this easy.

Serves 2
25g/8oz rump or fillet of beef
15ml/1 tbsp each light and dark
 soy sauce
15ml/1 tbsp rice wine or medium-
 dry sherry
5ml/1 tsp soft dark brown sugar
 or golden granulated sugar
90ml/6 tbsp vegetable oil
1 large onion, thinly sliced
2.5cm/1in piece fresh root ginger,
 peeled and grated
1 or 2 carrots, cut into
 matchsticks
2 or 3 fresh or dried chillies,
 halved, seeded (optional)
 and chopped
salt and ground black pepper
fresh chives, to garnish

1 Place the beef in the freezer for 30–40 minutes to firm up. With a sharp knife, slice the beef very thinly, then cut each slice into fine strips or shreds.

2 Mix together the light and dark soy sauces with the rice wine or medium-dry sherry and sugar in a bowl. Add the strips of beef and stir well to ensure they are evenly coated with the marinade.

3 Heat a wok and add half the oil. When it is hot, stir-fry the onion and ginger for 3–4 minutes, then transfer to a plate. Add the carrot, stir-fry for 3–4 minutes until slightly softened, then transfer to a plate and keep warm.

4 Heat the remaining oil in the wok, then quickly add the beef, with the marinade, followed by the chillies. Cook over high heat for 2 minutes, stirring all the time.

5 Return the fried onion and ginger to the wok and stir-fry for 1 minute more. Season with salt and pepper to taste, cover and cook for 30 seconds. Spoon the meat into two warmed bowls and add the strips of carrots. Garnish with fresh chives and serve immediately.

Energy 562kcal/2328kJ; Fat 43.8g; Saturated fat 8.2g; Carbohydrate 15.5g; Fibre 2.9g.

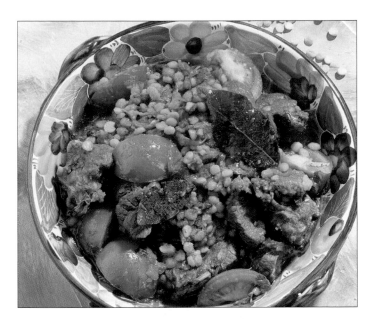

Beef Rendang

This spicy dish is usually served with the meat quite dry; if you prefer more sauce, add more water.

Serves 6–8

2 onions or 5 or 6 shallots, chopped
4 garlic cloves, chopped
2.5cm/1in piece fresh galangal, peeled and sliced, or 15ml/ 1 tbsp galangal paste
2.5cm/1in piece fresh root ginger, peeled and sliced
4–6 fresh red chillies, seeded and roughly chopped
lower part only of 1 lemon grass stalk, sliced
2.5cm/1in piece fresh turmeric, peeled and sliced, or 5ml/1 tsp ground turmeric
1kg/2¼lb prime beef in one piece
5ml/1 tsp coriander seeds, dry-fried
5ml/1 tsp cumin seeds, dry-fried
2 kaffir lime leaves, torn into pieces
2 × 400ml/14fl oz cans coconut milk
300ml/½ pint/1¼ cups water
30ml/2 tbsp dark soy sauce
5ml/1 tsp tamarind pulp, soaked in 60ml/4 tbsp warm water
8–10 small new potatoes, scrubbed
salt and ground black pepper
deep-fried onions, sliced fresh red chillies and spring onions (scallions), to garnish

1 Put the onions or shallots in a food processor. Add the garlic, galangal, ginger, chillies, sliced lemon grass and turmeric. Process to a fine paste or grind in a mortar, using a pestle.

2 Cut the meat into cubes using a large sharp knife, then place the cubes in a bowl. Grind the dry-fried coriander and cumin seeds, then add to the meat with the onion, chilli paste and kaffir lime leaves; stir well. Cover and leave in a cool place to marinate.

3 Pour the coconut milk and water into a wok, then stir in the spiced meat and the soy sauce. Strain the tamarind water and add to the wok. Stir over medium heat until the liquid boils, then simmer gently, half-covered, for 1½ hours. Add the potatoes and simmer for 20–25 minutes, or until meat and potatoes are tender. Add water if liked. Season and serve, garnished with deep-fried onions, chillies and spring onions.

Venison with Lentils & Tomatoes

Venison curries well and tastes good in this simple dish. Serve it with pilau rice, naan bread or bhaturas.

Serves 4

60ml/4 tbsp corn oil
1 bay leaf
2 cloves
4 black peppercorns
1 medium onion, sliced
450g/1lb diced venison
2.5ml/½ tsp ground turmeric
7.5ml/1½ tsp chilli powder
5ml/1 tsp garam masala
5ml/1 tsp crushed coriander seeds
2.5cm/1in cinnamon stick
5ml/1 tsp crushed garlic
5ml/1 tsp grated fresh root ginger
7.5ml/1½ tsp salt
1.5 litres/2½ pints/6 cups water
50g/2oz/⅓ cup split red lentils
2 medium tomatoes, quartered
2 fresh green chillies, chopped
15ml/1 tbsp chopped fresh coriander (cilantro)

1 Heat the oil in a karahi, wok or deep pan. Lower the heat slightly and add the bay leaf, cloves, peppercorns and onion slices. Fry for about 5 minutes, or until the onions are golden brown, stirring occasionally. Add the diced venison, turmeric, chilli powder, garam masala, coriander seeds, cinnamon stick, garlic, ginger and most of the salt, and stir-fry for about 5 minutes over a medium heat.

2 Pour in 900ml/1½ pints/3½ cups of the water and cover the pan with a lid. Simmer over a low heat for about 35–40 minutes, or until the water has evaporated and the meat is tender.

3 Put the lentils into a pan with the remaining 600ml/1 pint/ 2½ cups water and boil for about 12–15 minutes, or until the water has almost evaporated and the lentils are soft enough to mash. If the lentils are too thick, add up to 150ml/¼ pint/⅔ cup more water to loosen the mixture.

4 When the meat is tender, stir-fry the mixture using a wooden spoon, until some free oil begins to appear on the sides of the pan. Add the cooked lentils to the venison and mix together well. Add the tomatoes, chillies and fresh coriander and serve.

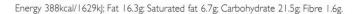

Energy 388kcal/1629kJ; Fat 16.3g; Saturated fat 6.7g; Carbohydrate 21.5g; Fibre 1.6g.

Energy 277kcal/1160kJ; Fat 13.9g; Saturated fat 2.6g; Carbohydrate 11.6g; Fibre 1.6g.

Balti Potatoes with Aubergines

Using baby potatoes adds to the attractiveness of this dish. Choose the smaller variety of aubergines, too, as they are tastier than the large ones, which contain a lot of water and little flavour. You can buy small aubergines from specialist grocers.

Serves 4
10–12 baby potatoes
6 small aubergines (eggplants)
1 medium red (bell) pepper
15ml/1 tbsp oil
2 medium onions, sliced

4–6 curry leaves
2.5ml/½ tsp onion seeds
5ml/1 tsp crushed coriander seeds
2.5ml/½ tsp cumin seeds
5ml/1 tsp grated fresh root ginger
5ml/1 tsp crushed garlic
5ml/1 tsp crushed dried red chillies
15ml/1 tbsp chopped fresh fenugreek leaves
5ml/1 tsp chopped fresh coriander (cilantro)
15ml/1 tbsp natural (plain) low-fat yogurt
fresh coriander leaves, to garnish

1 Cook the unpeeled potatoes in a pan of boiling water until they are just soft, but still whole.

2 Cut the aubergines into quarters if very small, or eighths if using larger aubergines.

3 Cut the pepper in half, remove the seeds and ribs, then slice the flesh into thin even strips.

4 Heat the oil in a karahi, wok or heavy pan and fry the sliced onions, curry leaves, onion seeds, crushed coriander seeds and cumin seeds until the onion slices are a soft golden brown, stirring constantly.

5 Add the ginger, garlic, crushed chillies and fenugreek, followed by the aubergines and potatoes. Stir everything together and cover the pan with a lid. Lower the heat and cook the vegetables for 5–7 minutes.

6 Remove the lid, add the fresh coriander followed by the yogurt and stir well. Serve garnished with coriander leaves.

Energy 183kcal/773kJ; Fat 4.42g; Saturated fat 0.70g; Carbohydrate 33.02g; Fibre 5.43g.

Balti Stir-fried Vegetables with Cashew Nuts

This quick and versatile stir-fry will accommodate most other combinations of vegetables – you do not have to use the selection suggested here.

Serves 4
2 medium carrots
1 medium red (bell) pepper, seeded
1 medium green (bell) pepper, seeded
2 courgettes (zucchini)

115g/4oz green beans
1 medium bunch spring onions (scallions)
15ml/1 tbsp oil
4–6 curry leaves
2.5ml/½ tsp cumin seeds
4 dried red chillies
10–12 cashew nuts
5ml/1 tsp salt
30ml/2 tbsp lemon juice
fresh mint leaves, to garnish

1 Prepare the vegetables: cut the carrots, peppers and courgettes into matchsticks, halve the beans and chop the spring onions. Set aside.

2 Heat the oil in a karahi, wok or heavy pan and fry the curry leaves, cumin seeds and dried red chillies for about 1 minute.

3 Add the vegetables and nuts, and stir them around gently. Add the salt and lemon juice. Continue to stir and cook for about 3–5 minutes.

4 Transfer the vegetables to a serving dish, garnish with fresh mint leaves and serve immediately.

> **Variation**
> Small florets of broccoli or cauliflower are delicious cooked in a stir-fry so that they retain their crunch. You could use them in place of the courgettes (zucchini). Or you could use mushrooms, mangetouts (snow peas) and beansprouts.

Energy 98kcal/406kJ; Fat 5.28g; Saturated fat 0.88g; Carbohydrate 10.36g; Fibre 3.94g.

Karahi Potatoes with Whole Spices

The potato is transformed into something quite exotic when it is cooked like this.

Serves 4
15ml/1 tbsp oil
5ml/1 tsp cumin seeds
3 curry leaves
5ml/1 tsp crushed dried
  red chillies
2.5ml/½ tsp mixed onion,
  mustard and fenugreek seeds
2.5ml/½ tsp fennel seeds
3 garlic cloves, sliced
2.5cm/1in piece fresh root ginger,
  grated
2 onions, sliced
6 new potatoes, thinly sliced
15ml/1 tbsp chopped fresh
  coriander (cilantro)
1 fresh red chilli, seeded
  and sliced
1 fresh green chilli, seeded
  and sliced

1 Heat the oil in a karahi, wok or heavy pan. Lower the heat slightly and add the cumin seeds, curry leaves, dried red chillies, mixed onion, mustard and fenugreek seeds, fennel seeds, garlic slices and ginger. Fry for 1 minute.

2 Add the onions and fry for a further 5 minutes, or until the onions are golden brown.

3 Add the potatoes, fresh coriander and sliced fresh red and green chillies and mix well. Cover the pan tightly with a lid or foil; if using foil, make sure that it does not touch the food. Cook over a very low heat for about 7 minutes or until the potatoes are tender.

4 Remove the pan from the heat, and take off the lid or foil cover. Serve hot straight from the pan.

Cook's Tip
Choose a waxy variety of new potato for this fairly hot vegetable dish; if you use a very soft potato, it will not be possible to cut it into thin slices without it breaking up. Suitable varieties are often labelled "salad potatoes" when sold at supermarkets. Leave the skin on for a tastier result.

Energy 110kcal/462kJ; Fat 3.6g; Saturated fat 0.39g; Carbohydrate 17.1g; Fibre 1.6g.

Balti Mushrooms in a Creamy Garlic Sauce

This is a simple and delicious Balti recipe which could be accompanied by bread or one of the rice side dishes from this book.

Serves 4
350g/12oz/4½ cups button
  (white) mushrooms
15ml/1 tbsp oil
1 bay leaf
3 garlic cloves, roughly chopped
2 green chillies, seeded and
  chopped
225g/8oz/1 cup low-fat fromage
  frais or ricotta cheese
15ml/1 tbsp chopped fresh
  mint
15ml/1 tbsp chopped fresh
  coriander (cilantro)
5ml/1 tsp salt
fresh mint and coriander leaves,
  to garnish

1 Cut the button mushrooms in half, or in quarters if large, and set aside.

2 Heat the oil in a karahi, wok or heavy pan, then add the bay leaf, chopped garlic and chillies, and quickly stir-fry for about 1 minute.

3 Add the mushrooms. Stir-fry for another 2 minutes.

4 Remove from the heat and stir in the fromage frais or ricotta cheese, followed by the mint, coriander and salt. Return to the heat and stir-fry for 2–3 minutes, then transfer to a warmed serving dish and garnish with mint and coriander leaves.

Cook's Tip
Balti curries have their origins in Baltistan, the area that is now North Pakistan. They are traditionally aromatic but not heavily flavoured with chilli, and bread is usually used to scoop up the food. However, rice also goes well with all the dishes.

Energy 76kcal/321kJ; Fat 3.4g; Saturated fat 0.55g; Carbohydrate 5.2g; Fibre 1.1g.

Balti Dhal with Spring Onions & Tomatoes

This rich-tasting dish is made using toor dhal, a shiny, yellow split lentil which resembles chana dhal. Fresh fenugreek leaves are perfect with pulses and impart a stunning aroma.

Serves 4

115g/4oz/½ cup toor dhal
 or yellow split peas
30ml/2 tbsp oil
1.5ml/¼ tsp onion seeds
1 medium bunch spring onions
 (scallions), roughly chopped
5ml/1 tsp crushed garlic
1.5ml/¼ tsp ground turmeric

7.5ml/1½ tsp grated fresh
 root ginger
5ml/1 tsp chilli powder
30ml/2 tbsp fresh fenugreek
 leaves
5ml/1 tsp salt
150ml/¼ pint/⅔ cup
 water
6–8 cherry tomatoes
30ml/2 tbsp fresh coriander
 (cilantro) leaves
½ green (bell) pepper, seeded
 and sliced
15ml/1 tbsp lemon juice
shredded spring onion tops
 and fresh coriander leaves,
 to garnish

1 Cook the dhal in a pan of boiling water for 40–45 minutes until soft and mushy. Drain and set aside.

2 Heat the oil with the onion seeds in a karahi, wok or heavy pan for a few seconds until hot.

3 Add the drained dhal to the wok or frying pan and stir-fry with the onion seeds for about 3 minutes.

4 Add the spring onions followed by the garlic, turmeric, ginger, chilli powder, fenugreek leaves and salt, and continue to stir-fry for 5–7 minutes.

5 Pour in just enough of the water to loosen the mixture.

6 Add the whole cherry tomatoes, coriander leaves, green pepper and lemon juice. Stir well and serve garnished with shredded spring onion tops and coriander leaves.

Balti Corn with Cauliflower & Mint

This quick and tasty vegetable side dish can be made with frozen corn, so it is an excellent store-cupboard standby. If you do not have any cauliflower, substitute broccoli or another vegetable such as slices of courgette.

Serves 4

3 small onions
1 fresh red chilli
15ml/1 tbsp oil
4 curry leaves
1.5ml/¼ tsp onion seeds
175g/6oz/1 cup frozen
 corn
½ small cauliflower, separated
 into florets
3–7 mint leaves

1 Using a sharp knife dice the onions finely. Slit the chilli, scrape out the seeds and then slice the flesh thinly.

2 Heat the oil in a karahi, wok or heavy pan and stir-fry the curry leaves and onion seeds for about 30 seconds.

3 Add the diced onions to the pan and fry them for 5–8 minutes until golden brown.

4 Add the chilli, frozen corn and cauliflower florets and stir-fry for 5–8 minutes more.

5 Toss with the mint leaves and serve immediately.

Cook's Tips

• It is best to eat this dish immediately after it has been cooked, as the flavour tends to spoil if it is kept warm.
• Whole mint leaves can be frozen in the summer when they are plentiful for use during the winter. They are then added while frozen to dishes such as this where they are mixed in with other ingredients. Frozen herbs are not suitable for garnishes, however.

Energy 152kcal/640kJ; Fat 6.1g; Saturated fat 0.9g; Carbohydrate 17.8g; Fibre 2.1g.

Energy 124kcal/519kJ; Fat 3.89g; Saturated fat 0.58g; Carbohydrate 19.31g; Fibre 2.56g.

Balti Dhal with Green & Red Chillies

The white urad dhal which is used in this recipe should ideally be soaked overnight as this makes it easier to cook. Serve with freshly made chapatis.

Serves 4
115g/4oz/½ cup urad
   dhal
10ml/2 tsp low-fat spread
10ml/2 tsp oil
1 bay leaf
2 onions, sliced

1 piece cinnamon stick
2.5cm/1in piece fresh root
   ginger, grated
2 garlic cloves
2 green chillies, seeded and
   sliced lengthways
2 red chillies, seeded and sliced
   lengthways
15ml/1 tbsp chopped
   fresh mint

1 Soak the dhal overnight in enough cold water to cover. Boil in water until the individual grains are soft enough to break into two. Set aside.

2 Heat the spread with the oil in a wok or heavy frying pan over a medium heat. Fry the bay leaf with the onions and the cinnamon.

3 Add the grated ginger, whole garlic cloves and half the green and red chillies.

4 Drain almost all the water from the lentils. Add the lentils to the wok or frying pan, then add the remaining green and red chillies and finally the chopped fresh mint. Heat through briefly and serve while piping hot.

Cook's Tip
If you like your curries milder, replace some of the chillies with some finely chopped green or red (bell) peppers.

Energy 159kcal/663kJ; Fat 3.19g; Saturated fat 0.51g; Carbohydrate 24.39g; Fibre 1.15g.

Chunky Fish Balti with Peppers

Try to find peppers in different colours to make this dish as colourful as possible.

Serves 2–4
450g/1lb cod, or any other firm
   white fish, such as haddock
7.5ml/1½ tsp ground cumin
10ml/2 tsp mango powder
   (amchur)
5ml/1 tsp ground coriander

2.5ml/½ tsp chilli powder
5ml/1 tsp salt
5ml/1 tsp grated fresh root ginger
45ml/3 tbsp cornflour
   (cornstarch)
150ml/¼ pint/⅔ cup corn oil
1 each green, orange and red
   (bell) peppers, seeded and
   chopped
8–10 cherry tomatoes

1 Skin the fish and cut it into small cubes. Put the cubes in a large mixing bowl and add the ground cumin, mango powder, ground coriander, chilli powder, salt, grated ginger and cornflour. Mix together thoroughly until the fish is well coated with the spice mix.

2 Heat the oil in a karahi, wok or large, deep pan. Lower the heat slightly and add the fish pieces, 3 or 4 at a time. Fry for about 3 minutes, turning constantly.

3 Drain the cooked fish pieces on kitchen paper and transfer to a serving dish. Keep hot while you fry the remaining fish pieces.

4 Fry the chopped peppers in the oil remaining in the pan for about 2 minutes. They should still be slightly crisp. Drain on kitchen paper.

5 Add the cooked peppers to the fish and garnish with the cherry tomatoes. Serve immediately.

Cook's Tip
Amchur is made from unripe mangoes and is used to add sourness.

Energy 495kcal/2058kJ; Fat 30g; Saturated fat 3.8g; Carbohydrate 13.3g; Fibre 3.4g.

Balti Fish Fillets in Spicy Coconut Sauce

Although coconut milk is a familiar ingredient in Indian fish dishes, it is quite unusual to find desiccated coconut in a starring role. It makes for a delicious and most unusual dish.

Serves 4
30ml/2 tbsp corn oil
5ml/1 tsp onion seeds
4 dried red chillies
3 garlic cloves, sliced
1 medium onion, sliced
2 medium tomatoes, sliced
30ml/2 tbsp desiccated
  (dry unsweetened shredded)
  coconut
5ml/1 tsp salt
5ml/1 tsp ground coriander
4 flat-fish fillets, such as plaice,
  sole or flounder, about 75g/
  3oz each
150ml/¼ pint/⅔ cup
  water
15ml/1 tbsp lime juice
15ml/1 tbsp chopped fresh
  coriander (cilantro)

1 Heat the oil in a karahi, wok or deep pan. Lower the heat slightly and add the onion seeds, dried red chillies, garlic slices and onion. Cook for 3–4 minutes, stirring once or twice.

2 Add the sliced tomatoes, coconut, salt and ground coriander and stir thoroughly.

3 Cut each fish fillet into 3 pieces. Drop the fish pieces into the mixture and turn them over gently until they are well coated.

4 Cook for 5–7 minutes, lowering the heat if necessary. Add the water, lime juice and fresh coriander and cook for a further 3–5 minutes until most of the water has evaporated. Serve immediately, with rice, if you like.

> **Cook's Tip**
> *Use fresh fish fillets to make this dish if you can, as the flavour and texture will probably be superior. If you must use frozen fillets, ensure that they are completely thawed before cooking.*

Energy 175kcal/731kJ; Fat 11.4g; Saturated fat 5g; Carbohydrate 4.9g; Fibre 2g.

Sizzling Balti Prawns in Hot Sauce

This sizzling prawn dish is cooked in a fiery hot and spicy sauce. This sauce not only contains chilli powder, but is further enhanced by the addition of ground fresh green chillies mixed with other spices. If the heat seems extreme, offer a cooling raita to moderate the piquant flavour.

Serves 4
2 medium onions, roughly
  chopped
30ml/2 tbsp tomato purée
  (paste)
5ml/1 tsp ground coriander
1.5ml/¼ tsp ground turmeric
5ml/1 tsp chilli powder
2 fresh green chillies
45ml/3 tbsp chopped fresh
  coriander (cilantro)
30ml/2 tbsp lemon juice
5ml/1 tsp salt
45ml/3 tbsp corn oil
16 cooked king prawns
  (jumbo shrimp)
sliced green chillies, to garnish
  (optional)

1 Put the onions, tomato purée, ground coriander, turmeric, chilli powder, 2 whole green chillies, 30ml/2 tbsp of the fresh coriander, the lemon juice and salt into the bowl of a food processor. Process for about 1 minute. If the mixture seems too thick, add a little water to loosen it.

2 Heat the oil in a karahi, wok or deep pan. Lower the heat slightly and add the spice mixture. Fry the mixture for 3–5 minutes or until the sauce has thickened slightly.

3 Add the prawns and stir-fry briefly over a medium heat.

4 As soon as the prawns are heated through, transfer them to a serving dish. Garnish with the rest of the fresh coriander and the chopped green chilli, if using. Serve immediately.

> **Cook's Tip**
> *Don't overcook the prawns or they will become tough.*

Energy 139kcal/578kJ; Fat 8.7g; Saturated fat 1.3g; Carbohydrate 5.9g; Fibre 1.1g.

Prawn & Vegetable Balti

This makes a delicious light lunch or supper, and is quick and simple to make.

Serves 4

175g/6oz frozen cooked
    peeled prawns (shrimp)
30ml/2 tbsp oil
1.5ml/¼ tsp onion seeds
4–6 curry leaves
115g/4oz/1 cup frozen peas
115g/4oz/⅔ cup frozen
    corn
1 large courgette (zucchini),
    sliced

1 medium red (bell) pepper,
    seeded and roughly diced
5ml/1 tsp crushed coriander
    seeds
5ml/1 tsp crushed dried
    red chillies
1.5ml/½ tsp salt
15ml/1 tbsp lemon juice
15ml/1 tbsp fresh coriander
    (cilantro) leaves, to garnish

1 Thaw the prawns and drain them of any excess liquid.

2 Heat the oil with the onion seeds and curry leaves in a karahi, wok or heavy frying pan.

3 Add the prawns to the spicy mixture in the wok and stir-fry until the liquid has evaporated.

4 Next, add the peas, corn, courgette and red pepper. Continue to stir for 3–5 minutes.

5 Finally, add the crushed coriander seeds and chillies, salt to taste and the lemon juice.

6 Serve immediately, garnished with fresh coriander leaves.

> **Cook's Tip**
> *Freshly crushed spices have a strong and vibrant flavour. The best way to crush whole seeds is to use an electric spice grinder or a small marble pestle and mortar.*

Energy 171kcal/714kJ; Fat 7.7g; Saturated fat 1.05g; Carbohydrate 11.8g; Fibre 2.8g.

Karahi Prawns & Fenugreek

The black-eyed beans, prawns and paneer in this recipe ensure that it is rich in protein. The combination of both ground and fresh fenugreek makes this a very fragrant and delicious dish. When preparing fresh fenugreek, use the leaves whole, but discard the stalks which would add a bitter flavour to the dish.

Serves 4–6

60ml/4 tbsp corn oil
2 medium onions, sliced
2 medium tomatoes, sliced
7.5ml/1½ tsp crushed garlic

5ml/1 tsp chilli powder
5ml/1 tsp grated fresh
    root ginger
5ml/1 tsp ground cumin
5ml/1 tsp ground coriander
5ml/1 tsp salt
150g/5oz paneer, cubed
5ml/1 tsp ground fenugreek
1 bunch fresh fenugreek leaves
115g/4oz cooked prawns
    (shrimp)
2 fresh red chillies, sliced
30ml/2 tbsp chopped fresh
    coriander (cilantro)
50g/2oz/⅓ cup canned
    black-eyed beans (peas),
    drained
15ml/1 tbsp lemon juice

1 Heat the oil in a karahi, wok or deep pan. Lower the heat slightly and add the onions and tomatoes. Fry for about 3 minutes.

2 Add the garlic, chilli powder, ginger, ground cumin, ground coriander, salt, paneer and the ground and fresh fenugreek. Lower the heat and stir-fry for about 2 minutes.

3 Add the prawns, red chillies, fresh coriander and black-eyed beans, and mix well. Toss over the heat for a further 3–5 minutes, or until the prawns are heated through. Sprinkle with the lemon juice and serve.

> **Cook's Tip**
> *Paneer is a type of cheese made with the curds from boiling milk which has been acidified with lemon juice. If you cannot locate paneer, tofu makes a good substitute.*

Energy 206kcal/858kJ; Fat 13g; Saturated fat 2.6g; Carbohydrate 10.7g; Fibre 2.3g.

Paneer Balti with Prawns

Paneer is a protein food and makes an excellent substitute for red meat. Here it is combined with king prawns to make a dish with unforgettable flavour.

Serves 4
12 cooked king prawns (jumbo shrimp)
175g/6oz paneer
30ml/2 tbsp tomato purée (paste)
60ml/4 tbsp Greek (US strained plain) yogurt
7.5ml/1½ tsp garam masala
5ml/1 tsp chilli powder
5ml/1 tsp crushed garlic
5ml/1 tsp salt
10ml/2 tsp mango powder (amchur)
5ml/1 tsp ground coriander
115g/4oz/½ cup butter
15ml/1 tbsp vegetable oil
3 fresh green chillies, chopped
45ml/3 tbsp chopped fresh coriander (cilantro)
150ml/¼ pint/⅔ cup single (light) cream

1 Peel and remove the black intestinal vein from the king prawns. Cut the paneer into small cubes.

2 Put the tomato purée, yogurt, garam masala, chilli powder, garlic, salt, mango powder and ground coriander in a mixing bowl. Mix to a paste and set aside.

3 Melt the butter with the oil in a karahi, wok or deep pan. Lower the heat slightly and quickly fry the paneer and prawns for about 2 minutes. Remove with a slotted spoon and drain on kitchen paper.

4 Pour the spice paste into the fat left in the pan and cook for about 1 minute, stirring constantly.

5 Add the paneer and prawns, and cook for 7–10 minutes, stirring occasionally, until the prawns are heated through.

6 Add the fresh chillies and most of the coriander, and pour in the cream. Heat through for about 2 minutes, garnish with the remaining coriander and serve.

Energy 416kcal/1720kJ; Fat 36g; Saturated fat 21.2g; Carbohydrate 5.4g; Fibre 0g.

Seafood Balti with Vegetables

In this dish, the spicy seafood is cooked separately and combined with the melange of vegetables at the last minute to give a truly delicious combination of flavours.

Serves 4
225g/8oz cod, or any other firm white fish
225g/8oz cooked prawns (shrimp)
6 seafood sticks, halved lengthways, or 115g/4oz white crab meat
15ml/1 tbsp lemon juice
5ml/1 tsp ground coriander
5ml/1 tsp chilli powder
5ml/1 tsp salt
5ml/1 tsp ground cumin
60ml/4 tbsp cornflour (cornstarch)
150ml/¼ pint/⅔ cup corn oil
lime slices, to garnish

For the vegetables
150ml/¼ pint/⅔ cup corn oil
2 medium onions, chopped
5ml/1 tsp onion seeds
½ medium cauliflower, cut into florets
115g/4oz green beans, cut into 2.5cm/1in lengths
175g/6oz/1 cup corn
5ml/1 tsp shredded fresh root ginger
5ml/1 tsp chilli powder
5ml/1 tsp salt
4 fresh green chillies, sliced
30ml/2 tbsp chopped fresh coriander (cilantro)

1 Skin the fish and cut into small cubes. Put into a medium mixing bowl with the prawns and seafood sticks or crab meat.

2 In a separate bowl, mix together the lemon juice, ground coriander, chilli powder, salt and ground cumin. Pour this over the seafood and mix together thoroughly, using your hands.

3 Sprinkle on the cornflour and mix again until the seafood is well coated. Place in the refrigerator for about 1 hour to allow the flavours to develop.

4 To make the vegetable mixture, heat the oil in a karahi, wok or deep pan. Add the onions and the onion seeds, and stir-fry until lightly browned.

5 Add the cauliflower, green beans, corn, ginger, chilli powder, salt, green chillies and fresh coriander. Stir-fry for about 7–10 minutes over a medium heat, making sure that the pieces of cauliflower retain their shape.

6 Spoon the fried vegetables around the edge of a shallow serving dish, leaving a space in the middle for the seafood, and keep hot.

7 Wash and dry the pan, then heat the oil to fry the seafood pieces. Fry the seafood pieces in 2 or 3 batches, until they turn a golden brown. Remove with a slotted spoon and drain on kitchen paper.

8 Arrange the seafood in the middle of the dish of vegetables and keep hot while you fry the remaining seafood. Garnish with lime slices and serve. Plain boiled rice and raita make ideal accompaniments for this dish.

Energy 279kcal/1165kJ; Fat 11g; Saturated fat 1.6g; Carbohydrate 18.5g; Fibre 4g.

Classic Balti Chicken

This recipe has a beautifully delicate flavour, and is probably the most popular of all Balti dishes. Choose a young chicken as it will be more flavoursome.

Serves 4–6

1–1.3kg/2¼–3lb chicken
45ml/3 tbsp corn oil
3 medium onions, sliced
3 medium tomatoes, halved
 and sliced
2.5cm/1in cinnamon stick

2 large black cardamom pods
4 black peppercorns
2.5ml/½ tsp black cumin seeds
5ml/1 tsp grated fresh root ginger
5ml/1 tsp crushed garlic
5ml/1 tsp garam masala
5ml/1 tsp chilli powder
5ml/1 tsp salt
30ml/2 tbsp natural (plain)
 yogurt
60ml/4 tbsp lemon juice
30ml/2 tbsp chopped fresh
 coriander (cilantro)
2 fresh green chillies, chopped

1 Skin the chicken, then use a sharp knife to cut it into eight pieces. Wash and trim the chicken pieces, and set to one side.

2 Heat the oil in a large karahi, wok or deep pan. Add the onions and fry until they are golden brown. Add the tomatoes and stir well.

3 Add the piece of cinnamon stick, cardamoms, peppercorns, black cumin seeds, ginger, garlic, garam masala, chilli powder and salt. Lower the heat and stir-fry for 3–5 minutes.

4 Add the chicken pieces, two at a time, and stir-fry for at least 7 minutes or until the spice mixture has completely penetrated the chicken pieces and they are beginning to brown. Add the yogurt to the chicken and mix well.

5 Lower the heat and cover the pan with a piece of foil, making sure that the foil does not touch the food. Cook very gently for about 15 minutes, checking once to make sure the food is not catching on the bottom of the pan.

6 Finally, add the lemon juice, fresh coriander and green chillies. Serve immediately, straight from the pan.

Energy 569kcal/2362kJ; Fat 38.2g; Saturated fat 9.5g; Carbohydrate 13.2g; Fibre 2.3g.

Sweet-&-sour Balti Chicken

This dish combines a sweet-and-sour flavour with a creamy texture. It is delicious served with pilau rice or naan bread.

Serves 4

45ml/3 tbsp tomato purée
 (paste)
30ml/2 tbsp Greek (US strained
 plain) yogurt
7.5ml/1½ tsp garam masala
5ml/1 tsp chilli powder
5ml/1 tsp crushed garlic

30ml/2 tbsp mango chutney
5ml/1 tsp salt
2.5ml/½ tsp granulated
 sugar
60ml/4 tbsp corn oil
675g/1½lb skinned boneless
 chicken, cubed
150ml/¼ pint/⅔ cup water
2 fresh green chillies,
 chopped
30ml/2 tbsp chopped fresh
 coriander (cilantro)
30ml/2 tbsp single (light)
 cream

1 Mix the tomato purée, Greek yogurt, garam masala, chilli powder, crushed garlic, mango chutney, salt and sugar in a medium mixing bowl. Stir well.

2 Heat the oil in a karahi, wok or deep pan. Lower the heat slightly and pour in the spice mixture. Bring to the boil and cook for about 2 minutes, stirring occasionally.

3 Add the chicken pieces and stir until they are well coated.

4 Stir in the water to thin the sauce slightly. Continue cooking for 5–7 minutes, or until the chicken is fully cooked and tender.

5 Finally, add the fresh chillies, coriander and cream, cook for a further 2 minutes over a low heat, then serve.

> **Variation**
> If you like, you could lightly fry 1 sliced green (bell) pepper and 115g/4oz/1½ cups whole small button (white) mushrooms in 15ml/1 tbsp oil and add to the spice mixture with the chicken pieces in step 3.

Energy 227kcal/957kJ; Fat 4.2g; Saturated fat 1.7g; Carbohydrate 6.7g; Fibre 0.3g.

Khara Masala Balti Chicken

Whole spices (*khara*) are used in this recipe, giving it a wonderful, rich flavour. This is a dry dish so it is best served with plenty of creamy raita.

Serves 4
3 curry leaves
1.5ml/¼ tsp mustard seeds
1.5ml/¼ tsp fennel seeds
1.5ml/¼ tsp onion seeds
2.5ml/½ tsp crushed dried
  red chillies
2.5ml/½ tsp white cumin seeds
1.5ml/¼ tsp fenugreek seeds

2.5ml/½ tsp crushed
  pomegranate seeds
5ml/1 tsp salt
5ml/1 tsp shredded fresh
  root ginger
3 garlic cloves, sliced
60ml/4 tbsp corn oil
4 fresh green chillies, slit
1 large onion, sliced
1 medium tomato, sliced
675g/1½lb skinless, boneless
  chicken, cubed
15ml/1 tbsp chopped fresh
  coriander (cilantro)

1 Mix together the curry leaves, mustard seeds, fennel seeds, onion seeds, crushed red chillies, cumin seeds, fenugreek seeds, crushed pomegranate seeds and salt in a large bowl.

2 Add the shredded ginger and garlic cloves to the spice mixture in the bowl and stir well.

3 Heat the oil in a medium karahi, wok or deep pan. Add the spice mixture, then tip in the green chillies.

4 Spoon the sliced onion into the pan and fry over a medium heat for 5–7 minutes, stirring constantly to flavour the onion with the spices.

5 Finally add the tomato and chicken pieces, and cook over a medium heat for about 7 minutes. The chicken should be cooked through and the sauce reduced.

6 Stir everything together over the heat for a further 3–5 minutes. Serve from the pan, garnished with chopped fresh coriander.

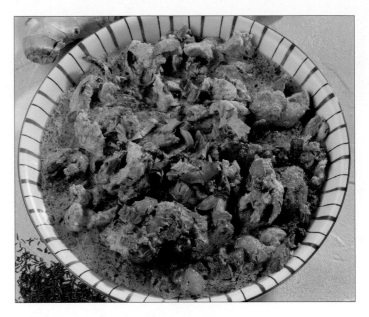

Balti Chicken Pasanda

Yogurt and cream give this tasty dish its characteristic richness. Serve it with garlic and coriander naan to complement the almonds.

Serves 4
60ml/4 tbsp Greek (US strained
  plain) yogurt
2.5ml/½ tsp black cumin seeds
4 cardamom pods
6 whole black peppercorns
10ml/2 tsp garam masala
2.5cm/1in cinnamon stick
15ml/1 tbsp ground almonds
5ml/1 tsp crushed garlic

5ml/1 tsp grated fresh root ginger
5ml/1 tsp chilli powder
5ml/1 tsp salt
675g/1½lb skinless, boneless
  chicken, cubed
75ml/5 tbsp corn oil
2 medium onions, diced
3 fresh green chillies, chopped
30ml/2 tbsp chopped fresh
  coriander (cilantro), plus extra
  to garnish
120ml/4fl oz/½ cup single (light)
  cream

1 Mix the Greek yogurt, black cumin seeds, cardamom pods, whole black peppercorns, garam masala and cinnamon stick together in a medium mixing bowl. Add the ground almonds, garlic, ginger, chilli powder and salt and mix together well.

2 Add the cubed chicken pieces, stir to coat, and leave in the spice mixture to marinate for about 2 hours.

3 Heat the oil in a large karahi, wok or deep pan. Add the onions and fry for 2–3 minutes.

4 Tip in the chicken mixture and stir until it is well blended with the onions.

5 Cook for 12–15 minutes over a medium heat until the sauce thickens and the chicken is cooked through.

6 Add the chopped green chillies and fresh coriander to the chicken in the wok, and pour in the single cream. Bring to the boil, stirring constantly, and serve the dish garnished with more coriander, if you like.

Energy 313kcal/1310kJ; Fat 13.7g; Saturated fat 2.3g; Carbohydrate 8.1g; Fibre 2.3g.

Energy 453kcal/1888kJ; Fat 26.8g; Saturated fat 8.7g; Carbohydrate 10.9g; Fibre 1.1g.

Balti Chicken Pieces with Cumin & Coriander

The potatoes are tossed in spices and cooked separately in the oven before being added to the chicken.

Serves 4
150ml/¼ pint/⅔ cup natural (plain) low-fat yogurt
25g/1oz/¼ cup ground almonds
7.5ml/1½ tsp ground coriander
2.5ml/½ tsp chilli powder
5ml/1 tsp garam masala
15ml/1 tbsp coconut milk
5ml/1 tsp crushed garlic
5ml/1 tsp grated fresh root ginger
30ml/2 tbsp chopped fresh coriander (cilantro)
1 fresh red chilli, seeded and chopped
225g/8oz skinned chicken breast fillets, cubed
15ml/1 tbsp oil
2 medium onions, sliced
3 green cardamom pods
2.5cm/1in cinnamon stick
2 cloves

For the potatoes
15ml/1 tbsp oil
8 baby potatoes, thickly sliced
1.5ml/¼ tsp cumin seeds
15ml/1 tbsp finely chopped fresh coriander (cilantro)

1 In a large bowl, mix together the first eight ingredients with half the fresh coriander and half the red chilli. Place the chicken pieces in the mixture, mix well, then cover and leave to marinate for about 2 hours.

2 Meanwhile, start to prepare the spicy potatoes. Heat the oil in a karahi, wok or heavy pan. Add the sliced potatoes, cumin seeds and fresh coriander and quickly stir-fry for 2–3 minutes.

3 Preheat the oven to 180°C/350°F/Gas 4. Spoon the potatoes into a baking dish, cover and bake for about 30 minutes or until they are cooked through.

4 Halfway through the potatoes' cooking time, heat the oil and fry the onions, cardamoms, cinnamon and cloves for 1½ minutes. Add the chicken mixture to the fried onions and stir-fry for 5–7 minutes. Lower the heat, cover and cook for 5–7 minutes. Top with the potatoes and garnish with coriander and red chilli.

Energy 2783kcal/1166kJ; Fat 10.76g; Saturated fat 1.58g; Carbohydrate 27.43g; Fibre 2.78g.

Chicken & Tomato Balti

If you like tomatoes, you will love this chicken recipe. It makes a delicious semi-dry Balti and is good served with a lentil dish and plain boiled rice.

Serves 4
60ml/4 tbsp corn oil
6 curry leaves
2.5ml/½ tsp mixed onion and mustard seeds
8 medium tomatoes, sliced
5ml/1 tsp ground coriander
5ml/1 tsp chilli powder
5ml/1 tsp salt
5ml/1 tsp ground cumin
5ml/1 tsp crushed garlic
675g/1½lb skinless, boneless chicken, cubed
150ml/¼ pint/⅔ cup water
15ml/1 tbsp sesame seeds, roasted
15ml/1 tbsp chopped fresh coriander (cilantro)

1 Heat the oil in a karahi, wok or deep round-bottomed frying pan. Add the curry leaves and mixed onion and mustard seeds.

2 Toss the seeds over the heat for 1–2 minutes so that they become fragrant. Do not let the seeds burn.

3 Lower the heat slightly and add the tomatoes.

4 While the tomatoes are gently cooking, mix together the ground coriander, chilli powder, salt, ground cumin and crushed garlic in a bowl.

5 Tip the spices on to the tomatoes in the wok or pan and stir well to mix thoroughly.

6 Add the chicken pieces and stir well. Stir-fry for about 5 minutes more.

7 Stir in the water and continue cooking, stirring occasionally, until the sauce thickens and the chicken is fully cooked and tender.

8 Sprinkle the roasted sesame seeds and chopped fresh coriander over the chicken and tomato Balti. Serve immediately, from the pan.

Energy 360kcal/1508kJ; Fat 18.3g; Saturated fat 3g; Carbohydrate 8.6g; Fibre 2.3g.

Balti Chicken in a Lentil Sauce

Traditionally, this dish is made with lamb, but it is equally delicious made with chicken breast.

Serves 4

30ml/2 tbsp chana dhal or yellow split peas
50g/2oz/¼ cup masoor dhal or red split peas
15ml/1 tbsp oil
2 medium onions, chopped
5ml/1 tsp crushed garlic
5ml/1 tsp grated fresh root ginger
2.5ml/½ tsp ground turmeric
7.5ml/1½ tsp chilli powder
5ml/1 tsp garam masala
2.5ml/½ tsp ground coriander

7.5ml/1½ tsp salt
175g/6oz skinned chicken breast fillets, cubed
45ml/3 tbsp fresh coriander (cilantro) leaves
1 or 2 fresh green chillies, seeded and chopped
30–45ml/2–3 tbsp lemon juice
300ml/½ pint/1¼ cups water
2 tomatoes, peeled and halved

For the tarka

5ml/1 tsp oil
2.5ml/½ tsp cumin seeds
2 garlic cloves
2 dried red chillies
4 curry leaves

1 Put the pulses in a pan with water and bring to the boil. Cook for 30–45 minutes until soft and mushy. Drain and set aside. Heat the oil in a karahi, wok or heavy frying pan and fry the onions until soft and golden brown. Stir in the garlic, ginger, turmeric, chilli powder, garam masala, ground coriander and salt.

2 Next, add the chicken pieces and fry for 5–7 minutes, stirring constantly over a medium heat to seal in the juices and lightly brown the meat.

3 Add half the fresh coriander, the green chillies, lemon juice and water and cook for 3–5 minutes. Stir in the cooked pulses, then add the tomatoes. Sprinkle over the remaining coriander leaves. Take the pan off the heat and set aside.

4 To make the tarka, heat the oil and add the cumin seeds, whole garlic cloves, dried red chillies and curry leaves. Heat for about 30 seconds then pour over the top of the chicken and lentils. Serve the dish immediately.

Energy 207kcal/868kJ; Fat 7.07g; Saturated fat 1.03g; Carbohydrate 20.37g; Fibre 2.84g.

Balti Chicken with Paneer & Peas

This is rather an unusual combination, but it really works well. Serve with plain boiled rice.

Serves 4

1 small chicken, about 675g/1½lb
30ml/2 tbsp tomato purée (paste)
45ml/3 tbsp natural (plain) low-fat yogurt
7.5ml/1½ tsp garam masala
5ml/1 tsp crushed garlic
5ml/1 tsp grated fresh root ginger
pinch of ground cardamom

15ml/1 tbsp chilli powder
1.5ml/¼ tsp ground turmeric
5ml/1 tsp salt
5ml/1 tsp granulated sugar
10ml/2 tsp oil
2.5cm/1in cinnamon stick
2 black peppercorns
300ml/½ pint/1¼ cups water
115g/4oz paneer, cubed
30ml/2 tbsp fresh coriander (cilantro) leaves
2 fresh green chillies, seeded and chopped
50g/2oz/¼ cup low-fat fromage frais or ricotta cheese
75g/3oz/¾ cup frozen peas, thawed

1 Skin the chicken and cut it into six to eight equal pieces.

2 Mix the tomato purée, yogurt, garam masala, garlic, ginger, cardamom, chilli powder, turmeric, salt and sugar in a bowl.

3 Heat the oil with the whole spices in a karahi, wok or heavy pan, then pour the yogurt mixture into the oil. Lower the heat and cook gently for about 3 minutes, then pour in the water and bring to a simmer.

4 Add the chicken pieces to the pan. Stir-fry for 2 minutes, then cover the pan and cook over medium heat for about 10 minutes.

5 Add the paneer cubes to the pan, followed by half the coriander and half the green chillies. Mix well and cook for a further 5–7 minutes.

6 Stir in the fromage frais or ricotta and peas, heat through and serve with the reserved coriander and chillies.

Energy 233kcal/977kJ; Fat 10.28g; Saturated fat 4.64g; Carbohydrate 8.14g; Fibre 1.49g.

Balti Chicken with Green & Red Chillies

Minced or ground chicken is seldom cooked in Indian homes. However, it works very well in this recipe.

Serves 4

275g/10oz skinned chicken
   breast fillet, cubed
2 plump fresh red chillies
3 plump fresh green chillies
30ml/2 tbsp oil
6 curry leaves
3 medium onions, sliced
7.5ml/1½ tsp crushed garlic
7.5ml/1½ tsp ground coriander
7.5ml/1½ tsp grated fresh
   root ginger
5ml/1 tsp chilli powder
5ml/1 tsp salt
15ml/1 tbsp lemon juice
30ml/2 tbsp chopped fresh
   coriander (cilantro)
chapatis and lemon wedges,
   to serve

1 Cook the chicken breast fillet in a pan of water for about 10 minutes until soft and cooked through. Remove with a slotted spoon and place in the bowl of a food processor fitted with a metal blade.

2 Roughly mince or grind the cooked chicken breast fillet.

3 Cut the chillies in half lengthways and remove the seeds, if you like. Cut the flesh into strips and set aside.

4 Heat the oil in a karahi, wok or heavy pan and fry the curry leaves and onions until the onions are a soft golden brown. Lower the heat and stir in the garlic, ground coriander, ginger, chilli powder and salt.

5 Add the minced (ground) chicken to the onion and spices, and stir-fry for 3–5 minutes.

6 Add the lemon juice, the prepared chilli strips and most of the fresh coriander. Stir-fry for a further 3–5 minutes.

7 Serve, garnished with the remaining fresh coriander and accompanied by warm chapatis and lemon wedges.

Energy 184kcal/767kJ; Fat 8.4g; Saturated fat 1.57g; Carbohydrate 10.1g; Fibre 1.3g.

Balti Chicken in Hara Masala Sauce

This chicken dish can be served as an accompaniment to any of the rice dishes in this book.

Serves 4

1 crisp green eating apple, peeled, cored and cut into small cubes
60ml/4 tbsp fresh coriander (cilantro) leaves
30ml/2 tbsp fresh mint leaves
120ml/4fl oz/½ cup natural (plain) low-fat yogurt
45ml/3 tbsp low-fat fromage frais or ricotta cheese
2 fresh green chillies, seeded and chopped
1 bunch spring onions (scallions), chopped
5ml/1 tsp salt
5ml/1 tsp granulated sugar
5ml/1 tsp crushed garlic
5ml/1 tsp grated fresh root ginger
15ml/1 tbsp oil
225g/8oz skinned chicken breast fillets, cubed
25g/1oz/2 tbsp sultanas (golden raisins)

1 Place the apple, 45ml/3 tbsp of the fresh coriander, the mint, yogurt, fromage frais or ricotta, chillies, spring onions, salt, sugar, garlic and ginger in a food processor and pulse for about 1 minute.

2 Heat the oil in a karahi, wok or heavy pan, pour in the yogurt mixture and cook over a low heat for about 2 minutes.

3 Next, add the chicken pieces and blend everything together. Cook over a medium to low heat for 12–15 minutes or until the chicken is fully cooked.

4 Stir in the sultanas and the remaining 15ml/1 tbsp fresh coriander leaves and serve.

> **Cook's Tip**
> This dish makes an attractive centrepiece for a dinner party.

Balti Butter Chicken

Butter Chicken is one of the most popular Balti chicken dishes, especially in the West. Cooked in butter, with aromatic spices, cream and almonds, this mild dish will be enjoyed by everyone. Serve with pilau rice.

Serves 4

150ml/¼ pint/⅔ cup natural (plain) yogurt
50g/2oz/½ cup ground almonds
7.5ml/1½ tsp chilli powder
1.5ml/¼ tsp crushed bay leaves
1.5ml/¼ tsp ground cloves
1.5ml/¼ tsp ground cinnamon
5ml/1 tsp garam masala
4 green cardamom pods
5ml/1 tsp grated fresh root ginger
5ml/1 tsp crushed garlic
400g/14oz/2 cups canned tomatoes
7.5ml/1¼ tsp salt
1kg/2¼lb skinless, boneless chicken, cubed
75g/3oz/6 tbsp butter
15ml/1 tbsp corn oil
2 medium onions, sliced
30ml/2 tbsp chopped fresh coriander (cilantro)
60ml/4 tbsp single (light) cream
coriander sprigs, to garnish

1 Put the yogurt in a bowl and add the ground almonds, chilli powder, crushed bay leaves, ground cloves, cinnamon, garam masala, cardamoms, ginger and garlic.

2 Chop the tomatoes and add them to the bowl with the salt. Mix thoroughly.

3 Put the chicken into a large mixing bowl and pour over the yogurt mixture. Set aside.

4 Melt together the butter and oil in a karahi, wok or deep pan. Add the onions and fry for about 3 minutes.

5 Add the chicken mixture and stir-fry for 7–10 minutes.

6 Sprinkle over about half of the coriander and mix well.

7 Pour over the single cream and stir in well. Heat through and serve, garnished with the remaining chopped fresh coriander and coriander sprigs.

Energy 158kcal/666kJ; Fat 4.37g; Saturated fat 1.69g; Carbohydrate 14.54g; Fibre 1.08g.

Energy 592kcal/2474kJ; Fat 32.2g; Saturated fat 13.7g; Carbohydrate 12.1g; Fibre 1.6g.

Balti Chicken in Thick Creamy Coconut Sauce

If you like the flavour of coconut, you will really love this aromatic curry.

Serves 4

15ml/1 tbsp ground almonds
15ml/1 tbsp desiccated (dry unsweetened shredded) coconut
75ml/2½fl oz/⅓ cup coconut milk
175g/6oz/⅔ cup low-fat fromage frais or ricotta cheese
7.5ml/1½ tsp ground coriander
5ml/1 tsp chilli powder
5ml/1 tsp crushed garlic
7.5ml/1½ tsp grated fresh root ginger
5ml/1 tsp salt
15ml/1 tbsp oil
225g/8oz skinned chicken fillet, cubed
3 green cardamom pods
1 bay leaf
1 dried red chilli, crushed
30ml/2 tbsp chopped fresh coriander (cilantro)

1 Using a heavy pan, dry-roast the ground almonds and desiccated coconut, stirring frequently, until they turn just a shade darker. Transfer the nut mixture to a mixing bowl.

2 Add the coconut milk, fromage frais or ricotta cheese, ground coriander, chilli powder, crushed garlic, ginger and salt to the mixing bowl.

3 Heat the oil in a karahi, wok or heavy pan and add the chicken cubes, cardamoms and bay leaf. Stir-fry for about 2 minutes to seal the chicken but not cook it.

4 Pour in the coconut milk mixture and blend everything together. Lower the heat, add the chilli and fresh coriander, cover and cook for 10–12 minutes, stirring occasionally. Uncover, then stir and cook for a further 2 minutes before serving, making sure the chicken is cooked.

Energy 166kcal/696kJ; Fat 8.30g; Saturated fat 2.84g; Carbohydrate 6.38g; Fibre 0.95g.

Balti Chicken in Saffron Sauce

This is a beautifully aromatic chicken dish that is partly cooked in the oven.

Serves 4

50g/2oz/¼ cup butter
30ml/2 tbsp corn oil
1.2–1.3kg/2½–3lb chicken, skinned and cut into 8 pieces
1 medium onion, chopped
5ml/1 tsp crushed garlic
2.5ml/½ tsp crushed black peppercorns
2.5ml/½ tsp crushed cardamom pods
2.5ml/¼ tsp ground cinnamon
7.5ml/1½ tsp chilli powder
150ml/¼ pint/⅔ cup natural (plain) yogurt
50g/2oz/½ cup ground almonds
15ml/1 tbsp lemon juice
5ml/1 tsp salt
5ml/1 tsp saffron strands
150ml/¼ pint/⅔ cup water
150ml/¼ pint/⅔ cup single (light) cream
30ml/2 tbsp chopped fresh coriander (cilantro)

1 Preheat the oven to 180°C/350°F/Gas 4. Melt the butter with the oil in a karahi, wok or deep pan. Add the chicken pieces and fry until lightly browned, about 5 minutes. Remove the chicken using a slotted spoon, leaving behind the fat.

2 Add the onion to the same pan, and fry over a medium heat. Meanwhile, mix together the next 10 ingredients in a bowl. When the onions are lightly browned, pour the spice mixture into the pan and stir-fry for about 1 minute.

3 Add the chicken pieces, and continue to fry for a further 2 minutes stirring constantly. Pour in the water and bring to a simmer. Transfer the contents of the pan to a casserole and cover with a lid, or, if using a karahi with heatproof handles, cover with foil. Transfer to the oven and cook for 30–35 minutes.

4 Once you are sure that the chicken is cooked right through, remove it from the oven. Transfer the mixture to a frying pan or place the karahi on the stove and stir in the cream.

5 Reheat gently for about 2 minutes. Garnish with fresh coriander and serve with a fruity pilau or plain boiled rice.

Energy 525kcal/2190kJ; Fat 33g; Saturated fat 13.3g; Carbohydrate 11g; Fibre 1.5g.

Balti Chicken with Vegetables

This is an excellent recipe for making a small amount of chicken go a long way. The carrots and courgettes add colour and boost the dish's nutritional value.

Serves 4–6

60ml/4 tbsp corn oil
2 medium onions, sliced
4 garlic cloves, thickly sliced
450g/1lb skinned chicken breast
  fillets, cut into strips
5ml/1 tsp salt
30ml/2 tbsp lime juice
3 fresh green chillies, chopped
2 medium carrots, cut into batons
2 medium potatoes, peeled and
  cut into 1cm/1/2in strips
1 medium courgette (zucchini),
  cut into batons
4 lime slices
15ml/1 tbsp chopped fresh
  coriander (cilantro)
2 fresh green chillies, cut into
  strips (optional)

1 Heat the oil in a large karahi, wok or deep pan. Lower the heat slightly and add the sliced onions. Fry until the onions are lightly browned and softened.

2 Add half the garlic slices and fry for a few seconds before adding the chicken strips and salt. Cook everything together, stirring, until all the moisture has evaporated and the chicken is lightly browned.

3 Add the lime juice, green chillies and all the vegetables to the pan. Increase the heat and add the rest of the garlic. Stir-fry for 7–10 minutes, or until the chicken is cooked through and the vegetables are just tender.

4 Transfer to a serving dish and garnish with the lime slices, fresh chopped coriander and green chilli strips, if you like. Serve the Balti immediately.

Cook's Tip
Try other fresh vegetables in this dish, such as green beans, mangetouts (snow peas) and (bell) peppers.

Energy 308kcal/1289kJ; Fat 13.1g; Saturated fat 2.1g; Carbohydrate 20.1g; Fibre 2.8g.

Balti Chilli Chicken

Hot and spicy would be the best way of describing this mouthwatering Balti dish. The smell of the fresh chillies while they are cooking is simply irresistible.

Serves 4–6

75ml/5 tbsp corn oil
8 large fresh green chillies, slit
2.5ml/1/2 tsp mixed onion seeds
  and cumin seeds
4 curry leaves
5ml/1 tsp grated fresh root ginger
5ml/1 tsp chilli powder
5ml/1 tsp ground coriander
5ml/1 tsp crushed garlic
5ml/1 tsp salt
2 medium onions, chopped
675g/1 1/2lb skinned chicken
  fillets, cubed
15ml/1 tbsp lemon juice
15ml/1 tbsp roughly chopped
  fresh mint
15ml/1 tbsp roughly chopped
  fresh coriander (cilantro)
8–10 cherry tomatoes

1 Heat the oil in a karahi, wok or deep pan. Lower the heat slightly and add the slit green chillies. Fry until the skin starts to change colour.

2 Add the onion seeds and cumin seeds, curry leaves, ginger, chilli powder, ground coriander, garlic, salt and onions, and fry for a few seconds, stirring continuously.

3 Add the chicken pieces to the pan. Stir-fry over a medium heat for 7–10 minutes, or until the chicken is cooked right through. Do not overcook the chicken or it will become tough in texture.

4 Sprinkle on the lemon juice and add the roughly chopped fresh mint and coriander. Dot with the cherry tomatoes and serve from the pan.

Cook's Tip
Frying the whole spices releases their lovely aromas.

Energy 346kcal/1448kJ; Fat 16.5g; Saturated fat 2.7g; Carbohydrate 9.9g; Fibre 1.3g.

Balti Chicken in Tamarind Sauce

The tamarind in this recipe gives the dish a sweet-and-sour flavour; this is also quite a hot Balti.

Serves 4–6
60ml/4 tbsp tomato ketchup
15ml/1 tbsp tamarind paste
60ml/4 tbsp water
7.5ml/1½ tsp chilli powder
7.5ml/1½ tsp salt
15ml/1 tbsp granulated sugar
7.5ml/1½ tsp grated fresh root ginger
7.5ml/1½ tsp crushed garlic
30ml/2 tbsp desiccated (dry unsweetened shredded) coconut
30ml/2 tbsp sesame seeds
5ml/1 tsp poppy seeds
5ml/1 tsp ground cumin
7.5ml/1½ tsp ground coriander
2 × 450g/1lb baby chickens, skinned and cut into 6–8 pieces each
75ml/5 tbsp corn oil
120ml/8 tbsp curry leaves
2.5ml/½ tsp onion seeds
3 large dried red chillies
2.5ml/½ tsp fenugreek seeds
10–12 cherry tomatoes
45ml/3 tbsp chopped fresh coriander (cilantro)
2 fresh green chillies, chopped

1 Put the tomato ketchup, tamarind paste and water into a large mixing bowl and use a fork to blend everything together. Add the chilli powder, salt, sugar, ginger, garlic, coconut, sesame and poppy seeds, cumin and coriander to the mixture. Stir to mix. Add the chicken pieces and stir until they are well coated with the spice mixture. Set aside.

2 Heat the oil in a karahi, wok or deep pan. Add the curry leaves, onion seeds, dried red chillies and fenugreek seeds and fry for about 1 minute.

3 Lower the heat to medium and add 2 or 3 chicken pieces at a time, with their sauce, mixing as you go. When all the pieces have been added to the pan, stir well, using a slotted spoon.

4 Simmer gently for about 12–15 minutes, or until the chicken is thoroughly cooked. Finally, add the tomatoes, fresh coriander and green chillies, and serve from the pan.

Energy 348kcal/1454kJ; Fat 19.9g; Saturated fat 6.4g; Carbohydrate 11.9g; Fibre 1.5g.

Balti Chicken Madras

This is a fairly hot chicken curry which is good served with either plain boiled rice, pilau rice or naan bread.

Serves 4
275g/10oz skinned chicken breast fillets
45ml/3 tbsp tomato purée (paste)
large pinch of ground fenugreek
1.5ml/¼ tsp ground fennel seeds
5ml/1 tsp grated fresh root ginger
7.5ml/1½ tsp ground coriander
5ml/1 tsp crushed garlic
5ml/1 tsp chilli powder
1.5ml/¼ tsp ground turmeric
30ml/2 tbsp lemon juice
5ml/1 tsp salt
300ml/½ pint/1¼ cups water
15ml/1 tbsp oil
2 medium onions, diced
2–4 curry leaves
2 fresh green chillies, seeded and chopped
15ml/1 tbsp fresh coriander (cilantro) leaves

1 Remove any visible fat from the chicken breasts and cut the meat into bitesize cubes.

2 Mix the tomato purée in a bowl with the fenugreek, fennel seeds, ginger, coriander, garlic, chilli powder, turmeric, lemon juice, salt and water.

3 Heat the oil in a karahi, wok or heavy pan and fry the diced onions together with the curry leaves until the onions are golden brown and softened.

4 Add the chicken pieces to the onions and stir over the heat for about 1 minute to seal the meat.

5 Next, pour in the prepared spice mixture and continue to stir the chicken for about 2 minutes.

6 Lower the heat and cook the spicy chicken for 8–10 minutes, stirring frequently to prevent the mixture from catching on the bottom of the pan.

7 Add the chopped chillies and fresh coriander leaves and serve the Balti immediately.

Energy 141kcal/591kJ; Fat 4.11g; Saturated fat 0.6g; Carbohydrate 8.6g; Fibre 1.53g.

Balti Lamb Tikka

This is a traditional tikka recipe, in which the lamb is marinated in yogurt and spices. The lamb is usually cut into cubes, but the cooking time can be halved by cutting it into strips.

Serves 4

450g/1lb lean boneless lamb, cut into strips
175ml/6fl oz/¾ cup natural (plain) yogurt
5ml/1 tsp ground cumin
5ml/1 tsp ground coriander
5ml/1 tsp chilli powder
5ml/1 tsp crushed garlic
5ml/1 tsp salt
5ml/1 tsp garam masala
30ml/2 tbsp chopped fresh coriander (cilantro)
30ml/2 tbsp lemon juice
30ml/2 tbsp corn oil
15ml/1 tbsp tomato purée (paste)
1 large green (bell) pepper, seeded and sliced
3 large fresh red chillies

1 Put the lamb strips, yogurt, ground cumin, ground coriander, chilli powder, garlic, salt, garam masala, fresh coriander and lemon juice into a large mixing bowl and stir thoroughly. Cover and marinate at cool room temperature for 1 hour.

2 Heat the oil in a karahi, wok or deep pan. Lower the heat slightly and stir in the tomato purée.

3 Add the lamb strips to the pan, a few at a time, leaving any excess marinade behind in the bowl.

4 Cook the lamb, stirring frequently, for 7–10 minutes or until it is well browned.

5 Finally, add the green pepper slices and the whole red chillies. Heat through, checking that the lamb is fully cooked, spoon into a serving dish and serve hot.

> **Cook's Tip**
> Coriander leaves can easily go soggy after washing, so dry them quickly on kitchen paper.

Balti Chicken Vindaloo

This version of a popular dish from Goa is not as fiery as some, but will still suit those who like their curry to have a definite spicy impact.

Serves 4

1 large potato
150ml/¼ pint/⅔ cup malt vinegar
7.5ml/1½ tsp crushed coriander seeds
5ml/1 tsp crushed cumin seeds
7.5ml/1½ tsp chilli powder
1.5ml/¼ tsp ground turmeric
5ml/1 tsp crushed garlic
5ml/1 tsp grated fresh root ginger
5ml/1 tsp salt
7.5ml/1½ tsp paprika
15ml/1 tbsp tomato purée (paste)
large pinch of ground fenugreek
300ml/½ pint/1¼ cups water
225g/8oz skinned chicken breast fillets, cubed
15ml/1 tbsp oil
2 medium onions, sliced
4 curry leaves
2 fresh green chillies, chopped

1 Peel the potato, cut it into large, irregular shapes, place these in a bowl of water and set aside.

2 In a bowl, mix the vinegar, crushed coriander seeds, cumin, chilli powder, turmeric, garlic, ginger, salt, paprika, tomato purée, fenugreek and water.

3 Pour this spice mixture over the chicken, stir and set aside.

4 Heat the oil in a karahi, wok or heavy pan and quickly fry the onions with the curry leaves for 3–4 minutes without burning.

5 Lower the heat and add the chicken mixture to the pan with the spices. Continue to stir-fry for a further 2 minutes.

6 Drain the potato pieces and add to the pan. Cover with a lid and cook over a medium to low heat for 5–7 minutes or until the sauce has thickened slightly and the chicken and potatoes are cooked through.

7 Stir in the chopped green chillies and serve.

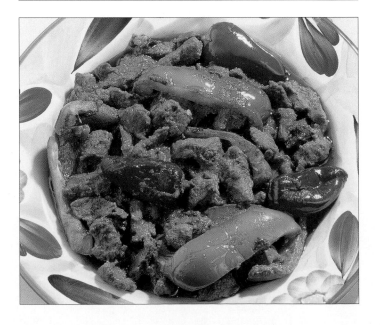

Energy 168kcal/704kJ; Fat 4.2g; Saturated fat 0.6g; Carbohydrate 17.65g; Fibre 2.04g.

Energy 289kcal/1207kJ; Fat 18.7g; Saturated fat 6.9g; Carbohydrate 6.1g; Fibre 0.7g.

Balti Lamb Koftas with Vegetables

These mouthwatering koftas look very attractive served on their bed of vegetables, especially if you make them quite small.

Serves 4
450g/1lb lean minced (ground) lamb
5ml/1 tsp garam masala
5ml/1 tsp ground cumin
5ml/1 tsp ground coriander
5ml/1 tsp crushed garlic
5ml/1 tsp chilli powder
5ml/1 tsp salt
15ml/1 tbsp chopped fresh coriander (cilantro)
1 small onion, finely diced
150ml/¼ pint/⅔ cup corn oil

For the vegetables
45ml/3 tbsp corn oil
1 bunch spring onions (scallions), roughly chopped

½ large red (bell) pepper, seeded and chopped
½ large green (bell) pepper, seeded and chopped
175g/6oz/1 cup corn
225g/8oz/1½ cups canned butter (lima) beans
½ small cauliflower, cut into florets
4 fresh green chillies, chopped

To garnish
5ml/1 tsp chopped fresh mint
15ml/1 tbsp chopped fresh coriander (cilantro)
15ml/1 tbsp shredded fresh root ginger
lime slices
15ml/1 tbsp lemon juice

1 Put the minced lamb into a food processor or blender and process for about 1 minute.

2 Transfer the lamb to a medium bowl. Add the dry spices, garlic, chilli powder, salt, fresh coriander and onion, and use your fingers to blend the kofta mixture thoroughly. Cover and set aside in the refrigerator.

3 Heat the oil for the vegetables in a karahi, wok or deep pan. Add the spring onions and stir-fry for 2 minutes.

4 Add the peppers, corn, butter beans, cauliflower and green chillies, and stir-fry over a high heat for about 2 minutes. Set to one side.

5 Using your hands, roll small pieces of the kofta mixture into round golf-ball size portions. You should have between 12 and 16 koftas.

6 Heat the oil for the koftas in a frying pan. Lower the heat slightly and add the koftas, a few at a time. Shallow-fry each batch, turning the koftas occasionally, until they are evenly browned. Remove from the oil with a slotted spoon, and drain on kitchen paper.

7 Put the vegetable mixture back over a medium heat, and add the cooked koftas. Stir the mixture gently for about 5 minutes, or until everything is heated through.

8 Garnish with the chopped mint and coriander, shredded ginger and lime slices. Just before serving, sprinkle over the lemon juice.

Energy 515kcal/2146kJ; Fat 35g; Saturated fat 9.9g; Carbohydrate 22g; Fibre 5.7g.

Balti Lamb with Potatoes & Fenugreek

The combination of lamb with fresh fenugreek works very well in this dish, which is delicious accompanied by plain boiled rice and Mango Chutney. Use only the fenugreek leaves, as the stalks can be rather bitter. This dish is traditionally served with rice.

Serves 4
450g/1lb lean minced (ground) lamb
5ml/1 tsp grated fresh root ginger
5ml/1 tsp crushed garlic
7.5ml/1½ tsp chilli powder
5ml/1 tsp salt

1.5ml/¼ tsp turmeric
45ml/3 tbsp corn oil
2 medium onions, sliced
2 medium potatoes, peeled, par-boiled and roughly diced
1 bunch fresh fenugreek, chopped
2 tomatoes, chopped
50g/2oz/½ cup frozen peas
30ml/2 tbsp chopped fresh coriander (cilantro)
3 fresh red chillies, seeded and sliced

1 Put the minced lamb, grated ginger, garlic, chilli powder, salt and turmeric into a large bowl, and mix together thoroughly. Set to one side.

2 Heat the oil in a karahi, wok or deep pan. Add the onion slices and fry for about 5 minutes until golden brown.

3 Add the minced lamb and fry over a medium heat for 5–7 minutes, stirring.

4 Stir in the potatoes, chopped fenugreek, tomatoes and peas and cook for a further 5–7 minutes, stirring continuously.

5 Just before serving, stir in the fresh coriander. Spoon into a large dish or on to individual plates and serve hot. Garnish with fresh red chillies.

Energy 386kcal/1610kJ; Fat 23.7g; Saturated fat 8.2g; Carbohydrate 20.3g; Fibre 2.5g.

Balti Mini Lamb Kebabs

In this unusual Balti dish the meat patties are cooked on skewers before being added to the karahi.

Serves 6
450g/1lb lean minced (ground) lamb
1 medium onion, finely chopped
5ml/1 tsp garam masala
5ml/1 tsp crushed garlic
2 medium fresh green chillies, finely chopped
30ml/2 tbsp chopped fresh coriander (cilantro), plus extra to garnish
5ml/1 tsp salt
15ml/1 tbsp plain (all-purpose) flour
60ml/4 tbsp corn oil
12 baby (pearl) onions
4 fresh green chillies, sliced
12 cherry tomatoes

1 Mix the lamb, onion, garam masala, garlic, green chillies, fresh coriander, salt and flour in a medium bowl, using your hands. Transfer the mixture to a food processor and process for about 1 minute, to make the mixture even finer in texture.

2 Put the mixture back into the bowl. Break off small pieces and wrap them around skewers to form small sausage shapes. Put about 2 of these shapes on each skewer.

3 Continue making up the sausage shapes until you have used up all the mixture. Preheat the grill (broiler) to its maximum setting. Baste the meat with 15ml/1 tbsp of the oil and grill (broil) the kebabs for 12–15 minutes, turning and basting occasionally, until the meat is evenly browned.

4 Heat the remaining 45ml/3 tbsp of the oil in a karahi, wok or deep pan. Lower the heat slightly and add the whole baby onions. As soon as they start to darken, add the fresh chillies and tomatoes.

5 Slide the lamb patties from their skewers and add them to the onion and tomato mixture. Stir gently for about 3 minutes to heat them through. Transfer to a serving dish and garnish with fresh coriander.

Energy 252kcal/1047kJ; Fat 17.6g; Saturated fat 5.7g; Carbohydrate 8.5g; Fibre 1.2g.

Balti Lamb with Cauliflower

This tasty curry is given a final tarka, a dressing of oil, cumin seeds and curry leaves, to enhance the flavour.

Serves 4
10ml/2 tsp oil
2 medium onions, sliced
7.5ml/1½ tsp grated fresh root ginger
5ml/1 tsp chilli powder
5ml/1 tsp crushed garlic
1.5ml/¼ tsp ground turmeric
2.5ml/½ tsp ground coriander
30ml/2 tbsp fresh fenugreek leaves
275g/10oz boneless lean spring lamb, cut into strips
1 small cauliflower, cut into small florets
300ml/½ pint/1¼ cups water
30ml/2 tbsp fresh coriander (cilantro) leaves
½ red (bell) pepper, seeded and sliced
15ml/1 tbsp lemon juice

For the tarka
10ml/2 tsp oil
2.5ml/½ tsp cumin seeds
4–6 curry leaves

1 Heat the oil in a karahi, wok or heavy pan and gently fry the onions until they are golden brown. Lower the heat and then add the ginger, chilli powder, garlic, turmeric and ground coriander. Stir well, then add the fenugreek leaves and mix well.

2 Add the lamb strips to the wok and stir-fry until the lamb is completely coated with the spices. Add half the cauliflower florets and stir the mixture well. Pour in the water, cover the wok, lower the heat and cook for 5–7 minutes until the cauliflower and lamb are almost cooked through.

3 Add the remaining cauliflower, half the fresh coriander, the red pepper and lemon juice and stir-fry for about 5 minutes, ensuring the sauce does not catch on the bottom of the pan. Check that the lamb is completely cooked, then remove the pan from the heat and set it aside.

4 To make the tarka, heat the oil and fry the seeds and curry leaves for about 30 seconds. While it is still hot, pour the seasoned oil over the cauliflower and lamb and serve garnished with the remaining fresh coriander leaves.

Energy 202kcal/839kJ; Fat 9.88g; Saturated fat 3.24g; Carbohydrate 10.86g; Fibre 2.88g.

Balti Bhoona Lamb

Bhooning is a very traditional way of stir-frying which simply involves semi-circular movements, scraping the bottom of the pan each time in the centre. Serve this dish of spring lamb with freshly made chapatis.

Serves 4
225–275g/8–10oz boneless lean spring lamb
3 medium onions
15ml/1 tbsp oil
15ml/1 tbsp tomato purée (paste)
5ml/1 tsp crushed garlic

7.5ml/1½ tsp finely grated fresh root ginger, plus 15ml/1 tbsp shredded
5ml/1 tsp salt
1.5ml/¼ tsp ground turmeric
600ml/1 pint/2½ cups water
15ml/1 tbsp lemon juice
15ml/1 tbsp chopped fresh coriander (cilantro)
15ml/1 tbsp chopped fresh mint
1 fresh red chilli, chopped

1 Using a sharp knife, remove any excess fat from the lamb and cut the meat into small cubes.

2 Dice the onions finely. Heat the oil in a karahi, wok or heavy pan and fry the onions until soft.

3 Meanwhile, mix together the tomato purée, garlic and ginger, salt and turmeric. Pour the spice mixture on to the onions in the pan and stir-fry for a few seconds.

4 Add the lamb and continue to stir-fry for about 2–3 minutes. Stir in the water, lower the heat, cover the pan and cook for 15–20 minutes, stirring occasionally.

5 When the water has almost evaporated, start bhooning over a medium heat, making sure that the sauce does not catch on the bottom of the pan. Continue for 5–7 minutes.

6 Pour in the lemon juice, followed by the shredded ginger, chopped fresh coriander, mint and red chilli. Stir to mix, then serve straight from the pan.

Energy 198kcal/825kJ; Fat 10.37g; Saturated fat 3.24g; Carbohydrate 11.05g; Fibre 1.84g.

Balti Lamb with Peas & Potatoes

Fresh mint leaves are used in this dish, but if they are unobtainable, use ready-minted frozen peas to bring an added freshness. Serve with plain rice.

Serves 4
225g/8oz boneless lean spring lamb
120ml/4fl oz/½ cup natural (plain) low-fat yogurt
1 cinnamon stick
2 green cardamom pods
3 black peppercorns
5ml/1 tsp crushed garlic
5ml/1 tsp grated fresh root ginger

5ml/1 tsp chilli powder
5ml/1 tsp garam masala
5ml/1 tsp salt
30ml/2 tbsp roughly chopped fresh mint
15ml/1 tbsp oil
2 medium onions, sliced
300ml/½ pint/1¼ cups water
1 large potato, diced
115g/4oz/1 cup frozen peas
1 firm tomato, peeled, seeded and diced

1 Using a sharp knife, trim any excess fat from the lamb and cut the meat into strips. Place it in a bowl.

2 Add the yogurt, cinnamon, cardamoms, peppercorns, garlic, ginger, chilli powder, garam masala, salt and half the mint. Stir well, cover the bowl and leave in a cool place to marinate for about 2 hours.

3 Heat the oil in a karahi, wok or heavy pan and fry the onions until golden brown. Stir in the lamb and the marinade and stir-fry for about 3 minutes.

4 Pour in the water, lower the heat and cook for about 15 minutes until the meat is cooked right through. Meanwhile, cook the potato in boiling water until just soft, but not mushy.

5 Add the peas and potato to the lamb and stir gently to mix.

6 Finally, add the remaining mint and the tomato and cook for a further 5 minutes before serving.

Energy 231kcal/968kJ; Fat 8.47g; Saturated fat 2.79g; Carbohydrate 22.72g; Fibre 3.73g.

Balti Lamb in Yogurt

The lamb is first marinated in spices then cooked slowly in a hot yogurt sauce. The dish is served with dried apricots which have been lightly sautéed in ghee with cinnamon and cardamom.

Serves 4

15ml/1 tbsp tomato purée (paste)
175ml/6fl oz/¾ cup natural (plain) low-fat yogurt
5ml/1 tsp garam masala
1.5ml/¼ tsp cumin seeds
5ml/1 tsp salt
5ml/1 tsp crushed garlic
5ml/1 tsp grated fresh root ginger
5ml/1 tsp chilli powder
225g/8oz boneless lean spring lamb, cut into strips
15ml/1 tbsp oil
2 medium onions, finely sliced
25g/1oz/2 tbsp ghee or unsalted (sweet) butter
2.5cm/1in cinnamon stick
2 green cardamom pods
5 dried apricots, quartered
15ml/1 tbsp fresh coriander (cilantro) leaves, to garnish

1 In a bowl blend together the tomato purée, yogurt, garam masala, cumin seeds, salt, garlic, ginger and chilli powder. Add the lamb to the sauce and mix well. Cover and leave to marinate in a cool place for about 1 hour.

2 Heat 10ml/2 tsp of the oil in a wok or heavy frying pan and fry the onions over a medium heat until they are crisp and golden brown. Remove the onions using a slotted spoon, allow to cool and then grind down by processing briefly in a food processor or with a pestle and mortar. Reheat the oil remaining in the pan and return the onions to the wok.

3 Add the lamb and stir-fry for about 2 minutes. Cover with a lid, lower the heat and cook, stirring occasionally, for about 15 minutes or until the meat is cooked through. If required, add about 150ml/¼ pint/⅔ cup water during the cooking. Remove from the heat and set aside.

4 Heat the ghee or butter with the remaining 5ml/1 tsp of oil and drop in the cinnamon stick and cardamoms. Add the dried apricots and stir over a low heat for about 2 minutes. Pour this over the lamb. Serve garnished with the fresh coriander leaves.

Energy 221kcal/922kJ; Fat 11.2g; Saturated fat 3.64g; Carbohydrate 14.6g; Fibre 1.8g.

Balti Lamb with Stuffed Vegetables

Aubergines and bright, mixed peppers are stuffed with an aromatic lamb filling and served on a bed of sautéed onions. The presentation is very attractive.

Serves 4–6

3 small aubergines (eggplants)
1 each red, green and yellow (bell) peppers

For the stuffing

45ml/3 tbsp corn oil
3 medium onions, sliced
5ml/1 tsp chilli powder
1.5ml/¼ tsp ground turmeric
5ml/1 tsp ground coriander
5ml/1 tsp ground cumin
5ml/1 tsp grated fresh root ginger
5ml/1 tsp crushed garlic
5ml/1 tsp salt
450g/1lb lean minced (ground) lamb
3 fresh green chillies, chopped
30ml/2 tbsp chopped fresh coriander (cilantro)

For the sautéed onions

45ml/3 tbsp corn oil
5ml/1 tsp mixed onion, mustard, fenugreek and white cumin seeds
4 dried red chillies
3 medium onions, roughly chopped
5ml/1 tsp salt
5ml/1 tsp chilli powder
2 medium tomatoes, sliced
2 fresh green chillies, chopped
30ml/2 tbsp chopped fresh coriander

1 Prepare the vegetables. Slit the aubergines lengthways up to the stalks; keep the stalks intact. Cut the tops off the peppers and remove the seeds.

2 Make the stuffing. Heat the oil in a medium pan. Add the onions and fry for about 3 minutes. Lower the heat and add the chilli powder, turmeric, ground coriander, ground cumin, ginger, garlic and salt, and stir-fry for about 1 minute. Add the lamb to the pan and increase the heat.

3 Stir-fry for 7–10 minutes or until the lamb is cooked, using a wooden spoon to scrape the bottom of the pan. Add the green chillies and fresh coriander towards the end. Remove from the heat, cover and set to one side.

4 Make the sautéed onions. Heat the oil in a karahi, wok or deep pan and add the mixed onion, mustard, fenugreek and white cumin seeds. Stir in the dried red chillies, and fry for about 1 minute. Add the onions and fry for about 2 minutes or until soft.

5 Add the salt, chilli powder, tomatoes, green chillies and fresh coriander. Cook for a further minute. Remove from the heat and set to one side.

6 The minced lamb should by now be cool enough to stuff the prepared aubergines and peppers. Fill the vegetables quite loosely with the meat mixture. As you stuff the vegetables, place them on top of the sautéed onions in the karahi. Cover with foil, making sure the foil doesn't touch the food, and cook over a low heat for about 15 minutes.

7 The dish is ready as soon as the aubergines and peppers are tender. Serve with a dish of plain boiled rice or a colourful pilau rice to complement the colours of the peppers.

Energy 606kcal/2521kJ; Fat 40.8g; Saturated fat 10.6g; Carbohydrate 35g; Fibre 7.4g.

Balti Lamb Chops with Potatoes

These chops are marinated before being cooked in a deliciously spicy sauce.

Serves 6–8
8 lamb chops, about
    50–75g/2–3oz each
30ml/2 tbsp olive oil
150ml/¼ pint/⅔ cup lemon juice
5ml/1 tsp salt
15ml/1 tbsp chopped fresh mint
    and coriander (cilantro)
150ml/¼ pint/⅔ cup corn oil
fresh mint sprigs and lime slices,
    to garnish

For the sauce
45ml/3 tbsp corn oil
8 medium tomatoes, roughly
    chopped
1 bay leaf
5ml/1 tsp garam masala
30ml/2 tbsp natural (plain)
    yogurt
5ml/1 tsp crushed garlic
5ml/1 tsp chilli powder
5ml/1 tsp salt
2.5ml/½ tsp black cumin seeds
3 black peppercorns
2 medium potatoes, peeled,
    roughly chopped and boiled

1 Put the chops into a large bowl. Mix together the olive oil, lemon juice, salt and fresh mint and coriander. Pour the oil mixture over the chops and rub it in well. Cover and leave to marinate for at least 3 hours in the refrigerator.

2 To make the sauce, heat the corn oil in a karahi, wok or deep pan. Lower the heat and add the chopped tomatoes. Stir-fry for about 2 minutes. Add the bay leaf, garam masala, yogurt, garlic, chilli powder, salt, black cumin seeds and black peppercorns, and stir-fry for a further 2–3 minutes. Lower the heat again and add the cooked potatoes, mixing everything together well. Remove from the heat and set to one side.

3 Heat 150ml/¼ pint/⅔ cup corn oil in a separate frying pan. Lower the heat slightly and fry the marinated chops until they are cooked through. This will take about 10–12 minutes. Remove and drain the cooked chops on kitchen paper.

4 Heat the sauce in the karahi, bringing it to the boil. Add the chops and lower the heat. Simmer for 5–7 minutes. Transfer to a warmed serving dish and garnish with the mint sprigs and lime slices.

Energy 327kcal/1367kJ; Fat 18.7g; Saturated fat 6.3g; Carbohydrate 14.8g; Fibre 2g.

Balti Beef

There's no marinating involved with this simple recipe, which can be prepared and cooked in under an hour.

Serves 4
1 red (bell) pepper
1 green (bell) pepper
15ml/1 tbsp oil
5ml/1 tsp cumin seeds
2.5ml/½ tsp fennel seeds
1 onion, cut into thick
    wedges
1 garlic clove, crushed
2.5cm/1in piece fresh root ginger,
    finely chopped
1 fresh red chilli, finely chopped
15ml/1 tbsp curry paste
2.5ml/½ tsp salt
675g/1½lb lean rump (round)
    or fillet steak (beef tenderloin),
    cut into thick strips
naan bread, to serve

1 Cut the red and green peppers into 2.5cm/1in chunks.

2 Heat the oil in a karahi, wok or frying pan and fry the cumin and fennel seeds for 2 minutes or until they begin to splutter. Add the onion, garlic, ginger and chilli and fry for a further 5 minutes.

3 Stir in the curry paste and salt and fry for a further 3–4 minutes.

4 Add the peppers and toss over the heat for about 5 minutes. Stir in the beef strips and continue to fry for 10–12 minutes or until the meat is tender. Serve from the pan, with warm naan bread.

Variations
• This recipe would also work well with chicken breast fillet.
• You could add mangetouts (snow peas), trimmed and left whole, to the dish for added crunch. As they need only the minimum amount of cooking, add them for the last 5 minutes of cooking only.

Energy 278kcal/1166kJ; Fat 11.6g; Saturated fat 3.52g; Carbohydrate 7.7g; Fibre 2.5g.

Aubergine Curry

A simple and delicious way of cooking aubergines which retains their full flavour.

Serves 4
2 large aubergines (eggplants)
115g/4oz/1½ cups button (white) mushrooms
15ml/1 tbsp oil
2.5ml/½ tsp black mustard seeds
1 bunch spring onions (scallions), finely chopped

2 garlic cloves, crushed
1 fresh red chilli, finely chopped
2.5ml/½ tsp chilli powder
5ml/1 tsp ground cumin
5ml/1 tsp ground coriander
1.5ml/¼ tsp ground turmeric
5ml/1 tsp salt
400g/14oz can chopped tomatoes
15ml/1 tbsp chopped fresh coriander (cilantro), plus a sprig to garnish

1 Preheat the oven to 200°C/400°F/Gas 6. Wrap each aubergine in foil and bake for 1 hour or until soft. Unwrap and leave to cool.

2 Cut the button mushrooms in half, or in quarters if large, and set aside.

3 While the aubergines are baking, heat the oil in a heavy pan and fry the mustard seeds for 2 minutes until they begin to splutter.

4 Add the spring onions, mushrooms, garlic and chilli and fry for 5 minutes. Stir in the chilli powder, cumin, ground coriander, turmeric and salt and fry for 3–4 minutes.

5 Add the tomatoes and simmer for 5 minutes.

6 Cut each of the cooked aubergines in half lengthways and scoop out the soft flesh into a mixing bowl. Mash the flesh roughly with a fork.

7 Add the mashed aubergines and chopped fresh coriander to the pan. Bring to the boil and simmer for 5 minutes or until the sauce thickens. Serve garnished with a fresh coriander sprig.

Energy 99kcal/413kJ; Fat 4.6g; Saturated fat 0.45g; Carbohydrate 10.4g; Fibre 6g.

Stuffed Aubergines in Seasoned Tamarind Juice

This spicy aubergine dish will add a refreshing tang to any meal.

Serves 4
12 baby aubergines (eggplants)
30ml/2 tbsp vegetable oil
1 small onion, chopped
10ml/2 tsp grated fresh root ginger
10ml/2 tsp crushed garlic
5ml/1 tsp coriander seeds
5ml/1 tsp cumin seeds

10ml/2 tsp white poppy seeds
10ml/2 tsp sesame seeds
10ml/2 tsp desiccated (dry unsweetened shredded) coconut
15ml/1 tbsp dry-roasted skinned peanuts
2.5–5ml/½–1 tsp chilli powder
5ml/1 tsp salt
6–8 curry leaves
1 or 2 dried red chillies, chopped
2.5ml/½ tsp concentrated tamarind paste

1 Make three deep slits lengthways on each aubergine, without cutting through, then soak in salted water for 20 minutes. Drain and dry on kitchen paper.

2 Heat half the oil in a pan and sauté the onion for 3–4 minutes. Add the ginger and garlic and cook for 30 seconds. Add the coriander and cumin seeds and sauté for 30 seconds, then add the poppy seeds, sesame seeds and coconut. Sauté for 1 minute, stirring constantly. Leave to cool slightly, then grind the spices in a food processor, adding 105ml/7 tbsp warm water. The mixture should form a thick, slightly coarse paste.

3 Mix the peanuts, chilli powder and salt into the paste. Stuff the aubergine slits with the spice and reserve any remaining paste.

4 Heat the remaining oil in a karahi, wok or large pan over a medium heat and add the curry leaves and chillies. Let the chillies blacken, then add the aubergines and the tamarind blended with 105ml/7 tbsp hot water. Add any remaining spice paste and stir to mix. Cover the pan and simmer gently for 15–20 minutes or until the aubergines are tender. Serve with chapatis and a meat or poultry dish, if you like.

Energy 141kcal/585kJ; Fat 12g; Saturated fat 1.7g; Carbohydrate 5.1g; Fibre 3.3g.

Aubergine & Sweet Potato Stew with Coconut Milk

Aubergines and sweet potatoes go well together and the coconut milk adds a mellow note.

Serves 6
400g/14oz baby aubergines (eggplants) or 2 standard aubergines
60ml/4 tbsp groundnut (peanut) oil
225g/8oz Thai red shallots or other small shallots or pickling onions
5ml/1 tsp fennel seeds, lightly crushed
4 or 5 garlic cloves, thinly sliced
25ml/1½ tbsp finely chopped fresh root ginger
475ml/16fl oz/2 cups vegetable stock
2 lemon grass stalks, outer layers discarded, finely chopped or minced (ground)
15g/½oz fresh coriander (cilantro), stalks and leaves chopped separately
3 kaffir lime leaves, lightly bruised
2 or 3 small fresh red chillies
45–60ml/3–4 tbsp Thai green curry paste
675g/1½lb sweet potatoes, peeled and cut into thick chunks
400ml/14fl oz/1⅔ cups coconut milk
2.5–5ml/½–1 tsp palm sugar or light muscovado (brown) sugar
250g/9oz/3½ cups mushrooms, thickly sliced
juice of 1 lime, to taste
salt and ground black pepper
boiled rice and 18 fresh Thai basil or ordinary basil leaves, to serve

1 Trim the aubergines. Slice baby aubergines in half lengthways. Cut standard aubergines into chunks.

2 Heat half the oil in a wide pan or deep, lidded frying pan. Add the aubergines and cook uncovered over medium heat, stirring occasionally, until lightly browned on all sides. Remove from the pan and set aside.

3 Slice 4 or 5 of the shallots. Cook the whole shallots in the oil remaining in the pan, adding a little more oil if necessary, until lightly browned. Set aside with the aubergines. Add the remaining oil to the pan and cook the sliced shallots, fennel seeds, garlic and ginger over a low heat for 5 minutes.

4 Pour in the vegetable stock, then add the lemon grass, chopped coriander stalks and any roots, lime leaves and whole chillies. Cover and simmer over a low heat for 5 minutes.

5 Stir in 30ml/2 tbsp of the curry paste and the sweet potatoes. Simmer gently for about 10 minutes, then return the aubergines and browned shallots to the pan and cook for a further 5 minutes.

6 Stir in the coconut milk and the sugar. Season to taste with salt and pepper, then stir in the mushrooms and simmer gently for 5 minutes, or until all the vegetables are cooked and tender. Stir in more curry paste and lime juice to taste, followed by the chopped coriander leaves. Adjust the seasoning, if necessary, and ladle the vegetables into warmed bowls. Sprinkle basil leaves over the stew and serve with rice.

Energy 225kcal/945kJ; Fat 10.3g; Saturated fat 1.4g; Carbohydrate 31.8g; Fibre 5.1g.

Aubergine & Pepper Tempura with Sweet Chilli Dip

These crunchy vegetables in a beautifully light batter are quick and easy to make and taste very good with the piquant dip.

Serves 4
2 aubergines (eggplants)
2 red (bell) peppers
vegetable oil, for deep-frying

For the tempura batter
250g/9oz/2¼ cups plain (all-purpose) flour
2 egg yolks
500ml/17fl oz/2¼ cups iced water
5ml/1 tsp salt

For the dip
150ml/¼ pint/⅔ cup water
10ml/2 tsp granulated sugar
1 fresh red chilli, seeded and finely chopped
1 garlic clove, crushed
juice of ½ lime
5ml/1 tsp rice vinegar
35ml/2½ tbsp Thai fish sauce
½ small carrot, finely grated

1 Slice the aubergines into thin batons. Halve and seed the peppers and slice them thinly. Mix together all the dip ingredients in a bowl and stir until the sugar has dissolved. Cover with clear film (plastic wrap) and set aside.

2 Set aside 30ml/2 tbsp of the flour for the tempura. Put the egg yolks in a bowl and beat in the iced water. Add the rest of the flour with the salt and stir briefly together – the mixture should be lumpy and not properly mixed. If it is too thick, add a little more iced water. Use the batter immediately. Heat the oil in a karahi, wok or deep-fryer to a temperature of 190°C/375°F, or until a cube of bread dropped in the oil browns in about 45 seconds.

3 Dust a few aubergine batons and pepper slices with the reserved flour, then dip into the batter and drop into the hot oil, taking care as the oil will froth up. Make two or three more fritters. Cook for 3–4 minutes, until golden and crisp all over, then lift out with a slotted spoon. Drain on kitchen paper. Repeat with the remaining vegetables. Serve with the dip.

Energy 410kcal/1722kJ; Fat 18.1g; Saturated fat 2.7g; Carbohydrate 56.4g; Fibre 5.4g.

Cauliflower & Coconut Milk Curry

A delicious vegetable stew which combines rich coconut milk with spices and is perfect as a vegetarian main course or as part of a buffet.

Serves 4

1 cauliflower
2 medium tomatoes
1 onion, chopped
2 garlic cloves, crushed

1 fresh green chilli, seeded
2.5ml/½ tsp ground turmeric
30ml/2 tbsp sunflower oil
400ml/14fl oz/1⅔ cups coconut milk
250ml/8fl oz/1 cup water
5ml/1 tsp granulated sugar
5ml/1 tsp tamarind pulp, soaked in 45ml/3 tbsp warm water
salt

1 Trim the stalk from the cauliflower and divide into tiny florets. Peel the tomatoes if you like, then chop them into 1–2.5cm/½–1in pieces.

2 Grind the chopped onion, garlic, green chilli and ground turmeric to a paste in a food processor.

3 Heat the oil in a karahi, wok or large frying pan and fry the spice paste to bring out the aromatic flavours, without allowing it to brown.

4 Add the cauliflower florets and toss well to coat in the spices. Stir in the coconut milk, water, sugar and salt to taste. Simmer for 5 minutes. Strain the tamarind and reserve the juice.

5 Add the tamarind juice and chopped tomatoes to the pan then cook for 2–3 minutes only. Taste and adjust the seasoning if necessary, then serve.

> **Cook's Tip**
> *Always be careful when preparing chillies as they can burn sensitive skin. Wear plastic gloves or wash hands thoroughly after preparation.*

Energy 119kcal/495kJ; Fat 6.7g; Saturated fat 1.1g; Carbohydrate 11.5g; Fibre 2.3g.

Parsnip, Aubergine & Cashew Biryani

Full of the flavours of India, this hearty supper dish is great for chilly winter evenings.

Serves 4–6

1 small aubergine (eggplant), sliced
275g/10oz basmati rice
3 parsnips
3 onions
2 garlic cloves
2.5cm/1in piece fresh root ginger, peeled
about 60ml/4 tbsp vegetable oil
175g/6oz/1½ cups unsalted cashew nuts

40g/1½oz/3 tbsp sultanas (golden raisins)
1 red (bell) pepper, seeded and sliced
5ml/1 tsp ground cumin
5ml/1 tsp ground coriander
2.5ml/½ tsp chilli powder
120ml/4fl oz/½ cup natural (plain) yogurt
300ml/½ pint/1¼ cups vegetable stock
25g/1oz/2 tbsp butter
salt and ground black pepper
2 hard-boiled eggs, quartered, and sprigs of fresh coriander (cilantro), to garnish

1 Sprinkle the aubergine with salt and leave for 30 minutes. Rinse, pat dry and cut into bite-size pieces. Soak the rice in a bowl of cold water for 40 minutes. Peel and core the parsnips. Cut into 1cm/½in pieces. Process 1 onion, the garlic and ginger in a food processor. Add 30–45ml/2–3 tbsp water and process to a paste.

2 Finely slice the remaining onions. Heat 45ml/3 tbsp of the oil in a large flameproof casserole and fry the onions gently for 10–15 minutes until they are soft and deep golden brown. Remove and drain. Add 40g/1½oz of the cashew nuts to the pan and stir-fry for 2 minutes, checking that they do not burn. Add the sultanas and fry until they swell. Remove and drain on kitchen paper. Add the aubergine and pepper to the pan and stir-fry for 4–5 minutes. Drain on kitchen paper. Fry the parsnips for 4–5 minutes. Stir in the remaining cashew nuts and fry for 1 minute. Set aside.

3 Add the remaining 15ml/1 tbsp of oil to the pan. Add the onion paste. Cook, stirring, over moderate heat for 4–5 minutes, until the mixture turns golden. Stir in the cumin, coriander and chilli powder. Cook, stirring, for 1 minute, then reduce the heat and add the yogurt.

4 Bring the mixture slowly to the boil and stir in the stock, parsnips, aubergine and peppers. Season with salt and pepper, cover and simmer for 30–40 minutes, until the parsnips are tender, and then transfer to an ovenproof casserole.

5 Preheat the oven to 150°C/300°F/Gas 2. Drain the rice and add to 300ml/½ pint/1¼ cups salted boiling water. Cook gently for 5–6 minutes, until the rice is tender but slightly undercooked.

6 Drain the rice and pile it in a mound on top of the parsnips. Make a hole from the top to the base using the handle of a wooden spoon. Sprinkle the reserved fried onions, cashew nuts and sultanas over the rice and dot with butter. Cover with a double layer of foil, then secure in place with a lid. Cook in the oven for 35–40 minutes. Serve garnished with eggs and coriander.

Energy 824kcal/3430kJ; Fat 40.7g; Saturated fat 9.4g; Carbohydrate 96.4g; Fibre 9.1g.

Mushroom Curry

This is a delicious way of cooking mushrooms. It goes well with meat dishes, but is also great served on its own.

Serves 4
30ml/2 tbsp oil
2.5ml/½ tsp cumin seeds
1.5ml/¼ tsp black peppercorns
4 green cardamom pods
1.5ml/¼ tsp ground turmeric
1 onion, finely chopped
5ml/1 tsp ground cumin
5ml/1 tsp ground coriander
2.5ml/½ tsp garam masala
1 fresh green chilli, finely chopped
2 garlic cloves, crushed
2.5cm/1in piece fresh root ginger, grated
400g/14oz can chopped tomatoes
1.5ml/¼ tsp salt
450g/1lb/6 cups button (white) mushrooms, halved
chopped fresh coriander (cilantro), to garnish

1 Heat the oil in a large, heavy pan and fry the cumin seeds, peppercorns, cardamom pods and turmeric for 2–3 minutes.

2 Add the onion and fry for about 5 minutes until golden. Stir in the cumin, ground coriander and garam masala and fry for a further 2 minutes.

3 Add the chilli, garlic and ginger and fry for 2–3 minutes, stirring all the time to prevent the spices from sticking to the pan. Add the tomatoes and salt. Bring to the boil and simmer for 5 minutes.

4 Add the mushrooms. Cover and simmer over a low heat for 10 minutes. Garnish with chopped coriander before serving.

Cook's Tip
The distinctive flavour of mushrooms goes well with this mixture of spices. If you don't want to use button (white) mushrooms, you can substitute any other mushrooms. Dried mushrooms can be added, if you like. Their intense flavour holds its own against the taste of the curry spices. Soak dried mushrooms before using, and add them to the recipe with the tomatoes.

Energy 113kcal/469kJ; Fat 6.9g; Saturated fat 0.88g; Carbohydrate 8.8g; Fibre 2.5g.

Mushrooms with Garlic & Chilli Sauce

When you are planning a barbecue for friends and family, it can be tricky finding something really special for the vegetarians in the party. These tasty mushroom kebabs are ideal because they look, smell and taste absolutely wonderful.

Serves 4
12 large field (portabello), chestnut or oyster mushrooms or a mixture, cut in half
4 garlic cloves, coarsely chopped
6 coriander (cilantro) roots, coarsely chopped
15ml/1 tbsp granulated sugar
30ml/2 tbsp light soy sauce
ground black pepper

For the dipping sauce
15ml/1 tbsp granulated sugar
90ml/6 tbsp rice vinegar
5ml/1 tsp salt
1 garlic clove, crushed
1 small fresh red chilli, seeded and finely chopped

1 If using wooden skewers, soak them in cold water for at least 30 minutes to prevent them burning over the barbecue or under the grill (broiler). You will need eight skewers.

2 Make the dipping sauce by heating the sugar, rice vinegar and salt in a small pan, stirring occasionally until the sugar and salt have dissolved. Add the garlic and chilli, pour into a serving dish and keep warm.

3 Thread three mushroom halves on to each skewer. Lay the filled skewers side by side in a shallow dish.

4 In a mortar or spice grinder pound or blend the garlic and coriander roots. Scrape into a bowl and mix with the sugar, soy sauce and a little pepper.

5 Brush the soy sauce mixture over the mushrooms and leave to marinate for 15 minutes. Prepare the barbecue or preheat the grill (broiler) and cook the mushrooms for 2–3 minutes on each side. Serve with the dipping sauce.

Energy 55kcal/231kJ; Fat 1.3g; Saturated fat 0.3g; Carbohydrate 6.2g; Fibre 3.1g.

Mushroom & Okra Curry

The sliced okra not only flavours this unusual curry, but thickens it, too.

Serves 4
4 garlic cloves, roughly chopped
2.5cm/1in piece fresh root ginger, roughly chopped
1 or 2 fresh red chillies, seeded and chopped
175ml/6fl oz/3/4 cup cold water
15ml/1 tbsp sunflower oil
5ml/1 tsp coriander seeds
5ml/1 tsp cumin seeds
5ml/1 tsp ground cumin
seeds from 2 green cardamom pods, ground
pinch of ground turmeric
400g/14oz can chopped tomatoes
450g/1lb/6 cups mushrooms, quartered if large
225g/8oz okra, trimmed and sliced
30ml/2 tbsp chopped fresh coriander (cilantro)
basmati rice, to serve

For the mango relish
1 large ripe mango, about 500g/11/4lb
1 small garlic clove, crushed
1 small onion, finely chopped
10ml/2 tsp grated fresh root ginger
1 fresh red chilli, seeded and finely chopped
a pinch each of salt and sugar

1 To make the mango relish, peel the mango, cut the flesh off the stone and chop it finely. Put it in a bowl. Mash with a fork and mix in the garlic, onion, ginger, chilli, salt and sugar. Set aside.

2 Put the garlic, ginger, chillies and 45ml/3 tbsp of the water in a blender or food processor and blend to a smooth paste.

3 Heat the oil in a large pan. Add the coriander and cumin seeds, and the ground cumin, ground cardamom and turmeric, and cook for 1 minute, until aromatic. Scrape in the garlic paste, then add the tomatoes, mushrooms and okra. Pour in the remaining water. Stir to mix well, and bring to the boil. Reduce the heat, cover and simmer the curry for 5 minutes.

4 Remove the lid, increase the heat slightly and cook for 5–10 minutes more, until the okra is tender. Stir in the fresh coriander and serve with the rice and the mango relish.

Mushrooms, Peas & Paneer

Paneer is a traditional cheese made from rich milk and is most popular with northern Indians. Rajasthani farmers eat this dish for lunch with thick parathas as they work in the fields.

Serves 4–6
75ml/6 tbsp ghee or vegetable oil
225g/8oz paneer, cubed
1 onion, finely chopped
a few fresh mint leaves, chopped
50g/2oz/2 cups fresh coriander (cilantro), chopped
3 fresh green chillies, chopped
3 garlic cloves, roughly chopped
2.5cm/1in piece fresh root ginger, sliced
5ml/1 tsp ground turmeric
5ml/1 tsp chilli powder (optional)
5ml/1 tsp garam masala
salt
225g/8oz/3 cups tiny button (white) mushrooms
225g/8oz/2 cups frozen peas, thawed and drained
175ml/6fl oz/3/4 cup natural (plain) yogurt, mixed with 5ml/1 tsp cornflour (cornstarch)
fresh mint sprig, to garnish

1 Heat the ghee or vegetable oil in a frying pan and fry the paneer cubes until they are golden brown on all sides. Remove and drain on kitchen paper.

2 Grind the onion, mint, coriander, chillies, garlic and ginger in a pestle and mortar or food processor to a fairly smooth paste. Remove and mix in the turmeric, chilli powder if using, garam masala and salt.

3 Remove the excess ghee or oil from the pan, leaving about 15ml/1 tbsp. Heat and fry the paste until the raw onion smell disappears and the oil separates.

4 Add the mushrooms, peas and paneer. Mix together well. Cool the mixture and gradually fold in the yogurt. Simmer for about 10 minutes. Garnish with a sprig of mint and serve hot.

Energy 152kcal/645kJ; Fat 4.4g; Saturated fat 0.7g; Carbohydrate 24.2g; Fibre 8g.

Energy 294kcal/1217kJ; Fat 20.3g; Saturated fat 3.7g; Carbohydrate 14g; Fibre 3.5g.

Okra with Green Mango & Lentils

If you like okra, you'll love this spicy tangy dish. Serve with rice for a main course.

Serves 4
115g/4oz/½ cup toor dhal or
   yellow split peas
450g/1lb okra
15ml/1 tbsp oil
2.5ml/½ tsp onion seeds
2 onions, sliced
2.5ml/½ tsp ground fenugreek
1.5ml/¼ tsp ground turmeric
5ml/1 tsp ground coriander
7.5ml/1½ tsp chilli powder
5ml/1 tsp grated fresh
   root ginger
5ml/1 tsp crushed garlic
1 green mango, peeled and sliced
7.5ml/1½ tsp salt
2 red chillies, seeded and sliced
30ml/2 tbsp chopped fresh
   coriander (cilantro)
1 tomato, sliced

1 Wash the toor dhal thoroughly to remove any grit and place in a large pan with enough cold water to cover. Bring to the boil and cook for 30–45 minutes until soft but not mushy.

2 Trim the okra and cut the pods into 1cm/½in pieces.

3 Heat the oil in a karahi, wok or heavy pan and fry the onion seeds until they begin to pop. Add the onions and fry until golden brown. Lower the heat and stir in the ground fenugreek, turmeric and coriander, and the chilli powder, ginger and garlic.

4 Add the mango slices and the okra pieces. Stir well and then add the salt, red chillies and fresh coriander. Stir-fry together for 3–4 minutes or until the okra is well cooked and tender.

5 Finally, add the cooked dhal and sliced tomato, and cook for a further 3 minutes. Serve hot.

> **Cook's Tip**
> *When buying okra, always choose small, bright-green ones with no brown patches. If cooking whole, trim off the conical cap, taking care not to pierce through to the seed pod where there are tiny edible seeds and a sticky juice.*

Energy 229kcal/963kJ; Fat 5g; Saturated fat 0.55g; Carbohydrate 36g; Fibre 8.1g.

Corn & Pea Curry

Tender corn cooked in a spicy tomato sauce makes a flavoursome curry. It is perfect served with chapatis.

Serves 4
6 frozen corn cobs, thawed
15ml/1 tbsp oil
2.5ml/½ tsp cumin seeds
1 onion, finely chopped
2 garlic cloves, crushed
1 fresh green chilli, finely chopped
15ml/1 tbsp curry paste
5ml/1 tsp ground coriander
5ml/1 tsp ground cumin
1.5ml/¼ tsp ground turmeric
2.5ml/½ tsp salt
2.5ml/½ tsp granulated
   sugar
400g/14oz can chopped
   tomatoes
15ml/1 tbsp tomato purée
   (paste)
150ml/¼ pint/⅔ cup
   water
115g/4oz/1 cup frozen peas,
   thawed
30ml/2 tbsp chopped fresh
   coriander (cilantro)
chapatis, to serve (optional)

1 Using a sharp knife, cut each piece of corn in half crossways to make 12 equal pieces in total.

2 Bring a large pan of water to the boil and cook the corn cob pieces for 10–12 minutes. Drain well.

3 Heat the oil in a large, heavy pan and fry the cumin seeds for 2 minutes or until they begin to splutter. Add the onion, garlic and chilli and fry for about 5–6 minutes until the onion is golden.

4 Add the curry paste and fry for 2 minutes. Stir in the remaining spices, the salt and sugar, and fry for a further 2–3 minutes, adding some water if the mixture is too dry.

5 Add the chopped tomatoes and tomato purée together with the water and simmer for 5 minutes or until the sauce thickens. Add the peas and cook for a further 5 minutes.

6 Stir in the pieces of corn and the fresh coriander and cook for 6–8 minutes more, until the corn and peas are tender. Serve with chapatis for mopping up the rich sauce, if you like.

Energy 159kcal/669kJ; Fat 5.2g; Saturated fat 0.48g; Carbohydrate 23g; Fibre 4.6g.

Corn & Cashew Nut Curry

A substantial curry, this combines all the essential flavours of southern Thailand. It is deliciously aromatic, but the flavour is fairly mild.

Serves 4

2 kaffir lime leaves
30ml/2 tbsp vegetable oil
4 shallots, chopped
90g/3¹/₂oz/scant 1 cup cashew nuts
5ml/1 tsp Thai red curry paste
400g/14oz potatoes, peeled and cut into chunks
1 lemon grass stalk, finely chopped
200g/7oz can chopped tomatoes
600ml/1 pint/2¹/₂ cups boiling water
200g/7oz/generous 1 cup drained canned whole kernel corn
4 celery sticks, sliced
15ml/1 tbsp tomato ketchup
15ml/1 tbsp light soy sauce
5ml/1 tsp palm sugar or light muscovado (brown) sugar
5ml/1 tsp Thai fish sauce
4 spring onions (scallions), thinly sliced
a small bunch of fresh basil, chopped

1 Remove the central rib from the kaffir lime leaves. Roll the leaves into tight cylinders and, using a sharp knife, slice through the cylinders to give thin strips.

2 Heat the oil in a large, heavy pan or wok. Add the shallots and stir-fry over a medium heat for 2–3 minutes, until softened. Add the cashew nuts and stir-fry for a few minutes until golden.

3 Stir in the red curry paste. Stir-fry for 1 minute, then add the potatoes, lemon grass, tomatoes and boiling water.

4 Bring back to the boil, then reduce the heat to low, cover and simmer gently for 15–20 minutes, or until the potatoes are tender.

5 Stir the corn, celery, lime leaves, tomato ketchup, soy sauce, sugar and fish sauce into the pan or wok. Simmer for a further 5 minutes, until heated through, then spoon into warmed serving bowls. Sprinkle with the sliced spring onions and chopped basil, and serve.

Energy 343kcal/1436kJ; Fat 18.1g; Saturated fat 3.2g; Carbohydrate 38.8g; Fibre 3.5g.

Sweet Pumpkin & Peanut Curry

A hearty, soothing curry that is perfect for autumn or winter evenings. Its cheerful colour alone will brighten you up – and it tastes terrific.

Serves 4

30ml/2 tbsp vegetable oil
4 garlic cloves, crushed
4 shallots, finely chopped
30ml/2 tbsp yellow curry paste
600ml/1 pint/2¹/₂ cups vegetable stock
2 kaffir lime leaves, torn
15ml/1 tbsp chopped fresh galangal
450g/1lb pumpkin, peeled, seeded and diced
225g/8oz sweet potatoes, diced
90g/3¹/₂oz/scant 1 cup peanuts, roasted and chopped
300ml/¹/₂ pint/1¹/₄ cups coconut milk
90g/3¹/₂oz/1¹/₂ cups chestnut mushrooms, sliced
15ml/1 tbsp soy sauce
30ml/2 tbsp Thai fish sauce
50g/2oz/¹/₃ cup pumpkin seeds, toasted, and fresh green chilli flowers, to garnish

1 Heat the oil in a large pan. Add the garlic and shallots and cook over a medium heat, stirring occasionally, for 10 minutes, until softened and golden. Do not let them burn.

2 Add the yellow curry paste and stir-fry over a medium heat for 30 seconds, until fragrant, then add the stock, lime leaves, galangal, pumpkin and sweet potatoes. Bring to the boil, stirring frequently, then reduce the heat to low and simmer gently for 15 minutes.

3 Add the peanuts, coconut milk and mushrooms. Stir in the soy sauce and fish sauce and simmer for 5 minutes more. Spoon into warmed individual serving bowls, garnish with the pumpkin seeds and chillies and serve.

> **Cook's Tip**
> The well-drained vegetables from any of these curries would make a very tasty filling for a pastry or pie. This may not be an Eastern tradition, but it is a good example of fusion food.

Energy 143kcal/603kJ; Fat 6.3g; Saturated fat 1g; Carbohydrate 20.6g; Fibre 3.2g.

Curried Stuffed Peppers

Hot, spicy and delicious, these fabulous peppers are often prepared for weddings in Hyderabad.

Serves 4–6
15ml/1 tbsp sesame seeds
15ml/1 tbsp white poppy seeds
5ml/1 tsp coriander seeds
60ml/4 tbsp desiccated (dry unsweetened shredded) coconut
1/2 onion, sliced
2.5cm/1 in piece fresh root ginger, sliced
4 garlic cloves, sliced
handful of fresh coriander (cilantro)
6 fresh green chillies
60ml/4 tbsp vegetable oil
2 potatoes, boiled and coarsely mashed
salt
2 each green, red and yellow (bell) peppers
30ml/2 tbsp sesame oil
5ml/1 tsp cumin seeds
60ml/4 tbsp tamarind juice

1 In a frying pan, dry-fry the sesame, poppy and coriander seeds, then add the coconut and continue to roast until the coconut turns golden brown. Add the onion, ginger, garlic, coriander, and 2 of the chillies, and roast for a further 5 minutes. Cool, and grind to a paste using a pestle and mortar or food processor. Set aside.

2 Heat 30ml/2 tbsp of the oil in a frying pan and fry the ground paste for 4–5 minutes. Add the potatoes and salt, and stir well until the spices have blended evenly into the potatoes.

3 Trim the bases of the peppers so that they stand, then slice off the tops and reserve. Remove the seeds and any white pith. Fill the peppers with equal amounts of the potato mixture and replace the tops.

4 Slit the remaining chillies and remove the seeds, if you like. Heat the sesame oil and remaining vegetable oil in a frying pan and fry the cumin seeds and the slit green chillies. When the chillies turn white, add the tamarind juice and bring to the boil. Place the peppers over the mixture, cover the pan and cook until the peppers are just tender. Serve immediately.

Energy 390kcal/1617kJ; Fat 27.3g; Saturated fat 10.4g; Carbohydrate 31.1g; Fibre 7.8g.

Stuffed Sweet Peppers

This is an unusual recipe where the stuffed peppers are steamed rather than baked, but the result is beautifully light and tender. The filling incorporates typical Thai ingredients such as red curry paste and fish sauce. Kaffir lime leaves also add a delicate citrus flavour.

Serves 4
3 garlic cloves
2 coriander (cilantro) roots
400g/14oz/3 cups mushrooms, quartered
5ml/1 tsp Thai red curry paste
1 egg, lightly beaten
15ml/1 tbsp Thai fish sauce
15ml/1 tbsp light soy sauce
2.5ml/1/2 tsp granulated sugar
3 kaffir lime leaves, finely chopped
4 yellow (bell) peppers, halved lengthways and seeded

1 Finely chop the garlic cloves and coriander roots. In a mortar or spice grinder pound or blend the garlic with the coriander roots. Scrape into a bowl.

2 Put the mushrooms in a food processor and pulse briefly until they are finely chopped.

3 Add to the garlic mixture, then stir in the Thai red curry paste, beaten egg and Thai fish sauce. Add the soy sauce, sugar and lime leaves.

4 Place the pepper halves in a single layer in a steamer basket. Spoon the mixture loosely into the pepper halves. Do not pack the mixture down tightly or the filling will dry out too much.

5 Bring the water in the steamer to the boil, then lower the heat to a simmer. Steam the peppers for 15 minutes, or until the flesh is tender. Serve hot.

Variations
Use red or orange (bell) peppers rather than yellow, if you prefer, or a combination of the two.

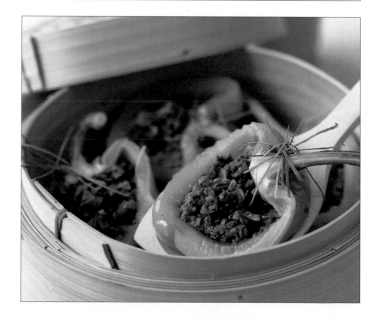

Energy 102kcal/425kJ; Fat 3.4g; Saturated fat 0.8g; Carbohydrate 12.8g; Fibre 4.2g.

Spinach & Potato Curry

Spinach, potatoes and traditional Indian spices are the main ingredients in this simple but authentic curry.

Serves 4

450g/1lb spinach
15ml/1 tbsp oil
5ml/1 tsp black mustard seeds
1 onion, thinly sliced
2 garlic cloves, crushed
2.5cm/1in piece fresh root ginger, finely chopped
675g/1½lb potatoes, cut into 2.5cm/1in chunks
5ml/1 tsp chilli powder
5ml/1 tsp salt
120ml/4fl oz/½ cup water

1 Wash and trim the spinach, then blanch it in a pan of boiling water for about 3–4 minutes.

2 Drain the spinach thoroughly and set aside. When it is cool enough to handle, use your hands to squeeze out any remaining liquid (see Cook's Tip) and set aside.

3 Heat the oil in a large, heavy pan and fry the mustard seeds for 2 minutes or until they splutter.

4 Add the sliced onion, garlic cloves and chopped ginger to the mustard seeds and fry for 5 minutes, stirring.

5 Add the potato chunks, chilli powder, salt and water, and cook for a further 8 minutes.

6 Add the drained spinach. Cover the pan with a lid and simmer for 10–15 minutes or until the potatoes are tender. Serve hot.

> **Cook's Tips**
> • To make certain that the spinach is completely dry, put it in a clean dish towel, roll up tightly and squeeze gently to remove any excess liquid.
> • Use a waxy variety of potato for this dish so that the pieces do not break up during cooking.

Spicy Potato & Tomato Curry

Diced potatoes are cooked gently in a fresh tomato sauce, which is flavoured with curry leaves, green chillies and ginger.

Serves 4

2 medium potatoes
15ml/1 tbsp oil
2 medium onions, finely chopped
4 curry leaves
1.5ml/¼ tsp onion seeds
1 fresh green chilli, seeded and chopped
4 tomatoes, sliced
5ml/1 tsp grated fresh root ginger
5ml/1 tsp crushed garlic
5ml/1 tsp chilli powder
5ml/1 tsp ground coriander
1.5ml/¼ tsp salt
5ml/1 tsp lemon juice
15ml/1 tbsp chopped fresh coriander (cilantro)
3 hard-boiled eggs, to garnish

1 Peel the potatoes and cut them into small cubes.

2 Heat the oil in a karahi, wok or heavy pan and stir-fry the onions, curry leaves, onion seeds and green chilli for about 40 seconds.

3 Add the tomatoes and cook for about 2 minutes over a low heat.

4 Add the ginger and garlic, chilli powder, ground coriander and salt to taste. Continue to stir-fry for 1–2 minutes, then add the potatoes and cook over a low heat for 5–7 minutes until the potatoes are tender.

5 Add the lemon juice and fresh coriander and stir to mix together.

6 Shell the hard-boiled eggs, cut into quarters, and add as a garnish to the finished dish.

> **Cook's Tip**
> Use vine-ripened tomatoes, if possible, for the best flavour. Locally grown tomatoes in season are also more likely to have a full flavour than those bought out of season.

Energy 203kcal/851kJ; Fat 4.6g; Saturated fat 0.65g; Carbohydrate 34.4g; Fibre 5.1g.

Energy 188kcal/790kJ; Fat 7.62g; Saturated fat 1.66g; Carbohydrate 23.41g; Fibre 3.1g.

Courgette Curry with Tomatoes

Thickly sliced courgettes are combined with authentic Indian spices for a tasty vegetable curry.

Serves 4
675g/1½lb courgettes (zucchini)
30ml/2 tbsp oil
2.5ml/½ tsp cumin seeds
2.5ml/½ tsp mustard seeds
1 onion, thinly sliced
2 garlic cloves, crushed
1.5ml/¼ tsp ground turmeric
1.5ml/¼ tsp chilli powder
5ml/1 tsp ground coriander
5ml/1 tsp ground cumin
2.5ml/½ tsp salt
15ml/1 tbsp tomato purée (paste)
400g/14oz can chopped tomatoes
150ml/¼ pint/⅔ cup water
15ml/1 tbsp chopped fresh coriander (cilantro)
5ml/1 tsp garam masala
rice or naan bread, to serve

1 Trim the ends from the courgettes and then cut them evenly into 1cm/½in thick slices.

2 Heat the oil in a large, heavy pan and fry the cumin and the mustard seeds for 2 minutes until they begin to splutter.

3 Add the sliced onion and crushed garlic to the seeds in the pan, and fry for about 5–6 minutes.

4 Add the turmeric, chilli powder, ground coriander, cumin and salt, and fry for 2–3 minutes.

5 Add the sliced courgettes all at once, and cook for 5 minutes, stirring so that they do not burn.

6 Mix together the tomato purée and chopped tomatoes and add to the pan with the water. Cover and simmer for 10 minutes until the sauce thickens.

7 Stir in the fresh coriander and garam masala, then cook for 5 minutes or until the courgettes are tender. Serve the curry with rice or naan bread.

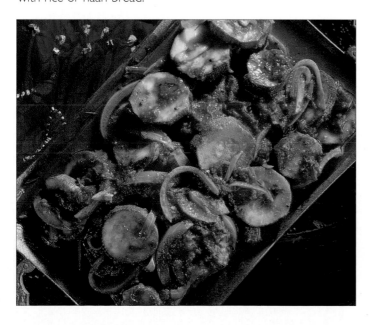

Energy 133kcal/550kJ; Fat 7.2g; Saturated fat 0.91g; Carbohydrate 11.6g; Fibre 2.8g.

Potatoes Stuffed with Cottage Cheese

This makes an excellent low-fat snack at any time of the day.

Serves 4
4 medium baking potatoes
225g/8oz/1 cup low-fat cottage cheese
10ml/2 tsp tomato purée (paste)
2.5ml/½ tsp ground cumin
2.5ml/½ tsp ground coriander
2.5ml/½ tsp chilli powder
2.5ml/½ tsp salt
15ml/1 tbsp oil
2.5ml/½ tsp mixed onion and mustard seeds
3 curry leaves
30ml/2 tbsp water

For the garnish
mixed salad leaves
fresh coriander (cilantro) sprigs
lemon wedges
2 tomatoes, quartered

1 Preheat the oven to 180°C/350°F/Gas 4. Wash each potato and pat dry. Make a slit in the middle of each potato. Prick the potatoes a few times with a fork or skewer, then wrap them individually in foil. Bake in the oven directly on the shelf for about 1 hour, or until soft. Put the cottage cheese into a heatproof dish and set aside.

2 In a separate bowl, mix the tomato purée, ground cumin, ground coriander, chilli powder and salt.

3 Heat the oil in a small pan for about 1 minute. Add the mixed onion and mustard seeds and the curry leaves. When the curry leaves turn a shade darker, pour the tomato purée mixture into the pan and turn the heat immediately to low. Add the water and mix well. Cook for a further minute, then pour the spicy tomato mixture on to the cottage cheese and stir together well.

4 Check that the baked potatoes are cooked right through, by inserting a knife or skewer into the middle of the flesh. If it is soft, unwrap the potatoes from the foil and divide the cottage cheese equally between them.

5 Garnish the filled potatoes with mixed salad leaves, coriander sprigs, lemon wedges and tomato quarters and serve hot.

Energy 175kcal/740kJ; Fat 4.3g; Saturated fat 0.43g; Carbohydrate 24.4g; Fibre 1.9g.

Spicy Root Vegetable Gratin

Subtly spiced, this rich gratin is substantial enough to serve on its own for lunch or supper.

Serves 4
2 large potatoes, total weight about 450g/1lb
2 sweet potatoes, total weight about 275g/10oz
175g/6oz celeriac
15ml/1 tbsp unsalted (sweet) butter
5ml/1 tsp curry powder
5ml/1 tsp ground turmeric
2.5ml/½ tsp ground coriander
5ml/1 tsp mild chilli powder
3 shallots, chopped
150ml/¼ pint/⅔ cup single (light) cream
150ml/¼ pint/⅔ cup milk
salt and ground black pepper
chopped fresh flat leaf parsley, to garnish

1 Peel the potatoes, sweet potatoes and celeriac and cut into thin, even slices using a sharp knife or the slicing attachment on a food processor. Immediately place the vegetables in a bowl of cold water to prevent them from discolouring.

2 Preheat the oven to 180°C/350°F/Gas 4. Heat half the butter in a heavy pan, add the curry powder, ground turmeric and coriander and half the chilli powder. Cook for 2 minutes, then leave to cool slightly. Drain the vegetables, then pat them dry with kitchen paper. Place in a bowl, add the spice mixture and the shallots, and mix well.

3 Arrange the vegetables in a shallow baking dish, seasoning well with salt and pepper between the layers. Mix the cream and milk together, pour the mixture over the vegetables, then sprinkle the remaining chilli powder on top.

4 Cover the dish with baking parchment and bake for 45 minutes. Remove the baking parchment, dot the vegetables with the remaining butter and bake for a further 50 minutes, or until the top is golden brown. Serve the gratin garnished with chopped parsley.

Energy 205kcal/863kJ; Fat 5.1g; Saturated fat 2.9g; Carbohydrate 36.9g; Fibre 4.7g.

Stuffed Baby Vegetables

The combination of potatoes and aubergines is popular in Indian cooking.

Serves 4
12 small potatoes
8 baby aubergines (eggplants)

For the stuffing
15ml/1 tbsp sesame seeds
30ml/2 tbsp ground coriander
30ml/2 tbsp ground cumin
2.5ml/½ tsp salt
1.5ml/¼ tsp chilli powder
2.5ml/½ tsp ground turmeric
10ml/2 tsp granulated sugar
1.5ml/¼ tsp garam masala
15ml/1 tbsp gram flour
2 garlic cloves, crushed
15ml/1 tbsp lemon juice
30ml/2 tbsp chopped fresh coriander (cilantro)

For the sauce
15ml/1 tbsp oil
2.5ml/½ tsp black mustard seeds
400g/14oz can chopped tomatoes
30ml/2 tbsp chopped fresh coriander
150ml/¼ pint/⅔ cup water

1 Preheat the oven to 200°C/400°F/Gas 6. Make deep slits in the potatoes and aubergines to hold the stuffing, ensuring that you do not cut right through.

2 Mix all the ingredients for the stuffing together on a plate.

3 Carefully spoon the spicy stuffing mixture into each of the slits in the potatoes and aubergines.

4 Arrange the stuffed potatoes and aubergines in a greased ovenproof dish, filling side up.

5 For the sauce, heat the oil in a heavy pan and fry the mustard seeds for 2 minutes until they begin to splutter, then add the canned tomatoes, chopped coriander and any leftover stuffing. Stir in the water. Bring to the boil and simmer for 5 minutes until the sauce thickens.

6 Pour the sauce over the potatoes and aubergines. Cover and bake in the oven for 25–30 minutes until the potatoes and aubergines are soft.

Energy 259kcal/1088kJ; Fat 7.6g; Saturated fat 0.73g; Carbohydrate 41.3g; Fibre 4g.

Mixed Vegetable Curry

You can use any combination of vegetables that are in season for this basic recipe.

Serves 4
15ml/1 tbsp oil
2.5ml/½ tsp black mustard seeds
2.5ml/½ tsp cumin seeds
1 onion, thinly sliced
2 curry leaves
1 fresh green chilli, finely chopped
2.5cm/1in piece fresh root ginger, finely chopped
30ml/2 tbsp curry paste

1 small cauliflower, broken into florets
1 large carrot, thickly sliced
115g/4oz green beans, cut into 2.5cm/1in lengths
1.5ml/¼ tsp ground turmeric
1.5ml/¼ tsp chilli powder
2.5ml/½ tsp salt
2 tomatoes, finely chopped
50g/2oz/½ cup frozen peas, thawed
150ml/¼ pint/⅔ cup vegetable stock
fresh curry leaves, to garnish

1 Heat the oil in a large, heavy pan and fry the mustard seeds and cumin seeds for 2 minutes until they begin to splutter. If they are very lively, put a lid on the pan.

2 Add the onion and the curry leaves and fry for 5 minutes.

3 Add the chopped chilli and fresh ginger and fry for 2 minutes. Stir in the curry paste, mix well and fry for 3–4 minutes.

4 Add the cauliflower florets, sliced carrot and beans, and cook for 4–5 minutes. Add the turmeric, chilli powder, salt and tomatoes and cook for 2–3 minutes.

5 Finally add the thawed peas and cook for a further 2–3 minutes. Pour in the stock. Cover and simmer over a low heat for 10–15 minutes until all the vegetables are tender. Serve garnished with curry leaves.

> **Variation**
> To turn this dish into a non-vegetarian main course, add some prawns (shrimp) or cubes of cooked chicken with the stock.

Energy 130kcal/540kJ; Fat 6.2g; Saturated fat 0.61g; Carbohydrate 12.3g; Fibre 6.2g.

Vegetable Korma

Here the aim is to produce a subtle, aromatic curry rather than an assault on the senses.

Serves 4
50g/2oz/¼ cup butter
2 onions, sliced
2 garlic cloves, crushed
2.5cm/1in piece fresh root ginger, grated
5ml/1 tsp ground cumin
15ml/1 tbsp ground coriander
6 cardamom pods
5cm/2in piece of cinnamon stick
5ml/1 tsp ground turmeric
1 fresh red chilli, seeded and finely chopped

1 potato, peeled and cut into 2.5cm/1in cubes
1 small aubergine (eggplant), chopped
115g/4oz/1½ cups mushrooms, thickly sliced
175ml/6fl oz/¾ cup water
115g/4oz green beans, cut into 2.5cm/1in lengths
60ml/4 tbsp natural (plain) yogurt
150ml/¼ pint/⅔ cup double (heavy) cream
5ml/1 tsp garam masala
salt and ground black pepper
fresh coriander (cilantro) sprigs, to garnish
boiled rice and poppadums, to serve

1 Melt the butter in a heavy pan. Add the onions and cook for 5 minutes until soft. Add the garlic and ginger and cook for 2 minutes, then stir in the cumin, coriander, cardamom pods, cinnamon stick, turmeric and finely chopped chilli. Cook, stirring constantly, for 30 seconds.

2 Add the potato cubes, aubergine and mushrooms and the water. Cover the pan, bring to the boil, then lower the heat and simmer for 15 minutes.

3 Add the beans and cook, uncovered, for 5 minutes. With a slotted spoon, remove the vegetables to a warmed serving dish and keep hot.

4 Allow the cooking liquid to bubble up until it has reduced a little. Season with salt and pepper to taste, then stir in the yogurt, double cream and garam masala. Pour the sauce over the vegetables and garnish with fresh coriander. Serve with boiled rice and poppadums.

Energy 361kcal/1494kJ; Fat 31.3g; Saturated fat 19.3g; Carbohydrate 16.7g; Fibre 3.2g.

Mixed Thai Vegetables in Coconut Milk

A most delicious way of cooking vegetables. If you don't like highly spiced food, use fewer red chilli peppers.

Serves 4–6
450g/1lb mixed vegetables, such as aubergines (eggplants), baby corn, carrots, snake beans and patty pan squash

8 red chillies, seeded
2 lemon grass stalks, chopped
4 kaffir lime leaves, torn
30ml/2 tbsp vegetable oil
250ml/8fl oz/1 cup coconut milk
30ml/2 tbsp fish sauce
salt
15–20 Thai basil leaves, to garnish

1 Cut the vegetables into similar-size shapes using a sharp knife.

2 Put the red chillies, lemon grass and kaffir lime leaves in a mortar and grind together with a pestle.

3 Heat the oil in a wok or large, deep frying pan. Add the chilli mixture and fry for 2–3 minutes.

4 Stir in the coconut milk and bring to the boil. Add the vegetables and cook for about 5 minutes or until they are tender. Season with the fish sauce and salt, and garnish with basil leaves.

Variation
For Broccoli and Courgettes in Coconut, steam or lightly boil 350g/12oz broccoli florets and 350g/12oz thickly sliced courgettes (zucchini). Stir-fry 15ml/1 tbsp black mustard seeds and 6 curry leaves for 1 minute and then add 225g/8oz sliced onion and 2 chopped fresh green chillies. Cook for 10 minutes until softened. Add 250ml/8fl oz/1 cup coconut milk and salt. Add a pinch of saffron threads and 30ml/2 tbsp fresh coriander (cilantro). Serve.

Mixed Vegetables in Coconut Sauce

A vegetable dish is an essential part of an Indian meal, even for a simple occasion, where one or two vegetable dishes may be served with a lentil dhal, a raita, and bread or boiled rice. There are many ways to make a vegetable curry, but this recipe, in which the vegetables are simmered in coconut milk, is typical of South India.

Serves 4
225g/8oz potatoes, cut into 5cm/2in cubes
115g/4oz green beans

150g/5oz carrots, scraped and cut into 5cm/2in cubes
500ml/17fl oz/2¼ cups hot water
1 small aubergine (eggplant), about 225g/8oz, quartered lengthways
75g/3oz coconut milk powder
5ml/1 tsp salt
30ml/2 tbsp vegetable oil
6–8 fresh or 8–10 curry leaves
1 or 2 dried red chillies, chopped into small pieces
5ml/1 tsp ground cumin
5ml/1 tsp ground coriander
2.5ml/½ tsp ground turmeric
Indian bread, to serve

1 Put the cubed potatoes, green beans and carrots in a large pan, add 300ml/½ pint/1¼ cups of the hot water and bring to the boil. Reduce the heat a little, cover the pan and continue to cook for 5 minutes.

2 Cut the aubergine quarters into 5cm/2in pieces. Rinse. Add to the pan.

3 Blend the coconut milk powder with the remaining hot water and add to the vegetables, with the salt. Bring to a slow simmer, cover and cook for 6–7 minutes.

4 In a small pan heat the oil over a medium heat and add the curry leaves and the dried red chillies. Immediately follow with the ground cumin, coriander and turmeric. Stir-fry the spices together for 15–20 seconds and pour the entire contents of the pan over the vegetables. Stir to distribute the spices evenly and remove the pan from the heat. Serve the mixed vegetables with any Indian bread.

Energy 80kcal/335kJ; Fat 6.1g; Saturated fat 0.9g; Carbohydrate 5.5g; Fibre 2.3g.

Energy 119kcal/499kJ; Fat 6.2g; Saturated fat 0.9g; Carbohydrate 14.8g; Fibre 2.9g.

Spiced Vegetables with Coconut

This spicy and substantial
stir-fry could be served as an
appetizer, or as a vegetarian
main course for two. Eat it
with spoons and forks, and
provide hunks of Granary
bread for mopping up the
delicious coconut milk.

Serves 2–4
1 red chilli
2 large carrots
6 celery sticks
1 fennel bulb
30ml/2 tbsp grapeseed oil
2.5cm/1in fresh root ginger,
    grated
1 garlic clove, crushed
3 spring onions (scallions), sliced
400ml/14fl oz can coconut
    milk
15ml/1 tbsp chopped fresh
    coriander (cilantro)
salt and ground black pepper
fresh coriander sprigs,
    to garnish

1 Halve, seed and finely chop the chilli. If necessary, wear
rubber gloves to protect your hands.

2 Thinly slice the carrots and the celery sticks on the diagonal.
Trim the fennel bulb and slice roughly, using a sharp knife.

3 Heat the wok, then add the oil. When the oil is hot, add the
chilli, fennel, carrots, celery, ginger, garlic and spring onions and
stir-fry for 2 minutes.

4 Stir in the coconut milk with a large spoon and bring the
mixture to the boil.

5 Stir in the coriander, and salt and pepper, and serve garnished
with coriander sprigs.

Cook's Tip
*When buying fennel, look for well-rounded bulbs; flatter ones
are immature and will not have developed their full aniseed-like
flavour. The bulbs should be white with overlapping ridged
layers. Avoid any that look damaged or bruised. The fennel
should be dry, but not desiccated.*

Energy 198kcal/827kJ; Fat 12.6g; Saturated fat 1.8g; Carbohydrate 19.3g; Fibre 6.4g.

Sweet-&-sour Vegetables with Paneer

The cheese used in this
recipe is Indian paneer,
which can be bought at
some Asian stores; tofu
can be used in its place.

Serves 4
1 green (bell) pepper, seeded
    and cut into squares
1 yellow (bell) pepper, seeded
    and cut into squares
8 cherry tomatoes
8 cauliflower florets
8 pineapple chunks
8 cubes paneer
plain, boiled rice,
    to serve

For the seasoned oil
15ml/1 tbsp oil
30ml/2 tbsp lemon juice
5ml/1 tsp salt
5ml/1 tsp crushed black
    peppercorns
15ml/1 tbsp clear honey
30ml/2 tbsp chilli sauce

1 Preheat the grill (broiler) to hot. Thread the pepper squares,
cherry tomatoes, cauliflower florets, pineapple chunks and
paneer cubes on to four skewers, alternating the ingredients.
Place the skewers on a flameproof dish or in a grill pan.

2 In a small bowl, combine all the ingredients for the seasoned
oil. If too thick, add 15ml/1 tbsp water.

3 Brush the vegetables with the seasoned oil. Grill (broil) for
about 10 minutes until the vegetables begin to darken slightly,
turning the skewers regularly to cook evenly. Serve on a bed
of plain boiled rice.

Cook's Tip
*Metal skewers are ideal for this recipe. Some of the traditional
Indian ones are very pretty, and will enhance the colour of the
dish. Wooden or bamboo skewers can be used instead, but
remember to soak them in water for at least 30 minutes
before threading them with the vegetables and paneer, or the
exposed tips may burn under the heat.*

Energy 75kcal/311kJ; Fat 3.3g; Saturated fat 0.38g; Carbohydrate 9.9g; Fibre 2.1g.

Spiced Vegetable Curry with Yogurt

This is a very delicately spiced vegetable dish that is particularly appetizing when served with plain yogurt. It is also a good accompaniment to a main course of heavily spiced curries.

Serves 4–6
350g/12oz mixed vegetables, such as beans, peas, potatoes, cauliflower, carrots, cabbage, mangetouts (snow peas) and mushrooms
30ml/2 tbsp vegetable oil
5ml/1 tsp cumin seeds, freshly roasted
2.5ml/½ tsp mustard seeds
2.5ml/½ tsp onion seeds
5ml/1 tsp ground turmeric
2 garlic cloves, crushed
6–8 curry leaves
1 dried red chilli
salt
5ml/1 tsp granulated sugar
150ml/¼ pint/⅔ cup natural (plain) yogurt mixed with 5ml/1 tsp cornflour (cornstarch)

1 Prepare all the vegetables you have chosen: string the beans; thaw the peas, if frozen; peel and cube the potatoes; cut the cauliflower into florets; dice the carrots; shred the cabbage; trim the mangetouts; wipe the mushrooms and leave whole.

2 Heat a large pan with enough water to cook all the vegetables and bring to the boil. First add the potatoes and carrots and cook until nearly tender then add all the other vegetables and cook until crisp-tender. All the vegetables should be crunchy except the potatoes. Drain.

3 Heat the oil in a frying pan and fry the cumin, mustard and onion seeds, the turmeric, garlic, curry leaves and dried chilli gently until the garlic is golden brown and the chilli nearly burnt. Reduce the heat.

4 Fold in the drained vegetables, add the sugar and salt and gradually add the yogurt and cornflour mixture. Heat until piping hot, and serve immediately.

Energy 99kcal/411kJ; Fat 6.1g; Saturated fat 0.9g; Carbohydrate 6.5g; Fibre 2g.

Vegetable Kashmiri

This is a wonderful vegetable curry, in which fresh mixed vegetables are cooked in a spicy aromatic yogurt sauce. The spicing is quite gentle, so it will appeal to most palates.

Serves 4
10ml/2 tsp cumin seeds
8 black peppercorns
seeds from 2 green cardamom pods
5cm/2in piece cinnamon stick
2.5ml/½ tsp grated nutmeg
30ml/2 tbsp oil
1 fresh green chilli, chopped
2.5cm/1in piece fresh root ginger, grated
5ml/1 tsp chilli powder
2.5ml/½ tsp salt
2 large potatoes, cut into 2.5cm/1in chunks
225g/8oz cauliflower, broken into florets
225g/8oz okra, trimmed and thickly sliced
150ml/¼ pint/⅔ cup natural (plain) low-fat yogurt
150ml/¼ pint/⅔ cup vegetable stock
toasted flaked (sliced) almonds and fresh coriander (cilantro) sprigs, to garnish

1 Grind the cumin seeds and peppercorns, cardamom seeds, cinnamon stick and nutmeg to a fine powder using a spice blender or a pestle and mortar.

2 Heat the oil in a large, heavy pan and fry the chilli and ginger for 2 minutes, stirring all the time.

3 Add the chilli powder, salt and ground spice mixture, and fry for about 2–3 minutes, stirring all the time to prevent the spices from sticking to the bottom of the pan.

4 Stir in the potatoes, cover and cook for 10 minutes over a low heat, stirring from time to time.

5 Add the cauliflower and okra and cook for 5 minutes.

6 Add the yogurt and stock. Bring to the boil, then reduce the heat. Cover and simmer for 20 minutes, or until all the vegetables are tender. Garnish with the toasted almonds and the coriander sprigs.

Energy 220kcal/920kJ; Fat 8.2g; Saturated fat 1.02g; Carbohydrate 29.1g; Fibre 4.7g.

Vegetable Biryani

This is a good-tempered dish made from everyday ingredients, and thus indispensable for the cook catering for an unexpected vegetarian guest.

Serves 4–6
175g/6oz/scant 1 cup long-grain
  rice, rinsed
2 whole cloves
seeds from 2 cardamom pods
450ml/³/₄ pint/scant 2 cups
  vegetable stock
2 garlic cloves
1 small onion, roughly chopped
5ml/1 tsp cumin seeds
5ml/1 tsp ground coriander
2.5ml/¹/₂ tsp ground turmeric
2.5ml/¹/₂ tsp chilli powder
1 large potato, cut into 2.5cm/
  1 in cubes
2 carrots, sliced
¹/₂ cauliflower, broken
  into florets
50g/2oz green beans, cut
  into 2.5cm/1 in lengths
30ml/2 tbsp chopped fresh
  coriander (cilantro), plus extra
  to garnish
30ml/2 tbsp lime juice
salt and ground black pepper

1 Put the rice, cloves and cardamom seeds into a large, heavy pan. Pour over the stock and bring to the boil. Reduce the heat, cover the pan and simmer for 20 minutes or until all the stock has been absorbed.

2 Meanwhile, put the garlic cloves, onion, cumin seeds, ground coriander, turmeric, chilli powder and seasoning into a blender or food processor together with 30ml/2 tbsp water. Blend to a smooth paste. Scrape the paste into a large flameproof casserole.

3 Preheat the oven to 180°C/350°F/Gas 4. Cook the spicy paste in the casserole over a low heat for 2 minutes, stirring occasionally. Add the potato cubes, carrots, cauliflower, beans and 90ml/6 tbsp water. Cover and cook over a low heat for 12 minutes, stirring occasionally. Add the chopped fresh coriander.

4 Remove the cloves from the rice. Spoon the rice over the vegetables. Sprinkle with the lime juice. Cover and cook in the oven for 25 minutes or until the vegetables are tender. Fluff up the rice with a fork before serving, garnished with coriander.

Energy 260kcal/1100kJ Fat 1.9g Saturated fat 0.07g Carbohydrate 55.8g Fibre 3.2g.

Broad Bean & Cauliflower Curry

This is a hot and spicy vegetable curry, tasty when served with cooked rice (especially a brown basmati variety), a few poppadums and cucumber raita.

Serves 4
2 garlic cloves, chopped
2.5cm/1 in piece fresh root ginger
1 fresh green chilli, seeded
  and chopped
30ml/2 tbsp oil
1 onion, sliced
1 large potato, chopped
15ml/1 tbsp curry powder,
  mild or hot
1 cauliflower, cut into small
  florets
600ml/1 pint/2¹/₂ cups vegetable
  stock
275g/10oz can broad (fava)
  beans
juice of ¹/₂ lemon (optional)
salt and ground black pepper
fresh coriander (cilantro) sprig,
  to garnish
plain rice, to serve

1 Blend the chopped garlic, ginger, chopped chilli and 15ml/1 tbsp of the oil in a food processor or blender until the mixture forms a smooth paste.

2 In a large, heavy pan, fry the sliced onion and chopped potato in the remaining oil for 5 minutes, then stir in the spice paste and curry powder. Cook for another minute.

3 Add the cauliflower florets to the onion and potato and stir well until they are thoroughly combined with the spicy mixture, then pour in the stock and bring to the boil over medium to high heat.

4 Season well, cover and simmer for 10 minutes. Add the beans with the liquid from the can and cook, uncovered, for a further 10 minutes.

5 Check the seasoning and adjust if necessary. Add a good squeeze of lemon juice, if you like, and serve hot, garnished with coriander and accompanied by plain boiled rice.

Energy 216kcal/906kJ; Fat 7.7g; Saturated fat 0.75g; Carbohydrate 25.8g; Fibre 7.9g.

Stir-fried Seeds & Vegetables

The contrast between the crunchy seeds and vegetables and the rich, savoury sauce is what makes this dish so delicious. Serve with rice.

Serves 4
30ml/2 tbsp vegetable oil
30ml/2 tbsp sesame seeds
30ml/2 tbsp sunflower seeds
30ml/2 tbsp pumpkin seeds
2 garlic cloves, finely chopped
2.5cm/1in piece fresh root ginger, peeled and finely chopped
2 large carrots, cut into batons
2 large courgettes (zucchini), cut into batons
90g/3½oz/1½ cups oyster mushrooms, torn in pieces
165g/5½oz watercress or spinach leaves, coarsely chopped
small bunch fresh mint or coriander (cilantro), leaves and stems chopped
60ml/4 tbsp black bean sauce
30ml/2 tbsp light soy sauce
15ml/1 tbsp palm sugar or light muscovado (brown) sugar
30ml/2 tbsp rice vinegar

1 Heat the oil in a wok or large frying pan. Add the seeds. Toss over a medium heat for 1 minute, then add the garlic and ginger, and stir-fry until the ginger is aromatic and the garlic is golden. Do not let the garlic burn or it will taste bitter.

2 Add the carrot and courgette batons and the torn mushrooms to the wok or pan and stir-fry over a medium heat for a further 5 minutes, or until all the vegetables are crisp-tender and are golden at the edges.

3 Add the watercress or spinach with the fresh herbs. Toss over the heat for 1 minute, then stir in the black bean sauce, soy sauce, sugar and vinegar. Stir-fry for 1–2 minutes, until combined and hot. Serve immediately.

Cook's Tip
Oyster mushrooms have acquired their name because of their texture, rather than flavour, which is quite superb. They are delicate, so it is usually better to tear them into pieces along the lines of the gills, rather than slice them with a knife.

Vegetable Forest Curry

This is a thin, soupy curry with lots of fresh green vegetables and robust flavours. In the forested regions of Thailand, where it originated, it would be made using edible wild leaves and roots. Serve it with rice or noodles for a simple lunch or supper.

Serves 2
600ml/1 pint/2½ cups water
5ml/1 tsp Thai red curry paste
5cm/2in piece fresh galangal or fresh root ginger
90g/3½oz/scant 1 cup green beans
2 kaffir lime leaves, torn
8 baby corn cobs, halved widthways
2 heads Chinese broccoli, chopped
90g/3½oz/1 cup beansprouts
15ml/1 tbsp drained bottled green peppercorns, crushed
10ml/2 tsp granulated sugar
5ml/1 tsp salt

1 Heat the water in a large pan. Add the red curry paste and stir until it has dissolved completely. Bring to the boil.

2 Meanwhile, using a sharp knife, peel and finely chop the fresh galangal or root ginger.

3 Add the galangal or ginger, green beans, lime leaves, baby corn, broccoli and beansprouts to the pan. Stir in the crushed peppercorns, sugar and salt. Bring back to the boil, then reduce the heat to low and simmer for 2 minutes. Serve immediately.

Cook's Tip
Galangal is a tuber (a kind of root), which looks similar to ginger. There are several different types; some are more peppery in flavour whereas others taste slightly of cardamoms. Galangal is used mostly in Thai and Indonesian cuisine. If you are not able to find fresh galangal you can substitute ginger in most recipes.

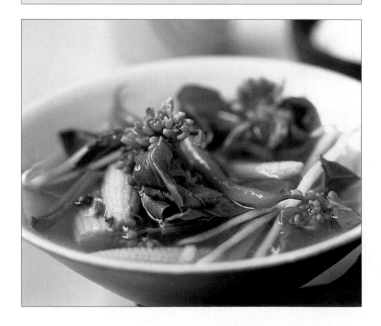

Curry with Lemon Grass Rice

Firm new potatoes, baby corn, broccoli, pepper and spinach make a fabulous combination cooked in a hot spicy curry. Fragrant jasmine rice, subtly flavoured with lemon grass and cardamom, is the perfect accompaniment.

Serves 4
10ml/2 tsp vegetable oil
400ml/14fl oz/1²/₃ cups
  coconut milk
300ml/½ pint/1¼ cups
  vegetable stock
225g/8oz new potatoes, halved
  or quartered, if large
8 baby corn cobs
5ml/1 tsp golden caster
  (superfine) sugar
185g/6½oz/1¼ cups broccoli florets
1 red (bell) pepper, seeded and
  sliced lengthways
115g/4oz spinach, tough stalks
  removed, leaves shredded
30ml/2 tbsp chopped fresh
  coriander (cilantro)
salt and ground black pepper

For the spice paste
1 fresh red chilli, seeded and
  chopped
3 fresh green chillies, seeded
  and chopped
1 lemon grass stalk, outer leaves
  removed and lower 5cm/2in
  finely chopped
2 shallots, chopped
finely grated rind of 1 lime
2 garlic cloves, chopped
5ml/1 tsp ground coriander
2.5ml/½ tsp ground cumin
1cm/½in piece fresh galangal,
  finely chopped, or 2.5ml/
  ½ tsp dried galangal (optional)
30ml/2 tbsp chopped fresh
  coriander
15ml/1 tbsp chopped fresh
  coriander roots and stems
  (optional)

For the rice
225g/8oz/1¼ cups jasmine
  rice, rinsed
6 cardamom pods, bruised
1 lemon grass stalk, outer leaves
  removed, cut into 3 pieces
475ml/16fl oz/2 cups water

1 Make the spice paste. Place all the ingredients in a food processor and process to a coarse paste. Heat the oil in a large, heavy pan. Add the paste and stir-fry over a medium heat for 1–2 minutes, until fragrant. Pour in the coconut milk and stock and bring to the boil. Reduce the heat, add the potatoes and simmer gently for about 15 minutes, until almost tender.

2 Meanwhile, put the rice into a large pan with the cardamoms and lemon grass. Pour in the water. Bring to the boil, reduce the heat, cover, and cook for 10–15 minutes, until the water has been absorbed and the rice is tender.

3 When the rice is cooked and slightly sticky, season to taste with salt, then replace the lid and leave to stand for 10 minutes.

4 Add the baby corn to the potatoes, season with salt and pepper to taste, then cook for 2 minutes. Stir in the sugar, broccoli and red pepper, and cook for 2 minutes more, or until the vegetables are tender.

5 Stir the shredded spinach and half the fresh coriander into the vegetable mixture. Cook for 2 minutes, then spoon the curry into a warmed serving dish.

6 Remove and discard the cardamom pods and lemon grass from the rice and fluff up the grains with a fork. Garnish with the remaining fresh coriander and serve with the rice.

Energy 347kcal/1455kJ; Fat 3.4g; Saturated fat 0.6g; Carbohydrate 68.9g; Fibre 4.5g.

Savoury Fried Rice

This is typical Thai street food, eaten at all times of the day. The recipe can be adapted to use whatever vegetables you have available, and you could also add meat or shellfish.

Serves 2
30ml/2 tbsp vegetable oil
2 garlic cloves, finely chopped
1 small fresh red chilli, seeded
  and finely chopped
50g/2oz/½ cup cashew nuts,
  toasted
50g/2oz/²/₃ cup desiccated
  (dry unsweetened shredded)
  coconut, toasted
2.5ml/½ tsp palm sugar or light
  muscovado (brown) sugar

30ml/2 tbsp light soy sauce
15ml/1 tbsp rice vinegar
1 egg
115g/4oz/1 cup green beans,
  sliced
½ spring cabbage or 115g/4oz
  spring greens (collards) or
  pak choi (bok choy), shredded
90g/3½oz/1 cup jasmine
  rice, cooked
lime wedges, to serve

1 Heat the oil in a wok or large, heavy frying pan. Add the garlic and cook over a medium to high heat until golden. Do not let it burn or it will taste bitter.

2 Add the red chilli, cashew nuts and toasted coconut to the wok or pan and stir-fry briefly, taking care to prevent the coconut from scorching. Stir in the sugar, soy sauce and rice vinegar. Toss over the heat for 1–2 minutes.

3 Push the stir-fry to one side of the wok or pan and break the egg into the empty side. When the egg is almost set stir it into the garlic and chilli mixture with a wooden spatula or spoon.

4 Add the green beans, greens and cooked rice. Stir over the heat until the greens have just wilted, then spoon into a dish to serve. Offer the lime wedges separately, for squeezing over the rice.

Energy 631kcal/2614kJ; Fat 42.6g; Saturated fat 18g; Carbohydrate 47g; Fibre 6.7g.

Spicy Chickpea & Aubergine Stew

Aubergines and chickpeas go particularly well with the warm spices in this substantial dish.

Serves 4

3 garlic cloves
2 large onions
3 large aubergines (eggplants), cubed
200g/7oz/1 cup chickpeas, soaked overnight
60ml/4 tbsp olive oil
2.5ml/½ tsp ground cumin
2.5ml/½ tsp ground cinnamon
2.5ml/½ tsp ground coriander
3 x 400g/14oz cans chopped tomatoes
salt and ground black pepper
boiled rice, to serve

For the garnish
30ml/2 tbsp olive oil
1 onion, sliced
1 garlic clove, sliced
sprigs of fresh coriander (cilantro)

1 Chop the garlic and onions and set aside. Cut the aubergines into bitesize cubes.

2 Place the aubergine cubes in a colander and sprinkle them with salt. Sit the colander in a bowl and leave for 30 minutes, to allow the bitter juices to escape. Rinse the aubergine with cold water and dry on kitchen paper.

3 Drain the chickpeas and put in a pan with enough water to cover. Bring to the boil and simmer for 1–1½ hours, or until tender. Drain.

4 Heat the oil in a large pan. Add the garlic and onion, and cook until soft. Add the spices and cook, stirring, for a few seconds. Add the aubergine and stir. Cook for 5 minutes.

5 Add the tomatoes and chickpeas and season with salt and pepper. Cover and simmer for 20 minutes.

6 To make the garnish, heat the oil in a frying pan and, when very hot, add the sliced onion and garlic. Fry until golden and crisp. Serve the stew with rice, topped with the onion and garlic and garnished with coriander.

Energy 384kcal/1613kJ; Fat 15.8g; Saturated fat 2.4g; Carbohydrate 47.5g; Fibre 14.8g.

Masala Chana

Chickpeas are used and cooked in a variety of ways all over the Indian subcontinent. Tamarind adds a sharp, tangy flavour.

Serves 4

225g/8oz/1¼ cups dried chickpeas, soaked overnight and drained
50g/2oz tamarind stick
120ml/4fl oz/½ cup boiling water
30ml/2 tbsp oil
2.5ml/½ tsp cumin seeds
1 onion, finely chopped
2 garlic cloves, crushed
2.5cm/1in piece fresh root ginger, grated
1 fresh green chilli, finely chopped
5ml/1 tsp ground cumin
5ml/1 tsp ground coriander
1.5ml/¼ tsp ground turmeric
2.5ml/½ tsp salt
225g/8oz tomatoes, peeled and finely chopped
2.5ml/½ tsp garam masala
chopped fresh chillies and chopped onion, to garnish

1 Place the chickpeas in a large pan with double the volume of cold water. Bring to the boil and boil vigorously for 10 minutes.

2 Skim off any scum that has risen to the surface of the liquid, using a slotted spoon. Lower the heat, cover the pan and simmer for 1½–2 hours or until the chickpeas are soft.

3 Meanwhile, break up the tamarind and soak in the boiling water for about 15 minutes. Rub the tamarind through a sieve into a bowl, discarding any stones and fibre left behind.

4 Heat the oil in a large, heavy pan and fry the cumin seeds for 2 minutes until they splutter. Add the onion, garlic, ginger and chilli, and fry for 5 minutes.

5 Stir in the cumin and coriander, with the turmeric and salt and fry for 3–4 minutes. Add the chopped tomatoes. Bring to the boil and then simmer for 5 minutes.

6 Drain the chickpeas and add to the tomato mixture together with the garam masala and tamarind pulp. Cover and simmer gently for about 15 minutes. Garnish with the chopped chillies and onion before serving.

Energy 313kcal/1317kJ; Fat 9.4g; Saturated fat 0.77g; Carbohydrate 44.6g; Fibre 1.5g.

Black-eyed Beans & Potato Curry

Nutty-flavoured black-eyed beans make a nutritious supper dish, especially when mixed with potatoes. This hot and spicy combination will be ideal for an autumn or winter evening.

Serves 4–6

2 potatoes
225g/8oz/1¼ cups black-eyed beans (peas), soaked overnight and drained
1.5ml/¼ tsp bicarbonate of soda (baking soda)
5ml/1 tsp five-spice powder
1.5ml/¼ tsp asafoetida
2 onions, finely chopped
2.5cm/1in piece fresh root ginger, crushed
a few fresh mint leaves
450ml/¾ pint/scant 2 cups water
60ml/4 tbsp vegetable oil
2.5ml/½ tsp each ground cumin, ground coriander, ground turmeric and chilli powder
4 fresh green chillies, chopped
75ml/5 tbsp tamarind juice
115g/4oz/4 cups fresh coriander (cilantro), chopped
2 firm tomatoes, chopped
salt

1 Cut the potatoes into cubes and boil in lightly salted water until tender.

2 Place the drained black-eyed beans in a heavy pan and add the bicarbonate of soda, five-spice powder and asafoetida. Add the chopped onions, crushed root ginger, mint leaves and the measured water. Simmer until the beans are soft. Remove any excess water and reserve.

3 Heat the oil in a frying pan. Gently fry the ground cumin and coriander, the turmeric and chilli powder with the green chillies and tamarind juice, until they are well blended.

4 Pour the spice mixture over the black-eyed beans and mix well.

5 Add the potatoes, fresh coriander, tomatoes and salt. Mix well, and, if necessary, thin with a little reserved water. Reheat and serve.

Boiled Egg Curry

This dish can be served on its own, with a biryani or pilau, and it also makes a good accompaniment to fried whole fish.

Serves 3–6

10ml/2 tsp white poppy seeds
10ml/2 tsp white sesame seeds
10ml/2 tsp whole coriander seeds
30ml/2 tbsp desiccated (dry unsweetened shredded) coconut
350ml/½fl oz/1½ cups tomato juice
10ml/2 tsp gram flour
5ml/1 tsp crushed fresh root ginger
5ml/1 tsp chilli powder
1.5ml/¼ tsp asafoetida
salt
5ml/1 tsp sugar
6 hard-boiled eggs, halved
30ml/2 tbsp sesame oil
5ml/1 tsp cumin seeds
4 dried red chillies
6–8 curry leaves
4 garlic cloves, finely sliced

1 Heat a frying pan and dry-fry the poppy, sesame and coriander seeds for 3–4 minutes. Add the desiccated coconut and dry-fry until it browns.

2 Cool and grind the ingredients together using a pestle and mortar or a food processor.

3 Take a little of the tomato juice and mix with the gram flour to a smooth paste. Add the ginger, chilli powder, asafoetida, salt and sugar and the ground spices. Add the remaining tomato juice, place in a pan and simmer gently for 10 minutes.

4 Add the hard-boiled eggs and cover with the sauce. Heat the oil in a frying pan and fry the remaining ingredients until the chillies turn dark brown. Pour the spices and oil over the egg curry, fold the ingredients together and reheat. Serve hot.

Cook's Tip
Gram flour, or besan, is made from ground chickpeas. It is less starchy than wheat flour and is used extensively in Indian cooking. For a recipe like this that uses a very tiny amount as a thickener, plain (all-purpose) flour can be substituted.

Energy 362kcal/1526kJ; Fat 12.4g; Saturated fat 1.6g; Carbohydrate 49.6g; Fibre 6.6g.

Energy 344kcal/1430kJ; Fat 28.5g; Saturated fat 10.1g; Carbohydrate 7g; Fibre 2.6g.

Eggs on Chipsticks

This is an unusual and delicious way of combining eggs with potato sticks, and is known as *sali pur eeda* in the Parsee language. The potato sticks are fried with chillies, turmeric and coriander. Eggs are then broken over the top and cooked until just set. It makes an unusual light lunch or supper dish and is incredibly quick to prepare and cook.

Serves 4–6
225g/8oz salted chipsticks
2 fresh green chillies, finely
   chopped
a few coriander (cilantro)
   sprigs, chopped
1.5ml/¼ tsp ground turmeric
60ml/4 tbsp vegetable oil
75ml/5 tbsp water
6 eggs
3 spring onions (scallions),
   finely chopped
salt and ground black pepper

1 In a large bowl, mix the salted chipsticks with the chopped chillies, coriander and turmeric.

2 Heat 30ml/2 tbsp of the oil in a heavy frying pan. Add the chipstick mixture and water. Cook until the chipsticks turn soft, and then crisp.

3 Place a dinner plate over the frying pan, and hold in place as you turn the pan over and carefully transfer the chipstick "pancake" on to the plate. Heat the remaining oil in the pan and slide the "pancake" back into the frying pan to brown the other side. Do this very gently, so that no chipsticks break off.

4 Gently break the eggs over the top, cover the frying pan and leave the eggs to set over a low heat. Season well and sprinkle with spring onions. Cook until the base is crisp. Serve hot for breakfast in the Parsee style, or with chapatis and a salad for lunch or supper.

> **Cook's Tip**
> As the chipsticks cook, the starch they contain will cause them to stick together. To encourage this, use a spoon to press them down.

Spicy Omelette

Another popular contribution by the Parsees, this irresistible omelette of potato, peas and corn is known to them as *poro*. Parsee cuisine offers some unique flavours, which appeal to both Eastern and Western palates.

Serves 4–6
30ml/2 tbsp vegetable oil
1 onion, finely chopped
2.5ml/½ tsp ground cumin
1 garlic clove, crushed

1 or 2 fresh green chillies,
   finely chopped
a few coriander (cilantro)
   sprigs, chopped, plus extra,
   to garnish
1 firm tomato, chopped
1 small potato, cubed
   and boiled
25g/1oz/¼ cup cooked peas
25g/1oz/¼ cup cooked corn,
   or drained canned corn
2 eggs, beaten
25g/1oz/¼ cup grated Cheddar
   cheese or Monterey Jack
salt and ground black pepper

1 Heat the oil in a karahi, wok or omelette pan, and add the onion, cumin, garlic, chillies, coriander, tomato, potato, peas and corn. Mix well.

2 Cook over a medium heat, stirring, for 5 minutes, until the potato and tomato are almost tender. Season well.

3 Preheat the grill (broiler) to high. Increase the heat under the pan and pour in the beaten eggs. Reduce the heat, cover and cook until the bottom layer is brown. Turn the omelette over and sprinkle with the grated cheese. Place under the hot grill and cook until the egg sets and the cheese has melted.

4 Garnish the omelette with sprigs of coriander and serve with salad for a light lunch. If you prefer, serve it for breakfast, in the typical Parsee style.

> **Variation**
> You can use any vegetable with the potatoes. Try thickly sliced button (white) mushrooms, which can be added in step 1.

Energy 482kcal/2008kJ; Fat 33.3g; Saturated fat 6.8g; Carbohydrate 36.6g; Fibre 1.6g.

Energy 167kcal/694kJ; Fat 11.3g; Saturated fat 3g; Carbohydrate 9.7g; Fibre 1.5g.

Scrambled Eggs with Chilli

This is a lovely way to liven up scrambled eggs. Prepare all the ingredients ahead so that the vegetables can be cooked quickly and retain crunch and colour.

Serves 4
30ml/2 tbsp sunflower oil
1 onion, finely sliced
225g/8oz Chinese leaves
(Chinese cabbage), finely sliced
or cut in diamonds
200g/7oz can corn
1 small fresh red chilli, seeded
and finely sliced
30ml/2 tbsp water
2 eggs, beaten
salt and ground black pepper
deep-fried onions, to garnish

1 Heat a karahi, wok or deep pan. Add the oil and, when it is hot, fry the onion until soft but not browned.

2 Add the Chinese leaves and toss the mixture over the heat until well mixed.

3 Add the corn, chilli and water. Cover with a lid and cook for 2 minutes.

4 Remove the lid and stir in the beaten eggs and seasoning. Stir constantly until the eggs are creamy and just set. Serve on warmed plates, sprinkled with crisp deep-fried onions.

Variations
• Chinese leaves give this dish a delicate flavour, which complements the corn and eggs well, but you could substitute other vegetables for a different flavour and appearance.
• Instead of Chinese leaves, you could try finely shredded spring greens (collards) or white cabbage. A mandolin is a useful implement for finely shredding vegetables such as these.
• Red, green or yellow (bell) peppers could also be used in place of the Chinese leaves and give the dish a bright appearance.

Energy 171kcal/711kJ; Fat 10.3g; Saturated fat 1.8g; Carbohydrate 13.7g; Fibre 2.1g.

Purée of Lentils with Baked Eggs

This unusual dish of brown lentils spiced with coriander and mint makes an excellent supper. For a nutty flavour you could add a 400g/14oz can of unsweetened chestnut purée to the lentil mixture.

Serves 4
450g/1lb/2 cups washed
brown lentils
3 leeks, thinly sliced
10ml/2 tsp coriander seeds,
crushed
15ml/1 tbsp chopped fresh
coriander (cilantro)
30ml/2 tbsp chopped fresh mint
15ml/1 tbsp red wine vinegar
1 litre/1¾ pints/4 cups vegetable
stock
4 eggs
salt and ground black pepper
generous handful of fresh parsley,
chopped, to garnish

1 Put the lentils in a deep pan. Add the leeks, coriander seeds, fresh coriander, mint, vinegar and stock. Bring to the boil, then lower the heat and simmer for 30–40 minutes, until the lentils are cooked and have absorbed all the liquid.

2 Preheat the oven to 180°C/350°F/Gas 4.

3 Season the lentils with salt and pepper, and mix well. Spread out in four lightly greased baking dishes.

4 Using the back of a spoon, make a hollow in the lentil mixture in each dish. Break an egg into each hollow. Cover the dishes with foil and bake for 15–20 minutes, or until the egg whites are set and the yolks are still soft. Sprinkle with plenty of parsley and serve at once.

Cook's Tip
If you prefer, the lentil mixture can be put into a large dish. Make four indentations in the mixture to hold the eggs.

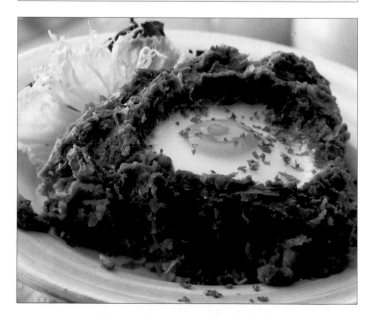

Energy 470kcal/1990kJ; Fat 7.9g; Saturated fat 1.9g; Carbohydrate 68.4g; Fibre 8.8g.

Indian Pilau Rice

This traditional spiced rice is the perfect accompaniment for meat, fish or vegetarian dishes.

Serves 4
225g/8oz/1¼ cups basmati
  rice
15ml/1 tbsp oil
1 small onion, finely chopped
1 garlic clove, crushed
5ml/1 tsp fennel seeds
15ml/1 tbsp sesame seeds
2.5ml/½ tsp ground turmeric
5ml/1 tsp ground cumin
1.5ml/¼ tsp salt
2 whole cloves
4 cardamom pods, lightly
  crushed
5 black peppercorns
450ml/¾ pint/scant 2 cups
  chicken stock
fresh coriander (cilantro),
  to garnish

1 Wash the rice well and leave to soak in water for 30 minutes. Heat the oil in a heavy pan, add the onion and garlic and fry gently for 5–6 minutes until softened.

2 Stir in the fennel and sesame seeds, the turmeric, cumin, salt, cloves, cardamom pods and peppercorns and fry for about a minute. Drain the rice well, add to the pan and stir-fry for a further 3 minutes.

3 Pour on the chicken stock. Bring to the boil, then cover. Reduce the heat to very low and simmer gently for 20 minutes, without removing the lid, until all the liquid has been absorbed.

4 Remove from the heat and leave to stand for 2–3 minutes. Fluff up the rice with a fork, garnish with coriander and transfer to a warmed dish to serve.

Plain Boiled Rice

Always use basmati rice for the best flavour and texture. It is easy to cook and produces an excellent finished result. It is slimmer than other long grain rice and has a delicate flavour. Although slightly more expensive, it is well worth buying as it is the perfect rice for accompanying curries.

Serves 4–6
150ml/1 tbsp ghee, unsalted
  (sweet) butter or olive oil
350g/12oz/1¾ cups basmati
  rice, washed and drained
450ml/¾ pint/scant 2 cups
  water
salt

1 Rinse the basmati rice well in cold water until most of the starch is removed and the water runs clear.

2 Heat the ghee, butter or oil in a pan and sauté the drained rice thoroughly for about 2–3 minutes.

3 Add the water and salt and bring to the boil. Reduce the heat to low, cover and cook gently for 10–15 minutes. To serve, fluff the grains gently with a fork.

Cook's Tips
• *Always test the rice after it has cooked for about 10 minutes; it should be just cooked.*
• *As a guide, 75g/3oz/scant ½ cup raw rice will give you an ample helping for one person.*

Variation
To make a fragrantly spiced version, sauté 4–6 green cardamom pods, 4 cloves, 5cm/2in piece cinnamon stick, 2.5ml/½ tsp black cumin seeds and 2 bay leaves. Add 350g/12oz/1¾ cups drained basmati rice and proceed as for plain boiled rice. For an even more luxurious rice, add 6–8 strands of saffron and sauté with the spices.

Cook's Tip
In South India, where large quantities of rice are eaten, people prefer a rice which will absorb the spicy flavours of seasonings. In this recipe, basmati rice is cooked in the traditional way to seal in all the flavour.

Energy 342kcal/1429kJ; Fat 3.5g; Saturated fat 2g; Carbohydrate 69.9g; Fibre 0g.

Energy 265kcal/1108kJ Fat 6g Saturated fat 0.68g Carbohydrate 49.5g Fibre 0.6g.

Colourful Pilau Rice

This lightly spiced rice makes an extremely attractive accompaniment to many Balti dishes, and is easily made.

Serves 4–6

450g/1lb/2⅓ cups basmati
  rice
75g/3oz/6 tbsp unsalted
  (sweet) butter
4 cloves
4 green cardamom pods
1 bay leaf
5ml/1 tsp salt
1 litre/1¾ pints/4 cups water
a few drops each of yellow, green
  and red food colouring

1 Wash the basmati rice twice, drain well and set aside in a sieve (strainer).

2 Melt the butter in a medium pan, and add the cloves, cardamoms, bay leaf and salt. Lower the heat and add the rice. Fry for about 1 minute, stirring constantly.

3 Add the water to the rice and spices and bring to the boil. As soon as it has boiled, cover the pan and reduce the heat. Cook for 10–15 minutes. Taste a grain of rice after 10 minutes; it should be slightly *al dente* (soft but with a bite in the centre).

4 Just before you are ready to serve the rice, pour a few drops of each colouring at different sides of the pan. Leave to stand for 5 minutes so that the colours can "bleed" into the rice. Mix gently with a fork and serve.

Variation
For Nut Pilau, fry 1.5ml/1/4 tsp cumin seeds with the cloves and cardamoms at step 2. When the rice has almost cooked, drain it and gently stir in a pinch of saffron threads and 15ml/ 1 tbsp ground almonds. Leave the rice to stand for a few minutes before serving. Omit the food colouring.

Energy 544kcal/2263kJ; Fat 16g; Saturated fat 9.8g; Carbohydrate 89.9g; Fibre 0g.

Fruity Pilau

Sultanas and almonds make this a flavoursome rice to serve alongside rich curries.

Serves 4–6

450g/1lb/2⅓ cups basmati
  rice
75g/3oz/6 tbsp unsalted
  (sweet) butter
15ml/1 tbsp corn oil
1 bay leaf
6 black peppercorns
4 green cardamom pods
5ml/1 tsp salt
75g/3oz/½ cup sultanas
  (golden raisins)
50g/2oz/½ cup flaked
  (sliced) almonds
1 litre/1¾ pints/4 cups
  water

1 Wash the basmati rice twice, drain well and set aside in a sieve (strainer).

2 Heat the butter and oil in a medium pan. Lower the heat and throw in the bay leaf, peppercorns and cardamoms, and fry for about 30 seconds.

3 Add the rice, salt, sultanas and flaked almonds. Stir-fry for about 1 minute, then pour in the water. Bring to the boil, then cover with a tightly fitting lid and lower the heat. Cook for 15–20 minutes. Taste a grain of rice after 10 minutes; it should be slightly *al dente* (soft but with a bite in the centre).

4 Turn off the heat and leave the rice to stand, still covered, for about 5 minutes. The rice will continue cooking gently during this time. Serve.

Variation
For Mushroom Pilau, boil the rice without any of the flavourings for 15 minutes and then drain. Stir-fry 10ml/2 tsp cumin seeds, 1.5ml/½ tsp fennel seeds and 1 star anise for 30 seconds. Add half a chopped onion and 75g/3oz/1 cup sliced mushrooms, and cook over medium-high heat for 5 minutes. Add to the rice and transfer to a casserole. Heat in the oven at 190°C/ 375°F/Gas 5 for 30 minutes.

Energy 696kcal/2901kJ; Fat 25.8g; Saturated fat 10.7g; Carbohydrate 103.8g; Fibre 1.3g.

Nut Pilau

Versions of this rice dish are cooked throughout Asia, always with the best-quality long grain rice. In India, basmati rice is the natural choice. In this particular interpretation of the recipe, walnuts and cashew nuts are added. Serve the pilau with a raita or yogurt.

Serves 4
15–30ml/1–2 tbsp vegetable oil
1 onion, chopped
1 garlic clove, crushed
1 large carrot, coarsely grated
225g/8oz/generous 1 cup
   basmati rice, soaked for
   20–30 minutes

5ml/1 tsp cumin seeds
10ml/2 tsp ground coriander
10ml/2 tsp black mustard seeds
4 green cardamom pods
450ml/ ¾ pint/scant 2 cups
   vegetable stock
1 bay leaf
75g/3oz/ ¾ cup unsalted walnuts
   and cashew nuts
salt and ground black pepper
fresh coriander (cilantro) sprigs,
   to garnish

1 Heat the oil in a karahi, wok or large pan. Fry the onion, garlic and carrot for 3–4 minutes. Drain the rice and add to the pan with the spices. Cook for 2 minutes, stirring to coat the grains in oil.

2 Pour in the stock, stirring. Add the bay leaf and season well.

3 Bring to the boil, lower the heat, cover and simmer very gently for 10–12 minutes without stirring.

4 Remove the pan from the heat without lifting the lid. Leave to stand for 5 minutes, then check the rice. If it is cooked, there will be small steam holes on the surface of the rice. Discard the bay leaf and the cardamom pods.

5 Stir in the walnuts and cashew nuts and check the seasoning. Spoon on to a warmed platter, garnish with the fresh coriander and serve.

Energy 376kcal/1562kJ; Fat 16g; Saturated fat 1.4g; Carbohydrate 50g; Fibre 1.6g.

Sultana & Cashew Pilau

The secret of a perfect pilau is to wash the rice thoroughly, then soak it briefly. This softens and moistens the grains, enabling the rice to absorb moisture during cooking, which results in fluffier rice.

Serves 4
600ml/1 pint/2 ½ cups hot
   chicken or vegetable stock
generous pinch of saffron threads
50g/2oz/ ¼ cup butter

1 onion, chopped
1 garlic clove, crushed
2.5cm/1in piece cinnamon stick
6 green cardamom pods
1 bay leaf
250g/9oz/1 ⅓ cups basmati
   rice, soaked in water for
   20–30 minutes
50g/2oz/ ⅓ cup sultanas
   (golden raisins)
15ml/1 tbsp vegetable oil
50g/2oz/ ½ cup cashew nuts
naan bread and tomato and
   onion salad, to serve

1 Pour the hot chicken stock into a jug (pitcher). Stir in the saffron threads and set aside.

2 Heat the butter in a pan and fry the onion and garlic for 5 minutes. Stir in the cinnamon stick, cardamoms and bay leaf and cook for 2 minutes.

3 Drain the rice and add to the pan, then cook, stirring, for 2 minutes more. Pour in the saffron stock and add the sultanas. Bring to the boil, stir, then lower the heat, cover and cook gently for 10 minutes or until the rice is tender and all the liquid has been absorbed.

4 Meanwhile, heat the oil in a wok, karahi or large pan and fry the cashew nuts until browned. Drain on kitchen paper, then sprinkle the cashew nuts over the rice. Serve with naan bread and tomato and onion salad.

Cook's Tip
Saffron powder can be used instead of saffron threads, if you prefer. Dissolve it in the hot stock.

Energy 462kcal/1922kJ Fat 19.5g Saturated fat 8g Carbohydrate 63.9g Fibre 1.2g.

Herby Rice Pilau

A quick and easy recipe to make, this simple pilau is delicious to eat. Serve with a main course meat, poultry or vegetarian curry accompanied by a selection of fresh seasonal vegetables such as broccoli florets, baby corn, asparagus and carrots.

Serves 4

1 onion
1 garlic clove
225g/8oz/generous 1 cup mixed brown basmati and wild rice
15ml/1 tbsp olive oil
5ml/1 tsp ground cumin
5ml/1 tsp ground turmeric
50g/2oz/¹/₃ cup sultanas (golden raisins)
750ml/1¹/₄ pints/3 cups vegetable stock
30–45ml/2–3 tbsp chopped fresh mixed herbs
salt and ground black pepper
sprigs of fresh herbs and 25g/1oz/¹/₄ cup pistachio nuts, chopped, to garnish

1 Chop the onion and crush the garlic cloves.

2 Wash the rice under cold running water until the water runs clear, then drain well.

3 Heat the oil, add the onion and garlic, and cook gently for 5 minutes, stirring occasionally.

4 Add the ground cumin and turmeric and drained rice and cook gently for 1 minute, stirring. Stir in the sultanas and vegetable stock, bring to the boil, cover and simmer gently for 20–25 minutes, stirring occasionally.

5 Stir in the chopped mixed herbs and season with salt and pepper to taste.

6 Spoon the pilau into a warmed serving dish and garnish with fresh herb sprigs and a sprinkling of chopped pistachio nuts. Serve immediately.

Tomato & Spinach Pilau

A tasty and nourishing dish for vegetarians and meat-eaters alike.

Serves 4

225g/8oz/generous 1 cup brown basmati rice
30ml/2 tbsp vegetable oil
15ml/1 tbsp ghee or unsalted (sweet) butter
1 onion, chopped
2 garlic cloves, crushed
3 tomatoes, peeled and chopped
10ml/2 tsp dhana jeera powder, or 5ml/1 tsp ground coriander and 5ml/1 tsp ground cumin
2 carrots, coarsely grated
900ml/1¹/₂ pints/3³/₄ cups vegetable stock
275g/10oz young spinach leaves
50g/2oz/¹/₂ cup unsalted cashew nuts
salt and ground black pepper
naan bread, to serve

1 Wash the basmati rice. Place it in a bowl, cover with cold water and leave to soak for 20 minutes. Drain the rice and place it in a large pan of boiling salted water, bring back to the boil and cook for 10 minutes.

2 Heat the oil and ghee or butter in a karahi, wok or large pan, and fry the onion and garlic for 4–5 minutes until soft. Add the tomatoes and cook for 3–4 minutes, stirring, until the mixture thickens. Drain the rice, add it to the pan and cook for a further 1–2 minutes, stirring, until the grains of rice are coated.

3 Stir in the dhana jeera powder or coriander and cumin, then add the carrots. Season with salt and pepper. Pour in the stock and stir well to mix.

4 Bring to the boil, then cover tightly and simmer over a very gentle heat for 20–25 minutes, until the rice is tender.

5 Lay the spinach on the surface of the rice, cover again, and cook for a further 2–3 minutes, until the spinach has wilted. Fold the spinach into the rest of the rice.

6 Dry-fry the cashew nuts until lightly browned and sprinkle over the rice mixture. Serve with naan bread.

Energy 271kcal/1133kJ; Fat 3.3g; Saturated fat 0.4g; Carbohydrate 55.1g; Fibre 1.1g.

Energy 402kcal/1687kJ Fat 17.1g Saturated fat 4.4g Carbohydrate 56.4g Fibre 4.8g.

Fragrant Meat Pilau

This rice dish acquires its delicious taste not only from the spices but the richly flavoured meat stock.

Serves 4–6
450g/1lb/2⅓ cups basmati rice
900g/2lb boned chicken pieces, or lean lamb, cubed
600ml/1 pint/2½ cups water
4 green cardamom pods
2 black cardamom pods
10 black peppercorns
4 cloves
1 medium onion, sliced
8–10 saffron strands
2 garlic cloves, crushed
5cm/2in piece fresh root ginger
5cm/2in piece cinnamon stick
salt
175g/6oz/1 cup sultanas (golden raisins) and sautéed blanched almonds, to garnish

1 Wash the rice under cold running water until the water runs clear. Drain the rice well and set aside.

2 In a large pan, cook the cubed chicken or lamb in the measured water with the cardamom pods, peppercorns, cloves, onion and salt, until the meat is cooked.

3 Remove the meat with a slotted spoon and keep warm. Strain the stock if you wish, and return to the pan.

4 Add the rice, saffron, garlic, ginger and cinnamon to the stock and bring the contents to the boil.

5 Quickly add the meat and stir well. Bring back to the boil, reduce the heat and cover. Cook covered for about 15–20 minutes.

6 Remove the pan from the heat and leave to stand for 5 minutes. Garnish with sultanas and sautéed blanched almonds and serve.

Tricolour Pilau

Most Indian restaurants in the West serve this popular vegetable pilau, which has three different vegetables. The effect is easily achieved with canned or frozen vegetables, but for entertaining or a special occasion dinner, you may prefer to use fresh produce.

Serves 4–6
225g/8oz/generous 1 cup basmati rice
30ml/2 tbsp vegetable oil
2.5ml/½ tsp cumin seeds
2 dried bay leaves
4 green cardamom pods
4 cloves
1 onion, finely chopped
1 carrot, finely diced
50g/2oz/½ cup frozen peas, thawed
50g/2oz/⅓ cup frozen corn, thawed
25g/1oz/¼ cup cashew nuts, lightly fried
475ml/16fl oz/2 cups water
1.5ml/¼ tsp ground cumin
salt

1 Wash the rice, then soak it in cold water for 20 minutes.

2 Heat the oil in a karahi, wok, or large pan over a medium heat, and fry the cumin seeds for 2 minutes. Add the bay leaves, cardamoms and cloves, and fry gently for 2 minutes more, stirring the spices from time to time.

3 Add the onion and fry until lightly browned. Stir in the diced carrot and cook, stirring, for 3–4 minutes.

4 Drain the soaked basmati rice and add to the contents in the pan. Stir well to mix. Add the peas, corn and fried cashew nuts.

5 Add the measured water and the ground cumin, and stir in salt to taste. Bring to the boil, cover and simmer for 15 minutes over a low heat until all the water is absorbed.

6 Leave to stand, covered, for 10 minutes. Fluff up the rice with a fork, transfer to a warmed dish and serve.

Energy 648kcal/2723kJ; Fat 3.1g; Saturated fat 0.7g; Carbohydrate 91g; Fibre 0.2g.

Energy 331kcal/1378kJ Fat 9.4g Saturated fat 1.4g Carbohydrate 54.1g Fibre 2g.

Pea & Mushroom Pilau

Tiny white mushrooms and petits pois, or baby peas, look great in this delectable rice dish.

Serves 6

450g/1lb/2¼ cups basmati rice
15ml/1 tbsp oil
2.5ml/½ tsp cumin seeds
2 black cardamom pods
2 cinnamon sticks
3 garlic cloves, sliced
5ml/1 tsp salt
1 medium tomato, sliced
50g/2oz/⅔ cup button (white) mushrooms
75g/3oz/¾ cup petits pois (baby peas)
750ml/1¼ pints/3 cups water

1 Wash the rice well and leave it to soak in water for 30 minutes.

2 In a medium, heavy pan, heat the oil and add the cumin seeds, cardamom, cinnamon sticks, garlic and salt.

3 Add the tomato and mushrooms and stir-fry for 2–3 minutes.

4 Tip the rice into a colander and drain it thoroughly. Add it to the pan with the peas. Stir gently, making sure that you do not break up the grains of rice.

5 Add the water and bring to the boil. Lower the heat, cover and continue to cook for 15–20 minutes. Just before serving, remove the lid from the pan and fluff up the rice with a fork. Spoon into a dish and serve immediately.

> **Cook's Tip**
> *Petits pois are small green peas, picked when very young. The tender, sweet peas inside the immature pods are ideal for this delicately flavoured rice dish. However, if you can't find petits pois, garden peas can be used instead.*

Rice with Seeds & Spices

Toasted sunflower and sesame seeds impart a rich, nutty flavour to rice spiced with turmeric, cardamom and coriander, for this delicious change from plain boiled rice, and a colourful accompaniment to serve with spicy curries. Basmati rice gives the best texture and flavour, but you can use ordinary long grain rice instead, if you prefer.

Serves 4

5ml/1 tsp sunflower oil
2.5ml/½ tsp ground turmeric
6 cardamom pods, lightly crushed
5ml/1 tsp coriander seeds, lightly crushed
1 garlic clove, crushed
200g/7oz/1 cup basmati rice
400ml/14fl oz/1⅔ cups vegetable stock
115g/4oz/½ cup natural (plain) yogurt
15ml/1 tbsp toasted sunflower seeds
15ml/1 tbsp toasted sesame seeds
salt and ground black pepper
coriander (cilantro) leaves, to garnish

1 Heat the oil in a non-stick frying pan and fry the turmeric, cardamom pods, coriander seeds and garlic for about 1 minute, stirring constantly.

2 Add the rice and stock, bring to the boil, then cover and simmer for 15 minutes, or until just tender.

3 Stir in the yogurt and the toasted sunflower and sesame seeds. Season with salt and pepper and serve hot, garnished with coriander leaves.

> **Cook's Tip**
> *Seeds are particularly rich in minerals, so they are a good addition to all kinds of dishes. Light toasting will improve their fine flavour.*

Energy 423kcal/1768kJ; Fat 3.8g; Saturated fat 0.39g; Carbohydrate 92.9g; Fibre 1.3g.

Energy 248kcal/1036kJ; Fat 5.4g; Saturated fat 0.7g; Carbohydrate 42.8g; Fibre 0.5g.

Saffron Rice

The saffron crocus is a perennial bulb that flowers for only two weeks of the year, and each stigma has to be removed by hand and dried with care. Consequently, saffron is said to be worth its weight in gold. Kashmir in the northern region of India is a major producer, so it isn't surprising that the subcontinent has some wonderful recipes for this beautifully fragrant spice.

Serves 6
450g/1lb/2⅓ cups basmati
   rice
750ml/1¼ pints/3 cups water
3 green cardamom pods
2 cloves
5ml/1 tsp salt
45ml/3 tbsp semi-skimmed
   (low-fat) milk
2.5ml/½ tsp saffron threads,
   crushed

1 Wash the rice, put it in a bowl and pour over water to cover. Leave to soak for 20 minutes.

2 Drain the basmati rice and put it in a large pan with the measured water. Add the cardamoms, cloves and salt. Stir, then bring to the boil. Lower the heat, cover the pan tightly, and simmer for 5 minutes.

3 Meanwhile, place the milk in a small pan. Add the saffron threads and heat through gently.

4 Pour the saffron milk over the rice and stir. Cover again and continue cooking over a low heat for 5–6 minutes.

5 Remove the pan from the heat without lifting the lid. Leave the rice to stand for about 5 minutes, then fork through just before serving.

> **Cook's Tip**
> *Washing and soaking the rice before cooking makes it fluffier.*

Energy 273kcal/1141kJ Fat 0.5g Saturated fat 0.1g Carbohydrate 60.2g Fibre 0g.

Jasmine Fried Rice

This substantial and tasty dish is based on coconut-flavoured jasmine rice. Diced chicken, red pepper and corn add colour and extra flavour.

Serves 4
475ml/16fl oz/2 cups water
50g/2oz/½ cup coconut
   milk powder
350g/12oz/1¾ cups jasmine
   rice, rinsed
30ml/2 tbsp groundnut
   (peanut) oil
2 garlic cloves, chopped
1 small onion, finely chopped
2.5cm/1in piece fresh root
   ginger, grated
225g/8oz skinned chicken breast
   fillets, cut into 1cm/½in dice
1 red (bell) pepper, seeded
   and sliced
115g/4oz/1 cup drained
   canned corn
5ml/1 tsp chilli oil
5ml/1 tsp hot curry powder
2 eggs, beaten
salt
spring onion (scallion) shreds,
   to garnish

1 Pour the water into a pan and whisk in the coconut milk powder. Add the rice and bring to the boil. Reduce the heat, cover and cook for 12 minutes, or until the rice is tender and the liquid has been absorbed. Spread the rice on a baking sheet and leave until completely cold.

2 Heat the oil in a wok, add the garlic, onion and ginger, and stir-fry over a medium heat for 2 minutes.

3 Push the onion mixture to the sides of the wok, add the chicken to the centre and stir-fry for 2 minutes. Add the rice and toss well. Stir-fry over a high heat for about 3 minutes more, until the chicken is cooked through.

4 Stir in the sliced red pepper, corn, chilli oil and curry powder, with salt to taste. Toss over the heat for 1 minute. Stir in the beaten eggs and cook for 1 minute more. Garnish with the spring onion shreds and serve.

Energy 524kcal/2193kJ; Fat 10.7g; Saturated fat 1.8g; Carbohydrate 82.1g; Fibre 1.3g.

Basmati Rice with Vegetables

Serve this delectable dish with roast chicken, lamb cutlets or pan-fried fish. Add the vegetables near the end of cooking so that they retain their crispness and colour.

Serves 4
1 onion
2 garlic cloves
350g/12oz/1¾ cups basmati rice
45ml/3 tbsp vegetable oil
750ml/1¼ pints/3 cups water or vegetable stock
115g/4oz/⅔ cup fresh or drained canned corn
1 red or green (bell) pepper, seeded and chopped
1 large carrot, grated
fresh chervil sprigs, to garnish

1 Chop the onion and crush the garlic cloves.

2 Wash the rice in a sieve (strainer), and then soak in cold water for 20 minutes. Drain very thoroughly.

3 Heat the oil in a large pan and fry the onion for a few minutes over a medium heat until it starts to soften.

4 Add the rice to the pan and fry for about 10 minutes, stirring constantly to prevent the rice from sticking to the base of the pan. Stir in the crushed garlic.

5 Pour in the water or stock and stir into the rice well. Bring to the boil, then lower the heat. Cover the pan and simmer for 10 minutes.

6 Sprinkle the corn over the rice, spread the chopped pepper on top and sprinkle over the grated carrot.

7 Cover tightly and steam over a low heat until the rice is tender, then mix with a fork.

8 Pile the vegetables and rice on to a serving plate and garnish with chervil sprigs.

Energy 454kcal/1897kJ Fat 9.7g Saturated fat 1.2g Carbohydrate 82.7g Fibre 2.3g.

Caramelized Basmati Rice

This dish is the traditional accompaniment to a dhansak curry. Sugar is caramelized in hot oil before the rice is added, along with whole spices.

Serves 4
225g/8oz/generous 1 cup basmati rice
45ml/3 tbsp vegetable oil
20ml/4 tsp granulated sugar
4 or 5 green cardamom pods, bruised
2.5cm/1in piece cinnamon stick
4 cloves
1 bay leaf, crumbled
2.5ml/½ tsp salt
475ml/16fl oz/2 cups hot water

1 Wash the rice, put it in a bowl and pour over water to cover. Leave to soak for 20 minutes.

2 Drain the rice in a colander, shaking it a little as you do so. Run the washed grains through your fingers to check that there is no excess water trapped between them. Set aside.

3 In a large pan, heat the vegetable oil over a medium heat. When the oil is hot, sprinkle the granulated sugar over the surface and wait until it has caramelized. Do not stir.

4 Reduce the heat to low and add the spices and bay leaf. Allow to sizzle for 15–20 seconds, then add the rice and salt. Fry gently, stirring, for 2–3 minutes.

5 Pour in the water and bring to the boil. Let it boil steadily for 2 minutes then reduce the heat to very low. Cover the pan and cook for 8 minutes.

6 Remove the rice from the heat and leave to stand for 6–8 minutes. Fluff up the rice with a fork and serve.

Cook's Tip
Watch the sugar carefully so that it does not burn.

Energy 276kcal/1150kJ Fat 8.5g Saturated fat 1g Carbohydrate 44.9g Fibre 0g.

Basmati Rice with Potato

Rice is eaten at all meals in Indian and Pakistani homes. There are several ways of cooking rice, and mostly whole spices are used. Always choose a good-quality basmati rice.

Serves 4
300g/11oz/1½ cups basmati rice
15ml/1 tbsp oil
1 small cinnamon stick
1 bay leaf
1.5ml/¼ tsp black cumin seeds
3 green cardamom pods
1 medium onion, sliced
5ml/1 tsp grated fresh root ginger
5ml/1 tsp crushed garlic
1.5ml/¼ tsp ground turmeric
7.5ml/1½ tsp salt
1 large potato, roughly diced
475ml/16fl oz/2 cups water
15ml/1 tbsp chopped fresh coriander (cilantro)

1 Wash the rice well and leave it to soak in water for 20 minutes. Heat the oil in a heavy pan, add the cinnamon, bay leaf, black cumin seeds, cardamoms and onion and cook for about 2 minutes.

2 Add the ginger, garlic, turmeric, salt and potato, and cook for 1 minute.

3 Drain the rice thoroughly. Add it to the potato and spices in the pan.

4 Stir to mix, then pour in the water followed by the coriander. Cover the pan with a lid and cook for 15–20 minutes. Remove from the heat and leave to stand, still covered, for 5–10 minutes before serving.

> **Cook's Tip**
> It is important to observe the standing time of this dish before serving. Use a slotted spoon to serve the rice and potato mixture and handle it gently to avoid breaking the delicate grains of rice.

Basmati Rice & Peas with Curry Leaves

This is a very simple rice dish, but it is full of flavour and can make a useful quick main course.

Serves 4
300g/11oz/1½ cups basmati rice
15ml/1 tbsp oil
6–8 curry leaves
1.5ml/¼ tsp mustard seeds
1.5ml/¼ tsp onion seeds
30ml/2 tbsp fresh fenugreek leaves
5ml/1 tsp crushed garlic
5ml/1 tsp grated fresh root ginger
5ml/1 tsp salt
115g/4oz/1 cup frozen peas
475ml/16fl oz/2 cups water

1 Wash the rice well and leave it to soak in a bowl of water for 30 minutes.

2 Heat the oil in a heavy pan and add the curry leaves, mustard seeds, onion seeds, fenugreek leaves, garlic, ginger and salt and stir-fry for 2–3 minutes.

3 Drain the rice, add it to the pan and stir gently.

4 Add the frozen peas and water and bring to the boil. Lower the heat, cover with a lid and cook for 15–20 minutes. Remove from the heat and leave to stand, still covered, for 10 minutes.

5 When ready to serve, fluff up the rice with a fork. Spoon the mixture on to serving plates and serve immediately.

> **Cook's Tip**
> Fenugreek is an important spice in Indian cuisine. It has a strong distinctive curry aroma while cooking and imparts a rich flavour to dishes. The leaves are available fresh and dried from Indian markets and stores, and are used sparingly in dishes, as the flavour is intense.

Energy 371kcal/1572kJ Fat 5.72g Saturated fat 1.03g Carbohydrate 77.36g Fibre 1.62g.

Energy 336kcal/1425kJ; Fat 5.96g; Saturated fat 1.09g; Carbohydrate 67.67g; Fibre 1.83g.

Red Fried Rice

This vibrant rice dish owes its appeal as much to the bright colours of its ingredients – red onion, red pepper and cherry tomatoes – as it does to their flavours.

Serves 2
130g/4½oz/¾ cup basmati rice
30ml/2 tbsp groundnut (peanut) oil

1 small red onion, chopped
1 red (bell) pepper, seeded and chopped
225g/8oz cherry tomatoes, halved
2 eggs, beaten
salt and ground black pepper

1 Wash the rice several times under cold running water. Drain well.

2 Bring a large pan of water to the boil. Add the rice and cook for 10–12 minutes.

3 Meanwhile, heat the oil in a wok until very hot. Add the onion and red pepper and stir-fry for 2–3 minutes.

4 Add the cherry tomatoes and continue stir-frying for 2 minutes more.

5 Pour in the beaten eggs all at once. Cook for 30 seconds without stirring, then stir to break up the egg as it sets.

6 Drain the cooked rice thoroughly. Add to the wok and toss it over the heat with the vegetables and egg mixture for 3 minutes. Season with salt and pepper, and serve immediately.

> **Variation**
> *To add even more colour to this bright dish, you could replace the red (bell) pepper with an orange or green variety.*

Tomato Biryani

Although generally served as an accompaniment to meat, poultry or fish dishes, this tasty rice dish can also be eaten as a complete meal on its own.

Serves 4
400g/14oz/2 cups basmati rice
15ml/1 tbsp oil
2.5ml/½ tsp onion seeds
1 medium onion, sliced

2 medium tomatoes, sliced
1 orange or yellow (bell) pepper, seeded and sliced
5ml/1 tsp grated fresh root ginger
5ml/1 tsp crushed garlic
5ml/1 tsp chilli powder
30ml/2 tbsp chopped fresh coriander (cilantro)
1 medium potato, diced
7.5ml/1½ tsp salt
50g/2oz/½ cup frozen peas
750ml/1¼ pints/3 cups water

1 Wash the rice well and leave it to soak in water for 30 minutes. Heat the oil in a heavy pan and fry the onion seeds for about 30 seconds. Add the sliced onion and fry for 5 minutes, stirring occasionally to prevent the slices from sticking to the pan.

2 Add the sliced tomatoes and peppers, ginger, garlic and chilli powder. Stir-fry for 2 minutes.

3 Add the fresh coriander, potato, salt and peas and stir-fry over a medium heat for a further 5 minutes.

4 Transfer the rice to a colander and drain it thoroughly. Add it to the spiced tomato and potato mixture and stir-fry for 1–2 minutes.

5 Pour in the water and bring to the boil, then lower the heat to medium. Cover and cook the rice for 12–15 minutes. Leave to stand for 5 minutes and then serve.

> **Cook's Tip**
> *Plain rice can look a bit dull; it is greatly enhanced by adding colourful ingredients such as tomatoes, peppers and peas.*

Energy 472kcal/1964kJ; Fat 17.3g; Saturated fat 2.9g; Carbohydrate 65.8g; Fibre 1.8g.

Energy 409kcal/1710kJ; Fat 3.7g; Saturated fat 0.44g; Carbohydrate 89.7g; Fibre 2.4g.

Festive Rice

This pretty dish is traditionally shaped into a cone and surrounded by a variety of accompaniments before being served.

Serves 8
450g/1lb/2⅓ cups jasmine rice
60ml/4 tbsp oil
2 garlic cloves, crushed
2 onions, thinly sliced
2.5ml/½ tsp ground turmeric

750ml/1¼ pints/3 cups water
400ml/14fl oz can coconut milk
1 or 2 lemon grass stalks, bruised

For the accompaniments
omelette strips
2 fresh red chillies, seeded and shredded
cucumber chunks
tomato wedges
deep-fried onions
prawn (shrimp) crackers

1 Put the jasmine rice in a large strainer and rinse it thoroughly under cold water. Drain well.

2 Heat the oil in a frying pan with a lid. Cook the garlic, onions and turmeric over a low heat for 2–3 minutes, until the onions have softened. Add the rice and stir well to coat in oil.

3 Pour in the water and coconut milk and add the lemon grass. Bring to the boil, stirring. Cover the pan and cook gently for 12 minutes, or until all the liquid has been absorbed by the rice.

4 Remove the pan from the heat and lift the lid. Cover with a clean dish towel, replace the lid and leave to stand in a warm place for 15 minutes. Remove the lemon grass, mound the rice mixture in a cone on a serving platter and garnish with the accompaniments, then serve.

Cook's Tip
Lemon grass is the stalk of a perennial grass, and is widely available in supermarkets. It can also be grown in a pot indoors.

Fragrant Harbour Fried Rice

Fragrant Harbour is the Chinese name for Hong Kong, the crossroads for so many styles of cooking.

Serves 4
225g/8oz/generous 1 cup long grain rice
about 90ml/6 tbsp vegetable oil
2 eggs, beaten
4 Chinese dried mushrooms, soaked for 30 minutes in warm water to cover
8 shallots or 2 small onions, sliced
115g/4oz peeled cooked prawns (shrimp), thawed if frozen

3 garlic cloves, crushed
115g/4oz cooked pork, cut into thin strips
115g/4oz Chinese sausage
30ml/2 tbsp light soy sauce
115g/4oz/1 cup frozen peas, thawed
2 spring onions (scallions), shredded
1 or 2 fresh or dried red chillies, seeded (optional)
salt and ground black pepper
fresh coriander (cilantro) leaves, to garnish

1 Bring a large pan of lightly salted water to the boil. Add the rice and cook for 12–15 minutes until just tender. Drain and leave to become cold. Ideally use the next day.

2 Heat about 15ml/1 tbsp of the oil in a large frying pan over a medium heat, pour in the beaten eggs and allow to set without stirring. Slide the omelette on to a plate, roll it up and cut into fine strips. Set aside.

3 Drain the mushrooms, cut off and discard the stems, and slice the caps finely. Heat a wok, add 15ml/1 tbsp of the remaining oil and, when hot, stir-fry the shallots or onions until crisp and golden brown. Remove with a slotted spoon and set aside.

4 Add the prawns and garlic to the wok, with a little more oil if needed, and fry for 1 minute. Remove the prawns and garlic and set aside. Add 15ml/1 tbsp more oil to the wok.

5 Stir-fry the shredded pork and mushrooms for 2 minutes; lift out and reserve. Steam the Chinese sausage in a colander for 5 minutes or until it plumps up. Trim and slice at an angle.

6 Wipe the wok, reheat with the remaining oil and stir-fry the rice, adding more oil if needed so the grains are coated. Stir in the soy sauce, salt and pepper, plus half the cooked ingredients.

7 Add the peas and half the spring onions and toss over the heat until the peas are cooked. Pile the fried rice on a heated platter and arrange the remaining cooked ingredients on top, with the remaining spring onions. Add the chilli, if using, and the coriander leaves, to garnish.

Cook's Tip
Dried mushrooms often have a more intense flavour than fresh, but they are inclined to be a little gritty. Before using, soak in lukewarm water for 5 minutes, then rinse in a strainer before soaking for 30 minutes to soften them for use.

Energy 303kcal/1263kJ; Fat 8.6g; Saturated fat 2g; Carbohydrate 49.5g; Fibre 0.5g.

Energy 567kcal/2359kJ; Fat 27g; Saturated fat 5.5g; Carbohydrate 56g; Fibre 2.3g.

Coconut Rice

This rich dish is usually served with a tangy papaya salad to balance the sweetness of the coconut milk and sugar. It is one of those comforting treats that everyone enjoys.

Serves 4–6
250ml/8fl oz/1 cup water
475ml/16fl oz/2 cups coconut milk
2.5ml/½ tsp salt
30ml/2 tbsp granulated sugar
450g/1lb/2⅔ cups jasmine rice

1 Place the measured water, coconut milk, salt and sugar in a heavy pan. Wash the jasmine rice in several changes of cold water until it runs clear.

2 Add the rice to the pan, cover tightly with a lid and bring to the boil over medium heat.

3 Reduce the heat to low and simmer gently, without lifting the lid unnecessarily, for 15–20 minutes, until the rice is tender and cooked through. Test it by biting a grain; it should be slightly *al dente* (soft but with a bite in the centre).

4 Turn off the heat and leave the rice to rest in the pan, still covered with the lid, for a further 5–10 minutes.

5 Gently fluff up the rice grains with a fork before transferring it to a warmed dish and serving.

Cook's Tip
Jasmine rice, or Thai fragrant rice, is an aromatic long grain rice with a subtle flavour. It is slightly sticky when cooked.

Variation
For a special occasion serve in a halved papaya and garnish with thin shreds of fresh coconut. Use a vegetable peeler to pare the coconut finely, as you would when making curls of Parmesan cheese.

Rice with Lime & Lemon Grass

It is unusual to find brown rice given the Thai treatment, but the nutty flavour of the grains is enhanced by the fragrance of limes and lemon grass in this delicious dish.

Serves 4
2 limes
1 lemon grass stalk
225g/8oz/generous 1 cup brown long grain rice
15ml/1 tbsp olive oil
1 onion, chopped
2.5cm/1in piece fresh root ginger, finely chopped
7.5ml/1½ tsp coriander seeds
7.5ml/1½ tsp cumin seeds
750ml/1¼ pints/3 cups vegetable stock
60ml/4 tbsp chopped fresh coriander (cilantro)
spring onion (scallion) green and toasted coconut strips, to garnish
lime wedges, to serve

1 Pare the limes, using a cannelle knife (zester) or fine grater, taking care to avoid cutting the bitter pith. Set the rind aside.

2 Finely chop the lower portion of the lemon grass stalk and set it aside.

3 Rinse the rice in plenty of cold water until the water runs clear. Tip it into a sieve (strainer) and drain thoroughly.

4 Heat the oil in a large pan. Add the onion, ginger, coriander and cumin seeds, lemon grass and lime rind and cook over a low heat for 2–3 minutes.

5 Add the rice to the pan and cook, stirring constantly, for 1 minute, then pour in the stock and bring to the boil. Reduce the heat to very low and cover the pan. Cook gently for 30 minutes, then check the rice. If it is still crunchy, cover the pan and cook for 3–5 minutes more. Remove from the heat.

6 Stir in the fresh coriander, fluff up the rice grains with a fork, cover the pan and leave to stand for 10 minutes. Transfer to a warmed dish, garnish with spring onion and toasted coconut strips, and serve with lime wedges.

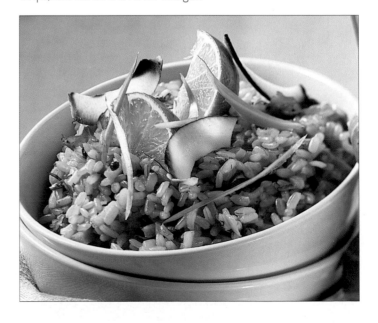

Energy 460kcal/1929kJ; Fat 0.9g; Saturated fat 0.2g; Carbohydrate 103.4g; Fibre 0g.

Energy 232kcal/969kJ; Fat 3.1g; Saturated fat 0.4g; Carbohydrate 46.1g; Fibre 0.2g.

Tarka Dhal

Probably the most popular Indian lentil dish found today, Tarka Dhal is served in most Indian and Pakistani restaurants.

Serves 4
115g/4oz/¹/₂ cup masoor dhal
  (red split lentils)
50g/2oz/¹/₄ cup mung dhal or
  yellow split peas
600ml/1 pint/2¹/₂ cups water
5ml/1 tsp grated fresh root ginger
5ml/1 tsp crushed garlic
1.5ml/¹/₄ tsp ground turmeric
2 fresh green chillies, chopped
7.5ml/1¹/₂ tsp salt

For the tarka
30ml/2 tbsp oil
1 onion, sliced
1.5ml/¹/₄ tsp mixed mustard
  and onion seeds
4 dried red chillies
1 tomato, sliced

For the garnish
15ml/1 tbsp chopped fresh
  coriander (cilantro)
1 or 2 fresh green chillies,
  seeded and sliced
15ml/1 tbsp chopped fresh
  mint

1 Boil all the masoor dhal and mung dhal or yellow split peas in the water with the ginger and garlic, turmeric and chopped green chillies for 15–20 minutes, or until soft.

2 Pound the mixture with a rolling pin or mash with a fork until it has the consistency of a creamy chicken soup.

3 If the lentil mixture looks too dry, add a little more water. Season with the salt. To prepare the tarka, heat the oil in a heavy pan and fry the onion with the mustard and onion seeds, dried red chillies and tomato for 2 minutes.

4 Spoon the mashed lentils into a serving dish and pour the tarka over. Garnish with fresh coriander, green chillies and mint, and serve immediately.

Cook's Tip
Use 1 or 2 red chillies if you want a milder tarka for the dhal.

Lentils Seasoned with Fried Spices

A simple supper dish for family or friends using traditional Indian lentils and peas.

Serves 4–6
115g/4oz/¹/₂ cup red gram
  (pigeon peas)
50g/2oz/¹/₄ cup Bengal gram
4 fresh green chillies
5ml/1 tsp ground turmeric
1 large onion, sliced
400g/14oz can chopped tomatoes

60ml/4 tbsp vegetable oil
2.5ml/¹/₂ tsp mustard seeds
2.5ml/¹/₂ tsp cumin seeds
1 garlic clove, crushed
6 curry leaves
2 dried red chillies
salt
deep-fried onions and fresh
  coriander (cilantro),
  to garnish

1 Place the red gram and bengal gram in a heavy pan and pour in 350ml/12fl oz/1¹/₂ cups water. Add the chillies, turmeric and onion slices and bring to the boil. Simmer, covered, until the lentils are soft and the water has evaporated.

2 Mash the lentils with the back of a spoon. When nearly smooth, add the tomatoes and salt to taste, and mix well. If necessary, thin with a little hot water.

3 Heat the oil in a frying pan. Fry the remaining ingredients until the garlic browns. Pour the oil and spices over the lentils and cover. After 5 minutes, mix well, garnish, and serve.

Cook's Tips
• Red gram, or pigeon peas, are the fruit of a small shrub but are used as a vegetable. They form a staple food in India as well as Africa and the Caribbean, and you will find them in Asian and Caribbean stores and markets.
• Bengal gram, or channa, is a small variety of chickpea, which is commonly used in Indian cuisine.

Green Lentils & Rice

Also known as continental lentils, green lentils retain their shape and colour when cooked. They are an important source of protein and add a robust flavour to dishes such as this. Chillies, ginger, cardamoms and cinnamon make this a lively main-course rice, excellent served with a vegetable curry or a simple salad.

Serves 4–6
350g/12oz/1¾ cups patna
   rice
175g/6oz/¾ cup green lentils
50g/2oz/¼ cup ghee
1 onion, finely chopped
2 garlic cloves, crushed
2.5cm/1in piece fresh root
   ginger, shredded
4 fresh green chillies,
   chopped
4 cloves
2.5cm/1in piece cinnamon stick
4 green cardamom pods
5ml/1 tsp ground turmeric
600ml/1 pint/2½ cups water
salt

1 Wash the rice and lentils, then soak them in a bowl of cold water for 20 minutes.

2 Gently heat the ghee in a large, heavy pan with a tight-fitting cover and fry the onion, garlic, ginger, chillies, cloves, cinnamon, cardamoms, turmeric and salt to taste until the onion is soft and translucent.

3 Drain the rice and lentils and add them to the spices in the pan. Sauté for 2–3 minutes. Add the water and bring the mixture to the boil.

4 Reduce the heat, cover and cook for about 20–25 minutes, or until all the water has been absorbed.

5 Take the pan off the heat and leave to rest with the lid on for 5 minutes.

6 Just before serving, gently toss the rice and lentils with a flat spatula, taking care not to break the delicate grains.

Energy 669kcal/2793kJ Fat 23.5g Saturated fat 15g Carbohydrate 97.4g Fibre 2.7g.

Courgettes with Split Lentils & Tomatoes

The nutty flavour of lentils goes particularly well with courgettes and tomatoes, perked up with a selection of aromatic spices. Serve with rice or bread for a filling and tasty supper.

Serves 4–6
225g/8oz courgettes (zucchini)
1 large onion, finely sliced
2 garlic cloves, crushed
2 fresh green chillies,
   chopped
175g/6oz/⅔ cup mung dhal
   or yellow split peas
2.5ml/½ tsp ground turmeric
60ml/4 tbsp vegetable oil
2.5ml/½ tsp mustard seeds
2.5ml/½ tsp cumin seeds
1.5ml/¼ tsp asafoetida
a few fresh coriander (cilantro)
   and mint leaves, chopped
6–8 curry leaves
2.5ml/½ tsp granulated sugar
200g/7oz can chopped tomatoes
60ml/4 tbsp lemon juice
salt

1 Cut the courgettes into wedges. Finely slice the onion and crush the garlic. Chop the green chilles.

2 In a pan, simmer the lentils and turmeric in 300ml/½ pint/1¼ cups water, until cooked but not mushy. Drain the cooked lentils, retaining the cooking liquid, and set aside while you cook the vegetables.

3 Heat the oil in a frying pan and add the courgette wedges, sliced onion, crushed garlic and chopped chillies. Add the mustard and cumin seeds, asafoetida, fresh coriander and mint, and stir in the curry leaves and sugar. Fry the ingredients together, stirring occasionally, and then add the chopped tomatoes. Mix well and add salt to taste.

4 Cover and cook until the courgettes are nearly tender but still crunchy.

5 Fold in the drained lentils and the lemon juice. If the dish is too dry, add some of the reserved cooking water. Reheat thoroughly and serve immediately.

Energy 278kcal/1165kJ Fat 12g Saturated fat 1.5g Carbohydrate 31.9g Fibre 3.9g.

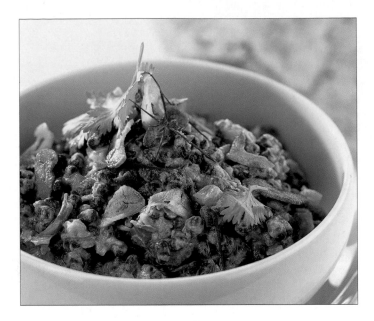

Creamy Black Lentils

Black lentils, or urad dhal, are available whole, split, and skinned and split.

Serves 4–6
175g/6oz/³/₄ cup black lentils, soaked
50g/2oz/¹/₄ cup red split lentils
120ml/4fl oz/¹/₂ cup double (heavy) cream, plus extra to serve
120ml/4fl oz/¹/₂ cup natural (plain) yogurt
5ml/1 tsp cornflour (cornstarch)

40g/1¹/₂oz/3 tbsp ghee or vegetable oil
1 onion, finely chopped
5cm/2in piece fresh root ginger, crushed
4 fresh green chillies, chopped
1 tomato, chopped
2.5ml/¹/₂ tsp chilli powder
2.5ml/¹/₂ tsp ground turmeric
2.5ml/¹/₂ tsp ground cumin
2 garlic cloves, sliced
salt
coriander (cilantro) sprigs and sliced fresh red chilli, to garnish

1 Drain the black lentils and place in a large pan with the red lentils. Cover with water and bring to the boil. Reduce the heat, cover the pan and simmer until tender. Mash with a spoon, and cool.

2 In a bowl, mix together the cream, yogurt and cornflour, and stir into the lentils in the pan.

3 Heat 15g/¹/₂oz/1 tbsp of the ghee or oil in a karahi, wok or large pan, and fry the onion, ginger, half the green chillies and the tomato until the onion is soft.

4 Add the ground spices and salt, and fry for a further 2 minutes. Stir into the lentil mixture and mix well. Reheat, transfer to a heatproof serving dish and keep warm.

5 Heat the remaining ghee or oil in a frying pan over a low heat and fry the garlic slices and remaining chillies until the garlic slices are golden brown.

6 Pour over the lentils, and fold in the garlic and chilli just before serving. Garnish and serve with extra cream so that diners can add more as they eat, if they wish.

Energy 431kcal/1800kJ Fat 26.5g Saturated fat 16.2g Carbohydrate 35g Fibre 2.9g.

Lentils Seasoned with Garlic Oil

This dish is popular in southern India, where there are numerous variations. A single vegetable can be added to the lentils, or a combination of two or more. It is traditionally served with steamed rice dumplings or stuffed rice pancakes. The garlic-flavoured lentils are also extremely satisfying with plain boiled rice.

Serves 4–6
120ml/4fl oz/¹/₂ cup vegetable oil
2.5ml/¹/₂ tsp mustard seeds
2.5ml/¹/₂ tsp cumin seeds
2 dried red chillies
1.5ml/¹/₄ tsp asafoetida
6–8 curry leaves

2 garlic cloves, crushed, plus 2 sliced
30ml/2 tbsp desiccated (dry unsweetened shredded) coconut
225g/8oz/1 cup red lentils, washed and drained
10ml/2 tsp sambhar masala or other curry powder
2.5ml/¹/₂ tsp ground turmeric
450ml/³/₄ pint/scant 2 cups water
450g/1lb mixed vegetables, such as okra, courgettes (zucchini), aubergine (eggplant), cauliflower, shallots and (bell) peppers, chopped
60ml/4 tbsp tamarind juice
4 firm tomatoes, quartered
a few coriander (cilantro) leaves, chopped

1 Heat half the oil in a karahi, wok, or large pan, and stir-fry the next seven ingredients until the coconut begins to brown.

2 Stir in the prepared red lentils with the masala and turmeric. Stir-fry for 2–3 minutes and add the water. Bring to the boil and reduce the heat to low.

3 Cover the pan and leave to simmer for 25–30 minutes, or until the lentils are mushy. Add the chopped mixed vegetables, tamarind juice and tomato quarters. Cook until the vegetables are just tender.

4 Heat the remaining oil in a small pan over a low heat, and fry the garlic slices until golden. Stir in the fresh coriander leaves, then pour over the lentils and vegetables. Mix together at the table before serving.

Energy 477kcal/1994kJ Fat 28.7g Saturated fat 7.1g Carbohydrate 38.6g Fibre 6.8g.

Lentils & Rice

Here, lentils are cooked with whole and ground spices, potato, rice and onion to produce a tasty and nutritious meal.

Serves 4

150g/5oz/¾ cup tuvar dhal or
  red split lentils
115g/4oz/½ cup basmati rice
1 large potato
1 large onion
30ml/2 tbsp oil
4 whole cloves
1.5ml/¼ tsp cumin seeds
1.5ml/¼ tsp ground turmeric
10ml/2 tsp salt
300ml/½ pint/1¼ cups water

1 Wash the tuvar dhal or red split lentils and rice in several changes of cold water. Put into a bowl and cover with water. Leave to soak for 15 minutes, then transfer to a strainer and drain well.

2 Peel the potato, then cut it into 2.5cm/1in chunks. Using a sharp knife, thinly slice the onion and set aside for later.

3 Heat the oil in a heavy pan and fry the cloves and cumin seeds for 2 minutes until the seeds are beginning to splutter.

4 Add the onion and potato chunks and fry for 5 minutes. Add the lentils, rice, turmeric and salt and fry for a further 3 minutes.

5 Add the water. Bring to the boil, cover and simmer gently for 15–20 minutes until all the water has been absorbed and the potato chunks are tender. Leave to stand, covered, for about 10 minutes before serving.

> **Cook's Tip**
> *Red split lentils are widely available in most supermarkets. Before cooking they are salmon-coloured and they turn a pale, dull yellow during cooking. They have a mild, pleasant, nutty flavour. Soaking them in water speeds up the cooking process but isn't strictly necessary.*

Energy 332kcal/1396kJ; Fat 6.7g; Saturated fat 0.76g; Carbohydrate 58.6g; Fibre 3.4g.

Spinach Dhal

Many different types of dhal are eaten in India and each region has its own speciality. This is a delicious, lightly spiced dish with a mild nutty flavour from the yellow lentils, which combine well with the spinach.

Serves 4

175g/6oz/1 cup chana dhal
  or yellow split peas
175ml/6fl oz/¾ cup water
15ml/1 tbsp oil
1.5ml/¼ tsp black mustard
  seeds
1 onion, thinly sliced
2 garlic cloves, crushed
2.5cm/1in piece fresh root
  ginger, grated
1 fresh red chilli, finely chopped
275g/10oz frozen spinach,
  thawed
1.5ml/¼ tsp chilli powder
2.5ml/½ tsp ground coriander
2.5ml/½ tsp garam masala
2.5ml/½ tsp salt

1 Wash the chana dhal or split peas in several changes of cold water. Put into a bowl and cover with plenty of water. Leave to soak for 30 minutes.

2 Drain the pulses and put them in a large pan with the water. Bring to the boil, cover and simmer for 20–25 minutes, or until they are soft.

3 Meanwhile, heat the oil in a large, heavy pan and fry the mustard seeds for 2 minutes until they begin to splutter.

4 Add the onion, garlic, ginger and chilli and fry for 5–6 minutes until softened but not coloured.

5 Add the spinach and cook for 10 minutes or until the spinach is dry and the liquid has been absorbed. Stir in the remaining spices and salt, and cook for 2–3 minutes.

6 Drain the split peas, add them to the spinach mixture and cook for about 5 minutes. Transfer to a warmed serving dish and serve immediately.

Energy 183kcal/778kJ Fat 2g Saturated fat 0.44g Carbohydrate 30.3g Fibre 4.9g.

South Indian Lentils & Vegetables

Pulses are perfect for easy, inexpensive meals. Choose a selection of your favourite vegetables, such as potato, cauliflower, carrots and beans for this tasty dish.

Serves 4–6

60ml/4 tbsp vegetable oil
2.5ml/½ tsp mustard seeds
2.5ml/½ tsp cumin seeds
2 dried red chillies
1.5ml/¼ tsp asafoetida
6–8 curry leaves
2 garlic cloves, crushed
30ml/2 tbsp desiccated (dry unsweetened shredded) coconut

225g/8oz/1 cup masoor dhal or red split lentils
10ml/2 tsp sambhar masala or garam masala
2.5ml/½ tsp ground turmeric
450g/1lb mixed vegetables, in bitesize pieces
60ml/4 tbsp tamarind juice
4 firm tomatoes, quartered
60ml/4 tbsp vegetable oil
2 garlic cloves, finely sliced
handful fresh coriander (cilantro), chopped

1 Heat the oil in a heavy pan. Fry the mustard seeds, cumin seeds, dried red chillies, asafoetida, curry leaves, crushed garlic and desiccated coconut until the coconut browns.

2 Mix in the masoor dhal or red split lentils, sambhar masala and ground turmeric. Stir in 450ml/¾ pint/scant 2 cups water.

3 Simmer the mixture until the lentils are mushy. Add the mixed vegetables, tamarind juice and tomatoes. Cook so that the vegetables are crunchy.

4 In the oil, fry the garlic slices and fresh coriander. Pour over the lentils and vegetables. Mix at the table before serving.

Cook's Tip
Courgettes (zucchini), aubergines (eggplants), (bell) peppers, mangetouts (snow peas) and broccoli would also taste wonderful in this curry.

Rice Layered with Bengal Gram

This rice and lentil dish is served with a gourd curry, or palida, which is prominently flavoured with fenugreek and soured with dried mangosteen.

Serves 4–6

175g/6oz/⅔ cup Bengal gram or lentils of your choice
600ml/1 pint/2½ cups water
2.5ml/½ tsp ground turmeric
50g/2oz deep-fried onions, crushed
45ml/3 tbsp green masala paste
a few fresh mint and coriander (cilantro) leaves, chopped
350g/12oz/1¾ cups basmati rice, cooked
30ml/2 tbsp ghee
salt

For the curry

60ml/4 tbsp vegetable oil
1.5ml/¼ tsp fenugreek seeds
15g/½oz dried fenugreek leaves
2 garlic cloves, crushed
5ml/1 tsp ground coriander
5ml/1 tsp cumin seeds
5ml/1 tsp chilli powder
60ml/4 tbsp gram flour mixed with 60ml/4 tbsp water
450g/1lb bottle gourd, peeled, pith and seeds removed and cut into bitesize pieces, or marrow (large zucchini) or firm courgettes (zucchini) prepared in the same way
175ml/6fl oz/¾ cup tomato juice
6 dried mangosteen (kokum), or juice of 3 lemons
salt

1 For the rice, boil the Bengal gram in the water with the turmeric until the grains are soft. Drain and reserve the water for the curry. Toss the Bengal gram gently with the deep-fried onions, green masala paste, mint and coriander. Add salt to taste.

2 Grease a heavy pan and place a layer of rice in the bottom. Add the bengal gram mixture and another layer of the remaining rice. Place small knobs (pats) of ghee on top, sprinkle with a little water and heat gently until steam rises from the mixture.

3 To make the curry, heat the oil in a pan and fry the fenugreek seeds and leaves and the garlic until the garlic turns golden brown. Mix the ground coriander, cumin and chilli powder to a paste with a little water. Add to the pan and simmer until all the water has evaporated. Add the gram-flour paste, gourd and the tomato juice. Add the mangosteen and salt. Cook until the gourd is soft. Serve hot.

Energy 459kcal/1917kJ; Fat 28.1g; Saturated fat 7g; Carbohydrate 37.3g; Fibre 5.8g.

Energy 536kcal/2250kJ; Fat 14g; Saturated fat 1.8g; Carbohydrate 82.3g; Fibre 4.9g.

Lentil Dhal with Roasted Garlic & Whole Spices

This spicy lentil dhal makes a sustaining and comforting meal when served with rice or Indian breads and any dry-spiced dish, particularly a cauliflower or potato dish. The spicy garnish offers a contrast in texture and flavour.

Serves 4–6
40g/1½oz/3 tbsp butter or ghee
1 onion, chopped
2 fresh green chillies, seeded and chopped
15ml/1 tbsp chopped fresh root ginger
225g/8oz/1 cup yellow or red lentils
900ml/1½ pints/3¾ cups water
45ml/3 tbsp roasted garlic purée
5ml/1 tsp ground cumin
5ml/1 tsp ground coriander
200g/7oz tomatoes, peeled and diced
a little lemon juice
salt and ground black pepper
30–45ml/2–3 tbsp coriander (cilantro) sprigs, to garnish

For the spicy garnish
30ml/2 tbsp groundnut (peanut) oil
4 or 5 shallots, sliced
2 garlic cloves, thinly sliced
15g/½oz/1 tbsp butter or ghee
5ml/1 tsp cumin seeds
5ml/1 tsp mustard seeds
3 or 4 small dried red chillies
8–10 fresh curry leaves

1 First begin the spicy garnish. Heat the oil in a large, heavy pan. Add the shallots and fry them over a medium heat, stirring occasionally, until they are crisp and browned. Add the garlic and cook, stirring frequently, for a moment or two until the garlic colours slightly. Use a slotted spoon to remove the mixture from the pan and set it aside in a bowl.

2 Melt the butter or ghee in the pan and cook the onion, chillies and ginger for 10 minutes, until golden. Stir in the lentils and water, then bring to the boil, reduce the heat and part-cover the pan. Simmer, stirring occasionally, for 50–60 minutes, until similar to a very thick soup.

3 Stir in the roasted garlic purée, cumin and ground coriander, then season with salt and pepper to taste. Cook for a further 10–15 minutes, uncovered, stirring frequently. Stir in the tomatoes and then adjust the seasoning, adding a little lemon juice to taste if necessary.

4 Finish the spicy garnish. Melt the butter or ghee in a frying pan. Add the cumin and mustard seeds and fry until the mustard seeds pop. Stir in the chillies, curry leaves and the shallot mixture, then immediately swirl the mixture into the cooked dhal. Garnish with coriander and serve.

> **Cook's Tip**
> *Ghee is a type of clarified butter that has had all the milk solids removed by heating. Because the milk solids have been removed, ghee has a high smoking point and can therefore be cooked at higher temperatures than ordinary butter.*

Energy 340kcal/1424kJ; Fat 16.3g; Saturated fat 7.5g; Carbohydrate 36.3g; Fibre 3.8g.

Bengal Gram & Bottle Gourd Curry

Tamarind gives this lentil and vegetable dish a lemony flavour. Rice or Indian bread is all you need to go with it.

Serves 4–6
450g/1lb bottle gourd, marrow (large zucchini)
175g/6oz/⅔ cup Bengal gram
scant 60ml/4 tbsp vegetable oil
2 fresh green chillies, chopped
1 onion, chopped
2 garlic cloves, crushed
5cm/2in piece fresh root ginger, crushed
6–8 curry leaves
5ml/1 tsp chilli powder
5ml/1 tsp ground turmeric
60ml/4 tbsp tamarind juice
2 tomatoes, chopped
chopped fresh coriander (cilantro)
salt

1 Peel the bottle gourd making sure that the pith is removed. Slice the gourd flesh thickly.

2 Put the Bengal gram in a pan with 450ml/¾ pint/scant 2 cups water, cook the lentils in the water until the grains are tender but not mushy. Set aside, without draining away any of the excess water.

3 Heat the vegetable oil in a large pan and fry the chopped green chillies and onion, crushed garlic, crushed ginger, curry leaves, chilli powder and ground turmeric. Add salt to taste.

4 Add the gourd slices and cook until soft.

5 Add the lentils to the gourd mixture in the pan and any water remaining in the pan. Bring to the boil. Stir in the tamarind juice, chopped tomatoes and fresh chopped coriander.

6 Simmer gently until the gourd is cooked. Serve hot with rice.

Energy 280kcal/1173kJ; Fat 12.2g; Saturated fat 1.6g; Carbohydrate 31.1g; Fibre 4.2g.

Cucumber Curry

Served hot, this unusual curry is good with fish dishes and can also be served cold with cooked meats.

Serves 4–6
120ml/4fl oz/½ cup water
115g/4oz creamed coconut
   (120ml/4fl oz/½ cup coconut
   cream)
2.5ml/½ tsp ground turmeric
5ml/1 tsp sugar
1 large cucumber, cut into
   small pieces

1 large red (bell) pepper,
   cut into small pieces
50g/2oz/½ cup salted peanuts,
   crushed
60ml/4 tbsp vegetable oil
2 dried red chillies
5ml/1 tsp cumin seeds
5ml/1 tsp mustard
   seeds
4–6 curry leaves
4 garlic cloves, crushed
salt
a few whole salted peanuts,
   to garnish

1 Bring the water to the boil in a heavy pan and add the creamed coconut, turmeric, sugar and salt. Simmer until the coconut dissolves and the mixture becomes a smooth, thick sauce.

2 Add the cucumber, red pepper and crushed peanuts and simmer for about 5 minutes. Transfer to a heatproof serving dish and keep hot.

3 Heat the oil in a karahi, wok or frying pan. Fry the chillies and cumin with the mustard seeds until they start to pop.

4 Reduce the heat, add the curry leaves and garlic and fry for 2 minutes. Pour over the cucumber mixture and stir well. Garnish with whole peanuts and serve hot.

Cook's Tip
The mustard seeds used extensively in Indian cooking are black and not yellow (which are ground and used to prepare English mustard). They are always fried to release their sweet aroma and flavour.

Energy 385kcal/1588kJ; Fat 37.6g; Saturated fat 19.6g; Carbohydrate 6.4g; Fibre 1.7g.

Spicy Cabbage

Another spicy twist on a Western favourite. This nutritious side dish is a great way to jazz up the flavour of cabbage for those not usually keen on the vegetable. Note the colourful variations.

2 medium carrots, grated
50g/2oz/¼ cup ghee or
   butter
2.5ml/½ tsp white cumin
   seeds
3–8 dried red chillies, to taste
2.5ml/½ tsp salt
30ml/2 tbsp lemon juice

Serves 4
225g/8oz/2½ cups shredded
   cabbage
1 small onion, sliced

1 Use a mandolin, if you have one, to shred the cabbage finely. Alternatively, use a sharp knife to slice through the layers of the cabbage.

2 Slice the onion and grate the carrots coarsely.

3 Melt the ghee or butter in a medium pan and fry the cumin seeds and dried chillies for about 30 seconds.

4 Add the onion and fry for about 2 minutes.

5 Add the cabbage and carrots and stir-fry for a further 5 minutes or until the cabbage is soft.

6 Finally, stir in the salt and lemon juice and serve immediately.

Variations
You will get a different appearance as well as flavour if you use different kinds of cabbage for this recipe. White cabbage has a delicate taste, whereas Savoy cabbage and spring greens (collards) have a fuller flavour. You could also try red cabbage and use a red onion as well for a colourful alternative.

Energy 91kcal/376kJ; Fat 5.5g; Saturated fat 1.27g; Carbohydrate 8.5g; Fibre 2.4g.

Curried Cauliflower

In this dish the creamy coconut sauce complements the flavour of the spiced cauliflower.

Serves 4–6
15ml/1 tbsp gram flour
120ml/4fl oz/½ cup water
5ml/1 tsp chilli powder
15ml/1 tbsp ground coriander
5ml/1 tsp ground cumin
5ml/1 tsp mustard powder
5ml/1 tsp ground turmeric
60ml/4 tbsp vegetable oil
6–8 curry leaves
5ml/1 tsp cumin seeds
1 cauliflower, broken into florets
175ml/6fl oz/¾ cup thick
    coconut milk
juice of 2 lemons
salt
lime wedges, to serve

1 Put the gram flour in a small bowl and stir in enough of the water to make a smooth paste.

2 Add the chilli, coriander, cumin, mustard, turmeric and salt. Add the remaining water and keep mixing to blend all the ingredients well.

3 Heat the oil in a frying pan, and add the curry leaves and cumin seeds. Add the spice paste and simmer for about 5 minutes, stirring frequently. If the sauce has become too thick, add a little hot water.

4 Add the cauliflower florets and the coconut milk. Bring the mixture to the boil and then reduce the heat. Cover with a lid and cook until the cauliflower is tender but still retains a bit of a crunch. (If you like your cauliflower more tender, cook for a little longer.)

5 Add the lemon juice, mix well and serve the curry hot with the wedges of lime to squeeze over.

> **Variation**
> This sauce also goes well with broccoli. For a pretty presentation use whole miniature vegetables.

Karahi Shredded Cabbage with Mangetouts & Corn

This is one of the best ways to cook cabbage, stir-fried with butter and crushed spices. This side dish makes a wonderful accompaniment to many meat or vegetable dishes.

Serves 4
15ml/1 tbsp corn oil
50g/2oz/¼ cup ghee or butter
2.5ml/½ tsp crushed coriander
    seeds
2.5ml/½ tsp white cumin seeds
6 dried red chillies
1 small Savoy cabbage, shredded
12 mangetouts (snow peas)
3 fresh red chillies, seeded
    and sliced
12 baby corn cobs
salt
25g/1oz/¼ cup flaked (sliced)
    almonds, toasted, and 15ml/
    1 tbsp chopped fresh coriander
    (cilantro), to garnish

1 Heat the oil and butter in a deep round-bottomed frying pan or a karahi and add the crushed coriander seeds, white cumin seeds and dried red chillies.

2 Add the shredded cabbage and mangetouts, and stir-fry for about 5 minutes.

3 Add the sliced fresh red chillies, baby corn and salt, and fry for a further 3 minutes.

4 Garnish with the toasted almonds and fresh coriander and serve hot.

> **Cook's Tip**
> This dish is strongly spiced with red chillies, both fresh and dried, but the recipe also works well with fewer chillies if you prefer a milder flavour. If you have large dried red chillies in your store cupboard (pantry) you might want to reduce the quantity to just one.

Energy 184kcal/759kJ; Fat 16.9g; Saturated fat 7.2g; Carbohydrate 4.3g; Fibre 3g.

Energy 160kcal/663kJ; Fat 12.1g; Saturated fat 1.6g; Carbohydrate 9g; Fibre 2g.

VEGETABLE SIDE DISHES

Spiced Aubergine

Chunks of aubergine are coated in a rich sauce and sprinkled with sesame seeds to make an unusual side dish that is quick to cook. This straightforward yet versatile vegetarian dish can be served hot, warm or cold, as the occasion demands.

Serves 4–6

2 aubergines, total weight
  about 600g/1lb 6oz, cut
  into large chunks
15ml/1 tbsp salt
5ml/1 tsp chilli powder, or
  to taste

75–90ml/5–6 tbsp sunflower
  oil
15ml/1 tbsp rice wine or
  medium-dry sherry
100ml/3½fl oz/scant ½ cup
  water
75ml/5 tbsp chilli bean sauce
  (see Cook's Tip)
salt and ground black pepper
a few toasted sesame seeds,
  to garnish

1 Place the aubergine chunks on a plate, sprinkle them with the salt and leave to stand for 15–20 minutes. Rinse well, drain and dry thoroughly on kitchen paper. Toss the aubergine cubes in the chilli powder.

2 Heat a wok and add the oil. When the oil is hot, add the aubergine chunks, with the rice wine or sherry. Stir constantly until the aubergine chunks start to turn a little brown. Stir in the water, cover the wok and steam for 2–3 minutes. Add the chilli bean sauce and cook for 2 minutes. Season to taste, then spoon on to a serving dish, sprinkle with sesame seeds and serve.

Cook's Tip
If you can't get hold of chilli bean sauce, use 15–30ml/ 1–2 tbsp chilli paste mixed with 2 crushed garlic cloves, 15ml/1 tbsp each dark soy sauce and rice vinegar, and 10ml/2 tsp light soy sauce.

Energy 193kcal/798kJ; Fat 17.1g; Saturated fat 2.1g; Carbohydrate 8.7g; Fibre 3.2g.

Carrot & Cauliflower Stir-fry

Slicing the carrots into thin batons helps them cook quickly. This dish has a crunchy texture and uses only a few whole spices.

Serves 4
2 large carrots
1 small cauliflower
15ml/1 tbsp oil
1 bay leaf

2 cloves
1 small cinnamon stick
2 cardamom pods
3 black peppercorns
5ml/1 tsp salt
50g/2oz/½ cup frozen peas,
  thawed
10ml/2 tsp lemon juice
15ml/1 tbsp chopped fresh
  coriander (cilantro), plus
  fresh leaves to garnish

1 Cut the carrots into thin batons about 2.5cm/1in long. Separate the cauliflower into small florets.

2 Heat the oil in a karahi, wok or heavy pan and add the bay leaf, cloves, cinnamon stick, cardamom pods and peppercorns. Quickly stir-fry over a medium heat for 30–35 seconds, then add the salt.

3 Next add the carrot batons and cauliflower florets and continue to stir-fry for 3–5 minutes.

4 Add the peas, lemon juice and chopped coriander and cook for a further 4–5 minutes. Serve garnished with the whole coriander leaves.

Variation
Substitute broccoli or sliced courgette (zucchini) for the cauliflower, if you like.

Cook's Tip
As both carrots and cauliflower can be eaten raw, they need only minimal cooking or they will lose their crunchy texture.

Energy 84kcal/349kJ; Fat 3.75g; Saturated fat 0.6g; Carbohydrate 9.05g; Fibre 3.67g.

Cauliflower & Potato Curry

Potatoes and cauliflower
make a wonderful
combination for a curry, and
a substantial side dish. Here
they are combined with
the mild flavours of cumin,
coriander and turmeric with
just enough chilli to give the
dish that little extra punch.

Serves 4
450g/1lb potatoes, cut into
  2.5cm/1in chunks
30ml/2 tbsp oil
5ml/1 tsp cumin seeds
1 fresh green chilli, finely chopped
450g/1lb cauliflower, broken
  into florets
5ml/1 tsp ground coriander
5ml/1 tsp ground cumin
1.5ml/¼ tsp chilli powder
2.5ml/½ tsp ground turmeric
2.5ml/½ tsp salt
chopped fresh coriander (cilantro),
  to garnish
tomato and onion salad and
  pickle, to serve

1 Par-cook the potatoes in a large pan of boiling water for
about 10 minutes. Drain well and set aside.

2 Heat the oil in a large, heavy pan. Add the cumin seeds and
fry them for 2 minutes until they begin to splutter. Add the chilli
and fry for a further 1 minute.

3 Add the cauliflower florets and fry, stirring, for 5 minutes.

4 Add the potatoes and the ground spices and salt and cook
for a further 7–10 minutes, or until both the vegetables are
tender. Garnish with fresh coriander and serve with tomato and
onion salad and pickle.

Variation
*Use sweet potatoes instead of ordinary potatoes for a curry
with a sweeter flavour.*

Energy 189kcal/791kJ; Fat 7.4g; Saturated fat 0.77g; Carbohydrate 24.6g; Fibre 3.5g.

Spicy Potatoes & Cauliflower

This dish is simplicity itself
to make and can be eaten
as a main meal with Indian
breads or rice, a raita such
as cucumber and yogurt,
and a fresh mint relish.

Serves 2
225g/8oz potatoes
75ml/5 tbsp groundnut
  (peanut) oil
5ml/1 tsp ground cumin
5ml/1 tsp ground coriander
1.5ml/¼ tsp ground turmeric
1.5ml/¼ tsp cayenne pepper
1 fresh green chilli, seeded
  and finely chopped
1 medium cauliflower, broken
  into small florets
5ml/1 tsp cumin seeds
2 garlic cloves, cut into
  shreds
15–30ml/1–2 tbsp fresh
  coriander (cilantro),
  finely chopped
salt

1 Cook the potatoes in their skins in boiling salted water
for about 20 minutes, until just tender. Drain and leave to
cool. When cool enough to handle, peel and cut into
2.5cm/1in cubes.

2 Heat 45ml/3 tbsp of the oil in a frying pan or wok.
When hot, add the ground cumin, coriander, turmeric, cayenne
pepper and chilli. Let the spices sizzle for a few seconds.

3 Add the cauliflower and about 60ml/4 tbsp water. Cook over
medium heat, stirring continuously, for 6–8 minutes. Add the
potatoes and stir-fry for 2–3 minutes. Season with salt, then
remove from the heat.

4 Heat the remaining oil in a small frying pan. When hot, add
the cumin seeds and garlic, and cook until lightly browned. Pour
the mixture over the vegetables. Sprinkle with the chopped
coriander and serve at once.

Cook's Tip
*Divide the cauliflower into small florets so that it will cook
evenly and quickly.*

Energy 409kcal/1698kJ; Fat 29.7g; Saturated fat 3.8g; Carbohydrate 26.6g; Fibre 5.4g.

Potatoes in Tomato Sauce

This delicious curry makes an excellent accompaniment to almost any other savoury dish, but goes particularly well with Balti dishes. Served with rice, it makes a great vegetarian main course.

Serves 4
10ml/2 tsp oil
1.5ml/¼ tsp onion seeds
4 curry leaves

2 medium onions, diced
400g/14oz can tomatoes
5ml/1 tsp ground cumin
7.5ml/1½ tsp ground coriander
5ml/1 tsp chilli powder
5ml/1 tsp grated fresh root ginger
5ml/1 tsp crushed garlic
1.5ml/¼ tsp ground turmeric
5ml/1 tsp salt
15ml/1 tbsp lemon juice
15ml/1 tbsp chopped fresh
    coriander (cilantro)
2 medium potatoes, diced

1 Heat the oil in a karahi, wok or heavy pan and add the onion seeds, curry leaves and diced onions. Fry over a medium heat for a few minutes, stirring occasionally and being careful not to burn the onions.

2 Meanwhile, place the canned tomatoes in a bowl and add the ground cumin and coriander, chilli powder, ginger, garlic, turmeric, salt, lemon juice and fresh coriander. Mix the ingredients together until well blended.

3 Pour this mixture into the pan and stir for about 1 minute to mix thoroughly with the onions.

4 Finally, add the diced potatoes, cover the pan and cook gently for 7–10 minutes over low heat. Check that the potatoes are properly cooked through, then serve.

Variations
This curry is also delicious if you add a few cauliflower or broccoli florets with the potatoes, or if you substitute diced parsnips for the potatoes. To emphasize the tomato flavour, stir in 15ml/1 tbsp tomato purée (paste).

Energy 119kcal/502kJ; Fat 2.27g; Saturated fat 0.24g; Carbohydrate 22.91g; Fibre 2.88g.

Potatoes in Red Sauce

This is a lightly spiced dish, perfect for children or those who like mild curries.

Serves 4–6
450g/1lb small new potatoes
7.5ml/1½ tsp coriander
    seeds
7.5ml/1½ tsp cumin seeds
4 garlic cloves
90ml/6 tbsp vegetable oil

45ml/3 tbsp thick tamarind
    juice (see Cook's Tip)
60ml/4 tbsp tomato purée
    (paste)
4 curry leaves
salt
5ml/1 tsp granulated sugar
coriander (cilantro) sprig,
    to garnish

1 Boil the potatoes until they are fully cooked but still retain their shape. To test, insert a thin sharp knife into the potatoes. It should come out clean when the potatoes are fully cooked. Drain well.

2 Grind the coriander seeds with the cumin seeds and garlic to a coarse paste using a mortar and pestle or food processor.

3 Heat the oil in a karahi, wok or frying pan. Fry the paste, tamarind juice, tomato purée, curry leaves, salt and sugar until the oil separates.

4 Add the potatoes and stir to coat them in the spicy tomato mixture. Reduce the heat, cover the pan and simmer for about 5 minutes. Garnish and serve.

Cook's Tip
You can buy tamarind concentrate or break off a piece of tamarind slab equivalent to 15ml/1 tbsp. Soak in 150ml/ ¼ pint/⅔ cup hot water for 10 minutes. Mash the tamarind into a paste and pass it through a sieve (strainer). The fine pulp and juice will go through, leaving behind the fibrous husk. Strain the juice. Tamarind pods have a long shelf life and they require soaking to release their juice.

Energy 231kcal/962kJ; Fat 16.8g; Saturated fat 2.1g; Carbohydrate 19.2g; Fibre 1.1g.

India is blessed with over 18 varieties of spinach. If you have access to an Indian or Chinese grocer, look out for some of the more unusual varieties.

Serves 4–6
225g/8oz potatoes
60ml/4 tbsp vegetable oil
2.5cm/1in piece fresh root ginger, crushed
4 garlic cloves, crushed
1 onion, chopped
2 fresh green chillies, chopped
2 dried red chillies, chopped
5ml/1 tsp cumin seeds
225g/8oz fresh spinach, trimmed, washed and chopped, or 225g/8oz frozen spinach, thawed and drained
salt
2 firm tomatoes, roughly chopped, to garnish

1 Wash the potatoes and cut into quarters. If using small new potatoes, leave them whole. Heat the oil in a frying pan and fry the potatoes until brown on all sides. Remove and put aside.

2 Remove the excess oil, leaving about 15ml/1 tbsp in the pan. Fry the ginger, garlic, onion, green chillies, dried red chillies and cumin seeds until the onion is golden brown.

3 Add the potatoes and salt, and stir well. Cover the pan and cook over a medium heat, stirring occasionally, until the potatoes are tender when pierced with a sharp knife.

4 Add the spinach and stir well. Using two wooden spoons or spatulas, toss the mixture over the heat until the spinach is tender and all the excess fluid has evaporated.

5 Spoon into a heated serving dish or on to individual plates and garnish with the chopped tomatoes. Serve hot.

> **Variation**
> This recipe also tastes very good if you substitute sweet potatoes for ordinary potatoes. Slice them just before cooking, or they may discolour.

Bombay Potatoes

This authentic dish belongs to the Gujarati, a totally vegetarian sect and the largest population group in the city of Mumbai.

Serves 4–6
2 onions
2 fresh green chillies
50g/2oz/2 cups fresh coriander (cilantro)
450g/1lb new potatoes
5ml/1 tsp turmeric
60ml/4 tbsp vegetable oil
2 dried red chillies
6–8 curry leaves
1.5ml/¼ tsp asafoetida
2.5ml/½ tsp each cumin, mustard, onion, fennel and nigella seeds
lemon juice, to taste
salt

1 Chop the onions and chillies finely, and coarsely chop the coriander.

2 Scrub the potatoes under cold running water and cut them into small pieces.

3 Boil the potatoes in water with a little salt and 2.5ml/½ tsp of the turmeric for 10–15 minutes, or until tender. Drain the potatoes well then mash them and set aside.

4 Heat the oil in a frying pan and fry the dried chillies and curry leaves until the chillies are nearly burnt.

5 Add the sliced onions, green chillies, fresh coriander and remaining turmeric to the pan, add the asafoetida, cumin, mustard, onion, fennel and nigella seeds. Cook, stirring occasionally, until the onions are soft.

6 Fold in the potatoes and add a few drops of water. Cook over a low heat for about 10 minutes, stirring well to ensure the spices are evenly mixed.

7 Add lemon juice to taste, and serve immediately.

Energy 207kcal/865kJ; Fat 11.6g; Saturated fat 1.4g; Carbohydrate 24.3g; Fibre 2.2g.

Energy 177kcal/734kJ; Fat 11.8g; Saturated fat 1.4g; Carbohydrate 15g; Fibre 2.9g.

Fiery Spiced Potatoes

The quantity of red chillies used here may be too fiery for some palates. For a milder version, seed the chillies, use fewer, or substitute them with a roughly chopped sweet red pepper instead.

Serves 4

12–14 baby new potatoes, peeled and halved
15ml/1 tbsp oil
2.5ml/½ tsp crushed dried red chillies
2.5ml/½ tsp cumin seeds
2.5ml/½ tsp fennel seeds
2.5ml/½ tsp crushed coriander seeds
1 medium onion, sliced
3 or 4 fresh red chillies, chopped
15ml/1 tbsp chopped fresh coriander (cilantro)
salt

1 Boil the potatoes in a pan of salted water until just cooked but still firm. Remove from the heat and drain off the water.

2 In a karahi, wok or deep pan, heat the oil quickly over high heat, then turn down the heat to medium. Add the crushed chillies, cumin, fennel and coriander seeds and a little salt and quickly stir-fry for about 30–40 seconds.

3 Add the onion and fry gently until golden brown. Then add the new potatoes, fresh red chillies and fresh coriander.

4 Cover and cook for 5–7 minutes over a very low heat. Serve hot.

Cook's Tip
Baby new potatoes have a wonderful flavour and texture, which are absolutely perfect for this dish. If you want to try older potatoes, choose ones that retain their shape well and cut them into large chunks. Watch them carefully so that they do not overcook and fall apart.

Energy 122kcal/513kJ; Fat 3.5g; Saturated fat 0.37g; Carbohydrate 21.2g; Fibre 1.5g.

Spiced Potatoes & Carrots Parisienne

Ready-prepared "parisienne" vegetables have recently become available in many supermarkets. These are simply root vegetables that have been peeled and cut into perfectly spherical shapes. This dish looks very fresh and appetizing and is delicious. If you can't locate "parisienne" vegetables, you can simply dice the potatoes and carrots yourself, or cut them into batons.

Serves 4

175g/6oz carrots parisienne
175g/6oz potatoes parisienne
115g/4oz green beans, sliced
75g/3oz/6 tbsp butter
15ml/1 tbsp vegetable oil
1.5ml/¼ tsp onion seeds
1.5ml/¼ tsp fenugreek seeds
4 dried red chillies
2.5ml/½ tsp mustard seeds
6 curry leaves
1 medium onion, sliced
5ml/1 tsp salt
4 garlic cloves, sliced
4 fresh red chillies
15ml/1 tbsp chopped fresh coriander (cilantro)
15ml/1 tbsp chopped fresh mint, plus 1 mint sprig to garnish

1 Drop the carrots, potatoes and green beans into a pan of boiling water, and cook for about 7 minutes, or until they are just tender but not overcooked. Drain in a colander, then refresh under cold water to arrest the cooking process. Drain again and set to one side.

2 Heat the butter and oil in a deep frying pan or a large karahi and add the onion seeds, fenugreek seeds, dried red chillies, mustard seeds and curry leaves. When these have sizzled for a few seconds, add the onion and fry for 3–5 minutes, stirring the mixture occasionally.

3 Add the salt, garlic and fresh chillies, followed by the cooked vegetables, and stir gently for about 5 minutes, over a medium heat.

4 Add the fresh coriander and mint, and serve hot, garnished with a sprig of mint.

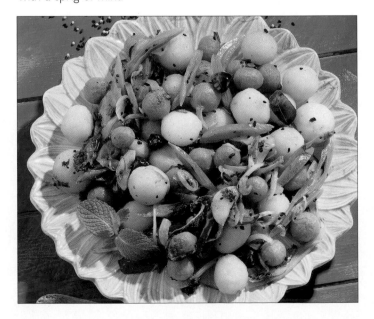

Energy 232kcal/961kJ; Fat 18.6g; Saturated fat 10.2g; Carbohydrate 15g; Fibre 2.7g.

Masala Mashed Potatoes

This delightfully simple variation on the popular Western side dish can be used as an accompaniment to just about any main course dish, not just Indian food. There are easily obtainable alternatives to mango powder if you cannot get hold of any (see Cook's Tip).

Serves 4

3 medium potatoes
15ml/1 tbsp chopped fresh mint
    and coriander (cilantro), mixed
5ml/1 tsp mango powder
    (amchur)

5ml/1 tsp salt
5ml/1 tsp crushed black
    peppercorns
1 fresh red chilli, chopped
1 fresh green chilli, chopped
50g/2oz/1/4 cup butter

1 Boil the potatoes until soft and then mash them down using a masher or potato ricer.

2 Stir the remaining ingredients together in a small bowl.

3 Stir the spice mixture into the mashed potatoes. Mix together thoroughly with a fork and serve warm as an accompaniment.

Cook's Tip
Mango powder, also known as amchur, is the unripe green fruit of the mango tree ground to a powder. The sour mangoes are sliced and dried in the sun, turning a light brown, before they are ground. Mango powder adds a fruity sharpness and a slightly resinous bouquet to a dish. It is widely used with vegetables and is usually added towards the end of the cooking time. If mango powder is unavailable, the nearest substitute is lemon or lime juice, in double or treble quantity.

Energy 100kcal/416kJ; Fat 5.3g; Saturated fat 1.25g; Carbohydrate 11.4g; Fibre 0.8g.

Potatoes in Yogurt Sauce

It is nice to use tiny new potatoes with the skins on for this recipe. The yogurt adds a tangy flavour to this fairly spicy dish, which is delicious served with plain or wholemeal chapatis.

Serves 4
small bunch fresh coriander
    (cilantro)
12 new potatoes, halved

275g/10oz/1 1/4 cups natural
    (plain) low-fat yogurt
300ml/1/2 pint/1 1/4 cups water
1.5ml/1/4 tsp ground turmeric
5ml/1 tsp chilli powder
5ml/1 tsp ground coriander
2.5ml/1/2 tsp ground cumin
5ml/1 tsp soft brown sugar
1.5ml/1/4 tsp salt
15ml/1 tbsp oil
5ml/1 tsp cumin seeds
2 green chillies, sliced

1 Cut off the roots and any thick stalks from the coriander and chop the leaves finely. Set aside.

2 Boil the potatoes in salted water with their skins on until they are just tender, then drain and set aside.

3 Mix together the yogurt, water, turmeric, chilli powder, ground coriander, ground cumin, sugar and salt in a bowl. Set aside.

4 Heat the oil in a medium, heavy pan and stir in the cumin seeds. Fry for 1 minute.

5 Reduce the heat, stir in the spicy yogurt mixture and cook for about 3 minutes over medium heat.

6 Add the chopped fresh coriander, green chillies and cooked potatoes. Blend everything together and cook for a further 5–7 minutes, stirring from time to time. Serve hot.

Cook's Tip
If new potatoes are unavailable, use 450g/1lb ordinary waxy potatoes instead. Peel them and cut into large chunks, then cook as described above.

Energy 169kcal/712kJ; Fat 4.3g; Saturated fat 0.78g; Carbohydrate 27.6g; Fibre 1.2g.

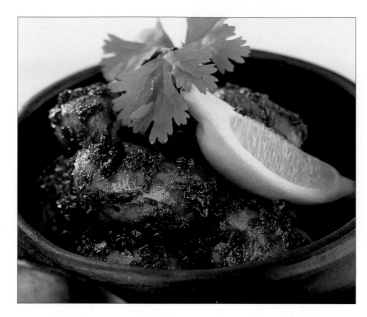

Potatoes in Chilli Tamarind Sauce

In this favourite potato dish from the state of Karnataka, the combination of chilli and tamarind awakens the taste buds immediately. This version adapts the traditional recipe slightly, to reduce the customary pungency and enhance the fiery appearance of this delicious combination.

Serves 4–6
450g/1lb small new potatoes, washed and dried
25g/1oz whole dried red chillies, preferably Kashmiri
7.5ml/1½ tsp cumin seeds
4 garlic cloves, chopped
90ml/6 tbsp vegetable oil
60ml/4 tbsp thick tamarind juice
30ml/2 tbsp tomato purée (paste)
4 curry leaves
5ml/1 tsp granulated sugar
1.5ml/¼ tsp asafoetida
salt
coriander (cilantro) sprigs and lemon wedges, to garnish

1 Boil the new potatoes until they are fully cooked, ensuring they do not break. To test, insert a thin sharp knife into the potatoes. It should come out clean when they are fully cooked. Drain and cool the potatoes in iced water to prevent them from cooking further.

2 Soak the chillies for 5 minutes in warm water. Drain and grind with the cumin seeds and garlic to a coarse paste, either using a mortar and pestle or in a food processor.

3 Heat the oil and fry the paste, tamarind juice, tomato purée, curry leaves, sugar, asafoetida and salt until the oil can be seen to have separated from the spice paste.

4 Add the potatoes and stir to coat. Reduce the heat, cover and simmer for 5 minutes. Garnish and serve.

Variation
Chunks of large potatoes can be used as an alternative to new potatoes. Alternatively, try this dish with sweet potatoes. The spicy sweet-and-sour taste works very well in this variation.

Energy 227kcal/945kJ; Fat 16.8g; Saturated fat 2.1g; Carbohydrate 18.1g; Fibre 1.1g.

Potatoes with Roasted Poppy Seeds

Poppy seeds are used in Indian cooking as thickening agents, and to lend a nutty taste to sauces.

Serves 4
45ml/3 tbsp white poppy seeds
45–60ml/3–4 tbsp vegetable oil
675g/1½lb potatoes, peeled and cut into 1cm/½in cubes
2.5ml/½ tsp black mustard seeds
2.5ml/½ tsp onion seeds
2.5ml/½ tsp cumin seeds
2.5ml/½ tsp fennel seeds
1 or 2 dried red chillies, chopped or broken into small pieces
2.5ml/½ tsp ground turmeric
2.5ml/½ tsp salt
150ml/¼ pint/⅔ cup warm water
fresh coriander (cilantro) sprigs, to garnish
pooris and natural (plain) yogurt, to serve

1 Preheat a karahi, wok or large pan over a medium setting. When the pan is hot, reduce the heat slightly and add the poppy seeds. Stir them around in the pan until they are just a shade darker. Remove from the pan and leave to cool.

2 In the pan, heat the vegetable oil over a medium heat and fry the cubes of potato until they are light brown. Remove them with a slotted spoon and drain on kitchen paper.

3 To the same oil, add the mustard seeds. As soon as they begin to pop, add the onion, cumin and fennel seeds and the chillies. Let the chillies blacken, but remove them from the pan before they burn.

4 Stir in the turmeric and follow quickly with the fried potatoes and salt. Stir well and add the warm water. Cover the pan with the lid and reduce the heat to low. Cook for 8–10 minutes, or until the potatoes are tender.

5 Grind the cooled poppy seeds in a mortar and pestle or spice grinder. Stir the ground seeds into the potatoes. It should form a thick paste which should cling to the potatoes. If there is too much liquid, continue to stir over a medium heat until you have the right consistency. Transfer to a serving dish. Garnish with coriander and serve with pooris and natural yogurt.

Energy 201kcal/842kJ; Fat 13.5g; Saturated fat 1.6g; Carbohydrate 29g; Fibre 2.2g.

Spiced Coconut Mushrooms

Here is a simple and delicious way to cook mushrooms. They can be served with almost any Indian meal as well as with traditional Western grilled or roasted meats and poultry.

Serves 4
30ml/2 tbsp groundnut (peanut) oil
2 garlic cloves, finely chopped
2 fresh red chillies, seeded and sliced into rings
3 shallots, finely chopped
225g/8oz/3 cups brown cap (cremini) mushrooms, thickly sliced
150ml/¼ pint/⅔ cup coconut milk
30ml/2 tbsp chopped fresh coriander (cilantro)
salt and ground black pepper

1 Heat a karahi, wok or shallow pan until hot, add the oil and swirl it around. Add the garlic and chillies, then stir-fry for a few seconds.

2 Add the shallots and stir-fry them for 2–3 minutes until softened. Add the mushrooms and stir-fry for 3 minutes.

3 Pour in the coconut milk and bring to the boil. Boil rapidly over a high heat until the liquid has reduced by about half and coats the mushrooms. Season to taste with salt and pepper.

4 Sprinkle over the chopped coriander and toss the mushrooms gently to mix. Serve immediately.

Variations
• Use chopped fresh chives instead of chopped fresh coriander (cilantro), if you wish.
• White (button) mushrooms or field (portabello) mushrooms would also work well instead of brown cap (cremini) mushrooms.
• Sprinkle some chopped toasted cashew nuts over the mushrooms before serving, if you like.

Energy 67kcal/280kJ; Fat 5.9g; Saturated fat 1.2g; Carbohydrate 2.4g; Fibre 0.8g.

Spinach with Mushrooms

A tasty vegetable that is often overlooked, spinach is highly nutritious. Cooked in this way it tastes wonderful. Serve with chapatis.

Serves 4
450g/1lb fresh or frozen spinach, thawed
30ml/2 tbsp oil
2 medium onions, diced
6–8 curry leaves
1.5ml/¼ tsp onion seeds
5ml/1 tsp crushed garlic
5ml/1 tsp grated fresh root ginger
5ml/1 tsp chilli powder
5ml/1 tsp salt
7.5ml/1½ tsp ground coriander
1 large red (bell) pepper, seeded and sliced
115g/4oz/1½ cups mushrooms, roughly chopped
225g/8oz/1 cup low-fat fromage frais or ricotta cheese
30ml/2 tbsp fresh coriander (cilantro) leaves

1 If using fresh spinach, blanch it briefly in boiling water and drain thoroughly. If using frozen spinach, drain well. Set aside.

2 Heat the oil in a karahi, wok or heavy pan and fry the onions with the curry leaves and the onion seeds for 1–2 minutes. Add the garlic, ginger, chilli powder, salt and ground coriander. Stir-fry for a further 2–3 minutes.

3 Add half the red pepper slices and all the mushrooms and continue to stir-fry for 2–3 minutes.

4 Add the spinach and stir-fry for 4–6 minutes, then add the fromage frais or ricotta and half the fresh coriander, followed by the remaining red pepper slices. Stir-fry for a further 2–3 minutes before serving, garnished with the remaining coriander.

> **Cook's Tip**
> Whether you use fresh or frozen spinach, make sure it is well drained, otherwise the stir-fried mixture will be too wet when you add the fromage frais or ricotta. Tip the spinach into a colander, and press it against the sides of the colander with a wooden spoon to extract as much liquid as possible.

Energy 188kcal/778kJ; Fat 11.57g; Saturated fat 5.99g; Carbohydrate 14.71g; Fibre 4.68g.

Courgettes with Mushrooms in a Yogurt Sauce

The slightly tart flavour of yogurt makes a creamy sauce which is delicious with cooked mushrooms and courgettes.

Serves 4
15ml/1 tbsp oil
1 medium onion, roughly chopped
5ml/1 tsp ground coriander
5ml/1 tsp ground cumin
5ml/1 tsp salt
2.5ml/½ tsp chilli powder

225g/8oz/3 cups mushrooms, sliced
2 courgettes (zucchini), sliced
45ml/3 tbsp natural (plain) low-fat yogurt
15ml/1 tbsp chopped fresh coriander (cilantro)

1 Heat the oil in a heavy pan and fry the onion until golden brown. Lower the heat to medium, add the ground coriander, cumin, salt and chilli powder and stir together well.

2 Once the onion and the spices are well blended, add the mushrooms and courgettes, and stir-fry gently for about 5 minutes until soft. If the mixture is too dry, add just a little water to loosen.

3 Finally, add the yogurt and mix it well into the vegetables.

4 Sprinkle with chopped fresh coriander and serve immediately.

Cook's Tip
Yogurt has a great affinity with stir-fried vegetables and this lovely combination of sliced courgettes (zucchini) and mushrooms would make a tasty accompaniment to serve with poultry or lamb dishes. If you prefer, you could use aubergines (eggplants) or mushrooms instead.

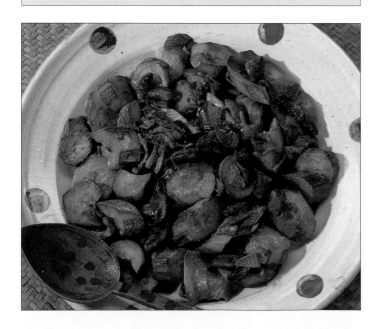

Energy 64kcal/265kJ; Fat 3.70g; Saturated fat 0.58g; Carbohydrate 4.80g; Fibre 1.40g.

Stuffed Okra

A delicious accompaniment to any dish, this can also be served on a bed of strained yogurt which gives an excellent contrast in flavour.

Serves 4–6
225g/8oz large okra
15ml/1 tbsp mango powder (amchur)

2.5ml/½ tsp ground ginger
2.5ml/½ tsp ground cumin
2.5ml/½ tsp chilli powder (optional)
2.5ml/½ tsp turmeric
a few drops of vegetable oil
30ml/2 tbsp cornflour (cornstarch), placed in a plastic bag
vegetable oil, for frying
salt

1 Wash the okra and dry on kitchen paper. Carefully trim off the tops without making a hole. Using a sharp knife, make a slit lengthways in the centre of each okra but do not cut all the way through.

2 In a bowl, mix the mango powder, ginger, cumin, chilli if using, turmeric and salt with a few drops of oil. Leave the mixture to rest for 1–2 hours.

3 Using your fingers, part the slit of each okra carefully and fill each with as much of the spice filling as possible.

4 Put all the okra into the plastic bag with the cornflour and shake the bag carefully to coat the okra evenly.

5 Fill a frying pan with enough oil to sit 2.5cm/1in deep, heat it and fry the okra in small batches for about 5–8 minutes, or until they are brown and slightly crisp. Serve hot.

Cook's Tip / Variation
Dusting the okra in cornflour before frying helps to ensure that none of the sticky liquid escapes and keeps the pods perfectly crisp.

Energy 176kcal/734kJ; Fat 12.4g; Saturated fat 1.6g; Carbohydrate 15.5g; Fibre 2.3g.

Okra in Yogurt

This tangy vegetable dish can be served as an accompaniment, but it also makes an excellent vegetarian meal if served with tarka dhal and warm, freshly made chapatis.

Serves 4
450g/1lb okra
15ml/1 tbsp oil
2.5ml/½ tsp onion seeds
3 medium fresh green
  chillies, chopped
1 medium onion, sliced
1.5ml/¼ tsp ground
  turmeric
2.5ml/½ tsp salt
15ml/1 tbsp natural (plain)
  low-fat yogurt
2 medium tomatoes, sliced
15ml/1 tbsp chopped fresh
  coriander (cilantro)
chapatis, to serve

1 Wash and trim the okra, cut into 1cm/½in pieces and place in a bowl. Set aside.

2 Heat the oil in a medium, heavy pan, add the onion seeds, green chillies and onion, and fry for about 5 minutes until the onion has turned golden brown.

3 Reduce the heat. Add the ground turmeric and salt to the onions and fry for about 1 minute.

4 Next, add the prepared okra, turn the heat to medium-high and quickly stir-fry the okra until they are lightly golden.

5 Stir in the yogurt, tomatoes and, finally, the coriander. Cook for a further 2 minutes.

6 Transfer the okra to a serving dish and serve immediately with freshly made chapatis.

Cook's Tip
It is always wise to wear plastic or rubber gloves when preparing chillies as they contain a strong irritant that will sting open cuts or eyes if it comes into contact with them.

Energy 82kcal/342kJ; Fat 4.2g; Saturated fat 0.41g; Carbohydrate 7.6g; Fibre 5.3g.

Masala Okra

Okra, or "lady's fingers", are a very popular Indian vegetable. Here the pods are stir-fried with a dry masala mixture to make a tasty side dish.

Serves 4
450g/1lb okra
2.5ml/½ tsp ground turmeric
5ml/1 tsp chilli powder
15ml/1 tbsp ground cumin
15ml/1 tbsp ground coriander
1.5ml/¼ tsp salt
1.5ml/¼ tsp granulated sugar
15ml/1 tbsp lemon juice
30ml/2 tbsp chopped fresh
  coriander (cilantro)
15ml/1 tbsp oil
2.5ml/½ tsp cumin seeds
2.5ml/½ tsp black mustard
  seeds
chopped fresh tomatoes,
  to garnish
poppadums, to serve

1 Wash, dry and trim the stalks away from the top of the okra, being careful not to pierce the pod itself, otherwise the sticky juices will be released and will affect the final dish. Set the okra aside. In a bowl, mix together the turmeric, chilli powder, cumin, ground coriander, salt, sugar, lemon juice and fresh coriander.

2 Heat the oil in a large, heavy pan. Add the cumin seeds and mustard seeds, and fry for about 2 minutes or until they start to splutter.

3 Scrape in the spice mixture and continue to fry for 2 minutes.

4 Add the okra, cover and cook over a low heat for 10 minutes, or until tender. Garnish with chopped fresh tomatoes and serve with poppadums.

Cook's Tip
When buying okra, choose firm, brightly coloured pods that are less than 10cm/4in long; larger ones can be stringy.

Energy 102kcal/424kJ; Fat 5.4g; Saturated fat 0.4g; Carbohydrate 8.6g; Fibre 4.7g.

Stir-fried Paneer with Mushrooms & Peas

Indian cheese, known as paneer, is a very versatile ingredient. It is used in both sweet and savoury dishes. Indian housewives generally make this cheese at home, although in recent years it has become available commercially.

Serves 4–6

90ml/6 tbsp ghee or vegetable oil
225g/8oz paneer, cubed
1 onion, finely chopped
a few fresh mint leaves, chopped, plus extra sprigs to garnish
50g/2oz/1 cup chopped fresh coriander (cilantro)
3 fresh green chillies, chopped
3 garlic cloves
2.5cm/1in piece fresh root ginger, sliced
5ml/1 tsp ground turmeric
5ml/1 tsp chilli powder (optional)
5ml/1 tsp garam masala
225g/8oz/3 cups tiny button (white) mushrooms, washed
225g/8oz/2 cups frozen peas, thawed
175ml/6fl oz/¾ cup natural (plain) yogurt, mixed with 5ml/1 tsp cornflour (cornstarch)
salt

1 Heat the ghee or oil in a karahi, wok or large pan, and fry the paneer cubes until they are golden brown on all sides. Remove and drain on kitchen paper.

2 Grind the onion, mint, coriander, chillies, garlic and ginger with a mortar and pestle or in a food processor to a fairly smooth paste. Remove and mix in the turmeric, chilli powder, if using, and garam masala, with salt to taste.

3 Remove the excess ghee or oil from the pan, leaving about 15ml/1 tbsp. Heat and fry the paste over a medium heat for 8–10 minutes, or until the raw onion smell disappears and the oil separates. Add the mushrooms, peas and paneer and mix well. Cool the mixture slightly and fold in the yogurt. Simmer for about 10 minutes, until the vegetables are tender and the flavours are well mixed. Garnish with fresh mint and serve.

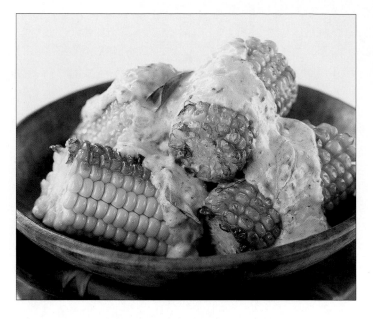

Corn on the Cob in a Rich Onion Sauce

Corn is grown extensively in the Punjab region, where it is used in many delicacies. Corn bread, *makki ki roti*, along with spiced mustard greens, *sarson ka saag*, is a combination that is hard to beat and it is what the Punjabis thrive on. Here, corn is cooked in a thick, rich onion sauce, in another classic Punjabi dish. It is excellent served with naan bread.

Serves 4–6

4 corn on the cob, thawed if frozen
vegetable oil, for frying
1 large onion, finely chopped
2 garlic cloves, crushed
5cm/2in piece fresh root ginger, crushed
2.5ml/½ tsp ground turmeric
2.5ml/½ tsp onion seeds
2.5ml/½ tsp cumin seeds
2.5ml/½ tsp chilli powder
6–8 curry leaves
2.5ml/½ tsp granulated sugar
200ml/7fl oz/scant 1 cup natural (plain) yogurt
chilli powder, to taste

1 Cut each corn cob in half, using a heavy knife or cleaver to make clean cuts and avoid damaging the kernels.

2 Heat the oil in a karahi, wok or large pan and fry the corn until golden brown. Remove the corn and set aside. Remove any excess oil, leaving about 30ml/2 tbsp in the wok.

3 Grind the onion, garlic and ginger to a paste using a mortar and pestle or in a food processor. Transfer the paste to a bowl and mix in the spices, curry leaves and granulated sugar.

4 Heat the oil and fry the onion paste mixture over a low heat for 8–10 minutes until all the spices have blended well and the oil separates from the sauce.

5 Cool the onion paste mixture and fold in the yogurt. Mix to a smooth sauce. Add the corn and mix well, so that all the pieces are covered with the sauce. Reheat gently for about 10 minutes. Serve hot.

Energy 280kcal/1162kJ; Fat 19.9g; Saturated fat 3.7g; Carbohydrate 11.7g; Fibre 3.7g.

Energy 214kcal/888kJ; Fat 15.1g; Saturated fat 2g; Carbohydrate 15.9g; Fibre 1.5g.

Peppers Filled with Vegetables

Nigella, or kalonji, has a mild, slightly nutty flavour and is best toasted for a few seconds in a dry frying pan before being used in a recipe. This helps to bring out its flavour.

Serves 6

6 large evenly shaped red or
   yellow (bell) peppers
500g/1¼lb waxy potatoes
1 small onion, chopped
4 or 5 garlic cloves, chopped
5cm/2in piece fresh root
   ginger, chopped
1 or 2 fresh green chillies,
   seeded and chopped
105ml/7 tbsp water
90–105ml/6–7 tbsp vegetable oil
1 aubergine (eggplant), diced
10ml/2 tsp cumin seeds
5ml/1 tsp nigella seeds
2.5ml/½ tsp ground turmeric
5ml/1 tsp ground coriander
5ml/1 tsp ground toasted
   cumin seeds
cayenne pepper
about 30ml/2 tbsp lemon juice
sea salt and ground black pepper
30ml/2 tbsp chopped fresh
   coriander (cilantro), to garnish

1 Cut the tops off the peppers, then remove and discard the seeds. Cut a thin slice off the base of any wobbly peppers so that they stand upright. Bring a large pan of lightly salted water to the boil. Add the peppers and cook for 5–6 minutes. Drain and leave them upside down in a colander.

2 Cook the potatoes in lightly salted, boiling water for 10–12 minutes until just tender. Drain, cool and peel, then cut into 1cm/½in dice.

3 Put the onion, garlic, ginger and green chillies in a food processor or blender with 60ml/4 tbsp of the water and process to a purée.

4 Heat 45ml/3 tbsp of the vegetable oil in a large, deep frying pan and cook the aubergine, stirring occasionally, until it is evenly browned. Remove the aubergine from the pan using a slotted spoon and set aside. Add another 30ml/2 tbsp of the vegetable oil to the pan, add the potatoes and cook until lightly browned. Remove the potatoes from the pan and set aside.

5 If necessary, add another 15ml/1 tbsp sunflower oil to the pan, then add the cumin and nigella seeds. Fry briefly until the seeds darken, then add the turmeric, coriander and ground cumin. Cook for 15 seconds. Stir in the onion and garlic purée and fry, scraping the pan with a spatula, until the onions begin to brown.

6 Return the potatoes and aubergine to the pan, season with salt, pepper and 1 or 2 pinches of cayenne. Add the remaining water and 15ml/1 tbsp lemon juice and then cook, stirring, until the liquid evaporates. Preheat the oven to 190°C/375°F/Gas 5.

7 Fill the peppers with the spiced vegetable mixture and place on a lightly greased baking tray. Brush the peppers with a little oil and bake for 30–35 minutes until they are cooked. Leave to cool a little, then sprinkle with a little more lemon juice. Garnish with the coriander and serve.

Energy 221kcal/923kJ; Fat 12.1g; Saturated fat 1.6g; Carbohydrate 26.1g; Fibre 4.4g.

Asparagus with Galangal & Chilli

This is an excitingly different way of cooking asparagus. The crunchy texture is retained and the flavour is complemented by the addition of galangal and fresh red chilli.

Serves 4

350g/12oz asparagus
30ml/2 tbsp vegetable oil
1 garlic clove, crushed
15ml/1 tbsp sesame seeds,
   toasted
2.5cm/1in piece fresh galangal,
   finely shredded
1 fresh red chilli, seeded and
   finely chopped
15ml/1 tbsp Thai fish sauce
15ml/1 tbsp light soy sauce
45ml/3 tbsp water
5ml/1 tsp palm sugar or light
   muscovado (brown) sugar

1 Snap the asparagus stalks. They will break naturally at the junction between the woody base and the more tender portion of the stalk when you bend the stems. Discard the woody parts of the stems.

2 Heat the oil in a wok and stir-fry the garlic, sesame seeds and shredded galangal for 3–4 minutes, until the garlic is just beginning to turn golden.

3 Add the asparagus stalks and chilli, toss to mix, then add the fish sauce, soy sauce, water and sugar.

4 Using two spoons, toss the mixture over the heat for a further 2 minutes, or until the asparagus just begins to soften and the liquid is reduced by half.

5 Carefully transfer the asparagus and sauce to a warmed serving platter and serve immediately.

> **Variations**
> *Try this with broccoli or pak choi (bok choy). The sauce also works very well with green beans.*

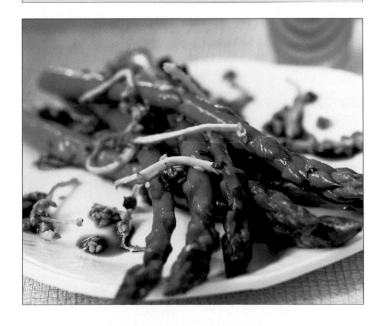

Energy 96kcal/394kJ; Fat 8.3g; Saturated fat 1.1g; Carbohydrate 1.9g; Fibre 1.8g.

Steamed Morning Glory with Fried Garlic & Shallots

Morning glory goes by various names, including water spinach, water convolvulus and swamp cabbage. It is a green leafy vegetable with long jointed stems and arrow-shaped leaves. The stems remain pleasantly crunchy while the leaves wilt like spinach when cooked.

Serves 4

2 bunches morning glory, total weight about 250g/9oz, trimmed and coarsely chopped into 2.5cm/1in lengths
4 shallots, thinly sliced
6 large garlic cloves, thinly sliced
30ml/2 tbsp vegetable oil
1.5ml/¼ tsp dried chilli flakes
sea salt

1 Trim the morning glory and chop it coarsely. Thinly slice the shallots and garlic cloves.

2 Place the morning glory in a steamer and steam over a pan of boiling water for 30 seconds, until just wilted. If necessary, cook it in batches. Place the leaves in a bowl or spread them out on a large serving plate.

3 Heat the oil in a wok and stir-fry the shallots and garlic over medium to high heat until golden. Spoon the mixture over the morning glory, sprinkle with a little sea salt and the chilli flakes and serve immediately.

Cook's Tip
Morning glory can also be eaten raw and makes an unusual addition to salads.

Variations
Use spinach instead of morning glory, or substitute young spring greens (collards), sprouting broccoli or Swiss chard.

Energy 71kcal/290kJ; Fat 6g; Saturated fat 0.7g; Carbohydrate 2.2g; Fibre 1.5g.

Sweet Cinnamon Carrots

A honey and cinnamon coating makes these glazed carrots extra special.

Serves 4
450g/1lb carrots, peeled and cut into batons

25g/1oz/2 tbsp butter
2.5ml/½ tsp ground cinnamon
15ml/1 tbsp clear honey
15ml/1 tbsp chopped fresh coriander (cilantro)
salt and ground black pepper
sprig of fresh coriander, to garnish

1 Steam or boil the carrots for 5 minutes until crisply tender. Drain well and return to the pan.

2 Add the butter to the pan to melt and add the cinnamon and honey. Season to taste with salt and pepper.

3 Add the chopped fresh coriander and toss well to coat the carrots with the flavoured butter. Serve garnished with a sprig of fresh coriander.

Sweet-&-sour Onions

Cooked in this way, sweet baby onions make an unusual yet tasty side dish.

Serves 6
450g/1lb baby onions, peeled
50ml/2fl oz/¼ cup wine vinegar
45ml/3 tbsp olive oil

40g/1½oz/⅓ cup caster (superfine) sugar
45ml/3 tbsp tomato purée (paste)
1 bay leaf
2 parsley sprigs
65g/2½oz/½ cup raisins
salt and ground black pepper

1 Put all the ingredients in a pan with 300ml/½ pint/1¼ cups water. Bring to the boil and simmer gently, uncovered, for 45 minutes or until the onions are tender and most of the liquid has evaporated.

2 Remove the bay leaf and parsley, check the seasoning and transfer to a serving dish. Serve at room temperature.

Top: Energy 97kcal/402kJ; Fat 5.5g; Saturated fat 3.4g; Carbohydrate 11.8g; Fibre 2.7g.
Above: Energy 150kcal/628kJ; Fat 5.8g; Saturated fat 0.8g; Carbohydrate 24.1g; Fibre 2g.

Hot Pickled Shallots

Pickling shallots in this way demands some patience while the vinegar and spices work their magic, but the results are worth the wait. Thinly sliced, the shallots are often used as a condiment with South-east Asian meals.

Makes 2–3 jars
5 or 6 small red or green bird's eye chillies
500g/1¼lb Thai pink shallots, peeled
2 large garlic cloves, peeled, halved and green shoots removed

For the vinegar
40g/1½oz/3 tbsp granulated sugar
10ml/2 tsp salt
5cm/2in piece fresh root ginger, sliced
15ml/1 tbsp coriander seeds
2 lemon grass stalks, cut in half lengthways
4 kaffir lime leaves or pared strips of lime rind
600ml/1 pint/2½ cups cider vinegar
15ml/1 tbsp chopped fresh coriander (cilantro)

1 The chillies can be left whole, or halved and seeded. The pickle will be hotter if you leave the seeds in. If leaving the chillies whole, prick them several times with a cocktail stick (toothpick). Bring a large pan of water to the boil. Add the chillies, shallots and garlic. Blanch for 1–2 minutes, then drain. Rinse all the vegetables under cold water, then drain again.

2 Prepare the vinegar. Put the sugar, salt, ginger, coriander seeds, lemon grass and lime leaves or lime rind in a pan, pour in the vinegar and bring to the boil. Reduce the heat to low and simmer for 3–4 minutes. Leave to cool.

3 Remove and discard the ginger, then bring the vinegar back to the boil. Add the fresh coriander, garlic and chillies, and cook for 1 minute.

4 Pack the shallots into sterilized jars, distributing the lemon grass, lime leaves, chillies and garlic among them. Pour over the hot vinegar. Cool, then seal and store in a cool, dark place for 2 months before eating.

Energy 138kcal/587kJ; Fat 0.8g; Saturated fat 0g; Carbohydrate 29.8g; Fibre 4.8g.

Spicy Bitter Gourds

Bitter gourds are widely used in India, often combined with other vegetables in a curry. They are also known as karelas and resemble small cucumbers with a warty skin. Gourds that are about 10cm/4in long are usually slightly less bitter than the tiny ones.

Serves 4
675g/1½lb bitter gourds
15ml/1 tbsp oil
2.5ml/½ tsp cumin seeds
6 spring onions (scallions), finely chopped
5 tomatoes, finely chopped
2.5cm/1in piece fresh root ginger, finely chopped
2 garlic cloves, crushed
2 fresh green chillies, finely chopped
2.5ml/½ tsp chilli powder
5ml/1 tsp ground coriander
5ml/1 tsp ground cumin
45ml/3 tbsp soft dark brown sugar
15ml/1 tbsp gram flour
fresh coriander (cilantro) sprigs, to garnish
salt

1 Bring a large pan of lightly salted water to the boil. Peel the bitter gourds and halve them. Discard the seeds. Cut into 2cm/¾in pieces, then cook in the boiling water for about 10–15 minutes or until just tender. Drain well.

2 Heat the oil in a large, heavy pan and fry the cumin seeds for 2 minutes until they begin to splutter.

3 Add the spring onions and fry for 3–4 minutes. Add the tomatoes, ginger, garlic and chillies, and cook the mixture, stirring occasionally, for a further 5 minutes.

4 Add 2.5ml/½ tsp salt, the remaining spices and sugar to the pan and cook for a further 2–3 minutes. Add the bitter gourds to the pan and mix well.

5 Sprinkle over the gram flour. Cover and simmer over a low heat for 5–8 minutes or until all the gram flour has been absorbed into the sauce. Stir well, then serve garnished with fresh coriander sprigs.

Energy 120kcal/490kJ; Fat 3.5g; Saturated fat 0.41g; Carbohydrate 9.2g; Fibre 0.4g.

Green Beans with Corn

Frozen green beans are useful for this dish, as they are quick to cook. It makes an excellent vegetable accompaniment.

Serves 4
15ml/1 tbsp oil
1.5ml/¼ tsp mustard seeds
1 medium red onion, diced
50g/2oz/⅓ cup frozen corn
50g/2oz/¼ cup canned red
    kidney beans, drained
175g/6oz frozen green beans
1 fresh red chilli, seeded
    and diced
1 garlic clove, chopped

2.5cm/1in piece fresh root ginger,
    finely chopped
15ml/1 tbsp chopped fresh
    coriander (cilantro)
5ml/1 tsp salt
1 medium tomato, seeded and
    diced, to garnish

1 Heat the oil in a karahi, wok or heavy pan for about 30 seconds, then add the mustard seeds and onion. Stir-fry for 2–3 minutes.

2 Add the corn, red kidney beans and green beans. Stir-fry for 3–5 minutes.

3 Add the red chilli, chopped garlic and ginger, coriander and salt, and stir-fry for 2–3 minutes.

4 Remove the pan from the heat. Transfer the vegetables to a serving dish and garnish with the diced tomato.

Cook's Tip
This is a good stand-by dish as it uses frozen and canned ingredients. To make sure you have always got a chilli available for making this dish, or others like it, you can freeze whole fresh chillies, washed but not blanched.

Vegetables & Beans with Curry Leaves

Bright, shiny green curry leaves look like small bay leaves, although they are not as tough. A popular seasoning ingredient in Indian cooking, curry leaves add a spicy flavour to dishes such as this dry vegetable and bean curry.

Serves 4
3 fresh green chillies
1 medium carrot
50g/2oz green beans
1 medium red (bell) pepper

15ml/1 tbsp oil
6 curry leaves
3 garlic cloves, sliced
3 dried red chillies
1.5ml/¼ tsp onion seeds
1.5ml/¼ tsp fenugreek
    seeds
115g/4oz/½ cup drained
    canned red kidney beans
5ml/1 tsp salt
30ml/2 tbsp lemon juice

1 Cut the chillies in half lengthways. Remove the membranes and seeds and chop the flesh.

2 Cut the carrot into strips and slice the green beans diagonally. Remove the seeds and stalk from the pepper and cut the flesh into strips.

3 Heat the oil in a karahi, wok or deep heavy pan. Add the curry leaves, sliced garlic cloves, dried chillies, and onion and fenugreek seeds.

4 When these ingredients turn a shade darker, add the chillies, kidney beans, carrot strips, green beans and pepper strips, stirring constantly.

5 Stir in the salt and the lemon juice. Lower the heat, cover and cook for about 5 minutes.

6 Transfer the hot curry to a serving dish and serve immediately.

Energy 84kcal/349kJ; Fat 3.44g; Saturated fat 0.5g; Carbohydrate 11.13g; Fibre 2.7g.

Energy 79kcal/331kJ; Fat 3.3g; Saturated fat 0.37g; Carbohydrate 9.7g; Fibre 2.6g.

Kidney Bean Curry

This is a popular Punjabi-style dish using red kidney beans. You can replace the dried beans with a 400g/14oz can if you prefer. Other pulses also work well in this dish.

Serves 4

225g/8oz/scant 1 cup dried
    red kidney beans
30ml/2 tbsp oil
2.5ml/ 1/2 tsp cumin seeds
1 onion, thinly sliced
1 fresh green chilli, finely chopped
2 garlic cloves, crushed
2.5cm/1in piece fresh root
    ginger, grated
30ml/2 tbsp curry paste
5ml/1 tsp ground cumin
5ml/1 tsp ground coriander
2.5ml/ 1/2 tsp chilli powder
2.5ml/ 1/2 tsp salt
400g/14oz can chopped
    tomatoes
30ml/2 tbsp chopped fresh
    coriander (cilantro)

1 Leave the kidney beans to soak overnight in a bowl of cold water.

2 Drain the beans and put in a large pan with double the volume of water. Boil vigorously for 10 minutes. Skim off any scum. Cover and cook for 1–1½ hours or until the beans are soft. If you want to reduce the cooking time, cook the beans in a pressure cooker for 20–25 minutes. Alternatively, replace the dried beans with canned beans. Use a 400g/14oz can and drain it very thoroughly.

3 Meanwhile, heat the oil in a large, heavy frying pan and fry the cumin seeds for 2 minutes until they begin to splutter. Add the onion, chilli, garlic and ginger, and fry for 5 minutes. Stir in the curry paste, cumin, ground coriander, chilli powder and salt, and cook for 5 minutes.

4 Add the tomatoes and simmer for 5 minutes. Drain the beans and stir them in with the fresh coriander, reserving a little of the herb for the garnish. Cover and cook for 15 minutes, adding a little water if necessary. Serve garnished with the reserved fresh coriander.

Mung Beans with Potatoes

Small mung beans are one of the quicker-cooking pulses. They do not require soaking and are easy and convenient to use. In this recipe they are cooked with potatoes and Indian spices to give a tasty and nutritious dish.

Serves 4

175g/6oz/1 cup mung beans
750ml/1 1/4 pints/3 cups water
225g/8oz potatoes, cut into
    2cm/ 3/4in chunks
30ml/2 tbsp oil
2.5ml/ 1/2 tsp cumin seeds
1 fresh green chilli, finely
    chopped
1 garlic clove, crushed
2.5cm/1in piece fresh root
    ginger, finely chopped
1.5ml/ 1/4 tsp ground turmeric
2.5ml/ 1/2 tsp chilli powder
5ml/1 tsp salt
5ml/1 tsp granulated sugar
4 curry leaves
5 tomatoes, peeled and finely
    chopped
15ml/1 tbsp tomato purée
    (paste)
curry leaves, to garnish
plain rice, to serve

1 Wash the beans. Pour the water into a pan, add the beans and bring to the boil. Boil hard for 15 minutes, then reduce the heat, cover the pan and simmer until soft, about 30 minutes cooking time. Drain.

2 In a separate pan, par-boil the potatoes in boiling water for 10 minutes, then drain well.

3 Heat the oil in a heavy pan and fry the cumin seeds until they splutter. Add the chilli, garlic and ginger, and fry for 3–4 minutes.

4 Add the turmeric, chilli powder, salt and sugar, and cook for 2 minutes, stirring to prevent the mixture from sticking to the pan.

5 Add the 4 curry leaves, chopped tomatoes and tomato purée, and simmer for about 5 minutes until the sauce thickens. Mix the tomato sauce and the potatoes with the mung beans and heat through. Garnish with the extra curry leaves and serve with plain boiled rice.

Energy 258kcal/1087kJ; Fat 7.8g; Saturated fat 0.86g; Carbohydrate 33.7g; Fibre 11.7g.

Energy 254kcal/1070kJ; Fat 6.8g; Saturated fat 0.89g; Carbohydrate 36.9g; Fibre 6.3g.

Masala Beans with Fenugreek

The term masala refers to the blending of several spices to achieve a distinctive taste, with different spice-combinations being used to complement specific ingredients. Households will traditionally create their own blends, and many are unique.

Serves 4
1 onion
5ml/1 tsp ground cumin
5ml/1 tsp ground coriander
5ml/1 tsp sesame seeds
5ml/1 tsp chilli powder
2.5ml/½ tsp crushed garlic
1.5ml/¼ tsp ground turmeric
5ml/1 tsp salt
30ml/2 tbsp vegetable oil
1 tomato, quartered
225g/8oz/1½ cups green
   beans, blanched
1 bunch fresh fenugreek leaves,
   stems discarded
60ml/4 tbsp chopped fresh
   coriander (cilantro)
15ml/1 tbsp lemon juice

1 Roughly chop the onion. Mix together the cumin and coriander, sesame seeds, chilli powder, garlic, turmeric and salt.

2 Put the chopped onion and spice mixture into a food processor or blender, and process for 30–45 seconds until you have a rough paste.

3 In a karahi, wok or large pan, heat the oil over a medium heat and fry the spice paste for about 5 minutes, stirring the mixture occasionally.

4 Add the tomato quarters, blanched green beans, fresh fenugreek and chopped coriander.

5 Stir-fry the contents of the pan for about 5 minutes, then sprinkle in the lemon juice and serve.

Variation
Instead of fresh fenugreek, you can also use 15ml/1 tbsp dried fenugreek for this recipe. Dried fenugreek is readily available from Indian stores and markets.

Dry-cooked Green Beans with Ginger

Slim green beans are ideal for use in this quick and tasty recipe. 'Dry-cooked' means using no stock or water.

5ml/1 tsp sugar
10ml/2 tsp light soy sauce
salt and ground black pepper

Serves 6
175ml/6fl oz/¾ cup sunflower oil
450/1lb green beans, trimmed and
   cut in half
6cm/2½in piece fresh root ginger,
   peeled and cut into matchsticks

1 Heat the oil in a wok. When the oil is just beginning to smoke, carefully add the beans and stir-fry them for 1–2 minutes until just tender.

2 Lift out the green beans on to a plate lined with kitchen paper.

3 Using a ladle, carefully remove all but about 30ml/2 tbsp oil from the wok.

4 Reheat the remaining oil, add the ginger and stir-fry for a minute or two to flavour the oil.

5 Return the green beans to the wok, stir in the sugar, soy sauce and salt and pepper, and toss together quickly to ensure the beans are well coated. Serve the beans immediately.

Variation
This simple recipe works just as well with other fresh green vegetables such as baby asparagus spears and okra. If you use okra, be sure to trim the stalk only and not to pierce the pod itself. You could also cook courgettes (zucchini), cut into long batons, in this way.

Energy 80kcal/331kJ; Fat 5.9g; Saturated fat 0.8g; Carbohydrate 5.4g; Fibre 2g.

Energy 223kcal/917kJ; Fat 22.9g; Saturated fat 2.8g; Carbohydrate 3.1g; Fibre 1.7g.

Tofu Stir-fry

The use of tofu in this recipe creates a pleasant creamy texture, which contrasts delightfully with the crunchy stir-fried vegetables. Make sure you buy firm tofu which is easy to cut neatly.

Serves 2–4
115g/4oz hard white cabbage
2 green chillies
225g/8oz firm tofu
45ml/3 tbsp vegetable oil
2 garlic cloves, crushed
3 spring onions (scallions), chopped
175g/6oz green beans, topped and tailed
175g/6oz baby corn, halved
115g/4oz beansprouts
45ml/3 tbsp smooth peanut butter
25ml/1½ tbsp dark soy sauce
300ml/½ pint/1¼ cups coconut milk

1 Shred the white cabbage. Carefully remove the seeds from the chillies and chop them finely. Wear rubber gloves to protect your hands, if necessary.

2 Cut the tofu into strips.

3 Heat the wok, then add 30ml/2 tbsp of the oil. When the oil is hot, add the tofu, stir-fry for 3 minutes, then remove it and set it aside. Wipe out the wok with kitchen paper.

4 Add the remaining oil. When it is hot, add the garlic, spring onions and chillies and stir-fry for 1 minute. Add the green beans, corn and beansprouts and stir-fry for a further 2 minutes.

5 Add the peanut butter and soy sauce to the wok. Stir well to coat the vegetables. Add the tofu to the vegetables in the wok.

6 Pour the coconut milk over the vegetables, simmer for 3 minutes and serve immediately.

Energy 242kcal/1004kJ; Fat 17.3g; Saturated fat 2.9g; Carbohydrate 11.2g; Fibre 3.4g.

Madras Sambal

There are many variations of this popular dish but it is regularly cooked in one form or another in almost every south-Indian home. You can use any combination of vegetables that are in season.

Serves 4
225g/8oz/1 cup tuvar dhal or red split lentils
600ml/1 pint/2½ cups water
2.5ml/½ tsp ground turmeric
2 large potatoes, cut into 2.5cm/1in chunks
30ml/2 tbsp oil
2.5ml/½ tsp black mustard seeds
1.5ml/¼ tsp fenugreek seeds
4 curry leaves
1 onion, thinly sliced
115g/4oz green beans, cut into 2.5cm/1in lengths
5ml/1 tsp salt
2.5ml/½ tsp chilli powder
15ml/1 tbsp lemon juice
toasted coconut, to garnish
fresh Coriander Relish, to serve

1 Wash the tuvar dhal or lentils in several changes of water. Place in a heavy pan with the measured water and the turmeric. Bring to the boil, then reduce the heat, cover the pan and simmer for 30–35 minutes until the lentils are soft.

2 Par-cook the potatoes in a large pan of boiling water for 10 minutes. Drain well and set aside.

3 Heat the oil in a large frying pan and fry the mustard and fenugreek seeds and the curry leaves for 2–3 minutes until the seeds begin to splutter. Add the sliced onion and the green beans and stir-fry for 7–8 minutes. Add the par-boiled potatoes and cook for a further 2 minutes.

4 Drain the lentils. Stir them into the potato mixture with the salt, chilli powder and lemon juice. Simmer for 2 minutes or until heated through. Garnish with toasted coconut and serve with freshly made coriander relish.

Energy 335kcal/1414kJ; Fat 6.1g; Saturated fat 1.98g; Carbohydrate 55.7g; Fibre 5.6g.

Sambal Nanas

Side dishes are known as sambals in Indonesia and Malaysia, and can be paste-like mixtures used as flavourings or finely chopped or sliced cold vegetables or fruits. Here sweet pineapple and cucumber is dressed with a savoury sauce.

Serves 8–10

1 small or ½ large fresh ripe pineapple
½ cucumber, halved lengthways
50g/2oz dried shrimps
1 large fresh red chilli, seeded
1cm/½in cube shrimp paste, prepared (see Cook's Tip)
juice of 1 large lemon or lime
soft light brown sugar, to taste (optional)
salt

1 Cut off both ends of the pineapple. Stand it upright on a board, then slice off the skin from top to bottom, cutting out the spines. Slice the pineapple, removing the central core. Cut into thin slices and set aside.

2 Trim the ends from the cucumber and slice thinly. Sprinkle with salt and set aside. Place the dried shrimps in a food processor and chop fairly finely. Add the chilli, prepared shrimp paste and lemon or lime juice and process again to a paste.

3 Rinse the cucumber, drain and dry on kitchen paper. Mix with the pineapple and chill. Just before serving, spoon in the spice mixture with sugar to taste. Mix well and serve.

> **Cook's Tip**
> The pungent shrimp paste, also called blachan, is popular in many South-east Asian countries, and is available in Asian supermarkets. Because it can taste a bit raw in a sambal, dry-fry it before use by wrapping in foil and heating in a frying pan over a low heat for 5 minutes, turning from time to time. If the shrimp paste is to be fried with other spices, this preliminary cooking can be left out.

Energy 38kcal/163kJ; Fat 0.3g; Saturated fat 0g; Carbohydrate 5.4g; Fibre 0.8g.

Balti Baby Vegetables

There is a wide and wonderful selection of baby vegetables available in supermarkets these days, and this simple recipe does full justice to their delicate flavour and attractive appearance. Serve as part of a main meal or even as a light appetizer.

Serves 4–6

10 new potatoes, halved
12–14 baby carrots
12–14 baby courgettes (zucchini)
30ml/2 tbsp corn oil
15 baby onions
30ml/2 tbsp chilli sauce
5ml/1 tsp crushed garlic
5ml/1 tsp grated fresh root ginger
5ml/1 tsp salt
400g/14oz/scant 3 cups drained canned chickpeas
10 cherry tomatoes
5ml/1 tsp crushed dried red chillies
30ml/2 tbsp sesame seeds

1 Bring a medium pan of salted water to the boil and add the new potatoes and baby carrots. Cook for 12–15 minutes, then add the courgettes, and boil for a further 5 minutes or until all the vegetables are just tender. Take care not to overcook the vegetables, as they will be given a brief additional cooking time later.

2 Drain the vegetables well and put them in a bowl. Set aside.

3 Heat the oil in a karahi, wok or deep pan and add the baby onions. Fry until the onions turn golden brown. Lower the heat and add the chilli sauce, garlic, ginger and salt, taking care not to burn the mixture.

4 Stir in the chickpeas and stir-fry over a medium heat until the moisture has been absorbed.

5 Add the cooked vegetables and cherry tomatoes, and stir over the heat with a slotted spoon for about 2 minutes.

6 Sprinkle the crushed red chillies and sesame seeds evenly over the vegetable mixture and serve.

Energy 311kcal/1306kJ; Fat 8.5g; Saturated fat 1.3g; Carbohydrate 48.7g; Fibre 8.4g.

Vegetables with Almonds

Yogurt gives this dish a tangy flavour and also makes it creamy.

Serves 4
30ml/2 tbsp oil
2 medium onions, sliced
5cm/2in piece fresh root ginger, shredded
5ml/1 tsp crushed black peppercorns
1 bay leaf
1.5ml/¼ tsp ground turmeric
5ml/1 tsp ground coriander
5ml/1 tsp salt
2.5ml/½ tsp garam masala
175g/6oz/2½ cups mushrooms, thickly sliced

1 medium courgette (zucchini), thickly sliced
50g/2oz green beans, cut into 2.5cm/1in lengths
15ml/1 tbsp roughly chopped fresh mint
150ml/¼ pint/⅔ cup water
30ml/2 tbsp natural (plain) low-fat yogurt
25g/1oz/¼ cup flaked (sliced) almonds

1 Heat the oil in a heavy pan, and fry the onions, ginger, peppercorns and bay leaf for 3–5 minutes.

2 Lower the heat and stir in the turmeric, coriander, salt and garam masala. Gradually add the sliced mushrooms, courgette, green beans and mint. Stir gently to coat the vegetables, being careful not to break them up.

3 Pour in the water and bring to a simmer, then lower the heat and cook until the water has been totally absorbed by the vegetables.

4 Beat the yogurt lightly with a fork, then pour it on to the vegetables in the pan and mix together well until the vegetables are coated.

5 Cook the vegetables for a further 2–3 minutes, stirring occasionally. Spoon into a large serving dish or on to individual plates. Serve immediately, garnished with the flaked almonds.

Energy 140kcal/579kJ; Fat 9.8g; Saturated fat 1.13g; Carbohydrate 9g; Fibre 2.2g.

Spring Vegetable Stir-fry

A colourful, dazzling medley of fresh and sweet young vegetables.

Serves 4
15ml/1 tbsp groundnut (peanut) oil
1 garlic clove, sliced
2.5cm/1in piece fresh root ginger, finely chopped
115g/4oz baby carrots
115g/4oz patty pan squash
115g/4oz baby corn
115g/4oz green beans, trimmed
115g/4oz sugar snap peas, trimmed

115g/4oz young asparagus, cut into 7.5cm/3in pieces
8 spring onions (scallions), trimmed and cut into 5cm/2in pieces
115g/4oz cherry tomatoes

For the dressing
juice of 2 limes
15ml/1 tbsp clear honey
15ml/1 tbsp soy sauce
5ml/1 tsp sesame oil

1 Heat the groundnut oil in a wok or large frying pan.

2 Add the garlic and root ginger, and stir-fry over high heat for 1 minute.

3 Add the carrots, patty pan squash, baby corn and beans, and stir-fry for another 3–4 minutes.

4 Add the sugar snap peas, asparagus, spring onions and cherry tomatoes and stir-fry for a further 1–2 minutes.

5 Mix the dressing ingredients together and add to the pan.

6 Stir well and then cover the pan. Cook for 2–3 minutes more, until the vegetables are just tender but still crisp.

Cook's Tip
Stir-fries take only moments to cook, so prepare this dish at the last minute.

Energy 112kcal/464kJ; Fat 4.8g; Saturated fat 0.9g; Carbohydrate 12.5g; Fibre 4.5g.

Stuffed Bananas

Bananas are cooked with spices in many different ways in southern India. Some recipes contain large quantities of chillies, but the taste is skilfully mellowed by adding coconut milk and tamarind juice. Green bananas are available from Indian stores, or you can use plantains or unripe eating bananas that are firm to the touch.

Serves 4

1 bunch fresh coriander (cilantro)
4 green bananas or plantains
30ml/2 tbsp ground coriander
15ml/1 tbsp ground cumin
5ml/1 tsp chilli powder
2.5ml/½ tsp salt
1.5ml/¼ tsp ground turmeric
5ml/1 tsp granulated sugar
15ml/1 tbsp gram flour
90ml/6 tbsp vegetable oil
1.5ml/¼ tsp cumin seeds
1.5ml/¼ tsp black mustard seeds

1 Set aside two or three coriander sprigs for the garnish. If necessary, remove the roots and any thick stems from the remaining coriander, then chop the leaves finely.

2 Trim the bananas or plantains and cut each crossways into three equal pieces, leaving the skin on. Make a lengthwise slit along each piece of banana, without cutting all the way through the flesh.

3 On a plate mix together the ground coriander, cumin, chilli powder, salt, turmeric, sugar, gram flour, chopped fresh coriander and 15ml/1 tbsp of the oil. Use your fingers to combine well.

4 Carefully stuff each piece of banana with the spice mixture, taking care not to break the bananas in half.

5 Heat the remaining oil in a wok, karahi or large pan, and fry the cumin and mustard seeds for 2 minutes or until they begin to splutter. Add the bananas and toss gently in the oil.

6 Cover and simmer over a low heat for 15 minutes, stirring from time to time, until the bananas are soft but not mushy. Garnish with the fresh coriander sprigs, and serve immediately.

Energy 265kcal/1110kJ; Fat 16.8g; Saturated fat 2.1g; Carbohydrate 29.4g; Fibre 1.3g.

Steamed Vegetables with Spicy Dip

In Thailand, steamed vegetables are often partnered with raw ones to create the contrasting textures that are such a feature of the national cuisine. By happy coincidence, it is an extremely healthy way to serve them.

Serves 4

1 head broccoli, divided into
   florets
130g/4½oz/1 cup green beans,
   trimmed
130g/4½oz asparagus, trimmed
½ head cauliflower, divided
   into florets

8 baby corn cobs
130g/4½oz mangetouts (snow
   peas) or sugar snap peas
salt

For the dip
1 fresh green chilli, seeded
4 garlic cloves, peeled
4 shallots, peeled
2 tomatoes, halved
5 pea aubergines (eggplants)
30ml/2 tbsp lemon juice
30ml/2 tbsp soy sauce
2.5ml/½ tsp salt
5ml/1 tsp granulated sugar

1 Place the broccoli, green beans, asparagus and cauliflower in a steamer and steam over boiling water for about 4 minutes, until just tender but still with a "bite". Transfer to a bowl and add the baby corn and mangetouts or sugar snap peas. Season to taste with a little salt. Toss to mix, then set aside.

2 To make the dip, preheat the grill (broiler). Wrap the chilli, garlic cloves, shallots, tomatoes and aubergines in a foil package. Grill (broil) for 10 minutes, until the vegetables have softened, turning the package over once or twice.

3 Unwrap the foil and place its contents in a mortar or food processor. Add the lemon juice, soy sauce, salt and sugar. Pound with a pestle or process to a fairly liquid paste.

4 Scrape the spicy dip into a serving bowl or four individual bowls. Serve immediately, surrounded by the steamed and raw vegetables.

Energy 108kcal/454kJ; Fat 2.3g; Saturated fat 0.5g; Carbohydrate 10.7g; Fibre 7.6g.

Stir-fried Pineapple with Ginger

This dish makes an interesting accompaniment to grilled meat or strongly flavoured fish such as tuna or swordfish. If the idea seems strange, think of it as resembling a fresh mango chutney, but with pineapple as the principal ingredient.

Serves 4
1 pineapple
15ml/1 tbsp vegetable oil
2 garlic cloves, finely chopped
2 shallots, finely chopped
5cm/2in piece fresh root ginger, peeled and finely shredded
30ml/2 tbsp light soy sauce
juice of 1/2 lime
1 large fresh red chilli, seeded and finely shredded

1 Trim and peel the pineapple. Cut out the core and dice the flesh into small pieces.

2 Heat the oil in a wok or frying pan. Stir-fry the garlic and shallots over a medium heat for 2–3 minutes, until golden. Do not let the garlic burn or the dish will taste bitter.

3 Add the pineapple. Stir-fry for about 2 minutes, or until the pineapple cubes start to turn golden on the edges.

4 Add the ginger, soy sauce, lime juice and shredded chilli.

5 Toss the mixture together until well mixed. Cook over a low heat for a further 2 minutes. Serve the pineapple as an accompaniment.

> **Variation**
> *This also tastes excellent if peaches or nectarines are substituted for the diced pineapple. Use three or four, depending on their size.*

Chilli & Mustard-flavoured Pineapple

Pineapple is cooked with coconut milk and a blend of spices in this dish, which could be served with any meat, fish or vegetable curry. The chilli adds heat, and the mustard seeds lend a rich, nutty flavour that complements the sharpness of the pineapple, while the coconut milk provides a creamy sweetness.

Serves 4
1 pineapple
50ml/2fl oz/1/4 cup water
150ml/1/4 pint/2/3 cup coconut milk
2.5ml/1/2 tsp ground turmeric
2.5ml/1/2 tsp crushed dried chillies
5ml/1 tsp salt
10ml/2 tsp granulated sugar
15ml/1 tbsp groundnut (peanut) oil
2.5ml/1/2 tsp mustard seeds
2.5ml/1/2 tsp cumin seeds
1 small onion, finely chopped
1 or 2 dried red chillies, broken
6–8 fresh curry leaves

1 Using a sharp knife halve the pineapple lengthways, then cut each half lengthways into two, so that you end up with four boat-shaped wedges. Peel them and remove the eyes and the central core. Cut into bitesize pieces.

2 Put the pineapple in a karahi, wok or large pan and add the measured water, with the coconut milk, turmeric and crushed chillies. Bring to a slow simmer over low heat, and cook, covered, for 10–12 minutes, or until the pineapple is soft but not mushy. Add the salt and sugar, and cook, uncovered, until the sauce thickens.

3 Heat the oil in a second pan, and add the mustard seeds. As soon as they begin to pop, add the cumin seeds and the onion. Fry for 6–7 minutes, stirring regularly, until the onion is soft.

4 Add the chillies and curry leaves. Fry for 1–2 minutes more, then pour the entire contents over the pineapple. Stir well, then remove from the heat. Serve hot or at room temperature.

Energy 71kcal/300kJ; Fat 3g; Saturated fat 0.3g; Carbohydrate 11.3g; Fibre 1.4g.

Energy 60kcal/252kJ; Fat 3g; Saturated fat 0.6g; Carbohydrate 8.3g; Fibre 0.8g.

Nutty Salad

The smooth creamy dressing is perfect with the crunchy nuts.

25g/1oz/¼ cup peanuts
fresh coriander (cilantro) and lime
  wedges, to garnish

Serves 4
150g/5oz can red kidney beans
1 medium onion, cut into
  12 rings
1 medium green courgette
  (zucchini), sliced
1 medium yellow courgette
  (zucchini), sliced
50g/2oz/²⁄₃ cup pasta shells,
  cooked
50g/2oz/½ cup cashew
  nuts

For the dressing
115g/4oz/½ cup low-fat fromage
  frais or ricotta cheese
30ml/2 tbsp natural (plain)
  low-fat yogurt
1 fresh green chilli, chopped
15ml/1 tbsp chopped fresh
  coriander (cilantro)
salt and ground black pepper
2.5ml/½ tsp crushed dried
  red chillies
15ml/1 tbsp lemon juice

1 Drain the kidney beans. Arrange them with the onion rings, courgette slices and pasta in a salad dish and sprinkle the cashew nuts and peanuts over the top.

2 In a separate bowl, mix together the fromage frais or ricotta cheese, yogurt, green chilli, fresh coriander and salt and pepper to taste. Beat well using a fork until all the ingredients are thoroughly combined. You may find it easier to add the coriander leaves a few at a time and mix in, to allow their flavour to permeate the mixture and ensure the resulting dressing is smooth in texture.

3 Sprinkle the crushed red chillies and lemon juice over the dressing. Garnish the salad with fresh coriander and lime wedges, and serve with the dressing.

> **Cook's Tip**
> Make the dressing just before serving the salad, so that the flavour of the coriander will be at its most intense.

Yogurt Salad

If this salad looks and tastes familiar, it isn't surprising. It is very similar to coleslaw, except that yogurt is used instead of mayonnaise, and cashew nuts are added.

Serves 4
115g/4oz cabbage
350ml/12fl oz/1½ cups natural
  (plain) low-fat yogurt
10ml/2 tsp clear honey
2 medium carrots, thickly sliced
2 spring onions (scallions),
  roughly chopped
50g/2oz/⅓ cup sultanas
  (golden raisins)
50g/2oz/½ cup cashew nuts
  (optional)
16 white grapes, halved
2.5ml/½ tsp salt
5ml/1 tsp chopped fresh mint

1 Use a mandolin, if you have one, to shred the cabbage finely. Alternatively, use a sharp knife to slice through the layers of the cabbage.

2 Using a fork, beat the yogurt in a bowl with the honey.

3 In a separate bowl, which will be suitable for serving the salad, mix together the carrots, spring onions, cabbage, sultanas, cashew nuts (if you are using them), grapes, salt and the chopped fresh mint.

4 Pour the sweetened yogurt mixture over the salad, mix well and serve.

> **Variation**
> For Squash and Yogurt Salad, mix together 2.5ml/½ tsp dry mustard, 2.5ml/½ tsp ground cumin, 2.5ml/½ tsp salt, 5ml/ 1 tsp grated fresh root ginger and 150ml/¼ pint/²⁄₃ cup natural yogurt. Chop half a green (bell) pepper and add to the spicy yogurt. Peel 250g/9oz butternut squash, then slice it and boil or steam until tender. Add to the yogurt mixture and stir well.

Energy 119kcal/503kJ; Fat 0.9g; Saturated fat 0.49g; Carbohydrate 23.4g; Fibre 1.8g.

Energy 199kcal/829kJ; Fat 11.6g; Saturated fat 2.63g; Carbohydrate 15.2g; Fibre 2.9g.

Spinach & Mushroom Salad

This salad is especially good served with glazed garlic prawns or any other seafood curry.

Serves 4
10 baby corn cobs
115g/4oz/3 cups mushrooms
2 medium tomatoes
20 small spinach leaves
8–10 onion rings

salt and ground black pepper
fresh coriander (cilantro) sprigs
  and lime slices, to garnish
  (optional)

1 Halve the baby corn cobs and slice the mushrooms and tomatoes.

2 Arrange all the salad ingredients in a large serving bowl. Season with salt and pepper and garnish with fresh coriander and lime slices, if you like.

Tofu & Cucumber Salad

This is a nutritious and refreshing salad with a hot, sweet-and-sour dressing. It is ideal for a buffet.

Serves 4–6
1 small cucumber
oil, for frying
1 square fresh or 115g/4oz
  long-life tofu
115g/4oz beansprouts, trimmed
  and rinsed
salt

For the dressing
1 small onion, grated
2 garlic cloves, crushed
2.5ml/½ tsp chilli powder
30–45ml/2–3 tbsp dark soy
  sauce
15–30ml/1–2 tbsp rice wine
  vinegar
10ml/2 tsp dark brown sugar
salt
celery leaves, to garnish

1 Trim the ends from the cucumber and then cut it into neat cubes.

2 Sprinkle the trimmed cucumber with salt and set aside while you prepare the remaining ingredients.

3 Heat a little oil in a pan and fry the tofu on both sides until golden brown. Drain well on absorbent kitchen paper and cut into cubes.

4 Prepare the dressing by blending together the onion, garlic and chilli powder. Stir in the soy sauce, vinegar, sugar and salt to taste. You can do this in a screw-topped glass jar.

5 Just before serving, rinse the cucumber under cold running water. Drain and dry thoroughly.

6 Toss the cucumber, tofu and beansprouts together in a serving bowl and pour over the dressing. Garnish with the celery leaves and serve immediately.

Baby Vegetable Salad with a Chilli Dressing

Warm salads make a pleasant change, and the flavours of the dressing are enhanced. Take the opportunity in spring to use the new season's baby vegetables for this mouthwatering combination, which makes an excellent accompaniment to spicy meals or to grilled meat or fish.

Serves 6
10 baby potatoes, halved
15 baby carrots

10 baby courgettes (zucchini)
115g/4oz/1½ cups button
  (white) mushrooms

For the dressing
45ml/3 tbsp lemon juice
25ml/1½ tbsp oil
15ml/1 tbsp chopped fresh
  coriander (cilantro)
5ml/1 tsp salt
2 fresh green chillies,
  finely sliced

1 Boil the potatoes, carrots and courgettes in water until tender. Drain them and place in a serving dish with the mushrooms.

2 Make the dressing in a separate bowl. Mix together the lemon juice, oil, fresh coriander, salt and chillies.

3 Toss the vegetables thoroughly in the chilli dressing and transfer to a serving bowl.

> **Variation**
> *For a mild version of this dish replace the green chillies with finely chopped green (bell) pepper.*

> **Cook's Tip**
> *As well as looking extremely attractive, the tiny baby vegetables give this salad a lovely flavour. Other baby vegetables, such as leeks, baby corn or cauliflower florets, can be used just as well.*

Top: Energy 25kcal/103kJ; Fat 0.6g; Saturated fat 0.09g; Carbohydrate 2.8g; Fibre 1.8g.
Above: Energy 65kcal/269kJ; Fat 4.6g; Saturated fat 0.6g; Carbohydrate 3.7g; Fibre 0.5g.

Energy 73kcal/308kJ; Fat 3.1g; Saturated fat 0.39g; Carbohydrate 10.1g; Fibre 1.5g.

Mango, Tomato & Red Onion Salad

This salad makes a delicious appetizer. The under-ripe mango blends well with the tomato.

Serves 4

1 firm under-ripe mango
2 large tomatoes or 1 beefsteak
   tomato, sliced
$^{1}/_{2}$ red onion, sliced into
   rings
$^{1}/_{2}$ cucumber, peeled and thinly
   sliced
chopped chives, to garnish

For the dressing
30ml/2 tbsp vegetable oil
15ml/1 tbsp lemon juice
1 garlic clove, crushed
2.5ml/$^{1}/_{2}$ tsp hot pepper sauce
salt and ground black pepper

1 Using a sharp knife or peeler, remove the skin from the mango, then cut and slice the flesh into bite-size pieces.

2 Arrange the mango, tomatoes, onion and cucumber on a large serving plate.

3 Make the dressing. Blend the oil, lemon juice, garlic, pepper sauce and seasoning in a blender or food processor, or shake vigorously in a small screw-top jar.

4 Spoon the dressing over the salad. Garnish with the chopped chives and serve.

> **Cook's Tip**
> *When cutting a mango, first peel the skin off with a sharp knife or peeler. Next, cut the fleshy cheeks from each side. Trim carefully around the fruit, following the curvature of the stone (pit), to remove all the flesh. You will end up with the stone, two cheeks and two thinner strips of fruit, which can then be sliced.*

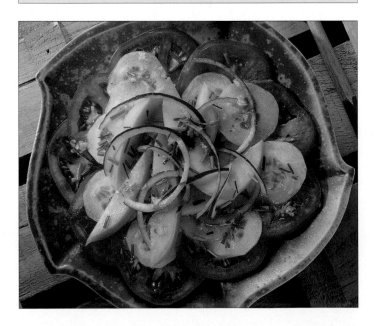

Energy 89kcal/370kJ; Fat 5.8g; Saturated fat 0.7g; Carbohydrate 8.6g; Fibre 1.9g.

Peppery Bean Salad

This pretty salad uses canned beans for speed and convenience.

Serves 4–6

425g/15oz can red kidney beans
425g/15oz can black-eyed beans
   (peas)
425g/15oz can chickpeas
$^{1}/_{4}$ red (bell) pepper
$^{1}/_{4}$ green (bell) pepper
6 radishes
15ml/1 tbsp chopped spring onion
   (scallion), plus extra to garnish

For the dressing
5ml/1 tsp ground cumin
15ml/1 tbsp tomato ketchup
30ml/2 tbsp olive oil
15ml/1 tbsp white wine
   vinegar
1 garlic clove, crushed
2.5ml/$^{1}/_{2}$ tsp hot pepper
   sauce

1 Drain the red kidney beans, black-eyed beans and chickpeas, and rinse under cold running water. Shake off the excess water and tip them into a large bowl.

2 Core, seed and chop the red and green peppers. Trim the radishes and slice thinly. Add the peppers, radishes and spring onion to the bowl.

3 To make the dressing, mix together the cumin, tomato ketchup, oil, white wine vinegar and crushed garlic in a small bowl. Add a little salt and hot pepper sauce to taste, and stir again thoroughly to combine.

4 Pour the dressing over the salad and mix. Cover the salad and chill for at least 1 hour before serving, garnished with the sliced spring onion.

> **Cook's Tip**
> *Look out for cans of mixed beans at the supermarket. These contain a colourful medley and would be perfect for this salad.*

Energy 430kcal/1814kJ; Fat 9.3g; Saturated fat 1.3g; Carbohydrate 64.8g; Fibre 19.8g.

Sweet Potato & Carrot Salad

This warm salad has a piquant flavour. As a main course, it will serve two.

Serves 4
1 medium sweet potato
2 carrots, cut into thick
　diagonal slices
3 medium tomatoes
8–10 iceberg lettuce leaves
75g/3oz/½ cup drained canned
　chickpeas

For the dressing
15ml/1 tbsp clear honey
90ml/6 tbsp natural (plain)
　low-fat yogurt
2.5ml/½ tsp salt
5ml/1 tsp coarsely ground
　black pepper

For the garnish
15ml/1 tbsp walnuts
15ml/1 tbsp sultanas
　(golden raisins)
1 small onion, cut into rings

1 Peel and dice the sweet potato. Cook in boiling water until soft but not mushy, remove from the heat, cover the pan and set aside.

2 Cook the carrots in a pan of boiling water for just a few minutes, making sure that they remain crunchy. Add the carrots to the sweet potatoes.

3 Drain the water from the sweet potatoes and carrots and mix them together in a bowl.

4 Slice the tops off the tomatoes, then scoop out and discard the seeds. Roughly chop the flesh.

5 Line a glass bowl with the lettuce leaves. Add the carrots, chickpeas and tomatoes to the potatoes and carrots. Mix lightly, then spoon the mixture into the lettuce-lined bowl.

6 Put all the dressing ingredients in a screw-top jar and shake well to combine, or put in a bowl and beat using a fork.

7 Garnish the salad with the walnuts, sultanas and onion rings. Pour the dressing over the salad or serve it in a separate bowl.

Energy 127kcal/532kJ; Fat 3.7g; Saturated fat 0.47g; Carbohydrate 20.6g; Fibre 3.1g.

Spicy Potato Salad

This tasty salad is quick to prepare, and makes a satisfying accompaniment to grilled or barbecued meat or fish.

Serves 6
900g/2lb potatoes
2 red (bell) peppers
2 celery sticks
1 shallot
2 or 3 spring onions (scallions)
1 fresh green chilli
1 garlic clove, crushed

10ml/2 tsp finely chopped
　fresh chives
10ml/2 tsp finely chopped
　fresh basil
15ml/1 tbsp finely chopped
　fresh parsley
30ml/2 tbsp single (light) cream
45ml/3 tbsp mayonnaise
5ml/1 tsp prepared mild mustard
7.5ml/1½ tsp granulated sugar
salt
chopped fresh chives, to garnish

1 Peel the potatoes. Boil in salted water for 10–12 minutes, until tender. Drain and cool, then cut into cubes and place in a large mixing bowl.

2 Halve the peppers, cut away and discard the core and seeds and cut the flesh into small pieces. Finely chop the celery, shallot and spring onions and slice the chilli very thinly, discarding the seeds. Add the vegetables to the potatoes together with the garlic and herbs.

3 Mix the cream, mayonnaise, mustard and sugar in a small bowl, stirring until the mixture is well combined.

4 Pour the dressing over the salad and stir gently to coat evenly. Serve, garnished with the chopped chives.

Cook's Tip
New potatoes would also work deliciously well in this recipe. Scrub them lightly to remove any earth and, unless they are very small, halve them. Cook them until just tender; test them with a knife.

Energy 185kcal/777kJ; Fat 6.7g; Saturated fat 1.3g; Carbohydrate 29.3g; Fibre 2.6g.

Fennel Coleslaw with Sultanas & Caraway Seeds

Another variation on traditional coleslaw in which the aniseed flavour of fennel plays a major role.

Serves 4
175g/6oz fennel
2 spring onions (scallions)
175g/6oz white cabbage
115g/4oz celery
175g/6oz carrots
50g/2oz/⅓ cup sultanas
    (golden raisins)
2.5ml/½ tsp caraway seeds
15ml/1 tbsp chopped fresh
    parsley
45ml/3 tbsp extra virgin olive oil
5ml/1 tsp lemon juice
shreds of spring onion (scallion),
    to garnish

1 Using a sharp knife, cut the fennel and spring onions into thin slices.

2 Cut the carrots into fine strips. Use a mandolin, if you have one, to slice the cabbage and celery finely. Alternatively, use a sharp knife.

3 Place in a bowl with the fennel and spring onions. Add the sultanas and caraway seeds, and toss lightly to mix.

4 Stir in the chopped parsley, olive oil and lemon juice, and mix all the ingredients very thoroughly. Cover and chill for 3 hours to allow the flavours to mingle. Serve garnished with shreds of spring onion.

> **Cook's Tip**
> The carrot can be coarsely grated if you prefer.

> **Variation**
> Use sour cream instead of olive oil for a creamier dressing.

Energy 146kcal/607kJ; Fat 8.7g; Saturated fat 1.2g; Carbohydrate 15.9g; Fibre 3.8g.

Carrot & Orange Salad

A fruit and a vegetable that could have been made for each other form the basis of this fresh-tasting salad.

Serves 4
450g/1lb carrots
2 large oranges
15ml/1 tbsp olive oil
30ml/2 tbsp lemon juice
pinch of granulated sugar
    (optional)
30ml/2 tbsp chopped
    pistachio nuts or toasted
    pine nuts
salt and ground black pepper

1 Peel the carrots and grate them into a large bowl.

2 Using a sharp knife, cut a thin slice of peel and pith from each end of the orange. Place cut side down on a plate and cut off the peel and pith in strips. Remove any remaining pith. Cut out each segment leaving the membrane behind. Squeeze the remaining juice from the membrane into a bowl.

3 Mix together the olive oil, lemon juice and orange juice from the bowl. Season with a little salt and pepper to taste, and granulated sugar if you like.

4 Toss the orange segments together with the carrots and pour the dressing over.

5 Sprinkle the salad with the pistachio nuts or pine nuts before serving.

> **Variation**
> Sliced eating apple would also work well in this recipe.

> **Cook's Tip**
> Be careful to remove all the pith from the orange segments so that you can easily cut just the segment away from the membrane.

Energy 148kcal/618kJ; Fat 7.4g; Saturated fat 1.1g; Carbohydrate 18.4g; Fibre 5g.

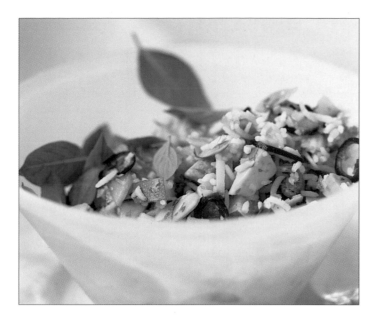

Rice Salad

The sky's the limit with this recipe. Use whatever fruit, vegetables and even leftover meat that you might have, mix with cooked rice and pour over the fragrant dressing.

Serves 4–6

350g/12oz/3 cups cooked rice
1 Asian pear, cored and diced
50g/2oz dried shrimp, chopped
1 avocado, peeled, stoned (pitted) and diced
1/2 medium cucumber, finely diced
2 lemon grass stalks, finely chopped
30ml/2 tbsp sweet chilli sauce

1 fresh green or red chilli, seeded and finely sliced
115g/4oz/1 cup flaked (sliced) almonds, toasted
small bunch fresh coriander (cilantro), chopped
fresh Thai sweet basil leaves, to garnish

For the dressing
300ml/1/2 pint/1 1/4 cups water
10ml/2 tsp shrimp paste
15ml/1 tbsp palm sugar or light muscovado (brown) sugar
2 kaffir lime leaves, torn into small pieces
1/2 lemon grass stalk, sliced

1 To make the dressing, put the measured water in a small pan with the shrimp paste, palm sugar or light muscovado sugar, kaffir lime leaves and sliced lemon grass.

2 Heat gently, stirring continuously, until the sugar dissolves, then bring to boiling point and simmer for 5 minutes. Strain into a bowl and set aside until cold.

3 Put the cooked rice in a large salad bowl and fluff up the grains with a fork. Add the cored and diced Asian pear, dried shrimp, diced avocado, cucumber, lemon grass and sweet chilli sauce. Mix well.

4 Add the sliced chilli, flaked almonds and chopped coriander to the bowl and toss well. Garnish the salad with Thai basil leaves and serve with the bowl of dressing to spoon over the top of individual portions.

Energy 398kcal/1663kJ; Fat 22.4g; Saturated fat 2.6g; Carbohydrate 34.9g; Fibre 4.1g.

Fried Egg Salad

Chillies and eggs may seem unlikely partners, but actually work very well together. The peppery flavour of the watercress makes it the perfect foundation for this tasty salad.

Serves 2
15ml/1 tbsp groundnut (peanut) oil
1 garlic clove, thinly sliced
4 eggs

2 shallots, thinly sliced
2 small fresh red chillies, seeded and thinly sliced
1/2 small cucumber, finely diced
1cm/1/2in piece fresh root ginger, peeled and grated
juice of 2 limes
30ml/2 tbsp soy sauce
5ml/1 tsp caster (superfine) sugar
small bunch coriander (cilantro)
bunch watercress or rocket (arugula), coarsely chopped

1 Heat the groundnut oil in a frying pan. Add the sliced garlic and cook over a low heat until it starts to turn golden.

2 Crack in the eggs. Break the yolks with a wooden spatula, then fry until the eggs are almost firm. Remove from the pan and set aside.

3 Mix the thinly sliced shallots, chillies, diced cucumber and grated ginger in a bowl.

4 In a separate bowl, whisk the lime juice with the soy sauce and sugar. Pour this dressing over the vegetables and toss lightly.

5 Set aside a few coriander sprigs for the garnish. Chop the remainder and add them to the salad. Toss it again.

6 Reserve a few watercress or rocket sprigs and arrange the remainder on two serving plates. Cut the fried eggs into slices and divide them between the watercress mounds.

7 Spoon the shallot mixture over the egg slices, and serve, garnished with the reserved coriander and watercress or rocket.

Energy 226kcal/938kJ; Fat 17g; Saturated fat 3.8g; Carbohydrate 5.3g; Fibre 1.1g.

Raw Vegetable Yam

In this context, the word "yam" does not refer to the starchy vegetable that resembles sweet potato, but rather to a unique style of Thai cooking. Yam dishes are salads made with raw or lightly cooked vegetables, dressed with a special spicy sauce.

Serves 4
50g/2oz watercress or baby spinach, chopped
½ cucumber, finely diced
2 celery sticks, finely diced
2 carrots, finely diced
1 red (bell) pepper, seeded and finely diced
2 tomatoes, seeded and finely diced
small bunch fresh mint, chopped
90g/3½oz cellophane noodles

For the yam
2 small fresh red chillies, seeded and finely chopped
60ml/4 tbsp light soy sauce
45ml/3 tbsp lemon juice
5ml/1 tsp palm sugar or light muscovado (brown) sugar
60ml/4 tbsp water
1 head pickled garlic, finely chopped, plus 15ml/1 tbsp vinegar from the jar
50g/2oz/scant ½ cup peanuts, roasted and chopped
90g/3½oz fried tofu, finely chopped
15ml/1 tbsp sesame seeds, toasted

1 Place the watercress or spinach, cucumber, celery, carrots, red pepper and tomatoes in a bowl. Add the chopped mint and toss together.

2 Soak the noodles in boiling water for 3 minutes, or according to the packet instructions, then drain well and snip with scissors into shorter lengths. Add them to the vegetables.

3 To make the yam, put the chopped chillies in a pan and add the soy sauce, lemon juice, sugar and water. Place over a medium heat and stir until the sugar has dissolved. Add the chopped garlic, with the pickling vinegar from the jar, then mix in the chopped nuts, tofu and toasted sesame seeds.

4 Pour the yam over the vegetables and noodles, toss together until well mixed, and serve immediately.

Energy 280kcal/1165kJ; Fat 12.6g; Saturated fat 1.6g; Carbohydrate 29g; Fibre 3.4g.

Mushroom Yam

The food of southern Thailand is notoriously hot, and the Muslim community have introduced richer curry flavours reminiscent of Indian food.

Serves 4
90g/3½oz Chinese leaves (Chinese cabbage), shredded
90g/3½oz/generous 1 cup beansprouts
90g/3½oz/scant 1 cup green beans, trimmed
90g/3½oz broccoli, preferably the purple sprouting variety, divided into florets
15ml/1 tbsp sesame seeds, toasted

For the yam
60ml/4 tbsp coconut cream
5ml/1 tsp Thai red curry paste
90g/3½oz/1¼ cups oyster mushrooms or field (portabello) mushrooms, sliced
60ml/4 tbsp coconut milk
5ml/1 tsp ground turmeric
5ml/1 tsp thick tamarind juice, made by mixing tamarind paste with warm water
juice of ½ lemon
60ml/4 tbsp light soy sauce
5ml/1 tsp palm sugar or light muscovado (brown) sugar

1 Steam the shredded Chinese leaves, beansprouts, green beans and broccoli separately or blanch them in boiling water for 1 minute per batch. Drain, place in a serving bowl and leave to cool.

2 To make the yam, pour the coconut cream into a wok or frying pan and heat gently for 2–3 minutes, until it separates. Stir in the red curry paste. Cook over a low heat for 30 seconds, until the mixture is fragrant. Increase the heat to high and add the mushrooms to the wok or pan. Cook for a further 2–3 minutes.

3 Pour in the coconut milk and add the ground turmeric, tamarind juice, lemon juice, soy sauce and sugar to the wok or pan. Mix thoroughly.

4 Pour the mixture over the prepared vegetables and toss well to combine. Sprinkle with the toasted sesame seeds and serve.

Energy 109kcal/451kJ; Fat 8g; Saturated fat 4.9g; Carbohydrate 5.6g; Fibre 2.4g.

Fruit & Vegetable Salad

This fruit salad is traditionally presented with the main course and serves as a cooler to counteract the heat of the chillies that will inevitably be present in the other dishes. It is a typically harmonious balance of flavours.

Serves 4–6

1 small pineapple
115g/4oz/1 cup green beans, trimmed and halved
1 small mango, peeled and sliced
1 green apple, cored and sliced
6 rambutans or lychees, peeled and stoned (pitted)
1 red onion, sliced
1 small cucumber, cut into short sticks
115g/4oz/1½ cups beansprouts
2 spring onions (scallions), sliced
1 ripe tomato, quartered
225g/8oz cos, romaine or iceberg lettuce leaves
salt

For the coconut dipping sauce

30ml/2 tbsp coconut cream
30ml/2 tbsp granulated sugar
75ml/5 tbsp boiling water
1.5ml/¼ tsp chilli sauce
15ml/1 tbsp Thai fish sauce
juice of 1 lime

1 To make the coconut dipping sauce, spoon the coconut cream, sugar and boiling water into a screw-top jar. Add the chilli and fish sauces and lime juice, close tightly and shake to mix.

2 Trim both ends of the pineapple with a serrated knife, then cut away the outer skin. Remove the central core with an apple corer. Alternatively, quarter the pineapple lengthways and remove the portion of core from each wedge with a knife. Chop the pineapple and set aside with the other fruits.

3 Bring a small pan of lightly salted water to the boil over a medium heat. Add the green beans and cook for 3–4 minutes, until just tender but still retaining some "bite". Drain, refresh under cold running water, drain well again and set aside.

4 To serve, arrange all the fruits and vegetables in small heaps on a platter or in a shallow bowl. Pour the coconut sauce into a small serving bowl and serve separately as a dip.

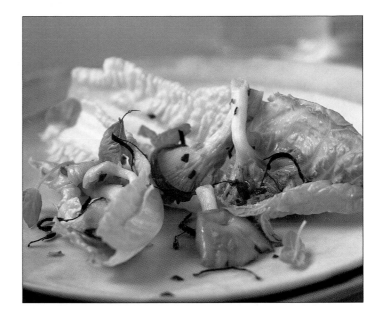

Fragrant Mushrooms in Lettuce Leaves

This quick and easy vegetable dish is served on lettuce leaf "saucers" so can be eaten with the fingers – a great treat for children.

Serves 2

30ml/2 tbsp vegetable oil
2 garlic cloves, finely chopped
2 baby cos or romaine lettuces, or 2 Little Gem (Bibb) lettuces
1 lemon grass stalk, finely chopped
2 kaffir lime leaves, rolled into cylinders and thinly sliced
200g/7oz/3 cups oyster or chestnut mushrooms, sliced
1 small fresh red chilli, seeded and finely chopped
juice of ½ lemon
30ml/2 tbsp light soy sauce
5ml/1 tsp palm sugar or light muscovado (brown) sugar
small bunch fresh mint, leaves removed from the stalks

1 Heat the oil in a wok or frying pan. Add the garlic and cook over a medium heat, stirring occasionally, until golden. Do not let it burn or it will taste bitter.

2 Meanwhile, separate the individual lettuce leaves and set aside while you cook the mushrooms.

3 Increase the heat under the wok or pan and add the lemon grass, lime leaves and sliced mushrooms. Stir-fry for about 2 minutes.

4 Add the finely chopped red chilli, lemon juice, soy sauce and palm or muscovado sugar to the wok or pan. Toss the mixture over the heat to combine the ingredients together thoroughly, then stir-fry for a further 2 minutes.

5 Arrange the lettuce leaves on a large plate. Spoon a small amount of the mushroom mixture on to each leaf, top with a mint leaf and serve.

Energy 151kcal/645kJ; Fat 1.1g; Saturated fat 0.2g; Carbohydrate 34.3g; Fibre 4.8g.

Energy 145kcal/600kJ; Fat 12.2g; Saturated fat 1.5g; Carbohydrate 5.5g; Fibre 2g.

Bamboo Shoot Salad

This hot, sharp-flavoured salad originated in north-eastern Thailand. Use canned whole bamboo shoots, if you can find them – they have more flavour than sliced ones.

Serves 4
400g/14oz canned bamboo
    shoots, in large pieces
25g/1oz/about 3 tbsp
    glutinous rice
30ml/2 tbsp chopped shallots
15ml/1 tbsp chopped garlic

45ml/3 tbsp chopped spring
    onions (scallions)
30ml/2 tbsp Thai fish sauce
30ml/2 tbsp fresh lime juice
5ml/1 tsp granulated sugar
2.5ml/½ tsp dried chilli flakes
20–25 small fresh mint leaves
15ml/1 tbsp toasted
    sesame seeds

1 Rinse the bamboo shoots under cold running water, then drain them and pat them thoroughly dry with kitchen paper. Set them aside.

2 Dry-roast the rice in a frying pan until it is golden brown. Leave to cool slightly, then tip into a mortar and grind to fine crumbs with a pestle.

3 Transfer the rice to a bowl and add the shallots, garlic, spring onions, fish sauce, lime juice, sugar, chillies and half the mint leaves. Mix well.

4 Add the bamboo shoots to the bowl and toss to mix. Serve sprinkled with the toasted sesame seeds and the remaining mint leaves.

Cook's Tip
Glutinous rice is an especially sticky rice when boiled, which makes it easy to eat using chopsticks. In this recipe, however, it is toasted and ground.

Energy 91kcal/383kJ; Fat 2.9g; Saturated fat 0.4g; Carbohydrate 11.7g; Fibre 2.2g.

Cabbage Salad

This is a simple and delicious way of serving a somewhat mundane vegetable. Classic Thai flavours permeate this colourful warm salad.

Serves 4–6
30ml/2 tbsp vegetable oil
2 large fresh red chillies, seeded
    and cut into thin strips

6 garlic cloves, thinly sliced
6 shallots, thinly sliced
1 small cabbage, shredded
30ml/2 tbsp coarsely chopped
    roasted peanuts, to garnish

For the dressing
30ml/2 tbsp Thai fish sauce
grated rind of 1 lime
30ml/2 tbsp fresh lime juice
120ml/4fl oz/½ cup coconut milk

1 To make the dressing, mix the fish sauce, lime rind and juice and coconut milk in a bowl. Whisk until thoroughly combined, then set aside.

2 Heat the vegetable oil in a wok. Stir-fry the thinly sliced chillies, garlic and shallots over medium heat for 3–4 minutes, until the shallots are brown and crisp. Remove with a slotted spoon and set aside.

3 Bring a large pan of lightly salted water to the boil. Add the cabbage and blanch for 2–3 minutes.

4 Tip the cabbage into a colander, drain well and put into a bowl.

5 Whisk the dressing again, add it to the warm cabbage and toss to mix.

6 Transfer the cabbage salad to a serving dish. Sprinkle with the fried shallot mixture and the chopped roasted peanuts. Serve immediately.

Variation
Other vegetables, such as cauliflower, broccoli and Chinese leaves (Chinese cabbage), can be prepared in this way.

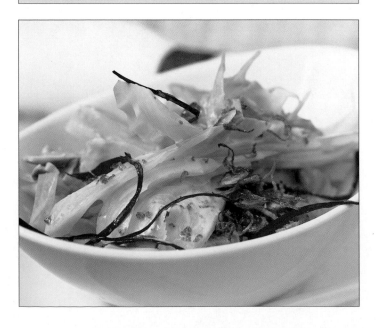

Energy 136kcal/565kJ; Fat 9.3g; Saturated fat 1.4g; Carbohydrate 9.8g; Fibre 3g.

Green Papaya Salad

This salad appears in many guises in South-east Asia. As green papaya is not always easy to get hold of, finely grated carrots, cucumber or even crisp green apple can be used instead. Alternatively, use very thinly sliced white cabbage.

Serves 4
1 green papaya
4 garlic cloves, coarsely chopped
15ml/1 tbsp chopped shallots
3 or 4 fresh red chillies, seeded and sliced
2.5ml/½ tsp salt

2 or 3 snake beans or 6 green beans, cut into 2cm/¾in lengths
2 tomatoes, cut into thin wedges
45ml/3 tbsp Thai fish sauce
15ml/1 tbsp caster (superfine) sugar
juice of 1 lime
30ml/2 tbsp crushed roasted peanuts
sliced fresh red chillies, to garnish

1 Cut the papaya in half lengthways. Scrape out the seeds with a spoon and discard. Using a swivel vegetable peeler or a small sharp knife remove the peel from the papaya. Shred the flesh finely in a food processor or using a grater.

2 Put the garlic, shallots, red chillies and salt in a large mortar and grind to a paste with a pestle. Add the shredded papaya, a small amount at a time, pounding with the pestle until it becomes slightly limp and soft.

3 Add the sliced snake or green beans and wedges of tomato to the mortar and crush them lightly with the pestle until they are incorporated.

4 Season the mixture with the fish sauce, sugar and lime juice. Transfer the salad to a serving dish and sprinkle with the crushed roasted peanuts.

5 Garnish with the sliced red chillies and serve the salad immediately.

Energy 115kcal/485kJ; Fat 3.8g; Saturated fat 0.7g; Carbohydrate 18g; Fibre 3.9g.

Sweet-&-sour Salad

Acar bening makes a perfect accompaniment to spicy dishes and curries, with its sharp, clean taste and bright colours.

Serves 8
1 small cucumber
1 onion, thinly sliced
1 small, ripe pineapple or 425g/15oz can pineapple rings
1 green (bell) pepper, seeded and thinly sliced

3 firm tomatoes, chopped
30ml/2 tbsp golden granulated sugar
45–60ml/3–4 tbsp white wine vinegar
120ml/4fl oz/½ cup water
salt
seeds of 1 or 2 pomegranates, to garnish

1 Halve the cucumber lengthways, remove the seeds, slice and spread on a plate with the onion. Sprinkle with salt. After 10 minutes, rinse and dry.

2 If using a fresh pineapple, peel and core it, removing all the eyes, then cut it into bitesize pieces. If using canned pineapple, drain the rings and cut them into small wedges. Place the pineapple in a bowl with the cucumber, onion, green pepper and tomatoes.

3 Heat the sugar, vinegar and measured water in a pan, stirring until the sugar has dissolved. Remove the pan from the heat and leave to cool. When cold, add a little salt to taste and pour over the fruit and vegetables. Cover and chill until required. Serve in small bowls, garnished with pomegranate seeds.

> **Variation**
> *To make an Indonesian-style cucumber salad, salt a salad cucumber as described in the recipe. Make half the dressing and pour it over the cucumber. Add a few chopped spring onions (scallions). Cover and chill. Serve the salad sprinkled with toasted sesame seeds.*

Energy 49kcal/211kJ; Fat 0.3g; Saturated fat 0.1g; Carbohydrate 11.7g; Fibre 1.5g.

Fruit & Raw Vegetable Gado-gado

A banana leaf can be used instead of the mixed salad leaves to line the platter for a special occasion.

Serves 6
$^1/_2$ cucumber
2 pears (not too ripe) or
    175g/6oz wedge of yam bean
1 or 2 eating apples
juice of $^1/_2$ lemon
mixed salad leaves
6 small tomatoes, cut into wedges
3 slices fresh pineapple, cored
    and cut into wedges
3 eggs, hard-boiled and shelled
175g/6oz egg noodles, cooked,
    cooled and chopped
deep-fried onions, to garnish

For the peanut sauce
2–4 fresh red chillies, seeded
    and ground, or 15ml/1 tbsp
    chilli sambal
300ml/$^1/_2$ pint/1$^1/_4$ cups
    coconut milk
350g/12oz/1$^1/_4$ cups crunchy
    peanut butter
15ml/1 tbsp dark soy sauce or
    dark brown sugar
5ml/1 tsp tamarind pulp, soaked
    in 45ml/3 tbsp warm water
coarsely crushed peanuts
salt

1 To make the peanut sauce, put the ground chillies or chilli sambal in a pan. Pour in the coconut milk, then stir in the peanut butter. Heat gently, stirring, until well blended.

2 Simmer gently until the sauce thickens, then stir in the soy sauce or sugar. Strain in the tamarind juice, add salt to taste, and stir well. Spoon into a bowl and sprinkle with a few coarsely crushed peanuts.

3 To make the salad, core the cucumber and peel the pears or wedge of yam bean. Cut them into matchsticks. Finely shred the apples and sprinkle them with the lemon juice. Spread a bed of lettuce leaves on a flat platter, then pile the fruit and vegetables on top.

4 Add the sliced or quartered hard-boiled eggs, the chopped noodles and the deep-fried onions. Serve immediately, with the peanut sauce.

Energy 558kcal/2323kJ; Fat 33.7g; Saturated fat 8.4g; Carbohydrate 45.1g; Fibre 5.7g.

Scented Fish Salad

For a tropical taste of the Far East, try this delicious fish salad scented with coconut, fruit and warm Thai spices.

Serves 4
350g/12oz fillet of red mullet,
    sea bream or snapper
1 cos or romaine lettuce
1 papaya or mango, peeled
    and sliced
1 pitaya, peeled and sliced
1 large ripe tomato, cut
    into wedges
$^1/_2$ cucumber, peeled and cut
    into batons
3 spring onions (scallions),
    sliced
salt

For the marinade
5ml/1 tsp coriander seeds
5ml/1 tsp fennel seeds
2.5ml/$^1/_2$ tsp cumin seeds
5ml/1 tsp caster (superfine) sugar
2.5ml/$^1/_2$ tsp hot chilli sauce
30ml/2 tbsp garlic oil

For the dressing
15ml/1 tbsp coconut cream
45ml/3 tbsp boiling water
60ml/4 tbsp groundnut (peanut) oil
finely grated rind and juice of
    1 lime
1 fresh red chilli, seeded and
    finely chopped
5ml/1 tsp granulated sugar
45ml/3 tbsp chopped fresh
    coriander (cilantro)

1 Cut the fish into even strips, removing any stray bones. Place it on a plate.

2 To make the marinade, put the coriander, fennel and cumin seeds in a mortar. Add the sugar and crush with a pestle. Stir in the chilli sauce, garlic oil, and salt to taste and mix to a paste. Spread the paste over the fish, cover and leave to marinate in a cool place for at least 20 minutes.

3 To make the dressing, place the coconut and salt in a screw-top jar. Stir in the water. Add the oil, lime rind and juice, chilli, sugar and coriander. Shake well.

4 Place the salad ingredients in a bowl and add the dressing.

5 Heat a large non-stick frying-pan, add the fish and cook for 5 minutes, turning once. Add the cooked fish to the salad, toss lightly and serve immediately.

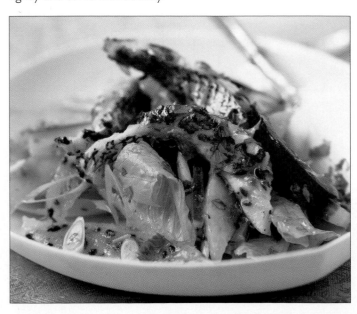

Energy 315kcal/1318kJ; Fat 20.5g; Saturated fat 4.1g; Carbohydrate 15.4g; Fibre 3.5g.

Aubergine Salad with Shrimp & Egg

An appetizing and unusual salad that you will find yourself making over and over again. Roasting the aubergines really brings out their flavour.

Serves 4–6

2 aubergines (eggplants)
15ml/1 tbsp vegetable oil
30ml/2 tbsp dried shrimp, soaked in warm water for 10 minutes
15ml/1 tbsp coarsely chopped garlic
1 hard-boiled egg, chopped
4 shallots, thinly sliced into rings
fresh coriander (cilantro) leaves and 2 fresh red chillies, seeded and sliced, to garnish

For the dressing

30ml/2 tbsp fresh lime juice
5ml/1 tsp palm sugar or light muscovado (brown) sugar
30ml/2 tbsp Thai fish sauce

1 Preheat the grill (broiler) to medium or preheat the oven to 180°C/350°F/Gas 4. Prick the aubergines several times with a skewer, then arrange on a baking sheet. Cook them under the grill for 30–40 minutes, or until they are charred and tender. Alternatively, roast them by placing them directly on the shelf of the oven for about 1 hour, turning them at least twice. Remove the aubergines and set aside until they are cool enough to handle.

2 Meanwhile, make the dressing. Put the lime juice, palm or muscovado sugar and fish sauce into a small bowl. Whisk well with a fork or balloon whisk. Cover with clear film (plastic wrap) and set aside until required. When the aubergines are cool enough to handle, peel off the skin and cut the flesh into medium slices.

3 Heat the oil in a small frying pan. Drain the dried shrimp thoroughly and add them to the pan with the garlic. Cook over a medium heat for about 3 minutes, until golden. Remove from the pan and set aside.

4 Arrange the aubergine slices on a serving dish. Top with the hard-boiled egg, shallots and dried shrimp mixture. Drizzle over the dressing and garnish with the coriander and red chillies.

Energy 91kcal/380kJ; Fat 5g; Saturated fat 0.9g; Carbohydrate 4.8g; Fibre 3.2g.

Seafood Salad with Fragrant Herbs

This is a spectacular salad. The luscious combination of prawns, scallops and squid makes it the ideal choice for a special celebration.

Serves 4–6

250ml/8fl oz/1 cup fish stock or water
350g/12oz squid
12 raw king prawns (jumbo shrimp), peeled and deveined, with tails intact
12 scallops
50g/2oz cellophane noodles, soaked in warm water for 30 minutes
½ cucumber, cut into thin batons
1 lemon grass stalk, finely chopped
2 kaffir lime leaves, finely shredded
2 shallots, thinly sliced
30ml/2 tbsp chopped spring onions (scallions)
30ml/2 tbsp fresh coriander (cilantro) leaves
12–15 fresh mint leaves, coarsely torn
4 fresh red chillies, seeded and cut into slivers
juice of 1 or 2 limes
30ml/2 tbsp Thai fish sauce
fresh coriander sprigs, to garnish

1 Wash the squid. Pull away the head and tentacles. Remove the ink sac and discard. Pull out all the innards and long transparent "pen", and discard with the thin body skin. Keep the two small side fins. Slice across the head just under the eyes, severing the tentacles. Discard the rest of the head. Squeeze the tentacles at the head end to push out the round beak and discard. Rinse the pouch and tentacles. Slice into rings.

2 Pour the fish stock or water into a medium pan, set over a high heat and bring to the boil. Cook each type of seafood separately in the stock for 3–4 minutes. Remove with a slotted spoon and set aside to cool.

3 Drain the noodles. Using scissors, cut them into short lengths, about 5cm/2in long. Place them in a serving bowl and add the cucumber, lemon grass, kaffir lime leaves, shallots, spring onions, coriander, mint and chillies.

4 Pour over the lime juice and fish sauce. Mix well, then add the seafood. Toss lightly. Garnish with the fresh coriander and serve.

Energy 224kcal/948kJ; Fat 2.7g; Saturated fat 0.6g; Carbohydrate 14.2g; Fibre 0.4g.

Tangy Chicken Salad

This fresh and lively dish typifies the character of Thai cuisine. It is ideal for a light lunch on a hot and lazy summer's day.

Serves 4–6

4 skinned chicken breast
   fillets
2 garlic cloves, crushed
30ml/2 tbsp soy sauce
30ml/2 tbsp vegetable oil
120ml/4fl oz/½ cup coconut
   cream
30ml/2 tbsp Thai fish sauce
juice of 1 lime
30ml/2 tbsp palm sugar or light
   muscovado (brown) sugar
115g/4oz/½ cup water
   chestnuts, sliced
50g/2oz/½ cup cashew nuts,
   roasted and coarsely chopped
4 shallots, thinly sliced
4 kaffir lime leaves, thinly sliced
1 lemon grass stalk, thinly sliced
5ml/1 tsp chopped fresh
   galangal
1 large fresh red chilli, seeded
   and finely chopped
2 spring onions (scallions),
   thinly sliced
10–12 fresh mint leaves, torn
1 lettuce, separated into leaves,
   to serve
2 fresh red chillies, seeded
   and sliced, to garnish

1 Place the chicken in a large dish. Rub with the garlic, soy sauce and 15ml/1 tbsp of the oil. Cover and leave to marinate for 1–2 hours.

2 Heat the remaining oil in a wok or frying pan and stir-fry the chicken for 3–4 minutes on each side, or until cooked. Remove and set aside to cool.

3 In a pan, heat the coconut cream, fish sauce, lime juice and sugar. Stir until the sugar has dissolved; set aside.

4 Tear the cooked chicken into strips and put it in a bowl. Add the sliced water chestnuts, roasted and chopped cashew nuts, shallots, kaffir lime leaves, lemon grass, galangal, red chilli, spring onions and mint leaves.

5 Pour the coconut dressing over the mixture and toss well. Serve the chicken on a bed of lettuce leaves and garnish with sliced red chillies.

Pomelo Salad

Peanuts, prawns, crab and pomelo make an unusual as well as refreshing and palate-cleansing salad to serve with a selection of other South-east Asian dishes.

Serves 4–6

30ml/2 tbsp vegetable oil
4 shallots, finely sliced
2 garlic cloves, finely sliced
1 large pomelo
15ml/1 tbsp roasted peanuts
115g/4oz cooked peeled
   prawns (shrimp)
115g/4oz cooked crab meat
10–12 small fresh mint leaves

For the dressing
30ml/2 tbsp Thai fish sauce
15ml/1 tbsp palm sugar or light
   muscovado (brown) sugar
30ml/2 tbsp fresh lime juice

For the garnish
2 spring onions (scallions), sliced
2 fresh red chillies, seeded and
   thinly sliced
fresh coriander (cilantro) leaves
shredded fresh coconut (optional)

1 To make the dressing, mix the fish sauce, sugar and lime juice in a bowl. Whisk well, then cover with clear film (plastic wrap) and set aside.

2 Heat the oil in a small frying pan, add the shallots and garlic, and cook over a medium heat until they are golden. Remove from the pan and set aside.

3 Peel the pomelo and break the flesh into small pieces, taking care to remove any membranes.

4 Grind the peanuts coarsely and put them in a salad bowl. Add the pomelo flesh, prawns, crab meat, mint leaves and the shallot mixture. Pour over the dressing, toss lightly and sprinkle with the spring onions, chillies and coriander leaves. Add the shredded coconut, if using. Serve immediately.

> **Cook's Tip**
> The pomelo is a large citrus fruit with pinkish-yellow flesh and a sharp taste.

Energy 336kcal/1412kJ; Fat 13.8g; Saturated fat 2.5g; Carbohydrate 13.9g; Fibre 1.2g.

Energy 150kcal/627kJ; Fat 7.8g; Saturated fat 1g; Carbohydrate 8.6g; Fibre 1.1g.

Beef & Mushroom Salad

All the ingredients for this traditional Thai dish – known as *yam nua yang* – are widely available in larger supermarkets.

Serves 4
675g/1½lb fillet or rump (round) steak
30ml/2 tbsp olive oil
2 small mild red chillies, seeded and sliced
225g/8oz/3¼ cups fresh shiitake mushrooms, stems removed and caps sliced

For the dressing
3 spring onions (scallions), finely chopped
2 garlic cloves, finely chopped
juice of 1 lime
15–30ml/1–2 tbsp Thai fish sauce
5ml/1 tsp soft light brown sugar
30ml/2 tbsp chopped fresh coriander (cilantro)

To serve
1 cos or romaine lettuce, torn into strips
175g/6oz cherry tomatoes, halved
5cm/2in piece cucumber, peeled, halved and thinly sliced
45ml/3 tbsp toasted sesame seeds

1 Preheat the grill (broiler) to medium, then cook the steak for 2–4 minutes on each side, depending on how well done you like it. (In Thailand, the beef is traditionally served quite rare.) Leave to cool for at least 15 minutes. Slice the meat as thinly as possible and place the slices in a bowl.

2 Heat the olive oil in a small frying pan. Add the seeded and sliced red chillies and the sliced shiitake mushroom caps. Cook for 5 minutes, stirring occasionally. Turn off the heat and add the steak slices to the pan. Stir well to coat the beef slices in the chilli and mushroom mixture.

3 To make the dressing, mix all the ingredients in a bowl, then pour it over the meat mixture and toss gently. Arrange the lettuce, tomatoes and cucumber on a serving plate. Spoon the steak mixture in the centre and sprinkle the sesame seeds over. Serve at once.

Coronation Potatoes

The connection between this recipe and traditional Indian cooking is tenuous, but coronation dressing is so popular that it would have been churlish to leave it out.

Serves 6
450g/1lb new potatoes
45ml/3 tbsp French dressing
3 spring onions (scallions), chopped
6 eggs, hard-boiled and halved
frilly lettuce leaves
¼ cucumber, cut into thin strips
6 large radishes, sliced
salad cress (optional)
salt and ground black pepper

For the coronation dressing
30ml/2 tbsp olive oil
1 small onion, chopped
15ml/1 tbsp mild curry powder or korma spice mix
10ml/2 tsp tomato purée (paste)
30ml/2 tbsp lemon juice
30ml/2 tbsp sherry
300ml/½ pint/1¼ cups mayonnaise
150ml/¼ pint/⅔ cup natural (plain) yogurt

1 Boil the potatoes in salted water until tender. Drain them, transfer to a large bowl and toss in the French dressing while they are still warm.

2 Stir in the spring onions and the salt and pepper, and leave to cool thoroughly.

3 Meanwhile, make the coronation dressing. Heat the oil in a small pan. Fry the onion for 3 minutes, until soft. Stir in the curry powder or spice mix and fry for a further 1 minute. Remove from the heat and mix in all the other dressing ingredients.

4 Stir the dressing into the potatoes, add the eggs, then chill.

5 Line a serving platter with lettuce leaves and pile the salad in the centre. Sprinkle over the cucumber and radishes with the cress, if using.

Energy 441kcal/1834kJ; Fat 28.5g; Saturated fat 8.3g; Carbohydrate 3.9g; Fibre 2.6g.

Energy 597kcal/2468kJ; Fat 53g; Saturated fat 8.8g; Carbohydrate 15.2g; Fibre 1.2g.

Spiced Yogurt

Yogurt is always a welcome accompaniment to hot curries. Here, it is topped with a hot spice mixture to provide a contrast in both taste and temperature.

Makes 450ml/¾ pint/ scant 2 cups
450ml/¾ pint/scant 2 cups natural (plain) yogurt

2.5ml/½ tsp freshly ground fennel seeds
salt
2.5ml/½ tsp granulated sugar
60ml/4 tbsp vegetable oil
1 dried red chilli
1.5ml/¼ tsp mustard seeds
1.5ml/¼ tsp cumin seeds
4–6 curry leaves
a pinch each of asafoetida and ground turmeric

1 In a heatproof serving dish, mix together the yogurt, fennel seeds, salt and sugar. Cover and chill until you are nearly ready to serve.

2 Heat the oil in a frying pan and fry the dried chilli, mustard and cumin seeds, curry leaves, asafoetida and turmeric.

3 When the chilli turns dark, pour the oil and spices over the yogurt. Fold the yogurt together with the spices at the table just before serving.

Variation
Asafoetida is quite bitter. Leave it out if you prefer.

Cook's Tip
You must keep asafoetida in an airtight container because its sulphurous odour will affect other foods and spices. It is most commonly available as a powder or granules, and is also sold in lumps that need to be crushed before using. It is a very powerful spice and should therefore be used in minute quantities. Even in its ground state, asafoetida lasts well over a year if stored properly, away from light and air.

Energy 36kcal/149kJ; Fat 2.6g; Saturated fat 0.4g; Carbohydrate 1.8g; Fibre 0g.

Grape & Walnut Raita

Refreshing raitas are served to cool the effect of hot curries. Cucumber and mint raita is the best known combination. Here is a refreshing fruit and nut version, which is particularly good with beef curries.

2 firm bananas
5ml/1 tsp granulated sugar
salt
5ml/1 tsp freshly ground cumin seeds
1.5ml/¼ tsp freshly roasted cumin seeds, chilli powder or paprika, to garnish

Serves 4
350ml/12fl oz/1½ cups natural (plain) yogurt
75g/3oz seedless grapes
50g/2oz/½ cup shelled walnuts

1 Place the yogurt in a chilled bowl and add the grapes and walnuts.

2 Slice the bananas directly into the bowl and fold in gently before they turn brown.

3 Add the sugar, salt and ground cumin, and gently mix together.

4 Chill, and just before serving, sprinkle on the cumin seeds, chilli powder or paprika.

Variations
• Instead of grapes, try kiwi fruit, peaches or nectarines.
• Almonds or hazelnuts can be used instead of or as well as the walnuts.
• For Coconut and Raisin Raita, coarsely grate half a fresh coconut by hand or using a food processor. Mix in a bowl with 225g/8oz natural (plain) yogurt and 2.5ml/½ tsp sugar. Stir in 25g/1oz chopped fresh coriander (cilantro) or mint, and add salt to taste. Transfer to a serving bowl.

Energy 184kcal/771kJ; Fat 9.6g; Saturated fat 1.2g; Carbohydrate 19.2g; Fibre 1g.

Sweet-&-sour Raita

This raita teams honey with mint sauce, chilli and fresh coriander to make a soothing mixture with underlying warmth. It goes well with biryanis.

Serves 4
475ml/16fl oz/2 cups natural (plain) low-fat yogurt
5ml/1 tsp salt
5ml/1 tsp granulated sugar
30ml/2 tbsp clear honey
7.5ml/1½ tsp mint sauce
30ml/2 tbsp roughly chopped fresh coriander (cilantro)
1 fresh green chilli, seeded and finely chopped
1 medium onion, diced
50ml/2fl oz/¼ cup water

1 Pour the yogurt into a bowl and whisk it well. Add the salt, sugar, honey and mint sauce.

2 Taste to check the sweetness and add more honey, if desired.

3 Reserve a little chopped coriander for the garnish and add the rest to the yogurt mixture, with the chilli, onion and water.

4 Whisk once again and pour into a serving bowl. Garnish with the reserved coriander and place in the refrigerator until ready to serve.

> **Variation**
> For Spinach Raita, finely chop 225g/8oz cooked spinach. Add to 450ml/¾ pint/scant 2 cups natural (plain) yogurt and mix in 2 chopped green chillies, 1.5ml/¼ tsp sugar, and salt and pepper to taste.

> **Cook's Tip**
> A 5–10cm/2–4in piece of peeled, seeded and grated cucumber can also be added to raita. Drain the cucumber in a colander, pressing it against the sides to extract excess liquid, which would dilute the raita.

Energy 128kcal/541kJ; Fat 1.18g; Saturated fat 0.64g; Carbohydrate 24.40g; Fibre 0.53g.

Sweet-&-sour Tomato & Onion Relish

This delicious relish can be served with any savoury meal. Choose vine-ripened tomatoes, if you can, as they have a superior flavour.

Serves 4
2 medium firm tomatoes
1 medium onion
1 fresh green chilli
15ml/1 tbsp fresh mint leaves
15ml/1 tbsp fresh coriander (cilantro) leaves
2.5ml/½ tsp Tabasco sauce
15ml/1 tbsp clear honey
2.5ml/½ tsp salt
30ml/2 tbsp lime juice
15ml/1 tbsp natural (plain) low-fat yogurt

1 Place the tomatoes in hot water for a few seconds. Lift each tomato out in turn, using a slotted spoon. The skins should have split, making it easy to remove them. Peel off carefully.

2 Cut the tomatoes in half, and squeeze out the seeds. Chop the flesh roughly. Set them aside while you prepare the other ingredients.

3 Using a sharp knife, roughly chop the onion, green chilli, mint and fresh coriander.

4 Place the herb mixture in a food processor with the Tabasco sauce, honey, salt and lime juice. Add the tomatoes to this and grind everything together for a few seconds.

5 Pour into a small serving bowl. Stir in the yogurt just before you serve the relish.

> **Cook's Tip**
> This relish will keep for up to 1 week in the refrigerator: prepare up to the end of step 4 but do not add the yogurt until just before you want to serve it.

Energy 43kcal/180kJ; Fat 0.29g; Saturated fat 0.06g; Carbohydrate 9.43g; Fibre 0.96g.

Fresh Coriander Relish

Delicious as an accompaniment to kebabs, samosas and bhajias, this relish can also be used as a spread for cucumber or tomato sandwiches.

Makes about 450g/1lb/ 2 cups
30ml/2 tbsp vegetable oil
1 dried red chilli
1.5ml/¼ tsp each cumin, fennel and onion seeds
1.5ml/¼ tsp asafoetida
4 curry leaves
115g/4oz/1⅓ cups desiccated (dry unsweetened shredded) coconut
10ml/2 tsp granulated sugar
salt
3 fresh green chillies, chopped
175–225g/6–8oz fresh coriander (cilantro), chopped
60ml/4 tbsp mint sauce
juice of 3 lemons

1 Heat the oil in a frying pan and add the dried chilli, the cumin, fennel and onion seeds, the asafoetida, curry leaves, desiccated coconut, sugar and salt. Fry, stirring often, until the coconut turns golden brown. Tip into a bowl and leave to cool.

2 Grind the spice mixture with the green chillies, fresh coriander and mint sauce. Moisten with lemon juice. Scrape into a bowl and chill before serving.

> **Cook's Tip**
> This may seem like a lot of coriander, but it is compacted when ground with the spices.

> **Variation**
> For Coriander and Walnut Relish, put 90ml/6 tbsp fresh coriander leaves, 2 garlic cloves, 50g/2oz chopped onion and 60ml/4 tbsp sugar into a food processor and grind until thick. Add 50g/2oz/½ cup chopped walnuts and mix well. Add salt and ground black pepper to taste.

Tomato Relish

This is a simple relish that can be served with most meals. It provides a contrast to hot curries, with its crunchy texture and refreshing ingredients.

Serves 4–6
2 small fresh green chillies
2 limes
2.5ml/½ tsp granulated sugar, or to taste
2 onions, finely chopped
4 firm tomatoes, finely chopped
½ cucumber, finely chopped
a few fresh coriander (cilantro) leaves, chopped
salt and ground black pepper
a few fresh mint leaves, to garnish

1 Using a sharp knife, cut both chillies in half. Scrape out the seeds, then chop the chillies finely and place them in a small bowl.

2 Squeeze the limes. Pour the juice into a glass bowl and add the sugar, with salt and pepper to taste. Set the bowl aside until the sugar and salt have dissolved, stirring the mixture occasionally.

3 Add the chopped chillies to the bowl, with the chopped onions, tomatoes, cucumber, chilli and fresh coriander leaves. Mix well.

4 Cover the bowl with clear film (plastic wrap) and place in the refrigerator for at least 3 hours, so that the flavours blend. Just before serving, taste the relish and add more salt, pepper or sugar if needed. Garnish with mint and serve.

> **Cook's Tip**
> For a milder flavour, use just one chilli, or dispense with the chilli altogether and substitute with a green (bell) pepper.

Energy 51kcal/211kJ; Fat 5.2g; Saturated fat 3.5g; Carbohydrate 0.8g; Fibre 0.9g.

Energy 47kcal/198kJ; Fat 0.5g; Saturated fat 0.1g; Carbohydrate 9.4g; Fibre 2.3g.

Fried Sesame Seed Chutney

This versatile chutney doubles as a dip, and also a sandwich filling with thin slices of cucumber.

Serves 4
175g/6oz/¾ cup sesame seeds
5ml/1 tsp salt
120–150ml/4–5fl oz/½–⅔ cup water
2 fresh green chillies, seeded and diced
60ml/4 tbsp chopped fresh coriander (cilantro)
15ml/1 tbsp chopped fresh mint
15ml/1 tbsp tamarind paste
30ml/2 tbsp granulated sugar
5ml/1 tsp oil
1.5ml/¼ tsp onion seeds
4 curry leaves
onion rings, sliced chillies and fresh coriander leaves, to garnish

1 Dry-roast the sesame seeds by putting them into a pan without adding any oil. Cook over medium to high heat, tossing them occasionally so that they brown evenly all over. Watch them carefully as they will burn if left. Leave the seeds to cool and then grind them in a coffee grinder until they become a grainy powder.

2 Transfer the sesame powder to a bowl. Add the salt, water, diced chillies, coriander, mint, tamarind paste and sugar, and use a fork to mix everything together.

3 Taste and adjust the seasoning, if necessary; the mixture should have a sweet-and-sour flavour. Add a little more tamarind paste if it needs to be more sour, or sugar to sweeten, if required.

4 Heat the oil in a heavy pan and fry the onion seeds and curry leaves together.

5 Tip the sesame seed paste into the pan and stir-fry for about 45 seconds. Transfer the chutney to a serving dish and leave to cool completely.

6 Garnish with onion rings, sliced green and red chillies and fresh coriander leaves and serve with your chosen curry.

Apricot Chutney

Chutneys can add zest to most meals, and in India you will usually find a selection of different kinds served in tiny bowls for people to choose from. Dried apricots are readily available from supermarkets and health food shops.

Makes about 450g/1lb/ 2 cups
450g/1lb/2 cups dried apricots, finely diced
5ml/1 tsp garam masala
275g/10oz/1¼ cups soft light brown sugar
450ml/¾ pint/scant 2 cups malt vinegar
5ml/1 tsp grated fresh root ginger
5ml/1 tsp salt
75g/3oz/½ cup sultanas (golden raisins)
450ml/¾ pint/scant 2 cups water

1 Put the dried apricots and garam masala into a medium pan and add the light brown sugar, malt vinegar, ginger, salt, sultanas and water. Mix thoroughly with a spoon.

2 Bring to the boil, then reduce the heat and simmer for 30–35 minutes, stirring occasionally.

3 When the chutney has thickened to a fairly stiff consistency, spoon it into 2–3 clean jam jars and leave to cool. This chutney should be stored in the refrigerator.

> **Variation**
> For Orchard Fruit Chutney, put 675g/1½lb peeled, cored and chopped cooking apples into a large pan with 115g/4oz/¼ cup each dried peaches and apricots and 50g/2oz/scant ½ cup raisins. Chop 5 garlic cloves and grate a 5cm/2in piece of fresh root ginger and add them to the pan. Add 350g/12oz soft light brown sugar, 400ml/14fl oz/1⅔ cups malt vinegar, 10ml/2 tsp salt and 5ml/1 tsp cayenne pepper. Bring the mixture to the boil and simmer for 30 minutes, stirring frequently.

Energy 347kcal/1438kJ; Fat 28.31g; Saturated fat 4.03g; Carbohydrate 25.31g; Fibre 3.63g.

Energy 118kcal/506kJ; Fat 0.2g; Saturated fat 0g; Carbohydrate 29.7g; Fibre 2g.

Fresh Tomato & Onion Chutney

Chutneys are served with most meat dishes in Indian cuisine. This one is lightly spiced and perfect to accompany a heavily spiced meal.

Serves 4
8 tomatoes
1 medium onion, chopped
45ml/3 tbsp light muscovado (brown) sugar
5ml/1 tsp garam masala
5ml/1 tsp ground ginger
175ml/6fl oz/³⁄₄ cup malt vinegar
5ml/1 tsp salt
15ml/1 tbsp clear honey
natural (plain) yogurt, sliced green chilli and fresh mint leaves, to garnish

1 Wash the tomatoes and cut them into quarters.

2 Place them with the onion in a heavy pan, and add the sugar, garam masala, ginger, vinegar, salt and honey.

3 Half-cover the pan with a lid and cook over a low heat for about 20 minutes.

4 Mash the tomatoes with a fork to break them up, then continue to cook them on a slightly higher heat until the chutney thickens.

5 Spoon the chutney into a bowl and leave to cool, then cover and place in the refrigerator until needed.

6 Serve chilled, garnished with yogurt, sliced chilli and mint leaves.

Cook's Tips
• *This chutney will keep for about 2 weeks in a covered container in the refrigerator. Add the garnish when ready to serve.*
• *Malt vinegar is generally used for chutneys that require a rich flavour as it has a fuller flavour than white wine vinegar.*
• *The sugar and vinegar give the chutney its flavour as well as its keeping qualities.*

Tomato Chutney with Cinnamon & Nigella

This delicious relish is especially suited to lentil dishes. If kept in a covered bowl in the refrigerator, it will keep for a week.

Makes 450–500g/1–1¼lb/ 2–2¼ cups
90ml/6 tbsp vegetable oil
5cm/2in piece cinnamon stick
4 cloves
5ml/1 tsp freshly roasted cumin seeds
5ml/1 tsp nigella seeds
4 bay leaves
5ml/1 tsp mustard seeds, crushed
4 garlic cloves
800g/1¾lb canned, chopped tomatoes
5cm/2in piece fresh root ginger, crushed
5ml/1 tsp chilli powder
5ml/1 tsp ground turmeric
60ml/4 tbsp brown sugar

1 Pour the oil into a frying pan, karahi or wok and place over a medium heat. When the oil is hot, fry the cinnamon, cloves, cumin and nigella seeds, bay leaves and mustard seeds for about 5 minutes.

2 Crush the garlic cloves and add them to the spice mixture. Fry until golden. Meanwhile, drain the tomatoes, reserving the juices.

3 Add the ginger, chilli powder, turmeric, sugar and the reserved tomato juices. Simmer until reduced, add the tomatoes and cook for 15–20 minutes. Cool and serve.

Cook's Tip
Nigella seeds, or kalonji, are frequently used in Indian cooking. They are small black oval-shaped seeds that have a delicate, slightly peppery flavour a little like oregano. They are most often seen sprinkled over naan breads. They have a strong flavour so should be used sparingly in cooking. They add depth to the flavour of this chutney but can be omitted if you are unable to find them.

Mint & Coconut Chutney

**Makes about 350ml/
12fl oz/1½ cups**
50g/2oz fresh mint leaves
*90ml/6 tbsp desiccated (dry
unsweetened shredded)
coconut*
15ml/1 tbsp sesame seeds
1.5ml/¼ tsp salt
*175ml/6fl oz/¾ cup natural
(plain) yogurt*

1 Finely chop the fresh mint leaves, using a sharp kitchen knife.

2 Put the mint with the desiccated coconut, sesame seeds, salt and yogurt into a food processor or blender and process until smooth. Transfer the chutney to a sterilized jar, cover and chill until needed.

Mango Chutney

Chutneys are usually served as an accompaniment to curry but this one is particularly nice served in a cheese sandwich or as a dip with poppadums.

Makes 450g/1lb/2 cups
60ml/4 tbsp malt vinegar
*2.5ml/½ tsp crushed dried
chillies*
6 cloves
6 peppercorns
5ml/1 tsp roasted cumin seeds
2.5ml/½ tsp onion seeds
salt
*175g/6oz/scant 1 cup
granulated sugar*
450g/1lb green (unripe) mangoes
*5cm/2in piece fresh root ginger,
thinly sliced*
2 garlic cloves, crushed
*thin rind of 1 orange or lemon
(optional)*

1 Use a sharp knife to cut two thick slices from either side of the large flat stone (pit) of the mango. Make criss-cross cuts in the flesh on each slice and then turn inside out. The cubes of flesh will stand proud of the skin. Cut these off close to the skin. Cut the remaining flesh from around the stone.

2 Pour the vinegar into a pan, and add the chillies, cloves, peppercorns, cumin and onion seeds, salt and sugar. Place over a low heat and simmer to infuse (steep) the spices in the vinegar – about 15 minutes.

3 Add the mango, ginger, garlic and peel, if using. Simmer until the mango is mushy and most of the vinegar has evaporated. When cool, pour into sterilized bottles. Cover and leave for a few days before serving.

> **Cook's Tip**
> *Fresh root ginger freezes very well, which can be handy if you find it difficult to get fresh ginger locally. It can be sliced or grated straight from the freezer and will thaw on contact with hot food.*

Tomato & Fresh Chilli Chutney

**Makes about 475ml/
16fl oz/2 cups**
1 red (bell) pepper
4 tomatoes, chopped
2 fresh green chillies, chopped
1 garlic clove, crushed
1.5ml/¼ tsp salt
2.5ml/½ tsp granulated sugar
5ml/1 tsp chilli powder
*45ml/3 tbsp tomato purée
(paste)*
*15ml/1 tbsp chopped fresh
coriander (cilantro)*

1 Halve the red pepper and remove the core and seeds. Roughly chop the red pepper halves.

2 Process the pepper with the tomatoes, chillies, garlic, salt, sugar, chilli powder, tomato purée and coriander with 30ml/ 2 tbsp water in a food processor until smooth. Transfer to a sterilized jar, cover and chill until needed.

> **Cook's Tip**
> *This chutney can be stored in the refrigerator for up to 5 days.*

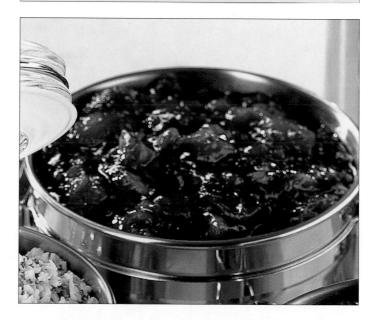

Energy 52kcal/224kJ; Fat 0g; Saturated fat 0g; Carbohydrate 13.7g; Fibre 0.7g.

Top: Energy 753kcal/3117kJ; Fat 66.6g; Saturated fat 50.2g; Carbohydrate 21.7g; Fibre 13.5g.
Above: Energy 187kcal/794kJ; Fat 2.5g; Saturated fat 0.5g; Carbohydrate 33.2g; Fibre 7.5g.

English Pickled Onions

The English love of pickled onions is famous, and at the time of the Raj the popular pickle was introduced into India. They should be stored in a cool, dark place for at least 6 weeks before being eaten.

Makes 3 or 4 450g/1lb jars
1kg/2¼lb pickling onions
115g/4oz/½ cup salt

750ml/1¼ pints/3 cups malt
  vinegar
15ml/1 tbsp granulated sugar
2 or 3 dried red chillies
5ml/1 tsp brown mustard seeds
15ml/1 tbsp coriander seeds
5ml/1 tsp allspice berries
5ml/1 tsp black peppercorns
5cm/2in piece fresh root ginger,
  sliced
2 or 3 blades of mace
2 or 3 fresh bay leaves

1 Trim off the root end of each onion, but leave the onion layers attached. Cut a thin slice off the top (neck) end of each onion. Place the onions in a bowl, then cover with boiling water. Leave to stand for about 4 minutes, then drain. Peel off the skin from each onion with a small, sharp knife.

2 Place the peeled onions in a bowl and cover with cold water, then drain the water off and pour it into a large pan. Add the salt and heat slightly to dissolve it, then cool before pouring the brine over the onions. Cover the bowl with a plate and weigh it down slightly so that all the onions are submerged in the brine. Leave the onions to stand in the salted water for 24 hours.

3 Pour the vinegar into a large pan. Wrap all the remaining ingredients, except the bay leaves, in a piece of muslin (cheesecloth) or sew them into a coffee filter paper. Add to the vinegar with the bay leaves. Bring to the boil, simmer for 5 minutes, then remove from the heat. Leave to infuse (steep) overnight.

4 Drain the onions, rinse and pat dry. Pack them into sterilized jars. Add some or all of the spice from the vinegar, but not the ginger slices. The pickle will get hotter if you add the chillies. Pour the vinegar over the onions to cover and add the bay leaves. Cover the jars with non-metallic lids.

Energy 120kcal/500kJ; Fat 0.7g; Saturated fat 0g; Carbohydrate 26.3g; Fibre 4.7g.

Fresh Coconut Chutney with Onion & Chilli

Serve a bowl of this tasty fresh chutney as an accompaniment for any Indian-style main course.

Serves 4–6
200g/7oz fresh coconut, grated
3 or 4 fresh green chillies, seeded
  and chopped
20g/¾oz fresh coriander
  (cilantro), chopped, plus
  2 or 3 sprigs to garnish
30ml/2 tbsp chopped fresh
  mint

30–45ml/2–3 tbsp lime juice
about 2.5ml/½ tsp salt
about 2.5ml/½ tsp caster
  (superfine) sugar
15–30ml/1–2 tbsp coconut
  milk (optional)
30ml/2 tbsp groundnut
  (peanut) oil
5ml/1 tsp nigella seeds
1 small onion, very finely
  chopped

1 Place the coconut, chillies, coriander and mint in a food processor. Add 30ml/2 tbsp of the lime juice, then process until thoroughly chopped.

2 Scrape the mixture into a bowl and add more lime juice to taste. Add salt and sugar to taste. If the mixture is dry, stir in 15–30ml/1–2 tbsp coconut milk.

3 Heat the oil in a small pan and fry the nigella seeds until they begin to pop, then reduce the heat and add the onion. Fry, stirring frequently, for 4–5 minutes, until the onion is soft.

4 Stir the onion mixture into the coconut mixture and leave to cool. Garnish with coriander before serving.

Cook's Tip
Nigella seeds, sometimes called black onion seeds or black cumin, can be found in Asian grocery stores, usually sold under the name kalonji.

Energy 168kcal/693kJ; Fat 17.2g; Saturated fat 11.1g; Carbohydrate 2.4g; Fibre 2.8g.

Red Onion, Garlic & Lemon Relish

This powerful relish is flavoured with spices and punchy preserved lemons. It reached India by way of Spain, being introduced by Jewish refugees forced to leave that country in the 15th century.

Serves 6
45ml/3 tbsp olive oil
3 large red onions, sliced
2 heads of garlic, separated into
    cloves and peeled
10ml/2 tsp coriander seeds,
    crushed but not finely ground
10ml/2 tsp light muscovado sugar,
    plus a little extra
pinch of saffron threads
5cm/2in piece cinnamon stick
2 or 3 small whole dried red
    chillies (optional)
2 fresh bay leaves
30–45ml/2–3 tbsp sherry vinegar
juice of ½ small orange
30ml/2 tbsp chopped preserved
    lemon
salt and ground black pepper

1 Heat the oil in a heavy pan. Add the onions and stir, then cover and reduce the heat to the lowest setting. Cook for 10–15 minutes, stirring occasionally, until the onions are soft and pale gold in colour.

2 Add the whole peeled garlic cloves and the crushed coriander seeds. Cover and cook for 5–8 minutes until the garlic is soft.

3 Add a pinch of salt, lots of pepper and the sugar. Stir, then cook, uncovered, for 5 minutes. Soak the saffron in about 45ml/3 tbsp warm water for 5 minutes, then add it to the onions, with the soaking water. Add the cinnamon stick, dried chillies, if using, and bay leaves. Stir in 30ml/2 tbsp of the sherry vinegar and the orange juice.

4 Cook over a low heat, uncovered, until the onions are very soft and most of the liquid has evaporated. Stir in the preserved lemon and cook gently for a further 5 minutes. Taste and adjust the seasoning, adding more salt, sugar and/or vinegar to taste. Serve warm or at room temperature. The relish tastes best if it is left to stand for 24 hours.

Onion, Mango & Peanut Chaat

Chaats are spiced relishes of vegetables and nuts, delicious with many savoury Indian dishes.

Serves 4
90g/3½oz/scant 1 cup
    unsalted peanuts
15ml/1 tbsp peanut oil
1 onion, chopped
½ cucumber, seeded and diced
1 mango, peeled, stoned (pitted)
    and diced
1 fresh green chilli, seeded
    and chopped
30ml/2 tbsp chopped fresh
    coriander (cilantro)
15ml/1 tbsp chopped fresh
    mint
15ml/1 tbsp lime juice
pinch of light muscovado
    (brown) sugar

For the chaat masala
10ml/2 tsp ground toasted
    cumin seeds
2.5ml/½ tsp cayenne pepper
5ml/1 tsp mango powder
    (amchur)
2.5ml/½ tsp garam masala
a pinch of ground asafoetida
salt and ground black pepper

1 To make the chaat masala, grind all the spices together, then season with 2.5ml/½ tsp each salt and pepper.

2 Fry the peanuts in the oil until lightly browned, then drain on kitchen paper until cool.

3 Mix the onion, cucumber, mango, chilli, fresh coriander and mint in a bowl. Sprinkle in 5ml/1 tsp of the chaat masala. Stir in the peanuts and then add lime juice and/or sugar to taste. Set the mixture aside for 20–30 minutes for the flavours to mature.

4 Spoon the mixture into a serving bowl, sprinkle another 5ml/1 tsp of the chaat masala over and serve.

> **Cook's Tip**
> *Any remaining chaat masala will keep in a sealed jar for 4–6 weeks.*

Energy 107kcal/442kJ; Fat 5.8g; Saturated fat 0.8g; Carbohydrate 12g; Fibre 2.2g.

Energy 187kcal/776kJ; Fat 13.3g; Saturated fat 2.5g; Carbohydrate 11.1g; Fibre 2.9g.

Hot Lime Pickle

A good lime pickle is not only delicious served with any meal, but it also increases the appetite and aids digestion.

Makes 450g/1lb/2 cups
25 limes
225g/8oz/1 cup salt
50g/2oz/½ cup fenugreek powder
50g/2oz/½ cup mustard powder
150g/5oz/½ cup chilli powder
15g/½oz/2 tbsp ground turmeric
600ml/1 pint/2½ cups mustard oil
5ml/1 tsp asafoetida
30ml/2 tbsp yellow mustard seeds, crushed

1 Cut each lime into 8 pieces and remove the seeds, if you like. Put the limes in a large sterilized jar or glass bowl.

2 Add the salt and toss with the limes. Cover and leave in a warm place for 1–2 weeks, until they become soft and dull brown in colour.

3 Mix together the fenugreek powder, mustard powder, chilli powder and turmeric, and add to the limes. Cover and leave to rest in a warm place for a further 2 or 3 days.

4 Heat the mustard oil in a frying pan and fry the asafoetida and mustard seeds. When the oil reaches smoking point, pour it over the limes.

5 Mix well, cover with a clean cloth and leave in a warm place for about 1 week before serving or bottling.

Cook's Tips
• *You will need to plan far ahead to make this pickle, as it requires at least three weeks to mature at various different stages of preparation before it can be eaten. This long process is essential for the flavours to develop fully, making a strong-tasting traditional pickle.*
• *To sterilize jars for bottling, boil in water for 10 minutes.*

Green Chilli Pickle

Southern India is the source of some of the hottest curries and pickles. You might imagine that eating them would be a case of going for the burn, but they actually cool the body.

**Makes 450–550g/1–1¼lb/
2–2½ cups**
50g/2oz/4 tbsp yellow mustard seeds, crushed
50g/2oz/4 tbsp freshly ground cumin seeds
25g/1oz/¼ cup ground turmeric
50g/2oz garlic cloves, crushed, plus 20 small garlic cloves, peeled but left whole
150ml/¼ pint/⅔ cup white vinegar
75g/3oz/6 tbsp granulated sugar
10ml/2 tsp salt
150ml/¼ pint/⅔ cup mustard oil
450g/1lb small fresh green chillies

1 Mix the mustard and cumin seeds, the turmeric, crushed garlic, vinegar, sugar and salt together in a sterilized glass bowl.

2 Cover with a cloth and leave to rest for 24 hours. This enables the spices to infuse and the sugar and salt to melt.

3 Heat the mustard oil in a frying pan and gently fry the spice mixture for about 5 minutes. (Keep a window open while cooking with mustard oil as it is pungent and the smoke may irritate the eyes.)

4 Add the whole, peeled garlic cloves and fry for a further 5 minutes.

5 Halve each fresh green chilli, washing your hands carefully afterwards. Add the chillies and cook gently until tender but still green in colour. This will take about 30 minutes over low heat.

6 Cool thoroughly, then pour into sterilized jars, ensuring that the oil is evenly distributed if you are using more than one jar. Leave to rest for a week before serving.

Energy 82kcal/336kJ; Fat 8.9g; Saturated fat 1.1g; Carbohydrate 0g; Fibre 0g.

Energy 54kcal/226kJ; Fat 5.7g; Saturated fat 0.6g; Carbohydrate 0.1g; Fibre 0g.

Bombay Duck Pickle

Boil (or bombil) is the name of a fish that is found off the west coast of India during the monsoon season. It is salted and dried in the sun and is characterized by a distinctive strong smell. How this fish acquired the name Bombay duck in the Western world is unknown. Bombay duck can be served hot or cold, and is usually eaten with Indian breads and vegetable dishes.

Serves 4–6
6–8 pieces boil (Bombay duck)
60ml/4 tbsp vegetable oil
2 fresh red chillies, chopped
15ml/1 tbsp granulated sugar
450g/1lb cherry tomatoes, halved
115g/4oz deep-fried onions
red onion rings, to garnish (optional)

1 Soak the fish in water for 5 minutes and then pat it dry using kitchen paper.

2 Heat the oil in a frying pan and fry the fish pieces for about 30–45 seconds on both sides until crisp. Be careful not to burn them or they will taste bitter. Drain well.

3 Transfer the drained fish pieces to a plate and leave to cool, and then break them into small pieces.

4 Cook the remaining ingredients until the tomatoes become pulpy and the onions are blended into a sauce. Fold in the Bombay duck and mix well.

5 Leave to cool, then garnish and serve. Alternatively, ladle into a hot sterilized jar, cover and leave to cool.

> **Cook's Tip**
> As an alternative to boil, try using skinned mackerel fillets, but don't fry them. You will need only 30ml/2 tbsp vegetable oil to make the sauce.

Energy 233kcal/973kJ; Fat 15.3g; Saturated fat 1.8g; Carbohydrate 11.5g; Fibre 2g.

Sweet-&-sour Pineapple

This may sound like a Chinese recipe, but it is a traditional Bengali dish known as *tok*. The predominant flavour is ginger, and the pieces of golden pineapple, dotted with plump, juicy raisins, have plenty of visual appeal with taste to match. It is equally delicious if made with mangoes instead of the pineapple.

2.5ml/½ tsp cumin seeds
2.5ml/½ tsp onion seeds
10ml/2 tsp grated fresh root ginger
5ml/1 tsp crushed dried chillies
50g/2oz/⅓ cup seedless raisins
115g/4oz/½ cup granulated sugar
7.5ml/1½ tsp salt

Serves 4
800g/1¾lb canned pineapple rings or chunks in natural juice
15ml/1 tbsp vegetable oil
2.5ml/½ tsp black mustard seeds

1 Drain the pineapple in a colander and reserve the juice. Chop the pineapple rings or chunks finely (you should have approximately 500g/1¼lb).

2 Heat the vegetable oil in a karahi, wok or large pan over a medium heat and immediately add the mustard seeds. As soon as they pop, add the cumin seeds, then the onion seeds. Add the ginger and chillies, and stir-fry the spices briskly for 30 seconds until they release their flavours.

3 Add the pineapple, raisins, sugar and salt. Add 300ml/ ½ pint/1¼ cups of the juice (made up with cold water if necessary) and stir into the pineapple mixture.

4 Bring the mixture to the boil, reduce the heat to medium and cook, uncovered, for 20–25 minutes.

Energy 264kcal/1124kJ; Fat 3.2g; Saturated fat 0.3g; Carbohydrate 61.5g; Fibre 2.7g.

Naan

Probably the most popular bread enjoyed with an Indian curry is naan, which was introduced from Persia. In Persian, the word "naan" means bread. Traditionally, naan is not rolled, but patted and stretched until the teardrop shape is achieved. You can, of course, roll it out to a circle, then gently pull the lower end, which will give you the traditional shape.

Makes 3

225g/8oz/2 cups unbleached strong white bread flour
2.5ml/½ tsp salt
15g/½oz fresh yeast
60ml/4 tbsp lukewarm milk
15ml/1 tbsp vegetable oil
30ml/2 tbsp natural (plain) yogurt
1 egg
30–45ml/2–3 tbsp melted ghee or butter, for brushing

1 Sift the flour and salt together into a large bowl. In a smaller bowl, cream the yeast with the milk. Set aside for 15 minutes. Add the yeast and milk mixture, vegetable oil, yogurt and egg to the flour. Combine the mixture using your hands until it forms a soft dough. Add a little more of the lukewarm water if the dough is too dry.

2 Turn the dough out on to a lightly floured surface and knead for about 10 minutes, or until it feels smooth. Return the dough to the bowl, cover and leave in a warm place for about 1 hour, or until it has doubled in size. Preheat the oven to its highest setting – it should not be any lower than 230°C/450°F/Gas 8.

3 Turn out the dough back on to the floured surface and knead for a further 2 minutes. Divide into three equal pieces, shape into balls and roll out into teardrop shapes 25cm/10in long, 13cm/5in wide and 5mm–8mm/¼–⅓in thick.

4 Preheat the grill (broiler) to its highest setting. Meanwhile, place the naan on preheated baking sheets and bake for 3–4 minutes, or until puffed up. Remove from the oven and place under the hot grill for a few seconds until the tops brown slightly. Brush with ghee or butter and serve warm.

Garlic & Coriander Naan

Traditionally cooked in a very hot clay oven known as a tandoor, naan are usually eaten with dry meat or vegetable dishes.

Makes 3

275g/10oz/2½ cups unbleached strong white bread flour
5ml/1 tsp salt
5ml/1 tsp dried yeast
60ml/4 tbsp natural (plain) yogurt
15ml/1 tbsp melted butter or ghee, plus 30–45ml/2–3 tbsp for brushing
1 garlic clove, finely chopped
5ml/1 tsp black onion seeds
15ml/1 tbsp fresh coriander (cilantro)
10ml/2 tsp clear honey

1 Sift the flour and salt together into a large bowl. In a smaller bowl, cream the yeast with the yogurt. Set aside for 15 minutes. Add the yeast mixture to the flour with the smaller quantity of melted butter or ghee, and add the chopped garlic, black onion seeds and chopped coriander, mixing to a soft dough.

2 Tip out the dough on to a lightly floured surface and knead for about 10 minutes until smooth and elastic. Place in a lightly oiled bowl, cover with lightly oiled clear film (plastic wrap) and leave to rise in a warm place for 45 minutes, or until the dough has doubled in bulk.

3 Preheat the oven to 230°C/450°F/Gas 8. Place three heavy baking sheets in the oven to heat. Turn the dough out on to a lightly floured surface and knock back (punch down). Divide into three equal pieces and shape each into a ball.

4 Cover two of the balls of dough with oiled clear film and roll out the third into a teardrop shape about 25cm/10in long, 13cm/5in wide and about 5mm–8mm/¼–⅓in thick. Preheat the grill (broiler) to its highest setting. Place the single naan on the hot baking sheets and bake for 3–4 minutes, or until puffy.

5 Remove the naan from the oven and place under the hot grill for a few seconds or until browned slightly. Wrap in a dish towel to keep warm while you roll out and cook the remaining naan. Brush with melted butter or ghee and serve warm.

Energy 197kcal/830kJ; Fat 8.2g; Saturated fat 5g; Carbohydrate 29.2g; Fibre 1.2g.

Energy 326kcal/1378kJ; Fat 6.8g; Saturated fat 1.3g; Carbohydrate 59.7g; Fibre 2.3g.

Spiced Naan

Another excellent recipe for naan bread, this time with fennel seeds, onion seeds and cumin seeds.

Makes 6

450g/1lb/4 cups strong white bread flour
5ml/1 tsp baking powder
2.5ml/½ tsp salt
1 sachet easy-blend (rapid-rise) dried yeast
5ml/1 tsp caster (superfine) sugar
5ml/1 tsp fennel seeds
10ml/2 tsp onion seeds
5ml/1 tsp cumin seeds
150ml/¼ pint/⅔ cup hand-hot milk
30ml/2 tbsp oil, plus extra for brushing
150ml/¼ pint/⅔ cup natural (plain) yogurt
1 egg, beaten

1 Sift the flour, baking powder and salt into a mixing bowl. Stir in the yeast, sugar, fennel seeds, onion seeds and cumin seeds. Make a well in the centre. Stir the hand-hot milk into the flour mixture, then add the oil, yogurt and beaten egg. Mix to form a ball of dough.

2 Tip the dough out on to a lightly floured surface and knead it for 10 minutes until smooth. Return to the clean, lightly oiled bowl and roll the dough to coat it with oil. Cover the bowl with clear film (plastic wrap) and set aside in a warm place until the dough has doubled in bulk.

3 Put a heavy baking sheet in the oven and preheat the oven to 240°C/475°F/Gas 9. Also preheat the grill (broiler). Knead the dough again lightly and divide it into six pieces. Keep five pieces covered while working with the sixth. Quickly roll the piece of dough out to a teardrop shape, brush lightly with oil and slap the naan on to the hot baking sheet. Repeat with the remaining dough.

4 Bake the naan in the oven for 3 minutes until puffed up, then place the baking sheets under the grill for about 30 seconds or until the naan are lightly browned. Serve hot or warm as an accompaniment to an Indian curry.

Energy 294kcal/1248kJ; Fat 2.6g; Saturated fat 0.8g; Carbohydrate 61.3g; Fibre 2.3g.

Chapatis

A chapati is an unleavened bread made from chapati flour, a ground wholemeal flour known as *atta*, which is finer than the Western equivalent. An equal quantity of standard wholemeal flour and plain flour will also produce satisfactory results, although chapati flour is available from Indian grocers. This is the everyday bread of the Indian home.

Makes 8–10

225g/8oz/2 cups chapati flour or wholemeal (whole-wheat) flour
2.5ml/½ tsp salt
175ml/6fl oz/¾ cup water

1 Sift the flour and salt into a mixing bowl. Make a well in the centre and gradually stir in the water, mixing well with your fingers.

2 Form a supple dough and knead for 7–10 minutes. Ideally, cover with clear film (plastic wrap) and leave to one side for 15–20 minutes to rest.

3 Divide the dough into 8–10 equal portions. Roll out each piece to a circle on a well-floured surface.

4 Place a tava (chapati griddle) or heavy frying pan over a high heat. When steam rises from it, lower the heat to medium and add the first chapati to the pan.

5 When the chapati begins to bubble, turn it over. Press down with a clean dish towel or a flat spoon and turn once again.

6 Remove the cooked chapati from the pan and keep warm in a piece of foil lined with kitchen paper while you cook the other chapatis.

7 Repeat the process until all the breads are cooked. Serve hot.

Energy 96kcal/408kJ; Fat 0.4g; Saturated fat 0.1g; Carbohydrate 21.9g; Fibre 0.9g.

Red Lentil Pancakes

This is a type of *dosa*, which is essentially a pancake from southern India, but used in the similar fashion to north Indian bread.

Makes 6
150g/5oz/3/4 cup long grain rice
50g/2oz/1/4 cup red lentils
250ml/8fl oz/1 cup warm water

5ml/1 tsp salt
2.5ml/1/2 tsp ground
 turmeric
2.5ml/1/2 tsp ground black
 pepper
30ml/2 tbsp chopped fresh
 coriander (cilantro)
oil, for frying and drizzling

1 Place the rice and lentils in a large bowl, cover with the warm water, cover and soak for at least 8 hours or overnight.

2 Drain off the water and reserve. Place the rice and lentils in a food processor and blend until smooth. Blend in the reserved water. Scrape into a bowl, cover with clear film (plastic wrap) and leave in a warm place to ferment for about 24 hours.

3 Stir in the salt, turmeric, pepper and coriander. Heat a heavy frying pan over a medium heat for a few minutes until hot. Smear with oil and add about 30–45ml/2–3 tbsp batter.

4 Using the rounded base of a soup spoon, gently spread the batter out, using a circular motion, to make a pancake that is about 15cm/6in in diameter.

5 Cook in the pan for 1½–2 minutes, or until set. Drizzle a little oil over the pancake and around the edges. Turn over and cook for about 1 minute, or until golden brown. Keep the cooked pancakes warm in a low oven or on a plate over simmering water while cooking the remaining pancakes. Serve warm.

Variation
Add 60ml/4 tbsp grated coconut to the batter just before cooking for a richer flavour.

Energy 190kcal/798kJ; Fat 8.5g; Saturated fat 1.1g; Carbohydrate 26.1g; Fibre 0.5g.

Parathas

Making a paratha is similar to making flaky pastry. The difference lies in the handling of the dough; this can be handled freely, unlike that for a flaky pastry.

50g/2oz/1/2 cup plain
 (all-purpose) flour
5ml/1 tsp salt
40g/1½oz/3 tbsp ghee or
 unsalted (sweet) butter
water, to mix

Makes 12–15
350g/12oz/3 cups chapati flour
 or an equal quantity of
 wholemeal (whole-wheat) flour
 and plain (all-purpose) flour,
 plus 50g/2oz/1/2 cup for dusting

1 Sift the flours and salt into a bowl. Make a well in the centre and add 10ml/2 tsp melted ghee or butter. Fold it into the flour to make a crumbly texture.

2 Gradually add water to make a soft, pliable dough. Knead until smooth. Cover and leave to rest for 30 minutes.

3 Melt the remaining ghee or butter over a low heat. Divide the dough into 12–15 equal portions and keep covered. Take one portion at a time and roll out on a lightly floured surface to about 10cm/4in in diameter.

4 Brush the dough with a little of the melted ghee or sweet butter and sprinkle with flour.

5 With a sharp knife, make a straight cut from the centre to the edge of the dough, then lift a cut edge and roll the dough into a cone shape. Lift it and flatten it again into a ball. Roll the dough out again on a lightly floured surface until it is 18cm/7in wide.

6 Heat a griddle and cook one paratha at a time, placing a little of the remaining ghee along the edges. Cook on each side until golden brown. Serve hot.

Energy 123kcal/521kJ; Fat 2.8g; Saturated fat 1.4g; Carbohydrate 21.9g; Fibre 2.8g.

Tandoori Rotis

Roti means bread and is the most common food eaten in central and northern India. *Tandoori roti* is traditionally baked in a tandoor, or clay oven, but it can also be made successfully in an electric or gas oven at the highest setting.

5ml/1 tsp salt
250ml/8fl oz/1 cup water
30–45ml/2–3 tbsp melted ghee
    or unsalted (sweet) butter

Makes 6
350g/12oz/3 cups chapati
    flour or wholemeal
    (whole-wheat) flour

1 Sift the flour and salt into a large mixing bowl. Add the water and mix to a soft, pliable dough.

2 Knead on a lightly floured surface for 3–4 minutes until smooth. Place the dough in a lightly oiled bowl, cover with lightly oiled clear film (plastic wrap) and leave to rest for about 1 hour.

3 Tip out the dough on to a lightly floured surface. Divide the dough into six pieces and shape each into a ball. Press out into a larger round with the palm of your hand, cover with lightly oiled clear film and leave to rest for about 10 minutes.

4 Meanwhile, preheat the oven to 230°C/450°F/Gas 8. Place three baking sheets in the oven to heat. Roll the rotis into 15cm/6in rounds, place two on each baking sheet and bake for 8–10 minutes. Brush with melted ghee or butter and serve warm.

> **Cook's Tip**
> *Chapati flour, known as* atta, *is a fine wholemeal flour used in Indian breads.*

Missi Rotis

This is a speciality from the Punjab. Gram flour, also known as besan, is used instead of the usual chapati flour. In the Punjab, *missi rotis* are very popular with a glass of lassi, a refreshing yogurt drink.

Makes 4
115g/4oz/1 cup gram flour
115g/4oz/1 cup wholemeal
    (whole-wheat) flour

1 fresh green chilli, seeded
    and chopped
1/2 onion, finely chopped
15ml/1 tbsp chopped fresh
    coriander (cilantro)
2.5ml/1/2 tsp ground
    turmeric
2.5ml/1/2 tsp salt
15ml/1 tbsp vegetable oil
120–150ml/4–5fl oz/1/2–2/3 cup
    lukewarm water
30–45ml/2–3 tbsp melted
    unsalted (sweet) ghee or butter

1 Mix the two types of flour, the chilli, onion, coriander, turmeric and salt together in a large bowl. Stir in the oil.

2 Mix in sufficient water to make a pliable soft dough. Tip out the dough on to a lightly floured surface and knead until smooth.

3 Place the dough in a lightly oiled bowl, cover with lightly oiled clear film (plastic wrap) and leave to rest for 30 minutes.

4 Place the dough on to a lightly floured surface. Divide into four equal pieces and shape into balls in the palms of your hands. Roll out each ball into a thick round about 15–18cm/6–7in in diameter.

5 Heat a griddle or heavy frying pan over a medium heat for a few minutes until hot.

6 Brush both sides of one roti with a little melted ghee or butter. Add it to the griddle or frying pan and cook for about 2 minutes, turning after 1 minute. Brush the cooked roti lightly with melted ghee or butter again, slide it on to a plate and keep warm in a low oven while cooking the remaining rotis in the same way. Serve the rotis warm.

Energy 226kcal/958kJ; Fat 3.5g; Saturated fat 0.5g; Carbohydrate 45.9g; Fibre 2g.

Energy 181kcal/769kJ; Fat 1.3g; Saturated fat 0.2g; Carbohydrate 37.3g; Fibre 5.3g.

Bhaturas

These leavened and deep-fried breads are from the Punjab, where the local people enjoy them with a bowl of spicy chickpea curry. The combination has become a classic over the years and is known as *choley bhature*. Bhaturas must be eaten hot and cannot be reheated.

Makes 10

15g/½oz fresh yeast
5ml/1 tsp granulated sugar
120ml/4fl oz/½ cup lukewarm
    water
200g/7oz/1¾ cups strong white
    bread flour
50g/2oz/⅓ cup semolina
2.5ml/½ tsp salt
15g/½oz/1 tbsp ghee or butter
30ml/2 tbsp natural (plain) yogurt
oil, for frying

1 Mix the yeast with the sugar and water in a jug (pitcher).

2 Sift the flour into a large bowl and stir in the semolina and salt. Rub in the butter or ghee.

3 Add the yeast mixture and yogurt, and mix to a dough. Turn out on to a lightly floured surface and knead for 10 minutes, or until smooth and elastic.

4 Place the dough in an oiled bowl, cover with oiled clear film (plastic wrap) and leave to rise in a warm place for about 1 hour, or until doubled in bulk.

5 Turn the dough out on to a lightly floured surface and knock back (punch down). Divide into ten equal pieces and shape each into a ball. Flatten into discs with the palm of your hand. Roll out on a lightly floured surface into 13cm/5in rounds.

6 Pour oil to a depth of 1cm/½in into a deep frying pan. Heat, and slide one bhatura into the oil. Fry for about 1 minute, turning over after 30 seconds.

7 Drain the bhatura well on kitchen paper. Keep each bhatura warm in a low oven while frying the remaining bhaturas. Serve immediately, while hot.

Pooris

These delicious little deep-fried breads, shaped into discs, make it temptingly easy to overindulge. In most areas, they are made of wholemeal flour, but in the east and north-east of India, they are made from plain refined flour, and are known as *loochis*.

Makes 12

115g/4oz/1 cup unbleached
    plain (all-purpose) flour
115g/4oz/1 cup wholemeal
    (whole-wheat) flour
2.5ml/½ tsp salt
2.5ml/½ tsp chilli powder
30ml/2 tbsp vegetable oil
100–120ml/3½–4fl oz/7–8 tbsp
    water
oil, for frying

1 Sift the flours, salt and chilli powder, if using, into a large mixing bowl. Add the vegetable oil then add sufficient water to mix to a dough.

2 Tip the dough out on to a lightly floured surface and knead for 8–10 minutes until smooth.

3 Place in an oiled bowl and cover with oiled clear film (plastic wrap). Leave for 30 minutes.

4 Place the dough on the floured surface. Divide into 12 pieces. Keeping the rest of the dough covered, roll one piece into a 13cm/5in round. Repeat with the remaining dough. Stack the pooris, layered between clear film, to keep them moist.

5 Pour the oil for frying to a depth of 2.5cm/1in in a deep frying pan and heat it to 180°C/350°F. Using a metal spatula, lift one poori and slide it into the oil; it will sink but then return to the surface and begin to sizzle. Gently press the poori into the oil. It will puff up. Turn the poori over after a few seconds and allow it to cook for a further 20–30 seconds.

6 Remove the poori from the pan and pat dry with kitchen paper. Place the cooked poori on a large baking tray and keep warm in a low oven while you cook the remaining pooris. Serve warm.

Energy 144kcal/605kJ; Fat 6.6g; Saturated fat 1.4g; Carbohydrate 19.7g; Fibre 0.7g.

Energy 79kcal/333kJ; Fat 2.2g; Saturated fat 0.3g; Carbohydrate 13.6g; Fibre 1.2g.

Ensaimadas

These sweet bread rolls are a popular snack in the Philippines and come with various fillings.

Makes 10–12

30ml/2 tbsp caster (superfine) sugar, plus extra for sprinkling
150ml/¼ pint/⅔ cup warm water
15ml/1 tbsp active dried yeast
450g/1lb/4 cups strong white bread flour
5ml/1 tsp salt
115g/4oz/½ cup butter, softened, plus 30ml/2 tbsp melted butter for the filling
4 egg yolks
90–120ml/6–8 tbsp warm milk
115g/4oz/1 cup grated Cheddar cheese (or similar well-flavoured hard cheese)

1 Dissolve 5ml/1 tsp of the sugar in the warm water, then sprinkle in the dried yeast. Stir, then set aside for 10 minutes or until frothy. Sift the flour and salt into a large bowl.

2 Cream the softened butter with the remaining sugar in a large bowl. When it is fluffy, beat in the egg yolks and a little of the sifted flour. Gradually stir in the remaining flour with the yeast mixture and enough milk to form a soft but not sticky dough. Transfer to an oiled plastic bag. Close the bag loosely, leaving plenty of room for the dough to rise. Leave in a warm place for about 1 hour, until the dough doubles in bulk.

3 On a lightly floured surface, knock back (punch down) the dough, then roll it out into a large rectangle. Brush the surface with half the melted butter, sprinkle with the cheese, then roll up from a long side like a Swiss (jelly) roll. Knead the dough thoroughly, then divide into 10–12 pieces.

4 Roll each piece of dough into a thin rope, 38cm/15in long. On greased baking sheets, coil each rope into a loose spiral. Leave to rise for about 45 minutes or until doubled in size. Preheat the oven to 220°C/425°F/Gas 7. Bake the ensaimadas for 15–20 minutes, until golden. Remove from the oven, then brush with the remaining melted butter and sprinkle with caster sugar. Serve warm.

Sugar Bread Rolls

These delicious sweet rolls make an unusual end to a meal.

Makes 10

350g/12oz/3 cups strong white bread flour
5ml/1 tsp salt
15ml/1 tbsp caster (superfine) sugar
5ml/1 tsp dried yeast
150ml/¼ pint/⅔ cup hand-hot water
3 egg yolks
50g/2oz/¼ cup unsalted (sweet) butter, softened, plus 25g/1oz/2 tbsp extra
75g/3oz Cheddar cheese or Monterey Jack, grated
50g/2oz/¼ cup granulated sugar

1 Sift the flour, salt and caster sugar into a food processor fitted with a dough blade or the bowl of an electric mixer fitted with a dough hook. Make a well in the centre. Dissolve the yeast in the hand-hot water and pour into the well. Add the egg yolks and leave for a few minutes until bubbles appear on the surface of the liquid.

2 Mix the ingredients for 30–45 seconds to form a firm dough. Add the softened butter and knead for 2–3 minutes in a food processor, or for 4–5 minutes with an electric mixer, until smooth. Transfer the dough out to a floured bowl, cover and leave in a warm place to rise until doubled in bulk.

3 Transfer the dough to a lightly floured surface and divide it into 10 pieces. Spread the grated cheese over the surface. Roll each of the dough pieces into a 13cm/5in length, incorporating the cheese as you do so. Coil into snail shapes and place on a lightly greased high-sided tray measuring 30 x 20cm/12 x 8in.

4 Cover the rolls with clear film (plastic wrap) and leave in a warm place for 45 minutes or until doubled in bulk.

5 Preheat the oven to 190°C/375°F/Gas 5 and then bake the rolls for 20–25 minutes. Melt the remaining butter, brush it over the rolls, sprinkle with the sugar and allow to cool. Separate the rolls before serving.

Energy 327kcal/1372kJ; Fat 16.2g; Saturated fat 9.3g; Carbohydrate 38.6g; Fibre 1.4g.

Energy 235kcal/986kJ; Fat 9.5g; Saturated fat 5.9g; Carbohydrate 33.7g; Fibre 1.1g.

Pears in Spiced Wine

Familiar Indian spices, infused in a red wine syrup, give pears a lovely warm flavour. The colour is beautiful, too.

Serves 4
1 bottle full-bodied red wine
1 cinnamon stick
4 cloves
2.5ml/ ½ tsp freshly grated
   nutmeg
2.5ml/ ½ tsp ground
   ginger
8 peppercorns
175g/6oz/scant 1 cup
   caster (superfine) sugar
thinly pared rind of ½ orange
thinly pared rind of ½ lemon
8 firm ripe pears

1 Pour the wine into a heavy pan into which the pears will fit snugly when standing upright.

2 Stir the cinnamon stick, cloves, nutmeg, ginger, peppercorns, caster sugar and citrus rinds into the wine.

3 Peel the pears, leaving the stalks intact, and stand them in the pan. The wine should only just cover the pears.

4 Bring the liquid to the boil, lower the heat, cover and simmer very gently for 30 minutes, or until the pears are tender. Using a slotted spoon, transfer the pears to a bowl.

5 Boil the poaching liquid until it has reduced by half and is thick and syrupy.

6 Strain the syrup over and around the pears and serve the dessert hot or cold.

Cook's Tip
Serve the pears with a mascarpone cream, made by combining equal quantities of mascarpone cheese and double (heavy) cream, and adding a little vanilla extract for flavour. They also taste good with yogurt or ice cream.

Energy 191kcal/806kJ; Fat 0.3g; Saturated fat 0g; Carbohydrate 43.1g; Fibre 6.6g.

Melon & Strawberry Salad

A beautiful and colourful fruit salad, this is suitable to serve as a refreshing appetizer or to round off a rich and spicy meal. Don't be tempted to chill the salad; it tastes best at room temperature.

Serves 4
1 Galia or Ogen melon
1 honeydew melon or other
   melon of your choice
   (see Cook's Tip)
½ watermelon
225g/8oz/2 cups
   strawberries
15ml/1 tbsp lemon juice
15ml/1 tbsp clear honey
15ml/1 tbsp chopped
   fresh mint

1 Prepare the melons by cutting them in half and discarding the seeds by scraping them out with a spoon.

2 Use a melon baller to scoop out the flesh into balls or a knife to cut it into cubes. Place these in a fruit bowl.

3 Rinse and take the stems off the strawberries, twisting them so that they remove the hull at the same time. If the hull remains inside, use a fine, sharp knife to cut it out. Cut the fruit in half and add them to the bowl.

4 Mix together the lemon juice and honey and add 15ml/ 1 tbsp water to make this easier to pour over the fruit. Mix into the fruit gently.

5 Sprinkle the chopped mint over the top of the fruit and serve.

Cook's Tip
Use whichever melons are available: replace Galia or Ogen with cantaloupe melon, or replace watermelon with charentais, for example. Try to choose three melons with a variation in colour for an attractive effect.

Energy 114kcal/482kJ; Fat 0.7g; Saturated fat 0g; Carbohydrate 26.5g; Fibre 1.6g.

Spiced Fruit Salad

Exotic fruits are becoming commonplace in supermarkets these days and it is fun to experiment with the different varieties. Look out in particular for physalis, star fruit, papaya and passion fruit.

Serves 4–6
75g/3oz/6 tbsp granulated
  sugar
300ml/½ pint/1¼ cups water
30ml/2 tbsp syrup from a jar
  of preserved stem ginger

2 pieces star anise
2.5cm/1in cinnamon
  stick
1 clove
juice of ½ lemon
2 fresh mint sprigs
1 mango
2 bananas, sliced
8 fresh or drained canned
  lychees
225g/8oz/2 cups strawberries,
  hulled and halved
2 pieces preserved stem ginger,
  cut into sticks
1 medium pineapple

1 Put the sugar, water, ginger syrup, star anise, cinnamon, clove, lemon juice and mint into a pan. Bring to the boil, then simmer for 3 minutes. Strain into a bowl and set aside to cool.

2 Remove the top and bottom from the mango and cut off the outer skin. Stand the mango on one end and remove the flesh in two pieces either side of the flat stone (pit). Slice evenly.

3 Add the mango slices to the syrup with the bananas, lychees, strawberries and stem ginger. Mix in well, making sure the fruits are well coated in the sugary liquid.

4 Cut the pineapple in half by slicing down the centre, using a very sharp knife. Loosen the flesh with a smaller, serrated knife, and remove the flesh by cutting around the rim and scooping it out. The pineapple halves will resemble two boat shapes. Do not discard the pineapple flesh, but cut it into chunks and add to the fruity syrup.

5 Spoon some of the fruit salad into the pineapple halves and serve on a large dish. There will be sufficient fruit salad in the bowl to refill the pineapple halves at least once.

Citrus Fruit Salad

This is a very appetizing and refreshing salad, with a typically Indian combination of citrus fruits seasoned with salt and pepper. It will provide the perfect ending to a heavy meal.

Serves 6
2 navel oranges
1 honeydew melon
½ watermelon
1 fresh mango
115g/4oz seedless green and
  black grapes

225g/8oz canned mandarin
  segments, drained
225g/8oz canned grapefruit
  segments, drained
juice of 1 lemon
salt and ground black pepper
2.5ml/½ tsp sugar
1.5ml/¼ tsp freshly ground
  cumin seeds

1 Using a sharp knife, cut a thin slice of peel and pith from each end of an orange. Place cut side down on a plate and cut off the peel and pith in strips. Remove any remaining pith. Cut out each segment leaving the membrane behind. Squeeze the remaining juice from the membrane. Repeat with the other orange.

2 Cut the honeydew melon in half and scrape out the seeds using a spoon. Remove the seeds from the watermelon in the same way. Use a melon baller to scoop out the flesh into balls or a knife to cut it into cubes.

3 Using a sharp knife take two thick slices from either side of the large flat stone (pit) of the mango without peeling the fruit. Make slices into the flesh and then turn the skin inside out. The slices of flesh will stand proud of the skin and can be easily cut off.

4 Place all the fruit in a large serving bowl and add the lemon juice. Toss gently to prevent damaging the fruit.

5 Mix together the remaining ingredients and sprinkle over the fruit. Gently toss, chill thoroughly and serve.

Energy 167kcal/710kJ; Fat 0.8g; Saturated fat 0.2g; Carbohydrate 39.5g; Fibre 3.1g.

Energy 110kcal/468kJ; Fat 0.3g; Saturated fat 0.1g; Carbohydrate 27.1g; Fibre 2.4g.

Mango & Coconut Stir-fry

Choose a ripe mango for this recipe. If you buy one that is a little underripe, leave it in a warm place for a day or two before using.

Serves 4

¼ coconut

1 large, ripe mango

juice and finely grated rind
   of 2 limes
15ml/1 tbsp sunflower oil
15g/½oz/1 tbsp butter
30ml/2 tbsp clear honey
crème fraîche or ice cream,
   to serve

1 Prepare the coconut if necessary. Drain the milk and remove the flesh. Peel with a vegetable peeler so that it forms flakes.

2 Peel the mango. Cut the stone (pit) out of the middle of the fruit. Cut each half of the mango into slices. Place the mango slices in a bowl and pour over the lime juice and rind. Set aside.

3 Meanwhile heat a karahi or wok, then add 10ml/2 tsp of the oil. When the oil is hot, add the butter. Once the butter has melted, stir in the coconut flakes and stir-fry for 1–2 minutes until the coconut is golden brown. Remove and drain on kitchen paper. Wipe out the pan. Strain the mango slices, reserving the juice.

4 Heat the pan again and add the remaining oil. When the oil is hot, add the mango and stir-fry for 1–2 minutes, then add the juice and leave to bubble and reduce for 1 minute.

5 Stir in the honey. When it has dissolved, spoon the mango and its juices into one large serving bowl or individual dishes. Sprinkle on the stir-fried coconut flakes and serve with crème fraîche or ice cream.

Variation

Nectarine or peach slices can be used instead of the mango.

Stewed Pumpkin in Coconut Cream

Fruit stewed in coconut milk is a popular dessert in Thailand. Pumpkins, bananas and melons can all be prepared in this simple but tasty way.

Serves 4–6

1kg/2¼lb kabocha
   pumpkin
750ml/1¼ pints/3 cups
   coconut milk
175g/6oz/scant 1 cup
   granulated sugar
pinch of salt
4–6 fresh mint sprigs,
   to decorate

1 Cut the pumpkin in half using a large, sharp knife, then cut away and discard the skin. Scoop out the seed cluster by scraping it out with a spoon.

2 Reserve a few seeds and throw away the remainder. Using a sharp knife, cut the pumpkin flesh into pieces that are about 5cm/2in long and 2cm/¾in thick.

3 Pour the coconut milk into a pan. Add the sugar and salt, and bring to the boil.

4 Add the pumpkin and simmer for about 10–15 minutes, or until it is tender.

5 Serve warm, in individual dishes. Decorate each serving with a mint sprig and toasted pumpkin seeds (see Cook's Tip).

Cook's Tip

To make the decoration, wash the reserved pumpkin seeds to remove any fibres, then pat them dry on kitchen paper. Roast them in a dry frying pan without any oil, or spread them out on a baking sheet and grill (broil) until golden brown, tossing them frequently to prevent them from burning. Watch them carefully as they will burn if left. These seeds can be prepared in advance and used cold to decorate the stewed pumpkin.

Energy 357kcal/1478kJ; Fat 32.7g; Saturated fat 24.1g; Carbohydrate 13.8g; Fibre 7g.

Energy 246kcal/1051kJ; Fat 1.1g; Saturated fat 0.6g; Carbohydrate 60.4g; Fibre 2.5g.

Mangoes with Sticky Rice

Sticky rice is just as good in desserts as in savoury dishes, and mangoes, with their delicate fragrance and velvety flesh, complement it especially well. You need to start preparing this dish the day before you intend to serve it.

Serves 4
175ml/6fl oz/ ¾ cup thick
    coconut milk
115g/4oz/ ⅔ cup white
    glutinous rice
45ml/3 tbsp granulated sugar
pinch of salt
2 ripe mangoes
strips of pared lime rind, to decorate

1 Pour the coconut milk into a bowl and leave to stand until the cream rises to the top.

2 Rinse the glutinous rice thoroughly in several changes of cold water until it runs clear, then leave to soak overnight in a bowl of fresh cold water.

3 Drain the rice well and spread it out evenly in a steamer lined with muslin (cheesecloth). Cover and steam over a double boiler or a pan of simmering water for about 20 minutes, or until the rice is tender.

4 Reserve 45ml/3 tbsp of the cream from the top of the coconut milk. Pour the remainder into a pan and add the sugar and salt. Heat, stirring constantly, until the sugar has dissolved, then bring to the boil. Remove the pan from the heat, pour the coconut milk into a bowl and leave to cool.

5 Tip the cooked rice into a bowl and pour over the cooled coconut milk mixture. Stir well, then leave the rice mixture to stand for 10–15 minutes.

6 Meanwhile, peel the mangoes, cut the flesh away from the central stones (pits) and cut into slices.

7 Spoon the rice on to individual serving plates. Arrange the mango slices on one side, then drizzle with the reserved coconut cream. Decorate with strips of lime rind and serve.

Energy 200kcal/846kJ; Fat 0.8g; Saturated fat 0.2g; Carbohydrate 46g; Fibre 2g.

Papayas in Jasmine Flower Syrup

The fragrant flower syrup can be prepared in advance, using fresh jasmine flowers from a houseplant or the garden. It tastes fabulous with papayas, but it is also good with all sorts of desserts. Try it with ice cream or spooned over lychees or mangoes.

Serves 2
105ml/7 tbsp water
45ml/3 tbsp palm sugar or
    light muscovado (brown)
    sugar
20–30 jasmine flowers, plus
    a few extra to decorate
    (optional)
2 ripe papayas
juice of 1 lime

1 Place the water and sugar in a small pan. Heat gently, stirring occasionally, until the sugar has dissolved, then simmer, without stirring, over a low heat for 4 minutes.

2 Pour into a bowl, leave to cool slightly, then add the jasmine flowers. Leave to infuse (steep) for at least 20 minutes.

3 Peel the papayas and slice in half lengthways. Scoop out and discard the seeds. Place the papayas on serving plates and squeeze over the lime.

4 Strain the syrup into a clean bowl, discarding the flowers. Spoon the syrup over the papayas. If you like, decorate with a few fresh jasmine flowers.

Variation
Slices of mango would work well in this recipe in place of papayas.

Cook's Tip
Although scented white jasmine flowers are perfectly safe to eat, it is important to be sure that they have not been sprayed with pesticides or other harmful chemicals. Washing them may not remove all the residue.

Energy 233kcal/990kJ; Fat 0.4g; Saturated fat 0g; Carbohydrate 58.7g; Fibre 8.8g.

Toffee Apples

A wickedly sweet way to end a meal, this dessert of crisp pieces of apple with a crunchy coating evokes memories of childhood.

Serves 4
4 firm eating apples
115g/4oz/1 cup plain
   (all-purpose) flour
about 120ml/4fl oz/½ cup water
1 egg, beaten
vegetable oil, for deep-frying, plus
   30ml/2 tbsp for the toffee
115g/4oz/½ cup granulated
   sugar

1 Peel and core each apple and cut into eight pieces. Dust each piece of apple with a little of the flour.

2 Sift the remaining flour into a mixing bowl, then slowly add the cold water and stir well to make a smooth batter.

3 Add the beaten egg and blend well.

4 Heat the oil in a karahi, wok or deep-fryer to a temperature of 190°C/375°F, or until a cube of bread dropped in the oil browns in about 45 seconds. Dip the apple pieces in the batter and deep-fry for about 3 minutes or until golden. Remove and drain on kitchen paper. Drain off the oil from the pan.

5 Heat the remaining oil in the pan, add the sugar and stir constantly until the sugar has caramelized. Quickly add the apple pieces and blend well so that each piece of apple is thoroughly coated with the toffee.

6 Dip the apple pieces in cold water to harden before serving.

> **Variation**
> *Try this recipe with bananas or pineapple pieces for a delicious change.*

Energy 410kcal/1723kJ; Fat 18.5g; Saturated fat 2.5g; Carbohydrate 60g; Fibre 2g.

Sesame Fried Fruits

For this deep-fried dessert you can use any firm fruit that are in season. Bananas are fantastic, but the batter also works well with pineapple and apple. Serve them as soon as they are fried so that they retain their crispness.

Serves 4
115g/4oz/1 cup plain
   (all-purpose) flour
2.5ml/½ tsp bicarbonate of soda
   (baking soda)
30ml/2 tbsp sugar
1 egg
90ml/6 tbsp water
15ml/1 tbsp sesame seeds
   or 30ml/2 tbsp desiccated
   (dry unsweetened shredded)
   coconut
4 firm bananas
oil, for deep-frying
salt
30ml/2 tbsp clear honey,
   to serve
fresh mint sprigs and lychees,
   to decorate

1 Sift the flour, bicarbonate of soda and a pinch of salt into a bowl. Stir in the sugar.

2 Whisk in the egg and just enough water to make a thin batter. Then whisk in the sesame seeds or the desiccated coconut.

3 Peel the bananas. Carefully cut each one in half lengthways, then cut in half crossways. Don't do this until you are ready to cook them, because once peeled, bananas will quickly discolour.

4 Heat the oil in a karahi, wok or deep-fryer to a temperature of 190°C/375°F, or until a cube of bread dropped in the oil browns in about 45 seconds. Dip the bananas in the batter, then gently drop a few pieces at a time into the hot oil. Fry until golden brown.

5 Remove the bananas from the oil and drain on kitchen paper.

6 Serve immediately with clear honey, and decorate with mint sprigs and lychees.

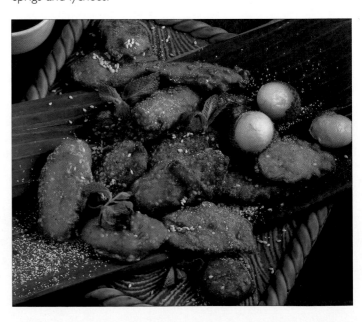

Energy 384kcal/1607kJ; Fat 20.7g; Saturated fat 6.3g; Carbohydrate 46g; Fibre 3g.

Coconut Fried Bananas

These deliciously sweet treats are a favourite with children and adults alike. In Thailand, you will find them on sale from portable roadside stalls and markets at almost every hour of the day and night.

Serves 4

115g/4oz/1 cup plain
  (all-purpose) flour
2.5ml/½ tsp bicarbonate of soda
  (baking soda)
pinch of salt
30ml/2 tbsp granulated
  sugar
1 egg, beaten
90ml/6 tbsp water
30ml/2 tbsp desiccated
  (dry unsweetened shredded)
  coconut or 15ml/1 tbsp
  sesame seeds
4 firm bananas
vegetable oil, for deep-frying
fresh mint sprigs, to decorate
30ml/2 tbsp clear honey,
  to serve (optional)

1 Sift the flour, bicarbonate of soda and salt into a large bowl. Stir in the granulated sugar and the egg, and whisk in just enough of the water to make quite a thin batter.

2 Whisk the coconut or sesame seeds into the batter so that they are evenly distributed.

3 Peel the bananas. Carefully cut each one in half lengthways, then in half crossways to make 16 pieces of about the same size. Don't do this until you are ready to cook them because, once peeled, bananas will quickly discolour.

4 Heat the oil in a karahi, wok or deep-fryer to a temperature of 190°C/375°F or until a cube of bread, dropped in the oil, browns in about 45 seconds. Dip the banana pieces in the batter, then gently drop a few into the oil.

5 Deep-fry until golden brown, then lift out and drain well on kitchen paper.

6 Cook the remaining banana pieces in the same way. Serve immediately with honey, if using, and decorated with sprigs of fresh mint.

Deep-fried Bananas

Fry these bananas at the last minute, so that the outer crust of batter is crisp in texture and the banana is soft and warm inside.

Serves 8

115g/4oz/1 cup self-raising
  (self-rising) flour
40g/1½oz/⅓ cup rice flour
2.5ml/½ tsp salt
200ml/7fl oz /scant 1 cup water
finely grated lime rind
8 small bananas
oil for deep-frying
caster (superfine) sugar and
  1 lime, cut into wedges,
  to serve

1 Sift the self-raising flour, the rice flour and the salt together into a bowl. Add just enough of the water to make a smooth, coating batter. Mix well, then stir in the lime rind.

2 Heat the oil in a karahi, wok or deep-fryer to a temperature of 190°C/375°F, or until a cube of bread dropped in the oil browns in about 45 seconds.

3 Peel the bananas and dip them into the batter two or three times.

4 Deep-fry the battered bananas in the hot oil until crisp and golden.

5 Drain and serve hot, dredged with sugar. Offer the lime wedges to squeeze over the bananas.

Variation

For Banana Fritters using evaporated (unsweetened condensed) milk, sift 115g/4oz/1 cup plain (all-purpose) flour and a pinch of salt into a bowl. Make a well in the centre and add 1 beaten egg. Blend the egg and the flour together, and as the mixture becomes thick, stir in a 175g/6oz can evaporated milk to make a smooth batter. Heat oil for deep-frying to 190°C/375°F and split 4 bananas in half lengthways. Dip them in the batter and deep-fry until golden. Roll in caster (superfine) sugar and serve.

Energy 412kcal/1725kJ; Fat 20.7g; Saturated fat 2.8g; Carbohydrate 53.4g; Fibre 2.3g.

Energy 201kcal/840kJ; Fat 10g; Saturated fat 1.3g; Carbohydrate 27.1g; Fibre 1.2g.

Fried Pineapple

A very simple and quick
dessert – fresh pineapple
fried in butter, brown sugar
and lime juice, and sprinkled
with toasted coconut.
The slightly sharp taste of
the fruit makes this a very
refreshing treat at the end
of a rich meal.

60ml/4 tbsp soft light
  brown sugar
60ml/4 tbsp fresh lime juice
lime slices, to decorate
thick and creamy natural (plain)
  yogurt, to serve

Serves 4
1 pineapple
40g/1½oz/3 tbsp butter
15ml/1 tbsp desiccated (dry
  unsweetened shredded)
  coconut

1 Using a sharp knife, cut the top off the pineapple and peel
off the skin, taking care to remove the eyes.

2 Cut the pineapple in half and remove and discard the woody
core. Cut the flesh lengthways into 1cm/½in wedges.

3 Heat the butter in a large, heavy frying pan or wok. When it
has melted, add the pineapple wedges and cook over a medium
heat for 1–2 minutes on each side, or until they have turned
pale golden in colour.

4 Meanwhile, dry-fry the desiccated coconut in a small frying pan
until lightly browned. Remove the pan from the heat and set aside.

5 Sprinkle the soft light brown sugar into the pan with the
pineapple, add the lime juice and cook, stirring constantly, until
the sugar has dissolved.

6 Divide the pineapple wedges among four bowls, sprinkle
with the coconut, decorate with the lime slices and serve with
the yogurt.

Energy 238kcal/1004kJ; Fat 11g; Saturated fat 7.2g; Carbohydrate 36.2g; Fibre 2.9g.

Honeyed Apples

These scrumptious treats
are best prepared for a
select number as they
require the cook's complete
attention. The honey coating
crispens when the fritters
are dipped in iced water.

Serves 4–5
4 crisp eating apples
juice of ½ lemon
25g/1oz/¼ cup cornflour
  (cornstarch)
sunflower oil, for deep-frying
toasted sesame seeds, for sprinkling

For the fritter batter
115g/4oz/1 cup plain
  (all-purpose) flour
generous pinch of salt
120–150ml/4–5fl oz/½–⅔ cup
  water
30ml/2 tbsp sunflower oil
2 egg whites

For the sauce
250ml/8fl oz/1 cup clear honey
120ml/4fl oz/½ cup sunflower oil
5ml/1 tsp white wine vinegar

1 Peel, core and cut the apples into eighths, brush each piece
lightly with lemon juice then dust with cornflour.

2 To make the sauce, heat the honey and oil in a pan, stirring
continuously until blended. Remove from the heat and stir in
the white wine vinegar.

3 Sift the flour and salt into a bowl, then stir in the water and
oil. Whisk the egg whites until stiff peaks form and then fold
them into the batter.

4 Heat the oil in a karahi, wok or deep-fryer to a temperature
of 190°C/375°F, or until a cube of bread dropped in the oil
browns in about 45 seconds. Spear each piece of apple in turn
on a skewer, dip in the batter and fry in the hot oil until golden.
Drain on kitchen paper. Place the fritters in a dish and pour the
sauce over.

5 Transfer the fritters to a lightly oiled serving dish, and sprinkle
with the toasted sesame seeds. Serve the honeyed fritters at
once, offering bowls of iced water for dipping to crispen the
honey coating.

Energy 564kcal/2361kJ; Fat 32.8g; Saturated fat 3.9g; Carbohydrate 67.8g; Fibre 2g.

Kheer

Both Muslim and Hindu communities prepare kheer, which is traditionally served in mosques and temples.

Serves 4–6
15g/½oz/1 tbsp ghee
5cm/2in piece cinnamon stick
175g/6oz/¾ cup soft
  brown sugar
115g/4oz/1 cup coarsely
  ground rice

1.2 litres/2 pints/5 cups
  full cream (whole) milk
5ml/1 tsp ground cardamom
50g/2oz/⅓ cup sultanas
  (golden raisins)
25g/1oz/¼ cup flaked
  (sliced) almonds
2.5ml/½ tsp freshly grated
  nutmeg, to serve

1 In a heavy pan, melt the ghee and fry the cinnamon stick and soft brown sugar. Watch carefully while frying and when the sugar begins to caramelize reduce the heat immediately, or remove the pan from the heat, as sugar can burn very quickly.

2 Return the pan to the heat and add the rice and half the milk. Bring to the boil, stirring constantly to avoid the milk boiling over. Reduce the heat and simmer until the rice is cooked, stirring regularly.

3 Stir in the remaining milk, with the ground cardamom, sultanas and almonds. Leave to simmer until the mixture thickens, stirring constantly to prevent the kheer from sticking to the base of the pan, about 1½ hours.

4 When the mixture is thick and creamy, spoon it into a serving dish or individual dishes. Serve the kheer hot or cold, sprinkled with the freshly grated nutmeg. Decorate with tinfoil, if you like.

> **Cook's Tip**
> Kheer is traditionally cooked twice: once until the rice grains disintegrate and then with the spices and flavourings. This recipe uses ground rice and so it will take less time to cook.

Energy 588kcal/2463kJ; Fat 20.6g; Saturated fat 11.1g; Carbohydrate 90.6g; Fibre 0.7g.

Sweet Fried Loops

These irresistible fritters are delicious served with hot chocolate or coffee.

Makes about 24
450ml/15fl oz/scant
  2 cups water
15ml/1 tbsp olive oil

15ml/1 tbsp caster (superfine)
  sugar, plus extra for
  dredging
2.5ml/½ tsp salt
150g/5oz/1¼ cups plain
  (all-purpose) flour
1 large egg
sunflower oil, for deep-frying

1 Mix the water, oil, sugar and salt in a large pan and bring to the boil. Remove from the heat, and then sift in the flour. Beat well with a wooden spoon until smooth.

2 Beat in the egg to make a smooth, glossy mixture with a piping consistency. Spoon into a pastry bag fitted with a large star nozzle.

3 Heat the oil in a karahi, wok or deep-fryer to a temperature of 190°C/375°F, or until a cube of bread dropped in the oil browns in about 45 seconds. Pipe loops of the mixture, two at a time, into the hot oil. Cook the loops for 3–4 minutes until they are golden.

4 Lift out the loops with a wire skimmer or slotted spoon and drain them on kitchen paper. Dredge them with caster sugar and serve warm.

> **Variation**
> Add 2.5ml/½ tsp cinnamon to the caster (superfine) sugar for sprinkling, if you like, to give the loops a warm, spicy flavour.

> **Cook's Tip**
> If you don't have a piping bag, you could fry teaspoons of mixture in the same way. Don't try to fry too many fritters at a time as they swell a little during cooking.

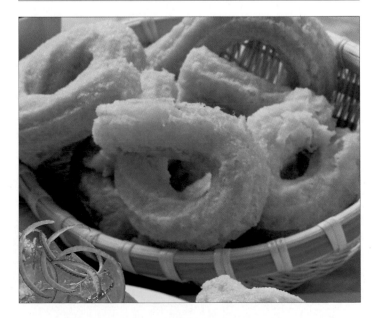

Energy 122kcal/507kJ; Fat 10.9g; Saturated fat 1.4g; Carbohydrate 5.5g; Fibre 0.2g.

Ground Rice Pudding

This delicious and light ground rice pudding is the perfect end to a spicy meal. It can be served either hot or cold.

Serves 4–6

50g/2oz/½ cup coarsely
   ground rice
4 green cardamom pods, crushed

900ml/1½ pints/3¾ cups
   semi-skimmed (low-fat) milk
90ml/6 tbsp granulated sugar
15ml/1 tbsp rose water
15ml/1 tbsp crushed pistachio
   nuts, to garnish

1 Place the ground rice in a pan with the cardamom pods.

2 Add 600ml/1 pint/2½ cups of the milk and bring to the boil over a medium heat, stirring occasionally.

3 Add the remaining milk and stir over a medium heat for about 10 minutes, or until the rice mixture thickens to the consistency of a creamy chicken soup.

4 Stir in the sugar and rose water and continue to cook for a further 2 minutes.

5 Garnish with the pistachio nuts and serve.

Variation
For an even richer version of this pudding, you could add 40g/1½oz ground almonds to the rice at step 1.

Cook's Tip
Rose water is a distillation of scented rose petals which has the intense fragrance and flavour of roses. It is a popular flavouring in Indian cooking. Use it cautiously, adding just enough to suit your taste.

Black Rice Pudding

This unusual rice pudding, flavoured with fresh root ginger, is quite delicious. When cooked, black rice still retains its husk and has a nutty texture. Serve in small bowls, with a little coconut milk or cream poured over each helping.

1cm/½in piece fresh root
   ginger, bruised
50g/2oz/¼ cup soft dark
   brown sugar
50g/2oz/¼ cup granulated
   sugar
300ml/½ pint/1¼ cups coconut
   milk or cream, to serve

Serves 6

115g/4oz/generous ½ cup black
   glutinous rice
475ml/16fl oz/2 cups water

1 Put the black glutinous rice in a sieve (strainer) and rinse well under cold running water.

2 Drain and put in a large pan, with the water. Bring to the boil and stir to prevent the rice from settling on the base of the pan. Cover and cook for about 30 minutes.

3 Add the ginger and both the brown and white sugar.

4 Cook for a further 15 minutes, adding a little more water if necessary, until the rice is cooked and porridge-like.

5 Remove the ginger and serve warm, in bowls, topped with coconut milk or cream.

Cook's Tip
Although black glutinous rice looks similar to wild rice, which is the seed of a rush plant, it is in fact a true rice. It has a particularly nutty flavour that is ideal for puddings and cakes. Long cooking makes the pudding thick and creamy, as the rice is naturally sticky.

Energy 260kcal/1102kJ; Fat 5.8g; Saturated fat 2.53g; Carbohydrate 46g; Fibre 0.3g.

Energy 146kcal/616kJ; Fat 0.5g; Saturated fat 0.1g; Carbohydrate 34.2g; Fibre 0g.

Baked Rice Pudding

Black glutinous rice, also known as black sticky rice, has long dark grains and a nutty taste reminiscent of wild rice. This baked pudding has a distinct character and flavour all of its own, as well as an intriguing appearance.

Serves 4–6
175g/6oz/scant 1 cup white or black glutinous rice
30ml/2 tbsp soft light brown sugar
475ml/16fl oz/2 cups coconut milk
250ml/8fl oz/1 cup water
3 eggs
30ml/2 tbsp granulated sugar

1 Combine the glutinous rice and brown sugar in a pan. Pour in half the coconut milk and the water.

2 Bring to the boil, reduce the heat to low and simmer, stirring occasionally, for 15–20 minutes, or until the rice has absorbed most of the liquid. Preheat the oven to 150°C/300°F/Gas 2.

3 Spoon the rice mixture into a single, large ovenproof dish or divide it among individual ramekins. Beat the eggs with the remaining coconut milk and sugar in a bowl.

4 Strain the egg mixture into a jug (pitcher), then pour it evenly over the par-cooked rice in the dish or ramekins.

5 Place the dish or individual ramekins in a roasting pan. Carefully pour in enough hot water to come halfway up the sides of the dish or ramekins.

6 Cover with foil and bake for about 35–60 minutes, or until the custard has set. Serve warm or cold.

Cook's Tip
Throughout South-east Asia, black glutinous rice is usually used for sweet dishes, whereas its white counterpart is more often used in savoury recipes.

Energy 298kcal/1252kJ; Fat 5.2g; Saturated fat 1.4g; Carbohydrate 54.3g; Fibre 0g.

Traditional Indian Vermicelli

Indian vermicelli, made from wheat, is much finer than Italian vermicelli and has a good texture in desserts. It is available from Asian stores.

Serves 4
115g/4oz/1 cup Indian vermicelli
1.2 litres/2 pints/5 cups water
2.5ml/½ tsp saffron threads
15ml/1 tbsp granulated sugar
60ml/4 tbsp low-fat fromage frais or Greek (US strained plain) yogurt, to serve

15ml/1 tbsp flaked (sliced) almonds
15ml/1 tbsp chopped pistachio nuts
15ml/1 tbsp granulated sugar

To decorate
15ml/1 tbsp shredded fresh or desiccated (dry unsweetened shredded) coconut

1 Crush the vermicelli in your hands and place it in a pan. Pour in the water, add the saffron and bring to the boil. Boil for about 5 minutes.

2 Stir in the sugar and continue cooking until the water has evaporated. Press through a sieve (strainer), if necessary, to remove any excess liquid.

3 Place the vermicelli in a serving dish and decorate with the coconut, almonds, pistachio nuts and sugar. Serve with fromage frais or yogurt.

Cook's Tip
You can use a variety of fruits instead of nuts to garnish this dessert. Try a few soft fruits such as blackberries, raspberries or strawberries, or add some chopped dried apricots or sultanas.

Energy 196kcal/822kJ; Fat 6.6g; Saturated fat 2.27g; Carbohydrate 31.8g; Fibre 0.8g.

Tapioca Pudding

This pudding, made from large pearl tapioca and coconut milk and served warm, is much lighter than the Western-style version. You can adjust the sweetness to your taste. Serve with lychees, or you could try the smaller, similar-tasting logans.

Serves 4
115g/4oz/²/₃ cup tapioca
475ml/16fl oz/2 cups water
175g/6oz/³/₄ cup granulated
   sugar
pinch of salt
250ml/8fl oz/1 cup coconut milk
250g/9oz prepared tropical fruits
finely shredded rind of 1 lime,
   to decorate

1 Soak the tapioca in warm water for 1 hour so that the grains swell. Drain.

2 Put the measured water in a pan and bring to the boil. Stir in the sugar and salt.

3 Add the tapioca and coconut milk and simmer for 10 minutes or until the tapioca turns transparent.

4 Serve warm with some tropical fruits and decorate with the finely shredded lime rind.

Cook's Tip
Sliced kiwi fruits, mangoes and strawberries would make a bright and tasty selection to serve with this pudding. Or you could try sliced bananas, nectarines and raspberries.

Variation
Serve this tapioca pudding with a refreshing peach salad for a change. Peel, stone (pit) and very thinly slice 8 peaches and put them in a serving bowl. Add 30ml/2 tbsp rose water, 20ml/4 tsp sugar, the juice of 1 lemon and 50ml/2fl oz/¼ cup freshly squeezed orange juice. Chill well before serving.

Fruit Vermicelli Pudding

This tasty dessert is prepared by Muslims early in the morning of Eid-ul-Fitr, the feast after the 30 days of Ramadan.

Serves 4–6
75g/3oz/6 tbsp ghee
115g/4oz/1 cup Indian vermicelli,
   coarsely broken
25g/1oz/¼ cup flaked
   (sliced) almonds
25g/1oz/¼ cup pistachio
   nuts, slivered
25g/1oz/¼ cup cuddapah
   nuts or almonds
50g/2oz/⅓ cup sultanas
   (golden raisins)
50g/2oz/⅓ cup dates, stoned
   (pitted) and thinly sliced
1.2 litres/2 pints/5 cups full cream
   (whole) milk
60ml/4 tbsp soft dark brown
   sugar
1 sachet saffron powder

1 Heat 50g/2oz/4 tbsp of the ghee in a frying pan and sauté the vermicelli until golden brown. (If you are using the Italian variety, sauté it for a little longer.) Remove and set aside.

2 Heat the remaining ghee in a separate pan and fry the almonds, pistachio and cuddapah nuts, sultanas and dates over a medium heat until the sultanas swell. Add the nuts and fruit to the vermicelli and mix gently.

3 Heat the milk in a large, heavy pan and add the sugar. Bring to the boil, add the vermicelli mixture and let the liquid return to the boil, stirring constantly.

4 Reduce the heat and simmer until the vermicelli is soft and you have a fairly thick pudding. Stir in the saffron powder and cook for 1 minute more. Serve hot or cold.

Cook's Tip
Cuddapah nuts taste a little like a combination of almonds and pistachio nuts and are also known as almondettes. If you can't locate them use extra almonds for this dish.

Energy 327kcal/1388kJ; Fat 0.6g; Saturated fat 0.2g; Carbohydrate 80.6g; Fibre 2.2g.

Energy 732kcal/3043kJ; Fat 44.6g; Saturated fat 23.6g; Carbohydrate 68.3g; Fibre 1.7g.

Pancakes Filled with Sweet Coconut

Traditionally, the pale green colour used for the pancake batter was obtained from the juice squeezed from fresh pandanus leaves. Green food colouring can be used instead.

Makes 12–15
175g/6oz/³⁄₄ cup soft dark brown sugar
450ml/³⁄₄ pint/scant 2 cups water
1 pandanus leaf, stripped through with a fork and tied into a knot
175g/6oz/2 cups desiccated (dry unsweetened shredded) coconut
oil, for frying
salt

For the pancake batter
225g/8oz/2 cups plain (all-purpose) flour, sifted
2 eggs, beaten
2 drops of edible green food colouring
few drops of vanilla extract
450ml/15fl oz/scant 2 cups water
45ml/3 tbsp groundnut (peanut) oil

1 Dissolve the sugar in the water with the pandanus leaf, in a pan over gentle heat, stirring all the time. Increase the heat and allow to boil gently for 3–4 minutes, until the mixture just becomes syrupy. Do not let it caramelize.

2 Put the coconut in a karahi or wok with a pinch of salt. Pour over the prepared sugar syrup and cook over a very gentle heat, stirring from time to time, until the mixture becomes almost dry; this will take 5–10 minutes. Set aside until required.

3 To make the batter, blend together the flour, eggs, food colouring, vanilla extract, water and oil either by hand or in a food processor.

4 Brush an 18cm/7in frying pan with oil and cook 12–15 pancakes. Keep the pancakes warm. Fill each pancake with a generous spoonful of the sweet coconut mixture, roll up and serve immediately.

Energy 191kcal/798kJ; Fat 13.1g; Saturated fat 8.5g; Carbohydrate 15.5g; Fibre 2.6g.

Coconut Pancakes

These light and sweet pancakes are often served as street food by the hawkers in Bangkok. They make a delightful coconut-flavoured dessert.

Makes 8
75g/3oz/²⁄₃ cup plain (all-purpose) flour, sifted
60ml/4 tbsp rice flour

45ml/3 tbsp caster (superfine) sugar
50g/2oz/²⁄₃ cup desiccated (dry unsweetened shredded) coconut
1 egg
275ml/9fl oz/generous 1 cup coconut milk
vegetable oil, for frying
lime wedges and maple syrup, to serve

1 Place the plain flour, rice flour, sugar and coconut in a bowl, stir to mix and then make a small well in the centre. Break the egg into the well and pour in the coconut milk.

2 With a whisk or fork, beat the egg into the coconut milk and then gradually incorporate the surrounding dry ingredients, whisking constantly until the mixture forms a batter. The mixture will not be entirely smooth, because of the coconut, but there shouldn't be any large lumps.

3 Heat a little oil in a 13cm/5in non-stick frying pan. Pour in about 45ml/3 tbsp of the mixture and spread to a thin layer with the back of a spoon. Cook over a high heat for about 30–60 seconds, until bubbles appear on the surface of the pancake, then turn it over and cook the other side until golden.

4 Slide the pancake on to a plate and keep it warm in a very low oven. Make more pancakes in the same way. Serve warm with lime wedges for squeezing and maple syrup for drizzling.

Variation
Serve with honey instead of maple syrup, if you like.

Energy 200kcal/837kJ; Fat 11.7g; Saturated fat 4.4g; Carbohydrate 21.9g; Fibre 1.3g.

Kulfi with Cardamom

The delicious, traditional Indian ice cream, kulfi, is always made with sweetened full cream milk and is a lovely refreshing way to end an Indian meal. Making kulfi is easy if you use yogurt pots or dariole moulds.

Serves 6
2 litres/3 1/2 pints/9 cups
   creamy milk
12 cardamoms
175g/6oz/scant 1 cup caster
   (superfine) sugar
25g/1oz/1/4 cup blanched
   almonds, chopped
toasted flaked (sliced) almonds
   and cardamoms, to decorate

1 Place the milk and cardamom pods in a large, heavy pan. Bring to the boil then simmer vigorously until reduced by one-third.

2 Strain the milk into a bowl, discarding the cardamoms, then stir in the caster sugar and chopped almonds until the sugar is dissolved. Leave to cool.

3 Pour the mixture into a freezerproof container, cover and freeze until almost firm, stirring every 30 minutes.

4 When almost solid, pack the ice cream into six kulfi moulds or clean yogurt pots. Return to the freezer until required, removing the pots about 10 minutes before serving and turning out the individual ices. Decorate with toasted almonds and cardamoms before serving.

Variation
Rose water is also a traditional flavouring for kulfi. Add 15ml/1 tbsp to the recipe, if you like.

Cook's Tip
Use a large pan for reducing the milk as there needs to be plenty of room for it to bubble up.

Energy 401kcal/1686kJ; Fat 19.3g; Saturated fat 11.2g; Carbohydrate 46.8g; Fibre 0.3g.

Leche Flan

Serve this delicious dessert hot or cold with whipped cream or crème fraîche.

Serves 8
5 large eggs
30ml/2 tbsp caster (superfine) sugar
few drops vanilla extract
400g/14oz can evaporated
   (unsweetened condensed) milk

300ml/1/2 pint/1 1/4 cups milk
5ml/1 tsp finely grated
   lime rind
strips of lime rind, to decorate

For the caramel
225g/8oz/generous 1 cup sugar
120ml/4fl oz/1/2 cup water

1 To make the caramel, put the sugar and water in a heavy pan. Stir to dissolve the sugar, then boil without stirring until the caramel is golden.

2 Quickly pour into eight individual ramekins, rotating them to coat the sides. Leave to one side to set.

3 Preheat the oven to 150°C/300°F/Gas 2. Beat the eggs, sugar and vanilla extract in a bowl.

4 Mix the evaporated milk and fresh milk in a pan. Heat to just below boiling point, then pour on to the egg mixture, stirring all the time. Strain the custard mixture into a jug (pitcher) and add the grated lime rind. Leave the custard to cool. Pour into the caramel-coated ramekins.

5 Place the ramekins in a roasting pan and pour in enough warm water to come halfway up the sides of the dishes.

6 Transfer the roasting pan to the oven and cook the custards for 35–45 minutes or until just set. They will just shimmer when the ramekins are gently shaken.

7 Serve the custards in their ramekin dishes. Alternatively, invert them on to serving plates. Break up the caramel into smaller pieces and use to decorate the custards. The custards can be served warm or cold, decorated with strips of lime rind.

Energy 229kcal/967kJ; Fat 6.2g; Saturated fat 2.7g; Carbohydrate 36.4g; Fibre 0g.

Steamed Coconut Custard

This popular dessert migrated to India from South-east Asia. Coconut milk makes marvellous custard. Here it is cooked with cellophane noodles and chopped bananas, a combination that works very well.

Serves 8

25g/1oz cellophane noodles
3 eggs
400ml/14fl oz can coconut
    milk
75ml/5 tbsp water
25g/1oz/2 tbsp granulated
    sugar
4 ripe bananas, peeled and
    cut into small pieces
salt
vanilla ice cream, to serve
    (optional)

1 Soak the cellophane noodles in a bowl of warm water for 5 minutes.

2 Beat the eggs in a bowl until pale. Whisk in the coconut milk, water and sugar.

3 Strain into a 1.75 litre/3 pint/7½ cup heatproof soufflé dish.

4 Drain the noodles well and cut them into small pieces with scissors. Stir the noodles into the coconut milk mixture, together with the chopped bananas. Add a pinch of salt and mix well.

5 Cover the dish with foil and place in a steamer for about 1 hour, or until set. A skewer inserted in the centre should come out clean. Serve hot or cold, on its own or topped with vanilla ice cream.

Cook's Tip
Cellophane noodles are translucent, thin dried noodles made from seaweed and mung bean flour. They make this dessert thick and creamy.

Steamed Custard in Nectarines

Steaming nectarines or peaches brings out their natural colour and sweetness, so this is a good way of making the most of underripe or less flavourful fruit.

Serves 4–6

6 nectarines
1 large (US extra large) egg
45ml/3 tbsp palm sugar or light
    muscovado (brown) sugar
30ml/2 tbsp coconut milk

1 Cut the nectarines in half. Using a teaspoon, scoop out the stones (pits) and a little of the surrounding flesh.

2 Lightly beat the egg, then add the sugar and the coconut milk. Beat until the sugar has dissolved.

3 Transfer the nectarines to a steamer and carefully fill the cavities three-quarters full with the custard mixture. Steam over a pan of simmering water for 5–10 minutes.

4 Remove from the heat and leave to cool completely before transferring to plates and serving.

Variations
• This recipe would also work well with peaches or pears. The pears might need a little longer to cook.
• A soft berry coulis would make a delicious accompaniment to the nectarines. Cook 350g/12oz/2 cups raspberries in a pan with 30ml/2 tbsp sugar and 15ml/1 tbsp water for about 10 minutes, or until the juices run. Press the raspberries through a fine sieve (strainer) to remove the seeds. Put a spoonful of coulis on to each plate beside the nectarines.

Cook's Tip
Palm sugar, also known as jaggery, is made from the sap of certain Asian palm trees, such as coconut and palmyrah. If you buy it as a cake or large lump, grate it before use.

Energy 115kcal/486kJ; Fat 2.8g; Saturated fat 0.9g; Carbohydrate 19.9g; Fibre 0.6g.

Energy 154kcal/658kJ; Fat 1.6g; Saturated fat 0.4g; Carbohydrate 32.4g; Fibre 2.7g.

Caramel Custard with Fresh Fruit

A creamy caramel dessert is a wonderful way to end a meal. It is light and delicious, and this recipe is very simple to make. Fresh fruit is the perfect accompaniment.

Serves 6
30ml/2 tbsp granulated sugar
30ml/2 tbsp water

For the custard
6 eggs
4 drops vanilla extract
115g/4oz/generous ½ cup
  granulated sugar
750ml/1¼ pints/3 cups
  semi-skimmed (low-fat) milk
fresh fruit, such as strawberries,
  blueberries, orange and banana
  slices, and raspberries, to serve

1 To make the caramel, place the sugar and water in a heavy pan and heat until the sugar has dissolved and the mixture is bubbling and pale gold in colour. Watch the sugar carefully, as it can quickly burn once it begins to caramelize. Pour carefully into a 1.2 litre/2 pint/5 cup soufflé dish. Leave the caramel to cool.

2 Preheat the oven to 180°C/350°F/Gas 4. To make the custard, break the eggs into a medium mixing bowl and whisk until frothy.

3 Stir the vanilla extract into the whisked eggs and gradually add the granulated sugar. Add the milk in a steady stream, whisking constantly.

4 Pour the custard over the top of the caramel.

5 Cook the custard in the oven for 35–40 minutes. Remove from the oven and leave to cool for 30 minutes or until the mixture is set.

6 Loosen the custard from the sides of the dish with a knife. Place a serving dish upside-down on top of the soufflé dish and invert, giving a gentle shake if necessary to turn out the custard on to the serving dish.

7 Arrange any fresh fruit of your choice around the custard on the serving dish and serve immediately.

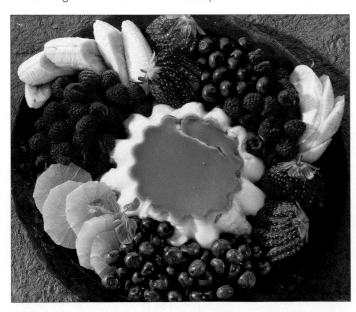

Energy 194kcal/823kJ; Fat 4.7g; Saturated fat 2.01g; Carbohydrate 32.9g; Fibre 0g.

Coconut Cream Diamonds

Although commercially ground rice can be used for this dish, grinding jasmine rice yourself – in a food processor – gives a much better result.

Serves 4–6
75g/3oz/scant ½ cup jasmine
  rice, soaked overnight in
  175ml/6fl oz/¾ cup water
350ml/12fl oz/1½ cups
  coconut milk
150ml/¼ pint/⅔ cup single
  (light) cream

50g/2oz/¼ cup caster
  (superfine) sugar
raspberries and fresh mint leaves,
  to decorate

For the coulis
75g/3oz/¾ cup blackcurrants,
  stalks removed
30ml/2 tbsp caster
  (superfine) sugar
75g/3oz/½ cup fresh or
  frozen raspberries

1 Put the rice and its soaking water into a food processor and process for a few minutes until the mixture is soupy. Heat the coconut milk and cream in a non-stick pan. When the mixture is on the point of boiling, stir in the rice mixture. Cook over a very gentle heat for 10 minutes, stirring constantly.

2 Stir the sugar into the coconut rice mixture and continue cooking for a further 10–15 minutes, or until the mixture is thick and creamy. Line a rectangular tin (pan) with baking parchment. Pour the coconut rice mixture into the pan, cool, then chill until the dessert is set and firm.

3 To make the coulis, put the blackcurrants in a bowl and sprinkle with the sugar. Set aside for 30 minutes. Transfer the blackcurrants and raspberries to a sieve (strainer) over a bowl. Using a spoon, press the fruit against the sieve so that the juices collect in the bowl. Taste the coulis and add more sugar if necessary.

4 Cut the coconut cream into diamonds. Spoon a little of the coulis on to each plate, arrange the diamonds on top and decorate with the raspberries and mint leaves.

Energy 248kcal/1043kJ; Fat 7.8g; Saturated fat 4.8g; Carbohydrate 42.2g; Fibre 1.2g.

Mango & Lime Fool

Canned mangoes are used here for convenience, but the dish tastes even better if made with fresh ones. Choose a variety like the voluptuous Alphonso mango, which is wonderfully fragrant and tastes indescribably delicious.

Serves 4
400g/14oz can sliced mango
grated rind of 1 lime
juice of ½ lime
150ml/¼ pint/⅔ cup double (heavy) cream
90ml/6 tbsp Greek (US strained plain) yogurt
fresh mango slices, to decorate (optional)

1 Drain the canned mango slices and put them in the bowl of a food processor.

2 Add the grated lime rind and the lime juice. Process until the mixture forms a smooth purée. Alternatively, mash the mango slices with a potato masher, then press through a sieve (strainer) into a bowl with the back of a wooden spoon. Stir in the lime rind and juice.

3 Pour the cream into a bowl and add the yogurt. Whisk until the mixture is thick and then quickly whisk in the mango mixture.

4 Spoon into four tall cups or glasses and chill for 1–2 hours. Just before serving, decorate each glass with fresh mango slices, if you like.

Cook's Tip
When mixing the cream and yogurt mixture with the mango purée, whisk just enough to combine, so as not to lose the lightness of the whipped cream mixture. If you prefer, fold the mixtures together lightly, so that the fool is rippled.

Energy 269kcal/1118kJ; Fat 22.6g; Saturated fat 13.8g; Carbohydrate 15.2g; Fibre 2.6g.

Coconut Custard

This traditional dessert can be baked or steamed and is often served with sweet sticky rice and a selection of fresh fruit. Mangoes and tamarillos go particularly well with the custard and rice. Rose or jasmine extract give the custard a distinctive flavour but vanilla also works well.

Serves 4
4 eggs
75g/3oz/6 tbsp soft light brown sugar
250ml/8fl oz/1 cup coconut milk
5ml/1 tsp vanilla, rose or jasmine extract
fresh mint leaves and icing (confectioners') sugar, to decorate
sliced fruit, to serve

1 Preheat the oven to 150°C/300°F/Gas 2.

2 Whisk the eggs and sugar in a bowl until smooth. Add the coconut milk and the vanilla, rose or jasmine extract and whisk well.

3 Strain the mixture into a jug (pitcher), then pour it into four individual heatproof glasses, ramekins or an ovenproof dish.

4 Stand the glasses, ramekins or dish in a roasting pan.

5 Fill the pan with hot water to reach halfway up the sides of the ramekins or dish.

6 Bake for about 35–40 minutes, or until the custards are set. Test with a fine skewer or cocktail stick (toothpick).

7 Remove the roasting pan from the oven, lift out the ramekins or dish and leave to cool.

8 If you like, turn out the custards on to a serving plate or plates. Decorate with the mint leaves and a dusting of icing sugar, and serve with sliced fruit such as ripe peaches, mangoes, papaya, star fruit (carambola) or kiwi fruit.

Energy 161kcal/681kJ; Fat 5.7g; Saturated fat 1.7g; Carbohydrate 22.7g; Fibre 0g.

Mango Sorbet with Sauce

After a heavy meal, this delightful sorbet makes a very refreshing dessert. Mango is said to be one of the oldest fruits cultivated in India, having been presented by Lord Shiva to his beautiful wife, Parvathi.

Serves 4–6
900g/2lb mango pulp
2.5ml/½ tsp lemon juice
grated rind of 1 orange and
   1 lemon

4 egg whites
50g/2oz/¼ cup caster
   (superfine) sugar
120ml/4fl oz/½ cup double
   (heavy) cream
50g/2oz/½ cup icing
   (confectioners') sugar

1 In a large, chilled bowl, mix half of the mango pulp with the lemon juice and the grated rind.

2 Whisk the egg whites until peaks form, then gently fold them into the mango mixture, with the caster sugar. Cover with clear film (plastic wrap) and place in the freezer for at least 1 hour.

3 Remove from the freezer and beat again. Transfer to an ice cream container, and freeze until fully set.

4 In a bowl, whip the double cream with the icing sugar and the remaining mango pulp. Cover and chill the sauce for 24 hours.

5 Remove the sorbet 10 minutes before serving. Scoop out individual servings and cover with a generous helping of mango sauce. Serve immediately.

Variation
Try this sorbet made with full-flavoured locally grown strawberries when in season for a delicious change.

Energy 387kcal/1631kJ; Fat 16.6g; Saturated fat 10.3g; Carbohydrate 58.4g; Fibre 5.9g.

Indian Ice Cream

Kulfi-wallahs (ice-cream vendors) have always made kulfi, and continue to this day, without using modern freezers. Kulfi is packed into metal cones sealed with dough and then churned in clay pots until set. Try this method – it works extremely well in an ordinary freezer.

Serves 4–6
3 × 400ml/14fl oz cans
   evaporated (unsweetened
   condensed) milk
3 egg whites

350g/12oz/3 cups icing
   (confectioners') sugar
5ml/1 tsp ground cardamom
15ml/1 tbsp rose water
175g/6oz/1½ cups pistachio
   nuts, chopped
75g/3oz/½ cup sultanas
   (golden raisins)
75g/3oz/¾ cup flaked
   (sliced) almonds
25g/1oz/3 tbsp glacé (candied)
   cherries, halved

1 Remove the labels from the cans of evaporated milk and lay the cans down in a pan with a tight-fitting cover. Fill the pan with water to reach three-quarters up the cans. Bring to the boil, cover and simmer for 20 minutes. (Don't leave the cans of evaporated milk unattended. Top up the water if necessary; the pan must never boil dry.) When cool, remove the cans and chill in the refrigerator for 24 hours. Chill a large bowl too.

2 Whisk the egg whites in another large bowl until peaks form. Open the cans and empty the milk into the chilled bowl. Whisk until doubled in quantity, then fold in the whisked egg whites and icing sugar.

3 Gently fold in the remaining ingredients, cover the bowl with clear film (plastic wrap) and place in the freezer for 1 hour.

4 Remove the ice cream from the freezer and mix well with a fork. Transfer to a serving container and return to the freezer for a final setting. Remove from the freezer 10 minutes before serving.

Energy 1123kcal/4722kJ; Fat 47.3g; Saturated fat 10.3g; Carbohydrate 144.2g; Fibre 5.1g.

Coconut & Lemon Grass Ice Cream

The combination of cream and coconut milk makes for a wonderfully rich ice cream. The lemon grass flavouring is very subtle, but quite delicious.

Serves 4
2 lemon grass stalks
475ml/16fl oz/2 cups double (heavy) cream
120ml/4fl oz/½ cup coconut milk
4 large (US extra large) eggs
105ml/7 tbsp caster (superfine) sugar
5ml/1 tsp vanilla extract

1 Cut the lemon grass stalks in half lengthways. Use a mallet or rolling pin to mash the pieces, breaking up the fibres so that all the flavour is released. Pour the cream and coconut milk into a pan. Add the lemon grass stalks and heat gently, stirring frequently, until the mixture starts to simmer.

2 Put the eggs, sugar and vanilla extract in a large bowl. Using an electric whisk, whisk until the mixture is very light and fluffy.

3 Strain the cream mixture into a heatproof bowl that will fit over a pan of simmering water. Whisk in the egg mixture, then place the bowl over the pan and continue to whisk until the mixture thickens. Remove it from the heat and leave to cool. Chill the coconut custard in the refrigerator for 3–4 hours.

4 Pour the mixture into a plastic tub or similar freezerproof container. Freeze for 4 hours, beating two or three times at hourly intervals with a fork to break up the ice crystals.

5 Alternatively, use an ice-cream maker. Pour the chilled mixture into the machine and churn until it is firm enough to scoop. Serve immediately, or scrape into a freezerproof container and place in the freezer. Allow the ice cream to soften in the refrigerator for 30 minutes before serving.

Energy 773kcal/3200kJ; Fat 69.4g; Saturated fat 41.3g; Carbohydrate 30.9g; Fibre 0g.

Coconut Ice Cream

This ice cream is easy to make in an ice-cream maker or by hand. Serve it with a spicy *gula melaka* sauce, hot, warm or cold.

Serves 6
400ml/14fl oz can coconut milk
400ml/14fl oz can condensed milk
2.5ml/½ tsp salt

For the gula melaka sauce
150g/5oz/¾ cup palm sugar or muscovado (molasses) sugar
150ml/¼ pint/⅔ cup water
1cm/½in slice fresh root ginger, bruised
1 pandanus leaf (if available)
coconut shells (optional) and thinly pared strips of coconut, to serve

1 Chill the cans of coconut and condensed milk thoroughly. In a bowl, mix the coconut milk with the condensed milk. Gently whisk together with the salt.

2 Pour the mixture into the frozen freezer bowl of an ice-cream maker (or follow the appliance instructions) and churn until thickened. (This will take 30–40 minutes.) Transfer the mixture to a lidded plastic tub, cover and freeze until the consistency is right for scooping.

3 If you do not have an ice-cream maker, pour the mixture into a shallow container and freeze on the coldest setting. When ice crystals form around the sides of the ice cream, beat the mixture, then return it to the freezer. Do this at least twice. The more you do it, the creamier the mixture will be.

4 To make the sauce, mix the sugar, measured water and ginger in a pan. Stir over medium heat until the sugar has dissolved, then bring the liquid to the boil. Add the pandanus leaf, if using, tying it into a knot so that it can easily be removed with the ginger before serving. Lower the heat and simmer for 3–4 minutes. Set aside until required.

5 Serve the ice cream in coconut shells or a bowl. Decorate with coconut and serve with the hot, warm or cold sauce.

Energy 237kcal/1001kJ; Fat 6.9g; Saturated fat 4.3g; Carbohydrate 40.3g; Fibre 0g.

Watermelon Ice

After a hot and spicy meal, the only thing more refreshing than ice-cold watermelon is this cooling watermelon ice. Making it is simplicity itself.

4 kaffir lime leaves, torn into small pieces
500g/1lb watermelon

Serves 4–6
90ml/6 tbsp caster (superfine) sugar
105ml/7 tbsp water

1 Put the caster sugar, water and kaffir lime leaves in a pan. Heat gently until the sugar has dissolved. Pour into a large bowl and set aside to cool.

2 Cut the watermelon into wedges with a large knife. Cut the flesh from the rind, remove the seeds and chop the flesh.

3 Spoon the watermelon into a food processor. Process to a slush, then mix with the sugar syrup. Chill the mixture in the refrigerator for 3–4 hours.

4 Strain the mixture into a freezerproof container. Freeze for 2 hours, then remove from the freezer and beat with a fork to break up the ice crystals. Return the mixture to the freezer and freeze for 3 hours more, beating the mixture at half-hourly intervals. Freeze until firm.

5 Alternatively, use an ice-cream maker. Pour the chilled mixture into the machine and churn until it is firm enough to scoop. Serve immediately, or scrape into a freezerproof container and store in the freezer.

6 About 30 minutes before serving, transfer the watermelon ice to the refrigerator so that it softens slightly. This allows the full flavour of the watermelon to be apparent and makes the ice easier to scoop.

Spiced Lassi

Lassi, or buttermilk, is prepared by churning yogurt with water and then removing the fat. To make this refreshing drink without churning, use low-fat natural yogurt instead.

300ml/½ pint/1¼ cups water
2.5cm/1in piece fresh root ginger, finely crushed
2 fresh green chillies, finely chopped
2.5ml/½ tsp ground cumin
salt and ground black pepper
a few fresh coriander (cilantro) leaves, chopped, to garnish

Serves 4
450ml/¾ pint/scant 2 cups natural (plain) yogurt

1 In a bowl, whisk the yogurt and water until well blended. The consistency should be that of full cream (whole) milk. Adjust by adding more water if necessary.

2 Add the ginger, chillies and ground cumin.

3 Season with the salt and black pepper, and mix well.

4 Pour into four serving glasses and chill. Garnish with chopped coriander before serving.

Cook's Tip
Lassi is often drunk with hot and spicy curries as it refreshes the palate well.

Variation
If you prefer an unspiced and cooler version, try Rose Water Lassi. Blend 300ml/½ pint/1¼ cups natural yogurt with 60ml/ 4 tbsp caster sugar, 400ml/14fl oz/1⅔ cups water and 15ml/ 1 tbsp rose water in a food processor or blender. Pour into individual glasses or a jug (pitcher) and add fresh mint leaves to decorate, if you like.

Energy 128kcal/545kJ; Fat 0.4g; Saturated fat 0.1g; Carbohydrate 32.4g; Fibre 0.1g.

Energy 63kcal/266kJ; Fat 1.1g; Saturated fat 0.6g; Carbohydrate 8.5g; Fibre 0g.

Pistachio Lassi

In India, lassi is not only made at home, but is also sold at roadside cafés, restaurants and hotels. There is no substitute for this drink, especially on a hot day. It is particularly good served with curries and similar hot dishes as it helps the body to digest spicy food.

Serves 4
300ml/½ pint/1¼ cups natural (plain) low-fat yogurt
5ml/1 tsp granulated sugar, or to taste
300ml/½ pint/1¼ cups water
30ml/2 tbsp puréed fruit (optional)
15ml/1 tbsp crushed pistachio nuts, to decorate

1 Place the natural yogurt in a jug (pitcher) and whisk until frothy. Add the granulated sugar.

2 Pour in the measured water and the puréed fruit, if using, and continue to whisk for 2 minutes.

3 Taste for sweetness and adjust as necessary. Pour the lassi into four serving glasses and serve chilled, decorated with crushed pistachio nuts.

Cook's Tips
• Refreshing, cooling drinks are the perfect accompaniment to spicy Indian dishes.
• A variety of fruit juices are often served as well as water flavoured with freshly squeezed limes or lemons and sweetened with sugar. Fresh fragrant mint is usually used to decorate and flavour the drinks.

Variation
To make a simple savoury lassi, omit the sugar and fruit and add lemon juice, ground cumin and salt. Garnish with fresh mint leaves.

Tea & Fruit Punch

This delicious punch can be served hot or cold. White wine or brandy may be added to taste.

Makes 4
600ml/1 pint/2½ cups water
1 cinnamon stick
4 cloves
12.5ml/2½ tsp Earl Grey tea leaves
175g/6oz/scant 1 cup granulated sugar
450ml/¾ pint/scant 2 cups tropical soft drink concentrate
1 lemon, sliced
1 small orange, sliced
½ cucumber, sliced

1 Bring the water to the boil in a pan with the cinnamon stick and cloves. Remove from the heat and add the tea leaves. Leave to brew for about 5 minutes. Stir and strain into a large bowl and chill in the refrigerator for 2–3 hours.

2 Add the sugar and the soft drink concentrate and allow to rest until the sugar has dissolved and the mixture cooled. Place the fruit and cucumber in a chilled punch bowl and pour over the tea mix. Chill for a further 24 hours before serving.

Almond Sherbet

Traditionally, this drink was always made in the month of Ramadan to break the Muslim fast. It should be served chilled.

Serves 4
50g/2oz/½ cup ground almonds
600ml/1 pint/2½ cups semi-skimmed (low-fat) milk
10ml/2 tsp granulated sugar, or to taste

1 Put the ground almonds into a serving jug (pitcher).

2 Pour in the semi-skimmed milk and add the sugar; stir to mix.

3 Taste for sweetness and adjust as necessary. Serve very cold in long glasses. Chilling the glasses first helps to keep the drink cold and adds a sense of occasion.

Energy 70kcal/296kJ; Fat 2.6g; Saturated fat 0.63g; Carbohydrate 7.5g; Fibre 0g.

Top: Energy 1108kcal/4737kJ; Fat 0g; Saturated fat 0g; Carbohydrate 294.5g; Fibre 0g;
Above: Energy 155kcal/651kJ; Fat 9.4g; Saturated fat 2.04g; Carbohydrate 11g; Fibre 0.9g.